Students learn best when they atten[d] and assignments...but learnin[g]

MyEconLab *Picks Up Whe[re]*

Instructors choose MyEconLab:

"MyEconLab's e-text is great. Particularly in that it helps offset the skyrocketing cost of textbooks. Naturally, students love that."

—**Doug Gehrke, Moraine Valley Community College**

"MyEconLab offers them a way to practice every week. They receive immediate feedback and a feeling of personal attention. As a result, my teaching has become more targeted and efficient."

—**Kelly Blanchard, Purdue University**

"Students tell me that offering them MyEconLab is almost like offering them individual tutors."

—**Jefferson Edwards, Cypress Fairbanks College**

"Chapter quizzes offset student procrastination by ensuring they keep on task. If a student is having a problem, MyEconLab indicates exactly what they need to study."

"MyEconLab helps both students and instructors. There's something there for everyone."

"Someone has already pulled out articles that relate to economics and to the chapter at hand. As much as MyEconLab helps the student, that helps the instructor."

—**Diana Fortier, Waubonsee Community College**

myeconlab

Get Ahead of the Curve

ectures and keep up with their reading
houldn't end when class is over.

Lectures and Office Hours Leave Off

Students choose MyEconLab:

In a Fall 2005 study, 87 percent of students who used MyEconLab regularly felt it improved their grade.

"It was very useful because it had EVERYTHING, from practice exams to exercises to reading. Very helpful."

—student, Northern Illinois University

"I like how every chapter is outlined by vocabulary and flash cards. It helped me memorize equations and definitions. It was like having a study partner."

—student, Temple University

Chart 2. Helpfulness of Study Plan Practice Questions and Feedback
From a fall 2005 nationwide survey of students using MyEconLab (conducted by Contemporary Solutions)

90% of students surveyed who used the Study Plan practice questions and feedback felt it helped them to prepare for tests.

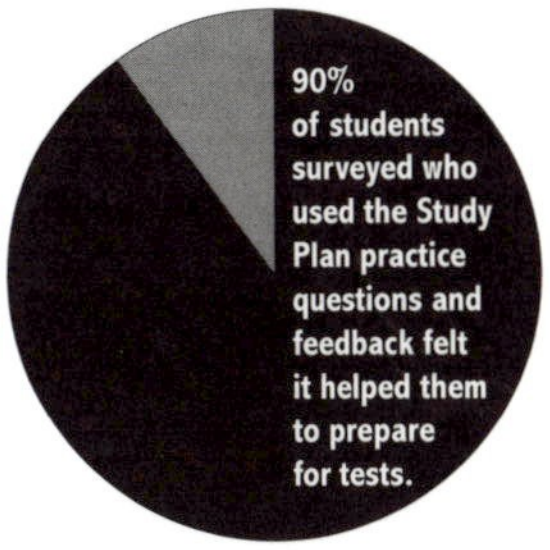

n = 227

"It made me look through the book to find answers so I did more reading."

—student, Northern Illinois University

"It was very helpful to get instant feedback. Sometimes I would get lost reading the book, and these individual problems would help me focus and see if I understood the concepts."

—student, Temple University

Chart 3. Recommendation to a Friend
From a fall 2005 survey of Texas A&M students using MyEconLab (conducted by Contemporary Solutions)

83.9% of students surveyed would recommend MyEconLab to a friend.

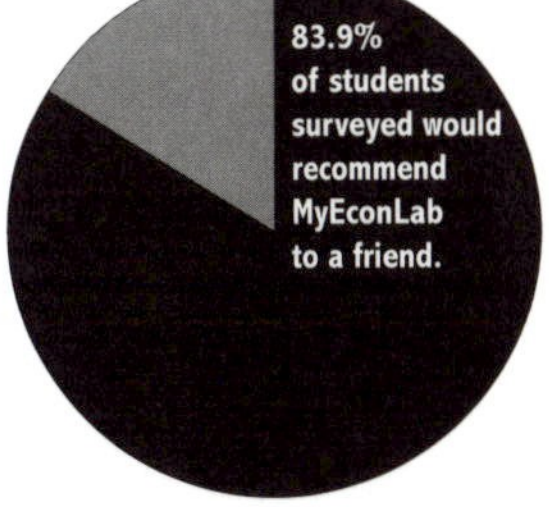

n = 33

"I really like the way MyEconLab took me through the graphs step-by-step. The Fast Track tutorials were the most helpful for the graph questions. I used the 1-2-3 buttons all the time."

—student, Stephen F. Austin State University

"I would recommend MyEconLab to a friend. It was really easy to use and helped in studying the material for class."

—student, Northern Illinois University

"I would recommend taking the quizzes on MyEconLab because it gives you a true account of whether or not you understand the material."

—student, Montana Tech

Microeconomics

PRINCIPLES, APPLICATIONS, AND TOOLS

FIFTH EDITION

Arthur O'Sullivan
Lewis and Clark College

Steven M. Sheffrin
University of California, Davis

Stephen J. Perez
California State University, Sacramento

Upper Saddle River, NJ 07458

Library of Congress Cataloging-in-Publication Data
O'Sullivan, Arthur
  Microeconomics / Arthur O'Sullivan, Steven M. Sheffrin.—5th ed.
    p. cm.
  ISBN 0-13-157283-0
  1. Microeconomics.   I. Sheffrin, Steven M.   II. Title.
HB172.5.O85 2007
338.5—dc22   2006032062

AVP/Executive Editor: *David Alexander*
VP/Editorial Director: *Jeff Shelstad*
VP/Director of Development: *Steve Deitmer*
Senior Development Editor: *Lena Buonanno*
Senior Media Project Manager: *Peter Snell*
AVP/Executive Marketing Manager: *Sharon Koch*
Marketing Assistant: *Patrick Barbera*
Associate Director, Production Editorial: *Judy Leale*
Production Editor: *Suzanne Grappi*
Permissions Coordinator: *Charles Morris*
Associate Director, Manufacturing: *Vinnie Scelta*
Manufacturing Buyer: *Diane Peirano*
Creative Director: *Maria Lange*

Design/Composition Manager: *Christy Mahon*
Interior Design: *MLM Graphics*
Cover Illustration/Photo: *Image Bank*
Illustration (Interior): *Rob Aleman*
Director, Image Resource Center: *Melinda Patelli*
Manager, Rights and Permissions: *Zina Arabia*
Manager, Visual Research: *Beth Brenzel*
Manager, Cover Visual Research & Permissions: *Karen Sanatar*
Image Permission Coordinator: *Angelique Sharps*
Photo Researcher: *Diane Austin*
Composition/Full-Service Project Management: *Prepare, Inc.*
Printer/Binder: *RR Donnelley*
Typeface: *Janson Text 10/12*

Credits and acknowledgments borrowed from other sources and reproduced, with permission, in this textbook appear on appropriate page within text (or on page 441).

Microsoft® and Windows® are registered trademarks of the Microsoft Corporation in the U.S.A. and other countries. Screen shots and icons reprinted with permission from the Microsoft Corporation. This book is not sponsored or endorsed by or affiliated with the Microsoft Corporation.

Pearson Education LTD.
Pearson Education Singapore, Pte. Ltd.
Pearson Education, Canada, Ltd.
Pearson Education–Japan

Pearson Education Australia PTY, Limited
Pearson Education North Asia Ltd
Pearson Educación de Mexico, S.A. de C.V.
Pearson Education Malaysia, Pte. Ltd

10 9 8 7 6 5 4 3 2 1

ISBN: 0-13-157283-0

TO OUR CHILDREN
CONOR, MAURA, MEERA, KIRAN, DAVIS, AND TATE

About the Authors

ARTHUR O'SULLIVAN

Is a professor of economics at Lewis and Clark College in Portland, Oregon. After receiving his B.S. in economics at the University of Oregon, he spent two years in the Peace Corps, working with city planners in the Philippines. He received his Ph.D. in economics from Princeton University in 1981 and has taught at the University of California, Davis, and Oregon State University, winning several teaching awards at both schools. He recently accepted an endowed professorship at Lewis and Clark College, where he teaches microeconomics and urban economics. He is the author of the best-selling textbook *Urban Economics*, currently in its sixth edition.

Professor O'Sullivan's research explores economic issues concerning urban land use, environmental protection, and public policy. His articles have appeared in many economics journals, including the *Journal of Urban Economics*, *Journal of Environmental Economics and Management*, *National Tax Journal*, *Journal of Public Economics*, and *Journal of Law and Economics*.

Professor O'Sullivan lives with his family in Lake Oswego, Oregon. For recreation, he enjoys hiking, boogie-boarding, paragliding, and squash.

STEVEN M. SHEFFRIN

Is dean of the division of social sciences and professor of economics at the University of California, Davis. He has been a visiting professor at Princeton University, Oxford University, and the London School of Economics and has served as a financial economist with the Office of Tax Analysis of the United States Department of the Treasury. He has been on the faculty of the University of California, Davis, since 1976 and has served as the chairman of the department of economics. He received his B.A. from Wesleyan University and his Ph.D. in economics from the Massachusetts Institute of Technology.

Professor Sheffrin is the author of 10 other books and monographs and over 100 articles in the fields of macroeconomics, public finance, and international economics. His most recent books include *Rational Expectations* (second edition) and *Property Taxes and Tax Revolts: The Legacy of Proposition 13* (with Arthur O'Sullivan and Terri Sexton).

Professor Sheffrin has taught macroeconomics at all levels, from large introduction to principles classes (enrollments of 400) to graduate classes for doctoral students. He is the recipient of the Thomas Mayer Distinguished Teaching Award in economics.

He lives with his wife Anjali (also an economist) in Davis, California, and has two daughters who have studied economics. In addition to a passion for current affairs and travel, he plays a tough game of tennis.

STEPHEN J. PEREZ

Is chair of the economics department at California State University, Sacramento. After receiving his B.A. in economics at the University of California, San Diego, he was awarded his Ph.D. in economics from the University of California, Davis, in 1994. He taught economics at Virginia Commonwealth University and Washington State University before coming to California State University, Sacramento, in 2001. He teaches macroeconomics at all levels as well as econometrics, sports economics, labor economics, and mathematics for economists.

Professor Perez's research explores most macroeconomic topics. In particular, he is interested in evaluating the ability of econometric techniques to discover the truth, issues of causality in macroeconomics, and sports economics. His articles have appeared in many economics journals, including the *Journal of Monetary Economics*, *Econometrics Journal*, *Economics Letters*, *Journal of Economic Methodology*, *Public Finance and Management*, *Journal of Economics and Business*, *Oxford Bulletin of Economics and Statistics*, *Journal of Money, Credit, and Banking*, *Applied Economics*, and *Journal of Macroeconomics*.

Brief Contents

Contents

ALTERNATIVE COURSE SEQUENCE

Alternative Microeconomics Sequence

The following chart helps you organize your syllabus based on your teaching preferences and objectives.

		Mix of Theory and Policy	Supply, Demand, and Policy	Supply, Demand, and Market Structure	Challenging Theory	Short Policy Course
1	Introduction: What Is Economics?	X	X	X	X	X
2	The Key Principles of Economics	X	X	X	X	X
3	Exchange and Markets	X	X	X	X	
4	Demand, Supply, and Market Equilibrium	X	X	X	X	X
5	Elasticity: A Measure of Responsiveness	X	X	X	X	X
6	Market Efficiency and Government Intervention	X	X	X	X	X
7	Consumer Choice Using Utility Theory				X	
8	Production Technology and Cost	X	X	X	X	
9	Perfect Competition	X	X	X	X	
10	Monopoly and Price Discrimination	X		X	X	
11	Market Entry and Monopolistic Competition	X		X	X	
12	Oligopoly and Strategic Behavior	X		X	X	
13	Controlling Market Power: Antitrust and Regulation	X		X	X	
14	Imperfect Information: Adverse Selection and Moral Hazard	X	X		X	X
15	Public Goods and Public Choice		X			X
16	External Costs and Environmental Policy		X			X
17	The Labor Market, Income, and Poverty	X	X		X	X
18	Unions, Monopsony, and Imperfect Information				X	
19	International Trade and Public Policy	X	X		X	

Preface

 APPLYING THE CONCEPTS

This is an applications-driven textbook. We carefully selected over 120 real-world Applications that help students develop and master essential economic concepts. We start each chapter with three to five thought-provoking questions that convey important economic concepts. Once we present the economic logic behind a concept, we illustrate its use with a real-world Application. For each Application, we provide exercises that test students' understanding of the concepts and give them opportunities to do their own economic analysis. Here is an example of our approach from Chapter 4, "Demand, Supply, and Market Equilibrium."

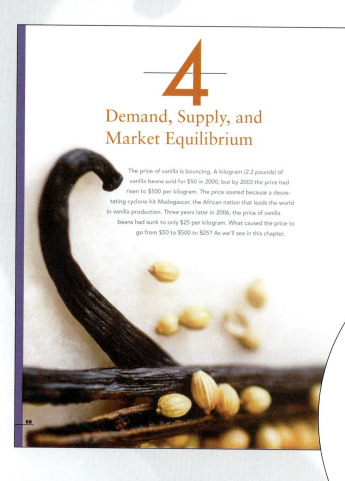

4
Demand, Supply, and Market Equilibrium

The price of vanilla is bouncing. A kilogram (2.2 pounds) of vanilla beans sold for $50 in 2000, but by 2003 the price had risen to $500 per kilogram. The price soared because a devastating cyclone hit Madagascar, the African nation that leads the world in vanilla production. Three years later in 2006, the price of vanilla beans had sunk to only $25 per kilogram. What caused the price to go from $50 to $500 to $25? As we'll see in this chapter,

APPLYING THE CONCEPTS

1 How do changes in demand affect prices?
Hurricane Katrina and Baton Rouge Housing Prices

2 What could explain a decrease in price?
Ted Koppel Tries to Explain Lower Drug Prices

3 How does the adoption of new technology affect prices?
Electricity from the Wind

4 How do changes in supply affect prices?
The Bouncing Price of Vanilla Beans

5 How do changes in one market affect other markets?
Platinum, Jewelry, and Catalytic Converters

the answer is "demand and supply." We'll use the model of demand and supply, the most popular tool of bouncing price of vanilla

4.7 | APPLICATIONS OF DEMAND AND SUPPLY

We can apply what we've learned about demand and supply to real markets. We can use the model of demand and supply to *predict* the effects of various events on equilibrium prices and quantities. We can also *explain* some observed changes in equilibrium prices and quantities.

1

A P P L I C A T I O N

HURRICANE KATRINA AND BATON ROUGE
HOUSING PRICES

● APPLYING THE CONCEPTS #1:
How do changes in demand affect prices?

In the late summer of 2005, Hurricane Katrina caused a storm surge and levee breaks that flooded much of New Orleans and destroyed a large fraction of the city's housing. Hundreds of thousands of residents were displaced, and about 250,000 relocated to nearby Baton Rouge. The increase in population was so large that Baton Rouge became the largest city in the state, and many people started calling the city "New Baton Rouge."

Figure 4.14 shows the effects of Hurricane Katrina on the housing market in Baton Rouge. Before Katrina, the average price of a single-family home was $130,000, as shown by point *a*. The increase in the city's population shifted the demand curve to the right, causing excess demand for housing at the original price. Just before the hurricane, there were 3,600 homes listed for sale in the city, but a wee[k...] only 500. The excess demand caused fierce competition a[...] supply of homes, increasing the price. Six months later, t[...] $156,000 as shown by point *b*. *Related to Exercises 7.1 a[...]*

SOURCE: Federal Deposit Insurance Corporation, *Louisiana State Profile—Fall 2[...]*

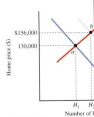

$156,000

130,000

Home price ($)

H_1 H_2
Number of h[...]

▲ FIGURE 4.14
Hurricane Katrina and Housing [...]
An increase in the population of Baton R[...]
demand for housing, shifting the deman[...]
librium price increases from $130,000 ([...]
(point *b*).

86

S U M M A R Y

In this chapter, we've seen how demand and supply determine prices. We also learned how to predict the effects of changes in demand or supply on prices and quantities. Here are the main points of the chapter:

1 A *market demand curve* shows the relationship between th quantity demanded and price, *ceteris paribus*.

2 A *market supply curve* shows the relationship between the quantity supplied and price, *ceteris paribus*.

3 *Equilibrium* in a market is shown by the intersection of the demand curve and the supply curve. When a market reaches equilibrium, there is no pressure to change the price.

4 A *change in demand* changes price and quantity in the same direction: An increase in demand increases the equilibrium price and quantity; a decrease in demand decreases the equilibrium price and quantity.

5 A *change in supply* changes price and quantity in opposite directions: An increase in supply decreases price and increases quantity; a decrease in supply increases price and decreases quantity.

K E Y   T E R M S

change in demand, p. 77
change in quantity demanded, p. 69
change in quantity supplied, p. 72
change in supply, p. 81
complements, p. 78
demand schedule, p. 68
excess demand (shortage), p. 75
excess supply (surplus), p. 76

individual demand curve, p. 69
individual supply curve, p. 72
inferior good, p. 77
law of demand, p. 69
law of supply, p. 72
market demand curve, p. 69
market equilibrium, p. 75
market supply curve, p. 73

minimum supply price, p. 72
normal good, p. 77
perfectly competitive market, p. 68
quantity demanded, p. 68
quantity supplied, p. 71
substitutes, p. 77
supply schedule, p. 71

E X E R C I S E S myeconlab

Get Ahead of the Curve

Visit www.myeconlab.com to complete these exercises online and get instant feedback.

4.1 | The Demand Curve

1.1 Arrow up or down: According to the law of demand, [...] the quantity [...]

[...] the variables that are [...]mand curve:

1.3 From the following list, choose the variables that change as we draw a market demand curve.
• The price of the product
• Consumer income
• The price of other related goods
• Consumer expectations about future prices
• The quantity of the product purchased

1.4 The market demand curve is the _____ (horizontal/vertical) sum of the individual demand curves.

4.7 | Applications of Demand and Supply

7.1 Arrow up or down: Hurricane Katrina _____ the demand for housing in Baton Rouge, so the price of housing _____ and the quantity of housing _____. (Related to Application 1 on page 86.)

7.2 Ted Koppel's analysis of the drug market was incorrect because he failed to notice that the _____ of drugs decreased at the same time that the _____ of drugs decreased. (Related to Application 2 on page 87.)

7.3 Innovations in wind technology decrease the price of electricity from wind from 50 cents per kilowatt-hour to _____ cents. (Related to Application 3 on page 88.)

7.4 Arrow up or down: The development of a sun-tolerant variety of the vanilla plant _____ the supply of vanilla and _____ its price. (Related to Application 4 on page 89.)

7.5 Arrow up or down: The increase in the price of platinum _____ recycling of used platinum and _____ the quantity of platinum used for jewelry. (Related to Application 5 on page 90.)

7.6 **Katrina Victims Move Back.** Suppose that 5 years after Hurricane Katrina, half the people who had relocated to Baton Rouge move back to a rebuilt New Orleans. Use a demand and supply graph of the

2003, the price of heroin decreased from $235 per gram to $76. Over the same period, the quantity of heroin consumed increased from 376 metric tons to 482 metric tons. Use a demand and supply graph to explain these changes in price and quantity. (Related to Application 2 on page 87.)

7.8 **Electricity from Fuel Cells.** Suppose that initially the cost of the capital required to generate electricity from fuel cells is $4,500 per kilowatt capacity, compared to $800 per kilowatt capacity for a diesel generator. The goal of the U.S. Department of Energy (DOE) is to cut the cost of fuel-cell generators to $400 per kilowatt capacity. Consider the market for electricity from fuel cells. Use a demand and supply graph to show the effects of meeting the DOE goal on the price and quantity of electricity from fuel cells. (Related to Application 3 on page 88.)

7.9 **Artificial Versus Natural Vanilla.** An artificial alternative to natural vanilla is cheaper to produce but doesn't taste as good. Suppose the makers of artificial vanilla discover a new recipe that improves its taste. Use a demand and supply graph to show the effects on the equilibrium price and quantity of natural vanilla. (Related to Application 4 on page 89.)

7.10 **Platinum Price and Jewelry.** Consider the market for platinum jewelry. Use a demand and supply graph to illustrate the following statement: "The increase

We tested our approach of using questions to open each chapter and related real-world applications with economics instructors. Here is what some of them had to say about our approach:

[The book] provides wonderful Applications for each principle presented. The introductory questions at the beginning of each chapter should create enough interest to get students to dig a little deeper into the subject.

ARLENA SULLIVAN, *Jones County Junior College*

The chapters have some incredible real-life examples that students will easily relate to; makes the math behind economics less scary and more approachable.

GRETCHEN MESTER, *Anne Arundel Community College*

I liked the use of the Katrina natural disaster [in Chapter 4] as a means of discussing the effect on market equilibrium price and quantity due to changes in demand, in the particular case of the textbook example of the housing market in "new" Baton Rogue.

CRAIG ROGERS, *Canisius College*

The Applications go beyond just illustrating concepts. They develop/reinforce the core principles by taking a nontechnical applied approach. Should enable students to understand the relevance of economics in everyday life and hopefully will arouse curiosity and interest.

RATHA RAMOO, *Diablo Valley College*

I think that the inclusion of this feature could both help the instructor in teaching and facilitate the understanding of the material by the students.

MIKAYEL VARDANYAN, *Oregon State University*

The book engages today's students by relating their world to economic theory. Our students of today need to know why the information is important before they undertake learning. Each chapter opens with intriguing, real-world resource allocation questions that economic principles can answer.

DAVID SHOROW, *Richland College*

 ## WHY FIVE KEY PRINCIPLES?

In Chapter 2, "The Key Principles of Economics," we introduce the following five key principles and then apply them throughout the book:

1   **The Principle of Opportunity Cost.** The opportunity cost of something is what you sacrifice to get it.

2   **The Marginal Principle.** Increase the level of an activity as long as its marginal benefit exceeds its marginal cost. Choose the level at which the marginal benefit equals the marginal cost.

3   **The Principle of Diminishing Returns.** If we increase one input while holding the other inputs fixed, output will increase, but at a decreasing rate.

4   **The Principle of Voluntary Exchange.** A voluntary exchange between two people makes both people better off.

5   **The Real–Nominal Principle.** What matters to people is the real value of money or income—its purchasing power—not the face value of money or income.

This approach of repeating five key principles gives students the big picture—the framework of economic reasoning. We make the key concepts unforgettable by using them repeatedly, illustrating them with intriguing examples, and giving students many opportunities to practice what they've learned. Throughout the text, economic concepts are connected to the five key principles:

 PRINCIPLE OF OPPORTUNITY COST
The opportunity cost of something is what you sacrifice to get it.

▶ | **HOW IS THE BOOK ORGANIZED?**

Chapter 1, "Introduction: What Is Economics?" uses three current policy issues—traffic congestion, poverty in Africa, and Japan's prolonged recession—to explain the economic way of thinking. Chapter 2, "The Key Principles of Economics," introduces the five principles we return to throughout the book. Chapter 3, "Exchange and Markets," is devoted entirely to exchange and trade. We discuss the fundamental rationale for exchange and introduce some of the institutions modern societies developed to facilitate trade.

Students need to have a solid understanding of demand and supply to be successful in the course. Many students have difficulty understanding movement along a curve versus shifts of a curve. To address this difficulty, we developed an innovative way to organize topics in Chapter 4, "Demand, Supply, and Market Equilibrium." We examine the law of demand and changes in quantity demanded, the law of supply and changes in quantity supplied, and then the notion of market equilibrium. After students have a firm grasp of equilibrium concepts, we explore the effects of changes in demand and supply on equilibrium prices and quantities. Here is what reviewers have said about our organization of Chapter 4:

> This treatment is innovative and effective. It covers equilibrium before changing demand and supply. This will greatly reduce the confusion about distinguishing between changes in quantity demanded and changes in demand (and, similarly, about changes in quantity supplied and changes in supply). . . . It makes good sense.
>
> GEOFFREY BLACK, *Boise State University*

> As I was reading the chapter, I thought to myself . . . this is a good approach: it takes one important economic idea to a conclusion: forces of demand and supply determine price and along the way, it covers quantity demanded, quantity supplied, demand curve, supply curve, etc. And now we're going to expand the model and look at the effects of the other determinants . . .
>
> RATHA RAMOO, *Diablo Valley College*

> The organization has the advantage of focusing attention early upon the key concept of market equilibrium, so that the reasons demand and supply shifts become important can be discussed before getting into the details of the shifts themselves . . .
>
> DAVID SCHUTTE, *Mountain View College*

See the "Alternative Microeconomics Sequence" chart on page xiii of this preface for organization options based on your teaching preferences.

Summary of the Microeconomics Chapters

A course in microeconomics starts with the first four chapters of the book, which provide a foundation for more detailed study of individual decision making and markets.

Part 2, "A Closer Look at Demand and Supply" (Chapters 5 through 7), provides a closer look at demand and supply, including elasticity, market efficiency, and consumer choice. Part 3, "Market Structures and Pricing" (Chapters 8 through 13) starts with a discussion of production and costs, setting the stage for an examination of alternative market structures, including the extremes of perfect competition and monopoly, as well as the middle ground of monopolistic competition and oligopoly. The last chapter in Part 3 discusses antitrust policy and deregulation. Part 4, "Externalities and Information" (Chapters 14 through 16), discusses the circumstances under which markets break down, including imperfect information, public goods, and environmental degradation.

Part 5, "The Labor Market and Income Distribution" (Chapters 17 and 18) explores the labor market, unions, poverty, discrimination, and the distribution of income. Part 6, "The International Economy" (Chapter 19), covers trade and public policy.

 ## WHAT'S NEW TO THIS EDITION?

Based on our teaching experiences and extensive feedback from economics instructors, we have revised selected key term definitions, added new graphs, updated existing graphs, and added new examples and Applications. For example, we now cover outsourcing, network externalities, globalization, and inflation targeting. We made three major revisions to the end-of-chapter exercises. First, we responded to market requests to group exercises together at the end of the chapter. Second, we revised the end-of-chapter exercises to correspond with new content and Applications in the chapters. Third, we give students the option of completing exercises online at www.myeconlab.com, where they receive instant feedback, tutorial instruction, and additional practice exercises.

A new coauthor, Steve Perez of California State University, Sacramento, joins the fifth edition. Professor Perez is the organizing force behind MyEconLab and ensured the seamless integration of MyEconLab with the book. He also served as advisor and coordinator for the extensive print and technology supplement package that accompanies the book. Professor Perez ensured that each supplement met the highest standards of quality. (For more on the supplements, please see pages xix–xxii.)

Key Changes to Microeconomics

We made two important organizational changes to the microeconomics chapters based on market feedback. First, instructors now have two options for covering consumer theory. Chapter 7 uses traditional utility theory, with the consumer's choice summarized by the equimarginal rule. In the appendix to Chapter 7, we present the alternative approach, modern consumer choice using indifference curves. Second, the chapters on production cost and market structure (Chapters 8 through 12) now appear right after the chapters on demand and supply.

There are 26 new Applications on topics such as outsourcing (Chapter 3), the connection between jewelry and catalytic converters (Chapter 4), why bumper crops are bad for farmers (Chapter 5), the cost of import restrictions (Chapter 6), the cost of producing the iPod (Chapter 8), competition between national brands and store brands (Chapter 11), genetic testing and insurance (Chapter 14), the external benefits from LoJack (Chapter 15), the external cost of young drivers (Chapter 16), the trade-offs from immigration (Chapter 17), and the effect of competition on trucker wages (Chapter 18).

 ## WHAT IS MYECONLAB?

Get Ahead of the Curve

Everyone benefits when students arrive to class confident and prepared. MyEconLab is the only online assessment system that gives students the tools they need to learn from their mistakes right at the moment they are struggling. MyEconLab has a variety of online features that solve problems for students and professors.

Problem Solving for Students

Each chapter in this text ends with a wide selection of summary and practice exercises to appeal to a variety of learning styles. Students have the option of completing these exercises online at www.myeconlab.com. MyEconLab identifies students' weak spots and provides tutorial help to master those areas:

- **Help Beyond Homework.** Student learning begins in the classroom. But instructors know that's only the start. Students need practice with theories and models to master key concepts. Instructors need a way to hold students accountable for getting that practice and to provide targeted support as they work through assessments.

- **Tests and Quizzes.** MyEconLab comes with two preloaded Sample Tests for each chapter so that students can self-assess their understanding of the material. Instructors can assign the Sample Tests or create their own from publisher-supplied content or their own custom exercises. Many Sample Test problems contain algorithmically generated values to increase practice opportunities.

- **Study Plan.** MyEconLab generates a Study Plan from each student's results on assigned and Sample Tests. Students can clearly see which topics they have mastered—and more importantly, where they need remediation. The Study Plan links them to additional practice problems and tutorial help on those topics.

- **Unlimited Practice.** Study Plan exercises and instructor-assigned Homework problems provide students with valuable opportunities for practice and remediation. Each problem includes links to learning resources so that students can focus on the concepts they need to master.

- **Learning Resources.** Students can get help from a host of interactive, targeted resources. Links to eText pages secure the connection between online practice and key chapter concepts. MyEconLab also has a suite of graphing tools that help students draw and interpret graphs and chapter-specific, current news articles that tie economic concepts to everyday topics.

Problem Solving for Instructors

Instructors choose how much, or how little, energy they want to spend setting up the course and gain back precious time with MyEconLab's automatic grading. MyEconLab helps instructors track student performance and assess their progress by offering:

- **Graded Homework.** Instructors can create and assign tests, quizzes, or graded homework assignments.

- **Graded Graphing Problems.** MyEconLab can even grade assignments that require students to *draw* a graph.

- **Gradebook.** MyEconLab saves time by automatically grading all questions and tracking results in an online grade book.

- **Supplementary Questions.** The complete *Test Banks* are also preloaded into MyEconLab, giving instructors ample material from which they can create assignments.

- **Weekly News Updates.** Weekly news feeds with links to related Web sites, accompanied by homework and discussion questions, are provided and archived for use in class or as homework.

- **Teaching Resources.** Once registered for MyEconLab, instructors have access to downloadable supplements such as Instructor's Manuals, PowerPoint® lecture notes, and *Test Banks*.

For more information about MyEconLab or to request an Instructor Access Code, visit www.myeconlab.com or ask your local Prentice Hall representative.

▶ WHAT INSTRUCTOR'S SUPPLEMENTS DID WE DEVELOP?

A fully integrated teaching and learning package is necessary for today's classroom. Our supplement package helps you provide new and interesting real-world Applications and assess student understanding of economics. The supplements are coordinated with the main text through the numbering system of the headings in each section. The major sections of the chapters are numbered (1.1, 1.2, 1.3, and so on), and that numbering system is used consistently in the supplements to make it convenient and flexible for instructors to develop assignments.

Two Test Banks

Microeconomics, Fifth Edition, is supported by two comprehensive test-item files. To ensure the highest level of quality, an accuracy review board of 30 professors carefully examined each test bank question for accuracy, consistency with the text, a balance of difficulty level and question type, and overall functionality for the purpose of testing student knowledge of the material. Ben Paris, Prentice Hall's executive producer of assessment programs, provided the test bank authors with guidance on how to write effective questions.

Each test bank offers multiple-choice, true/false, and short-answer questions. The questions are referenced by topic and are presented in sequential order. Each question is keyed by degree of difficulty as *easy, moderate*, or *difficult*. Easy questions involve straightforward recall of information in the text. Moderate questions require some analysis on the student's part. Difficult questions usually entail more complex analysis and may require the student to go one step further than the material presented in the text. Questions are also classified as *fact, definition, conceptual*, and *analytical*. Fact questions test the student's knowledge of factual information presented in the text. Definition questions ask the student to define an economic concept. Conceptual questions test the student's understanding of a concept. Analytical questions require the student to apply an analytical procedure to answer the question.

The test banks include tables and a series of questions asking students to solve for numeric values, such as profit or equilibrium output. There are also numerous questions based on graphs: Several questions ask students to either interpret data presented in a graph, draw a graph on their own and answer related questions.

New to the fifth edition test banks are several questions that support the Applications in the main book. Each test bank chapter also includes a *new* Application based on a newspaper, journal, or online news story. There are also new questions to support the updated and new content in the main book.

Test Bank 1, prepared by James Swofford of the University of South Alabama, includes approximately 3,000 multiple-choice, true/false, short-answer, and graphing questions. Test Bank 2, prepared by Hadley Hartman of Santa Fe Community College, contains over 2,000 multiple-choice, true/false, and short-answer questions. Both test banks are available in a computerized format using TestGen-EQ test-generating software.

TestGen

Test Item Files 1 and 2 appear in print and as computer files that may be used with this Test-Gen test-generating software. This test-generating program permits instructors to edit, add, or delete questions from the test bank; analyze test results; and organize a database of tests and student results. This software allows for flexibility and ease of use. It provides many options for organizing and displaying tests, along with a search and sort feature.

Instructor's Manual

The Instructor's Manual, revised by Daniel Condon of Dominican University, follows the textbook's organization, incorporating Applications and questions. The manual also provides detailed outlines (suitable for use as lecture notes) and solutions to all questions in the textbook. The solutions were prepared by David Schutte of Mountain View College. The Instructor's Manual is also designed to help the instructor incorporate applicable elements of the supplement package. Each manual contains the following for each chapter:

- Summary: provides a bullet list of key topics in the chapter
- Approaching the Material: Student-friendly examples to introduce the chapter
  - Chapter Outline: Summary of definitions and concepts
  - Teaching Tips on how to encourage class participation
  - Summary and discussion points for the Applications in the main text
- New Applications and discussion questions
- Solutions to All End-of-Chapter Exercises

The Instructor's Manual is also available for download from the Instructor's Resource Center.

PowerPoint® Lecture Presentation

Prepared by Fernando and Yvonn Quijano, with assistants Kyle Thiel and Aparna Subramanian, the comprehensive set of PowerPoint® slides can be used by instructors for class presentations or by students for lecture preview or review. The set includes all the graphs, tables, and equations in the textbook. It displays figures two versions—in step-by-step mode so you can build graphs as you would on a blackboard and in an automated mode, using a single click per slide.

Instructors and students may download these PowerPoint® presentations from www.prenhall.com/osullivan.

Color Transparencies

All figures and tables from *Microeconomics* have been reproduced as full-page, four-color acetates.

Instructor's Resource Center on CD-ROM

The Test Banks, Instructor's Manual, and PowerPoint® are also available on this CD-ROM. With this new, highly accessible menu, faculty can easily customize presentations or build their own online courses. By simply clicking on a chapter or searching for a key word, they can access an interactive library of resources. Faculty can pick and choose from the various supplements and export them to their hard drive.

Instructor's Resource Center Online

This password-protected site is accessible from www.prenhall.com/osullivan and hosts all of the resources listed above: Test Banks, Instructor's Manual, and PowerPoint®. Instructors can click on the "Help downloading Instructor Resources" link for easy-to-follow instructions on getting access or contact their sales representative for further information.

Online Courses: Blackboard and WebCT

Prentice Hall offers fully customizable course content for the Blackboard and WebCT course management systems that include a link to the MyEconLab software hosting all of the course materials.

Classroom Response Systems

Classroom Response Systems (CRS) is an exciting new wireless polling technology that makes large and small classrooms even more interactive because it enables instructors to pose questions to their students, record results, and display those results instantly. Students can answer questions easily using compact remote-control transmitters. Prentice Hall has partnerships with leading classroom response systems providers and can show you everything you need to know about setting up and using a CRS system. We'll provide the classroom hardware, text-specific PowerPoint® slides, software, and support, and we'll also show you how your students can benefit! Learn more at www.prenhall.com/crs.

▶ WHAT STUDENT SUPPLEMENTS DID WE DEVELOP?

To accommodate different learning styles and busy student lifestyles, we provide a variety of print and online supplements.

Study Guide

The Study Guide, created by David Eaton of Murray State University, reinforces economic concepts and Applications from the main book and helps students assess their learning. Each chapter of the study guide includes the following features:

- Chapter Summary: Provides a summary of the chapter, key term definitions, and review of the Applications from the main book.
- Study Tip: Provides students with tips on understanding key concepts
- Key Equation(s): Alert students to equations they are likely to see throughout the class.
- Caution!: Alerts students about potential pitfalls and key figures or tables that deserve special attention.
- Practice Test: Includes approximately 25 multiple-choice questions and 10 true or false questions that help students test their knowledge. Some of these questions support the Applications in the main book. Select questions include a graph or table for students to analyze.
- Solutions to the Practice Test

The Companion Web Site (www.prenhall.com/osullivan).

This free Web site, www.prenhall.com/osullivan, gives students access to select solutions to end-of-chapter problems, an interactive study guide with instant feedback, economics updates, and student PowerPoint® slides to promote success in the principles of economics course.

SafariX WebBooks

SafariX WebBooks (online versions of the printed texts) will be available for students to purchase in lieu of a standard print text, without any modifications needed to how the instructor or professor teaches the course. Learn more at www.prenhall.com/safariX.

VangoNotes

Students can study on the go with VangoNotes—chapter reviews from the text in downloadable MP3 format from www.vangonotes.com. Now wherever students are— whatever they're doing—they can study by listening to the following for each chapter of the book:

- **Big Ideas.** The "need to know" for each chapter
- **Practice Tests.** A gut check for the Big Ideas—tells students if they need to keep studying
- **Key Terms.** Audio "flashcards" to help students review key concepts and terms
- **Rapid Review.** A quick drill session that students can use right before a test

VangoNotes are **flexible**. Students can download all the material directly to their MP3 player or only the chapters they need. VangoNotes are also **efficient**. Students can use them in the car, at the gym, walking to class, wherever they want to go.

 ## HOW CAN YOU KEEP UP-TO-DATE WITH THE NEWS?

Analyzing current events is an important skill for economic students to develop. To sharpen this skill and further support the book's Application theme, Prentice Hall offers you and your students three news subscription.

The *Wall Street Journal* Print and Interactive Editions Subscription

Prentice Hall has formed a strategic alliance with the *Wall Street Journal*, the most respected and trusted daily source for information on business and economics. For a small additional charge, Prentice Hall offers your students a 10- or 15-week subscription to the *Wall Street Journal* print edition and the *Wall Street Journal* interactive edition.

Upon adoption of a special package containing the book and the subscription booklet, professors will receive a free one-year subscription of the print and interactive versions as well as weekly subject-specific *Wall Street Journal* educators' lesson plans.

The Financial Times

We are pleased to announce a special partnership with *The Financial Times*. For a small additional charge, Prentice Hall offers your students a 15-week subscription to *The Financial Times*. Upon adoption of a special package containing the book and the subscription booklet, professors will receive a free one-year subscription. Please contact your Prentice Hall representative for details and ordering information.

Economist.com

Through a special arrangement with Economist.com, Prentice Hall offers your students a 12-week subscription to Economist.com for a small additional charge. Upon adoption of a special package containing the book and the subscription booklet, professors will receive a free six-month subscription. Please contact your Prentice Hall representative for further details and ordering information.

▶ ACCURACY BOARD, CONSULTANTS, AND REVIEWERS

A long road exists between the initial vision of an innovative principles text and the final product. Along our journey we participated in a structured process to reach our goal. We wish to acknowledge the assistance of the many people who participated in this process.

Accuracy Board

A dedicated team of economics professors checked the figures, equations, and text in the book and supplements package:

DIANE ANSTINE,
North Central College

LEN ANYANWU,
Union County College

BHARATI BASU,
Central Michigan University

JAMES BRUMBAUGH,
Lord Fairfax Community College

MICHAEL COHICK,
Collin County Community College

DAVID EATON,
Murray State University

HAROLD ELDER,
University of Alabama-Tuscaloosa

MICHAEL GOODE,
Central Piedmont Community College

WILLIAM HALLAGAN,
Washington State University

HADLEY HARTMAN,
Santa Fe Community College

MICHAEL G. HESLOP,
Northern Virginia Community College

TONY LIMA,
California State University, Easy Bay

SOLINA LINDAHL,
California Polytechnic State University-San Luis Obispo

MICHAEL MCILHON,
Century College

SHAH MEHRABI,
Montgomery College

GRETCHEN MESTER,
Anne Arundel Community College
RANDY METHENITIS,
Richland College
JOHN S. MIN,
Northern Virginia Community College
LYDIA ORTEGA,
Palo Alto College
DEBORAH PAIGE,
Santa Fe Community College
TIM PAYNE,
Shoreline Community College
STANLEY J. PETERS,
Southeast Community College
JOHN L. PISCIOTTA,
Baylor University
RATHA RAMOO,
Diablo Valley College
CRAIG ROGERS,
Canisius College
JOSEPH SANTOS,
South Dakota State University
STEVEN M. SCHAMBER,
St. Louis Community College, Meramec
DAVID SCHUTTE,
Mountain View College
JERRY SCHWARTZ,
Broward Community College
MOURAD SEBTI,
Central Texas College
PETER SHAW,
Tidewater Community College
ROBERT L. SHOFFNER, III
Central Piedmont Community College
LARRY SINGELL,
University of Oregon
ARLENA SULLIVAN,
Jones County Junior College
ERIC TAYLOR,
Central Piedmont Community College
KEITH ULRICH,
Valencia Community College
MICHAEL VARDANYAN,
Binghamton University
ROBERT WHAPLES,
Wake Forest University
MARK WEINSTOCK,
Pace University
WENDY WYSOCKI,
Monroe County Community College

 CONSULTANT BOARD

We received guidance on content, organization, figure treatment, and design from a dedicated Consultant Board:

GEOFFREY BLACK,
Boise State University
JEFF BOOKWALTER,
University of Montana
AMY CRAMER,
Pima Community College and University of Arizona
HERB ELLIOTT,
Allan Hancock College
HARRY ELLIS,
University of North Texas
WILLIAM HALLAGAN,
Washington State University
R. PETER PARCELLS,
Whitman College
TED SCHEINMAN,
Mount Hood Community College
DAVID SCHUTTE,
Mountain View College
PETER MARK SHAW,
Tidewater Community College

 **REVIEWERS OF THE CURRENT EDITION**

The guidance and recommendations from the following professors helped us develop the revision plans for this new edition:

California

ANTONIO AVALOS,
California State University, Fresno
PETER BOELMAN-LOPEZ,
Riverside Community College
PEGGY CRANE,
Southwestern College
JOSE L. ESTEBAN,
Palomar College
RATHA RAMOO,
Diablo Valley College
GREG ROSE,
Sacramento City College
E. B. GENDEL,
Woodbury University

Florida

ERIC CHIANG,
Florida Atlantic University

GEORGE GREENLEE,
St. Petersburg College, Clearwater

STEPHEN MORRELL,
Barry University

CARL SCHMERTMANN,
Florida State University

MICHAEL VIERK,
Florida International University

ANDREA ZANTER,
Hillsborough Community College

Georgia

ASHLEY HARMON,
Southeastern Technical College

Illinois

DIANE ANSTINE,
North Central College

ROSA LEA DANIELSON,
College of DuPage

CHUCK SICOTTE,
Rock Valley College

Iowa

SAUL MEKIES,
Kirkwood Community College, Iowa City

Maryland

GRETCHEN MESTER,
Anne Arundel Community College

Massachusetts

BRIAN DEURIARTE,
Middlesex Community College

MARLENE KIM,
University of Massachusetts, Boston

Michigan

BHARATI BASU,
Central Michigan University

SCANLON ROMER,
Delta College

WENDY WYSOCKI,
Monroe Community College

Minnesota

MIKE MCILHON,
Augsburg College

RICHARD MILANI,
Hibbing Community College

Mississippi

ARLENA SULLIVAN,
Jones County Junior College

Missouri

DENISE KUMMER,
St. Louis Community College

STEVEN M. SCHAMBER,
St. Louis Community College, Meramec

ELIAS SHUKRALLA,
St. Louis Community College, Meramec

KEITH ULRICH,
Webster University

Nebraska

THEODORE LARSEN,
University of Nebraska, Kearney

TIMOTHY R. MITTAN,
Southeast Community College

Nevada

CHARLES OKEKE,
College of Southern Nevada

New Jersey

LEN ANYANWU,
Union County College

RICHARD COMERFORD,
Bergen Community College

BRIAN DE URIARTE
Middlesex County College

New York

FARHAD AMEEN,
State University of New York, Westchester Community College

BARBARA CONNELLY,
Westchester Community College

SERGE S. GRUSHHCHIN,
ASA College of Advanced Technology

MARIE KRATOCHVIL,
Nassau Community College

CRAIG ROGERS,
Canisius College

MICHAEL VARDANYAN,
Binghamton University

North Carolina

MICHAEL G. GOODE,
Central Piedmont Community College

DIANE TYNDALL,
Craven Community College

Ohio

JEFF ANKROM,
Wittenberg University

Oregon

LARRY SINGELL,
University of Oregon

South Carolina

FRANK GARLAND,
Tri-County Technical College

WOODROW W. HUGHES, JR.
Converse College

Tennessee

NIRMALENDU DEBNATH,
Lane College

QUENTON PULLIAM,
Nashville State Technical College

ROSE RUBIN,
University of Memphis

Texas

JACK BUCCO,
Austin Community College

MICHAEL I. DUKE,
Blinn College

S. AUN HASSAN,
Texas Tech University

RANDY METHENITIS,
Richland College

LYDIA ORTEGA,
Palo Alto College

JOSHUA PICKRELL,
South Plains College

JOHN PISCIOTTA,
Baylor University

DAVE SHORROW,
Richland College

INSKE ZANDVLIET,
Brookhaven College

Utah

ALI HEKMAT,
College of Eastern Utah

Virginia

JAMES BRUMBAUGH,
Lord Fairfax Community College, Middleton Campus

MICHAEL HESLOP,
North Virginia Community College

GEORGE HOFFER,
Virginia Commonwealth University

JOHN MIN,
North Virginia Community College, Alexandria

SHANNON K. MITCHELL,
Virginia Commonwealth University

Washington

WILLIAM HALLAGAN,
Washington State University

MARK WYLIE,
Spokane Falls Community College

▶ REVIEWERS OF PREVIOUS EDITIONS

We benefited from the assistance of many dedicated professors who reviewed all or parts of previous editions in various stages of development:

Alabama

JAMES SWOFFORD,
University of South Alabama

Alaska

PAUL JOHNSON,
University of Alaska, Anchorage

Arizona

PETE MAVROKORDATOS,
Tarrant County College/University of Phoenix

EVAN TANNER,
Thunderbird, The American Graduate School of International Management

DONALD WELLS,
University of Arizona

California

COLLETTE BARR,
Santa Barbara Community College

MATTHEW BROWN,
Santa Clara University

PEGGY CRANE,
San Diego State University

ALBERT B. CULVER,
California State University, Chico

CHARLES W. HAASE,
San Francisco State University

JOHN HENRY,
California State University, Sacramento

GEORGE JENSEN,
California State University, Los Angeles

JANIS KEA,
West Valley College

ROSE KILBURN,
Modesto Junior College

PHILIP KING,
San Francisco State University

ANTHONY LIMA,
California State University, Hayward

BRET MCMURRAN,
Chaffey College

JON J. NADENICHEK,
California State University, Northridge

ALEX OBIYA,
San Diego City College

JACK W. OSMAN,
San Francisco State University

STEPHEN PEREZ,
California State University, Sacramento

KURT SCHWABE,
University of California, Riverside

TERRI SEXTON,
California State University, Sacramento

XIAOCHUAN SONG,
San Diego Mesa College

ED SORENSEN,
San Francisco State University

RODNEY SWANSON,
University of California, Los Angeles

DANIEL VILLEGAS,
California Polytechnic State University

Connecticut

JOHN A. JASCOT,
Capital Community Technical College

Delaware

LAWRENCE STELMACH,
Delaware Valley College

Florida

IRMA DE ALONSO,
Florida International University

JAY BHATTACHARYA,
Okaloosa-Walton Community College

EDWARD BIERHANZL,
Florida A&M University

MARTINE DUCHATELET,
Barry University

MARTIN MARKOVICH,
Florida A&M University

THOMAS MCCALEB,
Florida State University

GARVIN SMITH,
Daytona Beach Community College

NOEL SMITH,
Palm Beach Community College

VIRGINIA YORK,
Gulf Coast Community College

Georgia

STEVEN F. KOCH,
Georgia Southern University

L. WAYNE PLUMLY, JR.,
Valdosta State University

GREG TRANDEL,
University of Georgia

Hawaii

BARBARA ROSS-PFEIFFER,
Kapiolani Community College

Idaho

CHARLES SCOTT BENSON JR.,
Idaho State University

TESA STEGNER,
Idaho State University

Illionois

SEL DIBOOGLU,
Southern Illinois University

LINDA GHENT,
Eastern Illinois University

GARY LANGER,
Roosevelt University

NAMPEANG PINGKARAWAT,
Chicago State University

DENNIS SHANNON,
Belleville Area College

Indiana

JOHN L. CONANT,
Indiana State University

MOUSUMI DUTTARAY,
Indiana State University

JAMES T. KYLE,
Indiana State University

VIRGINIA SHINGLETON,
Valparaiso University

Iowa

JONATHAN O. IKOBA,
Scott Community College

Kansas

CARL PARKER,
Fort Hays State University

JAMES RAGAN,
Kansas State University

TRACY M. TURNER,
Kansas State University

Kentucky

DAVID EATON,
Murray State University

JOHN ROBERTSON,
University of Kentucky

Louisiana

JOHN PAYNE BIGELOW,
Louisiana State University

SANG LEE,
Southeastern Louisiana University

RICHARD STAHL,
Louisiana State University

Maine

GEORGE SCHATZ,
Maine Maritime Academy

Maryland

IRVIN WEINTRAUB,
Towson State University

Massachusetts

DAN GEORGIANNA,
University of Massachusetts, Dartmouth

JAMES E. HARTLEY,
Mount Holyoke College

MARK SIEGLER,
Williams College

GILBERT WOLFE,
Middlesex Community College

Michigan

CHRISTINE AMSLER,
Michigan State University

NORMAN CURE,
Macomb Community College

SUSAN LINZ,
Michigan State University

ROBERT TANSKY,
St. Clair County Community College

Missouri

DUANE EBERHARDT,
Missouri Southern State College

DAVID GILLETTE,
Truman State University

BRAD HOPPES,
Southwest Missouri State University

Nebraska

STANLEY J. PETERS,
Southeast Community College

BROCK WILLIAMS,
Metropolitan Community College

Nevada

STEPHEN MILLER,
University of Nevada, Las Vegas

New Jersey

JOHN GRAHAM,
Rutgers University

PAUL C. HARRIS, JR.,
Camden County College

CALVIN HOY,
County College of Morris

TAGHI RAMIN,
William Paterson University

New Mexico

CARL ENOMOTO,
New Mexico State University

New York

KARIJIT K. ARORA,
Le Moyne College

ALEX AZARCHS,
Pace University

KATHLEEN K. BROMLEY,
Monroe Community College

SUSAN GLANZ,
St. John's University

ROBERT HERMAN,
Nassau Community College

MARIANNE LOWERY,
Erie Community College

JEANNETTE MITCHELL,
Rochester Institute of Technology

TED MUZIO,
St. John's University

FRED TYLER,
Fordham University

North Carolina

KATIE CANTY,
Cape Fear Community College

LEE CRAIG,
North Carolina State University

HOSSEIN GHOLAMI,
Fayetteville Technical Community College

CHARLES M. OLDHAM, JR.,
Fayetteville Technical Community College

RANDALL PARKER,
East Carolina University

CHESTER WATERS,
Durham Technical Community College

JAMES WHEELER,
North Carolina State University

North Dakota

SCOTT BLOOM,
North Dakota State University

Ohio

FATMA ABDEL-RAOUF,
Cleveland State University

TAGHI T. KERMANI,
Youngstown State University

Oklahoma

JEFF HOLT,
Tulsa Community College

MARTY LUDLUM,
Oklahoma City Community College

DAN RICKMAN,
Oklahoma State University

Oregon

TOM CARROLL,
Central Oregon Community College

JOHN FARRELL,
Oregon State University

DAVID FIGLIO,
University of Oregon

RANDY R. GRANT,
Linfield College

Pennsylvania

KEVIN A. BAIRD,
Montgomery County Community College

ED COULSON,
Pennsylvania State University

TAHANY NAGGAR,
West Chester University

ABDULWAHAB SRAIHEEN,
Kutztown University

South Carolina

DONALD BALCH,
University of South Carolina

CALVIN BLACKWELL,
College of Charleston

JANICE BOUCHER BREUER,
University of South Carolina

CHARLOTTE DENISE HIXSON,
Midlands Technical College

MIREN IVANKOVIC,
Southern Wesleyan University

CHIRINJEV PETERSON,
Greenville Technical College

DENISE TURNAGE,
Midlands Technical College

CHAD TURNER,
Clemson University

South Dakota

JOSEPH SANTOS,
South Dakota State University

Texas

RASHID AL-HMOUD,
Texas Technical University

MAHAMUDU BAWUMIA,
Baylor University

CINDY CANNON,
North Harris College

DAVID L. COBERLY,
Southwest Texas State University

GHAZI DUWAJI,
University of Texas, Arlington

HARRY ELLIS,
University of North Texas

THOMAS JEITSCHKO,
Texas A&M University

JESSICA McCRAW,
University of Texas, Arlington

WILLIAM NEILSON,
Texas A&M University

MICHAEL NELSON,
Texas A&M University

PAUL OKELLO,
University of Texas, Arlington

JAMES R. VANBEEK,
Blinn College

Utah

LOWELL GLENN,
Utah Valley State College

Virginia

BRUCE BRUNTON,
James Madison University

MELANIE MARKS,
Longwood College

THOMAS J. MEEKS,
Virginia State University

Australia

HAK YOUN KIM,
Monash University

 ## CLASS TESTERS

A special acknowledgment goes to the instructors who were willing to class-test drafts of early editions in different stages of development. They provided us with instant feedback on parts that worked and parts that needed changes:

SHERYL BALL,
Virginia Polytechnic Institute and State University

JOHN CONSTANTINE,
University of California, Davis

JOHN FARRELL,
Oregon State University

JAMES HARTLEY,
Mt. Holyoke College

KAILASH KHANDKE,
Furman College

PETER LINDERT,
University of California, Davis

LOUIS MAKOWSKI,
University of California, Davis

BARBARA ROSS-PFEIFFER,
Kapiolani Community College

Our greatest appreciation goes out to Carlos Aguilar and his economics students from El Paso Community College, who gave us their feedback and evaluations with comparable textbooks. The students provided us with positive feedback and constructive criticism that helped us prepare the third edition:

ERIK ACONA

ERICA AVILA

JAIME BERMUDEZ

ISRAEL CASTILLO

MARIBELL CASTILLO

SARAH DAVIS

REBEKAH DENNIS

MICHELE DONOHOE

EMMANUEL ECK

PATRICK ESPINOZA

EDWARD ESTRADA

KIM GARDNER

ALEISA GARZA

DANIEL HEITZ

LAURA HEREBIA

HILDA HOWARD

MELANIE JOHNSON

BRENDA JORDAN

EUGENE JORDAN

VANESSA LARA

HARMONY LOPEZ

STACEY LUCAS

MARIA LYNCH

SINDY MCELVANY

ROGER MITCHELL

BENNY ONTIVEROS

LOUIE ORTEGA

KAREN SEITZ

ANA SMITH

BEVERLY STEPHENS

ADRIAN TERRAZAS

CHRIS WRIGHT

▶ **FOCUS GROUPS**

We want to thank the participants who took part in the focus groups for the first and second editions; they helped us see the manuscript from a fresh perspective:

CARLOS AQUILAR,
El Paso Community College

JIM BRADLEY,
University of South Carolina

THOMAS COLLUM,
Northeastern Illinois University

DAVID CRAIG,
Westark College

JEFF HOLT,
Tulsa Junior College

THOMAS JEITSCHKO,
Texas A & M University

GARY LANGER,
Roosevelt University

MARK MCCLEOD,
Virginia Polytechnic Institute and State University

TOM MCKINNON,
University of Arkansas

AMY MEYERS,
Parkland Community College

HASSAN MOHAMMADI,
Illinois State University

JOHN MORGAN,
College of Charleston

NORM PAUL,
San Jancinto Community College

NAMPEANG PINGKARATWAT,
Chicago State University

SCANLAN ROMER,
Delta Community College

BARBARA ROSS-PFEIFFER,
Kapiolani Community College

ZAHRA SADERION,
Houston Community College

VIRGINIA SHINGLETON,
Valparaiso University

JIM SWOFFORD,
University of South Alabama

JANET WEST,
University of Nebraska–Omaha

LINDA WILSON,
University of Texas–Arlington

MICHAEL YOUNGBLOOD,
Rock Valley Community College

A WORLD OF THANKS . . .

We would also like to acknowledge the team of dedicated authors who contributed to the various ancillaries that accompany this book: Daniel Condon of Dominican University, David Eaton of Murray State University, Hadley Hartman of Santa Fe Community College, Randy Methenitis of Richland College, David Schutte of Mountain View College, James Swofford of the University of South Alabama, and Fernando Quijano of Dickinson State University.

For the Fifth Edition, Suzanne Grappi and Maria Lange turned our manuscript pages into a beautifully published book. Ben Paris, executive producer of assessment programs, critiqued the test-item files and helped the supplement authors improve the quality of those supplements. Karen Misler coordinated the extensive supplement package that accompanies this book. We want to single out two people for special mention. Our development editor, Lena Buonanno, did a terrific job identifying parts of the book that could be improved for the fifth edition, and had many suggestions on how to improve it. Finally, we are indebted to David Alexander, executive editor at Prentice Hall, who guided the project from start to finish.

From the start, Prentice Hall provided us with first-class support and advice. Over the first four editions, many people contributed to the project, including Leah Jewell, Rod Banister, P. J. Boardman, Marie McHale, Gladys Soto, Lisa Amato, Victoria Anderson, Cynthia Regan, Kathleen McLellan, Sharon Koch, David Theisen, Steve Deitmer, and Christopher Bath.

Last but not least, we must thank our families, who have seen us disappear, sometimes physically and other times mentally, to spend hours wrapped up in our own world of principles of economics. A project of this magnitude is very absorbing, and our families have been particularly supportive in this endeavor.

ARTHUR O'SULLIVAN

STEVEN SHEFFRIN

STEPHEN PEREZ

1

Introduction: What Is Economics?

Economics is the science of choice, exploring the choices made by individuals and organizations. Over the last few centuries, these choices have led to substantial gains in the standard of living around the globe. The typical American household today has roughly seven times the income and purchasing power of a household 100 years ago. Our prosperity is the result of choices made by all sorts of people, including inventors, workers, entrepreneurs, and the people who saved money and loaned it to others to invest in machines and other tools of production. One reason we have prospered is greater efficiency: We have discovered better ways to use our resources—raw materials, time, and energy—to produce the goods and services we value.

As an illustration of changes in the standard of living and our growing prosperity, let's compare the way people listened to music in 1891 with how we listen today. You can buy an iPod nano for $199 and fill it with 1,000 songs at $0.99 each. If you earn a wage of $15 per hour, it would take you about 80 hours of work to earn enough money to purchase and then fill an iPod. Back in 1891, the latest technological marvel was Thomas Edison's cylinder phonograph, which played music recorded on 4-inch cylinders. Imagine that you lived back then and wanted to get just as much music as you could fit on an iPod. Given the wages and prices in 1891, it would take you roughly 800 hours of work to earn enough money to buy the phonograph and all the cylinders. And if you wanted to keep your music with you, you would need 14 backpacks to carry all the cylinders.

Although prosperity and efficiency are widespread, they are not universal. In some parts of the world, many people live in poverty. For example, in sub-Saharan Africa 290 million people—almost half the population—live on less than $1 per day. And in all nations of the world, inefficiencies still exist, with valuable resources being wasted. For example, each year the typical urban commuter in the United States wastes more than 47 hours and $84 worth of gasoline trapped in rush hour traffic.

• **scarcity**
The resources we use to produce goods and services are limited.

• **economics**
The study of choices when there is scarcity.

• **factors of production**
The resources used to produce goods and services; also known as *production inputs*.

• **natural resources**
Resources provided by nature and used to produce goods and services.

• **labor**
The physical and mental effort people use to produce goods and services.

• **physical capital**
The stock of equipment, machines, structures, and infrastructure that is used to produce goods and services.

• **human capital**
The knowledge and skills acquired by a worker through education and experience.

• **entrepreneurship**
The effort used to coordinate the factors of production—natural resources, labor, physical capital, and human capital—to produce and sell products.

Economics provides a framework to diagnose all sorts of problems faced by society and then helps create and evaluate various proposals to solve them. Economics can help us develop strategies to replace poverty with prosperity, and to replace waste with efficiency. In this chapter, we explain what economics is and how we all can use economic analysis to think about practical problems and solutions.

1.1 | WHAT IS ECONOMICS?

Economists use the word **scarcity** to convey the idea that resources—the things we use to produce goods and services—are limited, while human wants are unlimited. Therefore, we cannot produce everything that everyone wants. In the words of the Rolling Stones, "You can't always get what you want." **Economics** studies the choices we make when there is scarcity; it is all about trade-offs. Here are some examples of scarcity and the trade-offs associated with making choices:

• You have a limited amount of time. If you take a part-time job, each hour on the job means one less hour for study or play.

• A city has a limited amount of land. If the city uses an acre of land for a park, it has one less acre for housing, retailers, or industry.

• You have limited income this year. If you spend $17 on a music CD, that's $17 less you have to spend on other products or to save.

People produce goods (music CDs, houses, and parks) and services (the advice of physicians and lawyers) by using one or more of the following five **factors of production**, or *production inputs*, or simply *resources*:

• **Natural resources** are provided by nature. Some examples are fertile land, mineral deposits, oil and gas deposits, and water. Some economists refer to all types of natural resources as *land*.

• **Labor** is the physical and mental effort people use to produce goods and services.

• **Physical capital** is the stock of equipment, machines, structures, and infrastructure that is used to produce goods and services. Some examples are forklifts, machines, computers, factories, airports, roads, and fiber-optic cables.

• **Human capital** is the knowledge and skills acquired by a worker through education and experience. Every job requires some human capital: To be a surgeon, you must learn anatomy and acquire surgical skills. To be an accountant, you must learn the rules of accounting and acquire computer skills. To be a musician, you must learn to play an instrument.

• **Entrepreneurship** is the effort used to coordinate the factors of production—natural resources, labor, physical capital, and human capital—to produce and sell products. An entrepreneur comes up with an idea for a product, decides how to produce it, and raises the funds to bring it to the market. Some examples of entrepreneurs are Bill Gates of Microsoft, Steve Jobs of Apple Computer, Inc., Howard Schultz of Starbucks, and McDonald's founder Ray Kroc.

Given our limited resources, we make our choices in a variety of ways. Sometimes we make our decisions as individuals, and other times we participate in collective decision making, allowing the government and other organizations to choose for us. Many of our choices happen within *markets*, institutions or arrangements that enable us to buy and sell things. For example, most of us participate in the labor market, exchanging our time for money, and we all participate in consumer markets, exchanging money for food and clothing. But we make other choices outside markets—from our personal decisions about everyday life to our political choices about matters that concern society as a whole. What unites all these decisions is the notion of scarcity: We can't have it all; there are trade-offs.

Economists are always reminding us that there is scarcity—that there are trade-offs in everything we do. Suppose that in a conversation with your economics instructor you share your enthusiasm about an upcoming launch of the space shuttle. The economist may tell you that the resources used for the shuttle could have been used instead for an unmanned mission to Mars.

By introducing the notion of scarcity into your conversation, your instructor is simply reminding you that there are trade-offs, that one thing (a shuttle mission) is sacrificed for another (a Mars mission). Talking about alternatives is the first step in a process that can help us make better choices about how to use our resources. For example, we could compare the scientific benefits of a shuttle mission to the benefits of a Mars mission and choose the mission with the greater benefit.

Positive Versus Normative Analysis

Economics doesn't tell us what to choose—shuttle mission or Mars mission—but simply helps us to understand the trade-offs. President Harry S. Truman once remarked,

> All my economists say, "On the one hand, . . .; On the other hand, . . ." Give me a one-handed economist!

An economist might say, "On the one hand, we could use a shuttle mission to do more experiments in the gravity-free environment of Earth's orbit; on the other hand, we could use a Mars mission to explore the possibility of life on other planets." In using both hands, the economist is not being evasive, but simply doing economics, discussing the alternative uses of our resources. The ultimate decision about how to use our resources—shuttle mission or Mars exploration—is the responsibility of citizens or their elected officials.

Most modern economics is based on **positive analysis**, which predicts the consequences of alternative actions by answering the question "What *is*?" or "What *will be*?" A second type of economic reasoning is normative in nature. **Normative analysis** answers the question "What *ought to be*?"

In Table 1.1, we compare positive questions to normative questions. Normative questions lie at the heart of policy debates. Economists contribute to policy debates by conducting positive analyses of the consequences of alternative actions. For example, an economist could predict the effects of an increase in the minimum wage on the number of people employed nationwide, the income of families with minimum-wage workers, and consumer prices. Armed with the conclusions of the

- **positive analysis**
  Answers the question "What is?" or "What will be?"

- **normative analysis**
  Answers the question "What *ought to be*?"

Table 1.1 | COMPARING POSITIVE AND NORMATIVE QUESTIONS

Positive Questions	Normative Questions
• If the government increases the minimum wage, how many workers will lose their jobs?	• Should the government increase the minimum wage?
• If two office-supply firms merge, will the price of office supplies increase?	• Should the government block the merger of two office-supply firms?
• How does a college education affect a person's productivity and earnings?	• Should the government subsidize a college education?
• How do consumers respond to a cut in income taxes?	• Should the government cut taxes to stimulate the economy?
• If a nation restricts shoe imports, who benefits and who bears the cost?	• Should the government restrict imports?

economist's positive analysis, citizens and policy makers could then make a normative decision about whether to increase the minimum wage. Similarly, an economist could study the projects that could be funded with $1 billion in foreign aid, predicting the effects of each project on the income per person in an African country. Armed with this positive analysis, policy makers could then decide which projects to support.

Economists don't always reach the same conclusions in their positive analyses. The disagreements often concern the magnitude of a particular effect. For example, most economists agree that an increase in the minimum wage will cause unemployment, but there is disagreement about how many people would lose their jobs. Similarly, economists agree that spending money to improve the education system in Africa will increase productivity and income, but there is disagreement about the size of the increase in income.

The Three Key Economic Questions: What, How, and Who?

Economic decisions are made at every level in society. Individuals decide what products to buy, what occupations to pursue, and how much money to save. Firms decide what goods and services to produce and how to produce them. Governments decide what projects and programs to complete and how to pay for them. The choices made by individuals, firms, and governments answer three questions:

1 *What products do we produce?* Trade-offs exist: If a hospital uses its resources to perform more heart transplants, it has fewer resources to care for premature infants.

2 *How do we produce the products?* Alternative means of production are available: Power companies can produce electricity with coal, natural gas, or wind power. Professors can teach in large lecture halls or small classrooms.

3 *Who consumes the products?* We must decide how the products of society are distributed. If some people earn more money than others, should they consume more goods? How much money should the government take from the rich and give to the poor?

As we'll see later in the book, most of these decisions are made in markets, with prices playing a key role in determining what products we produce, how we produce them, and who gets the products. In Chapter 3, we'll examine the role of markets in modern economies and the role of government in market-based economies.

Economic Models

Economists use *economic models* to explore the choices people make and the consequences of those choices. An economic model is a simplified representation of an economic environment, with all but the essential features of the environment eliminated. An **economic models** is an abstraction from reality that enables us to focus our attention on what really matters. As we'll see throughout the book, most economic models use graphs to represent the economic environment.

To see the rationale for economic modeling, consider an architectural model. An architect builds a scale model of a new building and uses the model to show how the building will fit on a plot of land and blend with nearby buildings. The model shows the exterior features of the building, but not the interior features. We can ignore the interior features because they are unimportant for the task at hand—seeing how the building will fit into the local environment.

Economists build models to explore decision making by individuals, firms, and other organizations. For example, we can use a model of a profit-maximizing firm to predict how a firm will respond to increased competition. If a new car-stereo

• **economic model**
A simplified representation of an economic environment, often employing a graph.

store opens up in your town, will the old firms be passive and simply accept smaller market shares, or will they aggressively cut their prices to try to drive the new rival out of business? The model of the firm includes the monetary benefits and costs of doing business, and assumes that firms want to make as much money as possible. Although there may be other motives in the business world—to have fun or help the world—the economic model ignores these other motives. The model focuses our attention on the profit motive and how it affects a firm's response to increased competition.

1.2 | ECONOMIC ANALYSIS AND MODERN PROBLEMS

Economic analysis provides important insights into real-world problems. To explain how we can use economic analysis in problem solving, we provide three examples. You'll see these examples again in more detail later in the book.

Economic View of Traffic Congestion

Consider first the problem of traffic congestion. According to the Texas Transportation Institute, the typical U.S. commuter wastes about 47 hours per year because of traffic congestion.[1] In some cities, the time wasted by the typical commuter is much greater: 93 hours in Los Angeles, 72 hours in San Francisco, and 63 hours in Houston. In addition to time lost, we also waste 2.3 billion gallons of gasoline and diesel fuel each year.

To an economist, the diagnosis of the congestion problem is straightforward. When you drive onto a busy highway during rush hour, your car takes up space and decreases the distance between the vehicles on the highway. The normal reaction to a shorter distance between moving cars is to slow down. So when you enter the highway, you force other commuters to spend more time on the highway. If each of your 900 fellow commuters spends just 2 extra seconds on the highway, you will increase the total travel time by 30 minutes. In deciding whether to use the highway, you will presumably ignore these costs that you impose on others. Similarly, your fellow commuters ignore the cost they impose on you and others when they enter the highway. Because no single commuter pays the full cost, too many people use the highway, and everyone wastes time.

One possible solution to the congestion problem is to force people to pay for using the road, just as they pay for gasoline and tires. The government could impose a congestion tax of $8 per trip on rush-hour commuters and use a debit card system to collect the tax: Every time a car passes a checkpoint, a transponder would charge the commuter's card. Traffic volume during rush hours would then decrease as travelers (a) shift their travel to off-peak times, (b) switch to ride sharing and mass transit, and (c) shift their travel to less congested routes. The job for the economist is to compute the appropriate congestion tax and predict the consequences of imposing the tax.

Economic View of Poverty in Africa

Consider next the issue of poverty in Africa. In the final two decades of the twentieth century, the world economy grew rapidly, and the average per capita income (income per person) increased by about 35 percent. By contrast, the economies of poverty-stricken sub-Saharan Africa shrank, and per capita income decreased by about 6 percent. Africa is the world's second-largest continent in both area and population and accounts for more than 12 percent of the world's human population. Figure 1.1 shows a map of Africa. The countries of sub-Saharan Africa are highlighted in yellow.

► **FIGURE 1.1**
Map of Africa
Africa is the world's second-largest continent in both area and population, and
accounts for more than 12 percent of the
world's human population. The countries
of sub-Saharan Africa are highlighted in
yellow.
*SOURCE: web.worldbank.org/WBSITE/
EXTERNAL/COUNTRIES/AFRICA*

Sub-Saharan
Africa

Economists have found that as a nation's economy grows, its poorest households
share in the general prosperity.[2] Therefore, one way to reduce poverty in sub-Saharan
Africa would be to increase economic growth. Economic growth occurs when a country expands its production facilities (machinery and factories), improves its public
infrastructure (highways and water systems), widens educational opportunities, and
adopts new technology.

The recent experience of sub-Saharan Africa is somewhat puzzling because in
the last few decades the region has expanded educational opportunities and
received large amounts of foreign aid. Some recent work by economists on the
sources of growth suggests that institutions such as the legal system and the regulatory environment play key roles in economic growth.[3] In sub-Saharan Africa, a
simple legal dispute about a small debt takes about 30 months to resolve, compared
to five months in the United States. In Mozambique, it takes 174 days to complete
the procedures required to set up a business, compared to just two days in Canada.
In many cases, institutions impede rather than encourage the sort of investment
and risk taking—entrepreneurship—that causes economic growth and reduces
poverty. As a consequence, economists and policy makers are exploring ways to
reform the region's institutions. They are also challenged with choosing among
development projects that will generate the biggest economic boost per dollar
spent—the biggest bang per buck.

Economic View of Japan's Economic Problems

Consider next the economic problems experienced by Japan in the last decade. Following World War II, Japan grew rapidly, with per capita income increasing by about
4 percent per year between 1950 and 1992. But in 1992, the economy came to a
screeching halt. For the next 10 years, per capita income either decreased or
increased slightly. In 1995, the prices of all sorts of goods—including consumer
goods and housing—actually started to decrease, and the downward slide continued
for years. In an economy with declining prices, consumers expect lower prices
tomorrow, so they are reluctant to buy goods and services today. Business managers

are reluctant to borrow money to invest in production facilities, because if the prices of their products drop they might not have enough money to repay the loans.

The challenge for economists was to develop a set of policies to get the Japanese economy moving again. Economists responded by designing policies to stimulate spending by consumers and businesses and to make needed changes to the Japanese financial system. Although it was a slow process, economic and political reforms have put the Japanese economy on a sound footing that will support future economic growth.

1.3 | THE ECONOMIC WAY OF THINKING

How do economists think about problems and decision making? The economic way of thinking is best summarized by British economist John Maynard Keynes (1883–1946)[4]:

> The theory of economics does not furnish a body of settled conclusions immediately applicable to policy. It is a method rather than a doctrine, an apparatus of the mind, a technique of thinking which helps its possessor draw correct conclusions.

Let's look at the four elements of the economic way of thinking.

1. Use Assumptions to Simplify

Economists use assumptions to make things simpler and focus attention on what really matters. If you use a road map to plan a car trip from Seattle to San Francisco, you make two unrealistic assumptions to simplify your planning:

- The earth is flat: The flat road map doesn't show the curvature of the earth.
- The roads are flat: The standard road map doesn't show hills and valleys.

Instead of a map, you could use a globe that shows all the topographical features between Seattle and San Francisco, but you don't need those details to plan your trip. A map, with its unrealistic assumptions, will suffice, because the curvature of the earth and the topography of the highways are irrelevant to your trip. Although your analysis of the road trip is based on two unrealistic assumptions, that does not mean your analysis is invalid. Similarly, if economic analysis is based on unrealistic assumptions, that doesn't mean the analysis is faulty.

What if you decide to travel by bike instead of by automobile? Now the assumption of flat roads really matters, unless of course you are eager to pedal up and down mountains. If you use a standard map, and thus assume there are no mountains between the two cities, you may inadvertently pick a mountainous route instead of a flat one. In this case, the simplifying assumption makes a difference. The lesson is that we must think carefully about whether a simplifying assumption is truly harmless.

2. Isolate Variables—*Ceteris Paribus*

Economic analysis often involves *variables* and how they affect one another. A **variable** is a measure of something that can take on different values. Economists are interested in exploring relationships between two variables—for example, the relationship between the price of apples and the quantity of apples consumers purchase. Of course, the quantity of apples purchased depends on many other variables, including the consumer's income. To explore the relationship between the quantity and price of apples, we must assume that the consumer's income—and anything else that influences apple purchases—doesn't change.

• **variable**
A measure of something that can take on different values.

- **ceteris paribus**
  The Latin expression meaning other variables being held fixed.

Alfred Marshall (1842–1924) was a British economist who refined the economic model of supply and demand and provided a label for this process.[5] He picked one variable that affected apple purchases (price) and threw the other variable (income) into what he called the "pound" (in Marshall's time, the "pound" was an enclosure for holding stray cattle; nowadays, a pound is for stray dogs). That variable waited in the pound while Marshall examined the influence of the first variable. Marshall labeled the pound **ceteris paribus**, the Latin expression meaning that other variables are held fixed:

> . . . the existence of other tendencies is not denied, but their disturbing effect is neglected for a time. The more the issue is narrowed, the more exactly can it be handled.

This book contains many statements about the relationship between two variables. For example, the quantity of computers produced by Dell depends on the price of computers, the wage of computer workers, and the cost of microchips. When we say, "An increase in the price of computers increases the quantity of computers produced," we are assuming that the other two variables—the wage and the cost of microchips—do not change. That is, we apply the *ceteris paribus* assumption.

3. Think at the Margin

- **marginal change**
  A small, one-unit change in value.

Economists often consider how a small change in one variable affects another variable and what impact that has on people's decision making. In other words, if circumstances change only slightly, how will people respond? A small, one-unit change in value is called a **marginal change**. The key feature of marginal change is that the first variable changes by only one unit. For example, you might ask, "If I study just one more hour, by how much will my exam score increase?" Economists call this process "thinking at the margin." Thinking at the margin is like thinking on the edge. You will encounter marginal thinking throughout this book. Here are some other marginal questions:

- If I study one more hour for an exam, by how much will my grade increase?
- If I stay in school and earn another degree, by how much will my lifetime earnings increase?
- If a car dealer hires one more sales associate, how many more cars will the dealer sell?

As we'll see in the next chapter, economists use the answer to a marginal question as a first step in deciding whether to do more or less of something.

4. Rational People Respond to Incentives

A key assumption of most economic analysis is that people act rationally, meaning that they act in their own self-interest. Scottish philosopher Adam Smith (1723–1790), who is also considered the founder of economics, wrote that he discovered within humankind:[6]

> a desire of bettering our condition, a desire which, though generally calm and dispassionate, comes with us from the womb, and never leaves us until we go to the grave.

Smith didn't say that people are motivated exclusively by self-interest, but rather that self-interest is more powerful than kindness or altruism. In this book, we will assume that people act in their own self-interest. Rational people respond to incentives. When the payoff, or benefit, from doing something changes, people change their behavior to get the benefit.

APPLICATION

PEDALING FOR TELEVISION TIME

APPLYING THE CONCEPTS #1: Do people respond to incentives?

To illustrate the notion that people are rational and respond to incentives, consider an experiment conducted by researchers at St. Luke's Roosevelt Hospital in New York City. The researchers addressed the following question: If a child must pedal a stationary bicycle to run a television set, will he watch less TV? The researchers randomly assigned obese children, ages 8 to 12, to two types of TVs. The first type of TV had a stationary bicycle in front of it, but the TV operated independently of the bicycle: No pedaling was required to operate the TV. In contrast, the second type of TV worked only if the child pedaled a bike facing the TV. The kids in the control group (no pedaling required) watched an average of 21 hours of TV per week, while the kids in the treatment group (pedaling required) watched only 2 hours per week. In other words, kids respond to incentives, watching less TV when the cost of watching is higher.
Related to Exercise 3.4.

SOURCE: Myles Faith et al., "Effects of Contingent Television on Physical Activity and Television Viewing in Obese Children," *Pediatrics*, vol. 107, May 2001, pp. 1043–1048; Nanci Hellmich, "Pedaling a Solution for Couch-Potato Kids," *USA Today*, April 19, 1999, p. 1.

1.4 | PREVIEW OF COMING ATTRACTIONS: MACROECONOMICS

The field of economics is divided into two categories: macroeconomics and microeconomics. **Macroeconomics** is the study of the nation's economy as a whole; it focuses on the issues of inflation, unemployment, and economic growth. These issues are regularly discussed on Web sites, in newspapers, and on television. Macroeconomics explains why economies grow and change and why economic growth is sometimes interrupted. Let's look at three ways we can use macroeconomics.

• **macroeconomics**
The study of the nation's economy as a whole; focuses on the issues of inflation, unemployment, and economic growth.

To Understand Why Economies Grow

As we discussed earlier in the chapter, the world economy has been growing in recent decades, with per capita income increasing by about 1.5 percent per year. Increases in income translate into a higher standard of living for consumers—better cars, houses, and clothing and more options for food, entertainment, and travel. People in a growing economy can consume more of all goods and services because the economy has more of the resources needed to produce these products. Macroeconomics explains why some of these resources increase over time and how an increase in resources translates into a higher standard of living. Let's look at a practical question about economic growth.

2

APPLICATION

LONDON SOLVES ITS CONGESTION PROBLEM

APPLYING THE CONCEPTS #2: What is the role of prices in allocating resources?

To illustrate the economic way of thinking, let's consider again how an economist would approach the problem of traffic congestion. Recall that each driver on the highway slows down other drivers but ignores these time costs when deciding whether to use the highway. If the government imposes a congestion tax to reduce congestion during rush hour, the question for the economist is: How high should the tax be?

To determine the appropriate congestion tax, an economist would assume that people respond to incentives and use the three other elements of the economic way of thinking:

- **Use assumptions to simplify.** To simplify the problem, we would assume that every car has the same effect on the travel time of other cars. Of course, this is unrealistic, because people drive cars of different sizes in different ways. But the alternative—looking at the effects of each car on travel speeds—would needlessly complicate the analysis.

- **Isolate variables—*ceteris paribus*.** To focus attention on the effects of a congestion tax on the number of cars using the highway, we would make the *ceteris paribus* assumption that everything else that affects travel behavior—the price of gasoline, bus fares, and consumer income—remains fixed.

- **Think at the margin.** To think at the margin, we would estimate the effects of adding one more car to the highway. The marginal question is: If we add one more car to the highway, by how much does the total travel time for commuters increase?

Once we answer this question, we could determine the cost imposed by the marginal driver. If the marginal driver forces each of the 900 commuters to spend two extra seconds on the highway, total travel time increases by 30 minutes. If the value of time is, say, $16 per hour, the appropriate congestion tax would be $8.

If the idea of charging people for using roads seems odd, consider the city of London, which for decades had experienced the worst congestion in Europe. In February 2003, the city imposed an $8 tax per day to drive in the city between 7:00 A.M. and 6:30 P.M. The tax reduced traffic volume and cut travel times for cars and buses in half. The congestion tax reduced the waste and inefficiency of congestion, and the city's economy thrived. Given the success of London's ongoing congestion tax, other cities, including Toronto, Singapore, and San Diego, have implemented congestion pricing. *Related to Exercise 3.5.*

Why do some countries grow much faster than others? Between 1960 and 2001, the economic growth rate was 2.2 percent per year in the United States, compared to 2.3 percent in Mexico and 2.7 percent in France. But in some countries, the economy actually shrank, and per capita income dropped. Among the countries with declining income were Romania, Sierra Leone, Haiti, and Zambia.

In the fastest-growing countries, citizens save a large fraction of the money they earn. Firms can then borrow the funds saved to purchase machinery and equipment that make their workers more productive. The fastest-growing countries also have well-educated workforces, allowing firms to quickly adopt new technologies that increase worker productivity.

To Understand Economic Fluctuations

All economies, including ones that experience a general trend of rising per capita income, are subject to economic fluctuations, including periods when the economy shrinks. During an economic downturn, some of the economy's resources—natural resources, labor, physical capital, human capital, and entrepreneurship—are idle. Some workers are unemployed, and some factories and stores are closed. By contrast, sometimes the economy grows too rapidly, causing prices to rise. Macroeconomics helps us understand why these fluctuations occur—why the economy sometimes cools and sometimes overheats—and what the government can do to moderate the fluctuations. Let's look at a practical question about economic fluctuations.

Should Congress and the president do something to reduce the unemployment rate? For example, should the government cut taxes to stimulate consumer spending and thus encourage firms to hire more workers to produce the additional goods and services? If unemployment is very high, the government may want to reduce it. However, it is important not to reduce the unemployment rate too much, because, as we'll see later in the book, a low unemployment rate will cause inflation.

To Make Informed Business Decisions

A third reason for studying macroeconomics is to make informed business decisions. As we'll see later in the book, the government uses various policies to influence interest rates and the inflation rate. A manager who intends to borrow money for a new factory or store could use knowledge of macroeconomics to predict the effects of current public policies on interest rates and then decide whether to borrow the money now or later. Similarly, a manager must keep an eye on the inflation rate to help decide how much to charge for the firm's products and how much to pay workers. A manager who studies macroeconomics will be better equipped to understand the complexities of interest rates and inflation and how they affect the firm.

1.5 | PREVIEW OF COMING ATTRACTIONS: MICROECONOMICS

Microeconomics is the study of the choices made by households (an individual or a group of people living together), firms, and government and how these choices affect the markets for goods and services. Let's look at three ways we can use microeconomic analysis.

• **microeconomics**
The study of the choices made by households, firms, and government and how these choices affect the markets for goods and services.

To Understand Markets and Predict Changes

One reason for studying microeconomics is to better understand how markets work and to predict how various events affect the prices and quantities of products in markets. In this book, we answer many practical questions about markets and how they operate. Let's look at one practical question that can be answered with some simple economic analysis.

How would a tax on beer affect the number of highway deaths among young adults? Research has shown that the number of highway fatalities among young adults is roughly proportional to the total amount of beer consumed by that group. A tax on beer would make the product more expensive, and young adults, like other beer drinkers, would therefore consume less of it. Consequently, a tax that decreases beer consumption by 10 percent will decrease highway deaths among young adults by about 10 percent, too.

To Make Personal and Managerial Decisions

On the personal level, we use economic analysis to decide how to spend our time, what career to pursue, and how to spend and save the money we earn. As workers, we use economic analysis to decide how to produce goods and services, how much to produce, and how much to charge for them. Let's use some economic analysis to look at a practical question confronting someone considering starting a business.

If the existing music stores in your city are profitable and you have enough money to start your own music store, should you do it? If you enter this market, the competition among the stores for consumers will heat up, causing some stores to drop their CD prices. In addition, your costs may be higher than the costs of the stores that are already established. It would be sensible to enter the market only if you expect a small drop in price and a small difference in costs. Indeed, entering what appears to be a lucrative market may turn out to be a financial disaster.

To Evaluate Public Policies

Although modern societies use markets to make most of the decisions concerning production and consumption, the government does fulfill several important roles. We can use economic analysis to determine how well the government performs its roles in the market economy. We can also explore the trade-offs associated with various public policies. Let's look at a practical question about public policy.

Like other innovations, prescription drugs are protected by government patents, giving the developer the exclusive right to sell the drug for a fixed period of time. Once the patent expires, other pharmaceutical companies can legally produce and sell generic versions of a drug, causing prices to drop. Should drug patents be shorter? Shortening the patent has trade-offs. The good news is that a shorter patent means that generic versions of the drug will be available sooner, so prices will be lower and more people will use the drug to improve their health. The bad news is that a shorter patent means that the pay-off from developing new drugs will be smaller, so pharmaceutical companies won't develop as many new drugs. The question is whether the benefit of shorter patents (lower prices) exceeds the cost (fewer drugs developed).

SUMMARY

This chapter explains what economics is and why it is useful. Economics is about making choices when options are limited. Options in an economy are limited because the factors of production are limited. We can use economic analysis to understand the consequences of our choices, as individuals, organizations, and society as a whole. Here are the main points of the chapter:

1 Most of modern economics is based on *positive analysis*, which answers the question "What *is*?" or "What *will be*?" Economists contribute to policy debates by conducting positive analyses about the consequences of alternative actions.

2 The choices made by individuals, firms, and governments answer three questions: What products do we produce?

How do we produce the products? Who consumes the products?

3 *Normative analysis* answers the question "What *ought to be*?"

4 To think like an economist, we (a) use assumptions to simplify, (b) use the notion of *ceteris paribus* to focus on the relationship between two variables, (c) think in marginal terms, and (d) assume that rational people respond to incentives.

5 We use *macroeconomics* to understand why economies grow, to understand economic fluctuations, and to make informed business decisions.

6 We use *microeconomics* to understand how markets work, to make personal and managerial decisions, and to evaluate the merits of public policies.

KEY TERMS

ceteris paribus, p. 10
economics, p. 4
economic model, p. 6
entrepreneurship, p. 4
factors of production, p. 4
human capital, p. 4

labor, p. 4
macroeconomics, p. 11
marginal change, p. 10
microeconomics, p. 13
natural resources, p. 4
normative analysis, p. 5

physical capital, p. 4
positive analysis, p. 5
scarcity, p. 4
variable, p. 9

EXERCISES

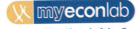

Get Ahead of the Curve

Visit www.myeconlab.com to complete these exercises online and get instant feedback.

1.1 | What Is Economics?

1.1 The three basic economic questions a society must answer are: _____ products do we produce? _____ do we produce the products? _____ consumes the products?

1.2 Which of the following statements is true?
   a. Positive statements answer questions like "What will happen if . . ."; normative economic statements answer questions like "What ought to happen to . . ."
   b. Normative statements answer questions like "What will happen if . . ."; positive economic statements answer questions like "What ought to happen to . . ."
   c. Most modern economics is based on normative analysis.

1.3. Indicate whether each of the following questions is normative or positive.
   a. Should your city build levees strong enough to protect the city from Class-5 hurricanes?

   b. How did Hurricane Katrina affect housing prices in New Orleans and Baton Rouge?
   c. Who should pay for a new skate park?
   d. Should a school district increase teachers' salaries by 20 percent?
   e. Would an increase in teachers' salaries improve the average quality of teachers?

1.2 | Economic Analysis and Modern Problems

2.1 What is the economist's solution to the congestion problem?
   a. Require people to carpool.
   b. Charge a toll during rush hour.
   c. Require people to move closer to their jobs.
   d. No economist would suggest any of the above.

2.2 Some recent work by economists on the sources of growth suggests that institutions such as the _____ and the _____ play key roles in economic growth.

3.1 A road map incorporates two unrealistic assumptions: (1) _____ and (2) _____

3.2 The four elements of the economic way of thinking are: (1) use _____ to simplify the analysis; (2) explore the relationship between two variables by _____; (3) think at the _____; and (4) rational people respond to _____.

3.3 Which of the following is the Latin expression meaning *other things being held fixed*?
  a. *ceteriferous proboscis*
  b. *ceteris paribus*
  c. *e pluribus unum*
  d. *tres grand fromage*

3.4 When researchers hooked TVs to stationary bikes as a power source, the cost of watching TV _____, and the kids responded by _____ the hours of TV watched. (Related to Application 1 on page 11.)

3.5 The city of London reduced traffic congestion and cut travel times for cars and buses in half by _____. (Related to Application 2 on page 12.)

NOTES

1. Texas Transportation Institute, *2005 Urban Mobility Study* (http://mobility.tamu.edu/ums/).

2. William Easterly, *The Elusive Quest for Growth* (Cambridge, MA: MIT Press, 2001), Chapter 1.

3. William Easterly, *The Elusive Quest for Growth* (Cambridge, MA: MIT Press, 2001); World Bank, *World Development Report 2000/2001: Attacking Poverty* (New York: Oxford University Press, 2000).

4. John Maynard Keynes, *The Collected Writings of John Maynard Keynes, Volume 7*, edited by Donald Moggridge (London: Macmillan, 1973), p. 856.

5. Alfred Marshall, *Principles of Economics*, 9th ed., edited by C.W. Guillebaud (London: Macmillan, 1961 [first published in 1920]), p. 366.

6. Adam Smith, *An Inquiry into the Nature and Causes of the Wealth of Nations* (First published in 1776; New York: Random House, 1973), Book 2, Chapter 3.

APPENDIX A
USING GRAPHS AND PERCENTAGES

Economists use several types of graphs to present data, represent relationships between variables, and explain concepts. In this appendix, we review the mechanics of graphing variables. We'll also review the basics of computing percentage changes and using percentages to compute changes in variables.

USING GRAPHS

A quick flip through the book will reveal the importance of graphs in economics. Every chapter has at least several graphs, and many chapters have more. Although it is possible to do economics without graphs, it's a lot easier with them in your toolbox.

Graphing Single Variables

As we saw earlier in Chapter 1, a *variable* is a measure of something that can take on different values. Figure 1A.1 shows two types of graphs, each presenting data on a single variable. Panel A uses a pie graph to show the breakdown of U.S. music sales by type of music. The larger the sales of a type of music, the larger the pie slice. For example, the most popular type is Rock music, comprising 24 percent of the market. The next largest type is Rap/Hip-hop, followed by R&B/Urban, Country, and so on. Panel B of Figure 1A.1 uses a bar graph to show the revenue from foreign sales (exports) of selected U.S. industries. The larger the revenue, the taller the bar. For example, the bar for computer software, with export sales of about $60 billion, is over three times taller than the bar for motion pictures, TV, and video, with export sales of $17 billion.

A third type of single-variable graph shows how the value of a variable changes over time. Panel A of Figure 1A.2 shows a time-series graph, with the total dollar

► **FIGURE 1A.1**
Graphs of Single Variables

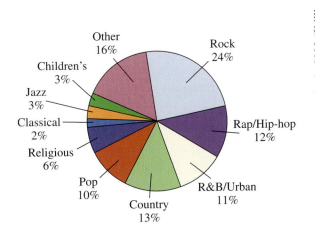

(A) Pie Graph for Types of Recorded Music Sold in the United States

SOURCE: Author's calculations based in Recording Industry Association of America, "2004 Consumer Profile."

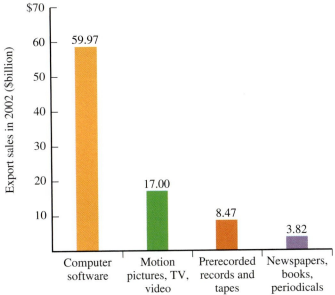

(B) Bar Graph for U.S. Export Sales of Copyrighted Products

SOURCE: Author's calculations based on International Intellectual Property Alliance, "Copyright Industries in the U.S. Economy, 2004 Report."

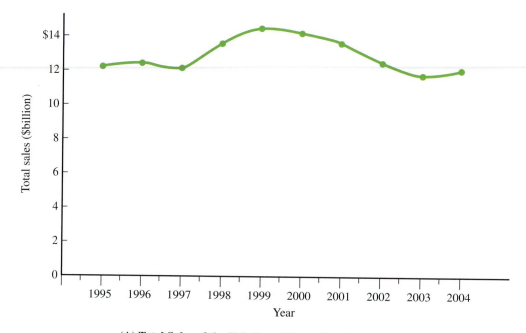

(A) Total Sales of the U.S. Sound Recording Industry, 1995–2004

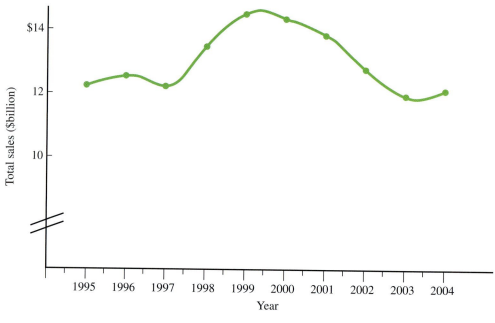

(B) Truncated Vertical Axis

value of the U.S. sound-recording industry from 1995 through 2004. Time is measured on the horizontal axis, and sales are measured on the vertical axis. The height of the line in a particular year shows the value in that year. For example, in 1995 the value was $12.32 billion. After reaching a peak of $14.59 billion in 1999, the value dropped over the next several years.

Panel B of Figure 1A.2 shows a truncated version of the graph in Panel A. The double hash marks in the lower part of the vertical axis indicate that the axis doesn't start from zero. The truncation of the vertical axis exaggerates the fluctuations in the value of production.

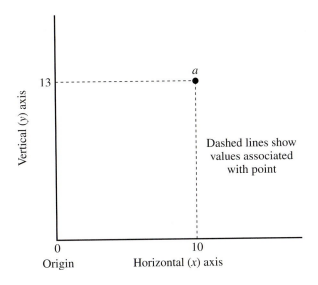

Basic Elements of a Two-Variable Graph
One variable is measured along the horizontal or *x* axis, while the other variable is measured along the vertical or *y* axis. The origin is defined as the intersection of the two axes, where the values of both variables are zero. The dashed lines show the values of the two variables at a particular point.

Graphing Two Variables

We can also use a graph to show the relationship between two variables. Figure 1A.3 shows the basic elements of a two-variable graph. One variable is measured along the horizontal, or *x*, axis, while the other variable is measured along the vertical, or *y*, axis. The *origin* is defined as the intersection of the two axes, where the values of both variables are zero. Dashed lines show the values of the two variables at a particular point. For example, for point *a*, the value of the horizontal, or *x*, variable is 10, and the value of the vertical, or *y*, variable is 13.

To see how to draw a two-variable graph, suppose that you have a part-time job and you are interested in the relationship between the number of hours you work and your weekly income. The relevant variables are the hours of work per week and your weekly income. In Figure 1A.4, the table shows the relationship between the hours

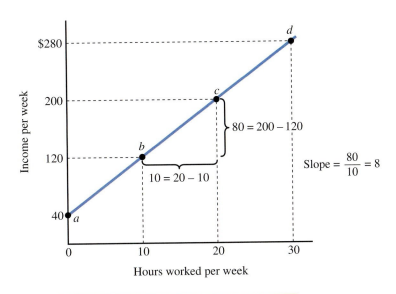

◄ FIGURE 1A.4
Relationship Between Hours Worked and Income
There is a positive relationship between work hours and income, so the income curve is positively sloped. The slope of the curve is $8: Each additional hour of work increases income by $8.

Hours Worked per Week	Income per Week	Point on the Graph
0	$ 40	*a*
10	120	*b*
20	200	*c*
30	280	*d*

worked and income. Let's assume that your weekly allowance from your parents is $40 and your part-time job pays $8 per hour. If you work 10 hours per week, for example, your weekly income is $120 ($40 from your parents and $80 from your job). The more you work, the higher your weekly income: If you work 20 hours, your weekly income is $200; if you work 30 hours, it is $280.

Although a table with numbers is helpful in showing the relationship between work hours and income, a graph makes it easier to see the relationship. We can use data in a table to draw a graph. To do so, we perform five simple steps:

1 Draw a horizontal line to represent the first variable. In Figure 1A.4, we measure hours worked along the horizontal axis. As we move to the right along the horizontal axis, the number of hours worked increases, from zero to 30 hours.

2 Draw a vertical line intersecting the first line to represent the second variable. In Figure 1A.4, we measure income along the vertical axis. As we move up along the vertical axis, income increases from zero to $280.

3 Start with the first row of numbers in the table, which shows that with zero hours worked, income is $40. The value of the variable on the horizontal axis is zero, and the value of the variable on the vertical axis is $40, so we plot point *a* on the graph. This is the *vertical intercept*—the point where the curve cuts or intersects the vertical axis.

4 Pick a combination with a positive number for hours worked. For example, in the second row of numbers, if you work 10 hours, your income is $120.

4.1 Find the point on the horizontal axis with that number of hours worked—10 hours—and draw a dashed line vertically straight up from that point.

4.2 Find the point on the vertical axis with the income corresponding to those hours worked—$120—and draw a dashed line horizontally straight to the right from that point.

4.3 The intersection of the dashed lines shows the combination of hours worked and income. Point *b* shows the combination of 10 hours worked and $120 in income.

5 Repeat step 4 for different combinations of work time and income shown in the table. Once we have a series of points on the graph (*a*, *b*, *c*, and *d*), we can connect them to draw a curve that shows the relationship between hours worked and income.

• **positive relationship**
A relationship in which two variables move in the same direction.

There is a **positive relationship** between two variables if they move in the same direction. As you increase your work time, your income increases, so there is a positive relationship between the two variables. In Figure 1A.4, as the number of hours worked increases, you move upward along the curve to higher income levels. Some people refer to a positive relationship as a *direct relationship*.

• **negative relationship**
A relationship in which two variables move in opposite directions.

There is a **negative relationship** between two variables if they move in opposite directions. For example, there is a negative relationship between the amount of time you work and the time you have available for other activities such as recreation, study, and sleep. Some people refer to a negative relationship as an *inverse relationship*.

Computing the Slope

• **slope of a curve**
The vertical difference between two points (the *rise*) divided by the horizontal difference (the *run*).

How sensitive is one variable to changes in the other variable? We can use the slope of the curve to measure this sensitivity. To compute the **slope of a curve**, we pick two points and divide the vertical difference between the two points (the *rise*) by the horizontal difference (the *run*):

$$\text{Slope} = \frac{\text{Vertical difference between two points}}{\text{Horizontal difference between two points}} = \frac{\text{rise}}{\text{run}}$$

To compute the slope of a curve, we take four steps:

1 Pick two points on the curve, for example, points b and c in Figure 1A.4.

2 Compute the vertical difference between the two points (the rise). For points b and c, the vertical difference between the points is \$80 (\$200 – \$120).

3 Compute the horizontal distance between the same two points (the run). For points b and c, the horizontal distance between the points is 10 hours (20 hours – 10 hours).

4 Divide the vertical distance by the horizontal distance to get the slope. The slope between points b and c is \$8 per hour:

$$\text{Slope} = \frac{\text{Vertical difference}}{\text{Horizontal difference}} = \frac{\$200 - 120}{20 - 10} = \frac{\$80}{10} = \$8$$

In this case, a 10-hour increase in time worked increases income by \$80, so the increase in income per hour of work is \$8, which makes sense because this is the hourly wage. Because the curve is a straight line, the slope is the same at all points along the curve. You can check this yourself by computing the slope between points c and d.

We can use some shorthand to refer to the slope of a curve. The mathematical symbol Δ (delta) represents the change in a variable. So the slope of the curve in Figure 1A.4 could be written as

$$\text{Slope} = \frac{\Delta \text{ Income}}{\Delta \text{ Work hours}}$$

In general, if the variable on the vertical axis is y and the variable on the horizontal axis is x, we can express the slope as

$$\text{Slope} = \frac{\Delta y}{\Delta x}$$

Moving Along the Curve Versus Shifting the Curve

Up to this point, we've explored the effect of changes in variables that cause movement along a given curve. In Figure 1A.4, we see the relationship between hours of work (on the horizontal axis) and income (on the vertical axis). Because the total income also depends on the allowance and the wage, we can make two observations about the curve in Figure 1A.4:

1 To draw this curve, we must specify the weekly allowance (\$40) and the hourly wage (\$8).

2 The curve shows that an increase in time worked increases the student's income, *ceteris paribus*. In this case, we are assuming that the allowance and the wage are both fixed.

A change in the weekly allowance will shift the curve showing the relationship between work time and income. In Figure 1A.5, when the allowance increases from \$40 to \$90, the curve shifts upward by \$50: For a given number of work hours, income increases by \$50. For example, the income associated with 10 hours of work is \$170 (point f), compared to \$120 with the original allowance (point b). The upward shift also means that to reach a given amount of income, fewer work hours are required. In other words, the curve shifts upward and to the left.

We can distinguish between movement along a curve and a shift of the entire curve. In Figure 1A.5, an increase in the hours worked causes movement along a single income curve. For example, if the allowance is \$40, we are operating on the lower of the two curves, and if the hours worked increases from 10 to 20, we move from point b to point c. In contrast, if something other than the hours worked changes, we shift the entire curve, as we've seen with an increase in the allowance.

Movement Along a Curve Versus Shifting the Curve

To draw a curve showing the relationship between hours worked and income, we fix the weekly allowance ($40) and the wage ($8 per hour). A change in the hours worked causes movement along the curve, for example, from point *b* to point *c*. A change in any other variable shifts the entire curve. For example, a $50 increase in the allowance (to $90) shifts the entire curve upward by $50.

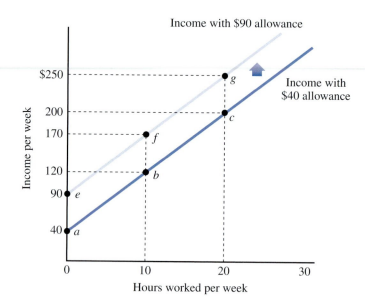

This book uses dozens of two-dimensional curves, each of which shows the relationship between *only two* variables. A common error is to forget that a single curve tells only part of the story. In Figure 1A.5, we needed two curves to explore the effects of changes in three variables. Here are some simple rules to keep in mind when you use two-dimensional graphs:

- A change in one of the variables shown on the graph causes movement along the curve. In Figure 1A.5, an increase in work time causes movement along the curve from point *a* to point *b*, to point *c*, and so on.

- A change in one of the variables that is not shown on the graph—one of the variables held fixed in drawing the curve—shifts the entire curve. In Figure 1A.5, an increase in the allowance shifts the entire curve upward.

Graphing Negative Relationships

We can use a graph to show a negative relationship between two variables. Consider a consumer who has an annual budget of $360 to spend on CDs at a price of $12 per CD and downloaded music at a price of $1 per song. The table in Figure 1A.6 shows the relationship between the number of CDs and downloaded songs. A consumer who doesn't buy any CDs has $360 to spend on downloaded songs and can get 360 of them at a price of $1 each. A consumer who buys 10 CDs at $12 each has $240 left to spend on downloaded songs (point *b*). Moving down through the table, as the number of CDs increases, the number of downloaded songs decreases.

The graph in Figure 1A.6 shows the negative relationship between the number of CDs and the number of downloaded songs. The vertical intercept (point *a*) shows that a consumer who doesn't buy any CDs can afford 360 downloaded songs. There is a negative relationship between the number of CDs and downloaded songs, so the curve is negatively sloped. We can use points *b* and *c* to compute the slope of the curve:

$$\text{Slope} = \frac{\text{Vertical difference}}{\text{Horizontal difference}} = \frac{240 - 120}{10 - 20} = \frac{120}{-10} = -12$$

The slope is 12 downloaded songs per CD: For each additional CD, the consumer sacrifices 12 downloaded songs.

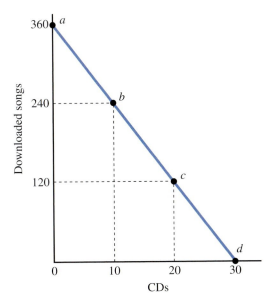

Number of CDs Purchased	Number of Songs Downloaded	Point on the Graph
0	360	a
10	240	b
20	120	c
30	0	d

▲ **FIGURE 1A.6**

Negative Relationship Between CD Purchases and Downloaded Songs

There is a negative relationship between the number of CDs and downloaded songs that a consumer can afford with a budget of $360. The slope of the curve is $12: Each additional CD (at a price of $12 each) decreases the number of downloadable songs (at $1 each) by 12 songs.

Graphing Nonlinear Relationships

We can also use a graph to show a nonlinear relationship between two variables. Panel A of Figure 1A.7 shows the relationship between hours spent studying for an exam and the grade on the exam. As study time increases, the grade increases, but at a decreasing rate. In other words, each additional hour increases the exam grade by a smaller and smaller amount. For example, the second hour of study increases the grade by 4 points—from 6 to 10 points—but the ninth hour of study increases the grade by only 1 point—from 24 points to 25 points. This is a nonlinear relationship: The slope of the curve changes as we move along the curve. In Figure 1A.7, the slope decreases as we move to the right along the curve: The slope is 4 points per hour between points *a* and *b* but only 1 point per hour between points *c* and *d*.

Another possibility for a nonlinear curve is that the slope increases as we move to the right along the curve. Panel B of Figure 1A.7 shows the relationship between the amount of grain produced on the horizontal axis and the total cost of production on the vertical axis. The slope of the curve increases as the amount of grain increases, meaning that production cost increases at an increasing rate. On the lower part of the curve, increasing output from 1 ton to 2 tons increases production cost by $5, from $10 to $15. On the upper part of the curve, increasing output from 10 to 11 tons increases production cost by $25, from $100 to $125.

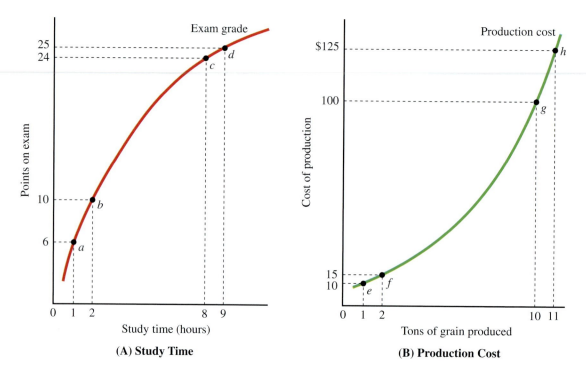

▲ **FIGURE 1A.7**
Nonlinear Relationships

(**A**) **Study time** There is a positive and nonlinear relationship between study time and the grade on an exam. As study time increases, the exam grade increases at a decreasing rate. For example, the second hour of study increased the grade by 4 points (from 6 points to 10 points), but the ninth hour of study increases the grade by only 1 point (from 24 points to 25 points).

(**B**) **Production cost** There is a positive and nonlinear relationship between the quantity of grain produced and total production cost. As the quantity increases, the total cost increases at an increasing rate. For example, to increase production from 1 ton to 2 tons, production cost increases by $5 (from $10 to $15) but to increase the production from 10 to 11 tons, total cost increases by $25 (from $100 to $125).

COMPUTING PERCENTAGE CHANGES AND USING EQUATIONS

Economists often express changes in variables in terms of percentage changes. This part of the appendix provides a brief review of the mechanics of computing percentage changes. It also reviews some simple rules for solving equations to find missing values.

Computing Percentage Changes

In many cases, the equations that economists use involve percentage changes. In this book, we use a simple approach to computing percentage changes: We divide the change in the variable by the initial value of the variable and then multiply by 100:

$$\text{Percentage change} = \frac{\text{New value} - \text{initial value}}{\text{Initial value}} \times 100$$

For example, if the price of a book increases from $20 to $22, the percentage change is 10 percent:

$$\text{Percentage change} = \frac{22 - 20}{20} \times 100 = \frac{2}{20} \times 100 = 10\%$$

Going in the other direction, suppose the price decreases from $20 to $19. In this case, the percentage change is −5 percent:

$$\text{Percentage change} = \frac{19 - 20}{20} \times 100 = -\frac{1}{20} \times 100 = -5\%$$

The alternative to this simple approach is to base the percentage change on the average value, or the midpoint, of the variable:

$$\text{Percentage change} = \frac{\text{New value} - \text{initial value}}{\text{Average value}} \times 100$$

For example, if the price of a book increases from $20 to $22, the computed percentage change under the midpoint approach would be 9.52 percent:

$$\text{Percentage change} = \frac{22 - 20}{(20 + 22) \div 2} \times 100 = \frac{2}{42 \div 2} \times 100 = \frac{2}{21} \times 100 = 9.52\%$$

If the change in the variable is relatively small, the extra precision associated with the midpoint approach is usually not worth the extra effort. The simple approach allows us to spend less time doing tedious arithmetic and more time doing economic analysis. In this book, we use the simple approach to compute percentage changes: If the price increases from $20 to $22, the price has increased by 10 percent.

If we know a percentage change, we can translate it into an absolute change. For example, if a price has increased by 10 percent and the initial price is $20, then we add 10 percent of the initial price ($2 is 10 percent of $20) to the initial price ($20), for a new price of $22. If the price decreases by 5 percent, we subtract 5 percent of the initial price ($1 is 5 percent of $20) from the initial price ($20), for a new price of $19.

Using Equations to Compute Missing Values

It will often be useful to compute the value of the numerator or the denominator of an equation. To do so, we use simple algebra to rearrange the equation to put the missing variable on the left side of the equation. For example, consider the relationship between time worked and income. The equation for the slope is

$$\text{Slope} = \frac{\Delta \text{Income}}{\Delta \text{Work hours}}$$

Suppose you want to compute how much income you'll earn by working more hours. We can rearrange the slope equation by multiplying both sides of the equation by the change in work hours:

$$\text{Work hours} \times \text{Slope} = \Delta \text{Income}$$

By swapping sides of the equation, we get:

$$\Delta \text{ Income} = \Delta \text{ Work hours} \times \text{Slope}$$

For example, if you work seven extra hours and the slope is $8, your income will increase by $56:

$$\Delta \text{ Income} = \Delta \text{Work hours} \times \text{Slope} = 7 \times \$8 = \$56$$

We can use the same process to compute the difference in work time required to achieve a target change in income. In this case, we multiply both sides of the slope equation by the change in work time and then divide both sides by the slope. The result is

$$\Delta \text{Work hours} = \frac{\Delta \text{ Income}}{\text{Slope}}$$

For example, to increase your income by $56, you need to work seven hours:

$$\Delta \text{Work hours} = \frac{\Delta \text{ Income}}{\text{Slope}} = \frac{\$56}{\$8} = 7$$

KEY TERMS

negative relationship, p. 20

positive relationship, p. 20

slope of a curve, p. 20

EXERCISES

Visit www.myeconlab.com to complete these exercises online and get instant feedback.

Get Ahead of the Curve

A1. Suppose you belong to a tennis club that has a monthly fee of $100 and a charge of $5 per hour to play tennis.

    a. Using Figure 1A.4 on page 19 as a model, prepare a table and draw a curve to show the relationship between the hours of tennis (on the horizontal axis) and the monthly club bill (on the vertical axis). For the table and graph, use 5, 10, 15, and 20 hours of tennis.

    b. The slope of the curve is _____ per _____.

    c. Suppose you start with 10 hours of tennis and then decide to increase your tennis time by 3 hours. On your curve, show the initial point and the new point. By how much will your monthly bill increase?

    d. Suppose you start with 10 hours and then decide to spend an additional $30 on tennis. On your curve, show the initial point and the new point. How many additional hours can you get?

A2. The following graph shows the relationship between the number of Frisbees produced and the cost of production. The vertical intercept is $____, and the slope of the curve is $_____ per Frisbee. Point *b* shows that the cost of producing _____ Frisbees is $____. The cost of producing 15 frisbees is $____.

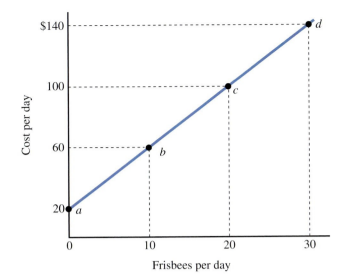

Cost per day

$140 ---------------------------- ● d

100 --------------------- ●
                          c

60 ------------- ●
                 b

20 ●
   a

0   10   20   30

Frisbees per day

A3. Suppose you have $120 to spend on CDs and movies. The price of a CD is $12, and the price of a movie is $6.
  a. Using Figure 1A.6 on page 23 as a model, prepare a table and draw a curve to show the relationship between the number of CDs (on the horizontal axis) and movies (on the vertical axis) you can afford to buy.
  b. The slope of the curve is _____ per _____.

A4. You manage Gofer Delivery Service. You rent a truck for $50 per day, and each delivery takes an hour of labor time. The hourly wage is $8.

  a. Draw a curve showing the relationship between the number of deliveries (on the horizontal axis) and your total cost (on the vertical axis). Draw the curve for between zero and 20 deliveries.
  b. The slope of the cost curve is _____ per _____.
  c. To draw the curve, what variables are held fixed?
  d. A change in _____ would cause a movement upward along the curve.
  e. Changes in _____ would cause the entire curve to shift upward.

A5. A change in a variable measured on an axis of a graph causes movement _____ a curve, while a change in a relevant variable that is not measured on an axis _____ the curve.

A6. Compute the percentage changes for the following :

Initial Value	New Value	Percentage Change
10	11	_____
100	98	_____
50	53	_____

A7. Compute the new values for the following changes.

Initial Value	Percentage Change	New Value
100	12%	_____
50	8	_____
20	15	_____

2

The Key Principles
of Economics

Your student film society is looking for an auditorium to use for an all-day Hitchcock film program and is willing to pay up to $200. Your college has a new auditorium that would be perfect for your event. However, according to the campus facility manager, "The daily rent on the auditorium is $450, an amount that includes $300 to help pay for the cost of building the auditorium, $50 to help pay for insurance, and $100 to cover the extra costs of electricity and janitorial services for a one-day event."

How should you respond to the facility manager? As we'll see, if you could persuade the manager to use the marginal principle—one of the five key principles of economics—you should be able to get the facility for an amount between $100 and $200.

• **opportunity cost**
What you sacrifice to get something.

In this chapter, we introduce five key principles that provide a foundation for economic analysis. A *principle* is a self-evident truth that most people readily understand and accept. For example, most people readily accept the principle of gravity. As you read through the book, you will see the five key principles of economics again and again as you do your own economic analysis.

2.1 | THE PRINCIPLE OF OPPORTUNITY COST

Economics is all about making choices, and to make good choices we must compare the benefit of something to its cost. **Opportunity cost** incorporates the notion of scarcity: No matter what we do, there is always a trade-off. We must trade off one thing for another because resources are limited and can be used in different ways. By acquiring something, we use up resources that could have been used to acquire something else. The notion of opportunity cost allows us to measure this trade-off.

PRINCIPLE OF OPPORTUNITY COST
The opportunity cost of something is what you sacrifice to get it.

Most decisions involve several alternatives. For example, if you spend an hour studying for an economics exam, you have one less hour to pursue other activities. To determine the opportunity cost of an activity, we look at what you consider the best of these "other" activities. For example, suppose the alternatives to studying economics are studying for a history exam or working in a job that pays $10 per hour. If you consider studying for history a better use of your time than working, then the opportunity cost of studying economics is the 4 extra points you could have received on a history exam if you studied history instead of economics. Alternatively, if working is the best alternative, the opportunity cost of studying economics is the $10 you could have earned instead.

The principle of opportunity cost can also be applied to decisions about how to spend money from a fixed budget. For example, suppose that you have a fixed budget to spend on music. You can either buy your music at a local music store for $15 per CD or you can buy your music online for $1 per song. The opportunity cost of 1 CD is 15 one-dollar online songs. A hospital with a fixed salary budget can increase the number of doctors only at the expense of nurses or physician's assistants. If a doctor costs five times as much as a nurse, the opportunity cost of a doctor is 5 nurses.

In some cases, a product that appears to be free actually has a cost. That's why economists are fond of saying, "There's no such thing as a free lunch." Suppose someone offers to buy you lunch if you agree to listen to a sales pitch for a time-share condominium. Although you don't pay any money for the lunch, there is an opportunity cost because you could spend that time in another way—such as studying for your economics or history exam. The lunch isn't free because you sacrifice an hour of your time to get it.

The Cost of College

What is the opportunity cost of a college degree? Consider a student who spends a total of $40,000 for tuition and books. Instead of going to college, the student could have spent this money on a wide variety of goods, including housing, stereo equipment, and world travel. Part of the opportunity cost of college is the $40,000 worth of other goods the student sacrifices to pay for tuition and books. Also, instead of going to college, the student could have worked as a bank clerk for $20,000 per year and earned

APPLICATION

THE OPPORTUNITY COSTS OF TIME AND INVESTED FUNDS

APPLYING THE CONCEPTS #1: What is the opportunity cost of running a business?

The principle of opportunity cost also applies to the cost of running a business. Suppose you inherit $10,000 and decide to use the money to start a lawn-care business. You purchase a truck and a mower for $10,000 and start mowing lawns. If your annual cost for fuel and other supplies is $2,000, what's your annual cost of doing business?

We can use the principle of opportunity cost to compute your costs. In addition to the $2,000 expense for fuel and other supplies, we must include two other sorts of costs:

- **Opportunity cost of funds invested.** You could have invested the $10,000 in a bank account. If the interest rate on a bank account is 8 percent, the annual cost of the truck and mower is the $800 you could have earned in a bank account during the year.

- **Opportunity cost of your time.** Suppose that you could have earned $30,000 in another job. The opportunity cost of your time is the $30,000 you sacrificed by being your own boss.

Adding the $800 cost of funds and the $30,000 cost of your time to the $2,000 fuel cost, the cost of doing business is $32,800 per year.
Related to Exercise 1.6.

$80,000 over four years. That makes the total opportunity cost of this student's college degree $120,000:

Opportunity cost of money spent on tuition and books	$ 40,000
Opportunity cost of college time (four years working for $20,000 per year)	80,000
Economic cost or total opportunity cost	$120,000

We haven't included the costs of food or housing in our computations of opportunity cost. That's because a student must eat and live somewhere even if he or she doesn't go to college. But if housing and food are more expensive in college, then we would include the extra costs of housing and food in our calculations.

There are other things to consider in a person's decision to attend college. As we'll see later, a college degree can increase a person's earning power, so there are benefits from a college degree. In addition, college offers the thrill of learning and the pleasure of meeting new people. To make an informed decision about whether to attend college, we must compare the benefits to the opportunity costs.

Opportunity Cost and the Production Possibilities Curve

Just as individuals face limits, so do entire economies. As we saw in Chapter 1, the ability of an economy to produce goods and services is determined by its factors of production, including labor, natural resources, physical capital, human capital, and entrepreneurship.

Figure 2.1 shows a production possibilities graph for an economy that produces wheat and steel. The horizontal axis shows the quantity of wheat produced by the economy, and the vertical axis shows the quantity of steel produced. The shaded area shows all the possible combinations of the two goods that can be produced. At point *a*,

► **FIGURE 2.1**
**Scarcity and the Production
Possibilities Curve**
The production possibilities curve illustrates
the principle of opportunity cost for an
entire economy. An economy has a fixed
amount of resources. If these resources
are fully employed, an increase in the production of wheat comes at the expense of
steel.

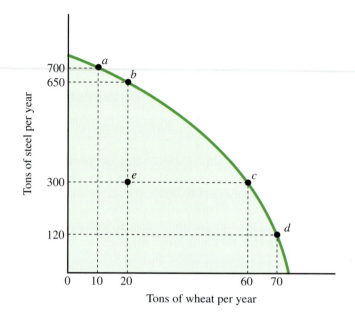

• **production possibilities curve**
A curve that shows the possible
combinations of products that an
economy can produce, given that its
productive resources are fully
employed and efficiently used.

for example, the economy can produce 700 tons of steel and 10 tons of wheat. In contrast, at point *e*, the economy can produce 300 tons of steel and 20 tons of wheat. The
set of points on the border between the shaded and unshaded area is called the **production possibilities curve** (or *production possibilities frontier*), because it separates the
combinations that are attainable from those that are not. The attainable combinations
are shown by the shaded area within the curve and the curve itself. The unattainable
combinations are shown by the unshaded area outside the curve. The points on the
curve show the combinations that are possible if the economy's resources are fully
employed.

The production possibilities curve illustrates the notion of opportunity cost. If
an economy is fully utilizing its resources, it can produce more of one product only if
it produces less of another product. For example, to produce more wheat, we must
take resources away from steel. As we move resources out of steel, the quantity of
steel will decrease. For example, if we move from point *a* to point *b* along the pro-

► **FIGURE 2.2**
**Shifting the Production
Possibilities Curve**
An increase in the quantity of resources or
technological innovation in an economy
shifts the production possibilities curve outward. Starting from point *f*, a nation could
produce more steel (point *g*), more wheat
(point *h*), or more of both goods (points
between *g* and *h*).

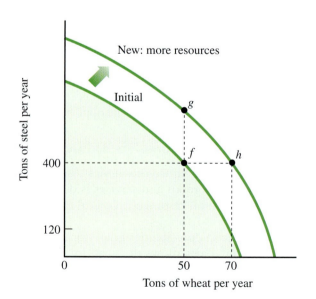

duction possibilities curve in Figure 2.1, we sacrifice 50 tons steel (700 tons − 650 tons) to get 10 more tons of wheat (20 tons − 10 tons). Further down the curve, if we move from point *c* to point *d*, we sacrifice 180 tons of steel to get the same 10-ton increase in wheat.

Why is the production possibilities curve bowed outward, with the opportunity cost of wheat increasing as we move down the curve? The reason is that resources are not perfectly adaptable for the production of both goods. Some resources are more suitable for steel production, while others are more suitable for wheat production. Starting at point *a*, the economy uses its most fertile land to produce wheat. A 10-ton increase in wheat reduces the quantity of steel by only 50 tons, because plenty of fertile land is available for conversion to wheat farming. As the economy moves downward along the production possibilities curve, farmers will be forced to use land that is progressively less fertile, so to increase wheat output by 10 tons, more and more resources must be diverted from steel production. In the move from point *c* to point *d*, the land converted to farming is so poor that increasing wheat output by 10 tons decreases steel output by 180 tons.

The production possibilities curve shows the production options for a given set of resources. As shown in Figure 2.2, an increase in the amount of resources available to the economy shifts the production possibilities outward. For example, if we start at point *f*, and the economy's resources increase, we can produce more steel (point *g*), more wheat (point *h*), or more of both goods (points between *g* and *h*). The curve will also shift outward as a result of technological innovations that enable us to produce more output with a given quantity of resources.

2.2 | THE MARGINAL PRINCIPLE

Economics is about making choices, and we rarely make all-or-nothing choices. For example, if you sit down to read a book, you don't read the entire book in a single sitting, but instead decide how many pages or chapters to read. Economists think in marginal terms, considering how a one-unit change in one variable affects the value of another variable and people's decisions. When we say *marginal*, we're looking at the effect of a small, or incremental, change.

The marginal principle is based on a comparison of the marginal benefits and marginal costs of a particular activity. The **marginal benefit** of an activity is the additional benefit resulting from a small increase in the activity. For example, the marginal benefit of keeping a bookstore open for one more hour equals the additional revenue from book sales. Similarly, the **marginal cost** is the additional cost resulting from a small increase in the activity. For example, the marginal cost of keeping a bookstore open for one more hour equals the additional expenses for workers and utilities. Applying the marginal principle, the bookstore should stay open for one more hour if the marginal benefit (the additional revenue) is at least as large as the marginal cost (the additional cost). For example, if the marginal benefit is $80 of additional revenue and the marginal cost is $30 of additional cost for workers and utilities, staying open for the additional hour increases the bookstore's profit by $50.

- **marginal benefit**
  The additional benefit resulting from a small increase in some activity.

- **marginal cost**
  The additional cost resulting from a small increase in some activity.

MARGINAL PRINCIPLE

Increase the level of an activity as long as its marginal benefit exceeds its marginal cost. Choose the level at which the marginal benefit equals the marginal cost.

Thinking at the margin enables us to fine-tune our decisions. We can use the marginal principle to determine whether a one-unit increase in a variable would make us better off. Just as a bookstore owner could decide whether to stay open for one

APPLICATION

THE OPPORTUNITY COST OF MILITARY SPENDING

APPLYING THE CONCEPTS #2: What are society's trade-offs between different goods?

We can also use the principle of opportunity cost to explore the cost of military spending. In 1992, Malaysia bought two warships. For the price of the warships, the country could have provided safe drinking water for 5 million citizens who lacked it. In other words, the opportunity cost of the warships was safe drinking water for 5 million people. The policy question is whether the benefits of the warships exceed their opportunity cost.

In the United States, economists have estimated that the cost of the Iraq War will be at least $540 billion. The economists' calculations go beyond the simple budgetary costs and quantify the opportunity cost of the war. For example, the resources used in the war could have been used in various government programs for children— to enroll more children in preschool programs, to hire more science and math teachers to reduce class sizes, or to immunize more children in poor countries. For example, each $100 billion spent on the war could instead support one of the following programs:

- Enroll 13 million preschool children in the Head Start program for one year.
- Hire 1.8 million additional teachers for one year.
- Immunize all the children in less-developed countries for the next 33 years.

The fact that the war had a large opportunity cost does not necessarily mean that it was unwise. The policy question is whether the benefits from the war exceed its opportunity cost. Taking another perspective, we can measure the opportunity cost of war in terms of its implications for domestic security. The resources used in the Iraq War could have been used to improve domestic security by securing ports and cargo facilities, hiring more police officers, improving the screening of airline passengers and baggage, improving fire departments and other first responders, upgrading the Coast Guard fleet, and securing our railroad and highway systems.

The cost of implementing the domestic-security recommendations of various government commissions would be about $31 billion, a small fraction of the cost of the war. The question for policy makers is whether money spent on domestic security would be more beneficial than money spent on the war.

Related to Exercises 1.5 and 1.7.

SOURCES: United Nations Development Program, *Human Development Report 1994* (New York: Oxford University Press, 1994); Linda Blimes and Joseph Stiglitz, "The Economic Costs of the Iraq War: An Appraisal Three Years After the Beginning of the Conflict," *Faculty Research Working Papers*, Harvard University, January 2006; Center for American Progress, "The Opportunity Costs of the Iraq War," August 25, 2004; Scott Wallsten and Katrina Kosec, "The Economic Costs of the War in Iraq," AEI-Brookings Joint Center for Regulatory Studies, September 2005.

more hour, you could decide whether to study one more hour for a psychology midterm. When we reach the level where the marginal benefit equals the marginal cost, we cannot do any better, and the fine-tuning is done.

How Many Movie Sequels?

To illustrate the marginal principle, let's consider movie sequels. When a movie is successful, its producer naturally thinks about doing another movie, continuing the story line with the same set of characters. If the first sequel is successful, too, the producer thinks about producing a second sequel, then a third, and so on. We can use the marginal principle to explore the decision of how many movies to produce.

Figure 2.3 shows the marginal benefits and marginal costs for movies. On the benefit side, a movie sequel typically generates about 30 percent less revenue than the original movie, and revenue continues to drop for additional movies. In the second column of the table, the first movie generates $300 million in revenue, the second generates $210 million, and the third generates $135 million. This is shown in the graph as a negatively sloped marginal-benefit curve, with the marginal benefit decreasing from $300 for the first movie (point *a*), to $210 (point *b*), and then to $135 (point *c*). On the cost side, the typical movie in the United States costs about $50 million to produce and about $75 million to promote.[1] In the third column of the table, the cost of the first movie (the original) is $125 million. In the graph, this is shown as point *d* on the marginal-cost curve. The marginal cost increases with the number of movies because film stars typically demand higher salaries to appear in sequels. For example, Angelina Jolie was paid more for *Tomb Raider 2* than for *Tomb Raider*, and the actors in *Charlie's Angels 2* received raises, too. In the table and the graph, the marginal cost increases to $150 million for the second movie (point *e*) and to $175 for the third (point *f*).

In this example, the first two movies are profitable, but the third is not. For the original movie, the marginal benefit ($300 million at point *a*) exceeds the marginal

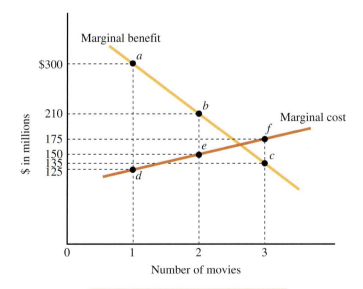

◄ **FIGURE 2.3**
The Marginal Principle and Movie Sequels
The marginal benefit of movies in a series decreases because revenue falls off with each additional movie, while the marginal cost increases because actors demand higher salaries. The marginal benefit exceeds the marginal cost for the first two movies, so it is sensible to produce two, but not three, movies.

Number of Movies	Marginal Benefit ($ millions)	Marginal Cost ($ millions)
1	$300	$125
2	210	150
3	135	175

cost ($125 million at point *d*), generating a profit of $175 million. Although the second movie has a higher cost and a lower benefit, it is profitable because the marginal benefit still exceeds the marginal cost, so the profit on the second movie is $60 million ($210 million − $150 million). In contrast, the marginal cost of the third movie of $175 million exceeds its marginal benefit of only $135 million, so the third movie *loses* $40 million. In this example, the movie producer should stop after the second movie.

Although this example shows that only two movies are profitable, other outcomes are possible. If the revenue for the third movie were larger, making the marginal benefit greater than the marginal cost, it would be sensible to produce the third movie. Similarly, if the marginal cost of the third movie were lower—if the actors didn't demand such high salaries—the third movie could be profitable. Many movies have had multiple sequels, such as *The Matrix* and *Star Wars*. Conversely, many profitable movies, such as *Rushmore* and *Groundhog Day*, didn't result in any sequels. In these cases, the expected drop-off in revenues and the run-up in costs for the second movie were large enough to make a sequel unprofitable.

Renting College Facilities

Recall the chapter opener about renting a college auditorium for your student film society. Suppose the society offers to pay $150 for using the auditorium. Should the college accept the offer? The college could use the marginal principle to make the decision.

To decide whether to accept your group's offer, the college should determine the marginal cost of renting out the auditorium. The marginal cost equals the extra costs the college incurs by allowing the student group to use an otherwise vacant auditorium. In our example, the extra cost is $100 for additional electricity and janitorial services. It would be sensible for the college to rent the auditorium, because the marginal benefit ($150 offered by the student group) exceeds the marginal cost ($100). In fact, the college should be willing to rent the facility for any amount greater than $100. If the students and the college's facility manager split the difference between the $200 the students are willing to pay and the $100 marginal cost, they would agree on a price of $150, leaving both parties better off by $50.

Most colleges do not use this sort of logic. Instead, they use complex formulas to compute the perceived cost of renting out a facility. In most cases, the perceived cost includes some costs that are unaffected by renting out the facility for the day. In our example, the facility manager included $300 worth of construction costs and $50 worth of insurance, for a total cost of $450 instead of just $100. Because many colleges include costs that aren't affected by the use of a facility, they overestimate the actual cost of renting out their facilities, missing opportunities to serve student groups and make some money at the same time.

Automobile Emissions Standards

We can use the marginal principle to analyze emissions standards for automobiles. The U.S. government specifies how much carbon monoxide a new car is allowed to emit per mile. The marginal question is: "Should the standard be stricter, with fewer units of carbon monoxide allowed?" On the benefit side, a stricter standard reduces health-care costs resulting from pollution: If the air is cleaner, people with respiratory ailments will make fewer visits to doctors and hospitals, have lower medication costs, and lose fewer work days. On the cost side, a stricter standard requires more expensive control equipment on cars and may also reduce fuel efficiency. Using the marginal principle, the government should make the emissions standard stricter as long as the marginal benefit (savings in health-care costs and work time lost) exceeds the marginal cost (the cost of additional equipment and extra fuel used).

APPLICATION

3

CONTINENTAL AIRLINES USES THE MARGINAL PRINCIPLE

APPLYING THE CONCEPTS #3: How do firms think at the margin?

In the 1960s, Continental Airlines puzzled observers of the airline industry and dismayed its stockholders by running flights with up to half the seats empty. The average cost of running a flight was about $4,000, and a half-full aircraft generated only $3,100 of revenue. So why did the airline run such flights? Were the managers of the airline irrational?

The managers of Continental Airlines ran half-full flights because they correctly applied the marginal principle. Although the average cost of a flight was $4,000, half of this cost involved fixed costs, such as airport fees and the cost of running the reservation system. The airline paid these costs regardless of how many flights it ran. The other half of the average cost involved costs that varied with the number of flights, including the cost of a flight crew, jet fuel, and food service. These other costs added up to $2,000 per flight. In other words, the marginal cost of a flight was only $2,000, so running a flight that generated $3,000 in revenue was sensible. Using the marginal principle, Continental ran flights with up to half the seats empty, earning profit in the process. *Related to Exercises 2.4 and 2.5.*

SOURCE: "Airline Takes the Marginal Bone," *BusinessWeek*, April 20, 1963, pp. 111–114.

2.3 | THE PRINCIPLE OF VOLUNTARY EXCHANGE

The principle of voluntary exchange is based on the notion that people act in their own self-interest. Self-interested people won't exchange one thing for another unless the trade makes them better off.

PRINCIPLE OF VOLUNTARY EXCHANGE

A voluntary exchange between two people makes both people better off.

Here are some examples.

- If you voluntarily exchange money for a college education, you must expect you'll be better off with a college education. The college voluntarily provides an education in exchange for your money, so the college must be better off, too.
- If you have a job, you voluntarily exchange your time for money, and your employer exchanges money for your labor services. Both you and your employer are better off as a result.

Exchange and Markets

Adam Smith stressed the importance of voluntary exchange as a distinctly human trait.[2] He noticed a propensity in human nature. . . to truck, barter, and exchange one thing for another. . . It is common to all men, and to be found in no other. . . animals. . . Nobody ever saw a dog make a fair and deliberate exchange of one bone for another with another dog.

As we saw in Chapter 1, a market is an institution or arrangement that enables people to exchange goods and services. If participation in a market is voluntary and people are well informed, both people in a transaction—buyer and seller—will be better off. The next time you see a market transaction, listen to what people say after money changes hands. If both people say "Thank you," that's the principle of voluntary exchange in action: The double thank you reveals that both people are better off.

The next chapter of the book explains the rationale for voluntary exchange. The alternative to exchange is *self-sufficiency:* Each of us could produce everything for ourselves. As we'll see in the next chapter, it is more sensible to specialize, doing what we do best and then buying products from other people, who in turn are doing what they do best. For example, if you are good with numbers but an awful carpenter, you could specialize in accounting and buy furniture from Woody, who could specialize in making furniture and pay someone to do his bookkeeping. In general, exchange allows us to take advantage of differences in people's talents and skills.

Online Games and Market Exchange

As another illustration of the power of exchange, consider the virtual world of online games. EverQuest is a role-playing game that allows thousands of people to interact online, moving their characters through a landscape of survival challenges. Each player constructs a character—called an *avatar*—by choosing some initial traits for it. The player then navigates the avatar through the game's challenges, where it acquires skills and accumulates assets, including clothing, weapons, armor, and even magic spells. The currency in EverQuest is a *platinum piece* (PP). Avatars can earn PPs by performing various tasks and use PPs to buy and sell assets.

The curious part about EverQuest is that players use real-life auction sites, including eBay and Yahoo! Auctions, to buy products normally purchased in the game with PPs.[3] Byron, who wants a piece of armor for his avatar (say, a Rubicite girdle), can use eBay to buy one for $50 from Selma. The two players then enter the online game, and Selma's avatar transfers the armor to Byron's avatar. It is even possible to buy another player's avatar, with all of its skills and assets. Given the time required to acquire various objects such as Rubicite girdles in the game versus the prices paid for them on eBay, the implicit wage earned by the typical online player auctioning them off is $3.42 per hour: That's how much the player could earn by first taking the time to acquire the assets in the game and then selling them on eBay.

2.4 | THE PRINCIPLE OF DIMINISHING RETURNS

Xena has a small copy shop, with one copying machine and one worker. When the backlog of orders piled up, she decided to hire a second worker, expecting that doubling her workforce would double the output of her copy shop from 500 pages per hour to 1,000. She was surprised when output increased to only 800 pages per hour. If she had known about the principle of diminishing returns, she would not have been surprised.

PRINCIPLE OF DIMINISHING RETURNS

Suppose output is produced with two or more inputs, and we increase one input while holding the other input or inputs fixed. Beyond some point—called the *point of diminishing returns*—output will increase at a decreasing rate.

APPLICATION

TIGER WOODS AND WEEDS

APPLYING THE CONCEPTS #4: What is the rationale for specialization and exchange?

Should Tiger Woods whack his own weeds? The swinging skills that make Tiger Woods one of the world's best golfers also make him a skillful weed whacker. His large estate has a lot of weeds, and it would take the best gardener 20 hours to take care of all of them. With his powerful and precise swing, Tiger could whack down all the weeds in just one hour. Since Tiger is 20 times more productive than the best gardener, should he take care of his own weeds?

We can use the principle of voluntary exchange to explain why Tiger should hire the less productive gardener. Suppose Tiger earns $1,000 per hour playing golf—either playing in tournaments or giving lessons. For Tiger, the opportunity cost of weed whacking is $1,000—the income he sacrifices by spending an hour cutting weeds rather than playing golf. If the gardener charges $10 per hour, Tiger could hire him to take care of the weeds for only $200. By switching one hour of his time from weed whacking to golf, Tiger earns $1,000 and incurs a cost of only $200, so he is better off by $800. Tiger Woods specializes in what he does best, and then buys goods and services from other people.
Related to Exercise 3.5.

Xena added a worker (one input) while holding the number of copying machines (the other input) fixed. Because the two workers shared a single copying machine, each worker spent some time waiting for the machine to be available. As a result, adding the second worker increased the number of copies, but did not double the output. With a single worker and a single copy machine, Xena has reached the point of diminishing returns: That is, as she increases the number of workers, output increases, but at a decreasing rate. The first worker increases output by 500 pages (from 0 to 500), but the second worker increases output by only 300 pages (from 500 to 800).

Diminishing Returns from Sharing a Production Facility

This principle of diminishing returns is relevant when we try to produce more output in an existing production facility (a factory, a store, an office, or a farm) by increasing the number of workers sharing the facility. When we add a worker to the facility, each worker becomes less productive because he or she works with a smaller piece of the facility: More workers share the same machinery, equipment, and factory space. As we pack more and more workers into the factory, total output increases, but at a decreasing rate.

It's important to emphasize that diminishing returns occurs because one of the inputs to the production process is fixed. When a firm can vary all of its inputs, including the size of the production facility, the principle of diminishing returns is not relevant. For example, if a firm doubled all of its inputs, building a second

APPLICATION

FERTILIZER AND CROP YIELDS

APPLYING THE CONCEPTS #5: Do farmers experience diminishing returns?

The notion of diminishing returns applies to all inputs to the production process. For example, one of the inputs in the production of corn is nitrogen fertilizer. Suppose a farmer has a fixed amount of land (an acre) and must decide how much fertilizer to apply. The first 50-pound bag of fertilizer will increase the crop yield by a relatively large amount, but the second bag is likely to increase the yield by a smaller amount, and the third bag is likely to have an even smaller effect. Because the farmer is changing just one of the inputs, the output will increase, but at a decreasing rate. Eventually, additional fertilizer will actually decrease output as the other nutrients in the soil are overwhelmed by the fertilizer.

Table 2.1 shows the relationship between the amount of fertilizer and the corn output. The first 50-pound bag of fertilizer increases the crop yield from 85 to 120 bushels per acre, a gain of 35 bushels. The next bag of fertilizer increases the yield by only 15 bushels (from 120 to 135), followed by a gain of 9 bushels (from 135 to 144) and then a gain of only 3 bushels (from 144 to 147). The farmer experienced diminishing returns because the other inputs to the production process are fixed.
Related to Exercises 4.5 and 4.6.

Table 2.1 FERTILIZER AND CORN YIELD

Bags of Nitrogen Fertilizer	Bushels of Corn Per Acre
0	85
1	120
2	135
3	144
4	147

factory and hiring a second workforce, we would expect the total output of the firm to at least double. The principle of diminishing returns does not apply when a firm is flexible in choosing all its inputs.

2.5 | THE REAL-NOMINAL PRINCIPLE

One of the key ideas in economics is that people are interested not just in the amount of money they have but also in how much their money will buy.

REAL-NOMINAL PRINCIPLE

What matters to people is the real value of money or income—its purchasing power—not the "face" value of money or income.

To illustrate this principle, suppose you work in your college bookstore to earn extra money for movies and newspapers. If your take-home pay is $10 per hour, is this a high wage or a low wage? The answer depends on the prices of the goods you buy. If

APPLICATION

THE DECLINING REAL MINIMUM WAGE

APPLYING THE CONCEPTS #6: How does inflation affect the real minimum wage?

Between 1974 and 2005, the federal minimum wage increased from $2.00 to $5.15. Was the typical minimum-wage worker better or worse off in 2005? We can apply the real-nominal principle to see what's happened over time to the real value of the federal minimum wage.

As shown in the first row of Table 2.2, the minimum wage was $2.00 per hour in 1974, and by 2005 it had risen to $5.15. These are nominal figures, indicating the face value of the minimum wage. By working 40 hours per week, a minimum-wage worker could earn $80 in 1974 and $206 in 2005. The third row of Table 2.2 shows the cost of a standard basket of consumer goods, which includes a standard mix of housing, food, clothing, and transportation. In 1974, consumer prices were relatively low, and the cost of buying all the goods in the standard basket was only $49. Between 1974 and 2005, consumer prices increased, and the cost of this standard basket of goods increased to $193.

The last row in Table 2.2 shows the purchasing power of the minimum wage in 1974 and 2005. In 1974, the $80 in weekly income could buy 1.63 standard baskets of goods. Between 1974 and 2005, the weekly income more than doubled, but the cost of the standard basket of goods nearly quadrupled, from $49 to $193. As a result, the weekly income of $206 in 2005 could buy only 1.07 baskets of goods. Because prices increased faster than the nominal wage, the real value of the minimum wage actually decreased over this period. *Related to Exercises 5.4 and 5.6.*

Table 2.2 | THE REAL VALUE OF THE MINIMUM WAGE, 1974–2005

	1974	2005
Minimum wage per hour	$2.00	$5.15
Weekly income from minimum wage	80.00	206.00
Cost of a standard basket of goods	49.00	193.00
Number of baskets per week	1.63	1.07

a movie costs $4 and a newspaper costs $1, with 1 hour of work you could afford to see 2 movies and buy 2 papers. The wage may seem high enough for you. But if a movie costs $8 and a newspaper costs $2, an hour of work would buy only 1 movie and 1 paper, and the same $10 wage doesn't seem so high. This is the real-nominal principle in action: What matters is not how many dollars you earn, but what those dollars will purchase.

The real-nominal principle can explain how people choose the amount of money to carry around with them. Suppose you typically withdraw $40 per week from an ATM to cover your normal expenses. If the prices of all the goods you purchase during the week double, you would have to withdraw $80 per week to make the same purchases. The amount of money people carry around depends on the prices of the goods and services they buy.

• **nominal value**
  The face value of an amount of money.

• **real value**
  The value of an amount of money in terms of what it can buy.

Economists use special terms to express the ideas behind the real-nominal principle:

• The **nominal value** of an amount of money is simply its face value. For example, the nominal wage paid by the bookstore is $10 per hour.

• The **real value** of an amount of money is measured in terms of the quantity of goods the money can buy. For example, the real value of your bookstore wage would fall as the prices of movies and newspapers increase, even though your nominal wage stayed the same.

Government officials use the real-nominal principle when they design public programs. For example, Social Security payments are increased each year to ensure that the checks received by the elderly and other recipients will purchase the same amount of goods and services, even if prices have increased.

The government also uses this principle when it publishes statistics about the economy. For example, when the government issues reports about changes in "real wages" in the economy over time, these statistics take into account the prices of the goods purchased by workers. Therefore, the real wage is stated in terms of its buying power, rather than its face value or nominal value.

7 APPLICATION

REPAYING STUDENT LOANS

APPLYING THE CONCEPTS #7: How does inflation affect lenders and borrowers?

Suppose you finish college with student loans that must be repaid in 10 years. Which is better for you, inflation (rising prices) or deflation (falling prices)? As an example, suppose you finish college this year with $20,000 in student loans and start a job that pays a salary of $40,000 in the first year. In 10 years, you will repay your college loans. Which would you prefer, stable prices, rising prices, or falling prices?

We can use the real-nominal principle to compute the real cost of repaying your loans. The first row of Table 2.3 shows the cost of the loan when all prices in the economy are stable—including the price of labor, your salary. In this case, your nominal salary in 10 years is $40,000, and the real cost of repaying your loan is the half year of work you must do to earn the $20,000. However, if all prices double over the 10-year period, your nominal salary will double to $80,000, and, as shown in the second row of Table 2.3, it will take you only a quarter of a year to earn $20,000 to repay the loan. In other words, a general increase in prices lowers the real cost of your loan. In contrast, if all prices decrease and your annual salary drops to $20,000, it will take you a full year to earn the money to repay the loan. In general, people who owe money prefer inflation to deflation.
Related to Exercises 5.5 and 5.8.

Table 2.3 | EFFECT OF INFLATION AND DEFLATION ON LOAN REPAYMENT

Change in Prices and Wages	Annual Salary	Years of Work to Repay $20,000 Loan
Stable	$40,000	1/2 year
Inflation: Salary doubles	80,000	1/4 year
Deflation: Salary cut in half	20,000	1 year

SUMMARY

This chapter covers five key principles of economics, the simple, self-evident truths that most people readily accept. If you understand these principles, you are ready to read the rest of the book, which will show you how to do your own economic analysis.

1 **Principle of opportunity cost.** The opportunity cost of something is what you sacrifice to get it.

2 **Marginal principle.** Increase the level of an activity as long as its marginal benefit exceeds its marginal cost.

Choose the level at which the marginal benefit equals the marginal cost.

3 **Principle of voluntary exchange.** A voluntary exchange between two people makes both people better off.

4 **Principle of diminishing returns.** Suppose that output is produced with two or more inputs, and we increase one input while holding the other inputs fixed. Beyond some point—called the *point of diminishing returns*—output will increase at a decreasing rate.

5 **Real-nominal principle.** What matters to people is the real value of money or income—its purchasing power—not the face value of money or income.

KEY TERMS

marginal benefit, p. 33
marginal cost, p. 33

nominal value, p. 42
opportunity cost, p. 30

production possibilities curve, p. 32
real value, p. 42

EXERCISES

Visit www.myeconlab.com to complete these exercises online and get instant feedback.

2.1 | The Principle of Opportunity Cost

1.1 Consider Figure 2.1 on page 32. Between points *c* and *d*, the opportunity cost of _____ tons of wheat is _____ tons of steel.

1.2 Arrow up or down: An increase in the wage for high-school graduates _____ the opportunity cost of college.

1.3 Arrow up or down: An increase in the market interest rate _____ the economic cost of holding a $500 collectible for a year.

1.4 Oprah just inherited a house with a market value of $200,000, and she does not expect the market value to change. Each year, she will pay $500 for utilities and $3,000 in taxes. She can earn 6 percent interest on money in a bank account. Her cost of living in the house for a year is $_____.

1.5 What is the cost of a pair of warships purchased by Malaysia? (Related to Application 2 on page 34.)

1.6 **The Cost of a Flower Business.** Jen left a job paying $50,000 per year to start her own florist shop in a building she owns. The market value of the building is $100,000. She pays $30,000 per year for flowers and other supplies, and has a bank account that pays 8 percent interest. What is the economic cost of Jen's business? (Related to Application 1 on page 31.)

1.7 **The Opportunity Cost of a Mission to Mars.** The United States has plans to spend billions of dollars on a mission to Mars. List some of the possible opportunity costs of the mission. What resources will be used to execute the mission, and what do we sacrifice by using these resources in a mission to Mars? (Related to Application 2 on page 34.)

1.8 **Interest Rates and ATM Trips.** Carlos, who lives in a country where interest rates are very high, goes to an ATM every day to get $10 of spending money. Art, who lives in a country with relatively low interest rates, goes to the ATM once a month to get $300 of spending money. Why does Carlos use the ATM more frequently?

1.9 **Correct the Cost Statements.** Consider the following statements about cost. For each incorrect statement, provide a correct statement about the relevant cost.

a. One year ago, I loaned a friend $100, and she just paid me back the whole $100. The loan didn't cost me anything.

b. Our sawmill bought a truckload of logs one year ago for $20,000. If we use the logs to build tables today, the cost of the logs is $20,000.

c. Our new football stadium was built on land donated to the university by a wealthy alum. The cost of the stadium equals the $50 million construction cost.

1.10 **Production Possibilities Curve.** Consider a nation that produces MP3 players and bicycles. The following table shows the possible combinations of the two products.

MP3 players (millions)	0	3	6	9	12
Bicycles (millions)	60	54	42	24	0

a. Draw a production possibilities curve with MP3 players on the horizontal axis and bicycles on the vertical axis.

b. Suppose the technology for producing MP3 players improves, meaning that fewer resources are needed for each MP3 player. In contrast, the technology for producing bicycles does not change. Draw a new production possibilities curve.

c. The opportunity cost of the first 3 million MP3 players is _____ million bicycles and the opportunity cost of the last 3 million MP3 players is _____ million bicycles.

2.2 | The Marginal Principle

2.1 If a bus company adds a third daily bus between two cities, the company's total cost will increase from $500 to $600 and its total revenue will increase by $150 per day. Should the company add the third bus? _____ (Yes/No)

2.2 In Figure 2.3 on page 35, suppose the marginal cost of movies is constant at $125 million. Is it sensible to produce the third movie? _____ (Yes/No)

2.3 Suppose that stricter emissions standards would reduce health-care costs by $50 million but increase the costs of fuel and emissions equipment by $30 million. Is it sensible to tighten the emissions standards? _____ (Yes/No)

2.4 Continental Airlines ran flights with up to half the seats empty because _____ was greater than _____. (Related to Application 3 on page 37.)

2.5 **Marginal Airlines.** Marginal Airlines runs 10 flights per day at a total cost of $50,000, including $30,000 in fixed costs for airport fees and the reservation system and $20,000 for flight crews and food service. (Related to Application 3 on page 37.)

a. If an 11th flight would have 25 passengers, each paying $100, would it be sensible to run the flight?

b. If the 11th flight would have only 15 passengers, would it be sensible to run the flight?

2.6 **How Many Police Officers?** In your city, each police officer has a budgetary cost of $40,000 per year. The property loss from each burglary is $4,000. The first officer hired will reduce crime by 40 burglaries, and each additional officer will reduce crime by half as much as the previous one. How many officers should the city hire? Illustrate with a graph with a marginal-benefit curve and a marginal-cost curve.

2.7 **How Many Hours at the Barber Shop?** Your opportunity cost of cutting hair at your barbershop is $20 per hour. Electricity costs $6 per hour, and your weekly rent is $250. You normally stay open nine hours per day.

a. What is the marginal cost of staying open for one more hour?

b. If you expect to give two haircuts in the 10th hour and you charge $15 per haircut, is it sensible to stay open for the extra hour?

2.8 **How Many Pints of Blackberries?** The pleasure you get from each pint of freshly picked blackberries is $2.00. It takes you 12 minutes to pick the first pint, and each additional pint takes an additional 2 minutes (14 minutes for the second pint, 16 minutes for the third pint, and so on). The opportunity cost of your time is $0.10 per minute.

a. How many pints of blackberries should you pick? Illustrate with a complete graph.

b. How would your answer to (a) change if your pleasure decreased by $0.20 for each additional pint ($1.80 for the second, $1.60 for the third, and so on)? Illustrate with a complete graph.

2.3 | The Principle of Voluntary Exchange

3.1 When two people involved in an exchange say "thank you" afterwards, they are merely being polite. _____ (True/False)

3.2 Consider a transaction in which a consumer buys a book for $15. The value of the book to the buyer is at least $_____, and the cost of producing the book is no more than $_____.

3.3 Arrow up or down: Andy buys and eats one apple per day, and smacks his lips in appreciation as he eats it. The greater his satisfaction with the exchange of money for an apple, the larger the number of smacks. If the price of apples decreases, the number of smacks per apple will _____.

3.4 Sally sells one apple per day to Andy, and says "ca-ching" to show her satisfaction with the transaction. The greater her satisfaction with the exchange, the louder her "ca-ching." If the price of apples decreases, her "ca-ching" will become _____. (louder/ softer)

3.5 **Should a Heart Surgeon Do Her Own Plumbing?** A heart surgeon is skillful at unplugging arteries and rerouting the flow of blood, and these skills also make her a very skillful plumber. She can clear a clogged drain in 6 minutes, about 10 times faster than the most skillful plumber in town. (Related to Application 4 on page 39.)
  a. Should the surgeon clear her own clogged drains? Explain.
  b. Suppose the surgeon earns $20 per minute in heart surgery, and the best plumber in town charges $50 per hour. How much does the surgeon gain by hiring the plumber to clear a clogged drain?

3.6 **Fishing Versus Boat Building.** Half the members of a fishing tribe catch 2 fish per day and half catch 8 fish per day. A group of 10 members could build a boat for another tribe in 1 day and receive a payment of 40 fish for the boat.
  a. Suppose the boat builders are drawn at random from the tribe. From the tribe's perspective, what is the expected cost of building the boat?
  b. How could the tribe decrease the cost of building the boat, thus making it worthwhile?

3.7 **Solving a Smoking Problem.** Consider a restaurant in a city with no restrictions on smoking. When one patron lights up a cigar in the full restaurant, an uproar occurs because other diners object to the smoke. You leave the restaurant, and when you return five minutes later the air is clear, but everyone is happy. On the table in front of the person who extinguished his cigar is a pile of cash. Use the principle of voluntary exchange to explain what happened.

2.4 | The Principle of Diminishing Returns

4.1 Consider the example of Xena's copy shop. If she added a third worker, her output would increase by fewer than _____ pages.

4.2 If a firm is subject to diminishing marginal returns, an increase in the number of workers decreases the quantity produced. _____ (True/False)

4.3 Fill in the blanks with "at least" or "less than": If a firm doubles one input but holds the other inputs fixed, we normally expect output to _____ double; if a firm doubles all inputs, we expect output to _____ double.

4.4 Fill in the blanks with "flexible" or "inflexible": Diminishing returns is applicable when a firm is _____ in choosing inputs, but does not apply when a firm is _____ in choosing its inputs.

4.5 Arrows up or down: As a farmer adds more and more fertilizer to the soil, the crop yield _____, but at a _____ rate. (Related to Application 5 on page 40.)

4.6 **Feeding the World from a Flowerpot?** Comment on the following statement: "If agriculture did not experience diminishing returns, we could feed the world using the soil from a small flowerpot." (Related to Application 5 on page 40.)

4.7 **When to Use the Principle of Diminishing Returns?** You are the manager of a firm that produces memory chips for mobile phones.
  a. In your decision about how much output to produce this week, would you use the principle of diminishing returns? Explain.
  b. In your decision about how much output to produce two years from now, would you use the principle of diminishing returns? Explain.

4.8 **Diminishing Returns in a Coffee Shop?** Your coffee shop produces espressos, using an espresso machine and workers.
  a. If you double the number of workers but don't add a second espresso machine, would you expect your output (espressos per hour) to double? Explain.
  b. If you double the number of workers and add a second espresso machine, would you expect your output (espressos per hour) to double? Explain.

4.9 **Diminishing Returns and the Marginal Principle.** Molly's Espresso Shop has become busy, and the more hours Ted works, the more espressos Molly can sell. The price of espressos is $2 and Ted's hourly wage is $11. Complete the following table.

Hours for Ted	Espressos Sold	Marginal Benefit from Additional Hour	Marginal Cost from Additional Hour
0	100	—	—
1	130	$60 = $2 × 30 additional espressos	$11 = hourly wage
2	154	_____	_____
3	172	_____	_____
4	184	_____	_____
5	190	_____	_____
6	193	_____	_____

If Molly applies the marginal principle, how many hours should Ted work?

5.1 Your savings account pays 4 percent per year: Each $100 in the bank grows to $104 over a one-year period. If prices increase by 3 percent per year, by keeping $100 in the bank for a year you actually gain $_____.

5.2 Suppose that over a one-year period, the nominal wage increases by 2 percent and consumer prices increase by 5 percent. Fill in the blanks: The real wage _____ by _____ percent.

5.3 Suppose you currently live and work in Cleveland, earning a salary of $60,000 per year and spending $10,000 for housing. You just heard that you will be transferred to a city in California where housing is 50 percent more expensive. In negotiating a new salary, your objective is to keep your real income constant. Your new target salary is $_____.

5.4 Between 1974 and 2005, the federal minimum wage increased from $2.00 to $5.15. Was the typical minimum-wage worker better off in 2005? _____ (Yes/No) (Related to Application 6 on page 41.)

5.5 Suppose you graduate with $20,000 in student loans and repay the loans 10 years later. Which is better for you, inflation (rising prices) or deflation (falling prices)? _____ (Related to Application 7 on page 42)

5.6 **Changes in Welfare Payments.** Between 1970 and 1988, the average monthly welfare payment to single mothers increased from $160 to $360. Over the same period, the cost of a standard basket of consumer goods (a standard bundle of food, housing, and other goods and services) increased from $39 to $118. Fill the blanks in the following table. Did the real value of welfare payments increase or decrease over this period? (Related to Application 6 on page 41.)

	1970	1988
Monthly welfare payment	$160	$360
Cost of a standard basket of goods	39	118
Number of baskets per week	_____	_____

5.7 **Changes in Wages and Consumer Prices.** The following table shows for 1980 and 2004 the cost of a standard basket of consumer goods (a standard bundle of food, housing, and other goods and services) and the nominal average wage (hourly earnings) for workers in several sectors of the economy.

Year	Cost of Consumer Basket	Nominal Wage: Manufacturing	Nominal Wage: Professional Services	Nominal Wage: Leisure and Hospitality	Nominal Wage: Information
1980	$82	$7.52	$7.48	$4.05	$9.83
2004	189	16.34	17.69	9.01	21.70
Percent change from 1980 to 2004					

a. Complete the table by computing the percentage changes of the cost of the basket of consumer goods and the nominal wages.

b. How do the percentage changes in nominal wages compare to the percentage change in the cost of consumer goods?

c. Which sectors experienced an increase in real wages, and which sectors experienced a decrease in real wages?

5.8 **Repaying a Car Loan.** Suppose you borrow money to buy a car and must repay $20,000 in interest and principal in 5 years. Your current monthly salary is $4,000. (Related to Application 7 on page 42.)

a. Complete the following table.

b. Which environment has the lowest real cost of repaying the loan?

Change in Prices and Wages	Monthly Salary	Months of Work to Repay $20,000 Loan
Stable	$4,000	
Inflation: Prices rise by 25%	_____	_____
Deflation: Prices drop by 50%	_____	_____

5.9 **Inflation and Interest Rates.** Len consumes only music, with an initial price of $10 per CD. Like other people, he prefers music now to music later and is willing to accept 1.10 units of music in 1 year for each unit of music he sacrifices today.

a. Suppose Len loans $100 to Barb, and Len sacrifices 10 CDs to make the loan. How much must Barb repay Len a year later to make him indifferent about making the loan? What is the implied interest rate?

b. Suppose that over the one-year period of the loan, all prices (including the price of CDs) increase by 20 percent. If Len and Barb anticipate the inflation, what is the appropriate loan arrangement? What is the implied interest rate?

ECONOMIC EXPERIMENT

Producing Fold-Its

Here is a simple economic experiment that takes about 15 minutes to run. The instructor places a stapler and a stack of paper on a table. Students produce "fold-its" by folding a page of paper in thirds and stapling both ends of the folded page. One student is assigned to inspect each fold-it to be sure that it is produced correctly. The experiment starts with a single student, or worker, who has 1 minute to produce as many fold-its as possible. After the instructor records the number of fold-its produced, the process is repeated with 2 students, 3 students, 4 students, and so on. The question is, "How does the number of fold-its change as the number of workers increases?"

NOTES

1. Colin Kennedy, "Lord of the Screens," *Economist: The World in 2003*, p. 29 (London, 2003).

2. Adam Smith, *An Inquiry into the Nature and Causes of the Wealth of Nations* (First published in 1776; New York: Random House, 1973), Book 1, Chapter 2.

3. Edward Castronova, *Synthetic Worlds: The Business and Culture of Online Games* (Chicago: University of Chicago Press, 2005).

3
Exchange and Markets

Mattel's Barbie, the most profitable doll in history, is sold in 140 countries around the world at a rate of two dolls per second. Annual sales are $1.7 billion.[1] Most people think the doll symbolizes American culture, but Barbie is really an international product. The dolls are designed in the United States, but most of the production occurs elsewhere. Saudi Arabia provides the oil used in Taiwanese factories to produce the vinyl plastic pellets that become Barbie's body. Japan supplies Barbie's nylon hair, and China provides her cotton clothes. The machinery used in Barbie factories in China, Indonesia, and Malaysia comes from Japan, Europe, and the United States. The United States provides the molds used to form the dolls and the pigments and oils used to paint them. Barbie dolls come in a box labeled "Made in China," but only about $0.33 of the $10 retail price goes to the factories in China that assemble the dolls. The rest goes to input suppliers around the world and to Mattel, which collects a $1 profit on each Barbie doll sold.

APPLYING THE CONCEPTS

1 How many jobs are lost to outsourcing—the shift of production to other countries?
Moving Jobs to Different States and Different Countries

2 Does the protection of one domestic industry harm another?
Candy Cane Makers Move to Mexico for Cheap Sugar

3 Why do markets develop wherever people go?
Markets in a Prisoner of War Camp

In Chapter 1, we saw that a society makes three types of economic decisions: what products to produce, how to produce them, and who gets them. In modern economies, most of these decisions are made in markets. Most of us participate in the labor market and are paid for jobs in which we produce goods and services for others. We participate in consumer markets, spending our incomes on food, clothing, housing, and other products. In this chapter, we explain why markets exist and then explore the virtues and the shortcomings of markets. We also examine the role of government in a market-based economy.

3.1 | COMPARATIVE ADVANTAGE AND EXCHANGE

As we saw earlier in the book, a market is an institution or arrangement that enables people to buy and sell things. The alternative to buying and selling in markets is to be self-sufficient, with each of us producing everything we need for ourselves. Rather than going it alone, most of us specialize: We produce one or two products for others and then exchange the money we earn for the products we want to consume.

Specialization and the Gains from Trade

We can explain how people can benefit from specialization and trade with a simple example of two people and two products. Suppose that the crew of the television show *Survivor* finishes filming a season of episodes on a remote tropical island, and when the crew returns to the mainland two people miss the boat and are left behind. The two real survivors produce and consume two goods, coconuts and fish. The first row of Table 3.1 shows their production possibilities. Each day Fred can either gather 2 coconuts or catch 6 fish, while Kate can either gather 1 coconut or catch 1 fish.

We'll show that the two survivors will be better off if each person specializes in one product and then exchanges with the other person. We can use one of the key principles to explore the rationale for specialization.

 # PRINCIPLE OF OPPORTUNITY COST

The opportunity cost of something is what you sacrifice to get it.

Fred's opportunity cost of a coconut is 3 fish—that's how many fish he could catch in the time required to gather 1 coconut. Similarly, his opportunity cost of a fish is one-third coconut, the number of coconuts he could gather in the time required to catch 1 fish. For Kate, the opportunity cost of a coconut is 1 fish, and the opportunity cost of a fish is 1 coconut.

Table 3.1 | PRODUCTIVITY AND OPPORTUNITY COSTS

| | Fred | | Kate | |
	Coconuts	Fish	Coconuts	Fish
Output per day	2	6	1	1
Opportunity cost	3 fish	1/3 coconut	1 fish	1 coconut

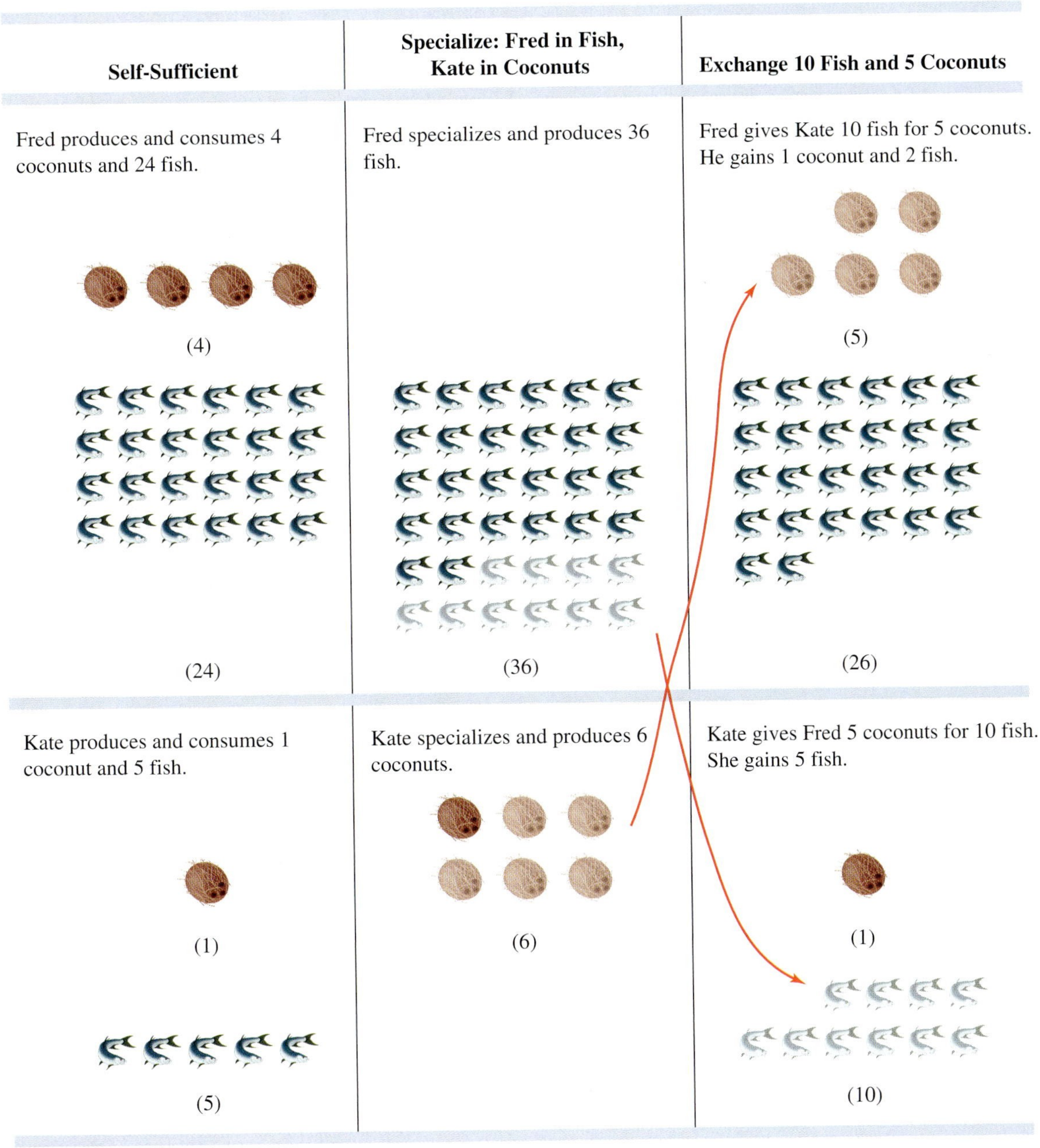

▲ **FIGURE 3.1**
Specialization and the Gains from Trade

To demonstrate the benefits of exchange, let's imagine that both people are initially self-sufficient, with each producing enough of both goods to satisfy their own desires. Suppose there are 6 workdays per week. If Fred initially devotes 2 days per week to gathering coconuts and 4 days per week to catching fish, he will produce and consume 4 coconuts (2 per day times 2 days) and 24 fish (6 per day times 4 days) per week. This is shown in the first column of Figure 3.1. If Kate initially devotes 1 day per week to coconuts and 5 days per week to fish, she will produce and consume 1 coconut and 5 fish per week.

• **comparative advantage**
The ability of one person or nation to produce a good at a lower opportunity cost than another person or nation.

Specialization will increase the total output of our little survivor economy. It is sensible for each person to specialize in the good for which he or she has a lower opportunity cost. We say that a person has a **comparative advantage** in producing a particular product if he or she has a lower opportunity cost than another person:

- Fred has a comparative advantage producing fish because his opportunity cost of fish is one-third coconut per fish, compared to 1 coconut per fish for Kate.

- Kate has a comparative advantage in coconuts because her opportunity cost of coconuts is 1 fish per coconut, compared to 3 fish per coconut for Fred.

The second column of Figure 3.1 shows what happens to production when the two people specialize: Fred produces 36 fish and Kate produces 6 coconuts. The total output of both goods increases: The number of coconuts increases from 5 to 6, and the number of fish increases from 29 to 36. Specialization increases the output of both goods because both people are focusing on what they do best.

If specialization is followed by exchange, both people will be better off. Suppose Fred and Kate agree to exchange 2 fish per coconut. Fred could give up 10 fish to get 5 coconuts. As shown in the third column of Figure 3.1, that leaves him with 5 coconuts and 26 fish. Compared to the self-sufficient outcome, he has more of both goods—one more coconut and 2 more fish. If Kate gives up 5 coconuts to get 10 fish, that leaves her with 1 coconut and 10 fish, which is better than her self-sufficient outcome of one coconut and 5 fish. Specialization and exchange make both people better off, illustrating one of the key principles of economics:

PRINCIPLE OF VOLUNTARY EXCHANGE

A voluntary exchange between two people makes both people better off.

Comparative Advantage Versus Absolute Advantage

We've seen that it is beneficial for each person to specialize in the product for which he or she has a comparative advantage—a lower opportunity cost. You may have noticed that Fred is more productive than Kate in producing both goods. Fred requires a smaller quantity of resources (less labor time) to produce both goods, so he has an **absolute advantage** in producing both goods. Despite his absolute advantage, Fred gains from specialization and trade because he has a comparative advantage in fish. Fred is twice as productive as Kate in producing coconuts, but six times as productive in producing fish. By relying on Kate to produce coconuts, Fred frees up time to spend producing fish, the good for which he has the larger productivity advantage over Kate. The lesson is that specialization and exchange result from comparative advantage, not absolute advantage.

• **absolute advantage**
The ability of one person or nation to produce a product at a lower resource cost than another person or nation.

The Division of Labor and Exchange

So far, we've seen that specialization and trade exploit differences in productivity across workers and make everyone better off. We've assumed that the differences in productivity are innate, not acquired. In his 1776 book *An Inquiry into the Nature and Causes of the Wealth of Nations*, Adam Smith noted that specialization actually increased productivity through the division of labor. He used the example of the pin factory to illustrate how the division of labor increased output:[2]

A workman . . . could scarce, perhaps with his utmost industry, make one pin a day, and certainly could not make twenty. But the way in which this business is now carried on . . . one man draws out the wire, another straightens it, a third cuts it, a fourth points it, a fifth grinds the top for receiving the head; to make the head requires two or three distinct operations. . . . The . . . making of a pin is, in this manner, divided into about eighteen distinct operations. . . . I have seen a small manufactory of this kind where ten men . . . make among them . . . upward of forty eight thousand pins in a day.

Smith listed three reasons for productivity to increase with specialization, with each worker performing a single production task:

1 *Repetition.* The more times a worker performs a particular task, the more proficient the worker becomes at that task.

2 *Continuity.* A specialized worker doesn't spend time switching from one task to another. This is especially important if switching tasks requires a change in tools or location.

3 *Innovation.* A specialized worker gains insights into a particular task that lead to better production methods. Smith believed that workers were innovators:[3]

A great part of the machines made use of in those manufactures in which labour is most subdivided, were originally the inventions of common workmen, who, being each of them employed in some simple operation, naturally turned their thoughts toward finding out easier and readier methods of performing it.

To summarize, specialization and exchange result from differences in productivity that lead to comparative advantage. Differences in productivity result from differences in innate skills and the benefits associated with the division of labor. Adam Smith wrote that "every man thus lives by exchanging, or becomes in some measure a merchant, and the society itself grows to be what is properly a commercial society."[4]

3.2 | COMPARATIVE ADVANTAGE AND INTERNATIONAL TRADE

The lessons of comparative advantage and specialization apply to trade between nations. Each nation could be self-sufficient, producing all the goods it consumes, or it could specialize in products for which it has a comparative advantage. Even if one nation is more productive than a second nation in producing all goods, trade will be beneficial if the first nation has a bigger productivity advantage in one product—that is, if one nation has a comparative advantage in some product. An **import** is a product produced in a foreign country and purchased by residents of the home country. An **export** is a product produced in the home country and sold in another country.

• **import**
A product produced in a foreign country and purchased by residents of the home country.

• **export**
A product produced in the home country and sold in another country.

Many people are skeptical about the idea that international trade can make everyone better off. President Abraham Lincoln expressed his discomfort with importing goods:[5]

I know if I buy a coat in America, I have a coat and America has the money—If I buy a coat in England, I have the coat and England has the money.

What President Lincoln didn't understand is that when he buys a coat in England, he sends dollars to England, and the dollars don't just sit there, but eventually are sent back to the United States to buy goods produced by American workers. In the words of economist Todd Buchholz, the author of *New Ideas from Dead Economists*:[6]

Money may not make the world go round, but money certainly goes around the world. To stop it prevents goods from traveling from where they are produced most inexpensively to where they are desired most deeply.

APPLICATION

MOVING JOBS TO DIFFERENT STATES AND DIFFERENT COUNTRIES

APPLYING THE CONCEPTS #1: How many jobs are lost to outsourcing—the shift of production to other countries?

When a domestic firm shifts part of its production to a different country, we say that the firm is *outsourcing* or *offshoring*. The chapter opener on Mattel's Barbie relates a classic example of outsourcing, with production occurring in Saudi Arabia, Taiwan, Japan, China, Indonesia, Malaysia, Europe, and the United States. In the modern global economy, transportation and communication costs are relatively low, so firms can spread production across many countries. By taking advantage of the comparative advantages of different countries, a firm can produce its product at a lower cost, charge a lower price, and sell more output.

In recent years, outsourcing has received a lot of attention as firms shift service functions overseas. The reduction of communication costs and the standardization of software have allowed firms to outsource business services such as customer service, telemarketing, document management, and medical transcription. Firms shift these functions overseas to reduce production costs, allowing them to sell their products at lower prices. Some recent studies of outsourcing have reached a number of conclusions:[8]

1 The loss of jobs is a normal part of a healthy economy, because technology and consumer preferences change over time. The number of jobs lost to outsourcing is a small fraction of the normal job loss experienced by a healthy economy. For example, in the first three months of 2004, a total of 239,361 workers were laid off, with 9,985 jobs moving to another location within the United States, 4,633 outsourced to another country, and the rest simply lost to the economy. This means that roughly 2 percent of the layoffs were caused by outsourcing.

2 The jobs lost to outsourcing are at least partly offset by jobs gained through *insourcing*, jobs that are shifted from overseas to the United States.

3 The cost savings from outsourcing are substantial, leading to lower prices for consumers and more output for firms. The jobs gained from increased output at least partly offset the jobs lost to outsourcing.

Related to Exercises 2.3 and 2.5.

SOURCE: U.S. Bureau of Labor Statistics, "Extended Mass Layoffs Associated with Domestic and Overseas Relocations, First Quarter 2004," June 2004.

Movie Exports

Although many people think of exports in terms of farm products, such as corn and wheat, and manufactured products, such as airplanes and satellites, one of the leading U.S. exports is movies. The U.S. film industry employs about 350,000 Americans, and almost two-thirds of its revenue comes from films exported to countries around the world. Figure 3.2

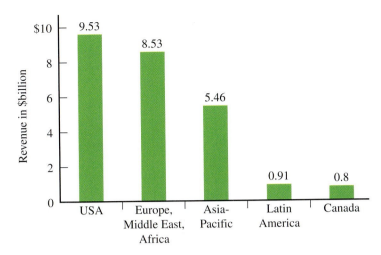

▲ FIGURE 3.2
International Box Office Revenue for U.S. Films, 2004
SOURCE: Author's computations based on MPA Worldwide Market Research, MPA Snapshot Report: 2004 International Theatrical Market (Motion Picture Association, March 2005).

APPLICATION

2

CANDY CANE MAKERS MOVE TO MEXICO FOR CHEAP SUGAR

APPLYING THE CONCEPTS #2: Does the protection of one domestic industry harm another?

About 90 percent of the world's candy canes are consumed in the United States, and until recently most candy canes were produced domestically. Domestic producers were closer to consumers, so they had lower transportation costs and lower prices than their foreign competitors. Domestic firms used their superior access to consumers to dominate the market.

In recent years, the domestic production of candy canes has decreased as firms have shut plants in the United States and opened new ones in Mexico. In 2003, Spangler Candy Company of Bryan, Ohio, shifted half of its production to a plant in Juarez, Mexico. The company opened the Mexico plant because the cost of sugar, the key ingredient in candy, is only $0.06 per pound in Mexico, compared to $0.21 in the United States. The shift to Mexico saves the firm about $2.7 million per year on sugar costs. The high price of sugar has caused other candy manufacturers to shift their operations overseas. Since 1998, the Chicago area, the center of the U.S. confection industry, has lost about 3,000 candy-production jobs.

Why is the price of sugar in the United States so high? The government protects the domestic sugar industry from foreign competition by restricting sugar imports. As a result, the supply of sugar in the United States is artificially low and the price is artificially high. In this case, the protection of jobs in one domestic industry reduces jobs in another domestic industry.
Related to Exercises 2.4 and 2.6.

SOURCE: "Sugar Costs Give Candy Cane Makers a Bitter Aftertaste," *Chicago Tribune,* December 25, 2003, p. 14.

shows the distribution of box office revenue from different parts of the world. Between 2001 and 2004, total export revenue from movies increased from $8.6 billion to $15.7 billion, with the largest increases in Europe and the Middle East.[7] By comparison, each year the United States exports about $25 billion worth of aircraft and spacecraft and about $12 billion worth of wheat, rice, and corn.

3.3 | MARKETS

Earlier in the chapter, we used a simple example of direct exchange to show the benefits of specialization and exchange. In a modern economy, people don't directly exchange goods like fish and coconuts, but instead rely on all sorts of markets to exchange goods and services, trading what they have for what they want. In a **market economy**, most people specialize in one productive activity, by picking an occupation, and use their incomes to buy most of the goods they consume. In addition to the labor and consumer markets, many of us participate in the market for financial capital: We earn interest from savings accounts and money-market accounts and pay interest on mortgages, car loans, and student loans. Friedrich Hayek, a famous twentieth-century economist, suggested that if the market system hadn't arisen naturally, it would have been proclaimed the greatest invention in human history.[8]

Although it appears that markets arose naturally, a number of social and government inventions have made them work better:

- **Contracts specify the terms of exchange, facilitating exchange between strangers.** If you have an AOL account, you expect to have reliable e-mail service as long as you pay your bill. If you operate a bookstore, you expect book wholesalers to deliver the books you've purchased. In both cases, a contract specifies the terms of exchange.

- **Insurance reduces the risk of entrepreneurs.** If you operate a bagel shop, fire insurance reduces your losses in the event of a fire.

- **Patents increase the profitability of inventions, encouraging firms to develop new products and production processes.** Pharmaceutical companies such as Bayer Pharmaceutical and Merck spend billions of dollars to create, test, and bring new products to the market. A patent prevents other companies from copying a new product, making it more likely that the revenue from a new product will be large enough to cover research and development costs.

- **Accounting rules provide potential investors with reliable information about the financial performance of a firm.** If you are thinking about investing in Apple Computer, you could use publicly available information to examine the company's financial history.

Virtues of Markets

To assess the virtues of the market system, imagine the alternative—a **centrally planned economy** in which a planning authority decides what products to produce, how to produce them, and who gets them. To make these decisions, a planner must first collect a huge amount of widely dispersed information about consumption desires (what products each individual wants), production techniques (what resources are required to produce each product), and the availability of factors of production (labor, human capital, physical capital, and natural resources). Then the planner must decide how to allocate the productive resources among the alternative products. Finally, the planner must divide the output among the economy's citizens. Clearly, a central planner has a formidable task.

• **market economy**
An economy in which people specialize and exchange goods and services in markets.

• **centrally planned economy**
An economy in which a government bureaucracy decides how much of each good to produce, how to produce the good, and who gets them.

Under a market system, decisions are made by the thousands of people who already have information about consumers' desires, production technology, and resources. These decisions are guided by prices of inputs and outputs. To illustrate, suppose you buy a wool coat. The dozens of people who contributed to the production of the coat—including the farmers who manage the sheep, the workers who transform raw wool into cloth and the cloth into a coat, the truckers who transport the inputs and the actual coat, and the merchant who sold the coat—didn't know you wanted a coat:

- The farmer knew that the price of wool was high enough to justify raising and shearing sheep.

- The workers knew that wages were high enough to make their efforts worthwhile.

- The merchant knew that the price of the coat was high enough to make it worthwhile to acquire the coat in anticipation of selling it.

3

APPLICATION

MARKETS IN A PRISONER OF WAR CAMP

APPLYING THE CONCEPTS #3: Why do markets develop wherever people go?

To illustrate the pervasiveness of exchange, consider the emergence of markets in prisoner of war (POW) camps in World War II, as documented by economist Roy Radner.

During World War II, the International Red Cross gave each Allied prisoner a weekly parcel, with the same mix of products—tinned milk, jam, butter, biscuits, corned beef, chocolate, sugar, and cigarettes. In addition, many prisoners received private parcels from family and friends. The prisoners used barter to exchange one good for another, and cigarettes emerged as the medium of exchange. Prisoners wandered through the camp calling out their offers of goods. For example, "cheese for seven" meant that the prisoner was willing to sell a cheese ration for seven cigarettes. In addition to food, the prisoners bought and sold clothing (80 cigarettes per shirt), laundry services (two cigarettes per garment), and hot cups of coffee (two cigarettes per cup).

The prices of products reflected their scarcity. The tea-drinking British prisoners demanded little coffee. Because the British were confined to their compound, packets of coffee beans sold for just a few cigarettes. Enterprising British prisoners bribed prison guards to permit them to travel to the French compound, where they could sell coffee for dozens of cigarettes. Religious groups such as the Sikhs didn't eat beef, and the excess supply of beef in the Sikh compound led to low beef prices. One prisoner who knew the Sikh language bought beef at a low price in the Sikh compound and sold it at a higher price in other compounds. Eventually, other people entered the Sikh beef trade, and beef prices across compounds became roughly equal.

Related to Exercises 3.2, 3.3, and 3.5.

SOURCE: R. A. Radford, "The Economic Organization of a P.O.W. Camp," *Economica*, November 1945, pp. 189–201.

In a market system, prices provide individuals the information they need to make decisions.

Prices provide signals about the relative scarcity of a product and help an economy respond to scarcity. For example, suppose wool becomes more scarce, either because a new use for wool is discovered or an old source of wool disappears. The greater scarcity will increase the price of wool, and producers and consumers will respond in ways that diminish scarcity:

- The higher price encourages fabric producers to use the available wool more efficiently and encourages farmers to produce more of it.
- The higher price also encourages consumers to switch to coats made from alternative fabrics.

These two responses help the economy accommodate an increase in scarcity. Consumers and producers don't need to know why wool is more scarce for these mechanisms to kick in—only that the price is higher.

The decisions made in markets result from the interactions of millions of people, each motivated by their own interests. Adam Smith used the metaphor of the "invisible hand" to explain that people acting in self-interest may actually promote the interest of society as a whole:[9]

> It is not from the benevolence of the butcher, the brewer, or the baker that we expect our dinner, but from their regard to their own interest. We address ourselves, not to their humanity but to their self-love, and never talk to them of our own necessities but of their advantages. . . . [Man is] led by an invisible hand to promote an end which was no part of this intention. . . . By pursuing his own interest he frequently promotes that of the society more effectually than when he really intends to promote it. . . . Nobody but a beggar chooses to depend chiefly upon the benevolence of his fellow citizens.

The market system works by getting each person, motivated by self-interest, to produce products for other people.

Entrepreneurs play a key role in a market economy. Prices and profits provide signals to entrepreneurs about what to produce. If a product suddenly becomes popular, competition among consumers will increase its price and increase the profits earned by firms producing the product. Entrepreneurs will enter the market and increase production to meet the higher demand, switching resources from the production of other products. As entrepreneurs enter the market, they compete for customers, driving the price back down to the level that generates just enough profit for them to remain in business. In contrast, if a product becomes less popular, the process is reversed. Producers will cut prices in order to sell the product to the smaller number of customers who want it. Entrepreneurs will leave the unprofitable market, finding other products to produce, and the price will eventually rise back to the level where profits are high enough for the remaining producers to justify staying in business.

One way to see the advantages of a market system is to see what happened in economies that were once centrally planned.[10] In the former Soviet Union, state-run auto repair shops, plagued by shortages of parts, were replaced by repair shops run by entrepreneurs with a profit incentive. In China, farmers moved away from the inefficient communal system and started selling their produce themselves.

3.4 | MARKET FAILURE AND THE ROLE OF GOVERNMENT

Although markets often operate efficiently, sometimes they do not. This phenomenon is known as *market failure*, which is what happens when markets fail to produce the most efficient outcomes on their own. Later in the book, we'll explore several sources of market failure and discuss possible responses by government. Here is a preview of the topics:

- **Pollution.** For markets to work efficiently, the people making the decisions about production and consumption must bear the full costs of their decisions. In some cases, however, other people bear some of the costs. For example, people living downwind from a paper mill breathe dirty air. The people who decide how much paper to produce will ignore these other costs, so they will produce too much paper. Similarly, people with asthma suffer from the emissions of cars and SUVs. Drivers ignore these other costs, so they drive too much. The role of government is to ensure that polluters bear the full cost of their production and consumption decisions.

- **Public goods.** Another requirement for market efficiency is that decision makers must reap the full benefits from their decisions. In the case of a public good such as a levee, the benefits go to everyone in the area protected from flooding, not just the person who builds the levee. The role of government is to facilitate the collective decision making for public goods such as levees, national defense, parks, and space exploration.

- **Imperfect information.** For markets to operate efficiently, people must have enough information to make informed decisions about how much to produce or consume. When they don't, the role of government is to disseminate information and promote informed choice.

- **Imperfect competition.** Some markets are dominated by a few large firms, and the lack of competition leads to high prices and small quantities. For example, DeBeers dominates the diamond market. The role of government is to foster competition, which leads to lower prices and more choices.

What are the other roles of government in a market-based economy? The government enforces property rights—protecting the property and possessions of individuals and firms from theft. The government uses the legal system—police, courts, and prisons—to enforce property rights. The protection of private property guarantees that people will keep the fruits of their labor, encouraging production and exchange. The government has two additional roles to play in a market economy:

- Establishing rules for market exchange and using its police power to enforce the rules.
- Reducing economic uncertainty and providing for people who have lost a job, have poor health, or experience other unforeseen difficulties and accidents.

Government Enforces the Rules of Exchange

The market system is based on exchanges between strangers. These exchanges are covered by implicit and explicit contracts that establish the terms of trade. For example, real-estate transactions are sealed with contracts that specify who pays what, and when. To facilitate exchange, the government helps to enforce contracts by maintaining a legal system that punishes people who violate contracts. This system allows people to trade with the confidence that the terms of the contract will be met.

In the case of consumer goods, the implicit contract is that the product is safe to use. The government enforces this implicit contract through product liability or tort law. If a consumer is harmed by using a particular product, the consumer can file a lawsuit and seek compensation for the harm done. For example, consumers who are injured in defective automobiles may be awarded settlements to cover the cost of medical care, lost work time, and pain and suffering.

The government also disseminates information on consumer products. The government requires firms to provide information about the features of their products, including warnings about potentially harmful uses of the product. For example, cigarettes have a warning label: "Quitting Smoking Now Greatly Reduces Serious Risks to Your Health." Some cold medications warn consumers to avoid driving while taking the medication.

As noted earlier in the chapter, one of the virtues of a market system is that competition among producers tends to keep prices low. As we'll see later in the book, the government uses antitrust policy to foster competition by (a) breaking up monopolies, (b) preventing firms from colluding to fix prices, and (c) preventing firms that produce competing products from merging into a single firm. In some markets, the emergence of a single firm—a monopolist—is inevitable, because the entry of a second firm would make both firms unprofitable. Some examples are the U.S. Postal Service and electricity producers. Governments regulate these firms, controlling the price of the products they produce.

Government Can Reduce Economic Uncertainty

A market economy provides plenty of opportunities to people, but there are risks. Your level of success in a market economy—how much income you earn and how much wealth you accumulate—will depend on your innate intelligence as well as your efforts. But there is also an element of luck: Your fate is affected by where you were born, what occupation you choose, and your genetic makeup and health. Chance events, such as natural disasters and human accidents, also can affect your prosperity. Finally, some people lose their jobs when the national economy is in a slump and firms layoff workers. Given the uncertainty of the market economics, most governments have a "social safety net" that provides for citizens who fare poorly in markets. The safety net includes programs that redistribute income from rich to poor, from the employed to the unemployed. The idea behind having a social safety net is to guarantee a minimum income to people who suffer from job losses, poor health, or bad luck.

Of course, there are private responses to economic uncertainty. For example, we can buy insurance to cover losses from fire and theft, to cover our medical expenses, and to provide death benefits to our survivors in the event of an accident or disaster. Private insurance works because only a fraction of the people who buy insurance file claims and receive reimbursements from insurance companies. In other words, the payments, or premiums, of many are used to pay the claims of a few. Private insurance works when enough low-risk people purchase insurance to cover the costs of reimbursing the high-risk people.

Some types of insurance are unavailable in the private insurance market. As a result, the government steps in to fill the void. For example, unemployment insurance (UI) is a government program that provides 26 weeks of compensation for people who lose their jobs. The insurance is financed by contributions from employers. Because UI is mandatory, all employers, including those facing low risks and high risks of unemployment, contribute to the system, thereby keeping the cost of the insurance down.

SUMMARY

This chapter explored specialization and exchange and the virtues and short-comings of markets. We also discussed the role of government in a market economy. Here are the main points of the chapter:

1 It is sensible for a person to produce the product for which he or she has a *comparative advantage,* that is, a lower opportunity cost than another person.

2 *Specialization* increases productivity through the division of labor, a result of the benefits of repetition, continuity, and innovation.

3 A system of international specialization and trade is sensible because nations have different opportunity costs of producing goods, giving rise to comparative advantages.

4 Under a *market system,* self-interested people, guided by prices, make the decisions about what products to produce, how to produce them, and who gets them.

5 Government roles in a market economy include establishing the rules for exchange, reducing economic uncertainty, and responding to market failures.

KEY TERMS

absolute advantage, p. 52
centrally planned economy, p. 56

comparative advantage, p. 52
export, p. 53

import, p. 53
market economy, p. 56

EXERCISES

 Get Ahead of the Curve

Visit www.myeconlab.com to complete these exercises online and get instant feedback.

3.1 | Comparative Advantage and Exchange

1.1 Consider an accounting firm with two accountants.
a. Fill the blanks in the following table.

	Quigley		Slokum	
	Financial Statements	Tax Returns	Financial Statements	Tax Returns
Output per hour	2	8	1	1
Opportunity cost				

b. Quigley has a comparative advantage in _____, while Slokum has a comparative advantage in _____.

1.2 Mike, the manager of a car wash, is more productive at washing cars than any potential workers he could hire. Should he wash all the cars himself? _____ (Yes/No)

1.3 Adam Smith listed three reasons for specialization to increase productivity: (1) _____; (2) _____; and (3) _____.

1.4 President Lincoln's discomfort with imports resulted from his failure to recognize that money sent to England eventually _____.

1.5 **Exchange in an Island Economy.** Robin and Terry are stranded on a deserted island and consume two products, coconuts and fish. In a day, Robin can catch 2 fish or gather 8 coconuts, and Terry can catch 1 fish or gather 1 coconut.
a. Use these numbers to prepare a table like Table 3.1 on page 50. Which person has a comparative advantage in fishing? Which person has a comparative advantage in gathering coconuts?
b. Suppose that each person is initially self-sufficient. In a six-day week, Robin produces and consumes 32

coconuts and 4 fish, and Terry produces and consumes 4 coconuts and 2 fish. Show that specialization and exchange (at a rate of 3 coconuts per fish) allows Robin to consume more coconuts and the same number of fish and allows Terry to consume more coconuts and the same number of fish. Illustrate your answer with a graph like Figure 3.1 on page 51.

1.6 **Technological Innovation and Exchange.** Recall the example of Fred and Kate shown in Table 3.1 on page 50. Suppose a technological innovation, such as a rope ladder, increases the coconut productivity of both people: Fred can now produce 3 coconuts per day, while Kate can now produce 2 coconuts per day. Their productivity for fish has not changed. Suppose they agree to trade 1 coconut for each fish. Will both people gain from specialization and trade?

1.7 **Comparative Advantage in Teaching.** Professor Kirby is a better teacher than Professor Jones for both an undergraduate course (U) and a graduate course (G). Teaching performance is measured by the average score on students' standardized tests:

	Professor Kirby	Professor Jones
Average Score in Undergraduate Course	48	24
Average Score in Graduate Course	60	20

   a. If each professor teaches one course and the objective is to maximize the sum of the test scores, which course should each professor teach?

   b. Is your answer to (a) consistent with Kirby teaching the course for which she has the larger productivity advantage over Jones?

3.2 | Comparative Advantage and International Trade

2.1 Outsourcing leads to _____ prices for consumers.

2.2 In the first three months of 2004, the number of jobs moving to another state was _____ (larger/smaller) than the number of jobs moving to another country.

2.3 Approximately what percentage of job losses in the first 3 months of 2004 were caused by outsourcing— 2, 10, or 25 percent? (Related to Application 1 on page 54.)

2.4 Candy cane manufacturers are shutting plants in the United States and moving to Mexico because import restrictions have caused higher _____ prices in the United States. (Related to Application 2 on page 55.)

2.5 **Outsourcing and Net Job Losses.** Consider a software firm that employs programmers and customer-service workers. Suppose the firm shifts its customer-service activities to a call center in another country, and 300 customer-service workers lose their jobs. In addition, suppose the outsourcing reduces the firm's overall production cost by 20 percent, allowing the company to cut the price of its software by 20 percent. Explain why the net loss of jobs from the firm's outsourcing will be fewer than 300 jobs. (Related to Application 1 on page 54.)

2.6 **The Steel Industry Versus the Appliance Industry.** Suppose the United States limits the imports of steel to protect its domestic steel industry. Explain the implications of the import restrictions on industries such as appliance manufacturers who use steel as an input. (Related to Application 2 on page 55.)

2.7 **Data on Exports and Imports.** Access the *Statistical Abstract of the United States* on the Internet and download the tables in the section entitled "Foreign Commerce and Aid." One of the tables lists U.S. exports and imports by selected Standard Industrial Trade Classification (SITC) commodity. Fill the blanks in the following table for the most recent year listed in the table.

Commodity	Export Value ($ millions)	Import Value ($ millions)	Net Exports = Exports – Imports ($ millions)
Coffee			
Corn			
Soybeans			
Airplanes			
Footwear			
Vehicles			
Crude oil			

2.8 **Trade Balances by Country.** Access the *Statistical Abstract of the United States* on the Internet and download the tables in the section entitled "Foreign Commerce and Aid." One of the tables lists U.S. exports and imports and merchandise trade balance by country. Fill the blanks in the following table for the most recent year listed in the table.

Country	Exports ($ millions)	General Imports ($ millions)	Merchandise Trade Balance ($ millions)
Australia			
China			
Italy			
Japan			
Mexico			
Netherlands			
Saudi Arabia			
Singapore			

3.3 | Markets

3.1 Four social inventions that support markets are (1) _____, which specify the terms of exchange; (2) _____, which reduce the risk of entrepreneurs; (3) _____, which increases the profitability of inventions; and (4) _____ rules, which provide potential investors with reliable information about the financial performance of firms.

3.2 A POW who didn't smoke might trade some of his Red Cross rations for cigarettes because they served as the _____ in World War II POW camps. (Related to Application 3 on page 57.)

3.3 Arrow up or down: Trade between different POW compounds ____ the difference in the price of beef across the compounds. (Related to Application 3 on page 57.)

3.4 To explain the virtues of markets, Adam Smith used the metaphor of the invisible pancreas. _____ (True/False)

3.5 **Coffee and Cheese Exchange in a POW Camp.** Suppose that in the British compound of a POW camp, the price of cheese is 6 cigarettes per cheese ration and the price of coffee beans is 3 cigarettes per coffee ration. In the French compound, the price of coffee beans is 24 cigarettes per ration. (Related to Application 3 on page 57.)

   a. Is there an opportunity for beneficial exchange?

   b. A British prisoner could exchange his cheese ration for ____ cigarettes, then exchange the extra cigarettes for _____ coffee rations in the British compound. If he travels to the French compound, he could exchange the extra coffee for ____ cigarettes. When he returns to the British compound, he can exchange the extra cigarettes for _____ cheese rations. In other words, his net gain from trade is _____ cheese rations.

3.6 **Extending Trade Outside the Camp.** Late in World War II, a German guard exchanged bread and chocolate at the rate of 1 loaf for 1 chocolate bar. Inside the Allied POW camp, the price of chocolate was 15 cigarettes per bar, and the price of bread was 40 cigarettes per loaf.

   a. Is there an opportunity for beneficial exchange?

   b. With the guard, a POW could exchange 3 chocolate bars for ____ loaves of bread. In the camp, the POW could exchange the extra loaves for _____ cigarettes, and then exchange the extra cigarettes for _____ chocolate bars. In other words, the POW's net gain from trade is ____ chocolate bars.

4.1 For markets to operate efficiently, the people making consumption and production decisions must bear the full _____ and reap the full _____ from their decisions.

4.2 Pollution from a paper mill is an example of market failure because people living downwind of the mill bear part of _____ of production.

4.3 Some markets are dominated by a few large firms, leading to high _____ and small _____.

4.4 By promoting competition, the government generates _____ product prices.

4.5 **Google Pirates Textbooks?** The government protects intellectual property rights by enforcing copyright rules on textbooks. Suppose Google scans the pages of this and other introductory economics textbooks and makes them available for downloading at no charge.

    a. As a current textbook consumer, would you be better off or worse off?

    b. What are the implications for the next generation of economics students?

4.6 **Unemployment Insurance.** Each worker employed by Risky Business has a 20 percent chance of losing his or her job in the next year. Each worker employed by Safe Business has a 2 percent chance of losing his or her job. You manage an insurance company that provides a lump sum of $10,000 for to each unemployed worker.

    a. What is the minimum amount you would charge Risky Business for each employee covered by the unemployment policy?

    b. What is the minimum amount you would charge Safe Business for each employee covered by the unemployment policy?

    c. Suppose you charge the same premium to both businesses. The companies have the same number of workers and are required to purchase unemployment insurance. What is the minimum amount you would charge?

NOTES

1. Rone Tempest, "Barbie and the World Economy," *Los Angeles Times*, September 22, 1996, p. A1. Available online: www.surferess.com/CEO/html/jill_barad.html.

2. Adam Smith, *An Inquiry into the Nature and Causes of the Wealth of Nations* (First published in 1776; New York: Random House, 1973), Book 1, Chapter 1.

3. Adam Smith, *An Inquiry into the Nature and Causes of the Wealth of Nations* (First published in 1776; New York: Random House, 1973), Book 1, Chapter 1.

4. Adam Smith, *An Inquiry into the Nature and Causes of the Wealth of Nations* (First published in 1776; New York: Random House, 1973), Book 1, Chapter 4.

5. Todd G. Buchholz, *New Ideas from Dead Economists* (New York: Penguin, 1999), p. 75.

6. Todd G. Buchholz, *New Ideas from Dead Economists* (New York: Penguin, 1999), p. 76.

7. MPA Worldwide Market Research, *MPA Snapshot Report: 2004 International Theatrical Market* (Motion Picture Association, March 2005).

8. Todd G. Buchholz, *New Ideas from Dead Economists* (New York: Penguin, 1999), p. 21.

9. Adam Smith, *An Inquiry into the Nature and Causes of the Wealth of Nations* (First published in 1776; New York: Random House, 1973), Book 4, Chapter 2.

10. Steven Greenhouse, "The Global March to Free Markets," *New York Times*, July 19, 1987, Sec. 3, p. 1.

4

Demand, Supply, and Market Equilibrium

The price of vanilla is bouncing. A kilogram (2.2 pounds) of vanilla beans sold for $50 in 2000, but by 2003 the price had risen to $500 per kilogram. The price soared because a devastating cyclone hit Madagascar, the African nation that leads the world in vanilla production. Three years later in 2006, the price of vanilla beans had sunk to only $25 per kilogram. What caused the price to go from $50 to $500 to $25? As we'll see in this chapter, the answer is "demand and supply." We'll use the model of demand and supply, the most popular tool of economic analysis, to explain the bouncing price of vanilla and other market phenomena.

• **perfectly competitive market**
A market with so many buyers and sellers that no single buyer or seller can affect the market price.

• **quantity demanded**
The amount of a product that consumers are willing and able to buy.

• **demand schedule**
A table that shows the relationship between the price of a product and the quantity demanded, *ceteris paribus*.

Our discussion of the virtues of exchange and markets in Chapter 3 has set the stage for this chapter, where we explore the mechanics of markets. We use the model of demand and supply—the most important tool of economic analysis—to see how markets work. We'll see how the prices of goods and services are affected by all sorts of changes in the economy, including bad weather, higher income, technological innovation, bad publicity, and changes in consumer preferences. This chapter will prepare you for the applications of demand and supply you'll see in the rest of the book.

The model of demand and supply explains how a perfectly competitive market operates. A **perfectly competitive market** has many buyers and sellers of a product, and no single buyer or seller can affect the market price. The classic example of a perfectly competitive firm is a wheat farmer, who produces a tiny fraction of the total supply of wheat. No matter how much wheat an individual farmer produces, the farmer can't change the market price of wheat.

4.1 | THE DEMAND CURVE

On the demand side of a market, consumers buy products from firms. The main question concerning the demand side of the market is: How much of a particular product are consumers willing to buy during a particular period? A consumer who is willing to buy a particular product is willing to sacrifice enough money to purchase it. The consumer doesn't merely have a desire to buy the good, but is willing and able to sacrifice something to get it. Notice that *demand* is defined for a particular period, for example, a day, a month, or a year.

We'll start our discussion of demand with the individual consumer. How much of a product is an individual willing to buy? It depends on a number of variables. Here is a list of the variables that affect an individual consumer's decision, using the pizza market as an example:

• The price of the product (for example, the price of a pizza)
• The consumer's income
• The price of substitute goods (for example, the prices of tacos or sandwiches)
• The price of complementary goods (for example, the price of lemonade)
• The consumer's preferences or tastes and advertising that may influence preferences
• The consumer's expectations about future prices

Together, these variables determine how much of a particular product an individual consumer is willing and able to buy, the **quantity demanded**. We'll start our discussion of demand with the relationship between the price and quantity demanded, a relationship that is represented graphically by the demand curve. Later in the chapter, we will discuss the other variables that affect the individual consumer's decision about how much of a product to buy.

The Individual Demand Curve and the Law of Demand

The starting point for a discussion of individual demand is a **demand schedule**, which is a table of numbers showing the relationship between the price of a particular product and the quantity that an individual consumer is willing to buy. The demand schedule shows how the quantity demanded by an individual changes with the price, *ceteris paribus* (everything else held fixed). The variables that are held fixed in the demand schedule are the consumer's income, the prices of substitutes and complements, the consumer's tastes, and the consumer's expectations about future prices.

The table in Figure 4.1 shows Al's demand schedule for pizza. At a price of $2, Al buys 13 pizzas per month. As the price rises, he buys fewer pizzas: 10 pizzas at a price of $4, 7 pizzas at a price of $6, and so on, down to only 1 pizza at a price of $10. It's important to remember that in a demand schedule, any change in quantity results from a change in price alone.

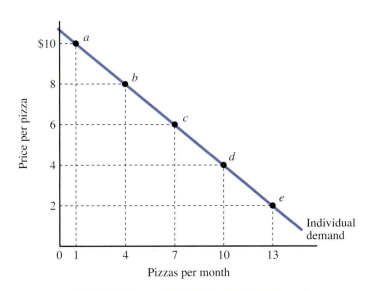

AL'S DEMAND SCHEDULE FOR PIZZAS

Point	Price	Quantity of Pizzas per Month
a	$10	1
b	8	4
c	6	7
d	4	10
e	2	13

The **individual demand curve** is a graphical representation of the demand schedule. By plotting the numbers in Al's demand schedule—various combinations of price and quantity—we can draw his demand curve for pizza. The demand curve shows the relationship between the price and the quantity demanded by an individual consumer, *ceteris paribus*. To get the data for a single demand curve, we change only the price of pizza and observe how a consumer responds to the price change. In Figure 4.1, Al's demand curve shows the quantity of pizzas he is willing to buy at each price.

Notice that Al's demand curve is negatively sloped, reflecting the **law of demand**. This law applies to all consumers:

There is a negative relationship between price and quantity demanded, **ceteris paribus.**

The words *ceteris paribus* remind us that to isolate the relationship between price and quantity demanded, we *must* assume that income, the prices of related goods such as substitutes and complements, and tastes are unchanged. As the price of pizza increases and nothing else changes, Al moves upward along his demand curve and buys a smaller quantity of pizza. For example, if the price increases from $8 to $10, Al moves upward along his demand curve from point *b* to point *a*, and he buys only 1 pizza per month, down from 4 pizzas at the lower price. A movement along a single demand curve is called a **change in quantity demanded**, a change in the quantity a consumer is willing to buy when the price changes.

From Individual Demand to Market Demand

The **market demand curve** shows the relationship between the price of the good and the quantity demanded by *all* consumers, *ceteris paribus*. As in the case of the individual demand curve, when we draw the market demand curve we assume that the other

• **individual demand curve**
A curve that shows the relationship between the price of a good and quantity demanded by an individual consumer, *ceteris paribus*.

• **law of demand**
There is a negative relationship between price and quantity demanded, *ceteris paribus*.

• **change in quantity demanded**
A change in the quantity consumers are willing and able to buy when the price changes; represented graphically by movement along the demand curve.

• **market demand curve**
A curve showing the relationship between price and quantity demanded by all consumers, *ceteris paribus*.

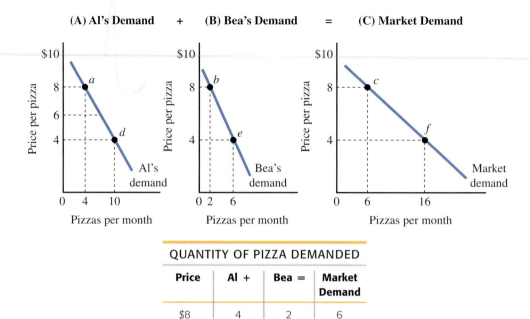

QUANTITY OF PIZZA DEMANDED			
Price	**Al +**	**Bea =**	**Market Demand**
$8	4	2	6
6	7	4	11
4	10	6	16
2	13	8	21

▲ **FIGURE 4.2**
From Individual to Market Demand
The market demand equals the sum of the demands of all consumers. In this case, there are only two consumers, so at each price, the market quantity demanded equals the quantity demanded by Al plus the quantity demanded by Bea. At a price of $8, Al's quantity is 4 pizzas (point *a*) and Bea's quantity is 2 pizzas (point *b*), so the market quantity demanded is 6 pizzas (point *c*). Each consumer obeys the law of demand, so the market demand curve is negatively sloped.

variables that affect individual demand (income, the prices of substitute and complementary goods, tastes, and price expectations) are fixed. In addition, we assume that the number of consumers is fixed.

Figure 4.2 shows how to derive the market demand curve when there are only 2 consumers. Panel A shows Al's demand curve for pizza, and Panel B shows Bea's demand curve. At a price of $8, Al will buy 4 pizzas (point *a*) and Bea will buy 2 pizzas (point *b*), so the total quantity demanded at this price is 6 pizzas. In Panel C, point *c* shows the point on the market demand curve associated with a price of $8. At this price, the market quantity demanded is 6 pizzas. If the price drops to $4, Al will buy 10 pizzas (point *d*) and Bea will buy 6 pizzas (point *e*), for a total of 16 pizzas (shown by point *f* on the market demand curve). The market demand curve is the horizontal sum of the individual demand curves.

The market demand is negatively sloped, reflecting the law of demand. This is sensible, because if each consumer obeys the law of demand, consumers as a group will too. When the price increases from $4 to $8, there is a change in quantity demanded as we move along the demand curve from point *f* to point *c*. The movement along the demand curve occurs if the price of pizza is the only variable that has changed.

4.2 | THE SUPPLY CURVE

On the supply side of a market, firms sell their products to consumers. Suppose you ask the manager of a firm, "How much of your product are you willing to produce and sell?" The answer is likely to be "it depends." The manager's decision about how much to produce depends on many variables, including the following, using pizza as an example:

- The price of the product (for example, the price per pizza)
- The wage paid to workers
- The price of materials (for example, the price of dough and cheese)
- The cost of capital (for example, the cost of a pizza oven)
- The state of production technology (for example, the knowledge used in making pizza)
- Producers' expectations about future prices
- Taxes paid to the government or *subsidies* (payments from the government to firms to produce a product)

Together, these variables determine how much of a product firms are willing to produce and sell, the **quantity supplied**. We'll start our discussion of market supply with the relationship between the price of a good and the quantity of that good supplied, a relationship that is represented graphically by the supply curve. Later in the chapter, we will discuss the other variables that affect the individual firm's decision about how much of a product to produce and sell.

- **quantity supplied**
  The amount of a product that firms are willing and able to sell.

The Individual Supply Curve and the Law of Supply

Consider the decision of an individual producer. The starting point for a discussion of individual supply is a **supply schedule**, a table that shows the relationship between the price of a particular product and the quantity that an individual producer is willing to sell. The supply schedule shows how the quantity supplied by an individual producer changes with the price, *ceteris paribus*. The variables that are held fixed in the supply schedule are input costs, technology, price expectations, and government taxes or subsidies.

- **supply schedule**
  A table that shows the relationship between the price of a product and quantity supplied, *ceteris paribus*.

The table in Figure 4.3 shows the supply schedule for pizza at Lola's Pizza Shop. At a price of $2, she doesn't produce any pizzas, indicating that a $2 price is not high enough to cover her cost of producing a pizza. In contrast, at a price of $4 she supplies

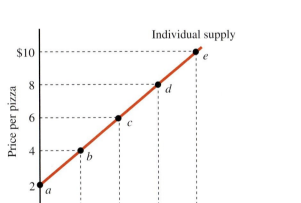

◄ FIGURE 4.3

The Individual Supply Curve

The supply curve of an individual supplier is positively sloped, reflecting the law of supply. As shown by point *a*, the quantity supplied is zero at a price of $2, indicating that the minimum supply price is just above $2. An increase in price increases the quantity supplied, to 100 pizzas at a price of $4, to 200 pizzas at a price of $6, and so on.

INDIVIDUAL SUPPLY SCHEDULE FOR PIZZA

Point	Price	Quantity of Pizzas per Month
a	$2	0
b	4	100
c	6	200
d	8	300
e	10	400

- **individual supply curve**
  A curve showing the relationship between price and quantity supplied by a single firm, *ceteris paribus*.

- **law of supply**
  There is a positive relationship between price and quantity supplied, *ceteris paribus*.

- **change in quantity supplied**
  A change in the quantity firms are willing and able to sell when the price changes; represented graphically by movement along the supply curve.

- **minimum supply price**
  The lowest price at which a product will be supplied.

100 pizzas. In this example, each $2 increase in price increases the quantity supplied by 100 pizzas—to 200 at a price of $6, to 300 at a price of $8, and so on. It's important to remember that in a supply schedule, a change in quantity results from a change in price alone.

The **individual supply curve** is a graphical representation of the supply schedule. By plotting the numbers in Lola's supply schedule—different combinations of price and quantity—we can draw her supply curve for pizza. The individual supply curve shows the relationship between the price of a product and the quantity supplied by a single firm, *ceteris paribus*. To get the data for a supply curve, we change only the price of pizza and observe how a producer responds to the price change.

Figure 4.3 shows the supply curve for Lola, which shows the quantity of pizzas she is willing to sell at each price. The individual supply curve is positively sloped, reflecting the **law of supply**, a pattern of behavior that we observe in producers:

There is a positive relationship between price and quantity supplied, **ceteris paribus**.

The words *ceteris paribus* remind us that to isolate the relationship between price and quantity supplied we assume that the other factors that influence producers are unchanged. As the price of pizza increases and nothing else changes, Lola moves upward along her individual supply curve and produces a larger quantity of pizza. For example, if the price increases from $6 to $8, Lola moves upward along her supply curve from point *c* to point *d*, and the quantity supplied increases from 200 to 300. A movement along a single supply curve is called a **change in quantity supplied**, a change in the quantity that a producer is willing and able to sell when the price changes.

The **minimum supply price** is the lowest price at which a product is supplied. A firm won't produce a product unless the price is high enough to cover the marginal cost of producing it. In the case of pizza, the price must be high enough to cover the cost of producing the first pizza. As shown in Figure 4.3, a price of $2 is not high enough to cover the cost of producing the first pizza, so Lola's quantity supplied is zero (point *a*). But when the price rises above $2, she produces some pizzas, indicating that her minimum supply price is just above $2.

Why Is the Individual Supply Curve Positively Sloped?

The individual supply curve is positively sloped, consistent with the law of supply. To explain the positive slope, consider how Lola responds to an increase in price. A higher price encourages a firm to increase its output by purchasing more materials and hiring more workers. To increase her workforce, Lola might be forced to pay overtime or hire workers who are more costly or less productive than the original workers. But the higher price of pizza makes it worthwhile to incur these higher costs.

The supply curve shows the marginal cost of production for different quantities produced. We can use the marginal principle to explain this.

MARGINAL PRINCIPLE

Increase the level of an activity as long as its marginal benefit exceeds its marginal cost. Choose the level at which the marginal benefit equals the marginal cost.

For Lola, the marginal benefit of producing a pizza is the price she gets for it. When the price is only $2.00, she doesn't produce any pizza, which tells us that the marginal cost of the first pizza must be greater than $2.00; otherwise, she would have produced it. But when the price rises to $2.01, she produces the first pizza because now the marginal benefit (the $2.01 price) exceeds the marginal cost. This tells us that the marginal cost of the first pizza is less than $2.01; otherwise, she wouldn't produce it at a price of $2.01. To summarize, the marginal cost of the first pizza is between $2.00 and $2.01, or just over $2.00. Similarly, point *b* on the supply curve in Figure 4.3 shows that Lola won't produce her 100th pizza at a price of $3.99, but will produce at a price of $4.00, indicating that her marginal cost of producing that pizza is between $3.99 and $4.00, or just under $4.00. In general, the supply curve shows the marginal cost of production.

From Individual Supply to Market Supply

The **market supply curve** for a particular good shows the relationship between the price of the good and the quantity that all producers together are willing to sell, *ceteris paribus*. To draw the market supply curve, we assume that the other variables that affect individual supply are fixed. The market quantity supplied is simply the sum of the quantities supplied by all the firms in the market. To show how to draw the market supply curve, we'll assume that there are only two firms in the market. Of course, a perfectly competitive market has a large number of firms, but the lessons from the two-firm case generalize to a case of many firms.

Figure 4.4 shows how to derive a market supply curve from individual supply curves. In Panel A, Lola has relatively low production costs, as reflected in her relatively low minimum supply price ($2 at point *a*). In Panel B, Hiram has higher production costs, so he has a higher minimum price ($6 at point *f*). As a result, his supply curve lies above Lola's. To draw the market supply curve, we add the individual supply curves horizontally. This gives us two segments for the market supply curve:

- **Prices between $2 and $6:** Segment connecting points *i* and *k*. Hiram's high-cost firm doesn't supply any output, so the market supply is the same as the individual supply from Lola. For example, at a price of $4 Lola supplies 100 pizzas (point *b*) and Hiram does not produce any pizzas, so the market supply is 100 pizzas (point *j*).

- **market supply curve**
  A curve showing the relationship between the market price and quantity supplied by all firms, *ceteris paribus*.

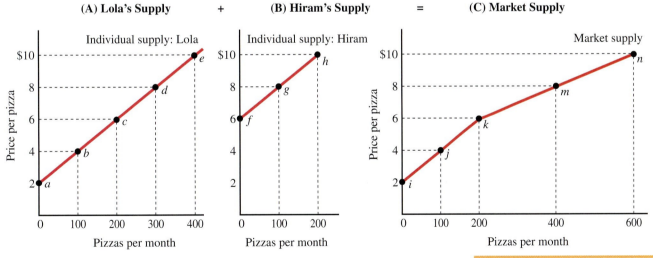

▲ **FIGURE 4.4**
From Individual to Market Supply
The market supply is the sum of the supplies of all firms. In Panel A, Lola is a low-cost producer who produces the first pizza once the price rises above $2 (shown by point *a*). In Panel B, Hiram is a high-cost producer who doesn't produce pizza until the price rises above $6 (shown by point *f*). To draw the market supply curve, we sum the individual supply curves horizontally. At a price of $8, market supply is 400 pizzas (point *m*), equal to 300 from Lola (point *d*) plus 100 from Hiram (point *g*)

QUANTITY OF PIZZA SUPPLIED			
Price	Lola +	Hiram =	Market Supply
2	0	0	0
4	100	0	100
6	200	0	200
8	300	100	400
10	400	200	600

► **FIGURE 4.5**

The Market Supply Curve with Many Firms

The market supply is the sum of the supplies of all firms. The minimum supply price is $2 (point *a*), and the quantity supplied increases by 10,000 for each $2 increase in price, to 10,000 at a price of $4 (point *b*), to 20,000 at a price of $6 (point *c*), and so on.

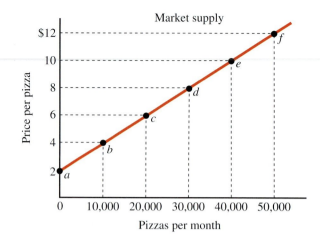

- **Prices above $6:** Segment above point *k*. At higher prices, the high-cost firm produces some output, and the market supply is the sum of the quantities supplied by the two firms. For example, at a price of $8 Lola produces 300 pizzas (point *d*) and Hiram produces 100 pizzas (point *g*), so the market quantity supplied is 400 pizzas (point *m*).

A perfectly competitive market has hundreds of firms rather than just two, but the process of going from individual supply curves to the market supply curve is the same. We add the individual supply curves horizontally by picking a price and adding up the quantities supplied by all the firms in the market. In the more realistic case of many firms, the supply curve will be smooth rather than kinked. This smooth line is shown in Figure 4.5. In this case, we assume that there are 100 firms identical to Lola's firm. The minimum supply price is $2, and for each $2 increase in price, the quantity supplied increases by 10,000 pizzas.

Why Is the Market Supply Curve Positively Sloped?

The market supply curve is positively sloped, consistent with the law of supply. To explain the positive slope, consider the two responses by firms to an increase in price:

- **Individual firm.** As we saw earlier, a higher price encourages a firm to increase its output by purchasing more materials and hiring more workers.
- **New firms.** In the long run, new firms can enter the market and existing firms can expand their production facilities to produce more output. The new firms may have higher production costs than the original firms, but the higher output price makes it worthwhile to enter the market even with higher costs.

Like the individual supply curve, the market supply curve shows the marginal cost of production for different quantities produced. In Figure 4.5, the marginal cost of the first pizza is the minimum supply price for the firm with the lowest cost (just over $2.00). Similarly, point *d* on the supply curve shows that the 30,000th pizza won't be produced at a price of $7.99, but will be produced at a price of $8.00. This indicates that the marginal cost of producing the 30,000th pizza is just under $8.00. Like the individual supply curve, the market supply curve shows the marginal cost of production.

4.3 | MARKET EQUILIBRIUM: BRINGING DEMAND AND SUPPLY TOGETHER

In Chapter 3, we saw that a market is an arrangement that brings buyers and sellers together. So far in this chapter, we've seen how the two sides of a market—demand and supply—work. In this part of the chapter, we bring the two sides of the market together to show how prices and quantities are determined.

When the quantity of a product demanded equals the quantity supplied at the prevailing market price, this is called a **market equilibrium**. When a market reaches an equilibrium, there is no pressure to change the price. For example, if pizza firms produce exactly the quantity of pizza consumers are willing to buy, there will be no pressure for the price of pizza to change. In Figure 4.6, the equilibrium price is shown by the intersection of the demand and supply curves. At a price of $8, the supply curve shows that firms will produce 30,000 pizzas, which is exactly the quantity that consumers are willing to buy at that price.

• **market equilibrium**
A situation in which the quantity demanded equals the quantity supplied at the prevailing market price.

Excess Demand Causes the Price to Rise

If the price is below the equilibrium price, there will be excess demand for the product. **Excess demand** (sometimes called a *shortage*) occurs when, at the prevailing market price, the quantity demanded exceeds the quantity supplied, meaning that consumers are willing to buy more than producers are willing to sell. In Figure 4.6, at a price of $6, there is an excess demand equal to 16,000 pizzas: Consumers are willing to buy 36,000 pizzas (point *c*), but producers are willing to sell only 20,000 pizzas (point *b*). This mismatch between demand and supply will cause the price of pizza to rise. Firms will increase the price they charge for their limited supply of pizza, and anxious consumers will pay the higher price to get one of the few pizzas that are available.

• **excess demand (shortage)**
A situation in which, at the prevailing price, the quantity demanded exceeds the quantity supplied.

An increase in price eliminates excess demand by changing both the quantity demanded and quantity supplied. As the price increases, the excess demand shrinks for two reasons:

- The market moves upward along the demand curve (from point *c* toward point *a*), decreasing the quantity demanded.
- The market moves upward along the supply curve (from point *b* toward point *a*), increasing the quantity supplied.

Because the quantity demanded decreases while the quantity supplied increases, the gap between the quantity demanded and the quantity supplied narrows. The price will continue to rise until excess demand is eliminated. In Figure 4.6, at a price of $8 the quantity supplied equals the quantity demanded, as shown by point *a*.

In some cases, government creates an excess demand for a good by setting a maximum price (sometimes called a *price ceiling*). If the government sets a maximum price that is less than the equilibrium price, the result is a permanent excess demand for the good. Later in the book, we will explore the market effects of such policies.

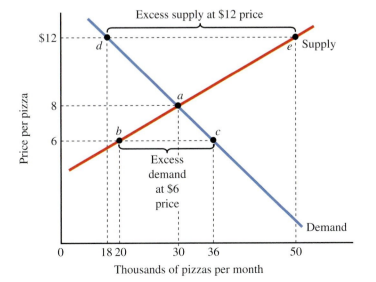

◀ **FIGURE 4.6**
Market Equilibrium
At the market equilibrium (point *a*, with price = $8 and quantity = 30,000), the quantity supplied equals the quantity demanded. At a price below the equilibrium price ($6), there is excess demand—the quantity demanded at point *c* exceeds the quantity supplied at point *b*. At a price above the equilibrium price ($12), there is excess supply—the quantity supplied at point *e* exceeds the quantity demanded at point *d*.

• **excess supply (surplus)**
A situation in which at the prevailing price the quantity supplied exceeds the quantity demanded.

Excess Supply Causes the Price to Drop

What happens if the price is above the equilibrium price? **Excess supply** (sometimes called a *surplus*) occurs when the quantity supplied exceeds the quantity demanded, meaning that producers are willing to sell more than consumers are willing to buy. This is shown by points *d* and *e* in Figure 4.6. At a price of $12, the excess supply is 32,000 pizzas: Producers are willing to sell 50,000 pizzas (point *e*), but consumers are willing to buy only 18,000 pizzas (point *d*). This mismatch will cause the price of pizzas to fall as firms cut the price to sell them. As the price drops, the excess supply will shrink for two reasons:

- The market moves downward along the demand curve from point *d* toward point *a*, increasing the quantity demanded.
- The market moves downward along the supply curve from point *e* toward point *a*, decreasing the quantity supplied.

Because the quantity demanded increases while the quantity supplied decreases, the gap between the quantity supplied and the quantity demanded narrows. The price will continue to drop until excess supply is eliminated. In Figure 4.6, at a price of $8, the quantity supplied equals the quantity demanded, as shown by point *a*.

The government sometimes creates an excess supply of a good by setting a minimum price (sometimes called a *price floor*). If the government sets a minimum price that is greater than the equilibrium price, the result is a permanent excess supply. We'll discuss the market effects of minimum prices later in the book.

4.4 | MARKET EFFECTS OF CHANGES IN DEMAND

We've seen that a market equilibrium occurs when the quantity supplied equals the quantity demanded, shown graphically by the intersection of the supply curve and the demand curve. In this part of the chapter, we'll see how changes on the demand side of the market affect the equilibrium price and equilibrium quantity.

Change in Quantity Demanded Versus Change in Demand

Earlier in the chapter, we listed the variables that determine how much of a particular product consumers are willing to buy. One of the variables is the price of the product. The demand curve shows the negative relationship between price and quantity demanded, *ceteris paribus*. In Panel A of Figure 4.7, when the price decreases from $8 to $6, we move down-

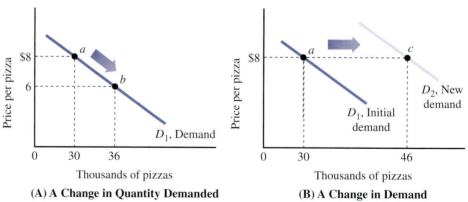

(A) A Change in Quantity Demanded

(B) A Change in Demand

▲ **FIGURE 4.7**

Change in Quantity Demanded Versus Change in Demand

(**A**) A change in price causes a change in quantity demanded, a movement along a single demand curve. For example, a decrease in price causes a move from point *a* to point *b*, increasing the quantity demanded.
(**B**) A change in demand, caused by changes in a variable other than the price of the good, shifts the entire demand curve. For example, an increase in demand shifts the demand curve from D_1 to D_2.

ward along the demand curve from point *a* to point *b*, and the quantity demanded increases. As noted earlier in the chapter, this is called a *change in quantity demanded*. Now we're ready to take a closer look at the other variables that affect demand besides price—income, the prices of related goods, tastes, advertising, and the number of consumers—and see how changes in these variables affect the demand for the product and the market equilibrium.

If any of these other variables change, the relationship between the product's price and quantity—shown numerically in the demand schedule and graphically in the demand curve—will change. That means we will have an entirely different demand schedule and an entirely different demand curve. In Panel B of Figure 4.7, this is shown as a *shift* of the entire demand curve from D_1 to D_2. This shift means that at any price consumers are willing to buy a larger quantity of the product. For example, at a price of $8 consumers are willing to buy 46,000 pizzas (point *c*), up from 30,000 with the initial demand curve. To convey the idea that changes in these other variables change the demand schedule and the demand curve, we say that a change in any of these variables causes a **change in demand**.

• **change in demand**
A shift of the demand curve caused by a change in a variable other than the price of the product.

Increases in Demand Shift the Demand Curve

What types of changes will increase the demand and shift the demand curve to the right, as shown in Figure 4.7? An increase in demand like the one represented in Figure 4.7 can occur for several reasons, which are listed in Table 4.1:

• **Increase in income.** Consumers use their income to buy products, and the more money they have, the more money they spend. For a **normal good**, there is a positive relationship between consumer income and the quantity consumed. When income increases, a consumer buys a larger quantity of a normal good. Most goods fall into this category—including new clothes, movies, and pizza.

• **normal good**
A good for which an increase in income increases demand.

• **Decrease in income.** An **inferior good** is the opposite of a normal good. Consumers buy larger quantities of inferior goods when their income *decreases*. For example, if you lose your job you might make your own coffee instead of buying it in a coffee shop, rent DVDs instead of going to the theater, and eat more macaroni and cheese. In this case, home-made coffee, DVDs, and macaroni and cheese are examples of inferior goods.

• **inferior good**
A good for which an increase in income decreases demand.

• **Increase in price of a substitute good.** When two goods are **substitutes**, an increase in the price of the first good causes some consumers to switch to the second good. Tacos and pizzas are substitutes, so an increase in the price of tacos increases the demand for pizzas as some consumers substitute pizza for tacos, which are now more expensive relative to pizza.

• **substitutes**
Two goods for which an increase in the price of one good increases the demand for the other good.

Table 4.1 | INCREASES IN DEMAND SHIFT THE DEMAND CURVE TO THE RIGHT

When this variable...	increases or decreases...	the demand curve shifts in this direction...
Income, with normal good	↑	
Income, with inferior good	↓	
Price of a substitute good	↑	
Price of complementary good	↓	
Population	↑	
Consumer preferences for good	↑	
Expected future price	↑	

An Increase in Demand Increases the Equilibrium Price

An increase in demand shifts the demand curve to the right: At each price, the quantity demanded increases. At the initial price ($8), there is excess demand, with the quantity demanded (point *b*) exceeding the quantity supplied (point *a*). The excess demand causes the price to rise, and equilibrium is restored at point *c*. To summarize, the increase in demand increases the equilibrium price to $10 and increases the equilibrium quantity to 40,000 pizzas.

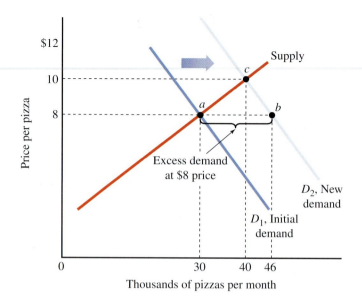

• **complements**
Two goods for which a decrease in the price of one good increases the demand for the other good.

• **Decrease in price of a complementary good.** When two goods are **complements**, they are consumed together as a package, and a decrease in the price of one good decreases the cost of the entire package. As a result, consumers buy more of both goods. Pizza and lemonade are complementary goods, so a decrease in the price of lemonade decreases the total cost of a lemonade-and-pizza meal, increasing the demand for pizza.

• **Increase in population.** An increase in the number of people means that there are more potential pizza consumers—more individual demand curves to add up to get the market demand curve—so market demand increases.

• **Shift in consumer preferences.** Consumers' preferences or tastes can change over time. If consumers' preferences shift in favor of pizza, the demand for pizza increases. One purpose of advertising is to change consumers' preferences, and a successful pizza advertising campaign will increase the demand for pizza.

• **Expectations of higher future prices.** If consumers think next month's pizza price will be higher than they had initially expected, they may buy a larger quantity today and a smaller quantity next month. That means that the demand for pizza today will increase.

We can use Figure 4.8 to show how an increase in demand affects the equilibrium price and equilibrium quantity. An increase in the demand for pizza resulting from one or more of the factors listed in Table 4.1 shifts the demand curve to the right, from D_1 to D_2. At the initial price of $8, there will be excess demand, as indicated by points *a* and *b*: Consumers are willing to buy 46,000 pizzas (point *b*), but producers are willing to sell only 30,000 pizzas (point *a*). Consumers want to buy 16,000 more pizzas than producers are willing to supply, and the excess demand causes upward pressure on the price. As the price rises, the excess demand shrinks because the quantity demanded decreases while the quantity supplied increases. The supply curve intersects the new demand curve at point *c*, so the new equilibrium price is $10 (up from $8), and the new equilibrium quantity is 40,000 pizzas (up from 30,000).

Decreases in Demand Shift the Demand Curve

What types of changes in the pizza market will decrease the demand for pizza? A decrease in demand means that at each price consumers are willing to buy a smaller quantity. In Figure 4.9, a decrease in demand shifts the market demand curve from D_1 to D_0. At the initial price of $8, the quantity demanded decreases

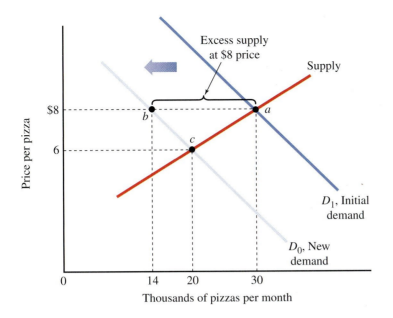

A Decrease in Demand Decreases the Equilibrium Price

A decrease in demand shifts the demand curve to the left: At each price, the quantity demanded decreases. At the initial price ($8), there is excess supply, with the quantity supplied (point *a*) exceeding the quantity demanded (point *b*). The excess supply causes the price to drop, and equilibrium is restored at point *c*. To summarize, the decrease in demand decreases the equilibrium price to $6 and decreases the equilibrium quantity to 20,000 pizzas.

from 30,000 pizzas (point *a*) to 14,000 pizzas (point *b*). A decrease in demand like the one represented in Figure 4.9 can occur for several reasons, which are listed in Table 4.2:

- **Decrease in income.** A decrease in income means that consumers have less to spend, so they buy a smaller quantity of each normal good.

- **Decrease in the price of a substitute good.** A decrease in the price of a substitute good such as tacos makes pizza more expensive relative to tacos, causing consumers to demand less pizza.

- **Increase in the price of a complementary good.** An increase in the price of a complementary good such as lemonade increases the cost of a lemonade-and-pizza meal, decreasing the demand for pizza.

- **Decrease in population.** A decrease in the number of people means that there are fewer pizza consumers, so the market demand for pizza decreases.

Table 4.2 | DECREASES IN DEMAND SHIFT THE DEMAND CURVE TO THE LEFT

When this variable...	increases or decreases...	the demand curve shifts in this direction...
Income, with normal good	↓	
Income, with inferior good	↑	
Price of a substitute good	↓	
Price of complementary good	↑	
Population	↓	
Consumer preferences for good	↓	
Expected future price	↓	

• **Shift in consumer tastes.** When consumers' preferences shift away from pizza in favor of other products, the demand for pizza decreases.

• **Expectations of lower future prices.** If consumers think next month's pizza price will be lower than they had initially expected, they may buy a smaller quantity today, meaning the demand for pizza today will decrease.

A Decrease in Demand Decreases the Equilibrium Price

We can use Figure 4.9 to show how a decrease in demand affects the equilibrium price and equilibrium quantity. The decrease in the demand for pizza shifts the demand curve to the left, from D_1 to D_0. At the initial price of $8, there will be an excess supply, as indicated by points *a* and *b*: Producers are willing to sell 30,000 pizzas (point *a*), but given the lower demand consumers are willing to buy only 14,000 pizzas (point *b*). Producers want to sell 16,000 more pizzas than consumers are willing to buy, and the excess supply causes downward pressure on the price. As the price falls, the excess supply shrinks because the quantity demanded increases while the quantity supplied decreases. The supply curve intersects the new demand curve at point *c*, so the new equilibrium price is $6 (down from $8), and the new equilibrium quantity is 20,000 pizzas (down from 30,000).

4.5 | MARKET EFFECTS OF CHANGES IN SUPPLY

We've seen that changes in demand shift the demand curve and change the equilibrium price and quantity. In this part of the chapter, we'll see how changes on the supply side of the market affect the equilibrium price and equilibrium quantity.

Change in Quantity Supplied Versus Change in Supply

Earlier in the chapter, we listed the variables that determine how much of a product firms are willing to sell. Of course, one of these variables is the price of the product. The supply curve shows the positive relationship between price and quantity, *ceteris paribus*. In Panel A of Figure 4.10, when the price increases from $6 to $8 we move

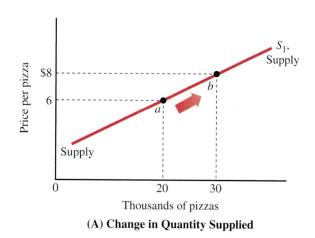

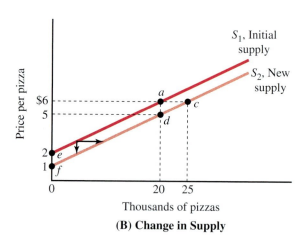

(A) **Change in Quantity Supplied**

(B) **Change in Supply**

▲ **FIGURE 4.10**

Change in Quantity Supplied Versus Change in Supply

(**A**) A change in price causes a change in quantity supplied, a movement along a single supply curve. For example, an increase in price causes a move from point *a* to point *b*.

(**B**) A change in supply (caused by a change in something other than the price of the product) shifts the entire supply curve. For example, an increase in supply shifts the supply curve from S_1 to S_2. For any given price (for example, $6), a larger quantity is supplied (25,000 pizzas at point *c* instead of 20,000 at point *a*). The price required to generate any given quantity decreases. For example, the price required to generate 20,000 pizzas drops from $6 (point *a*) to $5 (point *d*).

along the supply curve from point *a* to point *b*, and the quantity of the product supplied increases. As noted earlier in the chapter, this is called a *change in quantity supplied*. Now we're ready to take a closer look at the other variables that affect supply—including wages, material prices, and technology—and see how changes in these variables affect the supply curve and the market equilibrium.

If any of these other variables changes, the relationship between price and quantity—shown numerically in the supply schedule and graphically in the supply curve—will change. That means that we will have an entirely different supply schedule and a different supply curve. In Panel B of Figure 4.10, this is shown as a shift of the entire supply curve from S_1 to S_2. In this case, the supply curve shifts downward and to the right:

- The shift to the right means that at any given price (for example, $6), a larger quantity is produced (25,000 pizzas at point *c*, up from 20,000 at point *a*).

- The shift downward means that the price required to generate a particular quantity of output is lower. For example, the new minimum supply price is just over $1 (point *f*), down from just over $2 (point *e*). Similarly, the price required to generate 20,000 pizzas is $5 (point *d*), down from $6 (point *a*).

To convey the idea that changes in these other variables change the supply curve, we say that a change in any of these variables causes a **change in supply**.

- **change in supply**
  A shift of the supply curve caused by a change in a variable other than the price of the product.

Increases in Supply Shift the Supply Curve

What types of changes increase the supply of a product, shifting the supply curve downward and to the right? Consider first the effect of a decrease in the wage paid to pizza workers. A decrease in the wage will decrease the cost of producing pizza and shift the supply curve:

- **Downward shift.** When the cost of production decreases, the price required to generate any given quantity of pizza will decrease. In general, a lower wage means a lower marginal cost of production, so each firm needs a lower price to cover its production cost. In other words, the supply curve shifts downward.

- **Rightward shift.** The decrease in production costs makes pizza production more profitable at a given price, so producers will supply more at each price. In other words, the supply curve shifts to the right.

A decrease in the wage is just one example of a decrease in production costs that shifts the supply curve downward and to the right. These supply shifters are listed in Table 4.3. A reduction in the costs of materials (dough, cheese) or capital (pizza

Table 4.3 | CHANGES IN SUPPLY SHIFT THE SUPPLY CURVE DOWNWARD AND TO THE RIGHT

When this variable...	increases or decreases...	the supply curve shifts in this direction...
Wage	↓	
Price of materials or capital	↓	
Technological advance	↑	
Government subsidy	↑	
Expected future price	↓	
Number of producers	↑	

oven) decreases production costs, decreasing the price required to generate any particular quantity (downward shift) and increasing the quantity supplied at any particular price (rightward shift). An improvement in technology that allows the firm to economize on labor or material inputs cuts production costs and shifts the supply curve in a similar fashion. The technological improvement could be a new machine or a new way of doing business—a new layout for a factory or store, or a more efficient system of ordering inputs and distributing output. Finally, if a government subsidizes production by paying the firm some amount for each unit produced, the net cost to the firm is lowered by the amount of the subsidy, and the supply curve shifts downward and to the right.

Two other possible sources of increases in supply are listed in Table 4.3. First, if firms believe that next month's price will be lower than they had initially expected, they may try to sell more output now at this month's relatively high price, increasing supply this month. Second, because the market supply is the sum of the quantities supplied by all producers, an increase in the number of producers will increase market supply.

As summarized in Table 4.3, the language of shifting supply is a bit tricky. An increase in supply is represented graphically by a shift to the right (a larger quantity supplied at each price) and down (a lower price required to generate a particular quantity). The best way to remember this is to recognize that the *increase* in "increase in supply" refers to the increase in quantity supplied at a particular price—the horizontal shift of the supply curve to the right.

An Increase in Supply Decreases the Equilibrium Price

We can use Figure 4.11 to show the effects of an increase in supply on the equilibrium price and equilibrium quantity. An increase in the supply of pizza shifts the supply curve to the right, from S_1 to S_2. At the initial price of $8, the quantity supplied increases from 30,000 pizzas (point *a*) to 46,000 (point *b*).

The shift of the supply curve causes excess supply that eventually decreases the equilibrium price. At the initial price of $8 (the equilibrium price with the initial supply curve), there will be an excess supply, as indicated by points *a* and *b*: Producers are willing to sell 46,000 pizzas (point *b*), but consumers are willing to buy only 30,000 (point *a*). Producers want to sell 16,000 more pizzas than consumers are willing to buy, and the excess supply causes pressure to decrease the price. As the price

▶ **FIGURE 4.11**

An Increase in Supply Decreases the Equilibrium Price

An increase in supply shifts the supply curve to the right: At each price, the quantity supplied increases. At the initial price ($8), there is excess supply, with the quantity supplied (point *b*) exceeding the quantity demanded (point *a*). The excess supply causes the price to drop, and equilibrium is restored at point *c*. To summarize, the increase in supply decreases the equilibrium price to $6 and increases the equilibrium quantity to 36,000 pizzas.

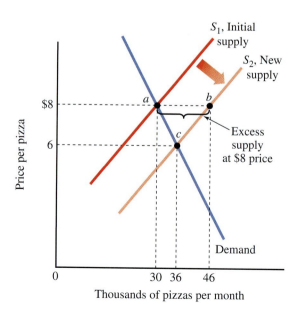

decreases, the excess supply shrinks, because the quantity supplied decreases while the quantity demanded increases. The new supply curve intersects the demand curve at point c, so the new equilibrium price is $6 (down from $8) and the new equilibrium quantity is 36,000 pizzas (up from 30,000).

Decreases in Supply Shift the Supply Curve

Consider next the changes that cause a decrease in supply. As shown in Table 4.4, anything that increases a firm's production costs will decrease supply. An increase in production cost increases the price required to generate a particular quantity (an upward shift of the supply curve) and decreases the quantity supplied at each price (a leftward shift). Production costs will increase as a result of an increase in the wage, an increase in the price of materials or capital, or a tax on each unit produced. As we saw earlier, the language linking changes in supply and the shifts of the supply curve is tricky. In the case of a decrease in supply, the *decrease* refers to the change in quantity at a particular price—the horizontal shift of the supply curve to the left.

A decrease in supply could occur for two other reasons. First, if firms believe next month's pizza price will be higher than they had initially expected, they may be willing to sell a smaller quantity today and a larger quantity next month. That means that the supply of pizza today will decrease. Second, because the market supply is the sum of the quantities supplied by all producers, a decrease in the number of producers will decrease market supply, shifting the supply curve to the left.

A Decrease in Supply Increases the Equilibrium Price

We can use Figure 4.12 to show the effects of a decrease in supply on the equilibrium price and equilibrium quantity. A decrease in the supply of pizza shifts the supply curve to the left, from S_1 to S_0. At the initial price of $8 (the equilibrium price with the initial supply curve), there will be an excess demand, as indicated by points a and b: Consumers are willing to buy 30,000 pizzas (point a), but producers are willing to sell only 14,000 pizzas (point b). Consumers want to buy 16,000 more pizzas than producers are willing to sell, and the excess demand causes upward pressure on the price. As the price increases, the excess demand shrinks because the quantity demanded decreases while the quantity supplied increases.

Table 4.4 | CHANGES IN SUPPLY SHIFT THE SUPPLY CURVE UPWARD AND TO THE LEFT

When this variable...	increases or decreases...	the supply curve shifts in this direction...
Wage	↑	
Price of materials or capital	↑	
Tax	↑	
Expected future price	↑	
Number of producers	↓	

▶ **FIGURE 4.12**

A Decrease in Supply Increases the Equilibrium Price

A decrease in supply shifts the supply curve to the left: At each price, the quantity supplied decreases. At the initial price ($8), there is excess demand, with the quantity demanded (point *a*) exceeding the quantity supplied (point *b*). The excess demand causes the price to rise, and equilibrium is restored at point *c*. To summarize, the decrease in supply increases the equilibrium price to $8 and decreases the equilibrium quantity to 24,000 pizzas.

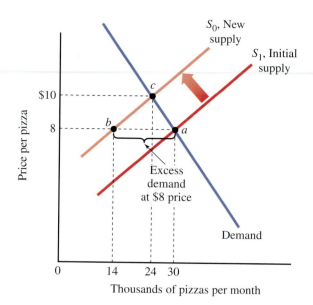

The new supply curve intersects the demand curve at point *c*, so the new equilibrium price is $10 (up from $8), and the new equilibrium quantity is 24,000 pizzas (down from 30,000).

Simultaneous Changes in Demand and Supply

What happens to the equilibrium price and quantity when both demand and supply increase? It depends on which change is larger. In Panel A of Figure 4.13, the increase in demand is larger than the increase in supply, meaning the demand curve shifts by a larger amount than the supply curve. The market equilibrium moves from point *a* to point *b*, and the equilibrium price increases from $8 to $9. This is sensible because an increase in demand tends to pull the price up, while an increase in supply tends to push the price down. If demand increases by a larger amount, the upward pull will be stronger than the downward push, and the price will rise.

We can be certain that when demand and supply both increase, the equilibrium quantity will increase. That's because both changes tend to increase the equilibrium quantity. In Panel A of Figure 4.13, the equilibrium quantity increases from 30,000 to 44,000 pizzas.

▶ **FIGURE 4.13**

Market Effects of Simultaneous Changes in Demand and Supply
(**A**) Larger increase in demand. If the increase in demand is larger than the increase in supply (if the shift of the demand curve is larger than the shift of the supply curve), both the equilibrium price and the equilibrium quantity will increase.
(**B**) Larger increase in supply. If the increase in supply is larger than the increase in demand (if the shift of the supply curve is larger than the shift of the demand curve), the equilibrium price will decrease and the equilibrium quantity will increase.

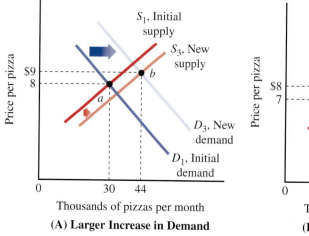

(A) Larger Increase in Demand

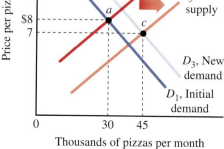

(B) Larger Increase in Supply

84

Panel B of Figure 4.13 shows what happens when the increase in supply is larger than the increase in demand. The equilibrium moves from point *a* to point *c*, meaning that the price falls from $8 to $7. This is sensible because the downward pull on the price resulting from the increase in supply is stronger than the upward pull from the increase in demand. As expected, the equilibrium quantity rises from 30,000 to 45,000 pizzas.

What about simultaneous *decreases* in demand and supply? In this case, the equilibrium quantity will certainly fall because both changes tend to decrease the equilibrium quantity. The effect on the equilibrium price depends on which change is larger, the decrease in demand, which pushes the price downward, or the decrease in supply, which pulls the price upward. If the decrease in demand is larger, the price will fall because the force pushing the price down will be stronger than the force pulling it up. In contrast, if the decrease in supply is larger, the price will rise because the force pulling the price up will be stronger than the force pushing it down.

4.6 | PREDICTING AND EXPLAINING MARKET CHANGES

We've used the model of demand and supply to show how equilibrium prices are determined and how changes in demand and supply affect equilibrium prices and quantities. Table 4.5 summarizes what we've learned about how changes in demand and supply affect equilibrium prices and quantities:

- When demand changes and the demand curve shifts, price and quantity change in the *same* direction: When demand increases, both price and quantity increase; when demand decreases, both price and quantity decrease.
- When supply changes and the supply curve shifts, price and quantity change in *opposite* directions: When supply increases, the price decreases but the quantity increases; when supply decreases, the price increases but the quantity decreases.

We can use these lessons about demand and supply to predict the effects of various events on the equilibrium price and equilibrium quantity of a product.

We can also use the lessons listed in Table 4.5 to explain the reasons for changes in prices or quantities. Suppose we observe changes in the equilibrium price and quantity of a particular good, but we don't know what caused these changes. Perhaps it was a change in demand, or maybe it was a change in supply. We can use the information in Table 4.5 to work backwards, using what we've observed about changes in prices and quantities to determine which side of the market—demand or supply—caused the changes:

- If the equilibrium price and quantity move in the same direction, the changes were caused by a change in demand.
- If the equilibrium price and quantity move in opposite directions, the changes were caused by a change in supply.

Table 4.5 | MARKET EFFECTS OF CHANGES IN DEMAND OR SUPPLY

Change in Demand or Supply	How does the equilibrium price change?	How does the equilibrium quantity change?
Increase in demand	↑	↑
Decrease in demand	↓	↓
Increase in supply	↓	↑
Decrease in supply	↑	↓

4.7 | APPLICATIONS OF DEMAND AND SUPPLY

We can apply what we've learned about demand and supply to real markets. We can use the model of demand and supply to *predict* the effects of various events on equilibrium prices and quantities. We can also *explain* some observed changes in equilibrium prices and quantities.

APPLICATION

HURRICANE KATRINA AND BATON ROUGE HOUSING PRICES

APPLYING THE CONCEPTS #1:
How do changes in demand affect prices?

In the late summer of 2005, Hurricane Katrina caused a storm surge and levee breaks that flooded much of New Orleans and destroyed a large fraction of the city's housing. Hundreds of thousands of residents were displaced, and about 250,000 relocated to nearby Baton Rouge. The increase in population was so large that Baton Rouge became the largest city in the state, and many people started calling the city "New Baton Rouge."

Figure 4.14 shows the effects of Hurricane Katrina on the housing market in Baton Rouge. Before Katrina, the average price of a single-family home was $130,000, as shown by point *a*. The increase in the city's population shifted the demand curve to the right, causing excess demand for housing at the original price. Just before the hurricane, there were 3,600 homes listed for sale in the city, but a week after the storm, there were only 500. The excess demand caused fierce competition among buyers for the limited supply of homes, increasing the price. Six months later, the average price had risen to $156,000 as shown by point *b*. **Related to Exercises 7.1 and 7.6.**

SOURCE: Federal Deposit Insurance Corporation, *Louisiana State Profile—Fall 2005*.

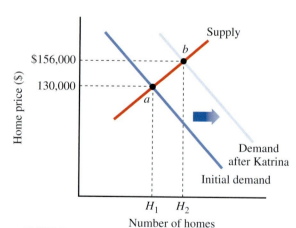

▲ **FIGURE 4.14**
Hurricane Katrina and Housing in Baton Rouge
An increase in the population of Baton Rouge increases the demand for housing, shifting the demand curve to right. The equilibrium price increases from $130,000 (point *a*) to $156,000 (point *b*).

APPLICATION

TED KOPPEL TRIES TO EXPLAIN LOWER DRUG PRICES

APPLYING THE CONCEPTS #2: What could explain a decrease in price?

Ted Koppel, host of the ABC news program *Nightline*, once said, "Do you know what's happened to the price of drugs in the United States? The price of cocaine, way down, the price of marijuana, way down. You don't have to be an expert in economics to know that when the price goes down, it means more stuff is coming in. That's supply and demand." According to Koppel, the price of drugs dropped because the government's efforts to control the supply of illegal drugs had failed. In other words, the lower price resulted from an increase in supply. According to the U.S. Department of Justice, the quantity of drugs consumed actually decreased during the period of dropping prices. Is Koppel's economic detective work sound?

In this case, both the price and the quantity decreased. As shown in the second row of Table 4.5, when both the price and the quantity decrease, that means demand has decreased. For example, in Figure 4.15, a decrease in demand shifts the demand curve to the left, and the market moves from point *a* (price = $15 and quantity = 400 units per day) to point *b* (price = $10 and quantity = 300 units per day). Koppel's explanation (an increase in supply) would be correct if the quantity of drugs increased at the same time that the price decreased. However, because the quantity of drugs consumed actually decreased during the period of dropping prices, Koppel's explanation is incorrect. Lower demand—not a failure of the government's drug policy and an increase in supply—was responsible for the decrease in drug prices.
Related to Exercises 7.2 and 7.7.

SOURCES: Kenneth R. Clark, "Legalize Drugs. A Case for Koppel," *Chicago Tribune*, August 30, 1988, sec. 5, p. 8; U.S. Department of Justice, "Drugs, Crime, and the Justice System" (Washington, DC: U.S. Government Printing Office, 1992), p. 30.

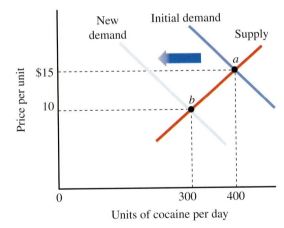

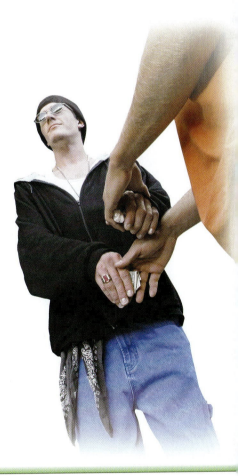

▲ **FIGURE 4.15**

Ted Koppel and the Falling Price of Drugs

At the same time that the price of cocaine decreased (from $15 to $10), the quantity of cocaine consumed decreased (from 400 to 300 units). Therefore the decrease in price was caused by a decrease in demand, not an increase in supply.

3

ELECTRICITY FROM THE WIND

APPLYING THE CONCEPT #3: How does the adoption of new technology affect prices?

In recent years, the supply of electricity generated from wind power has increased dramatically. Between 2000 and 2006, total wind power in the United States increased from 620 megawatts to 9,200 megawatts, enough power to serve the equivalent of 2.4 million households. Over the same period, the price of electricity generated from wind power decreased from 50 cents per kilowatt-hour to 4 cents.

Figure 4.16 shows the changes in the wind electricity market in recent years. Several design innovations, including the replacement of small, rapid rotors with large, slow-moving blades and the development of monitoring systems that change the direction and the angle of the blades to more efficiently harness the wind, have decreased the cost of producing electricity, shifting the supply curve downward and to the right. In Figure 4.16, the shift of the supply curve decreases the equilibrium price and increases the equilibrium quantity.

The innovations in wind generation have made wind power more competitive with conventional power sources such as coal and natural gas. The price of electricity from natural gas and coal is about 2 cents per kilowatt-hour. The producers of wind electricity receive a federal tax credit of almost 2 cents per kilowatt-hour, making the net price of wind power close to the price of conventional power.
Related to Exercises 7.3 and 7.8.

SOURCE: *Christian Science Monitor*, "A New Gust of Wind Projects Across the U.S.," January 19, 2006, p. 1.

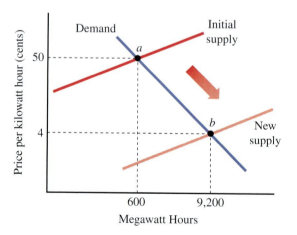

▲ **FIGURE 4.16**
Wind Power and Electricity
Technological innovations in generating electricity from the wind decreased production costs, shifting the supply curve downward and to the right. The equilibrium price decreased and the equilibrium quantity increased. (To represent the large changes in price and quantity, the graph is not drawn to scale.)

APPLICATION

4

THE BOUNCING PRICE OF VANILLA BEANS

APPLYING THE CONCEPTS #4: How do changes in supply affect prices?

As we saw in the chapter opener, the price of vanilla beans has been bouncing around a lot. The price was $50 per kilo (2.2 pounds) in 2000, then rose to $500 in 2003, then dropped to $25 in 2006. We can use the model of demand and supply to explain the bouncing price.

Figure 4.17 shows the changes in the vanilla market in recent years. Point *a* shows the initial equilibrium in 2000, with a price of $50 per kilo. The 2000 cyclone that hit Madagascar, the world's leading producer, destroyed that year's crop and a large share of the vines that produce vanilla beans. Although the vines were replanted, new plants don't bear usable beans for three to five years, so the supply effects of the cyclone lasted several years. In Figure 4.17, the cyclone shifted the supply curve upward and to the left, generating a new equilibrium at point *b*, with a higher price and a smaller quantity.

In Figure 4.17, the changes between 2003 and 2006 are shown by a shift of the supply curve downward and to the right. In 2006, the vines replanted in Madagascar in 2001 started to produce vanilla beans. In addition, other countries, including India, Papua New Guinea, Uganda, and Costa Rica, entered the vanilla market. The vines planted in these other countries started to produce beans in 2006, so the world supply curve for 2006 lies below and to the right of the original supply curve (in 2000). Given the larger supply of vanilla beans in 2006, the price dropped to about half of its 2000 level, to $25 per kilo. The increase in supply from other countries was facilitated by the development of a sun-tolerant variety of the vanilla plant that allows it to be grown as a plantation crop. The new variety is an example of technological progress. *Related to Exercises 7.4 and 7.9.*

SOURCES: Rhett Butler, "Collapsing Vanilla Prices Will Affect Madagascar," *mongabay.com* (May 9, 2005); Noel Paul, "Vanilla Sky High," *Christian Science Monitor* csmonitor.com (August 11, 2003); G.K. Nair, Vanilla prices fall on undercutting, *Hindu Business Line*, Apr. 03. 2006 [www.thehindubusinessline.com].

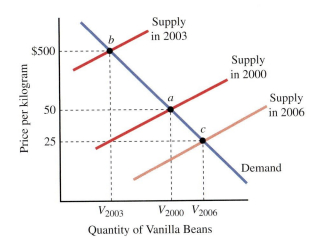

▲ **FIGURE 4.17**

The Bouncing Price of Vanilla Beans

A cyclone destroyed much of Madagascar's crop in 2000, shifting the supply curve upward and to the left. The equilibrium price increased from $50 per kilogram (point *a*) to $500 per kilogram (pont *b*). By 2005, the vines replanted in Madagascar—along with new vines planted in other countries— started producing vanilla beans, and the supply curve shifted downward and to the right, beyond the supply curve for 2000. The price dropped to $25 per kilogram (point *c*), half the price that prevailed in 2000. (To represent the large changes in price and quantity, the graph is not drawn to scale.)

5

APPLICATION

PLATINUM, JEWELRY, CATALYTIC CONVERTERS

APPLYING THE CONCEPTS #5: How do changes in one market affect other markets?

In early 2004, the price of platinum reached $937 per ounce—up from $440 in 1999 and $700 in 2003. The two largest sources of demand for platinum are jewelry and the catalytic converters used in automobiles to control emissions. In recent years, the tightening of emissions standards for automobiles and trucks increased the demand for platinum. In rapidly growing Asian countries, the demand for automobiles increased, and many countries adopted stricter emissions standards. In Latin America, Brazil and Chile recently mandated the use of catalytic converters in their automobiles.

Table 4.6 shows the changes in the demand for platinum from 1999 to 2004. The demand for platinum for use in catalytic converters more than doubled, from 1.19 million ounces to 2.81 million ounces. The increase in demand increased the equilibrium price of platinum. The other numbers in the table illustrate the laws of demand and supply:

1 *The law of demand for jewelry.* The increase in the price of platinum increased the equilibrium price of platinum jewelry, and consumers responded by purchasing less platinum jewelry. As a result, the amount of platinum used in jewelry decreased, from 2.88 million ounces to 2.20 million ounces.

2 *The law of supply for recycling.* The increase in the price of platinum increased the payoff from recycling used platinum, increasing the quantity of platinum supplied through recycling from 0.42 million ounces to 0.70 million ounces.

What's next for the platinum market? Another potential source of increased demand is the development of fuel cells. This environmentally friendly technology combines oxygen and hydrogen to produce electricity. Platinum is a core material in fuel cells, and if fuel cells emerge as an important source of electricity the resulting increase in the demand for platinum will increase its price.
Related to Exercises 7.5 and 7.10.

SOURCE: Johnson Matthy, *Platinum 2005* (London, 2005).

Table 4.6 | SOURCES OF DEMAND FOR PLATINUM

Source of Demand	1999 (million ounces)	2004 (million ounces)
Catalytic converters	1.19	2.81
Jewelry	2.88	2.20
Chemical and electrical	0.69	0.58
Other	0.83	0.99
Total	**5.59**	**6.58**
Supply from recycling	0.42	0.70

SUMMARY

In this chapter, we've seen how demand and supply determine prices. We also learned how to predict the effects of changes in demand or supply on prices and quantities. Here are the main points of the chapter:

1 A *market demand curve* shows the relationship between th quantity demanded and price, *ceteris paribus.*

2 A *market supply curve* shows the relationship between the quantity supplied and price, *ceteris paribus.*

3 *Equilibrium* in a market is shown by the intersection of the demand curve and the supply curve. When a market reaches equilibrium, there is no pressure to change the price.

4 A *change in demand* changes price and quantity in the same direction: An increase in demand increases the equilibrium price and quantity; a decrease in demand decreases the equilibrium price and quantity.

5 A *change in supply* changes price and quantity in opposite directions: An increase in supply decreases price and increases quantity; a decrease in supply increases price and decreases quantity.

KEY TERMS

change in demand, p. 77

change in quantity demanded, p. 69

change in quantity supplied, p. 72

change in supply, p. 81

complements, p. 78

demand schedule, p. 68

excess demand (shortage), p. 75

excess supply (surplus), p. 76

individual demand curve, p. 69

individual supply curve, p. 72

inferior good, p. 77

law of demand, p. 69

law of supply, p. 72

market demand curve, p. 69

market equilibrium, p. 75

market supply curve, p. 73

minimum supply price, p. 72

normal good, p. 77

perfectly competitive market, p. 68

quantity demanded, p. 68

quantity supplied, p. 71

substitutes, p. 77

supply schedule, p. 71

EXERCISES

Visit www.myeconlab.com to complete these exercises online and get instant feedback.

Get Ahead of the Curve

4.1 | The Demand Curve

1.1 Arrow up or down: According to the law of demand, an increase in price _____ the quantity demanded.

1.2 From the following list, choose the variables that are held fixed in drawing a market demand curve:
- The price of the product
- Consumer income
- The price of other related goods
- Consumer expectations about future prices
- The quantity of the product purchased

1.3 From the following list, choose the variables that change as we draw a market demand curve.
- The price of the product
- Consumer income
- The price of other related goods
- Consumer expectations about future prices
- The quantity of the product purchased

1.4 The market demand curve is the _____ (horizontal/vertical) sum of the individual demand curves.

1.5 **Draw a Demand Curve.** Your state has decided to offer its citizens vanity license plates for their cars and wants to predict how many vanity plates it will sell at different prices. The price of the state's regular license plates is $20 per year, and the state's per-capita income is $30,000. A recent survey of other states with approximately the same population (3 million people) generated the following data on incomes, prices, and vanity plates:

State	B	C	D	E
Price of vanity plate	$60	$55	$50	$40
Price of regular plates	20	20	35	20
Income	30,000	25,000	30,000	30,000
Quantity of vanity plates	6,000	6,000	16,000	16,000

a. Use the available data to identify some points on the demand curve for vanity plates and connect the points to draw a demand curve. Don't forget *ceteris paribus*.

b. Suppose the demand curve is linear. If your state set a price of $50, how many vanity plates would be purchased?

4.2 | The Supply Curve

2.1 Arrow up or down: According to the law of supply, an increase in price _____ the quantity supplied.

2.2 From the following list, choose the variables that are held fixed when drawing a market supply curve.
- The price of the product
- Wages paid to workers
- The price of materials used in production
- Taxes paid by producers
- The quantity of the product purchased

2.3 The minimum supply price is the _____ price at which a product is supplied.

2.4 The market supply curve is the _____ (horizontal/vertical) sum of the individual supply curves.

2.5 **Marginal Cost of Housing.** When the price of a standard three-bedroom house increases from $150,000 to $160,000, a building company increases its output from 20 houses per year to 21 houses per year. What does the increase in the quantity of housing reveal about the cost of producing housing?

2.6 Imports and Market Supply. Two nations supply sugar to the world market. Lowland has a minimum supply price of 10 cents per pound, while Highland

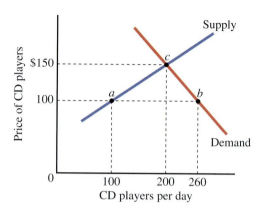

has a minimum supply price of 24 cents per pound. For each nation, the slope of the supply curve is 1 cent per million pounds.

a. Draw the individual supply curves and the market supply curve. At what price and quantity is the supply curve kinked?

b. The market quantity supplied at a price of 15 cents is _____ million pounds. The market quantity supplied at a price of 30 cents is _____ million pounds.

4.3 | Market Equilibrium: Bringing Demand and Supply Together

3.1 The market equilibrium is shown by the intersection of the _____ curve and the _____ curve.

3.2 Excess demand occurs when the price is _____ (less/greater) than the equilibrium price; excess supply occurs when the price is _____ (less/greater) than the equilibrium price.

3.3 Arrow up or down: An excess demand for a product will cause the price to _____. As a consequence of the price change, the quantity demanded will _____ and the quantity supplied will _____.

3.4 Arrow up or down: An excess supply of a product will cause the price to _____. As a consequence of the price change, the quantity demanded will _____, and the quantity supplied will _____.

3.5 **Interpreting the Graph.** The graph below shows the demand and supply curves for CD players. Complete the following statements.

a. At the market equilibrium (shown by point _____), the price of CD players is _____ and the quantity of CD players is _____.

b. At a price of $100, there would be excess _____, so we would expect the price to _____.

c. At a price exceeding the equilibrium price, there would be excess _____, so we would expect the price to _____.

3.6 **Draw and Find the Equilibrium.** The following table shows the quantities of corn supplied and demanded at different prices.

Price per Ton	Quantity Supplied	Quantity Demanded
$80	600	1,200
90	800	1,100
100	1,000	1,000
110	1,200	900

a. Draw the demand curve and the supply curve.

b. The equilibrium price of corn is _____, and the equilibrium quantity is _____.

4.4 | Market Effects of Changes in Demand

4.1 A change in demand causes a _____ (movement along/shift of) the demand curve. A change in quantity demanded causes a _____ (movement along/shift of) the demand curve.

4.2 Circle the variables that change as we move along the demand curve for pencils and cross out those that are assumed to be fixed.
- Quantity of pencils demanded
- Number of consumers
- Price of pencils
- Price of pens
- Consumer income

4.3 A decrease in the price of online music shifts the demand curve for CDs to the _____ (right/left); an increase in the price of CD players shifts the demand curve for CDs to the _____ (right/left).

4.4 Arrow up or down: The market demand curve for a product will shift to the right when the price of a substitute good _____, the price of a complementary good _____, consumer income _____, population _____.

4.5 Arrow up or down: An increase in demand for a product _____ the equilibrium price and _____ the equilibrium quantity.

4.6 **Market Effects of Increased Income.** Consider the market for restaurant meals. Use a demand and supply graph to predict the market effects of an increase in consumer income. Arrow up or down: The equilibrium price of restaurant meals will _____, and the equilibrium quantity of restaurant meals will _____.

4.7 **Public Versus Private Colleges.** Consider the market for private college education. Use a demand and supply graph to predict the market effects of an increase in the tuition charged by public colleges. Arrow up or down: The equilibrium price of a private college education will _____, and the equilibrium quantity will _____.

4.5 | Market Effects of Changes in Supply

5.1 A change in supply causes a _____ (movement along/shift of) the supply curve. A change in quantity supplied causes a _____ (movement along/shift of) the supply curve.

5.2 Circle the variables that change as we move along the supply curve for pencils and cross out those that are assumed to be fixed:
- Quantity of pencils supplied
- Price of wood
- Price of pencils
- Production technology

5.3 Arrow up or down: An increase in the price of wood shifts the supply curve for pencils _____; an improvement in pencil-production technology shifts the supply curve for pencils _____; a tax on pencil production shifts the supply curve for pencils _____.

5.4 Arrow up or down: An increase in the supply of a product _____ the equilibrium price and _____ the equilibrium quantity.

5.5 If both demand and supply increase simultaneously, the equilibrium price will increase if the change in _____ is relatively large.

5.6 **Effect of Weather on Prices.** Suppose a freeze in Florida wipes out 20 percent of the orange crop. How will this affect the equilibrium price and quantity of Florida oranges? Illustrate your answer with a graph.

5.7 **Immigration Control and Prices.** Consider the market for raspberries. Suppose a new law outlaws the use of foreign farm workers on raspberry farms, and the wages paid to farm workers increase as a result. Use a demand and supply graph to predict the effects of the higher wage on the equilibrium price and quantity of raspberries. Arrow up or down: The equilibrium price of raspberries will _____, and the equilibrium quantity of raspberries will _____.

5.8 **Market Effects of Import Ban.** Consider the market for shoes in a nation that initially imports half the shoes it consumes. Use a demand and supply graph to predict the market effect of a ban on shoe imports. Arrow up or down: The equilibrium price will _____, and the equilibrium quantity will _____.

5.9 **Market Effects of a Tax.** Consider the market for fish. Use a demand and supply graph to predict the effect of a tax paid by fish producers of $1 per pound of fish. Use a demand and supply graph to predict the market effect of the tax. Arrow up or down: The equilibrium price will _____, and the equilibrium quantity will _____.

5.10 **Innovation and the Price of Mobile Phones.** Suppose that the initial price of a mobile phone is $100 and that the initial quantity demanded is 500 phones per day. Use a graph to show the effects of a technological innovation that decreases the cost of producing mobile phones. Label the starting point with "*a*" and the new equilibrium with "*b*."

4.6 | Predicting and Explaining Market Changes

6.1 Fill the blanks in the following table. Note that the ordering of the first column has been scrambled.

Change in Demand or Supply	How does the equilibrium price change?	How does the equilibrium quantity change?
Increase in supply		
Decrease in demand		
Decrease in supply		
Increase in demand		

6.2 When _____ (supply/demand) changes, the equilibrum price and equilibrum price change in the same direction. When _____ (supply/demand) changes, the equilibrium price and equilibrium price change in opposite directions.

6.3 Suppose the equilibrium price of accordions recently increased while the equilibrium quantity decreased. These changes were caused by a(n) _____ (increase/decrease) in _____ (supply/demand).

6.4 Suppose the equilibrium price of housing recently increased, and the equilibrium quantity increased as well. These changes were caused by a(n) _____ (increase/decrease) in _____ (supply/demand).

6.5 **What Caused the Higher Gasoline Price?** In the last month, the price of gasoline increased by 20 percent. Your job is to determine what caused the increase in price, a change in demand or a change in supply. Ms. Info has all the numbers associated with the gasoline market, and she can answer a single factual question. (She cannot answer the question: "Was the higher price caused by a change in demand or a change in supply?")
a. What single question would you ask?
b. Provide an answer to your question that implies that the higher price was caused by a change in demand. Illustrate with a complete graph.
c. Provide an answer to your question that implies that the higher price was caused by a change in supply. Illustrate with a complete graph.

6.6 **Rising Price of Used Organs.** Over the last few years, the price of used organs (livers, kidneys, hearts) has increased dramatically. Why? What additional information about the market for used organs would allow you to prove that your explanation is the correct one?

6.7 **The Price of Summer Cabins.** As summer approaches, the equilibrium price of rental cabins increases and the equilibrium quantity of cabins rented increases. Draw a demand and supply graph that explains these changes.

6.8 **Simplest Possible Graph.** Consider the market for juice oranges. Draw the simplest possible demand and supply graph consistent with the following observations. You should be able to draw a graph with no more than 4 curves. Label each of your curves as "supply" or "demand" and indicate the year (1, 2, or 3).

Year	1	2	3
Price	$5	$7	$4
Quantity	100	80	110

6.9 **Zero Price for Used Newspapers.** In 1987, you could sell a ton of used newspaper for $60. Five years later, you couldn't sell them at any price. In other words, the price of used newspapers dropped from $60 to zero in just 5 years. Over this period, the quantity of used newspapers bought and sold increased. What caused the drop in price? Illustrate your answer with a complete graph.

4.7 | Applications of Demand and Supply

7.1 Arrow up or down: Hurricane Katrina _____ the demand for housing in Baton Rouge, so the price of housing _____ and the quantity of housing _____. (Related to Application 1 on page 86.)

7.2 Ted Koppel's analysis of the drug market was incorrect because he failed to notice that the _____ of drugs decreased at the same time that the _____ of drugs decreased. (Related to Application 2 on page 87.)

7.3 Innovations in wind technology decrease the price of electricity from wind from 50 cents per kilowatt-hour to _____ cents. (Related to Application 3 on page 88.)

7.4 Arrow up or down: The development of a sun-tolerant variety of the vanilla plant _____ the supply of vanilla and _____ its price. (Related to Application 4 on page 89.)

7.5 Arrow up or down: The increase in the price of platinum _____ recycling of used platinum and _____ the quantity of platinum used for jewelry. (Related to Application 5 on page 90.)

7.6 **Katrina Victims Move Back.** Suppose that 5 years after Hurricane Katrina, half the people who had relocated to Baton Rouge move back to a rebuilt New Orleans. Use a demand and supply graph of the Baton Rouge housing market to show the market effects of the return of people to New Orleans. (Related to Application 1 on page 86.)

7.7 **Decrease in the Price of Heroin.** Between 1990 and 2003, the price of heroin decreased from $235 per gram to $76. Over the same period, the quantity of heroin consumed increased from 376 metric tons to 482 metric tons. Use a demand and supply graph to explain these changes in price and quantity. (Related to Application 2 on page 87.)

7.8 **Electricity from Fuel Cells.** Suppose that initially the cost of the capital required to generate electricity from fuel cells is $4,500 per kilowatt capacity, compared to $800 per kilowatt capacity for a diesel generator. The goal of the U.S. Department of Energy (DOE) is to cut the cost of fuel-cell generators to $400 per kilowatt capacity. Consider the market for electricity from fuel cells. Use a demand and supply graph to show the effects of meeting the DOE goal on the price and quantity of electricity from fuel cells. (Related to Application 3 on page 88.)

7.9 **Artificial Versus Natural Vanilla.** An artificial alternative to natural vanilla is cheaper to produce but doesn't taste as good. Suppose the makers of artificial vanilla discover a new recipe that improves its taste. Use a demand and supply graph to show the effects on the equilibrium price and quantity of natural vanilla. (Related to Application 4 on page 89.)

7.10 **Platinum Price and Jewelry.** Consider the market for platinum jewelry. Use a demand and supply graph to illustrate the following statement: "The increase in the price of platinum increased the price of platinum jewelry, and consumers responded by purchasing less platinum jewelry." (Related to Application 5 on page 90.)

ECONOMIC EXPERIMENT

Market Equilibrium

This simple experiment takes about 20 minutes. We start by dividing the class into two equal groups: consumers and producers.

- The instructor provides each consumer with a number indicating the maximum amount he or she is willing to pay (WTP) for a bushel of apples: The WTP is a number between $1 and $100. Each consumer has the opportunity to buy 1 bushel of apples per trading period. The consumer's score for a single trading period equals the gap between the WTP and the price actually paid for apples. For example, if the consumer's WTP is $80 and he or she pays only $30 for apples, the consumer's score is $50. Each consumer has the option of not buying apples. This will be sensible if the best price the consumer can get exceeds the WTP. If the consumer does not buy apples, his or her score will be zero.

- The instructor provides each producer with a number indicating the cost of producing a bushel of apples (a number between $1 and $100). Each producer has the opportunity to sell 1 bushel per trading period. The producer's score for a single trading period equals the gap between the selling prices and the cost of producing apples. So if a producer sells apples for $20, and the cost is only $15, the producer's score is $5. Producers have the option of not selling apples, which is sensible if the best price the producer can get is less than the cost. If the producer does not sell apples, his or her score is zero.

Once everyone understands the rules, consumers and producers meet in a trading area to arrange transactions. A consumer may announce how much he or she is willing to pay for apples and wait for a producer to agree to sell apples at that price. Alternatively, a producer may announce how much he or she is willing accept for apples and wait for a consumer to agree to buy apples at that price. Once a transaction has been arranged, the consumer and producer inform the instructor of the trade, record the transaction, and leave the trading area.

Several trading periods are conducted, each of which lasts a few minutes. After the end of each trading period, the instructor lists the prices at which apples sold during the period. Then another trading period starts, providing consumers and producers another opportunity to buy or sell apples. After all the trading periods have been completed, each participant computes his or her score by adding the scores from the trading periods.

5

Elasticity: A Measure of Responsiveness

In every large city in the United States, the public bus system runs a deficit: Operating costs exceed revenues from passenger fares. Suppose your city wants to reduce its bus deficit and is trying to decide whether to increase fares by 10 percent. Consider the following exchange between two city officials:

BUSTER: "A fare increase is a great idea. We'll collect more money from bus riders, so revenue will increase, and the deficit will shrink."

BESSIE: "Wait a minute, Buster. Haven't you heard about the law of demand? The increase in the bus fare will decrease the number of passengers taking buses, so we'll collect less money, not more, and the deficit will grow."

Who is right? As we'll see in this chapter, we can't predict how an increase in price will affect total revenue unless we know just how responsive consumers are to an increase in price. Like other consumers, bus riders obey the law of demand, but that doesn't necessarily mean that total fare revenue will fall.

In Chapter 4, we discussed the law of demand, which states that an increase in price decreases the quantity demanded, *ceteris paribus*. The law of demand is useful, but sometimes we need to know the numbers behind the law of demand. That is, we need to know exactly how much less will be demanded at a higher price. In this chapter, we will quantify the law of demand, exploring the responsiveness of consumers to changes in price. Suppose your student film society has decided to increase the price for its tickets from $10 to $11. You know from the law of demand that you'll sell fewer tickets, but the question is: How many fewer tickets? As we'll see, you can use the concept of elasticity to predict how many tickets you'll sell and how much money you'll collect in total. Similarly, in the case of hiking the bus fare, we can use the concept of elasticity to determine whether Buster or Bessie is correct.

Switching to the supply side of the market, the law of supply tells us that an increase in price increases the quantity supplied, *ceteris paribus*. Sometimes the question is: By how much? We'll quantify the law of supply, showing how to predict just how much more of a product will be supplied at a higher price. For example, if the world price of oil increases from $70 to $80 per barrel, we know from the law of supply that domestic producers will supply more oil, but the question is: How much more? We can use the concept of elasticity to predict how much more domestic oil will be supplied at the higher price.

5.1 | THE PRICE ELASTICITY OF DEMAND

• **price elasticity of demand (E_d)**
A measure of the responsiveness of the quantity demanded to changes in price; equal to the absolute value of the percentage change in quantity demanded divided by the percentage change in price.

The **price elasticity of demand (E_d)** measures the responsiveness of the quantity demanded to changes in price. To compute the price elasticity of demand, we divide the percentage change in the quantity demanded by the percentage change in price, and then take the absolute value of the ratio:

$$E_d = \left| \frac{\text{percentage change in quantity demanded}}{\text{percentage change in price}} \right|$$

The vertical bars indicate that we take the absolute value of the ratio, so the price elasticity is always a positive number. For example, suppose the price of milk *increases* by 10 percent and the quantity demanded *decreases* by 15 percent. The price elasticity of demand is 1.5:

$$E_d = \left| \frac{\text{percentage change in quantity demanded}}{\text{percentage change in price}} \right| = \left| \frac{-15\%}{10\%} \right| = 1.50$$

The law of demand tell us that price and quantity demanded move in opposite directions. Therefore, the percentage change in quantity will always have the opposite sign of the percentage change in price. In our example, a positive 10-percent change in price results in a negative 15-percent change in quantity. The ratio of the percentage changes is −1.50, and taking the absolute value of this ratio, the elasticity is 1.50. Although it is conventional to use the absolute value to compute the price elasticity, the practice is not universal. So you may encounter a negative price elasticity, which means that the elasticity is reported as its numerical value rather than its absolute value.

When the price elasticity is listed as a positive number, the interpretation of the elasticity is straightforward. If the elasticity number is large, it means that the demand for the product is very elastic, or very responsive to changes in price. In contrast, a small number indicates that the demand for a product is very inelastic.

Computing Percentage Changes and Elasticities

As we saw in the Appendix to Chapter 1, a percentage change can be computed in two ways. Using the initial-value method, we divide the change in the value of a variable by its initial value. For example, if a price increases from $20 to $22, the percentage change is $2 divided by $20, or 10 percent:

$$\text{percent change with initial value} = \frac{22-20}{20} \times 100 = \frac{2}{20} \times 100 = 10\%$$

Alternatively, we could use the midpoint method. We divide the change in the variable by its average value, that is, the midpoint of the two values. For example, if the price increases from $20 to $22, the average or midpoint value is $21 and the percentage change is 9.52 percent:

$$\text{percent change with midpoint value} = \frac{2}{\dfrac{20+22}{2}} \times 100 = \frac{2}{21} \times 100 = 9.52\%$$

The advantage of the midpoint approach is that it generates the same absolute percentage change whether the variable has increased or decreased. That's because the denominator is the same in both cases. In contrast, the initial-value computation is based on the initial value, so it depends on the direction of the change—which of the two values is the initial value.

Table 5.1 shows the calculation of the price elasticity of demand with the two approaches. When the price increases from $20 to $22, the quantity demanded decreases from 100 to 80 units. Using the initial-value method, we get an elasticity of 2.0, equal to the 20-percent change in quantity divided by the 10-percent change in price. As shown in the lower part of the table, the midpoint method generates an elasticity of 2.33.

Why do the two approaches generate different elasticity numbers? The midpoint approach measures the percentage changes more precisely, so we get a more precise measure of price elasticity. In this case, the percentage changes are relatively small, so the two elasticity numbers are close to one another. If the percentage changes were larger, however, the elasticity numbers generated by the two approaches would be quite different, and it would be wise to use the midpoint approach. In this book, we use the initial-value approach because it generates nice round numbers and allows us to focus on economics rather than arithmetic. But anytime you want to be more precise, you can use the midpoint formula.

Table 5.1 | COMPUTING PRICE ELASTICITY WITH INITIAL VALUES AND MIDPOINTS

		Price	Quantity
Data	Initial	$20	100
	New	22	80

		Price	Quantity
Computation with Initial-value method	Percentage change	$10\% = \dfrac{\$2}{\$20} \times 100$	$-20\% = -\dfrac{20}{100} \times 100$
	Price elasticity of demand	$2.0 = \left\lvert \dfrac{-20\%}{10\%} \right\rvert$	

		Price	Quantity
Computation with Midpoint method	Percentage change	$9.52\% = \dfrac{\$2}{\$21} \times 100$	$-22.22\% = -\dfrac{20}{90} \times 100$
	Price elasticity of demand	$2.33 = \left\lvert \dfrac{-22.22\%}{9.52\%} \right\rvert$	

- **elastic demand**
  The price elasticity of demand is greater than one.

- **inelastic demand**
  The price elasticity of demand is less than one.

- **unit elastic demand**
  The price elasticity of demand is one.

- **perfectly inelastic demand**
  The price elasticity of demand is zero.

- **perfectly elastic demand**
  The price elasticity of demand is infinite.

Price Elasticity and the Demand Curve

Figure 5.1 shows five different demand curves, each with a different elasticity. We can divide products into five types, depending on their price elasticities of demand.

- **Elastic demand** (Panel A). In this case, a 20-percent increase in price (from $5 to $6) decreases the quantity demanded by 40 percent (from 20 to 12), so the price elasticity of demand is 2.0. When the price elasticity is greater than 1.0, we say that demand is "elastic," or highly responsive to changes in price. Some examples of goods with elastic demand are restaurant meals, air travel, and movies.

- **Inelastic demand** (Panel B). The same 20-percent increase in price decreases the quantity demanded by only 10 percent (from 20 to 18), so the price elasticity of demand is 0.50. When the elasticity is less than 1.0, we say that demand is *inelastic*, or not very responsive to changes in price. Some examples of goods with inelastic demand are salt, eggs, coffee and cigarettes.

- **Unit elastic demand** (Panel C). A 20-percent increase in price decreases the quantity demanded by exactly 20 percent, so the price elasticity of demand is 1.0. Some examples of goods with unit elasticity are housing and fruit juice.

- **Perfectly inelastic demand** (Panel D). When demand is perfectly inelastic, the quantity doesn't change as the price changes, so the demand curve is vertical at the fixed quantity. The price elasticity of demand is zero. This extreme case is rare because for most products, consumers can either switch to a substitute good or do without. For example, although there are no direct substitutes for household water, as the price of water rises, people install low-flow showerheads, water their lawns less frequently, and clean their cars less frequently. The rare cases of perfectly inelastic demand are medicines—such as insulin for diabetics—that have no substitutes.

- **Perfectly elastic demand** (Panel E). In this case, the price elasticity is infinite and the demand curve is horizontal, meaning that only one price is possible. At that price, the quantity demanded could be any quantity, from one unit to millions of units. If the price were to increase even a penny, the quantity demanded would drop to zero. As we'll see later in the book, firms in a perfectly competitive market face this sort of demand curve. For example, each wheat farmer can sell as much as he or she wants at the market price but would sell nothing at any price above the market price.

Elasticity and the Availability of Substitutes

The key factor in determining the price elasticity for a particular product is the availability of substitute products. Consider the substitution possibilities for insulin (a medicine for diabetics) and cornflakes. There are no good substitutes for insulin, so consumers are not very responsive to changes in price. When the price of insulin increases, diabetics cannot switch to another medicine, so the demand for insulin is inelastic. In contrast, there are many substitutes for cornflakes, including different types of corn cereals, as well as cereals made from wheat, rice, and oats. Faced with an increase in the price of cornflakes, consumers can easily switch to substitute products, so the demand for cornflakes is relatively elastic.

Table 5.2 on page 104 shows the price elasticities of demand for various products. The different elasticities illustrate the importance of substitutes in determining the price elasticity of demand. Because there are no good substitutes for water and salt, it is not surprising that the elasticities are small. For example, the price elasticity of demand for water is 0.20, meaning that a 10-percent increase in price decreases the quantity demanded by 2 percent. The demand for coffee is inelastic (0.30), because although there are alternative beverages and caffeine-delivery systems (tea, infused soft drinks, and pills), coffee provides a unique combination of taste and caffeine. Although there is an artificial substitute for eggs (for people concerned about dietary cholesterol), there are no natural substitutes, so the demand for eggs is relatively inelastic (0.30).

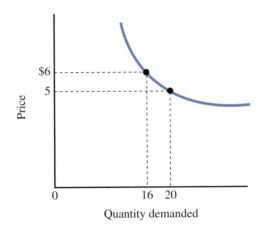

◀ **FIGURE 5.1**
Elasticity and Demand Curves

(A) Elastic Demand: $E_d = \left| \dfrac{-40\%}{20\%} \right| = 2.0 > 1$ **(B) Inelastic Demand:** $E_d = \left| \dfrac{-10\%}{20\%} \right| = 0.50 < 1$

(C) Unit Elastic Demand: $E_d = \left| \dfrac{-20\%}{20\%} \right| = 1$

(D) Perfectly Inelastic Demand: $E_d = \left| \dfrac{0\%}{20\%} \right| = 0$ **(E) Perfectly Elastic Demand:** $E_d = \infty$

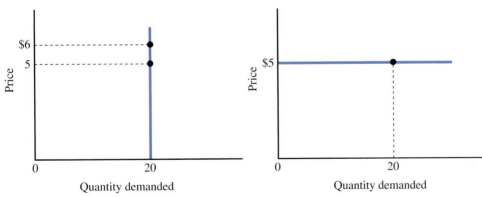

Alternative brands of a product are good substitutes for one another, so the demand for a specific brand of a product is typically elastic. For example, the elasticity of demand for a specific brand of coffee is 5.6, compared to an overall elasticity for coffee of 0.30. This means that a 10-percent increase in the price of coffee in general (all brands) will decrease the quantity of coffee sold by 3 percent, but a 10-percent increase in the price of a specific brand will decrease the quantity of that brand sold by 56 percent. Each brand of coffee is a substitute for the other

Table 5.2 PRICE ELASTICITIES OF DEMAND FOR SELECTED PRODUCTS

	Product	Price Elasticity of Demand
Inelastic	Salt	0.1
	Food (wealthy countries)	0.15
	Weekend canoe trips	0.19
	Water	0.2
	Coffee	0.3
	Physician visits	0.25
	Sport fishing	0.28
	Gasoline (short run)	0.3
	Eggs	0.3
	Cigarettes	0.3
	Food (poor countries)	0.34
	Shoes and footwear	0.7
	Gasoline (long run)	0.7
Unit elastic	Housing	1.0
	Fruit juice	1.0
Elastic	Automobiles	1.2
	Foreign travel	1.8
	Motorboats	2.2
	Restaurant meals	2.3
	Air travel	2.4
	Movies	3.7
	Specific brands of coffee	5.6

SOURCES: Frank Chaloupka, "Rational Addictive Behavior and Cigarette Smoking," *Journal of Political Economy*, August 1991, pp. 722–742; Gregory Chow, *Demand for Automobiles in the United States* (Amsterdam: North-Holland, 1957); David Ellwood and Mitchell Polinski, "An Empirical Reconciliation of Micro and Grouped Estimates of the Demand for Housing," *Review of Economics and Statistics*, vol. 61, 1979, pp. 199–205; H. F. Houthakker and Lester B. Taylor, *Consumer Demand in the United States: Analysis and Projections*, 2nd ed. (Cambridge, MA: Harvard University Press, 1970); John R. Nevin, "Laboratory Experiments for Estimating Consumer Demand: A Validation Study," *Journal of Marketing Research*, vol. 11, August 1974, pp. 261–268; Herbert Scarf and John Shoven, *Applied General Equilibrium Analysis* (New York: Cambridge University Press, 1984); Phil Goodwin, "Review of New Demand Elasticities with Special Reference to Short and Long Run Effects of Price Changes," *Journal of Transport Economics* 26 (1992), pp. 155–171; Chin-Fun Cling and James Peale, Jr., "Income and Price Elasticities," in *Advances in Econometrics Supplement*, edited by Henri Theil (Greenwich, CT: JAI Press, 1989); R. L. Adams, R. C. Lewis, and B. H. Drake, "Estimated Price Elasticity of Demand for Selected Outdoor Recreation Activities, United States," *Recreation Economic Decisions*, 2d ed., edited by J. B. Loomis and R. G. Walsh (State College, PA: Venture Publishing, Inc., 1973), p. 20; U.S. Army Corps of Engineers, Walla Walla District, "Sport Fishery Use and Value on the Lower Snake River Reservoirs," May 1999; Rand Health, "The Elasticity of Demand for Health Care: A Review of the Literature and Its Application to the Military Health System" (Santa Monica, CA, 2001).

brands, so consumers are very responsive to a change in the price of a specific brand. Similarly, the demand for specific brands of tires is more elastic than the demand for tires in general.

The availability of substitutes increases over time, so the longer the time consumers have to respond to a price change, the more elastic the demand. Because it often takes time for consumers to respond to price changes, the short-run price elasticity of demand is typically smaller than the long-run elasticity. For example, when the price of gasoline increases, consumers can immediately drive fewer miles in their existing cars or switch to public transportation. As shown in Table 5.2, the short-run price elasticity of demand for gasoline is 0.30. In the long run, consumers can buy more fuel-efficient cars and move closer to workplaces. As time passes, consumers have more options to cut gasoline consumption—more substitution possibilities—so demand becomes more elastic. In Table 5.2, the long-run price elasticity of demand for gasoline is 0.70, over twice as large as the short-run elasticity.

Other Determinants of the Price Elasticity of Demand

Two other factors help determine the price elasticity of demand for a product. First, the elasticity is generally larger for goods that take a relatively large part of a consumer's budget. If a good represents a small part of the budget of the typical consumer, demand is relatively inelastic. For example, suppose the price of pencils is 20 cents and then increases by 10 percent, or 2 cents. Because the price change is tiny compared to the income of the typical consumer, we would expect a relatively small decrease in the quantity of pencils demanded. In contrast, if the price of a car is $20,000 and then increases 10 percent ($2,000), we would expect a bigger response because the change in price is large relative to the income of the typical consumer.

International comparisons of the price elasticity of demand for food suggest that demand is more price elastic when the good represents a large part of the consumer's budget. As shown in Table 5.2, in wealthy countries such as the United States, Canada, and Germany, the price elasticity of demand for food is around 0.15. In poor countries such as India, Nigeria, and Bolivia, people spend a larger fraction of their budget on food, so they are more responsive to changes in food prices. In these poor countries, the price elasticity of demand is around 0.34.

Another factor in determining the elasticity of demand is whether the product is a necessity or a luxury good. As shown in Table 5.2, the demand for food, a necessity, is relatively low in both wealthy and poor countries. Similarly, the demand for physician visits is inelastic (elasticity = 0.25). In contrast, the elasticity of demand for luxury goods such as restaurant meals, foreign travel, and motorboats is relatively elastic. Of course, not all goods that are considered luxuries have elastic demand. For example, the price elasticity of demand for weekend canoe trips is 0.19, and the demand elasticity for sport fishing is 0.28. These elasticities suggest that one person's luxury is another person's necessity.

Table 5.3 summarizes our discussion of the determinants of the price elasticity of demand. Demand is relatively elastic if there are many good substitutes, if we allow consumers a long time to respond, if spending on the product is a large part of the consumer's budget, and if the product is a luxury as opposed to a necessity.

5.2 | USING PRICE ELASTICITY TO PREDICT CHANGES IN QUANTITY

The price elasticity of demand is a very useful tool for economic analysis. If we know the elasticity of demand for a particular good, we can quantify the law of demand, predicting the change in quantity resulting from a change in price.

If we have values for two of the three variables in the elasticity formula, we can compute the value of the third. The three variables are (1) the price elasticity of demand itself, (2) the percentage change in quantity, and (3) the percentage change in price. So if we know the values for the price elasticity and the percentage change in price, we can compute the value for the percentage change in quantity. Specifically, we can rearrange the elasticity formula:

$$\text{percentage change in quantity demanded} = \text{percentage change in price} \times E_d$$

Table 5.3 DETERMINANTS OF ELASTICITY

Factor	Demand is relatively elastic if . . .	Demand is relatively inelastic if . . .
Availability of substitutes	there are many substitutes.	there are few substitutes.
Passage of time	a long time passes.	a short time passes.
Fraction of consumer budget	is large.	is small.
Necessity	the product is a luxury.	the product is a necessity.

For example, suppose you run a campus film series and you've decided to increase your admission price by 15 percent. If you know the elasticity of demand for your movies, you could use it to predict how many fewer tickets you'll sell at the higher price. If the elasticity of demand is 2.0 and you increase the price by 15 percent, we would predict a 30-percent decrease in the quantity of tickets demanded:

$$\text{percentage change in quantity demanded} = \text{percentage change in price} \times E_d$$
$$= 15\% \times 2.0 = 30\%$$

1

APPLICATION

BEER TAXES AND HIGHWAY DEATHS

APPLYING THE CONCEPTS #1: How can we use the price elasticity of demand to predict the effects of taxes?

We can use the concept of price elasticity to predict the effects of a change in the price of beer on drinking and highway deaths among young adults. The law of demand tells us that an increase in the price of beer will decrease beer consumption, and if we know the price elasticity of demand for beer, we can predict just how much less beer will be consumed at the higher price.

The price elasticity of demand for beer among young adults is about 1.30. If a state imposes a beer tax that increases the price of beer by 10 percent, how will the price hike affect beer consumption among young adults? Using the elasticity formula, we predict that beer consumption will decrease by 13 percent:

$$\text{percentage change in quantity demanded} = \text{percentage change in price} \times E_d$$
$$= 10\% \times 1.30 = 13\%$$

The number of highway deaths among young adults is roughly proportional to their beer consumption, so the number of deaths will also decrease by 13 percent. Of course, if young adults switch from beer to other alcoholic beverages, the number of highway deaths will decrease by a smaller amount.

A recent study provides support for the notion that increasing the beer tax will reduce highway deaths. The authors predict that a doubling of the beer tax from $0.16 to $0.32 per six-pack would decrease highway deaths among 18- to 20-year-olds by about 12 percent. Larger taxes would decrease beer consumption and highway deaths by larger amounts. For example, raising the tax on beer to make it equivalent to the taxes on alcoholic spirits (rum, vodka, tequila) would cut highway deaths among young adults by 35 percent. Raising the beer tax back to where it was in 1951 would cut highway deaths by 32 percent. *Related to Exercises 2.1 and 2.5.*

SOURCES: Henry Saffer and Michael Grossman, "Beer Taxes, the Legal Drinking Age, and Youth Motor Vehicle Fatalities," *Journal of Legal Studies*, vol. 16, June 1987, pp. 351–374; Frank Chaloupka, Henry Saffer, and Michael Grossman, "Alcohol Control Policies and Motor Vehicle Fatalities," *Journal of Legal Studies*, vol. 22, January 1993, pp. 161–183.

APPLICATION

SUBSIDIZED MEDICAL CARE IN CÔTE D'IVOIRE AND PERU

APPLYING THE CONCEPTS #2: Does the responsiveness of consumers to changes in price vary by income?

If the price of medical care increases, how will consumers respond? The rising cost of medical care has forced many nations to take a closer look at programs that subsidize medical care for their citizens. If prices are increased to cover more of the costs of providing medical care, how will this affect poor and wealthy households?

Many developing nations subsidize medical care, charging consumers a small fraction of the cost of providing the services. If a nation were to cut its subsidies and thus increase the price of medical care for consumers, how would the higher price affect its poor and wealthy households? In Côte d'Ivoire in Africa, the price elasticity of demand for hospital services is 0.47 for poor households and 0.29 for wealthy households. This means that a 10-percent increase in the price of hospital services would cause poor households to cut back their hospital care by 4.7 percent:

$$\text{percentage change in quantity demanded} = 10\% \times 0.47 = 4.7\%$$

In contrast, wealthy households would cut back by only 2.9 percent:

$$\text{percentage change in quantity demanded} = 10\% \times 0.29 = 2.9\%$$

In Peru, the differences between poor and wealthy households are even larger: The price elasticity is 0.67 for poor households but only 0.03 for wealthy households. The same pattern occurs in the demand for the medical services provided in outpatient clinics. The poor are much more sensitive to price, so when prices increase, they experience much larger reductions in medical care. *Related to Exercises 2.2 and 2.8.*

SOURCE: Paul Gertler and Jacques van der Gaag, *The Willingness to Pay for Medical Care: Evidence from Two Developing Countries* (Baltimore, MD: Johns Hopkins University Press, 1990).

5.3 | PRICE ELASTICITY AND TOTAL REVENUE

Firms use the concept of price elasticity to predict the effects of changing their prices. A firm produces products to sell, and a firm's **total revenue** equals the money it generates from selling products. If a firm sells its product for the same price to every consumer, total revenue equals the price per unit times the quantity sold:

• **total revenue**
The money a firm generates from selling its product.

$$\text{total revenue} = \text{price per unit} \times \text{quantity sold}$$

3

APPLICATION

HOW TO CUT TEEN SMOKING BY 60 PERCENT

APPLYING THE CONCEPTS #3: How can we use the price elasticity of demand to predict the effects of public policies?

Under the 1997 federal tobacco settlement, if smoking by teenagers does not decline by 60 percent by the year 2007, cigarette makers will be fined $2 billion. The settlement increased cigarette prices by about 62 cents per pack, a percentage increase of about 25 percent. Will the price hike be large enough to meet the target reduction of 60 percent? The demand for cigarettes by teenagers is elastic, with an elasticity of 1.3. Therefore, a 25-percent price hike will reduce teen smoking by only 32.5 percent, far short of the target reduction:

$$\text{percentage change in quantity demanded} = 25\% \times 1.30 = 32.5\%$$

About half of the decrease in consumption occurs because fewer teenagers will become smokers, and the other half occurs because each teenage smoker will smoke fewer cigarettes. To meet the target reduction of teenage smoking, the price of cigarette prices must increase by about 46 percent:

$$\text{percentage change in quantity demanded} = 46\% \times 1.3 = 60\%$$

Tobacco companies recognize this problem and have taken other measures to reduce teen smoking, including antismoking campaigns aimed at teens.
Related to Exercises 2.3 and 2.9.

SOURCES: Michael M. Phillips and Suein L. Hwang, "Why Tobacco Pact Won't Hurt Industry," *Wall Street Journal*, September 12, 1997, p. A2; Frank J. Chaloupka and Michael Grossman, "Price, Tobacco Control Policies, and Smoking Among Young Adults," *Journal of Health Economics*, vol. 16, 1997, pp. 359–373.

Suppose a firm increases the price of its product. Will its total sales revenue increase or decrease? The answer depends on the price elasticity of demand for the product. If you know the price elasticity, you can determine whether a price hike will increase or decrease the firm's total revenue.

Let's return to the example of the campus film series. Suppose you are thinking about increasing the price of tickets by 10 percent, from $10 to $11. An increase in the ticket price brings good news and bad news:

- Good news. You get more money for each ticket sold.
- Bad news. You sell fewer tickets.

Your total revenue will decrease if the bad news (fewer tickets sold) dominates the good news (more money per ticket). The elasticity of demand tells us how the good news compares to the bad news. If demand is elastic, consumers will respond to the higher price by purchasing many fewer tickets, so although you will collect more money per ticket, you'll sell so few tickets that your total revenue will decrease.

Elastic Versus Inelastic Demand

The upper part of Table 5.4 shows an example of the effects of a price hike when the demand for a product is elastic. In this case, the price elasticity of demand is 2.0, so a 10-percent increase in price decreases the quantity demanded by 20 percent, from 100 to 80 tickets. Because the percentage decrease in quantity (the bad news) exceeds the percentage increase in price (the good news), total revenue decreases, from $1,000 to $880. In general, an elastic demand means that the percentage change in quantity (the bad news from a price hike) will exceed the percentage change in price (the good news), so an increase in price will decrease total revenue.

We get the opposite result if the demand for the good is inelastic: An increase in price increases total revenue. If demand is inelastic, consumers are not very responsive to an increase in price, so the good news (more money per unit sold) dominates the bad news (fewer units sold). The lower part of Table 5.4 shows an example of the effects of a price hike when demand is inelastic (equal to 0.50). Suppose that your campus bookstore starts with a textbook price of $100 and sells 10 books per minute. If the bookstore increases its price by 20 percent (from $100 to $120 per book) and the elasticity of demand for textbooks is 0.50, the quantity of textbooks sold will decrease by only 10 percent (from 10 to 9 per minute). Therefore, the store's total revenue will increase from $1,000 per minute ($100 × 10 books) to $1,080 per minute ($120 × 9 books). In general, an inelastic demand means that the percentage change in quantity will be smaller than the percentage change in price, so an increase in price will increase total revenue.

Table 5.5 summarizes the revenue effects of changes in prices for different types of goods:

- *Elastic demand.* The relationship between price and total revenue is negative: An increase in price decreases total revenue; a decrease in price increases total revenue.
- *Inelastic demand.* The relationship between price and total revenue is positive: An increase in price increases total revenue; a decrease in price decreases total revenue.
- *Unit elastic demand.* Total revenue does not vary with price.

Table 5.4 | PRICE AND TOTAL REVENUE WITH DIFFERENT ELASTICITIES OF DEMAND

Elastic Demand: $E_d = 2.0$

Price	Quantity Sold	Total Revenue
$10	100	$1,000
11	80	880

Inelastic Demand: $E_d = 0.50$

Price	Quantity Sold	Total Revenue
100	10	$1,000
120	9	1,080

Table 5.5	PRICE ELASTICITY AND TOTAL REVENUE	
Elastic Demand: $E_d > 1.0$		
If price . . .	**Total revenue . . .**	**Because the percentage change in quantity is . . .**
↑	↓	Larger than the percentage change in price.
↓	↑	Larger than the percentage change in price.
Inelastic: $E_d < 1.0$		
If price . . .	**Total revenue . . .**	**Because the percentage change in quantity is . . .**
↑	↑	Smaller than the percentage change in price.
↓	↓	Smaller than the percentage change in price.

We can use the relationships summarized in Table 5.5 to work backwards. If we observe the relationship between the price of a product and total sales revenue of the product, we can determine whether the demand for the product is elastic or inelastic. Suppose that when a music store increases the price of its CDs, its total revenue from CDs drops. The negative relationship between price and total revenue means that demand for the store's CDs is elastic: Total revenue decreases because consumers are very responsive to an increase in price, buying a much smaller quantity. In contrast, suppose that when a city increases the price it charges for water, the total revenue from water sales increases. The positive relationship between price and total revenue suggests that the demand for the city's water is inelastic: Total revenue increases because consumers are not very responsive to an increase in price.

Market Elasticity Versus Elasticity for a Firm

The manager of a DVD rental store has asked you to solve a puzzle. According to national studies of the DVD rental market, the price elasticity of demand for DVD rentals is 0.80: A 10-percent increase in price decreases the quantity of DVDs demanded by about 8 percent. In other words, the demand for DVDs is inelastic. Based on this information, the manager of the DVD store increased prices by 20 percent, expecting total revenue to increase. The manager expected the good news (more money per rental) to dominate the bad news (fewer rentals). But in fact total revenue decreased. Why?

The key to solving this puzzle is to recognize that the manager can't use the results of a national study to predict the effects of increasing a single store's price. The national study suggests that if all DVD stores in the nation increased their prices by 10 percent, the nationwide quantity of DVDs demanded would drop by 8 percent. But when a single DVD store in a city increases its price, consumers can easily rent DVDs at other competing stores in the city. As a result, a 10-percent increase in the price of DVD rentals at one store will decrease the quantity sold by that store by much more than 8 percent. The demand facing an individual store is elastic, so an increase in price will decrease total revenue.

Transit Fares and Deficits

At the beginning of the chapter, we considered the question of whether increasing the price of bus rides would reduce a city's transit deficit. Here is the exchange between two city officials:

- *Buster:* "A fare increase is a great idea. We'll collect more money from bus riders, so revenue will increase, and the deficit will shrink."

- *Bessie:* "Wait a minute, Buster. Haven't you heard about the law of demand? The increase in the bus fare will decrease the number of passengers taking buses, so we'll collect less money, not more, and the deficit will grow."

Who's right? It depends on the price elasticity of demand for bus ridership.

The price elasticity of demand for bus ridership in the typical city is 0.33, meaning that a 10-percent increase in fares will decrease ridership by only about 3.3 percent.[1] Because demand for bus travel is inelastic, the good news associated with a fare hike (10 percent more revenue per rider) will dominate the bad news (3.3 percent fewer riders), and total fare revenue will increase. In other words, an increase in fares will reduce the transit deficit, so Buster is right.

APPLICATION

A BUMPER CROP IS BAD NEWS FOR FARMERS

APPLYING THE CONCEPTS #4: If demand is inelastic, how does an increase in supply affect total expenditures?

Suppose that favorable weather generates a "bumper crop" for soybeans that is 30 percent larger than last year's harvest. The bumper crop generates good news and bad news for farmers. The good news is that they will sell more bushels of soybeans. The bad news is that the increase in supply will decrease the equilibrium price of soybeans, so they will get less money per bushel. Which will be larger, the increase in quantity or the decrease in price?

Unfortunately for farmers, the demand for soybeans and many other agricultural products is inelastic. Therefore, to increase the quantity demanded by 30 percent to meet the higher supply, the price must decrease by more than 30 percent. With inelastic demand, consumers need a large price reduction to buy more of the product. For example, if the price elasticity of demand is 0.75, the price must decrease by 40 percent to increase the quantity demanded by 30 percent. To show this, we can rearrange the elasticity formula:

$$\text{percentage change in price} = \frac{\text{percentage change in quantity demanded}}{E_d}$$

$$= \frac{30\%}{0.75} = 40\%$$

Although soybean farmers will sell 30 percent more bushels, they will receive 40 percent less per bushel, so their total revenue will decrease. In general, a bumper crop will make farmers worse off if the demand for their product is inelastic. *Related to Exercises 3.1 and 3.8.*

5

APPLICATION

DRUG PRICES AND PROPERTY CRIME

APPLYING THE CONCEPTS #5: If demand is inelastic, how does a decrease in supply affect total expenditures?

What's the connection between antidrug policies and property crimes such as robbery, burglary, and auto theft? The government uses search-and-destroy tactics to restrict the supply of illegal drugs. If this approach succeeds, drugs become scarce, and the price of drugs increases. Because the demand for illegal drugs is inelastic, the increase in price will increase total spending on illegal drugs. Many drug addicts support their habits by stealing personal property—robbing people, stealing cars, and burglarizing homes. This means that drug addicts will commit more property crimes to support the higher total spending level associated with pricier drugs. Given the inelastic demand for illegal drugs and the connection between drug consumption and property crime, there is a trade-off: A policy that increases drug prices will reduce drug consumption and the number of drug addicts, but will also increase the amount of property crime committed by addicts who continue to abuse drugs. *Related to Exercises 3.2 and 3.9.*

SOURCE: L. P. Silverman and N. L. Sprull, "Urban Crime and the Price of Heroin," *Journal of Urban Economics*, vol. 4, 1977, pp. 80–103.

5.4 | ELASTICITY AND TOTAL REVENUE FOR A LINEAR DEMAND CURVE

It is often useful to represent the demand for a product with a linear demand curve. A linear demand curve—a straight line—has a constant slope, but that does not mean that it has a constant elasticity of demand. In fact, the price elasticity of demand decreases as we move downward along a linear demand curve. On the upper half of a linear demand curve, demand is elastic; on the lower half of the curve, demand is inelastic. At the midpoint of a linear demand curve, demand is unit elastic.

Price Elasticity Along a Linear Demand Curve

We can use Panel A of Figure 5.2 to show how price elasticity varies along a linear demand curve. The slope of the demand curve is –$2 per unit quantity. We see this by picking any two points and computing the slope as the vertical difference between the two points (the "rise") divided by the horizontal difference between the two points (the "run"). For example, between points e and u, the vertical difference is –$30 and the horizontal difference is 15, so the slope is –$30/15 = –$2. That means a $2 decrease in price increases the quantity demanded by one unit.

Table 5.6 shows how to compute the price elasticity of demand with three starting points: e (for elastic demand), u (for unit elastic), and i (for inelastic). As shown in

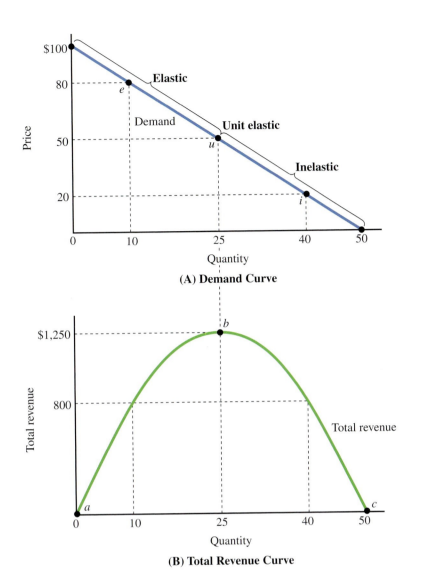

Price (y-axis)

$100, 80, 50, 20

e (Elastic), Demand, *u* (Unit elastic), Inelastic, *i*

Quantity (x-axis): 0, 10, 25, 40, 50

(A) Demand Curve

Total revenue (y-axis)

$1,250, 800

b, *a*, *c*, Total revenue

Quantity (x-axis): 0, 10, 25, 40, 50

(B) Total Revenue Curve

◄ **FIGURE 5.2**

Elasticity and Total Revenue Along a Linear Demand Curve

Demand is elastic along the upper half of a linear demand curve, so an increase in quantity from a decrease in price increases total revenue (between points *a* and *b* on the total-revenue curve). Demand is inelastic along the lower half of a linear demand curve, so an increase in quantity from a decrease in price decreases total revenue (between points *b* and *c*). Total revenue is maximized at the midpoint of a linear demand curve (point *u*), where demand is unit elastic.

Table 5.6 | ELASTICITY OF DEMAND ALONG A LINEAR DEMAND CURVE

A	B	C	D	E	F
Starting Point	Change in Price	Percentage Change in Price	Change in Quantity	Percentage Change in Quantity	Elasticity of Demand
e: Elastic	−$2	$\dfrac{-\$2}{\$80} = -2.5\%$	+1	$\dfrac{1}{10} = 10\%$	$\left\lvert\dfrac{10\%}{-2.5\%}\right\rvert = 4$
u: Unit elastic	−$2	$\dfrac{-\$2}{\$50} = -4\%$	+1	$\dfrac{1}{25} = 4\%$	$\left\lvert\dfrac{4\%}{-4\%}\right\rvert = 1$
i: Inelastic	−$2	$\dfrac{-\$2}{\$20} = -10\%$	+1	$\dfrac{1}{40} = 2.5\%$	$\left\lvert\dfrac{2.5\%}{-10\%}\right\rvert = 0.25$

columns B and D, a $2 reduction in price increases the quantity demanded by one unit.

- *Column C: Percentage change in price.* Starting from point *e*, we cut $2 off an $80 price, resulting in a 2.5-percent price cut. The same $2 price cut is larger in percentage terms farther down the demand curve, where the price is lower. For point *u*, the percentage change in price is –4 percent (equal to –$2/$50), and for point *i*, the percentage change in price is –10 percent (equal to –$2/$20).

- *Column E: Percentage change in quantity.* At point *e*, we start with 10 units, so a one-unit increase in quantity is a 10-percent increase. Moving down the column, the same one-unit increase in quantity is smaller in percentage terms as we move down the demand curve, where the quantity is larger. For point *u*, the percentage change in price is 4 percent (equal to 1/25), and for point *i* the percentage change in quantity is 2.5 percent (equal to 1/40).

- *Column F: Price elasticity of demand.* Starting from point *e*, the price elasticity is large (4.0) because the percentage change in quantity (10%) is four times the percentage change in price (2.5%). Starting at point *u*, demand is unit elastic because the percentage change in quantity equals the percentage change in price. Starting from point *i*, demand is inelastic (0.25), because the percentage change in quantity is one-fourth the percentage change in price.

Why does the price elasticity vary along a linear demand curve? It's tempting to think the elasticity will be constant because a straight line has a constant slope. But that's incorrect, because elasticity is measured by percentage changes, not absolute changes. As we move downward along the demand curve, we're moving in the direction of larger quantities, so the same absolute change in quantity (one unit) becomes a smaller *percentage* change in quantity. At the same time, as we move downward along the curve, we are moving to lower prices, so a $2 price reduction leads to a larger *percentage* change in price. As a result, the elasticity (the ratio of the percentage changes) decreases as we move downward along the demand curve.

Elasticity and Total Revenue for a Linear Demand Curve

Panel B of Figure 5.2 shows the relationship between total revenue and the quantity sold for the linear demand curve. Demand is elastic along the upper half of a linear demand curve, which means that a decrease in price will increase the quantity sold by a larger percentage amount. As a result, total revenue will increase, as shown by the positively sloped total-revenue curve between points *a* and *b*. In contrast, demand is inelastic along the lower half of a linear demand curve, which means that a decrease in price will increase the quantity sold by a smaller percentage amount. As a result, total revenue will decrease, as shown by the negatively sloped total-revenue curve between points *b* and *c*. The total-revenue curve reaches its maximum at the midpoint of the linear demand curve, where demand is unit elastic. In Figure 5.2, demand is unit elastic at point *u* on the demand curve, so total revenue reaches its maximum at $1,250 at point *b* on the total-revenue curve.

5.5 | OTHER ELASTICITIES OF DEMAND

We've seen that the price elasticity of demand measures the responsiveness of consumers to changes in the price of a particular good. Of course, the demand for a particular product also depends on other variables such as consumer income and the prices of related goods—substitutes and complements. We can use two other elasticities to measure the responsiveness of consumers to changes in these other variables that affect demand: income elasticity of demand and cross-price elasticity of demand.

Income Elasticity of Demand

We saw in Chapter 4 that the demand for a particular product depends in part on the consumer's income. The **income elasticity of demand** measures the responsiveness of demand to changes in income, indicating how much more or less of a particular product is purchased as income changes. The income elasticity of demand is defined as the percentage change in quantity demanded divided by the percentage change in income:

$$E_i = \frac{\text{percentage change in quantity demanded}}{\text{percentage change in income}}$$

For example, if a 10-percent increase in income increases the quantity of books demanded by 15 percent, the income elasticity of demand for books is 1.50 (equal to 15% divided by 10%).

We can use the income elasticities of demand for various products to categorize the products into different types. Recall from Chapter 4 that when a consumer's income increases, he or she buys more of a "normal" good. If the income elasticity is positive—indicating a positive relationship between income and demand—we say that the good is normal. New cars and new clothes are products that have positive income elasticities and are thus considered normal goods. In contrast, if the income elasticity is negative—indicating a negative relationship between income and demand—we say the good is "inferior." Some examples of inferior goods are intercity bus travel, used clothing, and used cars.

Cross-Price Elasticity of Demand

We saw in Chapter 4 that the demand for a particular product also depends in part on the prices of related goods—substitutes and complements. The **cross-price elasticity of demand** measures the responsiveness of demand to changes in the prices of other goods, indicating how much more or less of a particular product is purchased as other prices change. The cross-price elasticity is defined as the percentage change in quantity demanded of one good (X) divided by the percentage change in the price of another good (Y):

$$E_{xy} = \frac{\text{percentage change in quantity of } X \text{ demanded}}{\text{percentage change in price of } Y}$$

As we saw in Chapter 4, two goods are considered substitutes if there is a positive relationship between the quantity demanded of one good and the price of the other good. For example, an increase in the price of bananas increases the demand for apples as consumers substitute apples for the now relatively expensive bananas. For substitute goods, the cross-price elasticity is positive. In contrast, two goods are considered complements if there is a negative relationship between the quantity demanded of one good and the price of the other. For example, an increase in the price of ice cream increases the cost of apple pie with ice cream, causing consumers to demand fewer apples. For complementary goods, the cross-price elasticity is negative. Table 5.7 summarizes the signs (positive or negative) for different types of goods.

Table 5.7 | INCOME AND CROSS-PRICE ELASTICITIES FOR DIFFERENT TYPES OF GOODS

This elasticity	Is Positive for . . .	Is Negative for . . .
Income elasticity	Normal goods	Inferior goods
Cross-price elasticity	Substitute goods	Complementary goods

Estimates of cross-price elasticity of demand are useful to retailers in their pricing decisions. For example, when a grocery store cuts the price of peanut butter by 10 percent, the store will sell more peanut butter but will also sell more complementary goods such as jelly and bread. If the cross-price elasticity of demand for jelly is 0.5, a 10-percent decrease in the price of peanut butter will increase the demand for jelly by 5 percent. Retailers use coupons for one product to promote sales of that good as well as complementary goods. Armed with the relevant cross elasticities, retailers can predict just how much more of a complementary good consumers will buy.

5.6 | THE PRICE ELASTICITY OF SUPPLY

We've used the concept of elasticity to measure the responsiveness of consumers to changes in prices. We now look at elasticity on the supply side of the market. The **price elasticity of supply** measures the responsiveness of the quantity supplied to changes in price. We compute this elasticity by dividing the percentage change in quantity supplied by the percentage change in price:

$$E_s = \frac{\text{percentage change in quantity supplied}}{\text{percentage change in price}}$$

We can use some of the numbers in Figure 5.3 to compute the price elasticity of supply of milk. Consider Panel A, with a relatively steep supply curve. When the price of milk increases from $1.00 to $1.20, the quantity supplied increases from 100 million gallons (point *a*) to 102 million gallons (point *b*). The percentage change in quantity is the change (2) divided by the initial value (100), or 2 percent:

$$\text{percentage change in quantity supplied} = \frac{2}{100} = 2\%$$

price elasticity of supply
A measure of the responsiveness of the quantity supplied to changes in price; equal to the percentage change in quantity supplied divided by the percentage change in price.

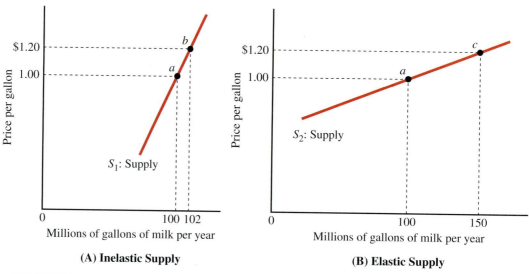

▲ **FIGURE 5.3**

The Slope of the Supply Curve and Supply Elasticity

(**A**) The supply curve is relatively steep. A 20% increase in price increases the quantity supplied by 2%, implying a supply elasticity of 0.10.

(**B**) The supply curve is relatively flat. A 20% increase in price increases the quantity supplied by 50%, implying a supply elasticity of 2.5.

The percentage change in price is the change ($0.20) divided by the initial value ($2.00), or 10 percent:

$$\text{percentage change in price} = \frac{\$0.20}{\$1.00} = 20\%$$

Dividing the percentage change in quantity supplied by the percentage change in price, the price elasticity of supply is 0.10:

$$E_s = \frac{\text{percentage change in quantity supplied}}{\text{percentage change in price}} = \frac{2\%}{20\%} = 0.10$$

What Determines the Price Elasticity of Supply?

What's the connection between the slope of the supply curve and the price elasticity of supply? With a steep curve, a given increase in price (in the denominator of the elasticity formula) generates a small increase in quantity supplied (in the numerator of the elasticity formula). In Panel A of Figure 5.3, an increase in price from $1.00 to $1.20 increases the quantity supplied from 100 to 102, so the price elasticity of supply is 0.10 (equal to 2% divided by 10%). In contrast, with a relatively flat supply curve the same increase in price generates a larger increase in quantity supplied, so the supply elasticity is relatively large. In Panel B of Figure 5.3, an increase in price from $1.00 to $1.20 increases the quantity supplied from 100 to 150, so the price elasticity of supply is 2.50 (equal to 50% divided by 20%).

Why is the market supply curve positively sloped? As we saw in Chapter 4, the market supply curve shows the marginal cost of production. A positively sloped supply curve tells us that the marginal cost of production increases as the total output of the industry increases. In other words, if we want to get more output out of an industry, the price must rise to cover the higher production costs associated with a larger industry. For example, as the total output of the gasoline industry increases, the worldwide demand for crude oil increases, pushing up its price. So to get more gasoline, the price of gasoline must increase to cover the higher cost of crude oil. The more rapidly crude-oil prices rise, the larger the increase in the gasoline price required to get more gasoline—and the steeper the gasoline supply curve.

The price elasticity of supply is determined by how rapidly production costs increase as the total output of the industry increases. If the marginal cost increases rapidly, the supply curve is relatively steep and the price elasticity is relatively low. For example, if crude-oil prices increase rapidly as the total amount of gasoline increases, the supply curve for gasoline will be relatively steep and the price elasticity of supply of gasoline will be relatively low. In contrast, as the output of the pencil industry increases the prices of wood and other inputs used to produce pencils are unlikely to increase by much, so the supply curve will be relatively flat and the price elasticity of supply will be relatively large.

The Role of Time: Short-Run Versus Long-Run Supply Elasticity

Time is an important factor in determining the price elasticity of supply for a product. As we saw in Chapter 4, the market supply curve is positively sloped because of two responses to an increase in price:

- *Short run.* A higher price encourages existing firms to increase their output by purchasing more materials and hiring more workers.
- *Long run.* New firms enter the market and existing firms expand their production facilities to produce more output.

The short-run response is limited because of the principle of diminishing returns.

PRINCIPLE OF DIMINISHING RETURNS

Suppose output is produced with two or more inputs, and we increase one input while holding the other input or inputs fixed. Beyond some point—called the *point of diminishing returns*—output will increase at a decreasing rate.

In the short run, the fixed input is the firm's production facility. Although a higher price will induce firms to produce more, the response is limited by the fixed capacity of the firms' production facilities. As a result, the short-run supply curve is relatively steep and the short-run supply elasticity is relatively small.

The long-run supply response to an increase in price is not limited by diminishing returns because production facilities are not fixed. Over time, new firms enter the market with new production facilities and old firms build new facilities. As a result, a given increase in price generates a larger increase in quantity supplied. The long-run supply curve will be relatively flat and the elasticity of supply will be relatively large.

The milk industry provides a good example of the difference between the short-run and long-run price elasticity of supply. In Panel A of Figure 5.3, the steep curve is a short-run supply curve, showing the relationship between price and quantity supplied over a one-year period. The price elasticity of supply over a one-year period is about 0.10: If the price of milk increases by 20 percent and stays there for a year, the quantity of milk supplied will rise by only 2 percent.[2] In the short run, dairy farmers can squeeze just a little more output from their existing production facilities.

In Panel B of Figure 5.3, the long-run supply curve shows the relationship between price and quantity supplied over a 10-year period. In the long run, dairy farmers can expand existing facilities and build new ones, so farmers are more responsive to a higher price—the supply curve is flatter and the supply elasticity is larger. The price elasticity of supply is 2.5, so the same 20-percent rise in price increases the quantity supplied by 50 percent.

Extreme Cases: Perfectly Inelastic Supply and Perfectly Elastic Supply

Figure 5.4 shows the extreme cases of supply elasticity. The supply curve in Panel A is a vertical line, indicating that regardless of price, the quantity supplied is 50 units. This is the case of **perfectly inelastic supply**, with a price elasticity of supply equal to zero. The numerator in the elasticity expression (the percentage change in quantity supplied) is zero, regardless of the percentage change in the price of the good. Land is

• **perfectly inelastic supply**
The price elasticity of supply equals zero.

▶ **FIGURE 5.4**
Perfectly Inelastic Supply and Perfectly Elastic Supply
In Panel A, the quantity supplied is the same at every price, so the price elasticity of supply is zero. In Panel B, the quantity supplied is infinitely responsive to changes in price, so the price elasticity of supply is infinite.

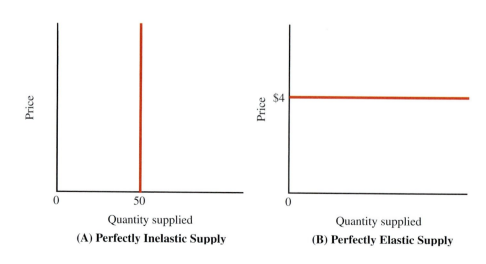

(A) Perfectly Inelastic Supply   **(B) Perfectly Elastic Supply**

an example of a product that has a perfectly inelastic supply. In the words of American humorist and author Will Rogers, "The trouble with land is that they're not making it any more."

The supply curve in Panel B of Figure 5.4 is a horizontal line, indicating that the quantity supplied is infinitely responsive to any change in price. This is the case of **perfectly elastic supply**, with a price elasticity of supply equal to infinity. The numerator in the elasticity expression (the percentage change in quantity supplied) is infinite, regardless of the percentage change in the price. One implication of this supply curve is that if the price were to drop below $4, the quantity supplied would fall to zero.

What is the economic logic behind a horizontal supply curve? Recall that the supply curve shows the marginal cost of production. A horizontal supply curve indicates that the marginal cost of production doesn't change as the total output of the industry increases. For example, if the production cost per pencil is $0.20 no matter how many pencils the industry produces, the supply curve will be horizontal at $0.20.

• **perfectly elastic supply**
The price elasticity of supply is equal to infinity.

Predicting Changes in Quantity Supplied

We can use the price elasticity of supply to predict the effect of price changes on the quantity supplied. For example, suppose that the elasticity of supply is 0.80 and the price increases by 5 percent. Rearranging the elasticity formula, we would predict a 4-percent increase in the quantity supplied:

$$\text{percentage change in quantity supplied} = E_s \times \text{percentage change in price}$$
$$= 0.80 \times 5\% = 4\%$$

As we saw in Chapter 4, many governments establish minimum prices for agricultural products. The higher the minimum price, the larger the quantity supplied, consistent with the law of supply. If we know the price elasticity of supply, we can predict just how much more will be supplied at a higher minimum price. For example, if the minimum price of cheese increases by 10 percent and the price elasticity is 0.60, the quantity of cheese supplied will rise by 6 percent:

$$\text{percentage change in quantity supplied} = E_s \times \text{percentage change in price}$$
$$= 0.60 \times 10\% = 6\%$$

5.7 | USING ELASTICITIES TO PREDICT CHANGES IN EQUILIBRIUM PRICE

When demand or supply changes—that is, when the demand curve or the supply curve shifts—we can draw a demand and supply graph to predict whether the equilibrium price will increase or decrease. In many cases, the simple graph will show all we need to know about the effects of a change in supply or demand. But what if we want to predict how much a price will increase or decrease? We can use a simple formula to predict the change in the equilibrium price resulting from a change in demand or a change in supply.

The Price Effects of a Change in Demand

In Figure 5.5, an increase in demand shifts the demand curve to the right and increases the equilibrium price. We explained in Chapter 4 that a demand curve shifts as a result of a change in something other than the price of the product—for example, a change in income, tastes, or the price of a related good. When demand increases, the immediate effect is excess demand: At the original price ($1.00), the quantity demanded exceeds the quantity supplied by 35 million gallons

An Increase in Demand Increases the Equilibrium Price

An increase in demand shifts the demand curve to the right, increasing the equilibrium price. In this case, a 35-percent increase in demand increases the equilibrium price by 10 percent. Using the price-change formula, 10% = 35%/(2.5 + 1.0).

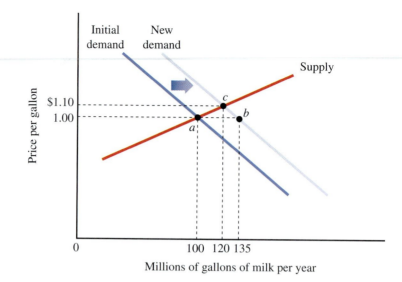

(135 million – 100 million). As the price increases, both consumers and producers help to eliminate the excess demand: Consumers buy less (the law of demand), and firms produce more (the law of supply).

Under what conditions will an increase in demand cause a relatively small increase in price?

- *Small increase in demand.* If the shift of the demand curve is relatively small, the gap between the new demand and the old supply will be relatively small, and the small excess demand can be eliminated with a relatively small increase in price.

- *Highly elastic demand.* If consumers are very responsive to changes in price, the increase in price caused by excess demand will cause a large reduction in the quantity demanded. As a result, the excess demand will be eliminated with a relatively small increase in price.

- *Highly elastic supply.* If producers are very responsive to changes in price, the increase in price caused by excess demand will cause a large increase in the quantity supplied. As a result, the excess demand will be eliminated with a relatively small increase in price.

We can use the following *price-change formula* to predict the change in the equilibrium price resulting from a change in demand. We divide the percentage change in demand by the sum of the price elasticities of supply and demand:

$$\text{percentage change in equilibrium price} = \frac{\text{percentage change in demand}}{E_s + E_d}$$

The numerator is the rightward shift of the demand curve in percentage terms. In Figure 5.5, the initial quantity demanded at a price of $1.00 is 100 million gallons (shown by the initial demand curve), and the new quantity demanded at the same price is 135 million gallons (shown by the new demand curve). The change in demand is 35 percent (35/100). The larger the increase in demand (the larger the rightward shift of the demand curve), the larger the increase in the equilibrium price. It makes sense that the change in demand is in the numerator of the price-change formula. The two price elasticities appear in the denominator. This is sensible because if consumers and producers are very responsive to changes in price (the elasticities are large numbers), excess demand will be eliminated with a relatively small increase in price.

We can use a simple example to see how to use the price-change formula. Suppose that demand increases by 35 percent (the demand curve shifts to the right by 35 percent). If the supply elasticity is 2.5 and the demand elasticity is 1.0, the predicted change in the equilibrium price is 10 percent:

$$\text{percentage change in equilibrium price} = \frac{35\%}{2.5+1.0} = \frac{35\%}{3.5} = 10\%$$

In Figure 5.5, the equilibrium price increases by 10 percent, from $1.00 to $1.10. If either demand or supply were less elastic (if either of the elasticity numbers were smaller), the predicted change in price would be larger. For example, if the supply elasticity were 0.75 instead of 2.5, we would predict a 20-percent increase in price (35% divided by 1.75).

What about the direction of the price change? We know from Chapter 4 that an increase in demand increases the equilibrium price, and a decrease in demand decreases the equilibrium price. Therefore, the percentage change in price is positive when the change in demand is positive (when demand increases and the demand curve shifts to the right), and negative when the change in demand is negative (when demand decreases and the demand curve shifts to the left). For example, suppose the demand for a product decreases by 12 percent (the demand curve shifts to the left by 12 percent). If the supply elasticity is 1.6 and the demand elasticity is 0.40, the price-change formula shows that the equilibrium price will decrease by 6 percent:

$$\text{percentage change in equilibrium price} = \frac{-12\%}{1.6+0.4} = \frac{-12\%}{2.0} = -6\%$$

The Price Effects of a Change in Supply

Consider next the effects of a change in supply on the equilibrium price. In Figure 5.6, a decrease in supply shifts the supply curve to the left and increases the equilibrium price. We explained in Chapter 4 that a change in supply results from

APPLICATION

METROPOLITAN GROWTH AND HOUSING PRICES

APPLYING THE CONCEPTS #6: How does population growth affect prices?

We can use the price-change formula to predict the effects of changes in demand on equilibrium prices. The Portland metropolitan area is expected to grow by 12 percent in the next decade. Suppose planners want to predict the effects of population growth on the equilibrium price of housing. At the metropolitan level, the price elasticity of supply is about 5.0 and the price elasticity of demand is 1.0. If the demand for housing is proportional to population, a 12-percent increase in population will increase the equilibrium price of housing by 2 percent:

$$\text{percentage change in equilibrium price} = \frac{12\%}{5.0 + 1.0}$$

$$= \frac{12\%}{6.0} = 2\%$$

Related to Exercises 7.5 and 7.6.

► **FIGURE 5.6**

A Decrease in Supply Increases the Equilibrium Price

An import restriction on shoes decreases the supply of shoes, shifting the market supply curve to the left and increasing the equilibrium price from $40 to $44. In this case, a 30% reduction in supply increases the equilibrium price by 10%. Using the price-change formula,

$10\% = -(-30\% / (2.3 + 0.70))$.

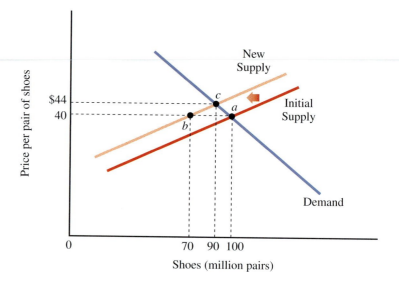

changes in something other than the price of the product—for example, a change in the cost of labor or raw materials, a change in production technology, or a change in the number of firms. The immediate effect of a decrease in supply is excess demand: At the original price, the quantity demanded exceeds the quantity supplied. In response to the excess demand, the price increases. Consumers respond to the higher price by purchasing less, and producers respond by producing more, so the gap between the quantity demanded and the quantity supplied narrows.

Under what conditions will a decrease in supply cause a relatively small increase in price?

- *Small decrease in supply.* If the shift of the supply curve is relatively small, the gap between the new supply and the old demand will be relatively small, and the small excess demand can be eliminated with a relatively small increase in price.

- *Highly elastic demand.* If consumers are very responsive to changes in price, the increase in price caused by excess demand will cause a large reduction in the quantity demanded. As a result, the excess demand will be eliminated with a relatively small increase in price.

- *Highly elastic supply.* If producers are very responsive to changes in price, the increase in price caused by excess demand will cause a large increase in the quantity supplied. As a result, the excess demand will be eliminated with a relatively small increase in price.

We can use a variation on the price-change formula to predict the price effects of a change in supply. We modify the numerator of the formula by substituting the percentage change in supply for the percentage change in demand and then add a minus sign. The minus sign indicates a negative relationship between supply and the equilibrium price: When supply decreases (when the supply curve shifts to the left), the price increases; when supply increases, the price decreases:

$$\text{percentage change in equilibrium price} = -\frac{\text{percentage change in supply}}{E_s + E_d}$$

APPLICATION

AN IMPORT BAN AND SHOE PRICES

APPLYING THE CONCEPTS #7: How do import restrictions affect prices?

We can use the supply version of the price-change formula to predict the effects of import restrictions on equilibrium prices. Consider a nation that limits shoe imports. Suppose the import restrictions decrease the supply of shoes by 30 percent. As shown in Figure 5.6, the policy shifts the supply curve to the left by 30 percent: At the original price of $40, the quantity supplied decreases from 100 million pairs (point *a*) to 70 million pairs (point *b*). The decrease in supply increases the equilibrium price, and the price-change formula tells us just how much the price will increase.

To use the price-change formula, we need the price elasticities of supply and demand. Suppose the supply elasticity is 2.3 and, as shown in Table 5.2, the demand elasticity is 0.70. Plugging these numbers into the price-change formula, we predict a 10-percent increase in price:

$$\text{percentage change in equilibrium price} = -\frac{-30\%}{2.3 + 0.70} = \frac{30\%}{3.0} = 10\%$$

In Figure 5.6, the price rises by 10 percent, from $40 to $44 per pair.
Related to Exercise 7.7.

SUMMARY

This chapter explored the numbers behind the laws of demand and supply. The law of demand tells us that an increase in price decreases the quantity demanded, *ceteris paribus*. If we know the price elasticity of demand for a particular product, we can determine just how much less of it will be purchased at the higher price. Similarly, if we know the price elasticity of supply for a product, we can determine just how much more of it will be supplied at a higher price. Here are the main points of the chapter:

1 The *price elasticity of demand*—defined as the percentage change in quantity demanded divided by the percentage change in price—measures the responsiveness of consumers to changes in price.

2 Demand is relatively elastic if there are good substitutes.

3 If demand is *elastic*, the relationship between price and total revenue is negative. If demand is *inelastic*, the relationship between price and total revenue is positive.

4 The *price elasticity of supply*—defined as the percentage change in quantity supplied divided by the percentage change in price—measures the responsiveness of producers to changes in price.

5 If we know the elasticities of demand and supply, we can predict the percentage change in price resulting from a change in demand or supply.

KEY TERMS

cross-price elasticity of demand, p. 115

elastic demand, p. 102

income elasticity of demand, p. 115

inelastic demand, p. 102

perfectly elastic demand, p. 102

perfectly elastic supply, p. 119

perfectly inelastic demand, p. 102

perfectly inelastic supply, p. 118

price elasticity of demand (E_d), p. 100

price elasticity of supply, p. 116

total revenue, p. 107

unit elastic demand, p. 102

EXERCISES

myeconlab

Get Ahead of the Curve

Visit www.myeconlab.com to complete these exercises online and get instant feedback.

5.1 | The Price Elasticity of Demand

1.1 To compute the price elasticity of demand, we divide the percentage change in _____ by the percentage change in _____ and then take the _____ value of the ratio.

1.2 If a 10-percent increase in price decreases the quantity demanded by 12 percent, the price elasticity of demand is _____.

1.3 When the price of CDs increased from $10 to $11, the quantity of CDs demanded decreased from 100 to 80. The price elasticity of demand for CDs is _____, and demand is _____ (elastic/inelastic).

1.4 As the number of substitutes for a particular product increases, the price elasticity of demand for the product _____ (increases/decreases).

1.5 Over time, the price elasticity of demand for gasoline _____ (increases/decreases).

5.2 | Using Price Elasticity to Predict Changes in Quantity

2.1 A doubling of the tax on beer will reduce the number of highway deaths among young adults by _____ percent. (Related to Application 1 on page 106.)

2.2 Suppose Peru increases the price of hospital care by 10 percent. The quantity of medical care demanded in low-income areas will _____ by _____ percent. (Related to Application 2 on page 107.)

2.3 A 20-percent increase in the price of cigarettes will reduce the quantity of cigarettes demanded by teenagers by _____ percent. (Related to Application 3 on page 108.)

2.4 If the price elasticity of demand is 0.60, a 10-percent increase in price will _____ the quantity demanded by _____ percent.

2.5 **MADD Beer Tax.** The organization Mothers Against Drunk Driving (MADD) has a target of reducing the number of highway deaths among young adults by 39 percent. Assume that the number of highway deaths for young adults is proportional to their beer consumption. By what percentage must the price of beer increase to meet the MADD target? (Related to Application 1 on page 106.)

2.6 **Use the Correct Elasticity.** Your company currently sells 50 units of salt per year and has decided to increase its price from $1.00 to $1.20. In a meeting, one person says, "As shown in Table 5.2 on page 104, the price elasticity of demand for salt is 0.10, so if we increase the price of salt by 20 percent, the quantity demanded will decrease by 2 percent." What's wrong with this statement?

2.7 **Projecting Transit Ridership.** As a transit planner, your job is to predict ridership and total fare revenue. Suppose the short-run elasticity of demand for commuter rail (over a one-month period) is 0.60, and the long-run elasticity (over a two-year period) is 1.60. The current ridership is 100,000 people per day. Suppose the transit authority decides to increase its fares from $2.00 to $2.20.

   a. Predict the changes in train ridership over a one-month period (the short run) and a two-year period (the long run).

   b. Over the one-month period, will total fare revenue increase or decrease? What about the two-year period?

2.8 **X-ray Film to Peru.** Last year your charitable organization donated 100 rolls of x-ray film to hospitals in low-income areas of Peru, just enough to meet the country's need for x-ray film in those areas. Suppose Peru increases the price of hospital care by 30 percent. How many rolls of x-ray film should you send to Peru this year? (Related to Application 2 on page 107.)

2.9 **Meeting the Teen Smoking Target with Prices and Persuasion.** Suppose an antismoking campaign reduces teen smoking by 8 percent, meaning that the price of cigarettes must increase by an amount large enough to reduce teenage smoking by 52 percent to achieve an overall reduction of 60 percent. The required percentage increase in price is _____ percent. (Related to Application 3 on page 108.)

5.3 | Price Elasticity and Total Revenue

3.1 A bumper crop is bad news for farmers because _____ is _____. (Related to Application 4 on page 111.)

3.2 A policy that limits the supply of illegal drugs increases the number of burglaries and robberies because _____ is _____. (Related to Application 5 on page 112.)

3.3 If demand is elastic, when the price increases, the percentage change in _____ (quantity/price) exceeds the percentage change in _____ (quantity/price).

3.4 If demand is elastic, an increase in price _____ (increases/decreases) total revenue; if demand is inelastic, an increase in price _____ (increases/decreases) total revenue.

3.5 If a decrease in the price of accordions increases total revenue from accordion sales, the demand for accordions is _____.

3.6 Suppose at the current price, the price elasticity of demand for a campus film series is 2.0. If the price is cut, total revenue will _____ (increase/decrease).

3.7 You observe a positive relationship between the price your store charges for CDs and the total revenue from CDs. The demand for your CDs is _____.

3.8 Revenue Effects of a Bumper Crop. Your job is to predict the total revenue generated by the nation's corn crop. Last year's crop was 100 million bushels, and the price was $5 per bushel. This year's weather was favorable throughout the country, and this year's crop will be 110 million bushels, or 10 percent larger than last year's. The price elasticity of demand for corn is 0.50. (Related to Application 4 on page 111.)
   a. Predict the effect of the bumper crop on the price of corn. Assume that the entire crop is sold this year, meaning that the price elasticity of supply is zero. Illustrate with a complete graph.
   b. Predict the total revenue from this year's corn crop.
   c. Did the favorable weather increase or decrease the total revenue from corn? Why?

3.9 The Price of Heroin and Property Crime. The price elasticity of demand for heroin is 0.27. Suppose that half of heroin users support their habits with property crime, so the loss from property crimes committed by heroin users equals half the total spending (total revenue) on the drug. Suppose the government reduces the supply of heroin, increasing the equilibrium price by 20 percent. Fill the blanks in the following table. (Related to Application 5 on page 112.)

Price	Quantity of Heroin	Total Spending (Total Revenue)	Property Crime
$10	1,000	$10,000	$5,000
12	____	____	____

3.10 Revenue from Mobile Phones. Consider the demand for mobile phones. Suppose the price elasticity of demand for the market as a whole is 0.80.
   a. If all mobile-phone companies simultaneously increased their prices, will total revenue in the industry increase or decrease?
   b. If a single mobile-phone company increased its price, would you expect the company's total revenue to increase or decrease? Explain.

3.11 Price Hikes and Cable TV Revenue. Four years ago the cable company in your city increased its price by 20 percent, and its total revenue increased. Last year, a new company started providing TV service with satellite dishes. This year, the cable company increased its price by 20 percent, but its total revenue decreased. Provide an explanation for the different revenue consequences of the cable company's price hikes.

5.4 | Elasticity and Total Revenue for a Linear Demand Curve

4.1 Demand is _____ on the upper portion of a linear demand curve and _____ on the lower portion of a linear demand curve.

4.2 Suppose we are on the upper portion of a linear demand curve. If the price increases by 10 percent, the quantity demanded will decrease by _____ (more/less) than 10 percent and total revenue will _____ (increase/decrease).

4.3 At the midpoint of a linear demand curve, the price elasticity of demand is _____ .

4.4 If we are on the lower part of a linear demand curve, a decrease in price _____ (increases/decreases) total revenue.

4.5 Revenue from Vanity Plates. The objective of your state is to maximize the total revenue from the sale of vanity license plates. The current price is $25. The demand for vanity license plates is linear, and a price of $80 would drive the quantity demanded to zero. What is the appropriate price? Illustrate with a complete graph.

4.6 Where on the Demand Curve? The demand curve for your firm's product is linear. Based on recent sales data, you have determined that at the current price, the price elasticity of demand is 0.80.
   a. Is the current price on the upper or lower portion of the demand curve?
   b. If you want to increase your total revenue, should you increase or decrease your price?
   c. Will you move upward or downward along the demand curve?

5.5 | Other Elasticities of Demand

5.1 The income elasticity of demand is _____ (positive/ negative) for normal goods and _____ (positive/ negative) for inferior goods.

5.2 If a 20-percent increase in income increases the quantity of iPods demanded by 30 percent, the income elasticity of demand is _____ .

5.3 The cross-price elasticity of demand is _____ (positive/negative) for substitute goods and _____ (positive/negative) for complementary goods.

5.4 If a 10-percent increase in the price of natural gas increases the quantity of residential electricity demanded by 18 percent, the cross-price elasticity of demand is _____ .

5.5 If a 10-percent increase in the price of tennis rackets decreases the quantity of tennis balls demanded by 15 percent, the cross-price elasticity of demand is _____ .

5.6 **Income and Starbucks Coffee Shops**. Starbucks just hired you to determine whether your city could support a new Starbucks coffee shop. There are currently four Starbucks coffee shops in the city, and each has just enough customers to survive. The average household income in the city is expected to increase by 10 percent per year for the next few years. Suppose the income elasticity of demand for Starbucks' coffee products is 1.25. The population of the city is constant.
   a. By what percentage will the demand for coffee increase each year?
   b. How soon will the area have enough demand to support a fifth Starbucks?

5.7 **iPods and iTunes**. You have been hired to predict the effects of increasing the price of iTunes songs by 10 percent, from $0.99 to $1.09. You are interested in the effects of the price hike on the number of songs downloaded legally from iTunes, the number of songs downloaded legally from other online music stores, the number of iPod players sold, and the number of CDs sold in stores. Given the hypothetical elasticities in the following table, fill in the blanks. Recall that conventional practice for the price elasticity of demand of a product uses the absolute value of the elasticity.

Product	Price Elasticity or Cross-Price Elasticity	Predicted Percentage Change in Quantity Demanded
iTunes songs	1.50 (absolute value)	_____
Songs from other online stores	+2.00	_____
iPod players	−0.70	_____
CDs in stores	+1.80	_____

5.6 | The Price Elasticity of Supply

6.1 When the price of paper increases from $100 to $104 per ton, the quantity supplied increases from 200 to 220 tons per day. The price elasticity of supply is _____ .

6.2 Suppose the price elasticity of a supply of cheese is 0.80. If the price of cheese rises by 20 percent, the quantity of cheese supplied will increase by _____ percent.

6.3 The short-run elasticity of supply is _____ (smaller/larger) than the long-run elasticity of supply because the principle of _____ is applicable in the short run.

6.4 As the supply curve becomes flatter, the price elasticity of supply _____ (increases/decreases).

5.7 | Using Elasticities to Predict Changes in Equilibrium Price

7.1 Assume that the elasticity of demand for chewing tobacco is 0.70 and the elasticity of supply is 2.30. Suppose an antichewing campaign decreases the demand for chewing tobacco by 18 percent. The equilibrium price of chewing tobacco will _____ (decrease/increase) by _____ percent.

7.2 Suppose the elasticity of demand for motel rooms is 1.0 and the elasticity of supply is 0.50. If the demand for motel rooms increases by 15 percent, the equilibrium price of motel rooms will _____ (decrease/increase) by _____ percent.

7.3 Suppose the price elasticity of demand for apples is 1.0 and the supply elasticity is 3.0. If the supply of apples decreases by 12 percent, the equilibrium price will _____ (decrease/increase) by _____ percent.

7.4 Suppose the price elasticity of demand for accordions is 2.0 and the supply elasticity is 3.0. If a subsidy on accordions increases supply by 20 percent, the equilibrium price will _____ (decrease/increase) by _____ percent.

7.5 **College Enrollment and Apartment Prices.** Consider a college town where the initial price of apartments is $400 and the initial quantity is 1,000 apartments. The price elasticity of demand for apartments is 1.0, and the price elasticity of supply of apartments is 0.50. (Related to Application 6 on page 121.)
   a. Use demand and supply curves to show the initial equilibrium, and label the equilibrium point *a*.
   b. Suppose that an increase in college enrollment is expected to increase the demand for apartments in a college town by 15 percent. Use your graph to show the effects of the increase in demand on the apartment market. Label the new equilibrium point *b*.

c. Predict the effect of the increase in demand on the equilibrium price of apartments.

7.6 **The Cost of Wood and the Price of Housing.** Suppose the price of wood increases the cost of building new houses by 4 percent and shifts the supply curve to the left by 12 percent. The initial price of new housing is $100,000, the price elasticity of demand is 1.0, and the price elasticity of supply is 3.0. Predict the effect of the higher wood prices on the equilibrium price of new housing. Illustrate your answer with a graph that shows the initial point (*a*) and the new equilibrium (*b*). (Related to Application 6 on page 121.)

7.7 **Import Restrictions and the Price of Steel.** Suppose import restrictions on steel decrease the supply of steel by 24 percent. The initial price of steel is $100 per unit, the elasticity of demand is 0.70, and the elasticity of supply is 2.3. Predict the effect of the import restrictions on the equilibrium price of steel. Illustrate your answer with a graph that shows the initial point (*a*) and the new equilibrium (*b*). (Related to Application 7 on page 123.)

NOTES

1. Kenneth A. Small, *Urban Transportation Economics* (Philadelphia, PA: Harwood Academic Publishers, 1992).

2. Richard Klemme and Jean-Paul Chavas, "The Effects of Changing Milk Price on Milk Supply and National Dairy Herd Size," *Economic Issues*, no. 92, June 1985, University of Wisconsin.

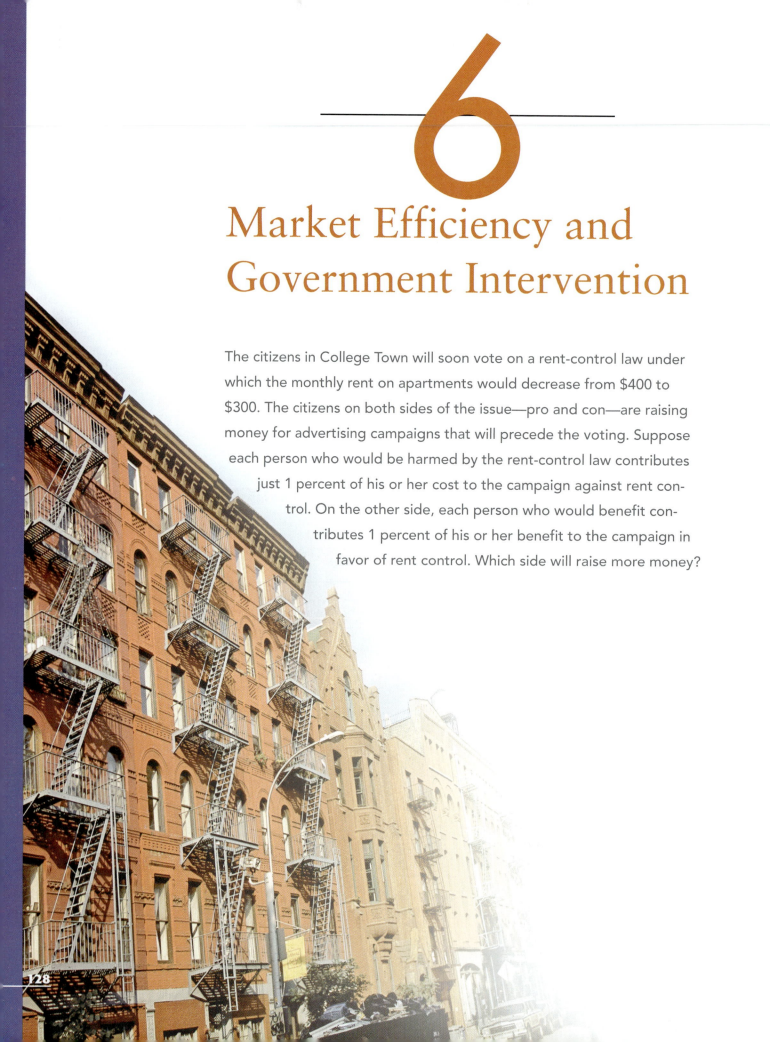

6

Market Efficiency and Government Intervention

The citizens in College Town will soon vote on a rent-control law under which the monthly rent on apartments would decrease from $400 to $300. The citizens on both sides of the issue—pro and con—are raising money for advertising campaigns that will precede the voting. Suppose each person who would be harmed by the rent-control law contributes just 1 percent of his or her cost to the campaign against rent control. On the other side, each person who would benefit contributes 1 percent of his or her benefit to the campaign in favor of rent control. Which side will raise more money?

APPLYING THE CONCEPTS

1 How does a minimum price (floor price) affect the market?
Milk Mountains

2 Who bears the cost of import restrictions?
U.S. and European Consumers Pay for Import Restrictions

3 What is the role of prices in allocating resources?
Supply and Demand for Human Organs

4 Who bears a tax on luxury goods?
Boat Workers and the Tax on Luxury Boats

5 How do taxes affect behavior?
Taxes and December Babies

As we'll see in this chapter, if everyone correctly anticipates the effects of rent control and contributes 1 percent of the personal cost or benefit, the campaign against rent control will raise more money. This tells us that although rent control produces winners and losers, the losses of the losers exceed the gains of the winners.

efficiency
A situation in which people do the best they can, given their limited resources.

When making choices, people strive for **efficiency**, trying to do the best they can, given their limited resources. The notion of efficiency applies to all sorts of decisions. A household decides how much to spend on consumer goods, how much to save, and how much to spend on a college education. The household tries to do the best it can, given its limited income. A Frisbee producer decides how many workers to hire and tries to make as much profit as possible, given the limitations of its factory. A government chooses between shuttle trips and Mars missions, and tries to generate as much scientific information as possible, given its space budget. As we'll see, economics provides a framework to guide us from inefficient choices to efficient ones.

In Chapter 3, we discussed the exchange principle, which conveys the simple idea that transactions make both the buyer and the seller better off.

PRINCIPLE OF VOLUNTARY EXCHANGE

A voluntary exchange between two people makes both people better off.

In this chapter, we will take a closer look at the benefits of exchange, examining the experiences of both buyers and sellers. We will see how to compute the surplus or net benefit from a market and see why the market equilibrium—where the quantity demanded equals the quantity supplied—*may* generate the largest possible surplus. We'll explore the logic behind Adam Smith's metaphor of the invisible hand—the idea that individual buyers and sellers, each acting in his or her own self-interest, *may* promote the social interest.

You'll notice that we use the word "may" in noting the virtues of markets and the invisible hand. A market equilibrium will generate the largest possible surplus when four conditions are met:

- *No external benefits:* The benefits of a product (a good or service) are confined to the person who pays for it.
- *No external costs:* The cost of producing a product is confined to the person who sells it.
- *Perfect information:* Buyers and sellers know enough about the product to make informed decisions about whether to buy or sell it.
- *Perfect competition:* Each firm produces such a small quantity that the firm cannot affect the price.

In this chapter, we discuss markets that meet these four conditions. As we'll see later in the book, when these conditions are not satisfied, free markets don't generate the largest possible surplus. A market that generates the largest possible surplus is efficient. A situation is *efficient* if we are doing the best we can, given our limited resources. In the case of a market, doing the best we can means getting the largest possible surplus. When that happens, we say that the market is efficient. Governments around the world intervene in markets, sometimes promoting efficiency, and other times preventing it. We'll see that when the four efficiency conditions are met, government intervention is inefficient in the sense that it decreases the total surplus of the market.

6.1 | CONSUMER SURPLUS AND PRODUCER SURPLUS

We'll begin our discussion of market efficiency by showing how to measure the benefits experienced by consumers and producers. We'll start with consumers and then look at producers.

The Demand Curve and Consumer Surplus

If you said "thank you" the last time you purchased a CD, did you mean it? If you were willing to pay more for the CD than the price you actually paid, you probably really *did* mean it when you said "thank you," because you got what you considered to be a good deal. Your **willingness to pay** for a product (a good or a service) is the maximum amount you are willing to pay for the product. Your **consumer surplus** is equal to your willingness to pay minus the price you actually pay. For example, if you are willing to pay $21 for a CD that you buy for $10, your consumer surplus is $11.

The market demand curve shows consumers' willingness to pay for a product. Consider the demand for lawn cutting in a small town; the market demand curve is shown in Figure 6.1. The demand curve shows that at a price of $25, no one will pay to have the lawn cut (point *t*), but if the price drops to $22, the first consumer (Juan) will pay for a lawn cut. This suggests that Juan is willing to pay up to $22 to have his lawn cut, but no more. Moving down the demand curve, the second consumer (Tupak) will pay for a lawn cutting when the price drops to $19, meaning that his willingness to pay is $19. As we continue to move downward along the demand curve, the price drops below the willingness to pay for more and more consumers, so more people have their lawns cut.

We can use the demand curve to measure just how much of a net benefit or surplus consumers get. Suppose that the price of a lawn cut is $10, and everyone in town pays this price. Juan's consumer surplus is $12, equal to his willingness to pay ($22) minus the price. Similarly, Tupak's consumer surplus is $9, equal to the difference between his willingness to pay ($19) and the market price. To compute the total consumer surplus in the lawn-cutting market, we simply add up the surpluses for each of the five consumers who buy lawn cutting at a price of $10. In this example, the market consumer surplus is $30, which is the sum of $12 (Juan) + $9 (Tupak) + $6 (Thurl) + $3 (Forest) + $0 (Fivola). The fifth consumer (Fivola) gets no consumer surplus, because the price equals her willingness to pay. The sixth person (Siggy) doesn't have his lawn cut because the amount he is willing to pay is less than the price.

The Supply Curve and Producer Surplus

Like consumers, the people who produce goods and services say "thank you" when they sell their products. This suggests that they receive a net benefit or surplus from voluntary transactions. A seller's **willingness to accept** is the minimum amount he or

• **willingness to pay**
The maximum amount a consumer is willing to pay for a product.

• **consumer surplus**
The amount a consumer is willing to pay for a product minus the price the consumer actually pays.

• **willingness to accept**
The minimum amount a producer is willing to accept as payment for a product; equal to the marginal cost of production.

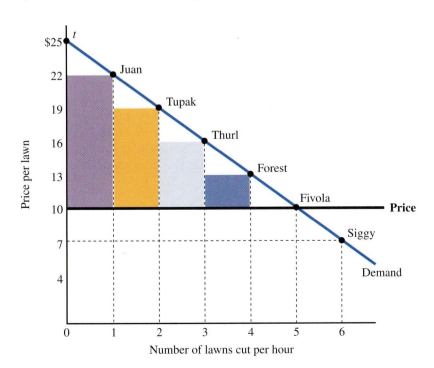

◄ **FIGURE 6.1**
The Demand Curve and Consumer Surplus
Consumer surplus equals the maximum amount a consumer is willing to pay (shown by the demand curve) minus the price paid. Juan is willing to pay $22, so if the price is $10, his consumer surplus is $12. The market consumer surplus equals the sum of the surpluses earned by all consumers in the market. In this case, the market consumer surplus is $30 = $12 + $9 + $6 + $3 + $0.

The Supply Curve and Producer Surplus

Producer surplus equals the market price minus the producer's willingness to accept or marginal cost (shown by the supply curve). Abe's marginal cost is $2, so if the price is $10, his producer surplus is $8. The market producer surplus equals the sum of the surpluses earned by all producers in the market. In this case, the market producer surplus is
$20 = $8 + $6 + $4 + $2 + $0.

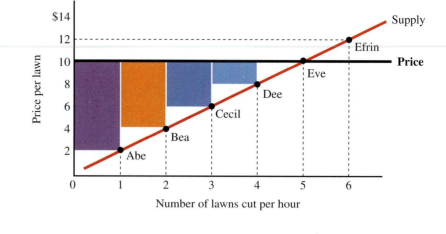

• **producer surplus**
The price a producer receives for a product minus the marginal cost of production.

she is willing to accept as payment for a product, and is equal to the marginal cost of production. For example, if your marginal cost of cutting a lawn is $4, you will be willing to accept any amount greater than or equal to $4. Of course, you'd prefer $10 to $4, but you'll accept as little as $4, because the lower amount covers all your costs, including the opportunity cost of your time. **Producer surplus** equals the price a producer receives for a product minus the marginal cost of production. For example, if your marginal cost for cutting a lawn is $4 and you do it for $10, your producer surplus is $6.

Figure 6.2 shows the market supply curve for lawn cutting in our small town. Let's imagine that up to six people are willing to cut lawns if the price is right, and each person can cut one lawn per hour. Each person incurs the same cost for renting a lawn mower but has a different opportunity cost for his or her time. The first producer (Abe) incurs a cost of $2, so he is willing to accept as little as $2 to cut a lawn. On the supply curve, if the price is $2, one person—Abe—will cut lawns. Bea has a higher opportunity cost of time, so her cost is $4, meaning that she won't cut a lawn unless she is paid at least $4. So if the price is $4, two people—Abe and Bea—will cut lawns. Moving upward along the supply curve, the other potential lawn cutters have even higher costs, so they don't start cutting until the price reaches their higher willingness to accept: $6 for Cecil, $8 for Dee, and so on. The higher the price, the larger the number of people willing to cut lawns.

We can use the supply curve to measure just how much of a net benefit or surplus producers get. If the price of lawn cutting is $10, Abe's producer surplus for cutting the lawn is $8, the price he receives minus his cost ($2). Similarly, Bea's producer surplus is $6, equal to the difference between the price and her cost ($4). To compute the total producer surplus in the lawn-cutting market, we simply add up the surpluses for each of the five producers who cut lawns at a price of $10. In this example, the market producer surplus is $20, which is the sum of $8 (Abe) + $6 (Bea) + $4 (Cecil) + $2 (Dee) + $0 (Eve). The fifth producer (Eve) gets no producer surplus because the price equals her cost, and the sixth potential producer (Efrin) doesn't cut any lawns because the price is less than his cost.

6.2 | MARKET EQUILIBRIUM AND EFFICIENCY

Figure 6.3 puts the demand and supply curves together to show the equilibrium in the market for lawn cutting. The demand curve intersects the supply curve at a price of $10 per lawn. At this price, five lawns are cut, meaning that there are five buyers and five sellers. The **total surplus** of a market is the sum of consumer surplus and producer surplus. In Figure 6.3, the consumer surplus is $30 and the producer surplus is $20, so the total surplus of the market—shown by the shaded areas—is $50. As we'll see in this part of the chapter, the market equilibrium generates the highest possible total

• **total surplus**
The sum of consumer surplus and producer surplus.

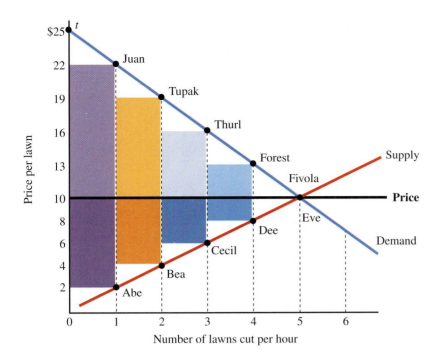

◀ **FIGURE 6.3**
Market Equilibrium and the Total Market Surplus
The total surplus of the market equals consumer surplus (the lightly shaded areas) plus producer surplus (the darkly shaded areas). The market equilibrium generates the highest possible total market value, equal to $50 = $30 (consumer surplus) + $20 (producer surplus).

surplus. That's why we say that the market equilibrium is efficient: We can't do any better in terms of the total surplus.

Total Surplus Is Lower with a Price Below the Equilibrium Price

To see why the market equilibrium maximizes the total surplus of the market, let's look at the total surplus of the market when the price is less than the equilibrium price. The government could set a maximum price, also known as a **price ceiling**.

Suppose the government imposes a maximum price of $4 on lawn cutting. As shown in Panel A of Figure 6.4, at this price only two people cut lawns—Abe and Bea. Abe's producer surplus is shown by the darkly shaded area between the price line and the supply curve. For Bea, the price equals her willingness to accept, so she participates in the market but gets no producer surplus, receiving a price just high enough to keep her in the market. Consumers can buy only as much as producers are willing to sell, so the market consumer surplus equals the surpluses of just the first two consumers—Juan and Tupak. This is shown as the lightly shaded areas between the price line and the demand curve. By comparing Panel A in Figure 6.4 to Figure 6.3, we see that the maximum price reduces the total surplus of the market. For the first two lawns, consumers simply gain at the expense of producers. The maximum price also eliminates the surpluses from the third and fourth lawns because these transactions don't happen. Therefore, the total surplus decreases.

The maximum price reduces the total surplus of the market because it prevents some mutually beneficial transactions. For example, the third consumer, Thurl, is willing to pay $16 to have his lawn cut, and the third producer, Cecil, is willing to cut a lawn if he is paid at least $6. Thurl is willing to pay more than Cecil requires, so cutting Thurl's lawn would generate a net benefit of $10. If they split the difference, agreeing on a price of $11, each would get a surplus of $5. The maximum price prevents Thurl and Cecil from executing their transaction. The same logic applies to the fourth lawn: The maximum price prevents Forest and Dee from executing a transaction that would generate a net benefit of $5, equal to Forest's willingness to pay ($13) minus Dee's marginal cost ($8).

• **price ceiling**
A maximum price set by the government.

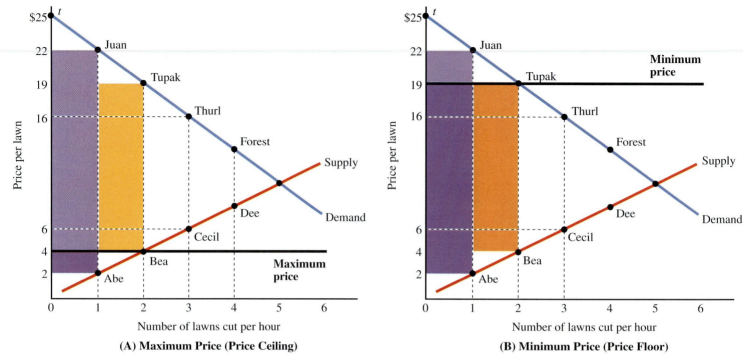

▲ **FIGURE 6.4**

Price Controls Decrease the Total Surplus of the Market

(**A**) A maximum price of $4 reduces the total surplus of the market. The first two consumers gain at the expense of the first two producers. The consumer and producer surpluses for the third and fourth lawns are lost entirely, so the total value of the market decreases.

(**B**) A minimum price of $19 reduces the total surplus of the market. The first two producers gain at the expense of the first two consumers. The consumer and producer surpluses for the third and fourth lawns are lost entirely, so the total value of the market decreases.

Total Surplus Is Lower with a Price Above the Equilibrium Price

To reinforce the notion that the market equilibrium maximizes the total surplus of the market, let's look at the total surplus of the market when the price exceeds the equilibrium price. The government could set a minimum price, also known as a **price floor**. Suppose the government sets a minimum price for lawn cutting at $19. As shown in Panel B of Figure 6.4, the demand curve indicates that at a price of $19, only two consumers, Juan and Tupak, will have their lawns cut. The total surplus of the market is the sum of consumer and producer surplus for these first two lawns, the same as it was under the maximum price. Again, this is lower than the total surplus that the consumer and producer could have gained, as shown by Figure 6.3. The difference between the two pricing policies is that under a maximum price, the first two consumers gain at the expense of the first two producers, whereas under the minimum price, the first two producers gain at the expense of the first two consumers. Like the maximum price, the minimum price prevents mutually beneficial transactions for the third, fourth, and fifth lawns.

Efficiency and the Invisible Hand

The market equilibrium maximizes the total surplus of the market because it guarantees that all mutually beneficial transactions will happen. Once we reach the market equilibrium at the intersection of the supply curve and demand curve, there are no more transactions that would benefit a buyer and a seller. The market demand curve tells us that the potential buyer of the sixth lawn cut (Siggy) is willing to pay only $7 for a lawn cut, and the supply curve tells us that the potential seller of the sixth lawn

• **price floor**
A minimum price set by the government.

cut (Efrin) has a marginal cost of $12. This transaction doesn't happen because the potential buyer is not willing to pay the cost of producing the good.

Our example of the market for lawn cutting illustrates a general lesson about markets. The typical market has thousands of buyers and thousands of sellers, each acting in his or her own self-interest. The market reaches the quantity that maximizes the total surplus of the market and is therefore efficient. Instead of using a bureaucrat to coordinate the actions of everyone in the market, we can rely on the actions of individual consumers and individual producers, each guided only by self-interest. This is Adam Smith's invisible hand in action.

Government Intervention in Efficient Markets

In most modern economies, governments take an active role in the economy. As we'll see later in the book, government action can be justified on efficiency grounds when one of the four efficiency conditions listed at the beginning of the chapter is not being met. But for a market that meets the four efficiency conditions, the market equilibrium generates the largest possible total surplus, so government intervention can only decrease the surplus and cause inefficiency. A government motivated exclusively by efficiency would not intervene in such a market, but instead would permit the invisible hand to guide consumers and producers to the market equilibrium.

So why would a government intervene in an efficient market? Sometimes the government's objective is not to promote efficiency—to maximize the size of the pie—but instead to slice the pie in favor of one group or another. For example, a government that restricts shoe imports prevents some domestic workers from losing their shoemaking jobs. Of course, limiting imports will decrease the supply of shoes, and consumers will pay higher prices. As we'll see, when the government intervenes in an efficient market to slice the pie in favor of one group, the pie shrinks, so there is a trade-off between efficiency (maximizing the size of the pie) and distributional concerns (slicing the pie).

What is the role of economic analysis in exploring government intervention in efficient markets? We will focus our attention on the inefficiencies of government intervention, looking at how much the pie shrinks. We will briefly discuss some of the distributional consequences of intervention—how the slices change. The decision about whether intervention in an efficient market is worthwhile—whether the changes in the slices are worth losing part of the pie—is made in the political sphere. Economic analysis shows the trade-offs associated with public policies.

Under some circumstances, groups of people who fare poorly in the market economy deserve special consideration. If a society decides that a particular group merits special treatment—for example, workers who lose their jobs because of imports—a more direct form of assistance is generally superior than intervention in efficient markets by the government. One alternative would be for the government to provide money for workers to get training for new jobs.

6.3 | CONTROLLING PRICES—MAXIMUM AND MINIMUM PRICES

We'll start our discussion of government intervention with policies that control product prices. The government could set a maximum price or a minimum price. In both cases, if the market meets the four efficiency conditions listed at the beginning of the chapter, government intervention reduces the total surplus of the market and causes inefficiency.

Setting Maximum Prices

We've already seen two different effects of a maximum price or price ceiling. In Chapter 4, we saw that when the government sets a maximum price that is less than the equilibrium price, the result is permanent excess demand for the product. The maximum price encourages firms to supply *less* and encourages consumers to buy *more*. So at the maximum price there is excess demand because consumers want to buy more than producers want to sell. In this chapter, we saw from Panel A in Figure 6.4 that a maximum price decreases the total surplus of the market: Some consumers gain at the expense of producers, and the total surplus decreases. Here are some examples of goods that have been subject to maximum prices or may be subject to maximum prices in the near future:

- *Rental housing.* During World War II, the federal government instituted a national system of rent controls. Although only New York City continued rent control after the war, during the 1970s rent control spread to dozens of cities.
- *Gasoline.* In response to sharp increases in the price of gasoline in the 1970s, the national government set a maximum price on gasoline.
- *Medical goods and services.* Some proposals to control medical costs include price controls for prescription drugs.

In all three cases, a maximum price will cause excess demand and reduce the total surplus of the market.

Rent Control

Figure 6.5 shows the effects of rent control on consumer and producer surplus. Panel A shows the market equilibrium, with a price (monthly rent) of $400 per apartment and a quantity of 1,000 apartments. The total surplus is the sum of the consumer surplus and producer surplus, shown as the area between the demand curve and the supply curve. Panel B shows the effect of a maximum price of $300 per apartment. The decrease in price causes movement downward along the supply curve to point *b*, and the quantity of apartments supplied decreases to 700. Because the policy decreases the number of apartments from 1,000 to 700, the total surplus of the market decreases. For the first 700 apartments, consumers gain at the expense of producers, paying $300 per apartment rather than $400. The 701st through the 1,000th apartments disappear from the market, so the surpluses associated with these apartments are lost entirely. The decrease in total surplus means that the market is inefficient.

Because rent control decreases the total surplus of the market, the policy generates a **deadweight loss**. In Figure 6.5, the deadweight loss is shown by the yellow triangle *abc*, the decrease in the total surplus of the market. This is a deadweight loss in the sense that it is not offset by a gain to anyone else. The consumers and producers

• **deadweight loss**
  The decrease in the total surplus of the market that results from a policy such as rent control.

► **FIGURE 6.5**
Rent Control Decreases Total Surplus
(**A**) In the market equilibrium, with a price of $400 and 1,000 apartments, the total surplus is the area between the demand curve and the supply curve.
(**B**) Rent control, with a maximum price of $300, reduces the quantity to 700 apartments and decreases the total surplus.

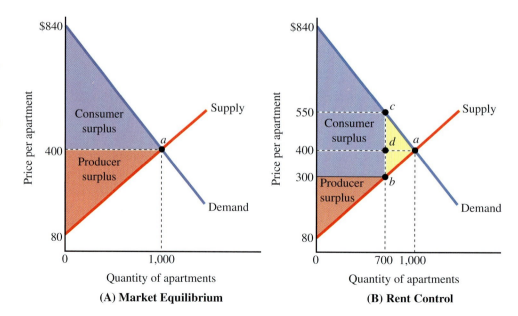

(A) Market Equilibrium   (B) Rent Control

who are excluded from the market by rent control lose the surpluses they could have received in the market.

Let's return to the chapter-opening story about citizens' contributions to the advertising campaigns for and against rent control. Recall that each citizen will contribute 1 percent of the personal gain or loss from rent control. We know from Figure 6.5 that rent control decreases the total surplus of the rental market because the losses of the losers exceed the gains of the winners. Therefore, the total contributions of the losers will exceed the total contributions of the winners, so the opponents of rent control will have a bigger campaign than the proponents.

Let's take a closer look at the gains and losses from rent control. There are 700 consumers and producers remaining in the market. The 700 consumers each gain $100 by paying $100 less for an apartment, while the 700 producers each lose $100 by receiving $100 less for an apartment. In other words, for the 700 apartments that remain in the market, the consumer gains exactly offset the producer losses. Rent control decreases the quantity of apartments in the market from 1,000 to 700, so there are 300 consumers and producers who are forced out of the market. These consumers and producers both lose their surpluses. The loss of consumer surplus is shown by triangle *cad*, and the loss of producer surplus is shown by triangle *dab*. Adding these together, we get the deadweight loss shown by triangle *abc*.

Another way to see the inefficiency of rent control is to apply the principle of voluntary exchange.

PRINCIPLE OF VOLUNTARY EXCHANGE
A voluntary exchange between two people makes both people better off.

As shown by the points between *c* and *a* on the demand curve, 300 consumers are willing to pay between $400 and $550 for an apartment. As shown by the points between points *b* and *a* on the supply curve, there are 300 producers who are willing to rent out an apartment for amounts between $300 and $400. Although the 300 excluded consumers are willing to pay more than these suppliers require to provide an apartment, the transactions are illegal under rent control. Because rent control outlaws transactions that would make both parties better off, it causes inefficiency.

Three more subtle effects associated with rent control add to its inefficiency:

- *Search costs.* At the artificially low maximum price, the number of people seeking apartments exceeds the number of apartments available. Consumers will spend more time searching for apartments, so an additional cost of rent control is the opportunity cost of the extra time spent searching for apartments.
- *Cheating.* Because rent control outlaws mutually beneficial transactions, many people violate the spirit and the letter of the law by cheating. In some rent-control cities, consumers pay extra money to property owners to outbid other consumers. These extra payments are often disguised as "nonrefundable security deposits" or as "key money"—thousands of dollars to get the keys to an apartment.
- *Decrease in quality of housing.* Given the lower payoff from providing apartments for rent, property owners will have less incentive to spend money on repair and maintenance, so the quality of apartments will decrease. In other words, lower rent is offset in part by lower housing quality.

Is rent control good for the poor? Rent control specifies a maximum rent for an apartment, regardless of who lives there. Rent-controlled apartments are occupied by the rich and the poor, so many wealthy people benefit from rent control. In other words, rent control is ineffective in helping the poor. As we explain later in the book, the government could use other policies to more effectively improve the economic circumstances of the poor.

APPLICATION

MILK MOUNTAINS

APPLYING THE CONCEPTS #1: How does a minimum price (floor price) affect the market?

Why is the U.S. government storing billions of pounds of powdered milk in warehouses and caves? The minimum price for powdered milk is $9.90 per hundred pounds. To prevent the market price from falling below $9.90, the U.S. government purchases any resulting surpluses at this price. In recent years, the market demand for powdered milk has been relatively low, so the government has purchased millions of pounds of powdered milk. By 2003, the government's stockpile of powdered milk reached 1.28 billion pounds. The mountains of dried milk are stored in warehouses across the United States and even in caves near Kansas City. Why doesn't the government just give all of its powdered milk away? The problem is that giving it away would ultimately reduce the amount of powder that farmers could sell to consumers. The government would then be forced to buy more unsold powder from farmers. *Related to Exercise 3.6.*

SOURCE: Tom Webb, "As Powdered Milk Piles Up, U.S. Taxpayers Pay $1 Billion," *Oregonian*, August 24, 2003, p. 1.

Setting Minimum Prices

We've already seen two different effects of a minimum price, or price floor. In Chapter 4, we saw that when the government sets a minimum price that exceeds the equilibrium price, the result is permanent excess supply. The increase in price encourages producers to produce *more* and encourages consumers to buy *less*. So at the minimum price, there is excess supply because producers want to sell more than consumers want to buy. In this chapter, we saw from Panel A in Figure 6.4 that a minimum price decreases the total surplus of the market: Some producers gain at the expense of consumers, and the total surplus decreases.

Governments around the world establish minimum prices for agricultural goods. Under a price-support program, a government sets a minimum price for an agricultural product and then buys any resulting surpluses at that price.

6.4 | CONTROLLING QUANTITIES—LICENSING AND IMPORT RESTRICTIONS

What happens when the government controls the quantity of a particular product instead of its price? We'll consider two policies that control quantities. In the domestic economy, many state and local governments limit the number of firms in particular markets by limiting the number of business licenses to operate in those markets. Many national governments restrict imports, using import bans or quotas on the quantity of a product—for example, shoes or cheese—that can be imported.

You may be surprised by the sheer number of state and local government business licensing programs. For example, many cities and states limit the number of taxicabs, dry cleaners, tobacco farms, liquor stores, bars, and even dog groomers. Some people defend licensing programs on the grounds that they protect consumers from low-quality products and poor service. But studies have shown that most licensing programs increase prices without improving the quality of products and service.[1] Another motive for cities to issue licenses is to limit the number of establishments that could be considered nuisances to some citizens, for example, bars, convenience stores, and gas stations.

Taxi Medallions

We can use the licensing of taxis to explain how the practice affects the market for taxi service and other markets in which licenses are common. Panel A of Figure 6.6 shows the market equilibrium in the taxi market. The demand curve intersects the supply curve at point *a*. The industry provides 10,000 miles of taxi service per day at a price of $3 per mile. Each taxi is capable of producing a maximum of 100 miles of service per day, and there are 100 taxicabs in the market. The total surplus of the market equals the sum of consumer surplus and producer surplus, shown by the area between the demand curve and the supply curve.

Now suppose that the city passes a law requiring each taxicab to have a license—also known as a taxi "medallion"—and limits the number of medallions to 80. The city then gives taxi medallions to the first 80 people who show up at City Hall. In Panel B of Figure 6.6, the vertical line at 8,000 miles of service shows that this policy fixes the quantity of taxi service at 8,000 miles per day (80 taxis times 100 miles per taxi per day). The medallion policy creates an excess demand for taxi service: At the original price ($3.00), the quantity demanded is 10,000 miles, but the city's 80 taxicabs provide only 8,000 miles of service. As a result, the market moves upward along the demand curve to point *c*, where the price is $3.60 per mile of service. The medallion policy increases the price and decreases the quantity of taxi services.

Licensing and Market Efficiency

The medallion policy decreases the total surplus of the taxi market. In Figure 6.6, we see that the total surplus in Panel B is less than the total surplus in Panel A. The medallion policy decreases consumer surplus, a result of the higher price and the smaller quantity supplied. Producer surplus could increase or decrease, depending on the shapes of the market supply and market demand curves. In this example, the producer surplus of taxi drivers with medallions actually increases by a small amount. As in the cases of a maximum price or a minimum price, the medallion policy decreases the quantity of goods sold, decreasing the total surplus of the market. The producers of the first 8,000 miles of service gain at the expense of consumers, but the

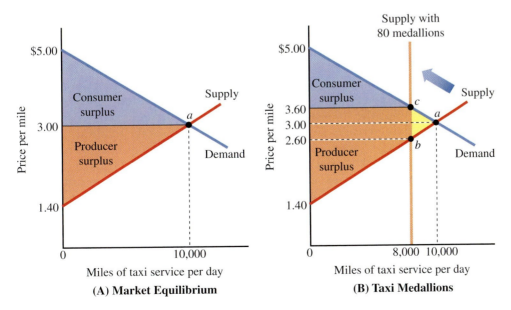

(A) Market Equilibrium

(B) Taxi Medallions

◀ **FIGURE 6.6**
The Market Effects of Tax Medallions
(**A**) The market equilibrium is shown by point *a*, with a price of $3.00 and a quantity of 10,000 miles of service per day (100 taxis and 100 miles per taxi). The total surplus is the area between the demand and supply curves.
(**B**) A medallion policy reduces the quantity of taxi service to 8,000 miles per day (80 taxis and 100 miles per taxi) and increases the price to $3.60 (point *c*). The producers of the first 8,000 miles gain at the expense of consumers, but the surpluses for between 8,000 and 10,000 miles are lost entirely. Therefore, the total surplus decreases.

surpluses that could have been gained between 8,000 and 10,000 miles are lost entirely, so the total surplus of the market decreases. The deadweight loss is shown by the area of yellow triangle *abc*.

Another way to see the inefficiency of taxi medallions is to look at just the consumers and producers who are excluded from the market and what they lose. Some of the excluded consumers would gladly pay the cost of providing taxi service. As shown by the points between points *c* and *a* on the demand curve, many consumers are willing to pay between $3.00 and $3.60 per mile for taxi service. Although there are plenty of drivers who would be willing to provide taxi service at these prices, they can't do so without a medallion. Because the medallion policy prevents these riders and drivers from executing mutually beneficial transactions, the policy causes inefficiency.

Our analysis of taxi medallions applies to any market subject to quantity controls. State and city governments use licensing to limit many types of small businesses. When an establishment such as a convenience store or dry cleaner would cause a nuisance to its neighbors, the inefficiency of the sort shown in Figure 6.6 may be at least partly offset by the benefit of controlling nuisances. Of course, the alternative policy is to control the nuisance directly by restricting the location of the establishment rather than simply limiting the number of establishments. In general, a policy that limits entry into a market increases price, decreases quantity, and causes inefficiency in the market. In evaluating such a policy, we must compare the possible benefits from controlling nuisances to the losses of consumer and producer surplus.

Winners and Losers from Licensing

Who benefits and who loses from licensing programs such as a taxi medallion policy? The losers are consumers, who pay more for taxi rides. The winners are the people who receive a free medallion and the right to charge an artificially high price for taxi service.

In some cities, people buy and sell taxi medallions. The market value of a medallion reflects the profits it can earn its owner. For example, the market price of a medallion is over $150,000 in New York City, $140,000 in Boston, and $100,000 in Toronto.[2] In cities such as Chicago, where medallions are more plentiful, the market price is much lower.

Why don't governments simply eliminate the taxi medallion system and allow free entry into the taxi market? Because doing so would decrease the price of taxi service and reduce the market value of medallions to zero. Some city governments are reluctant to eliminate medallions because owners use their political power to keep the system (and the value of their medallions) in place.

Import Restrictions

We've seen that the government can control the quantity of a good produced by issuing a limited number of business licenses to producers. Another way to control quantity is to limit the imports of a particular good. Like a licensing policy, an import restriction increases the market price and decreases the total surplus of the market.

To show the market effects of import restrictions, let's start with an unrestricted market. Panel A of Figure 6.7 shows the market equilibrium in the sugar market when there is free trade. The domestic supply curve shows the quantity supplied by domestic (U.S.) firms at different prices. Looking at point *m*, we see that U.S. firms will not supply any sugar unless the price is at least $0.26 per pound. The total supply curve, which shows the quantity supplied by both domestic and foreign firms, lies to the right of the domestic curve. At each price, the total supply exceeds the domestic supply because foreign firms also supply sugar. Point *a*

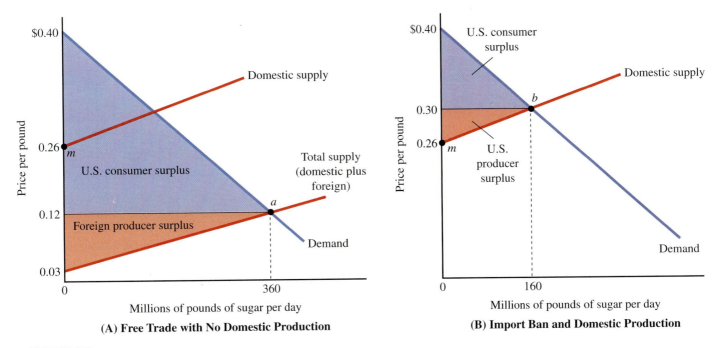

▲ **FIGURE 6.7**

The Effects of an Import Ban on U.S. Prices and Consumer and Producer Surplus
(**A**) With free trade, the demand intersects the total supply curve at point *a* with a price of $0.12
and a quantity of 360 million pounds. This price is below the minimum price of domestic suppliers ($0.26, as shown by point *m*), so domestic firms do not participate in the market. The total
surplus is shown by the shaded areas (U.S. consumer surplus and foreign producer surplus).
(**B**) If sugar imports are banned, the equilibrium is shown by the intersection of the demand curve
and the domestic (U.S.) supply curve (point *b*). The price increases to $0.30. Although the ban
generates a producer surplus for domestic producers, their gain is less than the loss of domestic
consumers.

shows the free-trade equilibrium: The domestic demand curve (which shows the
demand by U.S. consumers) intersects the total supply curve at a price of $0.12 per
pound and a quantity of 360 million pounds per day. Because this price is below the
minimum price for domestic firms, domestic firms do not supply any sugar to the
U.S. market.

What would happen if the United States banned sugar imports? Foreign suppliers would disappear from the market, so the total supply of sugar would consist
of only the domestic supply. In Panel B of Figure 6.7, the new equilibrium would
be shown by point *b*: The demand curve would intersect the domestic supply curve
at a price of $0.30 per pound and a quantity of 160 million pounds. The decrease
in supply resulting from the import ban would increase the price and decrease the
quantity. As a result, domestic firms would produce all the sugar for the domestic
market.

The import ban would ultimately decrease the total surplus in the sugar
market. The shaded areas in the two graphs show the consumer and producer
surpluses that would result with and without free trade. The import ban
decreases the U.S. consumer surplus, as shown by the two blue triangles in the
two graphs. The ban would also eliminate the producer surplus of foreign suppliers (shown by the red triangle in Panel A of Figure 6.7) and generate a producer surplus for domestic suppliers (shown by the red triangle in Panel B of
Figure 6.7). Therefore, the import ban would cause domestic producers to gain
at the expense of domestic consumers. Because consumers would lose more than
domestic producers would gain, the import ban would cause a net loss for people
in the United States.

APPLICATION

U.S. AND EUROPEAN CONSUMERS PAY FOR IMPORT RESTRICTIONS

APPLYING THE CONCEPTS #2: Who bears the cost of import restrictions?

Import restrictions are often defended on the grounds that they increase employment in the "protected" industries, such as apparel and steel. But the protection of these jobs increases consumer prices, so there is a trade-off: more jobs in the protected industry, but higher prices for consumers. According to one study, import restrictions in 1993 protected 56,464 jobs in the U.S. textile and apparel industries at a cost to consumers of about $178,000 per job and protected 3,419 jobs in the motor vehicle industry at a cost of about $271,000 per job. A study commissioned by the Swedish Ministry for Foreign Affairs concluded that import quotas imposed by the EU increased the cost of clothing for the typical family in the EU by about 270 euros per year. The quotas protected jobs in the domestic clothing industry, but the cost per job saved was about 41,000 euros per year.
Related to Exercises 4.1 and 4.12.

SOURCES: *The Economic Effects of Significant U.S. Import Restraints* (Washington, D.C.: U.S. International Trade Commission, initial report in 1993; update in 1996); Joseph F. François, Hans-Hinrich Glismann, Dean Spinanger, "The Cost of EU Trade Protection in Textiles and Clothing," Kiel Institute for World Economics, March 2000, p. 49.

6.5 | WHO REALLY PAYS TAXES?

In this part of the chapter, we'll look at the market effects of taxes and answer two important questions. First, who really bears the burden of a tax? As we'll see, it is not necessarily the person who actually pays the tax to the government. Second, is the total burden of a tax equal to the revenue collected by the government? As we'll see, a tax changes people's behavior, so the total burden actually exceeds the revenue collected.

Tax Shifting: Forward and Backward

We can use supply and demand curves to look at the market effects of taxes. Suppose that your city imposes a tax of $100 per apartment and collects the tax from housing firms— the firms that own apartment buildings and rent out the apartments. You may think the burden of the tax falls exclusively on the housing firm, because that's who mails the check to the government. But some simple supply and demand analysis will show why this is incorrect. The housing firm will charge more for apartments and pay less for its inputs, such as labor and land, so the tax will actually be paid by consumers and input suppliers.

Figure 6.8 shows the market effects of a $100 tax on apartments. As we saw earlier in the chapter, the market supply curve tells us how high the price must be to get producers to supply a particular quantity of output. The price must be high enough to cover all the costs of production. A unit tax increases the cost of production, so we need a higher price to get firms to produce any given quantity.

APPLICATION

3

SUPPLY AND DEMAND FOR HUMAN ORGANS

APPLYING THE CONCEPTS #3: What is the role of prices in allocating resources?

What is the economist's solution to the shortage of human organs for transplants? Sometimes governments go beyond simply reducing the quantity produced and outlaw market transactions entirely. Each year, thousands of Americans die waiting for replacement kidneys, hearts, livers, pancreases, and lungs. In the last decade, improvements in the effectiveness of organ transplants have increased the demand for used human organs. Because the supply hasn't increased along with demand, there are shortages of transplantable organs. In a normal market, the price would rise to eliminate the shortage, but because it is illegal to buy and sell human organs, there is no pricing mechanism to close the gap between the quantity supplied and the quantity demanded.

The conventional approach to the organ shortage is to appeal to people's generosity, urging them to commit their organs to the transplant program. The failure of this approach led Nobel-winning economist Gary Becker to suggest monetary incentives for organ donors. Under his proposal, the federal government would pay donors and their survivors for the organs they donate and would distribute the organs to hospitals for transplanting. This proposal raises all sorts of ethical questions and has not been embraced by many policy makers or health experts. *Related to Exercise 4.9.*

SOURCE: Gary S. Becker, "How Uncle Sam Could Ease the Organ Shortage," *BusinessWeek*, January 20, 1997, p. 18.

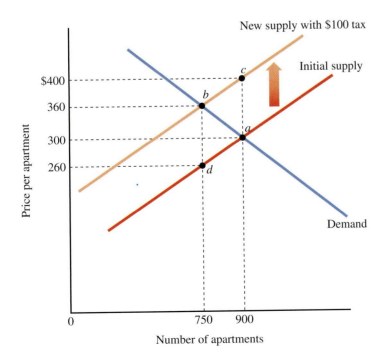

◀ **FIGURE 6.8**
The Market Effects of an Apartment Tax
A tax of $100 per apartment shifts the supply curve upward by the $100 tax, moving the market equilibrium from point *a* to point *b*. The equilibrium price increases from $300 to $360, and the equilibrium quantity decreases from 900 to 750 apartments.

In other words, the supply curve shifts upward by the amount of the tax. A unit tax of $100 per apartment increases a property owner's cost per apartment by $100, so the supply curve shifts upward by $100.

The shift of the supply curve increases the equilibrium price of apartments. At the $300 price, there will be an excess demand for apartments, and the price will increase to eliminate the excess demand. In Figure 6.8, the market moves from point *a* to point *b*: The demand curve intersects the new supply curve at a price of $360, compared to $300 before the tax. In other words, housing firms shift part of the tax forward onto consumers, who pay $60 of the $100 tax. Although housing firms pay the entire $100 tax in a legal sense, they get some of the money to pay the tax by charging consumers $60 more for apartments.

The apartment tax also affects the people who supply inputs such as land and labor to the housing industry. The tax decreases the output of the industry, so the industry needs smaller quantities of the inputs used to produce apartments. The resulting excess supply of inputs like labor and land will decrease land and labor prices, decreasing the cost of producing apartments. As a result, part of the $100 tax gets shifted backward onto input suppliers. Although housing firms pay the apartment tax in a legal sense, they get some of the money to pay the tax by paying less to workers and landowners.

Tax Shifting and the Price Elasticity of Demand

The amount of the tax shifted forward to consumers depends on the price elasticity of demand for the taxed good. If the demand for a taxed good is inelastic—meaning that consumers are not very responsive to price changes—we need a large price hike to eliminate the excess demand caused by the tax. Therefore, consumers will be hit by a large increase in price, and so they will pay the bulk of the tax. This is shown in Panel A of Figure 6.9. Demand is inelastic—that is, the demand curve is steep—so a $5 tax increases the equilibrium price by $4 (from $10 to $14). In other words, consumers pay four-fifths of the tax. In Panel B of Figure 6.9, demand is elastic—that is, the demand curve is relatively flat—so consumers pay just a small part of the tax. A $5 tax increases the equilibrium price by only $1 (from $10 to $11). In this case, consumers pay only one-fifth of the tax.

Why should we care about tax shifting? We've seen that a tax increases consumer prices and decreases input prices, so to determine who actually pays a tax, we must look beyond the actual taxpayer. As shown in the following application, the subtleties of tax shifting are often revealed by the objections of people who don't actually pay a tax in a legal sense.

► **FIGURE 6.9**

Elasticities of Demand and Tax Effects

If demand is inelastic (Panel **A**), a tax will increase the market price by a large amount, so consumers will bear a large share of the tax. If demand is elastic (Panel **B**), the price will increase by a small amount and consumers will bear a small share of the tax.

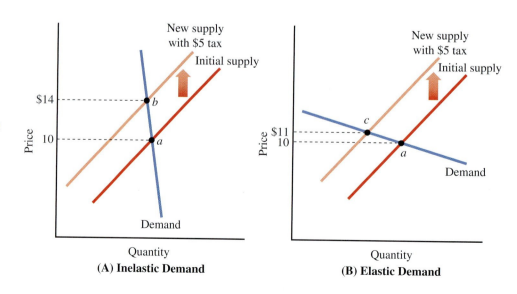

(A) Inelastic Demand

(B) Elastic Demand

Cigarette Taxes and Tobacco Land

In 1994, President Clinton proposed an immediate $0.75 per pack increase in the cigarette tax. The tax had two purposes: to generate revenue for Clinton's health-care reform plan and to decrease medical costs by discouraging smoking. Based on our discussion of the market effects of a tax, we would predict that the tax would be shared by consumers, who would pay higher prices, and the owners of land where tobacco is grown. It appears tobacco farmers and landowners understand the economics of cigarette taxes. Led by a group of representatives and senators from tobacco-growing areas in North Carolina, Kentucky, and Virginia, the Congress scaled back Clinton's proposed tax hike from $0.75 to $0.05. Although the government would have collected the tax from cigarette manufacturers, savvy tobacco farmers realized the tax would decrease the price of their tobacco-growing land.

Tax Burden and Deadweight Loss

We've seen that people respond to a tax by changing their behavior. As a result, the total burden of a tax will exceed the total amount of money the government actually collects from the tax. To see why, suppose the government imposes a tax on No. 3 pencils, and the tax is large enough that everyone who initially used No. 3 pencils switches to other types of pencils or other writing implements. If no one purchases No. 3 pencils, the tax won't raise any revenue for the government, but the tax still generates a burden because some people who would prefer to use No. 3 pencils have switched to other writing implements.

We'll use the fish market to explore the total burden of a tax. To simplify matters, let's assume that the supply curve for fish is horizontal, as shown in Figure 6.10. As we'll see later in the book, a supply curve will be horizontal if the prices of the inputs used in the industry don't change as the total output of the industry changes. For the fish market, this means that wages and the prices of bait and fuel don't change as the

4

APPLICATION

BOAT WORKERS AND THE TAX ON LUXURY BOATS

APPLYING THE CONCEPTS #4: Who bears the cost of a tax on luxury goods?

A lesson on backward shifting occurred when Congress passed a steep luxury tax on boats and other luxury goods in 1990. Under the new tax, a person buying a $300,000 boat paid an additional $20,000 in taxes. The burden of the tax was actually shared by consumers and input suppliers, including people who worked in boat factories and boatyards. The tax increased the price of boats, and consumers bought fewer boats. The boat industry produced fewer boats, and the resulting decrease in the demand for boat workers led to layoffs and lower wages for those who managed to keep their jobs. Although the idea behind the luxury tax was to "soak the rich," the tax actually harmed low-income workers in the boat industry. The tax was repealed a few years later.
Related to Exercise 5.5.

The Deadweight Loss or Excess Burden of a Tax

When the supply curve is horizontal, a tax increases the equilibrium price by the tax ($1 per pound in this example). Consumer surplus decreases by the areas *B* and *C*. Total tax revenue collected is shown by rectangle *B*, so the total burden exceeds tax revenue by triangle *C*. Triangle *C* is sometimes known as the deadweight loss or excess burden of the tax.

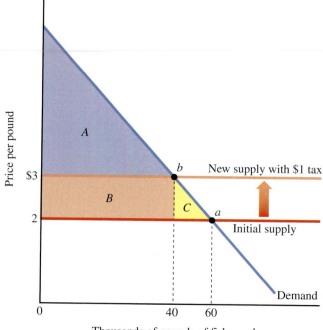

Thousands of pounds of fish per day

total fish harvest changes. The demand curve intersects the initial supply curve at point *a*, so the price is $2 per pound and the quantity is 60,000 pounds of fish per day.

Suppose the government imposes a tax of $1 per pound of fish, and the tax is paid in legal terms by producers. As we saw earlier, a unit tax shifts the market supply upward by the amount of the tax. As shown in Figure 6.10, a $1 tax on fish producers shifts the supply curve up by $1: Each firm now needs $3, not $2, to cover all of its costs, including the tax.

In Figure 6.10 the fish tax increases the equilibrium price of fish from $2 to $3. Why does the price increase by an amount equal to the tax? The supply curve is horizontal because input prices are fixed, regardless of how much output is produced. There is no opportunity to shift the tax backward onto input suppliers, so consumers bear the full cost of the tax.

We can use the concept of consumer surplus to determine just how much consumers lose as a result of the tax. Before the fish tax, the consumer surplus is shown by the area between the initial price line (and horizontal supply curve) and the demand curve, or areas *A*, *B*, and *C*. When the price increases to $3, the consumer surplus shrinks to the area of triangle *A*, so the loss of consumer surplus (the total burden of the tax) is shown by rectangle *B* and yellow triangle *C*. Let's take a closer look at these two areas.

- Rectangle *B* shows the extra money consumers must pay for the 40,000 pounds of fish they purchase. The tax increases the price by $1 per pound, so consumers pay an extra $40,000.

- Triangle *C* shows the loss of consumer surplus on the fish that are not consumed because of the tax. Consumers obey the law of demand, so when the price rises, they cut their purchases, buying 20,000 fewer pounds of fish. As a result, they give up the consumer surplus they would have received on these 20,000 pounds of fish.

How does the total burden of the tax compare to the tax revenue raised by the government? The total tax revenue is the tax per pound ($1) times the quantity consumed (40,000 pounds), or $40,000. This is shown by rectangle *B*: Part of the loss experienced by consumers is the revenue gain for government. But in addition to losing rectangle *B*, consumers also lose triangle *C*, so the consumer's total burden of the tax exceeds the tax revenue. Triangle *C* is sometimes known as the **deadweight loss from taxation** or the **excess burden of a tax**.

- **deadweight loss from taxation**
The difference between the total burden of a tax and the amount of revenue collected by the government.

- **excess burden of a tax**
Another name for deadweight loss.

APPLICATION

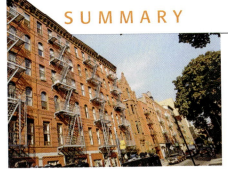

TAXES AND DECEMBER BABIES

APPLYING THE CONCEPTS #5: How do taxes affect behavior?

Why are so many babies born in the last week of December? The essential reason for excess burden is that taxes cause people to change their behavior, making choices to avoid taxes. The current tax law includes a tax credit for children: A child born on or before December 31 reduces the household's tax liability in that year and every subsequent year until the child reaches 18. A recent study shows that the higher the tax credit, the larger the percentage of children born in the last week of the year and the smaller the percentage of children born in the first week of the year. It appears that some couples time the births of their children to take advantage of the tax credit. The authors estimate that increasing the tax benefit of having a child by $500 raises the probability of having the child in the last week of December by about 27 percent. ***Related to Exercises 5.1 and 5.11.***

SOURCE: Stacy Dickert-Conlin and Amitabh Chandra, "Taxes and the Timing of Births," *Journal of Political Economy,* vol. 107, February 1999, pp. 161–77.

In the example shown in Figure 6.10, we used a horizontal supply curve to simplify matters and make the analysis of deadweight loss transparent. In a market with a positively sloped supply curve, a tax generates a deadweight loss, but the analysis is a bit more complex. For students interested in a challenge, one of the problems at the end of the chapter deals with deadweight loss for the apartment market, a market with a positively sloped supply curve.

SUMMARY

In this chapter, we discussed the efficiency of markets and the consequences of government intervention in perfectly competitive markets. In a market without external benefits or costs, government intervention prevents consumers and producers from executing beneficial transactions and thus decreases the total surplus of the market. We also saw that taxes affect the prices of consumer goods and inputs. To determine who actually bears the cost of a tax, we must look beyond the taxpayer. Here are the main points of the chapter:

1 The *total surplus* of a market equals the sum of consumer surplus and producer surplus.

2 In a market that meets the four efficiency conditions (no external cost, no external benefit, perfect information, perfect competition), the market equilibrium maximizes the total surplus and is therefore efficient.

3 Price controls reduce the total surplus of a market because they prevent mutually beneficial transactions.

4 Quantity controls (such as licensing and import restrictions) decrease consumer surplus and the total surplus of the market.

5 A tax on a good may be shifted forward onto consumers and backward onto input suppliers.

6 Because a tax causes people to change their behavior, the total burden of the tax exceeds the revenue generated by the tax.

KEY TERMS

consumer surplus, p. 131

deadweight loss, p. 136

deadweight loss from taxation, p. 146

efficiency, p. 130

excess burden of a tax, p. 146

price ceiling, p. 133

price floor, p. 134

producer surplus, p. 132

total surplus, p. 132

willingness to accept, p. 131

willingness to pay, p. 131

EXERCISES  Visit www.myeconlab.com to complete
Get Ahead of the Curve   these exercises online and get instant feedback.

6.1 | Consumer Surplus and Producer Surplus

1.1 Consumer surplus equals _____ minus _____.

1.2 Producer surplus equals _____ minus _____.

1.3 In Figure 6.1 on page 131, Tupak's consumer surplus is _____, compared to _____ for Thurl.

1.4 In Figure 6.2 on page 132, Bea's producer surplus is _____, compared to _____ for Dee.

1.5 As the market price increases, consumer surplus _____ (increases/decreases) and producer surplus _____ (increases/decreases).

1.6 For a given market price, a consumer who is on the high end of the demand curve has a _____ consumer surplus than a consumer on the low end of the demand curve.

1.7 For a given market price, a producer who is on the low end of the supply curve has a _____ producer surplus than a producer on the high end of the supply curve.

6.2 | Market Equilibrium and Efficiency

2.1 You are willing to pay $2,000 to have your house painted, and Pablo's marginal cost of painting a house is $1,400. If you agree to split the difference, the price is _____, your consumer surplus is _____, and Pablo's producer surplus is _____.

2.2 In Figure 6.4 on page 134, Forest is willing to pay _____ for the fourth cut lawn, and Dee's marginal cost is _____. If they split the difference, the price would be _____ and each would get a surplus of _____.

2.3 In Figure 6.4 on page 134, a maximum price of $4 prevents mutually beneficial transactions between Thurl and _____ and between Forest and _____.

2.4 Fill in the blanks with "consumers" or "producers." A maximum price below the equilibrium price generates benefits for some _____ and imposes costs on some _____ and some _____.

2.5 Fill in the blanks with "consumers" or "producers." A minimum price above the equilibrium price generates benefits for some _____ and imposes costs on some _____ and some _____.

2.6 **Identify the Surpluses.** The following graph shows a supply curve and a demand curve and several areas between the curves. Identify the areas on the figure that represent the following:

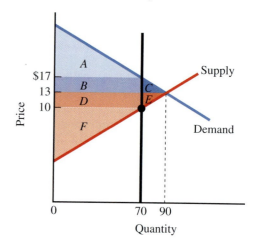

a. Consumer surplus in the market equilibrium

b. Producer surplus in the market equilibrium

c. Total surplus in the market equilibrium

d. Consumer surplus under a maximum price of $10

e. Producer surplus under a maximum price of $10

f. Total surplus under a maximum price of $10

g. Consumer surplus under a maximum quantity of 70

h. Producer surplus under a maximum quantity of 70

i. Total surplus under a maximum quantity of 70

6.3 | Controlling Prices—Maximum and Minimum Prices

3.1 Arrow up or down: In Figure 6.5 on page 136, rent control _____ the quantity of apartments, _____ producer surplus, _____ consumer surplus, and _____ the total market surplus.

3.2 In Figure 6.5 on page 136, rent control prevents a total of _____ mutually beneficial transactions for consumers on the demand curve between points _____ and _____ and producers on the supply curve between points _____ and _____.

3.3 In Figure 6.5 on page 136, suppose rent control is partly relaxed, with the maximum price rising from $300 to $350. The quantity of apartments on the market will increase from _____ to _____.

3.4 In Figure 6.5 on page 136, a consumer who is on the demand curve halfway between points *c* and *a* would be willing to pay $_____ above the controlled price to get an apartment.

3.5 In Figure 6.5 on page 136, a producer who is on the supply curve halfway between points *b* and *a* would be willing to supply an apartment at a price of $_____, or _____ above the maximum price.

3.6 **Excess Supply from a Minimum Milk Price.** In the equilibrium in the powdered milk market, the quantity is 100 million units and the price is $9.00 per unit. The price elasticity of demand is 0.80 and the price elasticity of supply is 2.50. Suppose the government imposes a minimum price of $9.90. (Related to Application 1 on page 138.)

a. Draw a graph to show the market effects of the minimum price.

b. At the minimum price, the quantity of powdered milk supplied is _____ million units, the quantity demanded is _____ million units, and the excess supply is _____ million units.

3.7 **No Deadweight Loss from Rent Control?** Like other fruit flies, Frudo has an expected life span of 37 days. According to Frudo, "If my assumptions are correct, a rent-control law implemented today will simply redistribute income from property owners to consumers. There will be no deadweight loss, at least not in my lifetime."

a. What is Frudo's key assumption?

b. Draw a complete graph to show his assumption and logic.

c. The typical elephant has an expected life span of 60 years. How would its analysis of rent control differ from Frudo's? Illustrate with a complete graph.

3.8 **Price Controls for Medical Care.** Consider a town where the equilibrium price of a doctor's visit is $60 and the equilibrium quantity supplied is 90 patient visits per hour. For suppliers (doctors), each $1 increase in price increases the quantity supplied by two visits. For consumers, each $1 increase in price decreases the quantity demanded by one visit. Suppose that in an attempt to control the rising costs of medical care the government imposes price controls, setting a maximum price of $50 per visit.

a. Use a completely labeled graph to show the effects of the maximum price on (i) the quantity of visits to doctors and (ii) the total surplus of the market.

b. What sort of inefficiencies does the price control cause?

c. Would you expect patients and doctors to find ways around the maximum price?

3.9 **Gasoline Price Controls.** The equilibrium price of gasoline is $3, and the equilibrium quantity is 100 million gallons per day. Suppose the government sets a maximum price of $2.90. For producers, each $0.01 increase in price increases the quantity supplied by 3 million gallons.

a. Draw a graph to show the effects of the maximum price on the gasoline market. Label the initial equilibrium point as *a* and the point that shows the quantity supplied under the maximum price as *b*.

b. How does the maximum price affect the quantity of gasoline sold?

6.4 | Controlling Quantities—Licensing and Import Restrictions

4.1 For each apparel job protected by import restrictions, consumers pay $_____ more for apparel. (Related to Application 2 on page 142.)

4.2 In Figure 6.6 on page 139, the taxi medallion policy changes consumer surplus from $_____ to $_____, changes producer surplus from $_____ to $_____ and changes the total surplus of the market from $_____ to $_____.

4.3 In Figure 6.6 on page 139, the deadweight loss is shown by the area of triangle _____, which equals $_____.

4.4 In Figure 6.6 on page 139, the taxi medallion policy prevents mutually beneficial transactions for consumers on the demand curve between points _____ and _____ and producers on the supply curve between points _____ and _____.

4.5 In Figure 6.6 on page 139, suppose the taxi medallion policy is tightened, with the number of medallions reduced from 80 to 60. The price of taxi service will increase from $_____ to $_____.

4.6 In Figure 6.6 on page 139, a consumer who is on the demand curve halfway between points *c* and *a* would be willing to pay $_____ for a mile of taxi service, while a supplier who is halfway between points *b* and *a* on the supply curve would be willing to supply a mile of taxi service at a price of $_____.

4.7 In Figure 6.7 on page 141, domestic firms will produce _____ tons of sugar a price of $0.15, _____ tons at a price of $0.30, and _____ tons at a price of $0.28.

4.8 Arrow up or down: An import ban _____ the price of sugar, _____ the total (market) quantity of sugar, and _____ the quantity of sugar produced by domestic firms.

4.9 **Equilibrium and Surplus in a Liver Market.** The following table shows different points on the linear supply curve and linear demand curve for livers for transplant. (Related to Application 3 on page 143.)

Price	Quantity Supplied	Quantity Demanded
$0	50	200
2,000	70	160
5,000	100	100
7,000	120	60
10,000	150	0

a. Draw the two curves and show the market equilibrium. The equilibrium price is $_____, and the equilibrium quantity is _____ livers.

b. On your graph, show the total surplus of the liver market—the sum of consumer and producer surplus.

c. Suppose the government bans the buying and selling of livers. On your graph, show the new equilibrium quantity of livers and the resulting loss in the total value of the market.

4.10 **Barber Licensing.** Consider the market for haircuts in a city. In the market equilibrium, the price per haircut is $6 and the quantity is 240 haircuts per day. For consumers, each $1 increase in price decreases the quantity demanded by 20 haircuts. For producers, each $1 increase in price increases the quantity supplied by 60 haircuts. In the market equilibrium, there are 24 barbers, each of whom produces 10 haircuts per day. Suppose the city passes a law requiring all barbers to have a license and then issues only 18 barber licenses. Each licensed barber continues to provide 10 haircuts per day. Use a completely labeled graph to show the effects of licensing on (a) the price of haircuts and (b) the total surplus in the haircut market.

4.11 **Bidding for a Boston Taxi Medallion.** In 1997, there were 1,500 taxi medallions in the city of Boston, and each medallion generated a profit of about $14,000 per year. In 1998, the city announced that it would issue 300 new taxi medallions, auctioning the new medallions to the highest bidders.[3] Even with the new medallions, the number of taxis in the city would still be less than the number that would occur in an unregulated market. Your job is to predict the annual profit from a medallion after the new medallions were issued. To predict the new annual profit, assume the following:

- The cost of providing taxi service is constant at $2.00 per mile of service.
- The initial price of taxi service (with 1,500 medallions issued) is $2.14 per mile.
- Each taxi (or medallion) provides 100,000 miles of service per year, so issuing the 300 new medallions increases the total quantity of taxi service from 150 million miles to 180 million miles.

- The slope of the demand curve is –$0.001 per million miles: For each $0.001 decrease in the price of taxi service, the quantity demanded increases by one million miles.

a. Compute the new price of taxi service.

b. Compute the new profit per medallion.

4.12 **Import Ban for Kiwi Fruit.** Initially, there are no restrictions on importing kiwi fruit. The minimum supply price of domestic producers is $0.26, while the minimum supply price of foreign suppliers is $0.08. Each supply curve is linear, with a slope of $0.01 per million pounds. In the initial equilibrium, the price is $0.18 and the quantity is 10 million pounds. The demand curve has a vertical intercept of $0.38 and a slope of –$0.02 per million pounds. (Related to Application 2 on page 142.)

a. Draw a graph showing the initial equilibrium.

b. Suppose imports are banned, raising the price to $0.30. Draw a graph to show the new equilibrium and identify the new equilibrium quantity.

c. Compute the consumer surplus before the import ban and after the ban.

d. Suppose the import ban protects 10 jobs in the kiwi fruit industry. What is the cost to consumers for each job protected?

6.5 | Who Really Pays Taxes?

5.1 The reason so many babies are born in the last week of December is that the government offers a _____ for each child born before the end of the year. (Related to Application 5 on page 147.)

5.2 A tax paid in legal terms by producers will be partly shifted forward onto _____ and partly shifted backward onto _____.

5.3 Arrow up or down: As the price elasticity of demand increases, the size of the price increase resulting from a tax _____ and the share of the tax borne by consumers _____.

5.4 The demand for coffee is relatively inelastic. Therefore, we would expect _____ to pay a relatively large share of a tax on coffee.

5.5 **The Employment and Wage Effects of a Luxury Boat Tax.** Suppose the luxury boat industry initially employs 1,000 workers and produces 100 boats per month. Suppose a tax on luxury boats increases the equilibrium price from $300,000 to $345,000. The price elasticity of demand for luxury boats is 2.0. (Related to Application 4 on page 145.)

a. The luxury tax increases the equilibrium price of boats by _____ percent, so it decreases the quantity of boats demanded from 100 to _____. If builders continue to employ 10 workers for each boat, the number of boat workers decreases from 1,000 to _____.

b. Suppose the workers in the industry respond to the luxury boat tax by agreeing to take a wage cut that decreases the cost of producing boats by 5 percent. In addition, suppose firms pass on the savings in labor costs to boat consumers. The wage reduction decreases the price of boats by _____ percent and increases the quantity of boats demanded from _____ to _____. If builders continue to employ 10 workers for each boat, the number of boat workers is _____.

5.6 **Shifting a Housecleaning Tax.** Consider a city where poor people clean the houses of rich people. Initially, housecleaning firms charge their customers $10 per hour, keep $1 per hour for administrative costs, and pay their workers $9 per hour. Like many luxury goods, the demand for housecleaning service is very elastic. Housecleaning workers are not very responsive to changes in the wage.
   a. Use supply and demand curves to show the initial equilibrium in the market for cleaning services (price = $10 per hour; quantity = 1,000 hours of cleaning per week), and label the equilibrium as point *a*.
   b. Suppose the city imposes a tax of $3 per hour of cleaning services, and one-third of the tax is shifted forward to consumers. Use your graph to show the effects of the tax on the housecleaning market. Label the new equilibrium as point *b*. What is the new price?
   c. Is it reasonable that only one-third of the tax is shifted forward? Explain.
   d. Suppose that firms continue to keep $1 per hour for administrative costs. Predict the new wage.
   e. Who bears the bulk of the housecleaning tax, wealthy households or poor ones?

5.7 **Effects of a Higher Fish Tax.** In Figure 6.10 on page 146, suppose the fish tax is $2 per pound of fish instead of $1. Draw a graph to show the effect of the $2 tax. In the new equilibrium, the price is $_____, the quantity is _____, and the deadweight loss from the tax is $_____.

5.8 **Projecting Tax Revenue.** You are a tax analyst in Washington, D.C., and have been asked to predict how much revenue will be generated by the city's gasoline tax. Suppose that initial quantity of gasoline is 100 million gallons per month and the price elasticity of demand for gasoline in the typical large city is 4.0. The tax, which is $0.10 per gallon, will increase the price of gasoline by 5 percent.
   a. How much revenue will the gasoline tax generate?
   b. In 1980, tax analysts in Washington, D.C., based their revenue predictions for a gasoline tax on the elasticity of demand for gasoline in the United States as a whole. Would you expect the analysts to overestimate or underestimate the revenue from the gasoline tax?

5.9 **Luxury Tax on Cars.** Under a special luxury tax passed by Congress, buyers of expensive cars pay a 10-percent tax on the portion of the purchase price above $30,000.
   a. Will the luxury car tax be paid exclusively by the wealthy consumers who buy expensive cars?
   b. What information do you need to determine the share of the taxes paid by wealthy consumers?

5.10 **Tax Eliminates a Market?** Use a supply and demand graph to show a situation in which a tax on No. 3 pencils reduces the equilibrium quantity of No. 3 pencils to zero.

5.11 **Donating a Car.** You have decided to get a new car and donate your old car to a charitable organization in either December or January. By donating your car, you'll get a tax deduction that will reduce that year's taxes by $3,000. Suppose the interest rate is 8 percent. If you could save $100 on the price of a new car by waiting until January, will you buy in December or wait until January? (Related to Application 5 on page 147.)

ECONOMIC EXPERIMENT

Government Intervention

Recall the market equilibrium experiment from Chapter 4. We can modify that experiment to show the various forms of government intervention in the market. After several trading periods without any government intervention, you can change the rules as follows:

- The instructor sets a maximum price for apples.
- The instructor sets a minimum price for apples.
- The instructor issues licenses to a few lucky producers.
- The instructor divides producers into domestic producers and foreign producers, and some of the foreign producers are excluded from the market.

NOTES

1. J. K. Smith, "An Analysis of State Regulations Governing Liquor Store Licensees," *Journal of Law and Economics*, October 1982, pp. 301–319; David Kirp and Eileen Soffer, "Taking Californians to the Cleaners," *Regulation*, September–October 1985, pp. 24–26.

2. D. W. Taylor, "The Economic Effects of Direct Regulation of Taxicabs in Metropolitan Toronto," *Logistics and Transportation Review*, June 1989, pp. 169–182; Laura Brown, "Hub Cabbie Hopefuls Cry: The Russians Are Coming!" *Boston Herald*, December 16, 1998, p. 1.

3. Laura Brown, "Hub Cabbie Hopefuls Cry: The Russians Are Coming!" *Boston Herald*, December 16, 1998, p. 1.

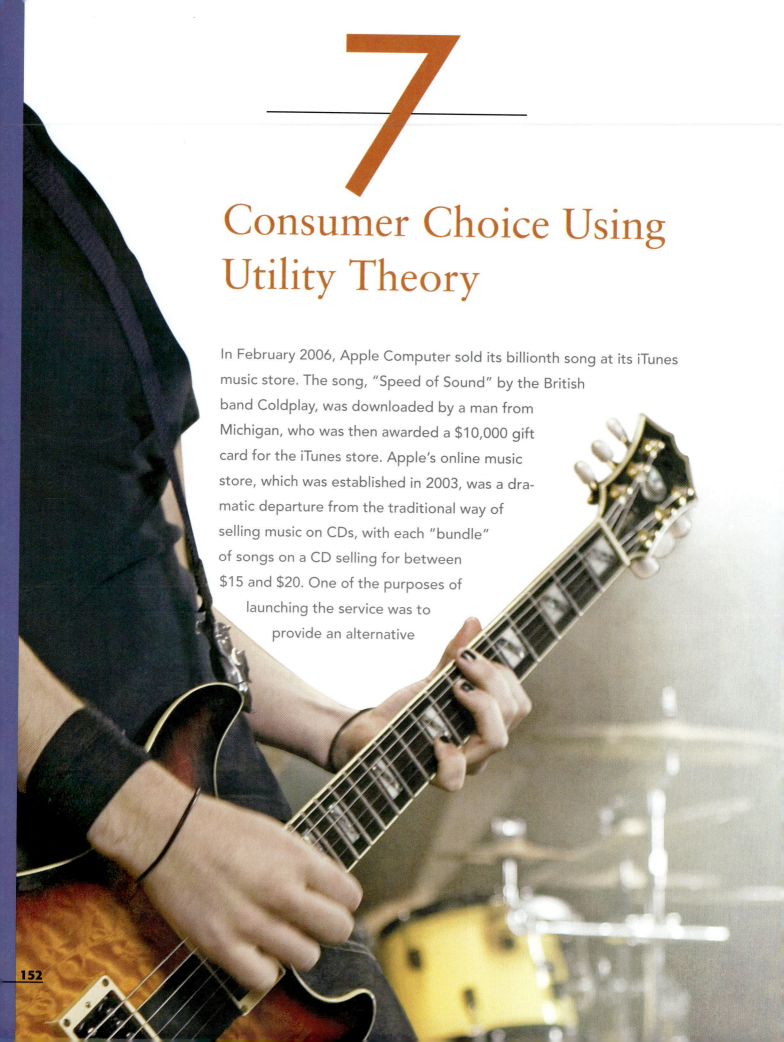

7

Consumer Choice Using Utility Theory

In February 2006, Apple Computer sold its billionth song at its iTunes music store. The song, "Speed of Sound" by the British band Coldplay, was downloaded by a man from Michigan, who was then awarded a $10,000 gift card for the iTunes store. Apple's online music store, which was established in 2003, was a dramatic departure from the traditional way of selling music on CDs, with each "bundle" of songs on a CD selling for between $15 and $20. One of the purposes of launching the service was to provide an alternative

APPLYING THE CONCEPTS

1 How does a tax on one good affect the demand for substitute goods?
   New Zealand's Tax on Light Spirits

2 Why do consumers dislike the bundling of goods?
   Online Music Stores and Piracy

3 How do consumers respond to offsetting changes in taxes?
   The Substitution Effect of a Gas Tax Decreases Gas Consumption

4 How does inflation affect the typical consumer?
   Inflation Doesn't Change Consumption or Utility

5 How could a firm use the insights from consumer theory to make decisions?
   Television Versus Radio Advertising

to Internet music piracy for people who wanted just a few songs, not an entire CD. In designing the online music store, the folks at Apple Computer applied some of the basic concepts of consumer choice, although they might not have realized it.

• **utility**
The satisfaction experienced from consuming a good.

• **util**
One unit of utility.

• **marginal utility**
The change in total utility from one additional unit of a good.

▶ **FIGURE 7.1**

Total Utility and Marginal Utility
In Panel A, the total utility or satisfaction from downloaded songs increases with the number of songs, but at a decreasing rate. In Panel B, the marginal utility from songs decreases as the number of songs increases.

I̲n Chapter 4, we introduced the law of demand and showed how it generates negatively sloped demand curves. In this chapter, we'll use the theory of consumer choice to provide the economic logic behind the law of demand and negatively sloped demand curves. The theory of consumer choice is based on the notion that consumers do the best they can, given the limitations dictated by their incomes and prices. As we'll see, every point on a demand curve represents the best choice for a consumer.

7.1 | TOTAL AND MARGINAL UTILITY

We'll start our discussion of consumer choice with the concept of **utility**, defined as the satisfaction experienced from consuming a good. Utility is difficult to measure: We can't hook a consumer up to a utility meter to determine how much happier she is after watching a movie. Nonetheless, suppose we can measure the consumer's benefit as the number of utils generated by the good (a **util** is one unit of utility or satisfaction).

Panel A of Figure 7.1 shows the relationship between the number of songs downloaded and the total utility from the songs. As the number of songs increases, total utility increases, but at a decreasing rate. When the consumer gets the first song, total utility increases from zero to 17 utils (point *a* on the total utility curve). For the second song, utility increases from 17 to 26 utils (point *b*), so the second song increases utility by 9 utils (26 utils – 17 utils). Moving upward along the curve from point *c* to point *d*, the ninth song increases utility by only 2 utils (46 utils – 44 utils).

Panel B of Figure 7.1 shows the consumer's marginal utility curve. **Marginal utility** is the change in total utility resulting from getting one additional unit of a good.

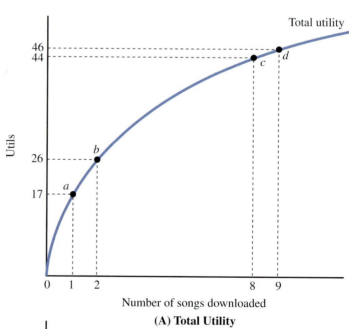

(A) Total Utility

(B) Marginal Utility

According to the **law of diminishing marginal utility**, as the consumption of a particular good increases, marginal utility decreases. In Panel B of Figure 7.1, the marginal utility drops from 17 utils (point *e* on the utility curve) for the first song, to 9 utils for the second song (point *f*), and so on down to 2 utils for the eighth song (point *g*).

7.2 | CONSUMER CHOICE

Let's consider the decisions of Maxine, a consumer who must decide how many movies and paperback books to buy each month. Maxine has a fixed income per month to spend on the two goods, so her options are limited by her budget. For every movie she watches, she sacrifices three books, and the opportunity cost of a movie is the foregone utility from the three books she could have bought instead. To decide how to spend her money, Maxine takes two steps:

1 She figures out her menu of options, the list of affordable combinations of books and movies.

2 She picks the affordable combination that generates the highest level of utility, or satisfaction. Her choice will reflect her own personal preferences and tastes.

We'll start with a discussion of Maxine's budget options, and then discuss her preferences.

Consumer Constraints: The Budget Line

Consider first the constraints faced by a consumer. Maxine's ability to purchase movies and other goods is limited by her income and the prices of movies and other products. Suppose Maxine has a fixed income of $30 per month, which she spends entirely on movies and used paperback books. The price of movies is $3 and the price of books is $1.

A consumer's **budget line** shows all the combinations of two goods that exhaust the consumer's budget. In Figure 7.2, if Maxine spends her entire $30 budget on books, she gets 30 books and no movies (point *a*). At the other extreme, she can spend her entire budget on movies, getting 10 of them at a price of $3 per movie (point *k*). The points between these two extremes are possible, too. For example, she could

◄ **FIGURE 7.2**
Budget Set and Budget Line
The budget set (the shaded triangle) shows all the affordable combinations of books and movies, and the budget line (with endpoints *a* and *k*) shows the combinations that exhaust the budget.

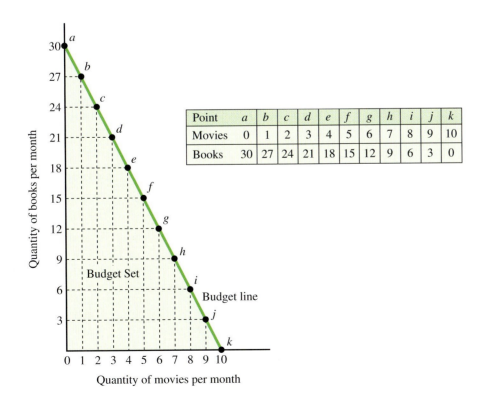

Point	a	b	c	d	e	f	g	h	i	j	k
Movies	0	1	2	3	4	5	6	7	8	9	10
Books	30	27	24	21	18	15	12	9	6	3	0

• **budget set**
The set of affordable combinations of two goods.

reach point *b* (1 movie and 27 books) by spending $3 on movies and $27 on books, or point *c* (2 movies and 24 books) by spending $6 on movies and $24 on books.

A consumer's **budget set** is the set of affordable combinations of two goods. The budget set includes the budget line—combinations that exhaust the budget—as well as combinations that cost less than the consumer has to spend, leaving the consumer with leftover money. In Figure 7.2, Maxine's budget set is shown as a shaded triangle. She can afford any combination on or below the budget line, but cannot afford combinations above it.

It's important to distinguish the budget line from a demand curve. Although the budget line may look similar to a consumer's demand curve, they are very different graphical tools. The budget line shows the different combinations of two goods that a consumer can buy. In contrast, the demand curve shows the quantity of a single good that a consumer is willing to buy at different prices.

Making Choices Using the Equimarginal Rule

• **equimarginal rule**
Pick the combination of two activities where the marginal benefit per dollar for the first activity equals the marginal benefit per dollar for the second activity.

Maxine's objective is to pick the point on her budget line that generates the highest level of satisfaction, or utility. To pick the best point, she can use the **equimarginal rule**.

$$\frac{\text{marginal utility of movies}}{\text{price per movie}} = \frac{\text{marginal utility of books}}{\text{price per book}}$$

EQUIMARGINAL RULE

Pick the combination of two activities where the marginal benefit per dollar for the first activity equals the marginal benefit per dollar for the second activity.

Table 7.1 shows how the equimarginal rule works for a consumer. The benefit of consuming a good is the utility generated by the good, so the marginal benefit of a good is the marginal utility. The second and third columns show different points on Maxine's budget line: As we move down through the table, we are moving downward along the budget line. The fourth column shows, for each point on the budget line, the marginal utility of movies. As we move down through the table, the quantity of movies increases. Under the assumption of diminishing marginal utility, the marginal utility of movies decreases as the number of movies increases. For example, the marginal utility of the first movie is 48 utils, and the marginal utility of the second movie is 45 utils.

The fifth column in Table 7.1 shows the marginal utility of books at different points on the budget line. At point *b*, Maxine gets a large number of books (27), so the marginal utility from an additional book is relatively low (6 utils). As we move down through the table, the quantity of books *decreases*, so the marginal utility of books

Table 7.1 | USING THE EQUIMARGINAL RULE

Point	Quantity		Marginal Utility		Marginal Utility per Dollar		Total Utility		
1	2	3	4	5	6	7	8	9	10
Point	Movies	Books	Movies	Books	Movies: Price = $3	Books: Price = $1	Movies	Books	Total
b	1	27	48	6	16	6	48	558	606
c	2	24	45	8	15	8	93	540	633
d	3	21	42	10	14	10	135	516	651
e	**4**	**18**	**36**	**12**	**12**	**12**	**171**	**486**	**657**
f	5	15	30	18	10	18	201	450	651
g	6	12	24	24	8	24	225	396	621
h	7	9	18	30	6	30	243	324	567
i	8	6	12	36	4	36	255	234	489
j	9	3	6	42	2	42	261	126	387

increases. The marginal utility of the 24th book is 8 utils (point *c*), compared to 10 utils for the 21st book (point *d*) and 24 utils for the 12th book (point *g*).

Columns 6 and 7 in Table 7.1 show the marginal utility per dollar for the two goods. At point *b*, the marginal utility of movies is 48 utils and the movie price is $3, so the marginal utility per dollar is $16. Moving downward through the table, the marginal utility per dollar decreases because the larger the number of movies, the smaller the marginal utility of movies. The marginal utility per dollar decreases to 14 utils for point *d*, to 12 utils for point *e*, and so on down to 8 utils for point *g*. As shown in column 7, because the price of books is $1, the marginal utility per dollar of books equals the marginal utility of books. As we move down through the table, the marginal utility per dollar *increases* as the quantity of books *decreases*. The popular term for the marginal utility per dollar is the "bang per buck."

We're now ready to find the best point on the budget line. Suppose we start at point *b* and see if Maxine could do better. At point *b* (1 movie and 27 books), the marginal utility per dollar on movies (16 utils) exceeds the marginal utility per dollar on books (6 utils). In other words, movies generate a larger bang per buck (16 utils versus 6 utils), so it would be sensible to buy more movies and fewer books. If Maxine moves to point *c* (2 movies and 24 books), the marginal utility per dollar of movies (15 utils) still exceeds the marginal utility per dollar of books (8 utils), so she should

APPLICATION

1

NEW ZEALAND'S TAX ON LIGHT SPIRITS

APPLYING THE CONCEPTS #1: How does a tax on one good affect the demand for substitute goods?

How did teenagers in New Zealand respond to a special tax on their favorite alcoholic beverage? We can use the equimarginal rule to explore New Zealand's recent experiences with taxing alcoholic beverages. Policy makers were concerned about teen drinking and discovered that the favored beverages among teens were "light spirits"—beverages with alcohol content between 14 and 24 percent. These light spirits provided the biggest alcoholic bang per buck for teens. For example, cheap rum with an alcohol content of 23 percent sold for $8, generating a bang per buck of 2.88 (equal to 23 divided by 8).

The government imposed a special tax on light spirits, nearly doubling the price of teens' favorite beverages, from $8 to $14. The tax decreased the bang per buck of light spirits to 1.64 (equal to 23 divided by 14) and teens responded by cutting back on light spirits. Producers responded by changing their beverage recipes, cutting the alcohol content to 13.9 percent to avoid the tax. Moreover, they priced these new "super-light" beverages below the prices of the original light beverages. For example, super-light rum with an alcohol content of 13.9 percent was priced at $7, yielding a bang per buck of 2.25—bigger than the 1.64 bang per buck from light beverages subject to the tax. Given the equimarginal rule, we would expect many teens to switch to super-light beverages, and that's exactly what happened. In addition, some teens went the other direction, switching to beverages that were too potent to be subject to the light-spirits tax.

The simple lesson is that consumers respond to taxes and changes in price. A tax decreases the bang per buck of the taxed good, causing consumers to switch to products that have a higher bang per buck than the taxed good. In the case of the light-spirit tax, the tax increased the consumption of beverages with lower and higher alcohol content.

Related to Exercises 2.1 and 2.9.

continue to move downward along the budget line. She will stop at point *e* because at this point (4 movies and 18 books), the marginal utility per dollar on the two goods is equal, at 12 utils per dollar:

$$\frac{\text{marginal utility of movies}}{\text{price per movie}} = \frac{\text{marginal utility of books}}{\text{price per book}}$$

$$\frac{36 \text{ utils}}{\$3} = \frac{12 \text{ utils}}{\$1}$$

In other words, the two goods generate the same bang per buck, so Maxine is maximizing her utility.

We can use the last three columns of Table 7.1 to verify that utility is maximized with 4 movies and 18 books. Column 8 shows the total utility from movies, which is 48 utils with one movie, 93 utils with two movies (equal to 48 for the first movie plus 45

APPLICATION

ONLINE MUSIC STORES AND PIRACY

APPLYING THE CONCEPTS #2: Why do consumers dislike the bundling of goods?

The chapter opener described the new online music stores, which provide an alternative to the traditional method of buying bundles of songs on CDs. We can use the theory of consumer choice to explain the logic behind this new development in the music business.

Consider Sam, who has $30 to spend on music and arcade games. In an ideal world, he could buy music by the song, just as he buys arcade games individually. Suppose the price of music in this ideal world is $1 per song and the price of arcade games is $0.50 per game. In Figure 7.3, Sam's budget line is the line connecting points *a* and *d* and all the points in between. He can spend his entire budget on games, getting 60 games (point *a*), or spend it all on songs, getting 30 songs (point *d*). Alternatively, he could divide his budget between the two goods. Suppose that in this ideal world, Sam's best point is *b*, where the marginal utility per dollar on songs equals the marginal utility per dollar on arcade games. At point *b*, Sam would get 6 songs and 48 arcade games.

Suppose that music cannot be purchased by the song but instead must be purchased on CDs. Each CD carries 15 songs and has a price of $15. In this case, Sam has only three options: He can spend his entire budget on games (60 games, as shown by point *a*), or he can get 1 CD with 15 songs and also get 30 games (point *c*), or he can spend his entire budget on 2 CDs (30 songs, point *d*). All of these points are inferior to point *b* because they all violate the equimarginal rule. His utility is maximized at point *b*, so if he must choose either zero songs or 15 songs, he will be worse off.

In the world of Internet file sharing, Sam actually has another option. He can use a swapping service to get songs for free. Of course, this swapping is illegal, and Sam risks a legal penalty and may also feel bad about breaking the law. If the benefit (free songs) exceeds the cost (risk of penalties and any bad feelings about breaking the law), he will engage in piracy.

Consider next the effects of iTunes and other online music services that sell single songs. Now Sam has a third alternative: He can get his ideal number of songs without any risk of criminal penalties. One motivation for online music stores is to reduce music piracy by people who want just a few songs off a particular CD. Of course, there are other motives for piracy, and piracy is expected to continue. But the experience with online music stores—over a billion songs sold—suggests that many consumers are willing to pay for music by the song. *Related to Exercises 2.2 and 2.10.*

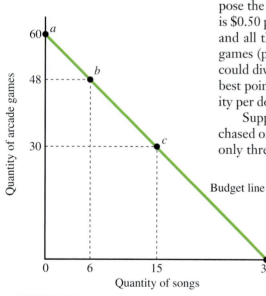

▲ **FIGURE 7.3**

Internet Music Piracy and iTunes
When music is sold as 15-song bundles on CDs, the consumer has three budget points (*a*, *c*, and *d*) rather than an entire budget line. If songs are sold individually, the consumer has a complete budget line and can legally reach his or her ideal combination of 6 songs and 48 arcade games (point *b*).

for the second), 135 utils for three movies, and so on. Column 9 shows the total utility from books. Starting at the bottom of the table, the utility from the first trio of books equals the marginal utility per book (42 utils) times 3 books, or 126 utils. Moving upward in column 9, the utility from books increases to 234 for 6 books (126 for the first trio of books plus 108 for the second trio), 324 utils for 9 books, and so on up to 558 for 27 books. Column 10 shows the total utility from movies and books together, the sum of the numbers in columns 8 and 9. The total utility reaches its maximum at point *e*, with 4 movies and 18 books. If we move from point *e* to point *f* (5 movies, 15 books), movie utility increases by 30 utils but book utility decreases by 36 utils, so total utility decreases by 6 utils, from 657 utils to 651 utils. Moving in the opposite direction from point *e*, we have fewer movies and more books, and utility again decreases. In other words, utility is maximized at point *e*, with 4 movies and 18 books.

What would happen if Maxine went too far, choosing point *f* instead of point *e*? At point *f* (5 movies, 15 books), books generate a larger bang per buck than movies. Once she noticed this, she would increase the number of books and reduce the number of movies, in the process moving upward along the budget line to point *e*. At this point, the two goods have the same bang per buck (marginal utility per dollar), so she cannot do any better.

7.3 | THE INDIVIDUAL DEMAND CURVE

As we saw in Chapter 4, the demand curve for an individual consumer is negatively sloped. The negative slope reflects the law of demand: The higher the price of a good, the smaller the quantity demanded. We can use the lessons from consumer theory to explain the economics behind the law of demand and the negatively sloped demand curve.

An individual demand curve shows the relationship between the price of a product and the quantity demanded by a rational consumer. In other words, the demand curve shows, for each price, the utility-maximizing quantity for the consumer. We already have one point on Maxine's demand curve for movies. When the price is $3, she maximizes utility by going to 4 movies. In Figure 7.4, this is shown by point *i* on her demand curve. This is the best Maxine can do when the price of movies is $3, her income is $30, and the price of books is $1.

The Income and Substitution Effects of a Price Change

Let's take a closer look at a consumer's response to a change in price. We will break down Maxine's response to a decrease in price into two effects:

- **Substitution effect.** A decrease in the price of movies decreases the price of movies relative to the price of other goods such as books. As movies become less costly relative to books, Maxine substitutes movies for books.

- **substitution effect**
The change in quantity consumed that is caused by a change in the relative price of the good, with real income held constant.

◄ **FIGURE 7.4**
The Individual Demand Curve
When the price of a movie is $3, Maxine maximizes utility at point *i*, with 4 movies. If the price drops to $2, she maximizes utility at point *j*, with 7 movies.

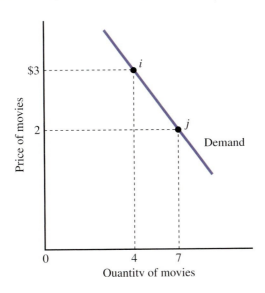

Table 7.2 | THE SUBSTITUTION EFFECT OF A PRICE CHANGE

For point *e* on the budget line: Movies = 4 and Books = 18

Marginal Utility		Marginal Utility per Dollar: Price of Movies = $3		Marginal Utility per Dollar: Price of Movies = $2	
Movies	Books	Movies	Books	Movies	Books
36	12	12	12	18	12

• **income effect**
The change in quantity consumed that is caused by a change in real income, with relative prices held constant.

- **Income effect.** A decrease in the price of movies increases Maxine's real income (the purchasing power of her nominal income), and she will buy more of all *normal* goods. If watching movies is a normal good, she will watch more movies.

To show the substitution effect, consider the following thought experiment. Suppose the price of movies decreases from $3 to $2 and at the same time Maxine's nominal income decreases from $30 to $26. In other words, her income drops by $4, which leaves her with just enough money that she can just afford her original bundle of 4 movies and 18 books:

$$\text{movie spending} = \$8 = 4 \text{ movies} \times \$2$$
$$\text{book spending} = \$18 = 18 \text{ books} \times \$1$$
$$\text{total spending} = \$26 = \$8 + \$18$$

Because the price reduction is exactly offset by a decrease in Maxine's nominal income, we say that her real income hasn't changed.

If Maxine can still afford her original bundle of goods, will she choose it? We can use the equimarginal rule to show that the bundle that was the best choice at a price of $3 is no longer the best choice when the price is only $2. In Table 7.2, the first four numbers (reading left to right) come from Table 7.1. When the price of movies is $3, Maxine chooses point *e*, where the marginal utility per dollar on movies equals the marginal utility per dollar on books (12 utils). The last two columns show what happens when the price of movies drops to $2. The marginal utility per dollar on movies is now higher (18 utils = 36 utils divided by $2), so Maxine's original choice no longer satisfies the equimarginal rule. Although she can still afford the original choice, she can do better. Given the larger bang per buck of movies, she will watch more movies and buy fewer books. In other words, given the lower relative price of movies, she substitutes movies for books—the substitution effect. For example, at the lower price she might watch 6 movies instead of only 4.

Consider next the income effect of a decrease in the price of movies. To observe the income effect, we simply restore Maxine's original nominal income of $30 and see how she responds. In other words, we "undo" the $4 reduction in income that we used to reveal the substitution effect. The change in movie consumption caused by the $4 increase in income is the income effect. When Maxine's income increases from $26 to $30, she will consume more of all normal goods. If watching movies is a normal good, she will use some of the extra money to watch more movies. For example, if she spends half of the additional $4 on movies, she will watch one more movie.

Points on the Demand Curve

We're ready to return to the individual demand curve shown in Figure 7.4. One point on the curve is point *i*, the combination of a price of $3 and a quantity of 4 movies. Given a movie price of $3, a book price of $1, and a budget of $30, that's the best Maxine can do, as shown in Table 7.1. Point *i* tells us that when the price of movies is $3, the utility-maximizing choice is 4 movies.

What happens when the price of movies decreases to $2? The net effect of the price change is the substitution effect *plus* the income effect. For example, suppose the substitution effect increases the quantity of movies from 4 to 6, and then the income effect increases the quantity of movies by 1 more. Adding the two effects, the decrease in price increases the quantity demanded by 3 movies, from 4 to 7. This is shown by a movement downward along the demand curve from point *i* to point *j*. The quantity demanded increases because the relative price of movies is lower (the substitution effect) and real income is higher (the income effect). For normal goods, the two effects work in the same direction, generating a negatively sloped demand curve that reflects the law of demand.

Although we haven't actually derived point *j* on the demand curve, we could do so by repeating the process that we used to derive point *i*. With a lower movie price of $2, Maxine would have a different budget line—a different set of affordable consumption

APPLICATION

THE SUBSTITUTION EFFECT OF A GAS TAX DECREASES GAS CONSUMPTION

APPLYING THE CONCEPTS #3: How do consumers respond to offsetting changes in taxes?

If the government raises the gasoline tax and cuts income taxes, will gasoline consumption decrease? Consider the following change in tax policy. Suppose the federal government imposes a new gasoline tax of $2 per gallon and simultaneously cuts income taxes. In other words, people will pay more in gasoline taxes, but less in income taxes. For the average taxpayer, the two changes in tax policy will exactly offset each other, leaving total taxes and net income after taxes unchanged. How will this change in tax policy affect gasoline consumption?

We can use a simple example to show the consumer response to the tax changes. Suppose the initial price of gasoline (before the tax) is $3 per gallon and the price of another good is $1 per unit. Consider a representative citizen, who initially maximizes utility by purchasing 1,000 gallons of gasoline per year. That's the quantity that satisfies the equimarginal rule. Because the price of gasoline is three times the price of the other good, the marginal utility of gasoline must be three times the marginal utility of the other good. For example, the marginal utility of gasoline is 12 utils, compared to 4 utils for the other good:

$$\frac{\text{marginal utility of gas}}{\text{price per gallon}} = \frac{\text{marginal utility of other good}}{\text{price per unit}}$$

$$\frac{12 \text{ utils}}{\$3} = \frac{4 \text{ utils}}{\$1}$$

How will the change in tax policy affect the citizen's utility-maximizing choice? Suppose the government combines the $2 gas tax with an income-tax cut of $2,000 per year, meaning that the citizen could still consume 1,000 gallons of gasoline and still have the same amount of money to spend on other goods: The $2,000 income-tax cut would exactly offset the $2,000 in extra gas taxes. Although the initial consumption bundle is affordable, the substitution effect tells us that the citizen won't choose it. Suppose the price of gasoline increases by the entire $2 tax, from $3 to $5. Using the equimarginal rule, the bang per buck of gasoline is now lower than the bang per buck for the other good, so the citizen will cut back on gasoline and spend more on the other good.

$$\frac{12 \text{ utils}}{\$5} < \frac{4 \text{ utils}}{\$1}$$

The decrease in gas consumption is the substitution effect in action. An increase in the relative price of gasoline, with real income held constant, reduces the consumption of gasoline as the consumer substitutes other goods for gasoline. The lesson from this application is that when a gas tax is combined with an offsetting cut in income taxes, the quantity of gasoline consumed will decrease because of the substitution effect.
Related to Exercises 3.1 and 3.6.

bundles. To find another point on the demand curve, we would create a new version of Table 7.1, and then find the combination of movies and books where the marginal utility per dollar for movies equals the marginal utility per dollar for books. That would give us the utility-maximizing quantity of movies when the price is $2—another point on the individual demand curve. In general, each point on a demand curve shows the utility-maximizing choice for a particular price.

7.4 | APPLICATIONS OF CONSUMER CHOICE

The theory of consumer choice explains the logic behind the law of demand and also provides a general framework for consumer decision making. In this part of the chapter, we use this framework to explore the consequences of inflation. We also show how the equimarginal rule could be used by a firm deciding how to split its advertising budget between radio and TV ads.

APPLICATION

INFLATION DOESN'T CHANGE CONSUMPTION OR UTILITY

APPLYING THE CONCEPTS #4: How does inflation affect the typical consumer?

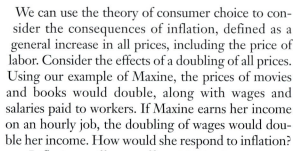

We can use the theory of consumer choice to consider the consequences of inflation, defined as a general increase in all prices, including the price of labor. Consider the effects of a doubling of all prices. Using our example of Maxine, the prices of movies and books would double, along with wages and salaries paid to workers. If Maxine earns her income on an hourly job, the doubling of wages would double her income. How would she respond to inflation?

Inflation will not affect Maxine's consumer decision because it won't affect her budget line. To see this, think about the horizontal and vertical intercepts of the budget line—the points where Maxine's budget line intersects the horizontal axis and the vertical axis. The horizontal intercept shows how many movies Maxine can buy if she spends her entire income on movies. Suppose inflation doubles her income from $30 to $60 and doubles the price of movies from $3 to $6. Before inflation, her $30 income could buy 10 movies at $3; after inflation, her $60 income can buy 10 movies at $6 each. Similarly, if the price of books doubles along with income, the vertical intercept won't change. Because her budget line doesn't change, her utility will be maximized at the same point, with the same combination of movies and books.

The implication of this analysis is that inflation doesn't harm or help Maxine. Inflation doesn't affect her budget set or her consumer choices, so she is just as well off as she was before inflation. This is an application of one of the five key principles of economics.

What matters to Maxine is her real income, which is unaffected by inflation because her nominal income doubles along with prices. *Related to Exercises 4.1 and 4.5.*

APPLICATION

5

TELEVISION VERSUS RADIO ADVERTISING

APPLYING THE CONCEPTS #5: How could a firm use the insights from consumer theory to make decisions?

The equimarginal rule is a general-purpose rule that can be used by any person or organization that has at least two alternative activities. For example, consider a firm that has a fixed amount of money to spend on advertising. The firm could use the equimarginal rule to pick the best mix of radio and television advertising. The benefit of advertising is the resulting increase in sales revenue, and the marginal benefit equals the increase in revenue from one more minute of airtime. Using the equimarginal rule, the firm would pick the combination of radio and TV advertisements where the bang per buck of radio equals the bang per buck of TV:

$$\frac{\text{marginal sales revenue from radio}}{\text{price of radio ad}} = \frac{\text{marginal sales revenue from TV}}{\text{price of TV ad}}$$

We can use a simple example to show how the firm could apply the equimarginal rule. Suppose the firm has a fixed advertising budget and initially uses 5 minutes of radio ads and 5 minutes of TV ads. Suppose an additional minute of radio advertising increases sales revenue by $5,000, and an additional minute of TV advertising increases sales revenue by $8,000. If the price of radio advertising is $1,000 per minute and the price of TV advertising is $4,000 per minute, the bang per buck of radio is 5, compared to only 2 for TV:

$$\frac{\$5,000}{\$1,000} > \frac{\$8,000}{\$4,000}$$

bang per buck for radio (5) > bang per buck for TV (2)

In this case, radio gives a bigger bang per buck, so it would be sensible to run more radio ads and fewer TV ads. The firm will continue to increase radio ads and decrease TV ads until the bang per buck for radio equals the bang per buck for TV. *Related to Exercises 4.2, 4.3, and 4.6.*

SUMMARY

In this chapter, we've used the theory of consumer choice to explain the economic logic behind the law of demand and the negatively sloped demand curve. The consumer's objective is to maximize utility, given an income and the prices of consumer goods. Here are the main points of the chapter:

1 The *law of diminishing marginal utility* says that as the consumption of a good increases, utility increases at a decreasing rate.

2 The theory of consumer choice has two steps: First, identify the affordable combinations of goods. Second, pick the affordable combination that maximizes utility.

3 The *equimarginal rule* tells us to pick the combination of two activities at which the marginal benefit per dollar for the first activity equals the marginal benefit per dollar for the second.

4 The individual demand curve is negatively sloped, reflecting the substitution effect and income effect of a change in price. A decrease in price decreases the relative price of the good, and consumers substitute the good for other goods (the *substitution effect*). A decrease in price also increases the consumer's real income, increasing the consumption of all normal goods (the *income effect*).

KEY TERMS

budget line, p. 155

budget set, p. 156

equimarginal rule, p. 156

income effect, p. 160

law of diminishing marginal utility, p. 155

marginal utility, p. 154

substitution effect, p. 159

util, p. 154

utility, p. 154

EXERCISES

Visit www.myeconlab.com to complete these exercises online and get instant feedback.

7.1 | Total and Marginal Utility

1.1 The total utility curve shows the relationship between _____ on the horizontal axis and _____ on the vertical axis.

1.2 In Figure 7.1 on page 154, if the total utility from 7 songs is 41 utils, the marginal utility of the eighth song is _____ utils, which is _____ than the marginal utility of the second song but _____ than the marginal utility of the ninth song.

1.3 Arrow up or down: As the consumption of a product increases, utility _____ at a _____ rate.

1.4 Arrow up or down: As we move upward along a total utility curve, the slope _____, meaning that marginal utility _____.

7.2 | Consumer Choice

2.1 Arrow up or down: When New Zealand imposed a tax on light beverages, the bang per buck of light beverages _____ and the bang per buck of super-light beverages _____. The consumption of super-light beverages _____. (Related to Application 1 on page 157.)

2.2 Arrow up or down: The selling of individual songs online rather than bundles of songs on CDs _____ the utility of the typical consumer and _____ the incentive for music piracy. (Related to Application 2 on page 158.)

2.3 Arrow up or down: Lawrence consumes harps (horizontal axis) and violins (vertical axis). As he moves downward along the budget line, the quantity of harps _____, the quantity of violins _____, marginal utility of harps _____, and the marginal utility of violins _____.

2.4 Lawrence maximizes his utility with 5 harps and 7 violins. The price of a violin is $100 and the price of a harp is $300. The marginal utility of harps is 600 utils. The marginal utility of violins is _____ utils.

2.5 Suppose a consumer has a fixed amount to spend each week on iTunes songs ($1 each) and movies ($6 each). For the combination she chose this week, the marginal utility of movies is 30 and the marginal utility of songs is 3. For next week she should _____ (increase/decrease) the number of songs and _____ (increase/decrease) the number of movies.

2.6 Rob has a weekly budget of $20 to spend on muffins (price = $2) and bagels (price = $1). This week he buys

4 muffins and _____ bagels. The marginal utility of muffins is 30 utils and the marginal utility of bagels is 10 utils. Next week, Rob should _____ (increase/decrease) the number of muffins and _____ (increase/decrease) the number of bagels.

2.7 In Table 7.1 on page 156, at point *g* the marginal utility of movies equals the marginal utility of books (at 24 utils). This is not the utility-maximizing point, because to maximize utility _____ is equal to _____.

2.8 Arrow up or down: A tax _____ the marginal utility per dollar on the taxed good, which _____ the consumption of the taxed good and _____ the consumption of untaxed goods.

2.9 **Choosing a Protein Beverage.** Consider a consumer who must choose between two protein drinks, A and B. The following table shows the protein content and prices for the two drinks. (Related to Application 1 on page 157.)
   a. Fill the blanks in the table. Which beverage generates the largest bang (protein content) per dollar? Which is the better choice for a consumer whose utility from the product depends only on the protein content?
   b. Suppose the government imposes a tax of $4 on beverage B, and the price increases by the amount of the tax. How will the consumer respond?

Drink	Protein Content	Price ($)	Bang per Buck
A	12	3	_____
B	30	6	_____

2.10 **Bundling TV Channels.** Your monthly budget for entertainment is $48, and your entertainment goods are cable TV and arcade games. The price of arcade games is $1 each. (Related to Application 2 on page 158.)
   a. Suppose the cable company has a price of $4 per channel. Draw your budget line.
   b. The following table shows the marginal utilities for different combinations of channels and games. Fill the blanks and find the utility-maximizing combination.

Quantity		Marginal Utility		Marginal Utility per Dollar	
Channels	Games	Channels	Games	Channels: Price = $4	Games: Price = $1
1	$44	6	50	_____	_____
2	40	8	44	_____	_____
3	**36**	**10**	**40**	_____	_____
4	32	12	36	_____	_____
5	28	18	32	_____	_____
6	24	24	28	_____	_____

c. Suppose the cable company switches from per-channel pricing to a bundle plan: you get 6 stations for a cost of $24 per month, but zero stations if you don't pay the full $24. In other words, the company tells you to take it (6 stations) or leave it (zero stations). Identify the new budget points on your graph. Does the switch make you worse off or better off?

2.11 **Utility-Maximizing Rides and Games.** Suppose the price of amusement rides is $2 and the price of a video arcade game is $1. The following table shows points on the budget line (given an income of $30) and the associated marginal utilities. Fill the blanks in the table. Then draw the budget line and find the utility-maximizing combination of rides and games.

Quantity		Marginal Utility		Marginal Utility per Dollar	
Rides	Games	Rides	Games	Rides: Price = $2	Games: Price = $1
1	28	10	50	_____	_____
2	26	14	42	_____	_____
3	24	18	36	_____	_____
4	22	26	26	_____	_____

2.12 **Consumer Consultant.** You have been hired to determine whether a consumer is maximizing his utility. He has a fixed budget of $2,500 per month to spend on food and housing. The price of food is $1 per pound, and the price of housing is $3 per square foot of living space. He currently lives in a 600-square foot apartment and spends $700 on food.
   a. You can ask your client two questions—only two. What are your questions?
   b. Your client's answers indicate that he is indeed maximizing utility. What are his answers?

2.13 **Consumer Metrics.** You are the economist for Consumer Metrics, a firm that has developed a device that measures the satisfaction level of a consumer before and after consuming a particular product. At the firm's annual holiday party, people ate cookies and punch, and the firm paid for everything. The price of a cookie is one-third the price of a unit of punch. By the end of the party, everything was consumed. Your job is to determine whether the firm spent its fixed party budget wisely, given its objective of maximizing the utility of the typical person at the party.
   a. If you could hook up the device to the typical person, what information would you collect?
   b. Give an example of information that would suggest the firm should have provided more cookies and less punch.

7.3 | The Individual Demand Curve

3.1 Arrow up or down: When a gasoline tax is offset by an income-tax cut that makes a consumer's original choice just affordable, gasoline consumption will _____ because the tax _____ the bang per buck of gasoline. (Related to Application 3 on page 161.)

3.2 An individual demand curve shows the relationship between _____ and _____, *ceteris paribus*.

3.3 Arrow up or down: The income effect is that a decrease in price _____ a consumer's real income and _____ the consumption of a normal good.

3.4 Arrow up or down: The substitution effect is that a decrease in the price of movies _____ the relative price of movies and _____ the consumption of movies.

3.5 Suppose Maxine initially watches 4 movies at a price of $3 and buys 18 books at a price of $1, and then the price of movies increases to $5. To make Maxine's original bundle just affordable, her income must increase to $_____. Her utility-maximizing consumption of movies will _____ because at the original bundle, _____ is now greater than _____.

3.6 **Response to the Gas Tax.** Petrov earns $10,000 in pretax income and initially pays $2,200 in income taxes and consumes 600 gallons of gasoline per year (at a price of $3 per gallon) and spends $6,000 on another good (at a price of $1 per unit). At the initial bundle of gas and the other good, the marginal utility of gas is 30 utils and the marginal utility of the other good is 10 utils. (Related to Application 3 on page 161.)

   a. Draw a complete graph showing Petrov's initial (before the gas tax) budget line and his initial choice. At his initial choice, the marginal utility per dollar on gasoline is _____ utils.

   b. Suppose the government imposes a new gasoline tax of $2 per gallon, and assume that the gas tax increases the price of gas to $5. To make his initial bundle of gasoline and other goods affordable after the $2 gas tax, Petrov's income tax must decrease by _____.

   c. After the tax changes, at his initial bundle, the bang per buck of gasoline is _____, compared to a bang per buck of _____ for the other good.

3.7 **Another Point on the Demand Curve.** Suppose the price of movies decreases from $3 to $2. Maxine's income is $30, and the price of books is $1. Fill the blanks in the following table. Then draw the budget line and find the utility-maximizing combination of movies and books.

Quantity		Marginal Utility		Marginal Utility per Dollar	
				Movies:	Books
Movies	Books	Movies	Books	Price = $2	Price = $1
1	____	54	3	____	____
2	____	50	5	____	____
3	____	46	7	____	____
4	____	42	9	____	____
5	____	38	11	____	____
6	____	34	13	____	____
7	____	30	15	____	____

3.8 **Shipping the Good Apples Out?** Suppose apples come in two quality levels, low and high. At a store in the apple-growing region, the price of low-quality apples is $1 per pound, and the price of high-quality apples is $4 per pound. Johnny lives in the apple-growing region, and buys 8 pounds of each type. His marginal utility of apples is 3 utils for low-quality apples and 12 utils for high-quality apples.

   a. Is Johnny maximizing his utility?

   b. Suppose Johnny moves to an area outside the apple-growing region. Shipping the apples to his new area adds $2 to the price of a pound of apples, for both low- and high-quality apples. To simplify matters, assume that his income increases by an amount large enough to fully offset the higher prices of apples. In other words, he can still afford the original bundle of 8 pounds of each type of apples. If he continues to buy 8 pounds of apples of each type, is he maximizing his utility? If not, how should he change his mix of high- and low-quality apples?

   c. What are the implications for the mix of high- and low-quality apples in apple-growing areas and other regions? Where will most of the high-quality apples be sold?

7.4 | Applications of Consumer Choice

4.1 Inflation does not affect a consumer's budget line because it increases _____ and _____ in the same proportions. (Related to Application 4 on page 162.)

4.2 If a firm has the best mix of radio and TV ads, _____ divided by _____ equals _____ divided by _____. (Related to Application 5 on page 163.)

4.3 Suppose the price of radio ads is $1,000 per minute and the price of TV ads is $4,000 per minute. Given a firm's tentative mix of radio and TV ads, the marginal sales revenue for radio is $3,000 and the marginal sales revenue for TV is $12,000. The bang per buck for radio is $_____ and the bang per buck of TV is $_____. The firm _____ (is/is not) satisfying the equimarginal rule. (Related to Application 5 on page 163)

4.4 If a firm's marginal benefit per dollar spent on Internet ads exceeds the marginal benefit per dollar spent on TV ads, a firm should _____ its use of Internet ads and _____ its use of TV ads.

4.5 **Higher Prices Versus Lower Income.** Recall the example of Maxine, who in January has an income of $30 and pays $3 per movie and $1 per book. (Related to Application 4 on page 162.)
   a. In February, the prices of movies and books double, but her income stays at $30. Draw her February budget line and shade her budget set.
   b. In March, her income is cut in half to $15, but the price of books returns to $1 and the price of movies returns to $3. Draw her March budget line and shade her budget set.
   c. Going from February to March, does her utility level increase, decrease, or stay the same? Explain.

4.6 **Allocating an Advertising Budget.** You are responsible for allocating a fixed advertising budget for your firm across seven different markets. Your budget is $12 million. The benefits and costs of advertising in the markets are shown in the following table (in millions of dollars):

Market	B	C	D	E	F	G	H
Benefit of advertising in market	$3	$14	$6	$15	$40	$30	$48
Cost of advertising in market	$1	$2	$2	$3	$4	$5	$6

   a. How would you allocate the fixed budget across the seven markets? What is the total benefit?
   b. Suppose you spent the $12 million budget in the markets with the least costly advertising campaigns. What is the total benefit? (Related to Application 5 on page 163.)

4.7 **Price and Income Changes.** Recall the example of Maxine, who has an income of $30 and pays $3 per movie and $1 per book. Use a graph to show the effects of the following changes on Maxine's budget line and budget set.
   a. The prices of both movies and books double, but her income doesn't change.
   b. The price of movies increases, but there are no changes in the price of books or her income.
   c. The price of movies increases to $5 and her income increases by $8. In this case, will her consumption of books increase, decrease, or stay the same?

APPLYING THE CONCEPTS

1 To determine whether a consumer is making the best choice, what single question can you ask?
What's Your MRS?

2 Why do consumers dislike the bundling of goods?
Online Music and Piracy

3 How does inflation affect the typical consumer?
Inflation Doesn't Change Consumption or Utility

4 How do consumers respond to offsetting changes in taxes?
The Substitution Effect of a Gas Tax Decreases Gas Consumption

In February 2006, Apple Computer sold its billionth song at its iTunes music store. The song, "Speed of Sound" by the British band Coldplay, was downloaded by a man from Michigan, who was then awarded a $10,000 gift card for the iTunes store. Apple's online music store, which was established in 2003, was a dramatic departure from the traditional way of selling music on CDs, with each "bundle" of songs on a CD selling for between $15 and $20. One of the purposes of launching the service was to provide an alternative to Internet music piracy for people who wanted just a few songs, not an entire CD. In designing the online music store, the folks at Apple Computer applied some of the basic concepts of consumer choice, although they might not have realized it.

In Chapter 4, we introduced the law of demand and showed how it generates negatively sloped demand curves. In this appendix, we'll use a model of consumer choice to provide the economic logic behind the law of demand and negatively sloped demand curves. The consumer-choice model is based on the notion that consumers do the best they can, given the limitations dictated by their incomes and prices. As we'll see, every point on a demand curve represents the best choice for a consumer.

7A.1 | CONSUMER CONSTRAINTS AND PREFERENCES

Let's consider the decisions of Maxine, a consumer who must decide how many movies and paperback books to buy each month. Maxine has a fixed income per month to spend on the two goods, so her options are limited by her budget. To decide how to spend her money, Maxine takes two steps:

1 She determines her menu of options, the list of alternative combinations of books and movies her budget allows.

2 She picks the combination of movies that generates the highest level of satisfaction.

To pick a combination from the menu, Maxine will carefully consider her own personal preferences and tastes. We'll start with a discussion of Maxine's budget options, and then discuss her preferences.

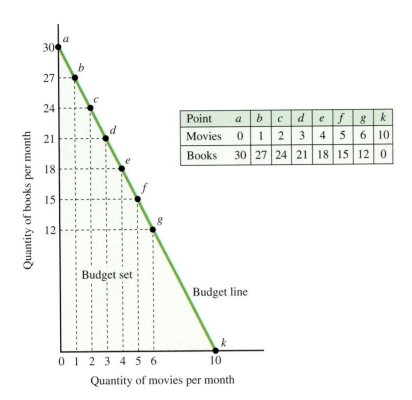

Point	a	b	c	d	e	f	g	k
Movies	0	1	2	3	4	5	6	10
Books	30	27	24	21	18	15	12	0

Budget Set and Budget Line
The budget set (the shaded triangle) shows all the affordable combinations of books and movies, and the budget line (with endpoints *a* and *k*) shows the combinations that exhaust the budget.

Consumer Constraints: The Budget Set and Budget Line

Consider first the constraints faced by a consumer. Maxine's ability to purchase movies and other goods is limited by her income and the prices of movies and other products. Suppose Maxine has a fixed income of $30 per month, which she spends entirely on movies and used paperback books. The price of movies is $3, and the price of books is $1.

A consumer's **budget line** shows all the combinations of two goods that exhaust the consumer's budget. In Figure 7A.1, if Maxine spends her entire $30 budget on books, she gets 30 books and no movies (point *a*). At the other extreme, she can spend her entire budget on movies, getting 10 of them (point *k*). The points between these two extremes are possible, too. For example, she could reach point *b* (one movie and 27 books) by spending $3 on movies and $27 on books, or point *c* (two movies and 24 books) by spending $6 on movies and $24 on books. Although the budget line may look similar to a consumer's demand curve, they are very different graphical tools. The budget line shows the different combinations of two goods that a consumer can buy.

A consumer's **budget set** is the set of all the affordable combinations of two goods. The budget set includes the budget line (combinations that exhaust the budget) as well as combinations that leave the consumer with leftover money. In Figure 7A.1, Maxine's budget set is shown as a shaded triangle. She can afford any combination below the budget line, but cannot afford combinations above it.

The budget line shows the market trade-off between books and movies. Starting from any point on the budget line, if Maxine buys one more movie, she diverts $3 from book purchases, reducing the number of $1 books she can purchase by three. The market trade-off equals the **price ratio**, the price of movies ($3) divided by the price of books ($1), or three books per movie. The market trade-off also equals the absolute value of the slope of the budget line, the "rise" (the change in books) divided by the "run" (the change in movies). Because all consumers pay the same price for the two goods, they all face the same market trade-off of three books per movie.

• **budget line**
The line connecting all the combinations of two goods that exhaust a consumer's budget.

• **budget set**
A set of points that includes all the combinations of two goods that a consumer can afford, given the consumer's income and the prices of the goods.

• **price ratio**
The price of the good on the horizontal axis divided by the price of the good on the vertical axis.

Consumer Preferences: Indifference Curves

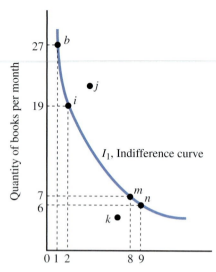

▲ **FIGURE 7A.2**

Indifference Curve and the Marginal Rate of Substitution

The indifference curve shows the different combinations of movies and books that generate the same utility level. The slope is the marginal rate of substitution (MRS) between the two goods. The MRS is eight books per movie between points *b* and *i*, but only one book per movie between points *m* and *n*.

- **indifference curve**
  A curve showing the different combinations of two goods that generate the same level of utility or satisfaction.

- **utility**
  The satisfaction experienced from consuming a good.

- **marginal rate of substitution (*MRS*)**
  The rate at which a consumer is willing to trade or substitute one good for another.

- **indifference curve map**
  A set of indifference curves, each with a different utility level.

We've seen the consumer's budget set, which shows what the consumer can afford. The next step in our discussion of consumer choice is to look at what the consumer wants, what makes the consumer happy. Once we have a means of representing consumer preferences, we can show how a consumer makes her choice, picking the best of the combinations shown by the budget set.

We can represent the consumer's preferences or tastes with indifference curves. An indifference curve represents the fundamental idea that there are different ways for a consumer to reach a particular level of satisfaction, or what economists call **utility**. An **indifference curve** shows the different combinations of two goods that generate the same level of utility or satisfaction. In Figure 7A.2, the indifference curve passing through points *b*, *i*, *m*, and *n* separates the combinations of books and movies into three groups:

1. *Superior combinations.* All of the combinations above the indifference curve generate higher utility than combinations on the curve. Maxine would prefer point *j* to point *i* because she gets more of both goods with point *j*.

2. *Inferior combinations.* All the combinations below the indifference curve generate lower utility than combinations on the curve. Maxine would prefer point *m* to point *k* because she gets more of both goods with point *m*.

3. *Equivalent combinations.* All combinations along the indifference curve generate the same utility level. Maxine is therefore indifferent between combinations *b*, *i*, *m*, and *n*.

An indifference curve shows the preferences of an individual consumer, so indifference curves vary from one consumer to another. Nonetheless, the indifference curves of all consumers share two characteristics: They are negatively sloped, and they become flatter as we move downward along an individual curve.

Why is the indifference curve negatively sloped? If we increased Maxine's movie consumption by one unit without changing her book consumption, her utility would increase. To restore the original utility level, we must take away some books, and that's what happens along an indifference curve. To keep utility constant, there is a negative relationship between books and movies, so the indifference curve is negatively sloped.

The slope of the curve is called the **marginal rate of substitution (*MRS*)** between the two goods; it is the rate at which a consumer is willing to trade or substitute one good for another. The *MRS* is the consumer's trade-off between the two goods, the number of books we must take from Maxine to offset the effect of giving her one more movie. In Figure 7A.2, if Maxine starts at point *b* and we give her one more movie, we take away eight books to keep her on the same indifference curve. Therefore, starting from point *b*, her marginal rate of substitution is eight books per movie.

The indifference curve becomes flatter as we move downward along the curve. This reflects the assumption that consumers prefer balanced consumption to extremes. As we move downward along Maxine's indifference curve, movie consumption increases while book consumption decreases. Starting from one extreme (few movies and many books), she is willing to sacrifice many books to get another movie: The *MRS* is large and the indifference curve is steep. For example, starting from point *b*, her *MRS* is eight books per movie. But as she gets more and more movies (and fewer and fewer books), she isn't willing to sacrifice many books to get more movies. As a result, her *MRS* decreases, and the indifference curve becomes flatter. For example, between points *m* and *n*, the *MRS* is one book per movie.

An **indifference curve map** is a set of indifference curves, each with a different level of utility. Figure 7A.3 shows three indifference curves: I_1, I_2, and I_3. As Maxine moves from a point on indifference curve I_1 to any point on I_2, her utility increases. This is sensible because she can get more of both goods on I_2, so she will be better off. For example, point *v* provides more of both goods than point *u*. In general, Maxine's utility increases as she moves in the northeasterly direction to a higher indifference curve (from I_1 to I_2 to I_3, and so on).

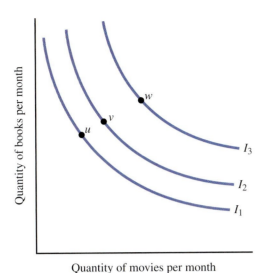

Indifference Curve Map
An indifference curve map shows a set of indifference curves, with utility increasing as we move northeasterly to higher indifference curves (from I_1 to I_2 to I_3).

7A.2 | MAXIMIZING UTILITY

We have now presented the two components of the consumer-choice model. The budget line represents the consumer's limitations or constraints, and the indifference curves represent the consumer's preferences or tastes. We can use the model to show how a consumer makes a rational choice. Maxine's objective is to maximize her utility, given her budget and the prices of movies and books. Maxine can pick from many affordable combinations of books and movies, and she will pick the one that generates the highest level of utility, or satisfaction. In graphical terms, Maxine will reach the highest indifference curve possible, given her budget set.

The Tangency Condition

In Figure 7A.4, Maxine maximizes her utility at point e, with four movies and 18 books. She achieves the utility level associated with indifference curve I_2. Why does she choose point e instead of other points, such as i, b, or w?

- **Point i.** Maxine doesn't choose this point for two reasons. First, it is not on the budget line, so it does not exhaust her budget: She would have some money left over. Second, it is on a lower indifference curve—and thus generates less utility—than point e.

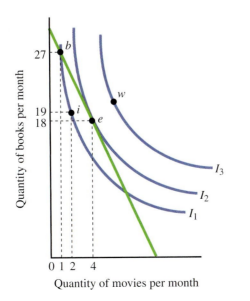

◄ **FIGURE 7A.4**
Maximizing Utility: *MRS* Equals the Price Ratio
To maximize utility, the consumer finds the combination of books and movies where an indifference curve is tangent to the budget line. At the utility-maximizing combination, the marginal rate of substitution (the consumer's own trade-off, shown by the slope of the indifference curve) equals the price ratio (the market trade-off, shown by the slope of the budget line).

- **Point *b*.** Although point *b* exhausts Maxine's budget, it lies on a lower indifference curve than *e*, so it generates less utility than point *e*. Starting from point *b*, Maxine could reallocate her budget and buy more movies and fewer books. As she moves down her budget line, she moves to progressively higher indifference curves, ultimately reaching point *e* on indifference curve I_2.
- **Point *w*.** Although point *w* is on a higher indifference curve than point *e* and thus would generate a higher utility level, it lies outside Maxine's budget set, so she cannot afford it.

At point *e*, Maxine reaches the highest indifference curve possible, given her budget set. Notice that at point *e*, the indifference curve touches—but does not pass through—the budget line. In other words, the indifference curve is tangent to the budget line.

The Utility-Maximizing Rule: MRS = Price Ratio

What is the economic interpretation of the tangency condition? At the point of tangency, the slope of the indifference curve equals the slope of the budget line. The slope of the budget line equals the price ratio, computed as the movie price ($3) divided by the book price ($1), or three books per movie. The slope of the indifference curve is the

APPLICATION

WHAT'S YOUR *MRS*?

APPLYING THE CONCEPTS #1: To determine whether a consumer is making the best choice, what single question can you ask?

We can use the utility-maximizing rule to determine whether consumers are doing the best they can. Suppose a firm has a fixed budget of $200 to spend on a punch and cookies for its holiday party. The price of punch is $2 per cup and the price of cookies is $1 per cookie; both goods will, of course, be provided free of charge to workers at the party. The firm's objective is to maximize the utility of the typical employee, and your job is to determine whether the company spent this year's party budget wisely. To simplify matters, assume that all employees have identical tastes for cookies and punch, so data from a single person will apply to every employee. You can ask the typical employee a single question. What's your question?

From the utility-maximizing rule, we know that when a consumer is maximizing utility, the marginal rate of substitution equals the price ratio. You know the price ratio for the holiday party is 2.0 (the price of punch is twice the price of cookies), so the question for the typical employee is, "What is your marginal rate of substitution?" Or in more familiar language, "How many cookies would you be willing to trade for one cup of punch?

If the answer is "two cookies per cup of punch," the *MRS* equals the price ratio, and the firm did the best it could. On the other hand, if the answer is "five cookies per cup of punch," the *MRS* exceeds the price ratio, and the firm could have generated higher utility with its $200 by providing more punch and fewer cookies. *Related to Exercises 2.1 and 2.9.*

APPLICATION

2

ONLINE MUSIC AND PIRACY

APPLYING THE CONCEPTS #2: Why do consumers dislike the bundling of goods?

The opening vignette described iTunes, one of the new online music stores. Online music stores provide an alternative to the traditional method of buying bundles of songs on CDs. We can use the consumer-choice model to explain the logic behind this new development in the music business.

Consider Sam, who has $30 to spend on music and arcade games. In an ideal world, he could buy music by the song, just as he buys arcade games individually. Suppose the price of music in this ideal world is $1 per song and the price of arcade games is $0.50 per game. In Figure 7A.5, Sam's budget line is the line connecting points a and d. He can spend his entire budget on games, getting 60 games (point a), or spend it all on songs, getting 30 songs (point d). Alternatively, he could split his budget between the two goods. With a price ratio of two games per song, the market trade-off is two games per song. Suppose that in this ideal world, Sam's best point is b, where an indifference curve is tangent to his budget line, meaning that his *MRS* equals the price ratio. At point b, Sam would have six songs and 48 arcade games.

Suppose that music cannot be purchased by the song but instead must be purchased on CDs. Each CD carries 15 songs and has a price of $15. In this case, Sam has only three options: He can spend his entire budget on games (60 games, as shown by point a), or he can get one CD with 15 songs and also get 30 games (point c), or he can spend his entire budget on two CDs (30 songs, point d). All of these points are below the indifference curve I_2 associated with point b, so his utility is lower at any of these other points. For example, the indifference curve going through point c is I_1, which is lower than I_2. He'd prefer point b (six songs and 48 games) to point c.

In the world of CDs and Internet file sharing, Sam actually has another option. He can use a swapping service to get songs for free. Of course, this is illegal, and Sam risks a penalty and may also feel bad about breaking the law. If the benefit (free songs) exceeds the cost (the risk of being penalized and the bad feelings about law breaking), he will engage in piracy.

Consider next the effects of iTunes and other online music services that sell single songs. Now Sam has a third option: He can get his ideal combination of goods without any risk of criminal penalties. One motivation for online music stores is to reduce music piracy by people who want just a few songs off a particular CD. Of course, there are other motives for piracy, and piracy is expected to continue. But the early experience with online music stores suggest that many consumers prefer the flexibility of buying music by the song and are willing to pay for it. *Related to Exercises 2.2 and 2.12.*

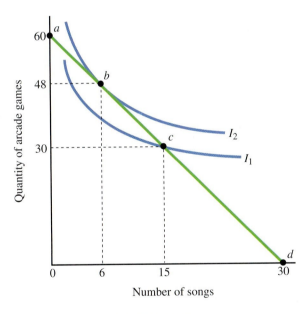

▲ **FIGURE 7A.5**

Internet Music Piracy and iTunes
When music is sold as 15-song bundles on CDs, the consumer has three budget points (*a, c,* and *d*) rather than an entire budget line. If songs are sold individually, the consumer has a full budget line and can legally reach his or her ideal combination of 6 songs and 48 arcade games (point *b*).

marginal rate of substitution (*MRS*), so if the two curves are tangent at point *e*, the *MRS* is also three books per movie. In other words, the consumer's trade-off between the two goods (the *MRS*) equals the market trade-off between the two goods (the price ratio). The **utility-maximizing rule** is to pick the combination such that

$$MRS = \frac{\text{price of good on horizontal axis}}{\text{price of good on vertical axis}}$$

To show why the tangent point is best, suppose Maxine tentatively chooses a point where the *MRS* is not equal to the price ratio. For example, suppose she started at point *b*, where the indifference curve is relatively steep and the *MRS* is eight books per movie. Starting at point *b*, she is willing to give up eight books to get a single movie. But given the market trade-off between the two goods, she can actually get that movie by sacrificing only three books. So she will move down her budget line and consume

3

APPLICATION

INFLATION DOESN'T CHANGE CONSUMPTION OR UTILITY

APPLYING THE CONCEPTS #3: How does inflation affect the typical consumer?

We can use the consumer-choice model to consider the consequences of inflation, defined as a general increase in all prices, including the price of labor. Consider the effects of a doubling of all prices. Using our example of Maxine, the prices of movies and books would double, along with wages and salaries paid to workers. If Maxine earns her income on an hourly job, the doubling of wages would double her income. How would she respond to inflation?

Inflation will not affect Maxine's consumer decision because it won't affect her budget line. To see this, think about the horizontal and vertical intercepts of the budget line—the points where Maxine's budget line crosses the horizontal axis and the vertical axis. The horizontal intercept shows how many movies Maxine can buy if she spends her entire income on movies. Suppose inflation doubles her income from $30 to $60 and doubles the price of movies from $3 to $6. Before inflation, her $30 income could buy 10 movies at $3; after inflation, her $60 income can buy 10 movies at $6 each. Similarly, if the price of books doubles along with income, the vertical intercept won't change. Because her budget line doesn't change, her utility will be maximized at the same point, with the same combination of movies and books.

The implication of this analysis is that inflation doesn't harm or help Maxine. Inflation doesn't affect her budget set or her consumer choices, so she is just as well off as she was before inflation. This is an application of one of the five key principles of economics.

THE REAL-NOMINAL PRINCIPLE

What matters to people is the real value of money or income, not the nominal value.

In our example, what matters to Maxine is her real income, or the purchasing power of her income. Although inflation doubles her income, it also doubles prices, leaving her real income the same. *Related to Exercise 2.3.*

more movies. The same argument applies to any combination for which the *MRS* (the consumer's own trade-off) is not equal to the price ratio (the market trade-off). Any time Maxine is willing to trade at a rate that is different from market trade-off, it will be in her best interest to do so. The benefits of trading will be exhausted when the *MRS* equals the price ratio. In Figure 7A.4, this happens at point *e*.

7A.3 | DRAWING THE INDIVIDUAL DEMAND CURVE

One of the purposes of this appendix is to explain the economic logic of the individual demand curve. We can use the model of consumer choice to show that every point on the individual demand curve is the result of utility maximization. Specifically, we can use the budget line and indifference curve for movies and books to draw Maxine's demand curve for just one of those products—say, movies. The exercise of drawing the curve reveals the logic of the law of demand.

The Negatively Sloped Demand Curve

We've already derived one point on Maxine's demand curve. Panel A in Figure 7A.6 shows the consumer-choice model, with indifference curves and a budget line. When the price of movies is $3, Maxine maximizes utility at point *e*, with four movies. Panel B shows her demand curve for movies, with the number of movies shown on the horizontal axis and the price of movies on the vertical axis. When the price is $3, her

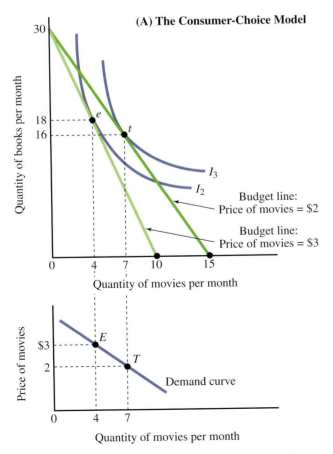

(A) The Consumer-Choice Model

(B) The Individual Demand Curve

◄ **FIGURE 7A.6**

Drawing the Demand Curve

A decrease in the price of movies tilts the budget line outward. In Panel A, the indifference curve is tangent to the new budget line at point *t*, with a larger quantity of movies (7 instead of 4). In Panel B, when the price of movies is $3, the consumer maximizes utility with 4 movies. A decrease in price to $2 increases the utility-maximizing number of movies to 7, illustrating the law of demand.

utility-maximizing choice is shown as point *e* in the upper panel and point *E* in the lower panel. In other words, the demand curve shows her utility-maximizing choice.

With so many curves floating around, it is worth reviewing their roles in consumer decision making:

- The *budget line* shows the affordable combinations of two goods, representing the consumer's constraints.
- An *indifference curve* shows the different combinations of two goods that generate the same utility level, representing the consumer's preferences.
- The *demand curve* shows how much of a *single* product a consumer is willing to buy at a particular price. To get the demand curve, we use both the budget line and indifference curves.

Panel A of Figure 7A.6 shows what happens to the budget line when the price of movies decreases to $2. The decrease in price tilts the budget line outward. The original vertical intercept (30 books) is still in the budget set, because if the entire budget is spent on books the price of movies is irrelevant. The horizontal intercept moves outward from 10 movies to 15 movies because with a lower movie price, a given budget will buy more movies. The price of movies decreases relative to the price of books, so the slope of the budget line—the price ratio—decreases.

How will Maxine respond to the lower price of movies? Given the new budget line and the same set of indifference curves, Maxine picks point *t*, where one of her indifference curves is tangent to the new budget line. Maxine responds to the decrease in price by consuming seven movies instead of four. With this combination, her *MRS* is equal to the new price ratio—two books per movie. The decrease in price decreases the market trade-off between the two goods from three to two, and Maxine chooses a new combination where her own trade-off matches the lower market trade-off.

Panel B of Figure 7A.6 shows the point on the demand curve associated with a movie price of $2 (point *T*). When the price is $2, Maxine consumes seven movies. This is consistent with the law of demand: The lower the price, the larger the quantity demanded, *ceteris paribus*. Recall that when we draw a demand curve, we use the *ceteris paribus* assumption that everything except the price of the product is fixed. To draw Maxine's demand curve for movies, we change the price of movies, holding her income and the price of books fixed. Because we are using a single set of indifference curves, we are also holding her personal preferences for the two goods fixed.

We've used the consumer-choice model to find two points on the individual demand curve. We could repeat the process for other prices to find other points on the demand curve. For each price, we find the quantity of movies that generates the highest possible utility level, given the consumer's budget and the price of the other good. Each point on the demand curve satisfies the utility-maximizing rule that the *MRS* (the consumer's own trade-off) equals the price ratio (the market trade-off).

The Income and Substitution Effects of a Price Change

Let's take a closer look at a consumer's response to a change in price. We will break down Maxine's response to a decrease in price into two effects:

- **Substitution effect**. A decrease in the price of movies decreases the price of movies relative to the price of other goods, such as books. As movies become less costly relative to books, Maxine substitutes movies for books.
- **Income effect**. A decrease in the price of movies increases Maxine's real income (the purchasing power of her nominal income), and she will buy more of all *normal* goods. If watching movies is a normal good, she will watch more movies.

- **substitution effect**
  The change in quantity consumed that is caused by a change in the relative price of the good, with real income held constant.

- **income effect**
  The change in quantity consumed that is caused by a change in real income, with relative prices held constant.

To show the substitution effect, consider the following thought experiment. Suppose the price of movies decreases from $3 to $2, and at the same time Maxine's nominal income (the face value of her income) decreases from $30 to $26. In other words, her nominal income drops by $4, which leaves her with just enough money that she can just afford her original bundle of four movies and 18 books:

$$\text{movie spending} = \$8 = 4 \text{ movies} \times \$2$$
$$\text{book spending} = \$18 = 18 \text{ books} \times \$1$$
$$\text{total spending} = \$26 = \$8 + \$18$$

Because the price reduction is exactly offset by a decrease in her nominal income, we say that her real income hasn't changed. In Figure 7A.7, the new budget line goes through her original utility-maximizing point *e* (four movies, 18 books).

Because the new budget line goes through point *e*, Maxine could continue to consume the original bundle. But will she? As we saw earlier, the *MRS* at point *e* is 3.0—the old price ratio. The new budget line, with a slope equal to the new price ratio of 2.0, is flatter than the original budget line. At point *e*, the indifference curve is steeper than the new budget line, meaning that the *MRS* (3.0) exceeds the new price ratio (2.0). Therefore, Maxine can do better, and can increase her utility level by moving downward along the new budget line, getting more movies and fewer books. Utility is maximized at point *s*, where the indifference curve I_4 is tangent to the new budget line. At this point, *MRS* equals the new price ratio of 2.0, so that's the best she can do. The quantity of movies increases from four to six.

Our little thought experiment has revealed the substitution effect of the decrease in price. The relative price of movies decreased from $3 to $2 while real income was unchanged, so the increase in quantity from four to six movies is due exclusively to the change in the relative price of movies. Although Maxine can just afford her original bundle, she doesn't choose it: The decrease in the relative price of movies causes her to substitute movies for books.

Consider next the income effect of a decrease in the price of movies. To observe the income effect, we simply restore Maxine's original nominal income of $30 and see how she responds. In other words, we "undo" the $4 reduction in income that we used

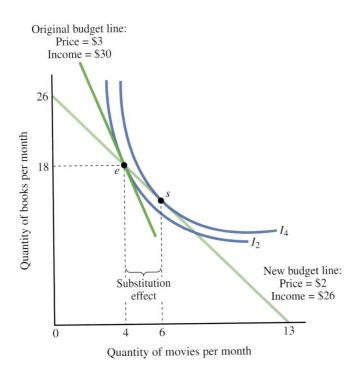

◀ **FIGURE 7A.7**

The Substitution Effect of a Decrease in Price

To observe the substitution effect, shown by the move from point *e* to point *s*, we offset the decrease in price of movies (from $3 to $2) by decreasing the consumer's income to $26, thereby making the original choice (point *e*) just affordable. At the original choice, the *MRS* (3 books per movie) exceeds the new price ratio (2 books per movie), so the consumer can do better. Moving from point *e* to point *s*, utility increases and the quantity of movies increases from 4 to 6.

4

THE SUBSTITUTION EFFECT OF A GAS TAX DECREASES GAS CONSUMPTION

APPLYING THE CONCEPTS #4: How do consumers respond to offsetting changes in taxes?

Consider the following change in federal tax policy. Suppose the federal government imposes a new gasoline tax of $2 per gallon and simultaneously cuts income taxes. Taxpayers will pay more in gasoline taxes, but less in income taxes. For the average taxpayer, the two changes in tax policy will exactly offset each other, leaving total taxes unchanged. How will this change in tax policy affect the consumption of gasoline?

We can use a simple example to show the consumer response to the tax changes. Consider a representative citizen, who initially (before the tax changes) buys 1,000 gallons of gasoline per year and pays $5,000 in income taxes. In Figure 7A.9, the citizen's initial choice is point a, where the original budget line—the flatter and darker curve—is tangent to the indifference curve I_1. The citizen buys 1,000 gallons of gasoline, because that's the affordable quantity where the MRS equals the price ratio.

The steeper and lighter budget line in Figure 7A.9 represents the new tax policy. In this example, the government combines a $2 gasoline tax with a $2,000 decrease in the income tax of the representative citizen. This means that the citizen could still consume 1,000 gallons of gasoline and have the same amount of money to spend on other goods: The $2,000 income-tax cut would exactly offset the $2,000 in extra gas taxes. In Figure 7A.9, the new budget line goes through the citizen's initial choice (point a), so the initial bundle is still affordable. Will the consumer still choose the initial bundle?

The substitution effect of the gasoline tax will reduce gasoline consumption. At point a, the indifference curve is flatter than the new budget line, so point a no longer maximizes utility. The MRS is less than the price ratio, and utility will increase as the citizen moves upward along the new budget line, buying less gasoline and more other goods. In Figure 7A.9, the new utility-maximizing point is b, with only 700 gallons of gasoline. Although the citizen could still afford to get 1,000 gallons of gasoline, the increase in the relative price of gasoline means that's not the best choice. Because of the substitution effect, when a gas tax is combined with an income tax cut, the quantity of gasoline consumed will decrease.
Related to Exercises 3.1, 3.2, and 3.8.

▲ **FIGURE 7A.9**
Increasing the Gas Tax and Decreasing the Income Tax
If a $2 gasoline tax is combined with a $2,000 decrease in the income tax, a person who initially buys 1,000 gallons (point a) can still afford the initial choice. But the increase in the relative price of gasoline means that the initial point no longer maximizes utility. At point a, the MRS is less than the new price ratio, and the substitution effect moves the consumer from point a to point b, reducing gasoline consumption from 1,000 to 700 gallons.

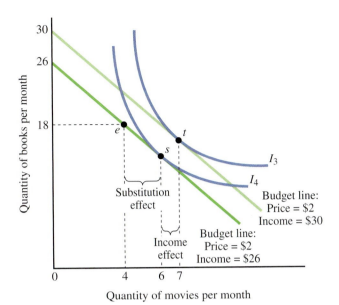

The Income Effect of a Decrease in Price
To observe the income effect, shown by the move from point s to point t, we restore the consumer's original nominal income of $30 (up from the $26 used to reveal the substitution effect) while keeping a price of $2 per movie. The budget line shifts outward, and the consumer maximizes utility at point t, so the quantity of movies increases from six to seven.

to reveal the substitution effect. In Figure 7A.8, starting at point *s* we restore the original nominal income by increasing nominal income by $4 while keeping the price of movies at $2 and the price of books at $1. The budget line shifts outward in a parallel fashion, and the increase in income allows Maxine to move to a higher indifference curve. She maximizes utility at point *t*, where the indifference curve I_3 is tangent to the higher budget line. When Maxine's nominal income increases from $26 back to $30, the utility-maximizing quantity of movies increases from six to seven. In other words, the income effect increases consumption by one movie.

Figure 7A.8 shows how to break down a consumer's response to a decrease in price into the substitution effect and the income effect. Point *e* shows the original choice, when nominal income is $30 and the price of movies is $3. Point *t* shows the utility-maximizing choice when nominal income is $30 and the price of movies is $2. We can break down this three-movie change into a substitution effect that increases the quantity from four to six movies (point *e* to point *s*) and an income effect that increases the quantity from six to seven movies (point *s* to point *t*).

SUMMARY

We've used the theory of consumer choice to explain the economic logic behind the law of demand and the negatively sloped demand curve. The consumer's objective is to maximize utility, given his or her income and the prices of consumer goods. Here are the main points of the appendix:

1 The theory of consumer choice has two steps: First, identify the affordable combinations of goods. Second, pick the affordable combination that maximizes utility.

2 To maximize utility, the consumer finds the bundle of goods at which an indifference curve is tangent to the budget line.

3 At the utility-maximizing combination of two goods, the marginal rate of substitution (the consumer's own trade-off between the two goods) equals the price ratio (the market trade-off).

4 The individual demand curve is negatively sloped, reflecting the substitution effect and income effect of a change in price. A decrease in price decreases the relative price of the good, and consumers substitute the good for other goods (the *substitution effect*). A decrease in price also increases the consumer's real income, increasing the consumption of all normal goods (the *income effect*).

KEY TERMS

EXERCISES

Visit www.myeconlab.com to complete
these exercises online and get instant feedback.

7A.1 | Consumer Constraints and Preferences

1.1 Rob has a budget of $120 and consumes ham (shown on the horizontal axis) and vermicelli (shown on the vertical axis). The price of ham is $6 per pound, and the price of vermicelli is $2 per pound. The vertical intercept of his budget line is _____ pounds of vermicelli; the horizontal intercept is _____ pounds of ham. The slope of the budget line is _____ pounds of _____ per pound of _____.

1.2 The budget line shows different combinations of two goods that have the same _____; an indifference curve shows the different combination of two goods that have the same _____.

1.3 As we move downward along an indifference curve, the slope of the curve _____ in absolute value, that is, the curve becomes _____ (steeper/flatter).

1.4 The marginal rate of substitution _____ (increases/decreases) as we move downward along an indifference curve.

1.5 As we move to a more northeasterly indifference curve, utility _____ (increases/decreases).

7A.2 | Maximizing Utility

2.1 If you know the price ratio and want to determine whether a consumer is making the best choice, ask the following question: What is your _____ ? (Related to Application 1 on page 172.)

2.2 Arrows up or down: The selling of individual songs online rather than bundles of songs on CDs _____ the utility of the typical consumer and _____ the incentive for music piracy. (Related to Application 2 on page 173.)

2.3 Inflation does not affect a consumer's budget line because it increases _____ and _____ in the same proportions. (Related to Application 3 on page 174.)

2.4 The utility-maximizing rule is that _____ equals _____.

2.5 Suppose Hattie tentatively picks a combination of hats (horizontal axis) and violets (vertical axis) at which the marginal rate of substitution is seven violets per hat. The price of violets is $3, and the price of hats is $12. Arrows up or down: To maximize utility, Hattie should _____ the consumption of violets and _____ the consumption of hats.

2.6 Sherman has a fixed budget to spend on sweaters (horizontal axis) and shirts (vertical axis). The price of shirts is $10 and the price of sweaters is $50. At his current consumption bundle, Sherman is willing to sacrifice two shirts to get one sweater. Arrows up or down: To maximize utility, Sherman should _____ the consumption of sweaters and _____ the consumption of shirts.

2.7 Suppose the price of amusement rides is $2 and the price of a video arcade game is $1. The following table shows points on the budget line (given an income of $30) and the associated *MRS*. To maximize utility, which point should the consumer choose?

	a	*b*	*c*	*d*
Quantity of rides	1	2	3	4
Quantity of video games	28	26	24	22
Marginal rate of substitution	5	3	2	1

2.8 When we use the consumer-choice model to find a point on a demand curve, we find the point at which a(n) _____ is tangent to the _____.

2.9 **Horsepower Versus Cubic Feet.** Carla has a fixed budget for a new car and has tentatively decided to buy a car with 80 horsepower (hp) and 100 cubic feet (cf) of interior space. Given the current selection of cars and their prices, the price of horsepower is one-third the price of cubic feet. After some prompting from a salesperson, Carla said, "To get an additional unit of horsepower, I would be willing to sacrifice two cubic feet of interior space." (Related to Application 1 on page 172.)

a. Does her tentative choice (80 hp and 100 cf) maximize her utility subject to her auto budget?

b. If not, should she choose an auto with more horsepower or less horsepower?

c. Illustrate the situation with a graph, with horsepower on the horizontal axis and cubic feet on the vertical axis.

2.10 **Ask the Consumer.** Recall the application "*What's Your MRS?*," which explored how to spend a firm's party budget on punch and cookies. Suppose the price of punch is $4 and the price of cookies is $1. When you ask the typical employee about her marginal rate of substitution, her answer is "three cookies per cup of punch."

a. Should your firm spend more on cookies or more on punch?

b. Illustrate your answer with a complete consumer-choice graph, with punch on the horizontal axis and cookies on the vertical axis.

2.11 **MPG Versus Mozart Speed.** Wolfgang has a fixed budget for a new car and has tentatively decided to buy a car that gets 20 miles per gallon (mpg) and has a performance level of 60 ms (the maximum speed at which a turntable can play Mozart's first symphony without skipping). A salesperson recently asked Wolfgang about his attitudes toward cars with different combinations of mpg and ms. Wolfgang would prefer a car with 19 mpg and 64 ms to his tentative choice, but would prefer his tentative choice to a car with 19 mpg and 62 ms. Suppose that the cost of an additional mpg is six times the cost of an additional unit of ms.

a. Does Wolfgang's tentative choice (20 mpg and 60 ms) maximize his utility, subject to his auto budget? If not, should he choose an auto with more or fewer mpg?

b. Illustrate your answer with a completely labeled graph. Label Wolfgang's tentative choice with a "T" and his utility-maximizing choice with a "U."

2.12 **Bundling TV Channels.** Your monthly budget for entertainment is $48, and your entertainment goods are cable TV and arcade games. Arcade games are $1 each. (Related to Application 2 on page 173.)

a. Suppose the cable company has a price of $4 per channel. Draw your budget line.

b. The table below shows the marginal rate of substitution for different combinations of channels and games. Find the utility-maximizing combination and show it on your graph with an indifference curve.

c. Suppose the cable company switches from per-channel pricing to a bundle plan: you get six stations for a cost of $24 per month, but zero stations if you don't pay the full $24. In other words, the company tells you to take it (six stations) or leave it (zero stations). Identify the new budget points on your graph. Does the switch make you better or worse off?

d. Suppose that you decide to take the bundled offer. On your graph, show that taking it is better than leaving it (picking zero channels).

Quantity		
Channels	Games	Marginal Rate of Substitution
1	$44	8
2	40	6
3	**36**	**4**
4	32	3
5	28	2
6	24	1

2.13 **Higher Prices Versus Lower Income.** Recall the example of Maxine, who in January has an income of $30 and pays $3 per movie and $1 per book.

a. In February, the prices of movies and books double, but her income stays at $30. Draw her February budget line and shade her budget set.

b. In March, her income is cut in half to $15, but the price of books returns to $1 and the price of movies returns to $3. Draw her March budget line and shade her budget set.

c. Going from February to March, does her utility level increase, decrease, or stay the same? Explain.

2.14 **Is the Average Bundle Better?** Biff consumes two entertainment goods, arcade games and CDs. When you ask him in week one, "How many arcade games are you wiling to sacrifice for one more CD?" he says, "two." When you ask him the same question a week later (week two), he says, "five." Over this period, his underlying preferences for arcade games and CDs haven't changed.

a. What could explain the change in his trade-off from week one to week two? Illustrate with a completely labeled graph, with CDs on the horizontal axis and arcade games on the vertical axis.

b. Suppose Biff reached the same utility levels in weeks one and two. In week three, you offer to provide Biff his average consumption bundle from weeks one and two, that is, the average number of

CDs and the average number of arcade games. Will he be better off, worse off, or equally well off compared to weeks one and two? Illustrate with a completely labeled graph.

7A.3 | Drawing the Individual Demand Curve

3.1 Arrows up or down: When a gasoline tax is offset by an income-tax cut that makes a consumer's original choice just affordable, the price ratio _____. To maximize utility, the consumer _____ the quantity of gasoline consumed. (Related to Application 4 on page 178.)

3.2 Suppose a gasoline tax is offset by an income-tax cut that makes a consumer's original choice just affordable. In this case, there is no _____ effect, and gasoline consumption _____ because of the _____ effect. (Related to Application 4 on page 178.)

3.3 Arrows up or down: A decrease in the price of the good shown on the horizontal axis _____ the slope of the budget line (the absolute value) and _____ the price ratio.

3.4 At every point on the demand curve, the marginal rate of substitution equals _____.

3.5 To show the substitution effect of a change in price, we change _____ while holding _____ constant.

3.6 To show the income effect of a change in price, we change _____ while holding _____ constant.

3.7 Suppose the gas tax increases and the income tax decreases to make a consumer's original bundle affordable. At the original bundle, the marginal rate of substitution _____ the price ratio, so the changes in taxes _____ the utility-maximizing quantity of gasoline.

3.8 **Response to the Gas Tax.** Petrov earns $10,000 in pretax income and initially pays $2,200 in income taxes, consumes 600 gallons of gasoline per year (at a price of $3 per gallon), and spends $6,000 on other goods (at a price of $1 per unit). (Related to Application 4 on page on page 178.)

   a. Draw a complete graph showing Petrov's initial (before the gas tax) budget line, indifference curve, and utility-maximizing quantities of gas and other goods (in $ spent). At his initial choice, the marginal rate of substitution is _____.

   b. Suppose the government imposes a new gasoline tax of $2 per gallon, and assume that the gas tax increases the price of gas to $5. To make his initial bundle of gasoline and other goods affordable after the $2 gas tax, Petrov's income tax must decrease by _____.

   c. On your graph, draw a new budget line for a policy that combines the $2 gas tax with the change in income tax you computed for part b.

   d. Use your graph to show whether the tax policy will increase, decrease, or not affect Petrov's gas consumption.

3.9 **Shipping the Good Apples Out?** Suppose apples come in two quality levels, low and high. At a store in the apple-growing region, the price of low-quality apples is \$1 per pound and the price of high-quality apples is \$4 per pound. Johnny lives in the apple-growing region, and maximizes utility, spending his \$25 income on five pounds of each type.

a. Use a complete consumer-choice graph to show Johnny's initial choice. Put high-quality apples on the horizontal axis and low-quality apples on the vertical axis.

b. Suppose Johnny moves to an area outside the apple-growing region, where his income is \$45 (up from \$25). Shipping the apples to his new area adds \$2 to the price of a pound of apples, for both low-quality and high-quality apples. Use a consumer-choice graph to show his new budget line and his new utility-maximizing choice of low-quality and high-quality apples.

c. What does this exercise suggest about the mix of high-quality and low-quality apples in apple-growing areas compared to the high-low mix in other areas? Will the proportion of high-quality apples be higher or lower in the apple-growing region?

8

Production Technology and Cost

A few years ago the price of a hardback version of *Encyclopedia Britannica*, the world's leading encyclopedia, was $1,600. Now you can get a CD version of the encyclopedia, along with a dictionary, thesaurus, and world atlas, for only $69.95. Why did the price drop to less than one-twentieth of its former value?

An encyclopedia is an information good because its production involves collecting information—facts, figures, and images—and packaging them for use by consumers. The cost of compiling the information for the first copy of an encyclopedia is huge, but the cost of reproducing the encyclopedia in digital format (CDs) is tiny. The move from hardback encyclopedias to digital ones decreased the cost of production, pulling down the price. In addition, heated competition among rival encyclopedia firms pulled the price down further.

- **economic profit**
  Total revenue minus economic cost.

- **economic cost**
  The opportunity cost of the inputs used in the production process; equal to explicit cost plus implicit cost.

- **explicit cost**
  The actual monetary payment for inputs.

- **implicit cost**
  The opportunity cost of inputs that do not require a monetary payment.

his chapter explores the relationship between the quantity of output produced and the cost of production. As we'll see, a firm's production cost is determined by its production technology—the way the firm combines capital, labor, and materials to produce output. After we explain the link between technology and costs, we'll look at the actual cost curves of several products, including aluminum, hospital services, wind power, truck freight, and airplanes.

As we saw in Chapter 2, economists distinguish between the short run and the long run. The long run is a period long enough that a firm is perfectly flexible in its choice of all inputs, including its production facility. In contrast, when a firm cannot modify its facility, it is operating in the short run. In this chapter, we'll explore both short-run and long-run costs. In later chapters, we'll show how firms use short-run and long-run cost curves to make decisions about whether to enter a market and how much output to produce.

8.1 | ECONOMIC COST AND ECONOMIC PROFIT

This is the first of several chapters on the decisions firms make. A firm's objective is to maximize its **economic profit**, which equals its total revenue minus its economic cost:

$$\text{economic profit} = \text{total revenue} - \text{economic cost}$$

As we saw earlier in the book, a firm's total revenue is the money it gets from selling its product. If a firm charges the same price to every consumer, its total revenue equals the price per unit of output times the quantity sold.

This chapter explores the firm's cost of production. A firm's **economic cost** equals the cost of all the inputs used in the production process; it is measured as the opportunity cost of the inputs. Recall the first key principle of economics.

PRINCIPLE OF OPPORTUNITY COST

The opportunity cost of something is what you sacrifice to get it.

To compute a firm's economic cost, we must determine what the firm sacrifices to use inputs in the production process. Economic cost is opportunity cost.

As shown in the first column of numbers in Table 8.1, a firm's economic cost can be divided into two types. A firm's **explicit cost** is its actual monetary payments for inputs. For example, if a firm spends a total of $10,000 per month on labor, capital, and materials, its explicit cost is $10,000. This is an opportunity cost because money spent on these inputs cannot be used to buy something else. A firm's **implicit cost** is the opportunity cost of the inputs that do not require a monetary payment. Here are two examples of inputs whose cost is implicit rather than explicit:

- *Opportunity cost of the entrepreneur's time.* If an entrepreneur could earn $5,000 per month in another job, the opportunity cost of the time spent running the firm is $5,000 per month.

Table 8.1 | ECONOMIC COST VERSUS ACCOUNTING COST

	Economic Cost	Accounting Cost
Explicit: monetary payments for labor, capital, materials	$10,000	$10,000
Implicit: opportunity cost of entrepreneur's time	5,000	—
Implicit: opportunity cost of funds	2,000	—
Total	17,000	10,000

- *Opportunity cost of the entrepreneur's funds.* Many entrepreneurs use their own funds to set up and run their businesses. If an entrepreneur starts a business with $200,000 withdrawn from a savings account, the opportunity cost is the interest income the funds could have earned, for example, $2,000 per month.

Economic cost equals explicit cost plus implicit cost:

$$\text{economic cost} = \text{explicit cost} + \text{implicit cost}$$

In the first column of Table 8.1, the firm's economic cost is $17,000, equal to $10,000 in explicit cost plus $7,000 in implicit cost.

Accountants have a different approach to computing costs. Their narrower definition of cost includes only the explicit cost of inputs:

$$\text{accounting cost} = \text{explicit cost}$$

In other words, **accounting cost** includes the monetary payments for inputs, but ignores the opportunity cost of inputs that do not require an explicit monetary payment. In the second column of Table 8.1, the accounting cost is the $10,000 in monetary payments for labor, capital, and materials. **Accounting profit** equals total revenue minus accounting cost:

$$\text{accounting profit} = \text{total revenue} - \text{accounting cost}$$

A firm's accounting cost is always lower than its economic cost, so its accounting profit is always *higher* than its economic profit. For the rest of this book, when we refer to cost and profit, we mean *economic* cost and *economic* profit.

- **accounting cost**
  The explicit costs of production.

- **accounting profit**
  Total revenue minus accounting cost.

8.2 | A FIRM WITH A FIXED PRODUCTION FACILITY: SHORT-RUN COSTS

Consider first the case of a firm with a fixed production facility. Suppose that you have decided to start a small firm to produce plastic paddles for rafts. The production of paddles requires a workshop where workers use molds to form plastic material into paddles. Before we can discuss the cost of production, we need information about the nature of the production process.

Production and Marginal Product

The table in Figure 8.1 shows how the quantity of paddles produced varies with the number of workers. A single worker in the workshop produces one paddle per day. Adding a second worker increases the quantity produced to five paddles per day. The **marginal product of labor** is the change in output from one additional unit of labor. In the table, the marginal product of the first worker is one paddle, compared to a marginal product of four paddles for the second worker.

Why does the marginal product increase as output increases? As we saw earlier in the book, when a firm increases its workforce, workers can specialize in production tasks. Productivity increases because of the benefits of continuity—each worker spends less time switching between production tasks. In addition, there are benefits from repetition—each worker becomes more proficient at an assigned task. A two-worker operation produces more than twice as many paddles as a one-person operation because the two workers can specialize, one being responsible for preparing the plastic for the mold and the other responsible for working the mold.

Starting with the third worker, the production process is subject to **diminishing returns**, one of the key principles of economics.

- **marginal product of labor**
  The change in output from one additional unit of labor.

- **diminishing returns**
  As one input increases while the other inputs are held fixed, output increases at a decreasing rate.

PRINCIPLE OF DIMINISHING RETURNS

Suppose that output is produced with two or more inputs and we increase one input while holding the other inputs fixed. Beyond some point—called the *point of diminishing returns*—output will increase at a decreasing rate.

The third worker adds three paddles to total output, down from four paddles for the second worker. As the firm continues to hire more workers, the marginal product drops to two paddles for the fourth worker and one paddle for the fifth worker. As we saw earlier in the book, diminishing returns occurs because workers share a production facility. A larger workforce means that each worker gets a smaller share of the production facility. In the paddle example, the workers share a mold; as the number of workers increases, they will spend more time waiting to use the mold.

Figure 8.1 shows the firm's **total-product curve**, which represents the relationship between the quantity of labor (on the horizontal axis) and output (on the vertical axis), *ceteris paribus*. The total-product curve shows the effects of labor specialization as well as diminishing returns. For the first two workers, output increases at an increasing rate because labor specialization increases the marginal product of labor. Starting with the third worker, however, total output increases at a decreasing rate because of diminishing returns.

• **total-product curve**
A curve showing the relationship between the quantity of labor and the quantity of output produced, ceteris paribus.

Short-Run Total Cost

We've seen the production relationship between labor input and output, so we're ready to show the relationship between output and production cost. Suppose the opportunity cost of your time is $50 per day, and you can hire workers for your workshop at the market wage of $50 per day. You can purchase your workshop, including the building and the paddle mold, for $365,000. If the interest rate you could have earned on that money is 10 percent per year, the opportunity cost of tying up your $365,000 in the workshop is $36,500 per year, or $100 per day.

▶ **FIGURE 8.1**

Total-Product Curve

The total-product curve shows the relationship between the quantity of labor and the quantity of output, given a fixed production facility. For the first 2 workers, output increases at an increasing rate because of labor specialization. Diminishing returns occurs for 3 or more workers, so output increases at a decreasing rate.

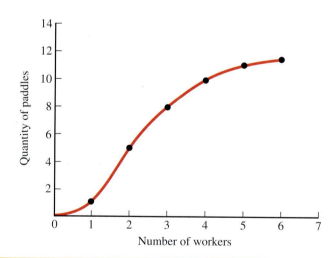

Labor	Quantity of Output Produced	Marginal Product of Labor
1	1	1
2	5	4
3	8	3
4	10	2
5	11	1
6	11.5	0.5

In the short-run analysis of costs, we divide production costs into two types, fixed cost and variable cost.

- **Fixed cost (FC)** is the cost that does not vary with the quantity produced. In our example, the fixed cost is the cost of the workshop, including the cost of the building and the mold. As shown in the third column of Table 8.2, the fixed cost is $100 per day, regardless of how much output is produced.

- **Variable cost (VC)** is the cost that varies with the quantity produced. For example, to produce more paddles, you must hire more workers. If the cost per worker is $50 per day, your daily variable cost is $50 times the number of workers, including you. As shown in the fourth column of Table 8.2, variable cost is $50 for one worker, $100 for two workers, and so on.

To compute the firm's total cost, we simply add the fixed and variable costs. The firm's **short-run total cost (TC)** equals the sum of fixed and variable costs:

$$TC = FC + VC$$

The fifth column in Table 8.2 shows the total cost for different quantities of output. For example, 1 worker produces 1 paddle at a total cost of $150, equal to the fixed cost of $100 plus a variable cost of $50. Hiring a second worker increases output to 5 paddles and increases total cost to $200, equal to $100 in fixed cost and $100 in variable cost. Moving down the fifth column, the total cost rises to $250 for 8 units of output, $300 for 10 units, and so on.

Figure 8.2 shows the short-run cost curves corresponding to columns 3, 4, and 5 of Table 8.2. The horizontal line on the graph shows the fixed cost of $100. The lower of the two positively sloped curves shows the variable cost (VC), and the higher of the two positively sloped curves is total cost (TC). Total cost is the sum of fixed cost and

- **fixed cost (FC)**
  Cost that does not vary with the quantity produced.

- **variable cost (VC)**
  Cost that varies with the quantity produced.

- **short-run total cost (TC)**
  The total cost of production when at least one input is fixed; equal to fixed cost plus variable cost.

Table 8.2 | SHORT-RUN COSTS

1	2	3	4	5	6	7	8	9
Labor	Output	Fixed Cost (FC)	Variable Cost (VC)	Total Cost (TC)	Average Fixed Cost (AFC)	Average Variable Cost (AVC)	Average Total Cost (ATC)	Marginal Cost (MC)
0	0	$100	$0	$100	—	—	—	—
1	1	100	$50	150	$100.00	$50.00	$150.00	$50.00
2	5	100	100	200	20.00	20.00	40.00	12.50
3	8	100	150	250	12.50	18.75	31.25	16.67
4	10	100	200	300	10.00	20.00	30.00	25.00
5	11	100	250	350	9.09	22.73	31.82	50.00
6	11.5	100	300	400	8.70	26.09	34.78	100.00

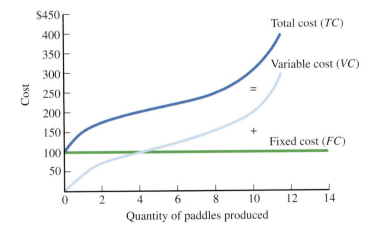

◄ FIGURE 8.2
Short-Run Costs: Fixed Cost, Variable Cost, and Total Cost
The short-run total-cost curve shows the relationship between the quantity of output and production costs, given a fixed production facility. Short-run total cost equals fixed cost (the cost that does not vary with the quantity produced) plus variable cost (the cost that varies with the quantity produced).

variable cost, so the vertical distance between the *TC* curve and the *VC* curve equals the firm's fixed cost. Notice that this distance is the same at any level of output.

Short-Run Average Costs

• **average fixed cost (AFC)**
Fixed cost divided by the quantity produced.

There are three types of average cost. **Average fixed cost (AFC)** equals the fixed cost divided by the quantity produced:

$$AFC = \frac{FC}{Q}$$

To compute *AFC* for our paddle company, we simply divide the fixed cost ($100) by the quantity of paddles produced. In Table 8.2, we divide the number in column 3 by the number in column 2. This calculation gives us the values for *AFC*, which are shown in column 6. For example, the output in the second row is 1 paddle, so the average fixed cost is $100 = $100/1. In the third row, output is 5 paddles, so the average fixed cost is $5 = $100/5. As output increases, the $100 fixed cost is spread over more units, so *AFC* decreases.

• **average variable cost (AVC)**
Variable cost divided by the quantity produced.

A firm's **average variable cost (AVC)** incorporates the costs that vary with the quantity produced. Average variable cost equals the variable cost divided by the quantity produced:

$$AVC = \frac{VC}{Q}$$

To compute *AVC* for our paddle company, we simply divide the number in column 4 of Table 8.2 by the number in column 2. That calculation gives us the values for *AVC*, shown in column 7. For example, the output in the third row is 5 paddles and the variable cost is $100, so the average variable cost is $100/5 paddles, or $20. Notice that for small quantities of output, the *AVC* decreases as the quantity produced increases—from $50 for one paddle, $20 for 2 paddles, and so on. The *AVC* declines because of the benefits of labor specialization. Adding workers to a small workforce makes workers more productive on average, so the amount of labor required per unit of output drops, pushing down the average variable cost. In contrast, for large quantities of output, average variable cost increases as output increases because of diminishing returns. Adding workers to a large workforce makes workers less productive on average, pulling up the average variable cost. In Figure 8.3, the *AVC* curve is negatively sloped for small quantities, but positively sloped for large quantities.

▶ **FIGURE 8.3**

Short-Run Average Costs

The short-run average-total-cost curve (*ATC*) is U-shaped. As the quantity produced increases, fixed costs are spread over more and more units, pushing down the average total cost. In contrast, as the quantity increases, diminishing returns eventually pulls up the average total cost. The gap between *ATC* and *AVC* is the average fixed cost (*AFC*).

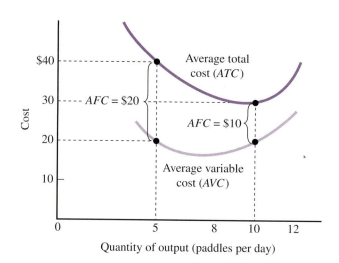

part 3

A firm's total cost is the sum of its fixed cost and variable cost, so the **short-run average total cost (ATC)**, or what we'll simply call "average cost," is the sum of the average fixed cost and the average variable cost:

$$ATC = \frac{TC}{Q} = \frac{FC}{Q} + \frac{VC}{Q} = AFC + AVC$$

- **short-run average total cost (ATC)**
  Short-run total cost divided by the quantity of output; equal to AFC plus AVC.

In Figure 8.3, we go from the *AVC* to *ATC* by adding the average fixed cost to *AVC*. For example, for five paddles *AFC* is $20 and *AVC* is $20, so *ATC* is equal to $40, the sum of $20 + $20. For 10 paddles, the average fixed cost is lower—only $10—while the average variable cost is $20, so *ATC* is $30, the sum of $10 + $20. In Figure 8.3, the gap between the *AVC* and *ATC* curves is the average fixed cost.

The *ATC* curve in Figure 8.2 is negatively sloped at quantities less than 10 paddles. The negative slope results from two forces that work together to push average cost down as output increases:

- *Spreading the fixed cost.* For small quantities of output, a one-unit increase in output reduces *AFC* by a large amount because the fixed cost is pretty "thick," being spread over just a few units of output. For example, going from 1 paddle to 5 paddles decreases *AFC* from $100 to $20 per paddle.
- *Labor specialization.* For small quantities of output, *AVC* decreases as output increases because labor specialization increases worker productivity.

These two forces both push *ATC* downward as output increases, so the curve is negatively sloped for small quantities of output.

What happens once the firm reaches the point at which the benefits of labor specialization are exhausted? As the firm continues to increase output beyond that point, the average variable cost increases because of diminishing returns. There is a tug-of-war between two forces: The spreading of fixed cost continues to push *ATC* down, while diminishing returns and rising average variable cost pull *ATC* up. The outcome of the tug-of-war varies with the quantity produced, giving the *ATC* curve its U shape:

- *Intermediate quantities of output, such as output between 3 and 10 paddles.* The tug-of-war is won by the spreading of fixed cost, because the fixed cost is still relatively "thick" and diminishing returns are not yet very strong. As a result, *ATC* decreases as output increases. For example, at 5 paddles *ATC* is $40, but at 10 paddles *ATC* drops to only $30.
- *Large quantities of output, such as 11 or more paddles.* The tug-of-war is won by diminishing returns and rising average variable cost. In this case, the reductions in *AFC* are relatively small because the fixed cost is already spread pretty thinly and diminishing returns are severe. As a result, *ATC* increases as output increases. For example, at 10 paddles *ATC* is $30, but at 11.5 paddles *ATC* jumps to $34.78.

Short-Run Marginal Cost

The **short-run marginal cost (MC)** is the change in short-run total cost per unit change in output. In other words, it is the increase in total cost resulting from a one-unit increase in output. Mathematically, marginal cost is calculated by dividing the change in total cost (*TC*) by the change in output (*Q*):

- **short-run marginal cost (MC)**
  The change in short-run total cost resulting from a one-unit increase in output.

$$MC = \frac{\Delta TC}{\Delta Q} = \frac{\text{change in } TC}{\text{change in output}}$$

The marginal cost of the first paddle is the increase in cost when the firm produces the first paddle. To produce the first unit of output, the firm hires a single worker at $50. As shown in column 9 of Table 8.2, the marginal cost of the first paddle is $50. Moving down the ninth column, hiring the second worker for $50 increases

► FIGURE 8.4

Short-Run Marginal and Average Cost

The marginal-cost curve (*MC*) is negatively sloped for small quantities of output, because of the benefits of labor specialization, and positively sloped for large quantities, because of diminishing returns. The *MC* curve intersects the average-cost curve (*ATC*) at the minimum point of the average curve. At this point *ATC* is neither falling nor rising.

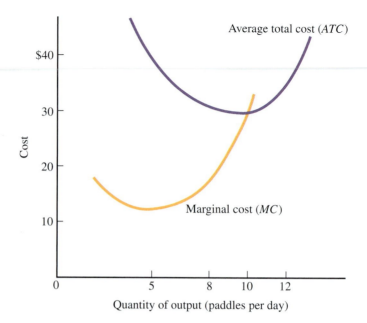

output to 5 paddles. A $50 increase in total cost increases output by 4 paddles, so the marginal cost is $12.50:

$$MC = \frac{\Delta TC}{\Delta Q} = \frac{\text{change in } TC}{\text{change in output}} = \frac{\$50}{4} = \$12.50$$

In this case, marginal cost decreases as output increases because of labor specialization and rising worker productivity. The first worker produces just one paddle, but adding a second worker increases output by four paddles. The $50 expense of adding the second worker translates into a $12.50 expense for each of the four extra paddles produced. We saw earlier that specialization leads to increasing marginal productivity. Now we know that specialization also leads to decreasing marginal cost. In Figure 8.4, the short-run marginal-cost curve is negatively sloped for the first five paddles.

The positively sloped portion of the marginal-cost curve is a result of diminishing returns. Hiring the third worker increases output from 5 to 8, so the $50 expense translates into a $16.67 expense for each of the 3 extra paddles produced. Diminishing returns has set in, so marginal cost increases as output increases. The marginal cost increases to $25 for between 8 and 10 paddles ($50/2 paddles), then increases to $50 for between 10 and 11 paddles ($50/1 paddle), and so on. In general, diminishing returns decreases labor productivity and causes rising marginal cost.

The Relationship Between Marginal Cost and Average Cost

Figure 8.4 shows the relationship between short-run marginal cost and short-run average total cost. Whenever the marginal cost is less than the average cost (for fewer than 10 paddles), the average cost is falling. In contrast, whenever the marginal cost exceeds the average cost (for more than 10 paddles), the average cost is rising. Finally, when the marginal cost equals the average cost, the average cost is neither rising nor falling. Therefore, the marginal-cost curve intersects the short-run average total cost curve at its minimum point.

We can use some simple logic to explain the relationship between average and marginal cost. Suppose that you start the semester with 9 completed courses and a cumulative grade-point average of 3.0. In the first row of Table 8.3, you have 27 grade points (4 points for each A, 3 points for each B, and so on), so your GPA is 3.0, which is 27 points divided by 9 courses. You enroll in a single course this semester—a history course. Your new GPA will depend on your grade in the history course, the marginal grade. There are three possibilities:

Table 8.3 | MARGINAL GRADE AND AVERAGE GRADE

	Marginal Grade	Number of Courses	Grade Points	Grade Point Average
Starting point	—	9	27	3.0 = 27/9
Marginal grade < GPA	D	10	28 = 27 + 1	2.8 = 28/10
Marginal grade = GPA	B	10	30 = 27 + 3	3.0 = 30/10
Marginal grade > GPA	A	10	31 = 27 + 4	3.1 = 31/10

- *Marginal grade less than the average grade.* In the second row of Table 8.3, if you get a D in history, your grade point total increases from 27 points to 28 points. Dividing the new total by 10 courses, your new GPA is 2.80. It's lower because your marginal grade of 1.0 is less than the old average grade of 3.0.

- *Marginal grade equal to the average grade.* In the second row of Table 8.3, if you get a B in history, your grade point total increases from 27 points to 30 points. Dividing the new total by 10 courses, your new GPA is 3.0. It hasn't changed because your marginal grade of 3.0 equals the old average grade of 3.0.

- *Marginal grade greater than the average grade.* In the second row of Table 8.3, if you get an A in history, your grade point total increases from 27 points to 31 points, so your new GPA is 3.10. It's higher because your marginal grade of 4.0 is greater than the old average grade of 3.0.

To summarize, whenever the marginal grade is less than the average grade, the average will fall; whenever the marginal grade exceeds the average grade, the average will rise; whenever the marginal grade equals the average grade, the average will not change.

8.3 | PRODUCTION AND COST IN THE LONG RUN

Up to this point, we've been exploring short-run cost curves, which show the cost of producing different quantities of output in a given production facility. We turn next to long-run cost curves, which show production costs in facilities of different sizes. The *long run* is defined as the period of time over which a firm is perfectly flexible in its choice of all inputs. In the long run, a firm can build a new production facility such as a factory, store, office, or restaurant. Another option in the long run is to modify an existing facility.

The key difference between the short run and the long run is that there are no diminishing returns in the long run. Recall that diminishing returns occur because workers share a fixed production facility, so the larger the number of workers in the facility, the smaller the share of the facility available for each worker. In the long run, a firm can expand its production facility as its workforce grows, so there are no diminishing returns.

Expansion and Replication

Continuing the example of paddle production, suppose that you have decided to replace your existing workshop with a new one. You have been producing 10 paddles per day at a total cost of $300 per day, or an average cost of $30 per paddle. Suppose a company that sponsors rafting adventures orders new paddles, and you decide to produce twice as much output in your new facility. What should you do?

One possibility is simply to double the original operation. You could build two workshops that are identical to the original shop and hire two workforces, each identical to the original workforce. In the table in Figure 8.5, your firm moves from the third row of numbers (4 workers and $100 worth of capital produces 10 paddles per

► **FIGURE 8.5**

The Long-Run Average-Cost Curve and Scale Economies

The long-run average-cost curve (*LAC*) is negatively sloped for up to 10 paddles per day, a result of indivisible inputs and the effects of labor specialization. If the firm replicates the operation that produces 10 paddles per day, the long-run average-cost curve will be horizontal beyond 10 paddles per day.

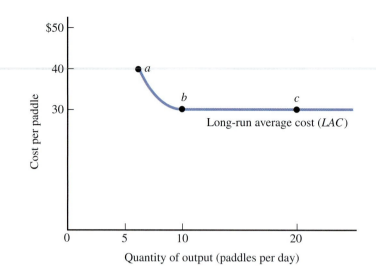

	1	2	3	4	5
Labor	Capital	Output	Labor Cost	Long-Run Total Cost (*LTC*)	Long-Run Average Cost (*LAC*)
1	$100	1	$50	$150	$150
2	100	5	100	200	40
4	100	10	200	300	30
8	200	20	400	600	30
12	300	30	600	900	30

• **long-run total cost (*LTC*)**
The total cost of production when a firm is perfectly flexible in choosing its inputs.

• **long-run average cost (*LAC*)**
The long-run cost divided by the quantity produced.

• **constant returns to scale**
A situation in which the long-run total cost increases proportionately with output, so average cost is constant.

day) to the fourth row, with twice as much labor, capital, and output. A firm's **long-run total cost (*LTC*)** is the total cost of production when the firm is perfectly flexible in choosing its inputs, including its production facility. As shown in column 5 of the table in Figure 8.5, if your firm doubles its output from 10 paddles to 20 paddles, the long-run total cost doubles too, from $300 to $600.

The firm's **long-run average cost (*LAC*)** equals the long-run cost divided by the quantity produced. As shown in column 6 of the table in Figure 8.5, doubling output from 10 to 20 paddles doesn't change the long-run average cost because doubling output by doubling both labor and capital increases costs proportionately. In the graph in Figure 8.5, point *b* shows the average cost with 10 paddles and point *c* shows the average cost with 20 paddles. As the quantity produced increases, the average cost doesn't change, so the average-cost curve is horizontal over this range of output. This is the case of **constant returns to scale**: As a firm scales up its operation, costs increase proportionately with output, so average cost is constant.

The same logic applies to larger output levels. Your firm could build a third workshop identical to the first two workshops, and its production costs will increase proportionately, from $600 to $900. In the table in Figure 8.5, the average cost for 30 paddles is $30, the same as for 10 and 20 paddles. In general, the replication process means the long-run total cost increases proportionately with the quantity produced, so the average cost is constant. In Figure 8.5, the long-run average-cost curve is horizontal for 10 or more paddles per day. In other words, there are constant returns to scale for output levels of 10 or more paddles.

We've seen that if a firm wants to double its output in the long run, replication is one option. By simply replicating an existing operation, a firm can double its output and its total costs, leaving average cost unchanged. Another possibility is to build a

194

single larger workshop, one that can produce twice as much output at a lower cost than would be possible by simply replicating the original. If so, the long-run average cost of producing 20 or 30 paddles would be less than $30 per paddle.

A firm's **long-run marginal cost (*LMC*)** is the change in long-run cost resulting from producing one more unit of output. In the long run, the firm is perfectly flexible in choosing its inputs. Therefore, *LMC* is the increase in cost when the firm can change its production facility as well as its workforce.

Reducing Output with Indivisible Inputs

What would happen if you decide to produce only 5 paddles per day instead of 10? Although it's tempting to think that your total costs would be cut in half, that's not necessarily the case. Remember that you use a single mold to produce 10 paddles per day. If you cut your output in half, you would still need the mold, so your capital costs won't be cut in half. In addition, if each mold requires a fixed amount of floor space, you would still need the same floor space. Therefore, cutting output in half wouldn't decrease the cost of your production facility at all. You would still have a cost of $100 per day for the mold and the workspace. Because cutting output in half doesn't cut capital costs in half, the average cost for producing 5 paddles will exceed the average cost for 10 paddles.

The mold is an example of an **indivisible input**, one that cannot be scaled down to produce a smaller quantity of output. When a production process requires the use of indivisible inputs, the average cost of production increases as output decreases, because the cost of the indivisible inputs is spread over a smaller quantity of output. Most production operations use some indivisible inputs, but the costs of these inputs vary. Here are some examples of firms and their indivisible inputs:

- A railroad company uses tracks to provide freight service between two cities. The company cannot scale down by laying a half set of tracks—a single rail.
- A shipping firm uses a large ship to carry TV sets from Japan to the United States. The company can't scale back by transporting TVs in rowboats.
- A steel producer uses a large blast furnace. The company can't scale back by producing steel in a toaster oven.
- A hospital uses imaging machines for x-rays, CAT scans, and MRIs. The hospital can't scale back by getting mini-MRI machines.
- A pizzeria uses a pizza oven. The company can't scale back by making pizza in a toaster oven.

The second row of the table in Figure 8.5 on page 194 shows labor and capital costs in the smaller operation. Suppose that to produce 5 paddles, you'll need 2 workers, including yourself. In this case, your labor cost will be $100. Adding the $100 cost of the indivisible input (the mold and shop space), the total cost of producing 5 paddles per day will be $200, or $40 per paddle. This cost exceeds the average cost of 10 paddles because in the smaller operation you still need the same amount of capital. In Figure 8.5 on page 194, point *a* shows that the average cost of 5 paddles per day exceeds the average cost for larger quantities.

Scaling Down and Labor Specialization

A second possible reason for higher average long-run costs in a smaller operation is that labor will be less specialized in the small operation. As we saw earlier in the chapter, the labor specialization—each worker specializing in an individual production task—makes workers more productive because of continuity and repetition. Reversing this process, when we reduce the workforce each worker will become less specialized, performing a wider variety of production tasks. The loss of specialization will decrease labor productivity, leading to higher average cost.

To see the role of labor specialization, consider the first row of numbers in the table in Figure 8.6. To produce one paddle per day, the firm needs a full day of work by one worker. The single worker performs all production tasks and is less productive than the specialized workers in larger operations. This is one reason for the relatively high average cost in a one-paddle operation ($150). The second reason is that the cost of the indivisible input is spread over fewer paddles.

Economies of Scale

• **economies of scale**
A situation in which the long-run average cost of production decreases as output increases.

A firm experiences **economies of scale** if the long-run average cost of production decreases as output increases, meaning that the long-run average-cost curve is negatively sloped. In Figure 8.5 on page 194, the paddle producer experiences economies of scale between points *a* and *b*. At point *a*, the long-run average cost is $40, compared to $30 at point *b* and beyond. An increase in output from 5 to 10 paddles decreases the long-run average cost of production because the firm spreads the cost of an indivisible input over a larger quantity, decreasing average cost. In other words, there are some economies—cost savings—associated with scaling up the firm's operation.

• **minimum efficient scale**
The output at which scale economies are exhausted.

One way to quantify the extent of scale economies in the production of a particular good is to determine the minimum efficient scale for producing the good. The **minimum efficient scale** is defined as the output at which scale economies are exhausted. In Figure 8.5, the long-run average-cost curve becomes horizontal at point *b*, so the minimum efficient scale is 10 paddles. If a firm starts out with a quantity of output below the minimum efficient scale, an increase in output will decrease the average cost. Once the minimum efficient scale has been reached, the average cost no longer decreases as output increases.

Diseconomies of Scale

• **diseconomies of scale**
A situation in which the long-run average cost of production increases as ouput increases.

A positively sloped long-run average-cost curve indicates the presence of **diseconomies of scale**. In this case, average cost increases as output increases. Diseconomies of scale can occur for two reasons:

• *Coordination problems.* One of the problems of a large organization is that it requires several layers of management to coordinate the activities of the different parts of the organization. A large organization requires more meetings, reports, and administrative work, leading to higher unit cost. If an increase in the firm's output requires additional layers of management, the long-run average-cost curve may be positively sloped.

• *Increasing input costs.* When a firm increases its output, it will demand more of each of its inputs and *may* be forced to pay higher prices for some of these inputs.

For example, an expanding construction firm may be forced to pay higher wages to attract more workers. Alternatively, an expanding firm may be forced to hire workers who are less skilled than the original workers. An increase in wages or a decrease in productivity will increase the average cost of production, generating a positively sloped long-run average-cost curve.

Firms recognize the possibility of diseconomies of scale and adopt various strategies to avoid them. An example of a firm that adjusts its operations to avoid diseconomies of scale is 3M, a global technology company that produces products ranging from Post-it® notes to pharmaceuticals and telecommunications systems. The company makes a conscious effort to keep its production units as small as possible to keep them flexible. When a production unit gets too large, the company breaks it apart.

Actual Long-Run Average-Cost Curves

Figure 8.6 shows the actual long-run average-cost curves for three products: aluminum production, truck freight, and hospital services.[1] In each case, the long-run average cost curve is negatively sloped for small quantities of output and relatively flat—almost horizontal—over a large range of output. In other words, these curves are

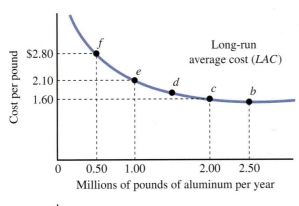

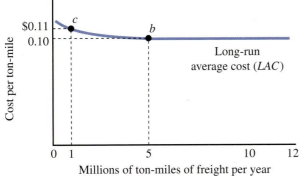

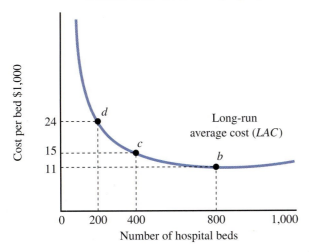

L-shaped. Other studies suggest that the long-run cost curves of a wide variety of goods and services have the same shape.

Why is the typical long-run average-cost curve L-shaped? The long-run average-cost curve is negatively sloped for small quantities of output because there are economies of scale resulting from indivisible inputs and labor specialization. As output increases, the average-cost curve eventually becomes horizontal and remains horizontal for a wide range of output. Over the horizontal portion of the cost curve, increases in inputs lead to proportionate increases in output, so the average cost doesn't change. In other words, the long-run average total cost (*LAC*) is constant and production is subject to constant returns to scale.

Short-Run Versus Long-Run Average Cost

Why is the firm's short-run average-cost curve U-shaped, while the long-run average-cost curve is L-shaped? For large quantities of output, the short-run curve is positively sloped because of diminishing returns and the resulting decrease in labor productivity and increase in marginal cost. If a firm increases its output while at least one input is held fixed, diminishing returns eventually occur, pulling up the average cost of production.

The difference between the short run and long run is a firm's flexibility in choosing inputs. In the long run, a firm can increase all of its inputs, scaling up its operation by building a larger production facility. As a result, the firm will not suffer from diminishing returns. In most cases, the long-run average-cost curve will be negatively sloped or horizontal. In some cases, firms experience diseconomies of scale, so the long-run average-cost curve will be positively sloped for high output levels. Nonetheless, the long-run average cost will not be as steep as the short-run curve, which is relatively steep because of diminishing returns.

8.4 | APPLICATIONS OF PRODUCTION COST

In this chapter, we've explored the links between production technology and the cost of production. We've seen the firm's short-run cost curves, which show how production costs vary with the quantity produced when at least one input is fixed. We've also seen the long-run cost average-cost curve, which shows how the average cost of production varies when the firm is perfectly flexible in choosing its inputs. In this part of the chapter, we look at actual production costs for several products.

APPLICATION

THE PRODUCTION COST OF AN iPOD NANO

APPLYING THE CONCEPTS #1: What are the cost components for electronic products?

What's the cost of producing an iPod Nano, the ultra-thin digital music player with a storage capacity of 2 GB? As shown in Table 8.4, the cost per iPod is $98, which is divided between flash memory, other electronic components, other materials and parts, and assembly cost. The largest part of the cost is the $54 spent on flash memory.

Apple has sold millions of iPods, and its large sales volume gives the company an advantage in negotiating with its suppliers. For example, the flash memory that costs Apple $54 would cost smaller companies about $90. The large volume also provides a large reward for cost cutting. When the company switched the computer chip controlling the click wheel from a $1 chip from Synaptics to a $0.55 chip from Cypress Semiconductor, it saved only $0.45 per iPod, but with millions of units sold, that small savings per unit added up to a large increase in profit. *Related to Exercises 4.1 and 4.6.*

Table 8.4 | THE AVERAGE COST OF AN IPOD NANO

Component	Cost per iPod
Flash memory	$54
Other electronic components	15
Other materials and parts	21
Assembly	8
TOTAL	**98**

SOURCE: Arik Hesseldahl, "Unpeeling Apple's Nano," *BusinessWeek Online*, September 22, 2005, available online at *www.businessweek.com/technology/*, accessed 06/27/2006.

APPLICATION

INDIVISIBLE INPUTS AND THE COST OF FAKE KILLER WHALES

APPLYING THE CONCEPTS #2: How do indivisible inputs affect production costs?

Sea lions off the Washington coast eat steelhead and other fish, depleting some species threatened with extinction and decreasing the harvest of the commercial fishing industry. Rick Funk is a plastics manufacturer who has offered to build a life-sized fiberglass killer whale, mount it on a rail like a roller-coaster, and send the whale diving through the water to scare off the sea lions, their natural prey. According to Funk, it would cost about $16,000 to make the first whale, including $11,000 for the mold and $5,000 for labor and materials. Once the mold is made, each additional whale would cost an additional $5,000. In other words, the cost of producing the first fake killer whale is more than three times the cost of producing the second. In terms of total cost, producing 2 whales would cost a total of $21,000, while 3 whales would cost a total of $26,000, and so on.

This little story illustrates the effects of indivisible inputs on the firm's cost curves. The mold is an indivisible input, because it cannot be scaled down and still produce whales. If Funk wants to cut his production from 2 whales per month down to 1, he still needs the mold; he cannot simply produce half as many whales with a mold that is half the size. The cost of producing the first whale, $16,000, includes the cost of the mold, the indivisible input. Once the firm has the mold, the marginal cost for each whale is only $5,000, so the average cost per whale decreases as the number of whales increases.
Related to Exercises 4.2 and 4.7.

SOURCE: Sandi Doughton, "Killer Whale Latest Idea on Sea Lions," *The Oregonian*, January 7, 1995, p. B2.

3

APPLICATION

SCALE ECONOMIES IN WIND POWER

APPLYING THE CONCEPTS #3: What are the sources of scale economies in production?

There are scale economies in the production of electricity from wind because electricity can be generated from turbines of different size. Although large wind turbines are more costly than small ones, the higher cost is more than offset by greater generating capacity. The scale economies occur because the cost of purchasing, installing, and maintaining a wind turbine increases less than proportionately with the turbine's generating capacity. Table 8.5 shows the costs of a small turbine (150-kilowatt capacity) and a large turbine (600-kilowatt capacity), each with an assumed lifetime of 20 years.

The large turbine has four times the generation capacity of the small turbine—20 million kilowatt hours versus 5 million kilowatt hours—but its purchase price is less than three times as much. The two turbines have the same installation cost, and the operating and maintenance cost of the larger turbine is less than twice as large. Adding the various costs, the larger turbine, with four times the generating capacity, has less than twice the cost. As a result, the average cost per kilowatt-hour is only $0.032 for the large turbine, compared to $0.065 for the smaller turbine. *Related to Exercises 4.3 and 4.8.*

Table 8.5 | WIND TURBINES AND THE AVERAGE COST OF ELECTRICITY

	Small Turbine (150 kilowatt)	Large Turbine (600 kilowatt)
Purchase price of turbine	$150,000	$420,000
Installation cost	$100,000	$100,000
Operating and maintenance cost	$75,000	$126,000
Total cost	**$325,000**	**$646,000**
Electricity generated (kilowatt-hours)	5 million	20 million
Average cost (per kilowatt-hour)	$0.065	$0.032

SOURCE: Danish Wind Turbine Manufacturers Association, "Guided Tour of Wind Energy" (2003), available online at *www.windpower.dk*, accessed 06/27/2006.

4

APPLICATION

INFORMATION GOODS AND FIRST-COPY COST

APPLYING THE CONCEPTS #4: What is the cost structure for information goods?

Consider the cost of producing an information good such as a music CD, a movie on DVD, or a book. In all three cases, the cost of producing the first copy is very high, but the marginal cost of reproduction is very low. Suppose that your band, Adam Smith and the Invisible Hands, has decided to produce a music CD. The cost of recording a set of songs is $100,000. This amount includes the band's opportunity cost of time spent in the recording studio and the cost of studio time at $200 per hour. Once the tracks are recorded and put in a digital format, you can have CDs burned at a cost of $1 per CD, regardless of the number burned.

The table in Figure 8.7 shows the relationships between the quantity of CDs produced and the production cost. In this case, you are using the production facilities of other firms, so the distinction between short run and long run is not important. The marginal cost is constant at $1, but the average cost decreases with the quantity produced. For example, the cost of the first CD is a whopping $100,001, but the average cost drops to $11 for the 10,000th CD and $3 for the 50,000th CD. In Figure 8.7, the average-cost curve is negatively sloped and gets closer and closer to the horizontal marginal-cost curve as the quantity produced increases. The gap decreases as the fixed recording cost is spread over a larger number of CDs. *Related to Exercises 4.4 and 4.9.*

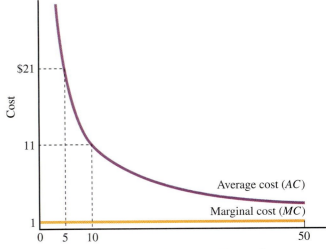

Quantity of CDs	Recording Cost	Burning Cost	Total Cost	Average Cost	Marginal Cost
0	$100,000	$0	$100,000	—	—
1	100,000	1	100,001	$100,001	$1
1,000	100,000	1,000	101,000	101	1
5,000	100,000	5,000	105,000	21	1
10,000	100,000	10,000	110,000	11	1
50,000	100,000	50,000	150,000	3	1

▲ **FIGURE 8.7**
Average-Cost Curve for an Information Good
For an information good such as a music CD, the cost of producing the first copy is very high, but the marginal cost of reproduction is low and constant.

APPLICATION

THE AVERAGE COST OF PRODUCING AIRPLANES

APPLYING THE CONCEPTS #5: Why does average cost decrease as the quantity produced increases?

Suppose you want to design and manufacture a new airplane, one with a performance level comparable to the Boeing 737. To get a rough idea of how much it would cost to design the new aircraft and then produce a particular quantity of airplanes, you could use the Airframe Cost Model developed by U.S. National Aeronautics and Space Administration (NASA).

Figure 8.8 shows the average cost of production for up to 100 airplanes. The fixed cost includes the cost of designing the aircraft and the cost of capital used in the production process, including the machine tools used to fabricate the components of the aircraft. Together these fixed costs add up to about $2.45 billion. The variable cost includes the costs of the materials and labor used to produce the components and then assemble the aircraft. The NASA cost model suggests that the average variable cost decreases as the number of airplanes increases because of labor specialization. The average-

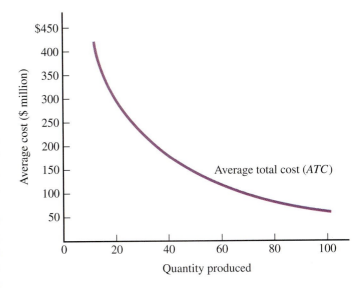

▲ **FIGURE 8.8**

Average-Cost Curve of Aircraft
The average cost per airplane decreases as the number produced increases because the cost of designing the aircraft and the cost of capital are spread over more units and labor specialization reduces variable cost.

cost curve in Figure 8.8 is negatively sloped because as the quantity of aircraft increases, the fixed cost is spread over more units *and* labor specialization pulls down the average variable cost. The average cost decreases from $435 million for a quantity of 10 aircraft, to $257 for 20 aircraft, and so on down to $86 million for 100 aircraft.

The average-cost curve is negatively sloped, implying that there are no diminishing returns in the production of airplanes. This occurs because the cost model assumes that as output increases, production occurs over a longer period of time. Diminishing returns normally occur if an increase in output requires an increase in the number of workers in a given production facility. In the normal case, each worker becomes less productive because each worker gets a smaller share of the production facility—plant and equipment such as machine tools. But if doubling output means that we operate a given production facility twice as long, diminishing returns won't occur: Each worker still gets the same share of the facility, but simply uses the facility for twice as much time.   *Related to Exercises 4.5 and 4.10.*

SOURCE: National Aeronautics and Space Administration, "Cost Estimating Web Site," available online at *cost.jsc.nasa.gov/airframe.html*, accessed 06/27/2006.

SUMMARY

In this chapter, we explored the cost side of a firm, explaining the shapes of the firm's short-run and long-run cost curves. Table 8.6 summarizes the definitions of various types of costs. Here are the main points of the chapter:

1 The negatively sloped portion of the *short-run marginal-cost curve (MC)* results from input specialization that causes increasing marginal returns.

2 The positively sloped portion of the short-run marginal-cost curve (MC) results from *diminishing returns*.

3 The *short-run average-total-cost curve (ATC)* is U-shaped because of the conflicting effects of (a) fixed costs being spread over a larger quantity of output and (b) diminishing returns.

4 The *long-run average-cost curve (LAC)* is horizontal over some range of output because replication is an option, so doubling output will no more than double long-run total cost.

5 The long-run average-cost curve (LAC) is negatively sloped for small quantities of output because (a) there are indivisible inputs that cannot be scaled down and (b) a smaller operation has limited opportunities for labor specialization.

6 *Diseconomies of scale* arise if there are problems in coordinating a large operation or higher input costs in a larger organization.

Table 8.6 | THE LANGUAGE AND MATHEMATICS OF COSTS

Type of Cost	Definition	Symbols and Equations
Economic cost	The opportunity cost of the inputs used in the production process; equal to explicit cost plus implicit cost	—
Explicit cost	The actual monetary payment for inputs	—
Implicit cost	The opportunity cost of inputs that do not require a monetary payment	—
Accounting cost	Explicit cost	—
Short-Run Costs		
Fixed cost	Cost that does not vary with the quantity produced	FC
Variable cost	Cost that varies with the quantity produced	VC
Short-run total cost	The total cost of production when at least one input is fixed	$TC = FC + VC$
Short-run marginal cost	The change in short-run total cost resulting from a one-unit increase in output	$MC = \Delta TC / \Delta Q$
Average fixed cost	Fixed cost divided by the quantity produced	$AFC = FC / Q$
Average variable cost	Variable cost divided by the quantity produced	$AVC = VC / Q$
Short-run average total cost	Short-run total cost divided by the quantity of output	$ATC = AFC + AVC$
Long-Run Costs		
Long-run total cost	The total cost of production when a firm is perfectly flexible in choosing its inputs	LTC
Long-run average cost	Long-run total cost divided by the quantity produced	$LAC = LTC / Q$
Long-run marginal cost	The change in long-run cost resulting from a one-unit increase in output	$LMC = \Delta LTC / \Delta Q$

KEY TERMS

accounting cost, p. 187
accounting profit, p. 187
average fixed cost (*AFC*), p. 190
average variable cost (*AVC*), p. 190
constant returns to scale, p. 194
diminishing returns, p. 187
diseconomies of scale, p. 196
economic cost, p. 186

economic profit, p. 186
economies of scale, p. 196
explicit cost, p. 186
fixed cost (*FC*), p. 189
implicit cost, p. 186
indivisible input, p. 195
long-run average cost (*LAC*), p. 194
long-run marginal cost (*LMC*), p. 195

long-run total cost (*LTC*), p. 194
marginal product of labor, p. 187
minimum efficient scale, p. 196
short-run average total cost
   (*ATC*), p. 191
short-run marginal cost (*MC*), p. 191
short-run total cost (*TC*), p. 189
total-product curve, p. 188
variable cost (*VC*), p. 189

EXERCISES

Visit www.myeconlab.com to complete these exercises online and get instant feedback.

Get Ahead of the Curve

8.1 | Economic Cost and Economic Profit

1.1 The computation of economic cost is based on the principle of _____.

1.2 A firm's implicit cost is defined as the _____ cost of nonpurchased inputs, such as the entrepreneur's _____ and _____.

1.3 Suppose a person quits a job earning $40,000 per year and starts a business with $100,000 withdrawn from a money-market account earning 8 percent per year. The implicit cost of the business is _____ for the entrepreneur's time plus _____ for the entrepreneur's funds.

1.4 The _____ run is defined as a period over which a firm cannot change its production facility.

1.5 When a firm is perfectly flexible in its choice of all inputs, the firm is operating in the _____ run.

1.6 **Computing Cost.** Edward the entrepreneur takes 2 hours to cut a lawn, and he cuts 1,000 lawns per year. He uses solar-powered equipment (truck and mower) that will last forever—and could be sold at any time for $20,000. Edward could earn $12 per hour as a pedicurist. The interest rate is 10 percent.
   a. Given his current output level, compute his marginal cost and average cost of cutting lawns.
   b. Suppose he decides to reduce the number of lawns cut by half, to 500 per year. Compute the new marginal cost and average cost.

8.2 | A Firm with a Fixed Production Facility: Short-Run Costs

2.1 The short-run marginal cost curve is shaped like the letter _____.

2.2 The negatively sloped portion of the short-run marginal-cost curve is explained by _____.

2.3 The positively sloped portion of the short-run marginal cost curve is explained by _____.

2.4 The short-run average cost curve is shaped like the letter _____.

2.5 Over the positively sloped portion of the short-run average-cost curve, the effect of _____ dominates the effect of _____.

2.6 At the current level of output, the marginal cost of chairs is less than the average cost. If you increase output, the average cost will _____ (increase/decrease).

2.7 A marginal-cost curve intersects the average-cost curve at the minimum point of the _____ cost curve.

2.8 The short-run average cost of production is the same for two different quantities. _____ (True/False).

2.9 **Compute the Costs.** Consider a firm that has a fixed cost of $60. Complete the following table:

Output	Fixed Cost (*FC*)	Variable Cost (*VC*)	Total Cost (*TC*)	Marginal Cost (*MC*)	Average Fixed Cost (*AFC*)	Average Variable Cost (*AVC*)	Average Total Cost (*ATC*)
1		$10	___	___	___	___	___
2		18	___	___	___	___	___
3		30	___	___	___	___	___
4		45	___	___	___	___	___
5		65	___	___	___	___	___

2.10 **Changing Costs.** Consider the paddle production example shown in Table 8.2 on page 189. Compute the short-run average cost for 10 paddles with the following changes.
   a. Your opportunity cost of work time triples, from $50 to $150.
   b. The interest rate for invested funds is cut in half, from 10 to 5 percent.
   c. Labor productivity—the quantity produced by each workforce—doubles.

2.11 Compute the Short-Run Costs. Consider a firm with the following short-run costs:

Quantity	Variable Cost (VC)	Total Cost (TC)	Marginal Cost (MC)	Average Variable Cost (AVC)	Average Total Cost (ATC)
1	$30	$90	____	____	____
2	50	110	____	____	____
3	90	150	____	____	____
4	140	200	____	____	____
5	200	260	____	____	____

a. What is the firm's fixed cost?
b. Compute short-run marginal cost (MC), short-run average variable cost (AVC), and short-run average total cost (ATC) for the different quantities of output.
c. Draw the three cost curves. Explain the relationship between the MC curve and the ATC curve and the relationship between the AVC curve and the ATC curve.

2.12 Same Average Cost with Different Quantities? Suppose there are two pencil producers with identical production facilities—identical factories and equipment. The firms pay the same wages and pay the same prices for materials. Sam has a small workforce and produces 1,000 pencils per minute; Marian has a medium-size workforce and produces 2,000 pencils per minute. The two firms have the same average total cost of 10 cents per pencil. Suppose you build a production facility identical to the ones used by the other firms and hire enough workers and buy enough materials to produce 2,500 pencils per minute. Would you expect your average cost to be 10 cents per pencil (like the other two firms), less than 10 cents, or more than 10 cents?

8.3 | Production and Cost in the Long Run

3.1 The presence of indivisible inputs explains the _____ portion of a long-run average-cost curve.

3.2 The notion of replication explains the _____ portion of a long-run average-cost curve.

3.3 Consider the information provided in Figure 8.6 on page 197. Suppose the output of a large aluminum firm drops from 2 million pounds to 1 million pounds per year. The long-run average cost of producing aluminum will go from $_____ to $_____.

3.4 The typical *short-run* average-cost curve is shaped like the letter U, while the typical *long-run* average-cost curve is shaped like the letter L because _____ are not applicable in the _____ run.

3.5 Deregulation and the Cost of Trucking. Suppose the government initially limits the number of trucking firms that can haul freight. The market for truck freight is initially served by a single firm that produces 5 million ton miles of service per year, where 1 ton mile is the hauling of 1 ton of freight 1 mile. The newly elected governor has proposed that other firms be allowed to enter the market. At a public hearing on the issue of eliminating the entry restrictions, the manager of the existing firm issued a grim warning: "If you allow entry into the market, 4 or 5 firms will enter, and the unit cost of truck freight will at least triple. There are big economies of scale in trucking services, so a single large firm is much more cost-efficient than several small firms would be." What's your reaction to this statement?

3.6 Draw the Long-Run Cost Curve. Consider the long-run production of shirts. The cost of the indivisible inputs used in the production of shirts is $400 per day. To produce 1 shirt per day, the firm must also spend a total of $5 on other inputs—labor, materials, and other capital. For each additional shirt, the firm incurs the same additional cost of $5.
a. Compute the average cost for 40 shirts, 100 shirts, 200 shirts, and 400 shirts.
b. Draw the long-run average-cost curve for 40 to 400 shirts per day.

3.7 Diminishing Returns Versus Diseconomies of Scale. Explain the difference between diseconomies of scale and diminishing returns. Based on the cost curves you've seen in this chapter, which is more likely in firms?

8.4 | Applications of Production Cost

4.1 The average cost of producing an iPod Nano is about $_____. (Related to Application 1 on page 198.)

4.2 The cost of producing the first fake killer whale is about three times the cost of producing the second because the firm uses _____ inputs. (Related to Application 2 on page 199.)

4.3 The average cost of electricity _____ (increases/decreases) as the size of the wind turbine increases. (Related to Application 3 on page 200.)

4.4 For information goods such as CDs and DVDs, the cost of producing the first copy is very _____, but the marginal cost of reproduction is _____. (Related to Application 4 on page 200.)

4.5 The average cost per airplane _____ (increases/decreases) as the number of airplanes produced increases. (Related to Application 5 on page 201.)

4.6 Changing the Cost of iPods. Suppose a new flash-memory chip for the iPod Nano has two-thirds the cost of the original chip. The new chip doubles the assembly cost. How does the cost of an iPod with the new chip compare to the cost of the iPod with the original chip? (Related to Application 1 on page 198.)

4.7 A Better Whale Mold? Suppose a new mold is developed for producing fake killer whales. The new mold has twice the cost of the original mold, but cuts the marginal cost of whales to $1,000.

   a. How does the cost of the first whale produced with the new mold compare to the cost with the original mold?

   b. At what quantity of whales will production with the new mold be less costly than production with the original mold? (Related to Application 2 on page 199.)

4.8 The Average Cost of a Super-Sized Turbine. Suppose a new super-sized wind turbine is developed. Fill the blanks in the following table.

	Super-Sized Turbine (1,000 kilowatt)
Purchase price of turbine	$500,000
Installation cost	$100,000
Operating and maintenance cost	$200,000
Total cost	_____
Electricity generated (kilowatt-hours)	40 million
Average cost (per kilowatt-hour)	_____

(Related to Application 3 on page 200.)

4.9 The Average Cost of Drama DVDs. You have been hired to produce a DVD of a play put on by a high-school drama club. It will take you about 50 hours to make the master that is stored on a hard drive on your computer. The opportunity cost of your time is $20 per hour. The marginal cost of burning DVDs is constant at $2. Draw the average-cost curve for producing the DVD, with quantities up to 100 DVDs. (Related to Application 4 on page 200.)

4.10 Limited Time to Produce Airplanes. Suppose you have one year to produce airplanes in a given production facility. Using Figure 8.8 on page 201 as a starting point, draw a hypothetical average cost for producing airplanes. Why does it differ from the curve shown in Figure 8.8? (Related to Application 5 on page 201.)

NOTES

1. Laurits Christensen and William H. Greene, "Economies of Scale in U.S. Electric Power Generation," *Journal of Political Economy*, vol. 84, 1976, pp. 655–676. Reprinted by permission of The University of Chicago Press; Joel P. Clark and Merton C. Flemings, "Advanced Materials and the Economy," *Scientific American*, vol. 255, October 1986, pp. 51–60. Copyright © 1986 by Scientific American, Inc. All rights reserved; Roger Koenker, "Optimal Scale and the Size Distribution of American Trucking Firms," *Journal of Transport Economics and Policy*, January 1977, p. 62; Harold A. Cohen, "Hospital Cost Curves with Emphasis on Measuring Patient Care Output," in *Empirical Studies in Health Economics*, edited by Herbert E. Klarman (Baltimore, MD: Johns Hopkins University Press, 1970); John Johnson, *Statistical Cost Analysis* (New York: McGraw-Hill, 1960).

9

Perfect Competition

In 1992, Hurricane Andrew struck the southeastern United States, leaving millions of people without electricity for several days. Refrigerators stopped working, and thousands of people suddenly needed a lot of ice to cool and preserve their food. The price of a bag of ice immediately rose from $1 to $5. Similar price hikes occurred for bottled

APPLYING THE CONCEPTS

1 What is the break-even price?
The Break-Even Price for a Corn Farmer

2 How do entry costs affect the number of firms in a market?
Wireless Women in Pakistan

3 How do producers respond to an increase in price?
Wolfram Miners Obey the Law of Supply

4 When production costs vary across producers, what are the implications for the market supply curve?
The Worldwide Supply of Sugar

5 When input prices increase with the total output of the industry, what are the implications for the market supply curve?
Zoning, Land Prices, and the Supply Curve for Apartments

water, chain saws to clear downed trees, and tarpaper for roof repairs.

If you had been the governor of Florida in 1992, what would you have

done about the price hikes?

• **perfectly competitive market**
A market with many sellers and buyers of a homogeneous product and no barriers to entry.

• **price taker**
A buyer or seller that takes the market price as given.

• **firm-specific demand curve**
A curve showing the relationship between the price charged by a specific firm and the quantity the firm can sell.

This is the first of four chapters exploring the decisions firms make in different types of markets. Markets differ in the number of firms that compete against one another for customers. In this chapter, we'll look at a perfectly competitive market. In a **perfectly competitive market**, hundreds, or even thousands, of firms sell a homogeneous product. Each firm is such a small part of the market that it takes the market price as given: Each firm is a **price taker**. For example, each soybean farmer takes the market price as given. There is no reason to cut the price to sell more soybeans, because the farmer can sell as much as he wants at the market price. There is no reason to increase the price, because the farmer would lose all of his customers to other farmers selling at the market price.

A perfectly competitive market has two other features. First, on the demand side of the market there are hundreds, or even thousands, of buyers, each of whom takes the market price as given. Second, there are no barriers to market entry, so firms can easily enter or exit the market. To summarize, here are the five features of a perfectly competitive market:

1 There are many sellers.
2 There are many buyers.
3 The product is homogeneous.
4 There are no barriers to market entry.
5 Both buyers and sellers are price takers.

If you're thinking that the model of perfect competition is unrealistic, you're right. Most firms have some flexibility over their prices. For example, when Target increases its price of DVDs, it will certainly sell fewer DVDs, but the quantity sold will probably not drop to zero. Although perfect competition is rare, it's a good starting point for analyzing a firm's decisions, because a price-taking firm's decisions are easy to understand. The firm doesn't have to pick a price; it just decides how much to produce, given the market price. Once you understand this simple case, you will be ready to tackle the more complex decisions made by firms that are *price makers*—able to affect prices. We'll discuss this scenario in later chapters.

In this chapter, we'll see how price-taking firms use information on revenues and costs to decide how much output to produce. The output decisions of price-taking firms underlie the market supply curve and the law of supply. In other words, this chapter reveals the economic logic behind the market supply curve and the law of supply.

9.1 | PREVIEW OF THE FOUR MARKET STRUCTURES

Before we delve into perfect competition, it will be useful to see how our discussion of perfect competition fits into the general scheme of the book. After discussing perfect competition in this chapter, we'll look at three other market structures in the next three chapters. The key difference between perfect competition and these other market structures is that perfectly competitive firms are price takers, while firms in these other market structures are price makers.

Let's start by distinguishing between a market demand curve and the demand curve for an individual firm. As we saw earlier in the book, the market demand curve shows the relationship between the price and the quantity that can be sold in the market, assuming that all firms charge the same price. In contrast, the **firm-specific demand curve** shows the relationship between the price charged by a specific firm and the quantity the firm can sell. In a *monopoly*, a single firm serves the entire market, so the firm-specific demand curve is the same as the market demand curve. As shown in Panel A of Figure 9.1, the monopolist can choose any point on the market demand curve, recognizing that the higher the price, the smaller the quantity the firm will sell.

As shown in Panel B of Figure 9.1, things are different for a perfectly competitive firm. The firm-specific demand curve is horizontal—perfectly elastic. A perfectly competitive firm can sell as much as it wants at the market price of $12, but if it raises its price even a penny, it will sell nothing.

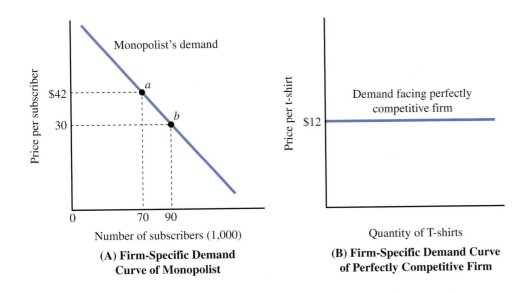

(A) Firm-Specific Demand Curve of Monopolist

(B) Firm-Specific Demand Curve of Perfectly Competitive Firm

◀ **FIGURE 9.1**
Monopoly Versus Perfect Competition
In Panel A, the demand curve facing a monopolist is the market demand curve. In Panel B, a perfectly competitive firm takes the market price as given, so the firm-specific demand curve is horizontal. The firm can sell all it wants at the market price, but would sell nothing if it charged a higher price.

Most markets lie between the extremes of monopoly and perfect competition. Table 9.1 provides a preview of three alternative market structures, which we discuss in the next three chapters:

- *Monopoly.* A single firm serves the entire market. A monopoly occurs when the barriers to market entry are very large. This can result from very large economies of scale or a government policy that limits the number of firms. Some examples of monopolies that result from large economies of scale are local phone service, cable TV, and electric power transmission. Some examples of monopolies established by government policy are drugs covered by patents, the selling of firewood in national parks, and the U.S. Postal Service.
- *Monopolistic competition.* There are no barriers to entering the market, so there are many firms, and each firm sells a slightly different product. For example, coffee shops in your city provide slightly different goods and compete for customers. Your local grocery store sells many brands of toothbrushes, with slight differences in size, shape, color, and style.
- *Oligopoly.* The market consists of just a few firms because economies of scale or government policies limit the number of firms. Some product examples are automobiles, computer processor chips, airline travel, and breakfast cereals. The large economies of scale in automobile production result from the large startup costs, with billions of dollars required to build a factory or assembly plant. Similarly, a fabrication plant for computer processor chips costs several billion dollars.

Table 9.1 | CHARACTERISTICS OF THE FOUR MARKET STRUCTURES

Characteristic	Perfect Competition	Monopolistic Competition	Oligopoly	Monopoly
Number of firms	Many	Many	Few	One
Type of product	Homogeneous	Differentiated	Homogeneous or differentiated	Unique
Firm-specific demand curve	Demand is perfectly elastic	Demand is elastic but not perfectly elastic	Demand is less elastic than demand facing monopolistically competitive firm	Firm faces market demand curve
Entry conditions	No barriers	No barriers	Large barriers from economies of scale or government policies	Large barriers from economies of scale or government policies
Examples	Corn, plain T-shirts	Toothbrushes, music stores, groceries	Air travel, automobiles, beverages, cigarettes, mobile phone service	Local phone service, patented drugs

9.2 | THE FIRM'S SHORT-RUN OUTPUT DECISION

We'll start our discussion of perfect competition with an individual firm's decision about how much output to produce. The firm's objective is to maximize *economic profit*, which as we saw in the previous chapter, equals total revenue minus economic cost. Recall that economic cost includes all the opportunity costs of production, including both explicit costs (cash payments) and implicit costs (the entrepreneur's opportunity costs). In the previous chapter, we saw that the cost of production varies with the quantity produced. In this chapter, we'll see how economic profit varies with the quantity produced and then show how a firm can pick the quantity that maximizes its economic profit.

It's important to note that economic profit differs from the conventional notion of profit. As we saw in Chapter 8, when accountants compute a firm's cost, they include explicit costs, but ignore implicit costs. Accountants focus on the flow of money into and out of a firm, so they ignore costs that do not involve explicit transactions. *Accounting profit* equals total revenue minus explicit costs. Because accountants ignore implicit costs, accounting profit usually exceeds economic profit.

We will use the market for plain T-shirts to illustrate decision making in a perfectly competitive market. Some plain T-shirts are sold directly to consumers, and others are sold to firms that imprint words and images on the T-shirts and then sell the finished shirts to consumers. Plain T-shirts are produced in countries around the world by a large number of producers.

The Total Approach: Computing Total Revenue and Total Cost

One way for a firm to decide how much to produce is to compute the economic profit at different quantities and then pick the quantity that generates the highest profit. As we've seen, economic profit equals total revenue minus economic cost. We looked at the cost side of the profit equation in Chapter 8. The revenue side for a perfectly competitive market is straightforward. A firm's total revenue is the money it gets by selling its product. Total revenue is equal to the price of the product times the quantity sold. For example, if a firm sells 8 T-shirts at $12 per shirt, total revenue is $96 (equal to 8 × $12). If our T-shirt producer has an economic cost of $63, the firm's profit would be $33 (equal to $96 − $63).

Table 9.2 shows the total revenue and total costs of a hypothetical producer of plain cotton T-shirts. Follow the row for an output of 8 shirts. As shown in the second and third columns, the fixed cost is $17, and the variable cost increases with the

Table 9.2 | DECIDING HOW MUCH TO PRODUCE WHEN THE PRICE IS $12

1	2	3	4	5	6	7	8
Output: Shirts per Minute (Q)	Fixed Cost (FC)	Variable Cost (VC)	Total Cost (TC)	Total Revenue (TR)	Marginal Revenue Profit = TR − TC	Marginal (Price) (MR)	Cost (MC)
0	$17	$0	$17	$0	−$17		
1	17	5	22	12	−10	$12	$5
2	17	6	23	24	1	12	1
3	17	9	26	36	10	12	3
4	17	13	30	48	18	12	4
5	17	18	35	60	25	12	5
6	17	25	42	72	30	12	7
7	17	34	51	84	33	12	9
8	**17**	**46**	**63**	**96**	**33**	**12**	**12**
9	17	62	79	108	29	12	16
10	17	83	100	120	20	12	21

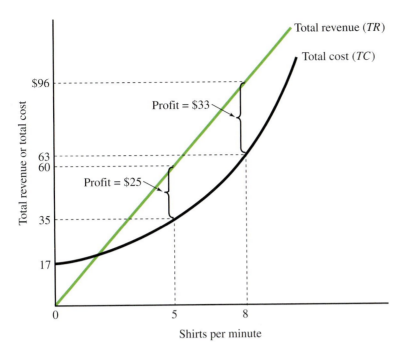

◀ **FIGURE 9.2**

Using the Total Approach to Choose an Output Level
Economic profit is shown by the vertical distance between the total-revenue curve and the total-cost curve. To maximize profit, the firm chooses the quantity of output that generates the largest vertical difference between the two curves.

amount produced. The fourth column shows total cost, the sum of the fixed and variable costs. As shown in the fifth column, at a price of $12 per shirt, the firm's total revenue is $12 times the number of shirts produced. The sixth column shows economic profit, equal to total revenue minus total cost.

Figure 9.2 shows one way to choose the quantity of output that maximizes profit. We're looking for the largest profit, shown by the biggest gap between total revenue and total cost. For example, for 5 shirts, the gap is $25: Total revenue (*TR*) equals $60, and total cost (*TC*) equals $35. Moving down the table and across the figure, we see that profit increases to $30 for 6 shirts:

$$TR - TC = \$72 - \$42 = \$30$$

Profit is maximized at $33 when the firm produces either 7 or 8 shirts:

$$TR - TC = 84 - 51 = \$33$$
$$TR - TC = 96 - 63 = \$33$$

When profit reaches its highest level with two different quantities (7 and 8 shirts in this example), we assume that the firm produces the larger quantity. When the firm produces 8 shirts, its total revenue is $96 and its total cost is $63, leaving a profit of $33.

The Marginal Approach

The other way for a firm to decide how much output to produce involves the marginal principle, the general decision-making rule that is one of the key principles of economics.

MARGINAL PRINCIPLE

Increase the level of an activity as long as its marginal benefit exceeds its marginal cost. Choose the level at which the marginal benefit equals the marginal cost.

Because our firm is in the business to make money, the "benefit" it gets from producing shirts is revenue. The *marginal* benefit—or **marginal revenue**—of producing shirts is the change in total revenue that results from selling one more shirt. A perfectly

• **marginal revenue**
The change in total revenue from selling one more unit of output.

competitive firm takes the market price as given, so the marginal revenue—the change in total revenue from one more shirt—is simply the price:

$$\text{marginal revenue} = \text{price}$$

The marginal principle tells us that the firm will maximize its profit by choosing the quantity at which price equals marginal cost:

> To maximize profit, produce the quantity where price = marginal cost

In Figure 9.3, the horizontal line shows the market price for T-shirts, which our shirt producer takes as given. The price line intersects the marginal-cost curve at 8 shirts per minute, so that's the quantity that satisfies the marginal principle and maximizes profit.

To see that an output of 8 shirts per minute maximizes the firm's profit, imagine the firm initially produced only 5 shirts per minute. Could the firm make more profit by producing more—that is, 6 shirts instead of 5?

- From the seventh row of numbers in Table 9.2 and point *c* in Figure 9.3, we know that the marginal cost of the sixth shirt is $7.
- The price of shirts is $12, so the marginal revenue is $12.

Because the extra revenue from the sixth shirt (price = $12) exceeds the extra cost (marginal cost = $7), the production and sale of the sixth shirt increases the firm's total profit by $5 (equal to $12 − $7). Therefore, it is sensible to produce the sixth shirt. The same logic applies, with different numbers for marginal cost, for the seventh shirt. For the eighth shirt, marginal revenue equals marginal cost, so the firm's profit doesn't change. To be consistent with the marginal principle, we'll assume that the firm produces to the point where marginal revenue equals marginal cost. In this case, the firm chooses point *a* and produces 8 shirts.

If the firm produced more than 8 shirts, it would earn less than the maximum profit. Imagine the firm initially produced 9 shirts. From Table 9.2 and the marginal-cost curve in Figure 9.3, we see that the marginal cost of the ninth shirt is $16 (point *d*), which exceeds the marginal revenue (the market price) of $12. The ninth shirt adds more to cost ($16) than it adds to revenue ($12), so producing the shirt decreases the firm's profit by $4. The marginal principle suggests that the firm should choose point *a*, with an output of 8 shirts. The output decision is the same whether the firm uses the marginal approach or the total approach.

The advantage of the marginal approach is that it is easier to apply. To use the total approach, a firm needs information on the total revenue and total cost for all possible

▶ **FIGURE 9.3**

The Marginal Approach to Picking an Output Level

A perfectly competitive firm takes the market price as given, so the marginal benefit, or marginal revenue, equals the price. Using the marginal principle, the typical firm will maximize profit at point *a*, where the $12 market price equals the marginal cost. Economic profit equals the difference between the price and the average cost ($4.125 = $12 − $7.875) times the quantity produced (8 shirts per minute), or $33 per minute.

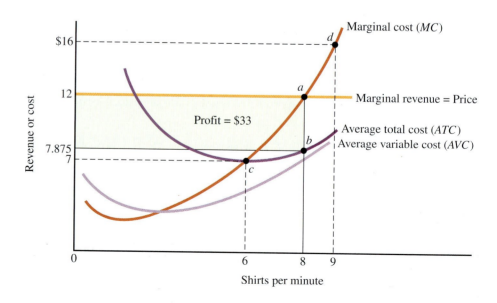

output levels. In contrast, a firm can apply the marginal principle by simply increasing its output by one unit and computing the marginal revenue (the price) and the marginal cost. Using the marginal principle, the firm should produce more output if the price exceeds the marginal cost, or produce less if the opposite is true. The firm can use the marginal principle to fine-tune its decision until the price equals the marginal cost.

Economic Profit and the Break-Even Price

We've seen that the perfectly competitive firm maximizes its profit by producing the quantity at which its marginal revenue (price) equals its marginal cost. How much profit does the firm earn? The firm's economic profit equals its total revenue minus its total cost. One way to compute a firm's total economic profit is to multiply the average profit per unit produced—the gap between the price and the average cost—by the quantity produced:

$$\text{economic profit} = (\text{price} - \text{average cost}) \times \text{quantity produced}$$

In Figure 9.3, the average cost of producing 8 shirts is $7.875 (point *b*), so the economic profit is $33:

$$\text{economic profit} = (\$12 - \$7.875) \times 8 = \$4.125 \times 8 = \$33$$

In Figure 9.3, the firm's profit is shown by the area of the shaded rectangle. The area of a rectangle is the height of the rectangle times its width. In Figure 9.3, the height of the profit rectangle is the average profit of $4.125 per shirt (equal to $12 − $7.875) and the width is the 8 shirts produced, so the profit is $33.

How would a decrease in price affect the firm's output decision? A decrease in price shifts the marginal-revenue (price) line downward, so it will intersect the marginal-cost curve at a smaller quantity. In Figure 9.3, suppose the price drops to $7. The marginal-revenue line will shift downward, causing it to intersect the marginal-cost curve at point *c*, so the firm will produce only 6 shirts per minute. In other words, when the price decreases from $12 to $7 the quantity produced decreases from 8 to 6 shirts. This is the law of supply in action: The lower the price, the smaller the quantity supplied.

What about the firm's economic profit at a price of $7? At point *c*, average total cost is $7, the same as the price. Therefore, economic profit is zero. We have discovered the **break-even price**, the price at which economic profit is zero. The break-even price is shown by the minimum point of the *ATC* curve, where marginal cost equals average total cost. Remember that zero economic profit means that the firm is making just enough money to cover all its costs, including the opportunity costs of the entrepreneur.

• **break-even price**
The price at which economic profit is zero; price equals average total cost.

9.3 | THE FIRM'S SHUT-DOWN DECISION

Consider next the decisions faced by a firm that is losing money. Suppose the price of shirts drops to $4, which is so low that the firm's total revenue is less than its total cost. In Table 9.3, the marginal principle tells the firm to produce 4 shirts at this price, but the firm's total cost of $30 exceeds its total revenue of $16, so the firm will lose $14 per minute. Should the firm continue to operate at a loss or shut down?

Total Revenue, Variable Cost, and the Shut-Down Decision

The decision to operate or shut down is a short-run decision, a day-to-day decision to temporarily halt production in response to market conditions. Suppose our shirt factory hires workers by the day, so the decision is made at the beginning of each day. The decision-making rule is:

operate if total revenue > variable cost
shut down if total revenue < variable cost

Table 9.3 **DECIDING HOW MUCH TO PRODUCE WHEN THE PRICE IS $4**

1	2	3	4	5	6	7	8
Output: Shirts per Minute (Q)	Fixed Cost (FC)	Variable Cost (VC)	Total Cost (TC)	Total Revenue (TR)	Marginal Revenue Profit (P)	Marginal (Price) (MR)	Cost (MC)
0	$17	$0	$17	$0	−$17		
1	17	5	22	4	−18	$4	$5
2	17	6	23	8	−15	4	1
3	17	9	26	12	−14	4	3
4	**17**	**13**	**30**	**16**	**−14**	**4**	**4**
5	17	18	35	20	−15	4	5
6	17	25	42	24	−18	4	7

As we saw in Chapter 8, a firm's variable cost includes all the costs that vary with the quantity produced. In the case of the shirt firm, it includes the costs of workers, raw materials, such as cotton, and the cost of heating and powering the factory for the day. The variable cost does not include the $17 fixed cost of the production facility—for example, the cost of the machines or the factory itself—because these costs are not affected by the decision to operate or shut down.

Although the decision is made at the beginning of each day, we can use the revenue and costs per minute to compare total revenue to variable cost. From Table 9.3, when the price is $4, the best quantity is 4 shirts and the variable cost is $13. The total revenue from selling 4 shirts at $4 per shirt is $16, which exceeds the $13 variable cost. By operating the factory, the firm pays $13 in variable cost to generate $16 in revenue, so the firm is better off operating the facility. The benefit of operating the facility exceeds the variable cost, so it is sensible to produce 4 shirts per minute.

Figure 9.4 shows the firm's choice when the price of shirts is $4. The marginal principle is satisfied at point *a*, where the price equals the marginal cost. As shown by point *b*, the average cost of producing 4 shirts is $7.50, so the firm loses $3.50 per shirt. The shaded rectangle shows the firm's loss of $14. The height of the rectangle is the $3.50 loss per shirt, and the width of the rectangle is the 4 shirts produced.

Of course, if the price drops to a low enough level, the firm will shut down the factory. For example, if the price drops to $1, the firm would be better off shutting the factory down for the day. In this case, the marginal principle is satisfied with 2 shirts

▶ **FIGURE 9.4**

The Shut-Down Decision and the Shut-Down Price

When the price is $4, marginal revenue equals marginal cost at 4 shirts (point *a*). At this quantity, average cost is $7.50, so the firm loses $3.50 on each shirt, for a total loss of $14. Total revenue is $16 and the variable cost is only $13, so the firm is better off operating at a loss rather than shutting down and losing its fixed cost of $17. The shut-down price, shown by the minimum point of the *AVC* curve, is $3.00.

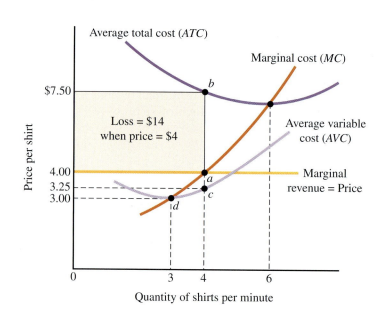

per day. At this quantity, the variable cost is $6, which exceeds $2 revenue ($1 per shirt times 2 shirts). With this low price, the firm's total revenue is not high enough to cover the firm's variable cost from operating the facility, so it is better to shut down for the day.

The Shut-Down Price

There is a shortcut to determine whether it is sensible to continue to operate—compare the price to the average variable cost. Total revenue equals the price times the quantity produced, and the variable cost equals the average variable cost times the quantity produced. Therefore, total revenue will exceed variable cost if the price exceeds the average variable cost. If that happens, the firm should continue to operate. Otherwise, the firm should shut down.

operate if price > average variable cost

shut down if price < average variable cost

In Figure 9.4, with a price of $4, the marginal principle is satisfied at point *a*, and the average variable cost of producing 4 shirts is $3.25 (point *c*). The price exceeds the average variable cost, so it is sensible to continue operating, even at a loss.

The firm's **shut-down price** is the price at which the firm is indifferent between operating and shutting down. To find the shut-down price, we find the minimum point on the *AVC* curve. In Figure 9.4, *AVC* reaches its minimum of $3 at a quantity of 3 shirts per minute, so the shut-down price is $3 (shown by point *d*). The average variable cost never drops below $3, so if the price drops below $3 it would be impossible to generate enough revenue to cover the firm's variable cost. When the price equals the shut-down price, the firm is generating just enough revenue to cover its variable costs, so it is just as well off either operating or shutting down.

How long will a firm continue to operate at a loss? Let's think about what happens when the firm must decide whether or not to build a new production facility. The firm will build a new facility—and stay in the market—only if the price of shirts exceeds the average total cost of production. In other words, the firm will stay in the market only if the market price is high enough for its total revenue to cover *all* the costs of production, including the cost of the new facility. In other words, the price must be greater than or equal to the firm's break-even price. Although a firm might make a short-run decision to operate an existing facility at a loss, the firm won't replace the facility unless a new facility will be profitable.

• **shut-down price**
The price at which the firm is indifferent between operating and shutting down; equal to the minimum average variable cost.

Fixed Costs and Sunk Costs

It's important to note that the decision whether to operate or shut down does not incorporate the fixed costs of the production facility. If we assume that the facility cannot be rented out to some other firm while the shirt firm isn't using it, the fixed cost is a **sunk cost**, a cost that a firm has already paid or committed to pay, so it cannot be recovered. Once the firm incurs this cost, it cannot be avoided by shutting down the factory. Therefore, the firm should ignore the cost of the facility when deciding whether to operate or shut down.

Rent is just one example of an irrelevant sunk cost. The marginal principle tells us that decisions are based on the costs that depend on what we do, not on costs that we can do nothing about. Suppose a dairy farmer spills two-thirds of a 300-gallon load of milk on the way to an ice-cream plant. Should the farmer return to the farm or deliver the remaining 100 gallons? As long as the marginal cost of delivering the milk—the opportunity cost of the farmer's time and the cost of fuel—is less than the amount the farmer will be paid for the remaining 100 gallons, it is sensible to deliver the milk. The spilt milk is a sunk cost that is irrelevant to the farmer's delivery decision. The farmer should not cry over spilt milk, but deliver the rest.

• **sunk cost**
A cost that a firm has already paid or committed to pay, so it cannot be recovered.

APPLICATION

THE BREAK-EVEN PRICE FOR A CORN FARMER

APPLYING THE CONCEPTS #1: What is the break-even price?

To illustrate the notions of break-even and shut-down prices, let's look at these prices for the typical corn farmer. The break-even, or zero-profit, price is $0.72 per bushel. At this price, the farmer will produce at the minimum point of the average total-cost curve, with the average cost equal to the market price of $0.72. At a higher price, the farmer will make a positive economic profit. For example, if the price is $0.92 per bushel and the farmer produces 50,000 bushels, the economic profit will be $10,000:

$$\text{economic profit} = (\$0.92 - \$0.72) \times 50{,}000 = \$0.20 \times 50{,}000 = \$10{,}000$$

The corn farmer's shut-down price is $0.44. At this price, total revenue equals the farmer's variable cost, so the farmer is indifferent about operating as opposed to shutting down. At a price between the shut-down price ($0.44) and the break-even price ($0.72), the farmer will lose money but will continue to operate at a loss because total revenue will exceed the variable cost of growing corn. For example, if the price is $0.50, the farmer will operate at a loss in the short run. However, if the price drops below the shut-down price of $0.44, the farmer will shut down, not bringing any crops to market in a particular year.

In the long run, farmers will exit the corn market if the price is not high enough to cover all the costs of growing corn, including the costs of the production facility. In the long run, the price must be high enough to cover the costs of land, machinery, and vehicles. In other words, farmers will exit the market if the price stays below the break-even price of $0.72. If the price is below this level, the farmer will not raise enough revenue to cover all the costs of growing corn and will exit the market. *Related to Exercises 3.5 and 3.6.*

SOURCE: Walter Adams, *The Structure of the American Economy,* 8th ed. (Upper Saddle River, NJ: Prentice Hall, 1990).

9.4 | SHORT-RUN SUPPLY CURVES

Now that we've explored the output decision of a price-taking firm, we're ready to show how a firm responds to changes in the market price of its product. We'll show the relationship between price and quantity supplied with two short-run supply curves, one for the individual firm and one for the entire market.

The Firm's Short-Run Supply Curve

• **short-run supply curve**
A curve showing the relationship between the market price of a product and the quantity of output supplied by a firm in the short run.

The firm's **short-run supply curve** shows the relationship between the market price and the quantity supplied by the firm in the short run, over a period of time during

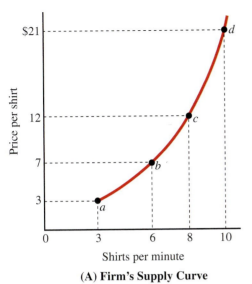

(A) Firm's Supply Curve

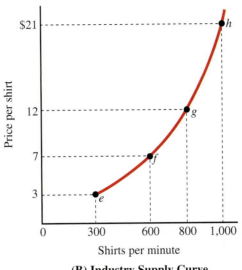

(B) Industry Supply Curve

◄ FIGURE 9.5
Short-Run Supply Curves
In Panel A, the firm's short-run supply curve is the part of the marginal-cost curve above the shut-down price. In Panel B, there are 100 firms in the market, so the market supply at a given price is 100 times the quantity supplied by the typical firm. At a price of $7, each firm supplies 6 shirts per minute (point *b*), so the market supply is 600 shirts per minute (point *f*).

which one input— the production facility—cannot be changed. In the case of shirt producers, the firm's supply curve answers the following question: At a given market price for shirts, how many shirts will the firm produce? In Figures 9.3 and 9.4, we used the marginal principle to answer this question for several different prices: At a price of $3, the quantity is 3 shirts; at a price of $7, the quantity is 6 shirts; at a price of $12, the quantity is 8 shirts.

The firm's short-run supply curve is the part of the firm's short-run marginal-cost curve above the shut-down price. The shut-down price for the shirt firm is $3, so as shown by point *a* in Figure 9.5 the short-run supply curve is the marginal-cost curve starting at $3. For any price above the shut-down price, the firm will choose the quantity at which price equals marginal cost, so we can read the firm's quantity supplied directly from its marginal-cost curve. If the price is $7, the firm will supply 6 shirts per minute (point *b*). As the price increases, the firm responds by supplying more shirts: 8 shirts at a price of $12 (point *c*) and 10 shirts at a price of $21 (point *d*).

What about prices below the shut-down price? If the price drops below the shut-down price, the firm's total revenue will not be high enough to cover its variable cost, so the firm will shut down and produce no output. In Panel A of Figure 9.5, the firm's supply curve starts at point *a*, indicating that the quantity supplied is zero for any price less than $3.

The Short-Run Market Supply Curve

The **short-run market supply curve** shows the relationship between the market price and the quantity supplied by firms as a whole in the short run. Panel B of Figure 9.5 shows the short-run market supply curve when there are 100 identical shirt firms. For each price, we get the quantity supplied for the entire market by multiplying the quantity supplied by the typical firm (from the individual supply curve) by 100. At a price of $7, each firm produces 6 shirts (point *b* in Panel A), so the market supply is 600 shirts (point *f* in Panel B). If the price increases to $12, each firm increases production to 8 shirts (point *c* in Panel A), so the market supply is 800 shirts (point *g* in Panel B).

What happens if firms are not identical but instead have different individual supply curves? To compute the market supply in this case, we would add the quantities supplied by the hundreds of firms in the market. The assumption that firms are identical is harmless: It makes it easier to derive the market supply curve from the supply curve of the typical firm, but it does not change the analysis.

• **short-run market supply curve**
A curve showing the relationship between market price and the quantity supplied in the short run.

Market Equilibrium

Figure 9.6 shows a perfectly competitive market in equilibrium. For a short-run equilibrium, two conditions are satisfied:

1 At the market level, the quantity of the product supplied equals the quantity demanded. The demand curve intersects the short-run market supply curve at a price of $7 and a quantity of 600 shirts per minute (Panel A).

2 The typical firm in the market maximizes its profit, given the market price. Given the market price of $7, each of the 100 firms maximizes profit by producing 6 shirts per minute (Panel B).

In Figure 9.6, the market has reached a short-run equilibrium because the price of $7 generates a total of 600 shirts per minute, exactly the quantity demanded by consumers at this price.

In the long run, firms can enter or leave an industry, and existing firms can modify their facilities or build new facilities. The market reaches a long-run equilibrium when the two conditions for short-run equilibrium are met, and a third long-run condition holds as well.

3 Each firm in the market earns zero economic profit, so there is no incentive for existing firms to leave the market and no incentive for other firms to enter the market.

In Figure 9.6, at the quantity chosen by the typical firm (6 shirts), the price ($7) equals the average total cost, so each firm makes zero economic profit, with total revenue equal to total cost. In other words, the market price equals the break-even price. When economic profit is zero, the firm's revenue is high enough to cover all its costs—including the opportunity costs of the entrepreneur—but not high enough to cause additional firms to enter the market. Each firm that is already in the market makes just enough money to stay in business, so there is no incentive for new firms to enter the market, and no incentive for existing firms to leave.

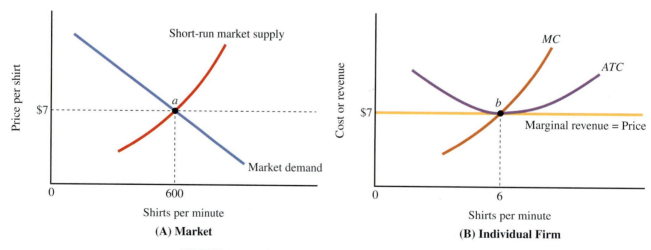

(A) Market   **(B) Individual Firm**

▲ **FIGURE 9.6**

Market Equilibrium

In Panel A, the market demand curve intersects the short-run market supply curve at a price of $7. In Panel B, given the market price of $7, the typical firm satisfies the marginal principle at point *b*, producing 6 shirts per minute. The $7 price equals the average cost at the equilibrium quantity, so economic profit is zero, and no other firms will enter the market.

APPLICATION

WIRELESS WOMEN IN PAKISTAN

APPLYING THE CONCEPTS #2: How do entry costs affect the number of firms in a market?

For another example of a competitive market, consider phone service in the developing world. In many parts of the developing world, people cannot afford their own phones and have traditionally relied on pay phones. The recent development of mobile phones has generated a new competitive industry in many developing nations.

In Pakistan, many poor villagers cannot afford their own phones, and phone service is provided by thousands of "wireless women," entrepreneurs who invest $310 in wireless phone equipment (transceiver, battery, charger), a signboard, a calculator, and a stopwatch. Then they sell phone service to their neighbors, charging by the minute and second. On average, their net income is about $2 per day, about three times the average per capita income in Pakistan. The market for phone service has the features of a perfectly competitive market, with easy entry, a standardized good, and a large enough number of suppliers that each takes the market price as given. In contrast, to enter the phone business in the United States, your initial investment would be millions, or perhaps billions, of dollars, so the market for phone service is not perfectly competitive. *Related to Exercise 4.5.*

SOURCE: TeleCommons Development Group, "Grameen Telecom's Village Phone Programme: A Multi-Media Case Study," 2000, available online at *www.telecommons.com/villagephone*, accessed 06/27/2006.

9.5 | THE LONG-RUN SUPPLY CURVE FOR AN INCREASING-COST INDUSTRY

Let's look at the **long-run market supply curve**, which shows the relationship between the market price and the quantity supplied by all firms in the long run, a period long enough that firms can enter or leave the market. Suppose the typical shirt firm produces 6 shirts per minute, using a standard set of inputs, including a factory, some workers, and raw materials of cotton and thread. In a perfectly competitive industry, there are no restrictions on entry, so anyone can use the standard set of inputs to produce 6 shirts per minute.

We'll start with the case of an **increasing-cost industry**, an industry in which the average cost of production increases as the total output of the industry increases. The average cost increases as the industry grows for two reasons:

- *Increasing input price.* As an industry grows, it competes with other industries for limited amounts of various inputs, and this competition drives up the prices of these inputs. For example, suppose that the shirt industry competes against other industries for a limited amount of cotton. To get more cotton to produce more shirts, firms in the shirt industry must outbid other industries for the limited amount available, and this drives up the price of cotton.

- **long-run market supply curve**
  A curve showing the relationship between the market price and quantity supplied in the long run.

- **increasing-cost industry**
  An industry in which the average cost of production increases as the total output of the industry increases; the long-run supply curve is positively sloped.

• *Less productive inputs.* A small industry will use only the most productive inputs, but as the industry grows, firms may be forced to use less productive inputs. For example, a small shirt industry will use only the most skillful workers, but as the industry grows, it will hire workers with lower skills. As the average skill level of the industry's workforce decreases, the average cost of production increases: A firm will require more labor time—and pay more in labor costs—to produce each shirt.

Another example of progressively less productive inputs is the production of agricultural products such as sugar. Because of variation in climate and soil conditions, it is cheaper to grow sugar in some areas than in others. As the quantity of sugar produced increases, growers are forced to produce sugar in areas with less favorable climates and soil conditions, and this results in higher costs.

Production Cost and Industry Size

Table 9.4 shows hypothetical data on the cost of producing shirts. Let's start with the first row, which shows the firm's production costs in an industry with 100 firms and a total of 600 shirts produced per day (6 shirts per firm). To compute the total cost for the typical firm, we add the cost of the firm's production facility (the cost of the shirt factory), the cost of labor, and the cost of materials. In the first row, the total cost of the typical firm producing 6 shirts per minute is $42, and the average cost is $7 per shirt ($42 divided by 6 shirts). In the second row, if the number of firms doubles to 200 and each firm continues to produce 6 shirts per minute, the total output of the industry will double to 1,200 shirts per minute. For the two reasons listed earlier (higher input prices and less productive inputs), the total cost per firm increases to $60, so the average cost per shirt increases to $10. In the last row, when the total output of the industry increases to 1,800 shirts per minute, the average cost per shirt increases to $13.

The shirt industry is an example of an increasing-cost industry. In the last column of Table 9.4, the average cost increases from $7 for an industry that produces 600 shirts, to $10 for an industry that produces 1,200 shirts, and so on. The average cost increases because firms in a larger industry pay higher input prices and use less productive inputs.

Drawing the Long-Run Market Supply Curve

The long-run supply curve tells us how much output will be produced at each price in the long run, when the number of firms in the market can change. Recall that in the long-run equilibrium, each firm makes zero economic profit, meaning that the price equals the average cost of production.

The data in Table 9.4 shows three points on the long-run supply curve. At a price of $7, a total of 100 firms will be in the market, with each producing 6 shirts per hour. This combination (price = $7 and quantity = 600 shirts) is on the long-run supply curve because the price equals the average cost. Each firm makes zero economic profit, so there is no incentive for firms to either enter or exit the market. This is shown by point *a* in Figure 9.7. Suppose the price of shirts increases. At the higher price, shirt making will be more profitable, and firms will enter the market, increasing total output. Firms will continue to enter the market until the economic profit becomes zero again, which happens when the average cost again equals the price. From Table 9.4, we see that entry will continue until the market reaches 200 firms producing 1,200 shirts at an average cost and price of $10. This is shown by point *b* in Figure 9.7. Point *c* shows another point on the long-run supply curve, with a price of $13 and a quantity of 1,800 shirts.

Table 9.4 | INDUSTRY OUTPUT AND AVERAGE PRODUCTION COST

Number of Firms	Industry Output	Shirts per Firm	Total Cost for Typical Firm	Average Cost per Shirt
100	600	6	$42	$7
200	1,200	6	60	10
300	1,800	6	78	13

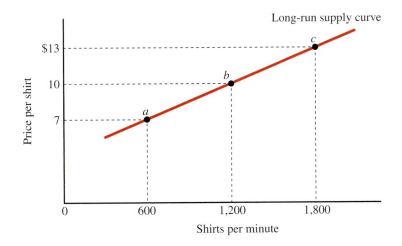

Long-run supply curve

◄ **FIGURE 9.7**
Long-Run Market Supply Curve
The long-run market supply curve shows the relationship between the price and quantity supplied in the long run, when firms can enter or leave the industry. At each point on the supply curve, the market price equals the long-run average cost of production. Because this is an increasing-cost industry, the long-run market supply curve is positively sloped.

The long-run supply curve in Figure 9.7 is positively sloped, as it will be for any increasing-cost industry. This is another example of the law of supply. An increase in the price of shirts initially makes shirt production profitable, so firms enter the market and produce more shirts. As industry-wide output increases, the greater demand for cotton and labor increases input prices, which in turn increases the average cost of producing shirts. Firms will continue to enter the market until the average cost rises to the point where it equals the price of shirts. The positively sloped supply curve tells us that the market won't produce a larger quantity of shirts unless the price rises to cover the higher average cost associated with the larger industry.

3

APPLICATION

WOLFRAM MINERS OBEY THE LAW OF SUPPLY

APPLYING THE CONCEPTS #3: How do producers respond to an increase in price?

For an example of the law of supply with market entry, consider the market for wolfram during World War II. Wolfram is an ore of tungsten, an alloy required to make heat-resistant steel for armor plate and armor-piercing shells. During World War II, the United States and its European allies bought up all the wolfram produced in Spain, thus denying the Axis powers—Germany and Italy—this vital military input. However, the wolfram-buying program was very costly to the Allied powers for two reasons:

- The Allied powers had to outbid the Axis powers for the wolfram, so the price increased from $1,144 per ton to $20,000 per ton.
- Spanish firms responded to the higher prices by supplying more wolfram. Workers poured into the Galatia area in Spain, where they used simple tools to gather wolfram from the widely scattered outcroppings of ore. Because of this market entry, the quantity of wolfram supplied increased tenfold. Because wolfram miners obeyed the law of supply, the Allied powers were forced to buy a huge amount of wolfram, much more than they had expected. *Related to Exercises 5.6 and 5.8.*

SOURCE: D. I. Gordon and R. Dangerfield, *The Hidden Weapon* (New York: Harper & Brothers, 1947), pp. 105–116.

4

APPLICATION

THE WORLDWIDE SUPPLY OF SUGAR

APPLYING THE CONCEPTS #4: When production costs vary across producers, what are the implications for the market supply curve?

The sugar industry is another example of an increasing-cost industry. If the price of sugar is only 11 cents per pound, sugar production is profitable in areas with relatively low production costs, including the Caribbean, Latin America, Australia, and South Africa. At a price of 11 cents, the world supply of sugar equals the amount produced in these areas. As the price increases, sugar production becomes profitable in areas where production costs are higher, and as these areas enter the world market, the quantity of sugar supplied increases. For example, at a price of 14 cents per pound, sugar production is profitable in some countries in the European Union too. At a price of 24 cents, production is profitable even in the United States. *Related to Exercises 5.7 and 5.9.*

SOURCE: Frederic L. Hoff and Max Lawrence, "Implications of World Sugar Markets, Policies, and Production Costs for U.S. Sugar," *Agricultural Economic Research Report* 543 (Washington, D.C.: U.S. Department of Agriculture, Economic Research Service, November 1985).

9.6 | SHORT-RUN AND LONG-RUN EFFECTS OF CHANGES IN DEMAND

We can use what we've learned about the short-run and long-run supply curves to get a deeper understanding of perfectly competitive markets. Let's use the two supply curves to explore the short-run and the long-run effects of a change in demand in a perfectly competitive market.

The Short-Run Response to an Increase in Demand

Figure 9.8 shows the short-run effects of an increase in the demand for shirts. Panel A shows what's happening at the market level. Let's start with the initial equilibrium shown by point *a*: The original demand curve intersects the short-run market supply curve at a price of $7 per shirt and a quantity of 600 shirts. When demand increases, the new demand curve intersects the supply curve at a price of $12 and a quantity of 800 shirts (point *b*). In Panel B, an increase in price from $7 to $12 increases the output per firm from 6 shirts to 8 shirts. At this quantity, the $12 price now exceeds the average total cost, so the typical firm makes an economic profit, as shown by the shaded rectangle.

Point *b* is not a long-run equilibrium, because each firm is making a positive economic profit. Firms will enter the profitable market, and as they compete for customers the price of shirts will decrease. New firms will continue to enter the market until the price drops to the point at which economic profit is zero. How far will the price drop?

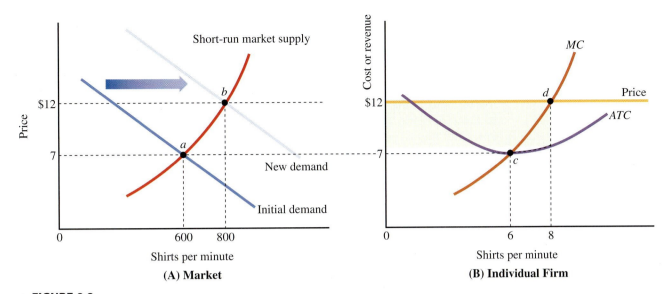

▲ **FIGURE 9.8**
Short-Run Effects of an Increase in Demand
An increase in demand for shirts increases the market price to $12, causing the typical firm to produce 8 shirts instead of 6. Price exceeds the average total cost at the 8-shirt quantity, so economic profit is positive. Firms will enter the profitable market.

The Long-Run Response to an Increase in Demand

We can use the long-run supply curve to determine the long-run price after an increase in demand. In Figure 9.9, the short-run effect of the increase in demand is shown by the move from point *a* to point *b*: The price increases from $7 to $12, and the quantity increases from 600 to 800. Economic profit is positive, so firms will enter the market. As shown by the long-run supply curve, entry will continue until the price drops to $10 and the quantity is 1,200 shirts per minute. The new long-run equilibrium is shown by point *c*, where the new demand curve intersects the long-run supply curve. At this price and quantity, each of the 200 firms produces six shirts per minute and earns zero economic profit.

Figure 9.9 shows how the price of shirts changes over time. An increase in demand causes a large upward jump in the price from $7 to $12 in the short run,

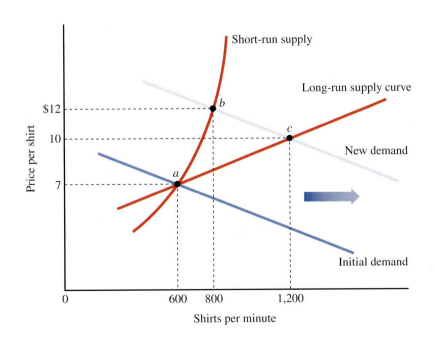

◄ **FIGURE 9.9**
Short-Run and Long-Run Effects of an Increase in Demand
The short-run supply curve is steeper than the long-run supply curve because of diminishing returns in the short run. In the short run, an increase in demand increases the price from $7 (point *a*) to $12 (point *b*). But in the long run, firms can enter the industry and build more production facilities, so the price eventually drops to $10 (point *c*). The large upward jump in price after the increase in demand is followed by a downward slide to the new long-run equilibrium price.

followed by a slide downward to the new long-run equilibrium price of $10. In the short run, firms respond to an increase in price by squeezing more output from their existing production facilities. Because of diminishing returns, it is very costly to increase output in the short run, so the price must increase by a large amount to cover these much higher production costs. The higher price causes new firms to enter the market, and as they enter, the price gradually drops to the point at which each firm makes zero economic profit. The long-run supply curve is relatively flat because firms enter the industry and build new factories, so there are no diminishing returns to increase production costs.

5

APPLICATION

ZONING, LAND PRICES, AND THE SUPPLY CURVE FOR APARTMENTS

APPLYING THE CONCEPTS #5: When input prices increase with the total output of the industry, what are the implications for the market supply curve?

In many communities, the rental-apartment industry is an increasing-cost industry. Most communities use zoning laws to restrict the amount of land available for apartments. As the industry expands by building more apartments, competition is fierce among firms for the small amount of land zoned for apartments. Housing firms bid up the price of land, increasing the cost of producing apartments. Producers can cover these higher production costs only by charging higher rents to tenants.

What are the implications of zoning for a market that experiences an increase in demand? In the short run, the stock of housing is fixed. An increase in demand for apartments will increase the price of apartments (the monthly rent), and firms will convert some owner-occupied houses to rental apartments. This short-run supply response will be relatively small, so the price will increase by a relatively large amount, just as we saw in Figure 9.9 as the movement from point *a* to point *b*. In the long run, firms will enter the market by building more apartments. As we saw at point *c* in Figure 9.9, the new long-run equilibrium is shown by the intersection of the new demand curve and the long-run supply curve. The increase in demand leads to a net increase in price because zoning restricts the supply of apartment land, leading to higher land prices and a higher cost of producing apartments.

Related to Exercises 6.4 and 6.5.

SOURCE: Frank De Leeuw and Nkanta Ekanem, "The Supply of Rental Housing," *American Economic Review*, vol. 61, 1971, pp. 806–817.

9.7 | LONG-RUN SUPPLY FOR A CONSTANT-COST INDUSTRY

So far we have examined products that are produced by increasing-cost industries, whose average cost increases as the industry expands. We turn next to a **constant-cost industry**, an industry whose average cost is constant—it doesn't change as the industry expands. That is, the prices of inputs such as labor and materials do not change as the total output of the industry increases. This happens when the industry uses a relatively small amount of the available labor and materials, meaning that events in the industry—increases or decreases in output—do not affect the price of the input. As a result, the average cost of production for the typical firm doesn't change as the industry grows. In Table 9.4, the shirt industry would be a constant-cost industry if the average cost of shirts were constant at $7, regardless of how many shirts were produced.

• **constant-cost industry**
An industry in which the average cost of production is constant; the long-run supply curve is horizontal.

Long-Run Supply Curve for a Constant-Cost Industry

As an example of a constant-cost industry, consider the production of birthday-cake candles. As the industry grows, it will use more workers, wicks, and wax, but because the industry is such a small part of the markets for labor and materials, the prices of these inputs won't change. As a result, the average cost of production won't change as the industry grows.

The long-run supply curve for a constant-cost industry is horizontal at the constant average cost of production. If the average cost of birthday-cake candles is $0.05 per candle, the long-run supply curve for candles will be horizontal at $0.05, as shown by Figure 9.10. At any lower price, the quantity of candles supplied would be zero, because in the long run no rational firm would provide candles at a price less than the average cost of production. At any higher price, firms would enter the candle industry in droves, and entry would continue until the price dropped to the constant average cost of $0.05 per candle.

Hurricane Andrew and the Price of Ice

For an example of the effects of an increase in demand in a constant-cost industry, let's look at the short-run and long-run effects of a hurricane. In 1992, Hurricane Andrew struck the southeastern United States, leaving millions of people without electricity for several days. Figure 9.11 shows the short-run and long-run effects of the hurricane on the price of ice, which was used to cool and preserve food in areas without electricity. Before the hurricane, the market was at point *a*, with a price of $1 per bag of ice. The long-run supply curve is horizontal, indicating that the ice industry is a constant-cost industry.

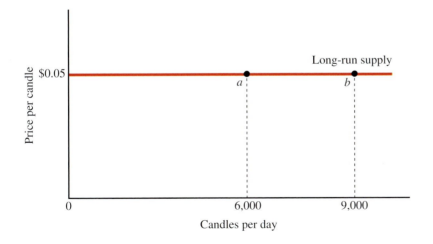

◄ **FIGURE 9.10**

Long-Run Supply Curve for a Constant-Cost Industry

In a constant-cost industry, input prices do not change as the industry grows. Therefore, the average production cost is constant and the long-run supply curve is horizontal. For the candle industry, the cost per candle is constant at $0.05, so the supply curve is horizontal at $0.05 per candle.

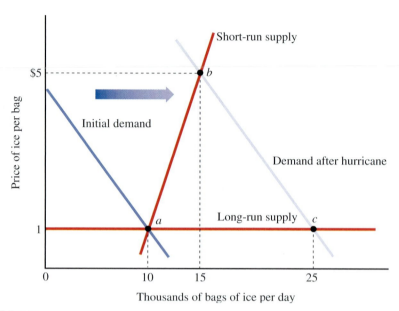

▲ **FIGURE 9.11**

Hurricane Andrew and the Price of Ice

A hurricane increases the demand for ice, shifting the demand curve to the right. In the short run, the supply curve is relatively steep, so the price rises by a large amount—from $1 to $5. In the long run, firms enter the industry, pulling the price back down. Because ice production is a constant-cost industry, the supply is horizontal, and the large upward jump in price is followed by a downward slide back to the original price.

In the short run (a day or two), the number of ice suppliers is fixed. The increase in demand caused by the hurricane moved the market from point *a* to point *b*, and the price rose to $5 per bag of ice. In the long run, firms responded to the higher price by entering the market. Many people trucked ice from distant locations and sold it from trucks parked on streets and highways. As these firms entered the ice market in the days after the hurricane, the price of ice gradually dropped, and the market eventually reached the intersection of the new demand curve and the long-run supply curve (point *c*), with a price equal to the prehurricane price. In the case of the retail ice industry, the long run is just a few days.

This pattern of price changes following the hurricane was observed in other markets. Immediately after the hurricane, $200 chain saws were sold for $900, but the price dropped steadily as new roadside firms entered the market. The same sort of price changes occurred for bottled water, tarpaper, and plywood. The basic pattern was a large upward jump in price followed by a downward slide to the long-run equilibrium price.

If you had been the governor of Florida in 1992, what would you have done about the price hikes? Public officials are often tempted to pass laws prohibiting what's called *price gouging*, charging high prices for scarce goods after a natural disaster. One effect of such laws is to slow the transition from the short run to the long run. The people who set up roadside stands to sell ice were motivated by the high price. If the price were controlled at $1 per bag, few people would have incurred the large expenses associated with trucking the ice from distant locations and setting up roadside stores. The result would have been less ice and more spoiled food. An alternative to a law regulating prices is to leave prices to the market and help to ease the transition from short run to long run by making it easier for entrepreneurs to enter the market.

SUMMARY

In this chapter, we explored the decisions made by perfectly competitive firms and the implications of these decisions for the supply side of the market. In the short run, a firm uses the marginal principle to decide how much output to produce. In the long run, a firm will enter a market if the price exceeds the average cost of production. Here are the main points of this chapter:

1 A *price-taking* firm should produce the quantity of output at which the marginal revenue (the price) equals the marginal cost of production.

2 An unprofitable firm should continue to operate if its total revenue exceeds its total variable cost.

3 The long-run supply curve will be positively sloped if the average cost of production increases as the industry grows.

4 The long-run supply curve is flatter than the short-run supply curve because there are diminishing returns in the short run, but not in the long run.

5 An increase in demand causes a large upward jump in price, followed by a downward slide to the new long-run equilibrium price.

KEY TERMS

break-even price, p. 213
constant-cost industry, p. 225
firm-specific demand curve, p. 208
increasing-cost industry, p. 219

long-run market supply curve, p. 219
marginal revenue, p. 211
perfectly competitive market, p. 208
price taker, p. 208

short-run supply curve, p. 216
short-run market supply curve, p. 217
shut-down price, p. 215
sunk cost, p. 215

EXERCISES

Get Ahead of the Curve

Visit www.myeconlab.com to complete these exercises online and get instant feedback.

9.1 | Preview of the Four Market Structures

1.1 The firm-specific demand curve shows the relationship between the _____ charged by the firm and the _____ by the firm.

1.2 For a perfectly competitive firm, the firm-specific demand curve is _____ (horizontal/negatively sloped).

1.3 For a monopolist, the firm-specific demand curve is the same as the _____ demand curve.

1.4 For a monopolist, the firm-specific demand curve is _____ (horizontal/negatively sloped).

9.2 | The Firm's Short-Run Output Decision

2.1 Economic profit equals _____ minus _____.

2.2 Economic cost equals _____ cost plus _____ cost.

2.3 For a perfectly competitive firm, marginal revenue equals _____.

2.4 A perfectly competitive firm produces the quantity of output at which _____ equals _____.

2.5 At the current output level, a farmer's marginal cost of producing sugar is $0.30. If the price of sugar is $0.22 per pound, the farmer should _____ (increase/decrease) production. If the price of sugar is $0.32 per pound, the farmer should _____ (increase/decrease) production.

2.6 A firm produces 20 units of output at a market price of $5, a marginal cost of $5, and an average cost of $3. The firm's economic profit is $_____, and the firm _____ (is/is not) maximizing its economic profit.

2.7 For the break-even price, _____ equals the price, so the firm earns _____ economic profit.

2.8 Your firm delivers packages by bicycle. If you want to determine whether you are maximizing your profit, you need to know your _____ and your _____.

2.9 **How Many Deliveries?** Consider a delivery firm that delivers packages by bicycle, charging $13 per package and paying each of its workers $12 per hour. One day, one of the workers was two hours late to work, and the number of packages delivered that day decreased by one package.
   a. Did the tardiness of the worker increase or decrease the firm's profit?

b. Based on the new information provided by the tardy worker, should the firm produce more deliveries by hiring more workers, or produce fewer deliveries by reducing its workforce? Explain, using the marginal principle.

2.10 Advice for a Firm. You've been hired as an economic consultant by a price-taking firm that produces scarves. The firm already has a factory, so it is operating in the short run. The price of scarves is $9, the hourly wage is $24, and each scarf requires $1 worth of material. The following table shows the relationship between the number of workers and the output of scarves.

Workers	10	11	12	13	14	15
Output	5	29	41	47	50	52
Labor cost	—	—	—	—	—	—
Material cost	—	—	—	—	—	—
Fixed cost	$2	$2	$2	$2	$2	$2
Total cost	—	—	—	—	—	—
Marginal cost	—	—	—	—	—	—

a. Fill the blanks in the table.
b. What is the profit-maximizing output?

9.3 | The Firm's Shut-Down Decision

3.1 A firm will shut down an unprofitable business if _____ revenue is less than _____ cost.

3.2 Your firm has a total revenue of $500, a total cost of $700, and a variable cost of $400. You should _____ (operate/shut down) because _____ exceeds _____.

3.3 A firm that is losing money should continue to operate in the short run if the market price exceeds _____.

3.4 Your firm has a price of $5, an average total cost of $7, and an average variable cost of $4. In the short run, you should _____ (operate/shut down) because _____ exceeds _____. In the long run, you should _____ (stay in the market/exit) because _____ exceeds _____.

3.5 The typical corn farmer makes zero economic profit at a price of $_____. (Related to Application 1 on page 216.)

3.6 Changes in the Break-Even and Shut-Down Prices. Consider a corn farmer whose initial production costs are the ones reported in the application, "The Break-Even Price for a Corn Farmer." For each of the following changes, explain the effects on the farmer's break-even price and shut-down price. Specifically, will the price increase, decrease, or remain the same? (Related to Application 1 on page 216.)
a. The fixed cost of production increases.
b. The cost of fertilizer increases.
c. The opportunity cost of the farmer's time increases.

3.7 Advice for an Unprofitable Firm. You've been hired as an economic consultant by a price-taking firm that produces baseball caps. The firm already has a factory, so it is operating in the short run. The price of caps is $5, the hourly wage is $12, and each cap requires $1 worth of material. The firm has experimented with different workforces and the results are shown in the first two columns of the table below.

Workers	Caps	Labor Cost	Material Cost	Variable Cost	Total Revenue	Marginal Cost of Caps
14	56	—	—	—	—	—
15	60	—	—	—	—	—

a. Fill the blanks in the table.
b. Is it sensible to continue to operate at a loss with 14 workers?
c. Would it be better to operate with 15 workers? Explain, using the marginal principle.

3.8 A Bluffing Farmer? Consider the following statement from a wheat farmer to his workers: "The price of wheat is very low this year, and the most I can get from the crop is $35,000. If I paid you the same amount as I paid you last year ($30,000), I'd lose money because I also have to worry about the $20,000 I paid three months ago for seed and fertilizer. I'd be crazy to pay a total of $50,000 to harvest a crop I can sell for only $35,000. If you are willing to work for half as much as last year ($15,000), my total cost will be $35,000, so I'll break even. If you don't take a pay cut, I won't harvest the wheat." Is the farmer bluffing, or will the farm workers lose their jobs if they reject the proposed pay cut?

9.4 | Short-Run Supply Curves

4.1 A firm's short-run supply curve shows the relationship between _____ (on the horizontal axis) and _____ (on the vertical axis).

4.2 To draw a firm's short-run supply curve, you need its _____ curve and its _____ price.

4.3 A perfectly competitive industry has 100 identical firms. At a price of $8, the typical firm supplies seven units of output, so the market quantity supplied is _____ units of output.

4.4 Figure 9.6 on page 218 shows a long-run equilibrium because (1) the quantity _____ equals the quantity _____; (2) the typical firm maximizes _____ by picking the quantity at which _____ equals _____; (3) each firm makes _____ economic profit because _____ equals _____.

4.5 In Pakistan, the market for phone service is perfectly _____, because a person can enter the market with a relatively small initial investment—only $310. (Related to Application 2 on page 219.)

4.6 Soybeans Versus Processor Chips. Why is the market for soybeans perfectly competitive, with thousands of soybean farmers, while the market for computer processor chips is dominated by a few large firms? (Related to Application 2 on page 219.)

4.7 Draw the Supply Curves. The following table shows short-run marginal costs for a perfectly competitive firm:

Output	100	200	300	400	500
Marginal cost	$5	$10	$20	$40	$70

a. Use this information to draw the firm's marginal-cost curve.
b. Suppose the shut-down price is $10. Draw the firm's short-run supply curve.
c. Suppose there are 100 identical firms with the same marginal-cost curve. Draw the short-run industry supply curve.

4.8 Maximizing the Profit Margin? According to the marginal principle, the firm should choose the quantity of output at which price equals marginal cost. A tempting alternative is to maximize the firm's profit margin, defined as the difference between price and short-run average total cost. Use the firm's short-run cost curves to evaluate this approach. Draw the firm's short-run supply curve and compare it to the supply curve of a firm that maximizes its profit.

4.9 Expand If Profit Margin Is Positive? Consider a firm that uses the following rule to decide how much output to produce: If the profit margin (price minus short-run average total cost) is positive, the firm will produce more output. Use the firm's short-run cost curves to evaluate this approach. Draw the firm's short-run supply curve and compare it to the short-run supply curve of a profit-maximizing firm.

9.5 | The Long-Run Supply Curve for an Increasing-Cost Industry

5.1 The long-run supply curve shows the relationship between _____ (on the horizontal axis) and _____ (on the vertical axis).

5.2 Arrows up or down: As the total output of an increasing-cost industry increases, the average cost of production _____ because input prices _____ and the productivity of inputs used by firms _____.

5.3 As the total output of an increasing-cost industry increases, the average cost of production _____ (increases/decreases), so the supply curve is _____ (horizontal/positively sloped/negatively sloped).

5.4 In Table 9.4 on page 220, suppose the relationship between industry output and the total cost for the typical firm is linear, and each firm produces six shirts. If there are 400 firms in the industry, the total cost for the typical firm is $_____, and the average cost per shirt is $_____. Another point on the supply curve is a price of $_____ and a quantity of _____ shirts.

5.5 An increase in the price of shirts will cause firms to _____ the industry, and as output increases the _____ cost of production increases. Entry will continue until _____ equals _____.

5.6 During World War II, the quantity of wolfram supplied increased because the Allies' buying program increased the _____ of wolfram. (Related to Application 3 on page 221.)

5.7 As the price of sugar increases, the quantity of sugar produced increases because areas with relatively high _____ enter the market. (Related to Application 4 on page 222.)

5.8 Wolfram Elasticity. Consider the Application, "Wolfram Miners Obey the Law of Supply." Suppose the initial equilibrium price is $1,144 per ton and the output is 100 tons. (Related to Application 3 on page 221.)
a. Using the numbers related in the application, draw a supply and demand graph showing the effects of the Allies' wolfram buying program. Your supply curve should be a long-run curve, which incorporates the entry and exit of firms.
b. Using the formula for the elasticity of supply in the earlier chapter on elasticity, compute the price elasticity of supply.

5.9 Sugar Import Ban. Suppose that initially there are no controls on sugar imported into the United States, so the price paid in the United States equals the prevailing world price. (Related to Application 4 on page 222.)
a. If the world price is 13 cents per pound, what areas of the world supply sugar to the world market and the United States?
b. Suppose the United States bans sugar imports. Predict the new price of sugar.

5.10 Long-Run Supply Curve of Lamps. Suppose each lamp manufacturer produces 10 lamps per hour. Complete the following table. Then use the data in the table to draw the long-run supply curve for lamps.

Number of Firms	Industry Output	Total Cost for Typical Firm	Average Cost per Lamp
40	_____	$300	_____
80	_____	360	_____
120	_____	420	_____

9.6 Short-Run and Long-Run Effects of Changes in Demand

6.1 The short-run supply curve is steeper than the long-run supply curve because of the principle of _____.

6.2 Arrows up or down: Suppose the demand for shirts increases. In the short run, the price _____ by a relatively large amount. As firms enter the market, the price _____. In the new long-run equilibrium, there is a net _____ in price relative to the old equilibrium.

6.3 An increase in demand causes a large initial upward _____ (jump/slide) in price, followed by a downward _____ (jump/slide) to the new long-run equilibrium price.

6.4 Land-use zoning that limits the amount of land for apartments generates a relatively _____ (flat/steep) supply curve for housing, so an increase in the demand for apartments leads to a relatively _____ (large/small) increase in price. (Related to Application 5 on page 224.)

6.5 **Market Effects of an Increase in Apartment Demand.** Consider the market for apartments in a small city. In the initial equilibrium, the monthly rent (the price) is $500, and the quantity is 10,000 apartments. Suppose that the population of the city suddenly increases by 24 percent. The price elasticity of demand for apartments is 1.0. The short-run price elasticity of supply is 0.20, and the long-run price elasticity of supply is 0.50. (Related to Application 5 on page 224.)
  a. Draw demand and supply graphs to show the short-run and long-run effects of the increase in population.
  b. Use the price-change formula from the elasticity chapter to compute the new prices in the short run and the long run.

9.7 Long-Run Supply for a Constant-Cost Industry

7.1 As the total output of a constant-cost industry increases, the _____ cost does not change, so the long-run supply curve is _____ (horizontal/positively sloped/negatively sloped).

7.2 A constant-cost industry consumes a relatively _____ (small/large) amount of inputs such as labor and materials, so as industry output increases the prices of these inputs _____ (increase/decrease/don't change).

7.3 Arrow up, down, or horizontal: In a constant-cost industry, when demand increases the long-run equilibrium price _____.

7.4 Arrows up, down, or horizontal: Hurricane Andrew _____ the demand for ice. In the short run, the price _____ by a relatively large amount. In the long run, the price _____ relative to the prehurricane price.

7.5 **The Price of Haircuts.** The haircutting industry in your city uses a tiny fraction of the electricity, scissors, and commercial space available on the market. In addition, the industry employs only about 100 of the 50,000 people who could cut hair.

a. Draw a long-run supply curve for haircutting in your city.

b. Suppose the initial equilibrium price of haircuts is $12. Draw demand and supply graphs to show the short-run and long-run effects of an increase in population. Does population growth affect the long-run equilibrium price of haircuts?

7.6 **Butter Prices.** Several years ago, people became concerned about the undesirable health effects of eating butter. The demand for butter dropped, decreasing its price. Some time later, the price of butter started rising steadily, although demand hadn't been changing. After several months of price hikes, the price of butter reached the price observed before demand decreased. According to a consumer watchdog organization, the rising price of butter was evidence of a conspiracy on the part of butter producers. Provide an alternative explanation for the rising price of butter and its eventual return to the original price.

10

Monopoly and Price Discrimination

The Coca-Cola Company recently built a new football scoreboard for a large state university. Now football fans can enjoy the latest in scoreboard graphics as they watch the game. In addition, Coca-Cola gave $2.3 million to remodel the university's student center, providing students with a comfortable place to meet, eat, talk, and relax.[1] What explains this outburst of apparent generosity? Does it have anything to do with the fact that Coca-Cola was recently given the exclusive right to sell beverages on campus—a monopoly? Who is really paying for the scoreboard and the student center?

APPLYING THE CONCEPTS

1 What happens when a monopoly ends?
Ending the Monopoly on Internet Registration

2 What is the value of a monopoly?
Bribing the Makers of Generic Drugs

3 When do firms have an opportunity to charge different prices to different consumers?
Paying for a Cold Soft Drink on a Hot Day

4 When does price discrimination work?
Movie Admission versus Popcorn

5 What types of consumers pay relatively high prices?
Hardback Editions Are Relatively Expensive

- **monopoly**
  A market in which a single firm sells a product that does not have any close substitutes.

- **market power**
  The ability of a firm to affect the price of its product.

- **barrier to entry**
  Something that prevents firms from entering a profitable market.

- **patent**
  The exclusive right to sell a new good for some period of time.

- **network externalities**
  The value of a product to a consumer increases with the number of other consumers who use it.

- **natural monopoly**
  A market in which the economies of scale in production are so large that only a single large firm can earn a profit.

In the previous chapter, we explored the decisions made by firms in a perfectly competitive market, a market in which there are many firms. This chapter deals with the opposite extreme: a **monopoly**, a market in which a single firm sells a product that does not have any close substitutes. In contrast with a perfectly competitive, or price-taking, firm, a monopolist controls the price of its product, so we can refer to a monopolist as a *price maker*. A monopolist has **market power**, the ability to affect the price of its product. Of course, consumers obey the law of demand, and the higher the monopolist's price, the smaller the quantity it will sell.

A monopoly occurs when a **barrier to entry** prevents a second firm from entering a profitable market. Among the possible barriers to entry are patents, network externalities, government licensing, the ownership or control of a key resource, and large economies of scale in production:

- A **patent** grants an inventor the exclusive right to sell a new product for some period of time, currently 20 years under international rules.

- When the value of a product to a consumer increases with the number of consumers who use it, **network externalities** are at work. For example, the larger the number of people on an online chat network, the greater the opportunities for interaction. Similarly, the larger the number of people using a software application such as a word processor, the greater the opportunities to share files. Network externalities provide an advantage to existing firms and may inhibit the entry of new ones.

- Under a licensing policy, the government chooses a single firm to sell a particular product. Some examples are licensing for radio and television stations, off-street parking in cities, and vendors in national parks.

- If a firm owns or controls a key resource, the firm can prevent entry by refusing to sell the input to other firms. The classic example is DeBeers, the South African company that controls about 80 percent of the world's production of diamonds. Before the 1940s, the Aluminum Company of America—ALCOA—had long-term contracts to buy most of the world's available bauxite, a key input to the production of aluminum.

- A **natural monopoly** occurs when the scale economies in production are so large that only a single large firm can earn a profit. The market can support only one profitable firm because if a second firm entered the market, both firms would lose money. Some examples are cable TV service, electricity transmission, and water systems.

In this chapter we will discuss "unnatural" monopolies, which result from artificial barriers to entry. Later in the book, we'll explore the reasons for natural monopolies and various public policies to control them.

This chapter examines the production and pricing decisions of a monopoly and explores the implications for society as a whole. As we'll see, monopoly is inefficient from society's perspective because it produces too little output. We'll also discuss the trade-offs with patents, which lead to monopoly and higher prices but also encourage innovation. We'll also explore the issue of price discrimination, which occurs when firms such as airlines and movie theaters charge different prices to different types of consumers. Although we discuss price discrimination in a monopoly, it also happens in markets with more firms, including oligopoly (a few firms) and monopolistic competition (many firms selling differentiated products).

10.1 | THE MONOPOLIST'S OUTPUT DECISION

Like other firms, a monopolist must decide how much output to produce, given its objective of maximizing its profit. We learned about production costs in an earlier chapter, so we start our discussion of the monopolist's output decision with the revenue side of the profit picture. Then we show how a monopolist picks the profit-maximizing quantity.

Total Revenue and Marginal Revenue

A firm's total revenue—the money it gets by selling its product—equals the price times the quantity sold. In this part of the chapter, we'll assume that the monopolist charges the same price to each customer. The table in Figure 10.1 shows how to use a demand schedule (in columns 1 and 2) to compute a firm's total revenue (in column 3). At a price of $16, the firm doesn't sell anything, so its total revenue is zero. To sell the first unit, the firm must cut its price to $14, so its total revenue is $14. To get consumers to buy 2 units instead of just 1, the firm must cut its price to $12, so the total revenue for selling 2 units is $24. As the price continues to drop and the quantity sold increases, total revenue increases for a while, but then starts falling. To sell 5 units instead of 4, the firm cuts its price from $8 to $6, and total revenue decreases from $32 to $30. The total revenue for selling 6 units is even lower, only $24.

The firm's marginal revenue is defined as the change in total revenue that results from selling one more unit of output. This is shown in column 4 of the table in Figure 10.1. For example, the marginal revenue for the third unit is $6, equal to the total revenue from selling 3 units ($30) minus the total revenue from selling only 2 units ($24). As shown in the table, marginal revenue is positive for the first 4 units sold. Beyond that point, selling an additional unit actually decreases total revenue, so marginal revenue is negative. For example, the marginal revenue for the fifth unit is −$2, and the marginal revenue for the sixth unit is −$6.

The table in Figure 10.1 illustrates the trade-offs faced by a monopolist in cutting the price to sell a larger quantity. When the firm cuts its price from $12 to $10, there is good news and bad news:

- Good news: The firm collects $10 from the new customer (the third), so revenue increases by $10.
- Bad news: The firm cuts the price for all its customers, so it gets less revenue from the customers who would have been willing to pay the higher price of $12. Specifically, the firm collects $2 less from each of the two original customers, so revenue from the original customers decreases by $4.

The combination of good news and bad news leads to a net increase in total revenue of only $6, equal to $10 gained from the new customer minus the $4 lost on the first two customers.

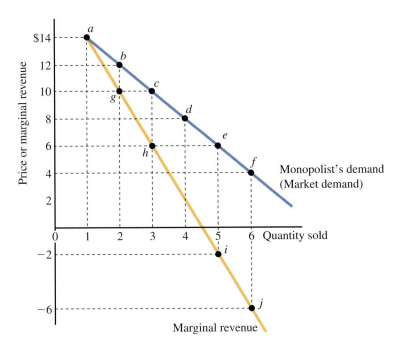

◄ FIGURE 10.1

The Demand Curve and the Marginal-Revenue Curve
Marginal revenue equals the price for the first unit sold, but is less than the price for additional units sold. To sell an additional unit, the firm cuts the price and receives less revenue on the units that could have been sold at the higher price. The marginal revenue is positive for the first 4 units, and negative for larger quantities.

(1) Price (P)	(2) Quamtity Sold (Q)	(3) Total Revenue (TR = P × Q)	(4) Marginal Revenue MR = Δ TR/Δ Q
$ 16	0	0	—
14	1	$14	$14
12	2	24	10
10	3	30	6
8	4	32	2
6	5	30	−2
4	6	24	−6

Our discussion of good news and bad news has revealed a key feature of a monopoly: *Marginal revenue is less than price.* To sell one more unit, the monopolist must cut its price, and the difference between marginal revenue and price is the bad news—the loss in revenue from consumers who would have bought the good at the higher price. In fact, this is true for any firm that must cut its price to sell more.

You may recall from the previous chapter that marginal revenue is different for a perfectly competitive firm, which can sell as much as it wants at the market price. If a perfectly competitive firm sells one unit at $12, it can sell a second unit at the same price, so its marginal revenue is $12 for the second unit sold, just as it was $12 for the first unit sold. For a perfectly competitive firm, marginal revenue is always equal to the price, no matter how many units the firm sells. A perfectly competitive firm does not cut the price to sell more, so there is no bad news associated with selling more.

A Formula for Marginal Revenue

We can use a simple formula to compute marginal revenue. The formula quantifies the good news and bad news from selling one more unit:

marginal revenue = new price + (slope of demand curve × old quantity)

The first part of the formula is the good news, the money received for the extra unit sold. The second part is the bad news from selling one more unit, the revenue lost by cutting the price for the original customers. The revenue change equals the price change required to sell one more unit—the slope of the demand curve, which is a negative number—times the number of original customers who get a price cut.

We can illustrate this formula with a few examples. Suppose the monopolist wants to increase the quantity sold from 2 to 3, so it cuts the price from $12 to $10. The new price is $10, the old quantity is 2 units, and the slope of the demand curve is –$2, so marginal revenue is $6:

marginal revenue = $10 – ($2 per unit × 2 units) = $6

Similarly, to sell the fifth unit, the firm would cut the price from $8 to $6, and marginal revenue is actually negative:

marginal revenue = $6 – ($2 per unit × 4 units) = –$2

Marginal revenue is negative because the $8 revenue lost from the original customers exceeds the $6 gain from the new customer. This happens because there are so many original customers who get a price cut. If a monopolist continues to cut its price, marginal revenue will eventually become negative because there will be so many consumers who get price cuts.

The graph in Figure 10.1 shows the demand curve and marginal-revenue curve for the data shown in the table. For the first unit sold, the marginal revenue equals the price. Because the firm must cut its price to sell more output, the marginal-revenue curve lies below the demand curve. For example, the demand curve shows that the firm will sell 3 units at a price of $10 (point *c*), but the marginal revenue for this quantity is only $6 (point *b*). The firm will sell 5 units at a price of $6 (point *e*), but the marginal revenue for this quantity is –$2 (point *i*). The marginal revenue is positive for the first 4 units and negative for larger quantities.

Using the Marginal Principle

A monopolist can use the marginal principle to decide how much output to produce. Suppose a firm called Curall holds a patent on a new drug that cures the common cold, and must decide how much of the drug to produce.

MARGINAL PRINCIPLE

Increase the level of an activity as long as its marginal benefit exceeds its marginal cost. Choose the level at which the marginal benefit equals the marginal cost.

The firm's activity is producing the cold drug, and it will pick the quantity at which the marginal revenue from selling one more dose equals the marginal cost of production.

In Figure 10.2, the first two columns of the table show the relationship between the price of the cold drug and the quantity demanded. We can use these numbers to draw the market demand curve, as shown in the graph in Figure 10.2. Because the firm is a monopolist—the only seller of the drug—the market demand curve shows how much the firm will sell at each price. The demand curve is negatively sloped, consistent with the law of demand. For example, at a price of $18 per dose, the quantity demanded is 600 doses per hour (point f), compared to 900 doses at a price of $15 (point b).

Like other monopolists, the firm must cut its price to sell a larger quantity, so marginal revenue is less than price. This is shown in the third column of the table as well as the graph. We can use the marginal-revenue formula explained earlier to compute marginal revenue for different quantities of output. The slope of the demand curve is $0.01 per dose. To simplify the arithmetic, rather than using the "new" price and "old" quantity, we can use a matched pair of price and quantities from the demand curve to get an approximation of marginal revenue. When the change in price is relatively small, for example, $0.01, the difference between the new and old price is small enough to be ignored. For example, at a price of $18, the quantity sold is 600 doses, so marginal revenue is $12:

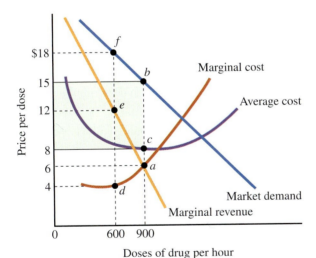

Doses of drug per hour

◄ **FIGURE 10.2**
The Monopolist Picks a Quantity and a Price
To maximize profit, the monopolist picks point a, where marginal revenue equals marginal cost. The monopolist produces 900 doses per hour at a price of $15 (point b). The average cost is $8 (point c), so the profit per dose is $7 (equal to the $15 price minus the $8 average cost) and the total profit is $6,300 (equal to $7 per dose times 900 doses). The profit is shown by the shaded rectangle.

(1) Price (P)	(2) Quantity Sold (Q)	(3) Marginal Revenue (MR = ΔTR/ΔQ)	(4) Marginal Cost (MC = ΔTC/ΔQ)	(5) Total Revenue (TR = P × Q)	(6) Total Cost (TC)	(7) Profit (TR − TC)
$18	600	$12	$4.00	$10,800	$5,710	$5,090
17	700	10	4.60	11,900	6,140	5,760
16	800	8	5.30	12,800	6,635	6,165
15	**900**	**6**	**6.00**	**13,500**	**7,200**	**6,300**
14	1,000	4	6.70	14,000	7,835	6,165
13	1,100	2	7.80	14,300	8,560	5,740
12	1,200	0	9.00	14,400	9,400	5,000

$$\text{marginal revenue} = \$18 - (\$0.01 \times 600 \text{ doses}) = \$12$$

Similarly, at a price of $15, the quantity is 900 doses and marginal revenue is $6:

$$\text{marginal revenue} = \$15 - (\$0.01 \times 900 \text{ doses}) = \$6$$

We're ready to show how a monopolist can use the marginal principle to pick a quantity to produce. To maximize its profit, the firm will produce the quantity at which the marginal revenue equals marginal cost. As shown in the fourth row in the table in Figure 10.2, this happens with a quantity of 900 doses. In the graph, the marginal-revenue curve intersects the marginal-cost curve at point *a*, with a quantity of 900 doses, so that's the quantity that maximizes profit. To get consumers to buy this quantity, the price must be $15 (point *b* on the demand curve). The average cost of production is $8 per dose (shown by point *c*).

We can compute the firm's profit in two ways. First, profit equals total revenue minus total cost:

$$\text{profit} = \text{total revenue} - \text{total cost}$$
$$\text{profit} = \$15 \text{ per dose} \times 900 \text{ doses} - \$8 \text{ per dose} \times 900 \text{ doses} = \$6,300$$

Second, we can compute the profit per dose and multiply it by the number of doses:

$$\text{profit} = \text{profit per dose} \times \text{quantity of doses}$$

The profit per dose is the price minus the average cost: $7 = $15 − $8:

$$\text{profit} = \$7 \text{ per dose} \times 900 \text{ doses} = \$6,300$$

To show that a quantity of 900 doses maximizes the firm's profit, let's see what would happen if the firm picked some other quantity. Suppose the firm decided to produce 599 doses per hour at a price just above $18 (just above point *f* on the demand curve). Could the firm make more profit by cutting the price by enough to sell one more dose? The firm should answer two questions:

• What is the extra cost associated with producing dose number 600? As shown by point *d* on the marginal-cost curve, the marginal cost of the 600th dose is $4.

• What is the extra revenue associated with dose number 600? As shown by point *e* on the marginal-revenue curve, the marginal revenue is $12.

If the firm wants to maximize its profit, it should produce the 600th dose because the $12 extra revenue exceeds the $4 extra cost, meaning that the firm's profit will increase by $8. The same argument applies, with different numbers for marginal revenue and marginal cost, for doses 601, 602, and so on, up to 900 doses. The firm should continue to increase the quantity produced as long as the marginal revenue exceeds the marginal cost. The marginal principle is satisfied at point *a*, with a total of 900 doses.

Why should the firm stop at 900 doses? Beyond 900 doses, the marginal revenue from an additional dose will be less than the marginal cost associated with producing it. Although the firm could cut its price and sell a larger quantity, an additional dose would add less to revenue than it adds to cost, so the firm's total profit would decrease. As shown in the fifth row in the table in Figure 10.2, the firm could sell 1,000 doses at a price of $14, but the marginal revenue at this quantity is only $4, while the marginal cost at this quantity is $6.70. Producing the 1,000th dose would decrease the firm's profit by $2.70. For any quantity exceeding 900 doses, the marginal revenue is less than the marginal cost. Therefore, the firm should produce exactly 900 doses.

Let's review what we've learned about how a monopolist picks a quantity and how to compute the monopoly profit. The three-step process is as follows:

1 Find the quantity that satisfies the marginal principle, that is, the quantity at which marginal revenue equals marginal cost. In the example shown in Figure

10.2, marginal revenue equals marginal cost at point *a*, so the monopolist produces 900 doses.

2 Using the demand curve, find the price associated with the monopolist's chosen quantity. In Figure 10.2, the price required to sell 900 doses is $15 (point *b*).

3 Compute the monopolist's profit. The profit per unit sold equals the price minus the average cost, and the total profit equals the profit per unit times the number of units sold. In Figure 10.2, the profit is shown by the shaded rectangle, with height equal to the profit per unit sold and width equal to the number of units sold.

10.2 | THE SOCIAL COST OF MONOPOLY

Why should we as a society be concerned about monopoly? Most people are not surprised to hear that a monopolist uses its market power to charge a relatively high price. If this were the end of the story, a monopolist would simply gain at the expense of consumers. In other words, a monopoly would change how we slice the economic "pie," with a bigger slice for producers and a smaller slice for consumers. As we'll see in this part of the chapter, the social consequences of monopoly go beyond a different slicing of the pie: A monopoly causes inefficiency and actually reduces the size of the pie, so there is less to divide among consumers and producers.

Deadweight Loss from Monopoly

How does a monopoly differ from a perfectly competitive market? To show the difference, let's consider an example of an arthritis drug that could be produced by a monopoly or a perfectly competitive industry. Let's take the long-run perspective—a period of time long enough that a firm is perfectly flexible in its choice of inputs and can enter or leave the market.

Consider the monopoly outcome first. Let's assume that the long-run average cost of producing the arthritis drug is constant at $8 per dose. As we saw in the chapter on production and cost, if average cost is constant, the marginal cost equals the average cost. In Panel A of Figure 10.3, the long-run marginal-cost curve is the same as the long-run average-cost curve. Given the demand and marginal-revenue curves in Panel A of Figure 10.3, the monopolist will maximize profit where marginal revenue equals marginal cost (point *a*), producing 200 doses per hour at a price of $18 per dose (point *b*). The monopolist's profit is $2,000 per hour—a $10 profit per dose ($18 − $8) times 200 doses.

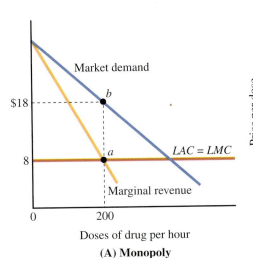

(A) Monopoly

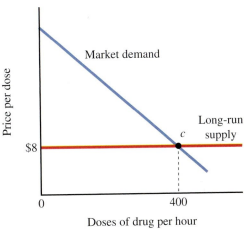

(B) Perfect Competition

◄ **FIGURE 10.3**
Monopoly Versus Perfect Competition: Its Effect on Price and Quantity
(**A**) The monopolist picks the quantity at which the long-run marginal cost equals marginal revenue—200 does per hour, as shown by point *a*. As shown by point *b* on the demand curve, the price required to sell this quantity is $18 per dose.
(**B**) The long-run supply curve of a perfectly competitive, constant-cost industry intersects the demand curve at point *c*. The equilibrium price is $8, and the equilibrium quantity is 400 doses.

► **FIGURE 10.4**

The Deadweight Loss from a Monopoly

A switch from perfect competition to monopoly increases the price from $8 to $18 and decreases the quantity sold from 400 to 200 doses. Consumer surplus decreases by an amount shown by the areas *B* and *D*, while profit increases by the amount shown by rectangle *B*. The net loss to society is shown by triangle *D*, the deadweight loss from monopoly.

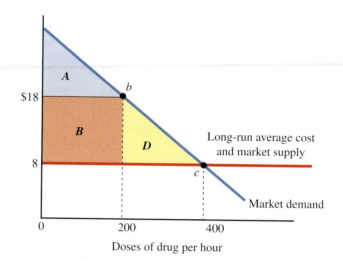

Doses of drug per hour

Consider next the market for the arthritis drug under perfect competition. We're assuming that the arthritis drug industry is a constant-cost industry: Input prices do not change as the industry grows, so the long-run market supply curve is horizontal at the long-run average cost of producing the drug, which is $8 per dose. In Panel B of Figure 10.3, the horizontal long-run supply curve intersects the demand curve at point *c*, with an equilibrium price of $8 and an equilibrium quantity of 400 doses per hour. Compared to a monopoly outcome, the perfectly competitive outcome has a lower price ($8 instead of $18 per dose) and a larger quantity (400 doses instead of 200).

To examine the social cost of monopoly power, let's imagine that we start with a perfectly competitive market, and then switch to a monopoly. Consumers will be worse off under monopoly, and we can use the concept of consumer surplus to determine just how much worse off they will be. As we saw in the chapter on market efficiency, consumer surplus is shown by the area between the demand curve and the horizontal price line. In Figure 10.4, the monopoly price is $18, so the consumer surplus with a monopoly is shown by triangle *A*. In contrast, the perfectly competitive price is $8, so the consumer surplus with perfect competition is shown by the larger triangle consisting of triangle *A*, rectangle *B*, and triangle *D*. In other words, a switch from perfect competition to monopoly decreases consumer surplus by the areas *B* and *D*.

We can use some simple geometry to compute the reduction in consumer surplus. The formula for the area of a rectangle is

$$\text{area of rectangle} = \text{base} \times \text{height}$$

In Figure 10.4, the base of rectangle *B* is 200 and the height is $10, so the area is $2,000:

$$\text{area of rectangle } B = 200 \text{ doses} \times \$10 \text{ per dose} = \$2,000$$

The switch to monopoly increases the price by $10 per dose, so consumers pay $10 extra on the 200 doses they buy from the monopolist, resulting in a loss of $2,000. The other part of the consumer loss is triangle *D*. The formula for the area of a triangle is

$$\text{area of triangle} = 1/2 \times \text{base} \times \text{height}$$

In Figure 10.4, the base of triangle *D* is 200 and the height is $10, so the area is $1,000:

$$\text{area of triangle } D = 1/2 \times 200 \text{ doses} \times \$10 \text{ per dose} = \$1,000$$

The switch to monopoly increases the price and decreases the quantity demanded because consumers obey the law of demand. Consumers lose consumer surplus on the doses they would have consumed at the lower price, and this $1,000 loss is shown by triangle *D*. The total loss of consumers is the sum of the areas of rectangle *B* and triangle *D*, or $3,000.

It's clear that consumers lose from monopoly, but what about the monopolist? Under perfect competition, each firm makes zero economic profit. In contrast, the monopolist earns positive economic profit, shown by rectangle *B* in Figure 10.4. The monopolist's profit per dose is $10, the $18 price minus the $8 average cost. The monopolist's profit is $2,000:

$$\text{profit} = \$10 \text{ per dose} \times 200 \text{ doses} = \$2,000$$

This $2,000 gain by the monopolist comes at the expense of consumers.

Because only part of the loss experienced by consumers is recovered by the monopolist, there is a net loss from switching to monopoly. Consumers lose rectangle *B* and triangle *D*, but the monopolist gains only rectangle *B*. That leaves triangle *D* as the net decrease in the market surplus, or **deadweight loss from monopoly**. The word *deadweight* indicates that this loss is not offset by a gain to anyone. Triangle *D* measures the consumer surplus lost because the monopoly produces less output than a perfectly competitive market. The monopolist prevents consumers from getting consumer surplus for the 201st through the 400th units of output, meaning that the monopolist reduces the size of the economic pie and causes inefficiency. The lesson is that monopoly is inefficient because it generates less output than a perfectly competitive market.

- **deadweight loss from monopoly**
  A measure of the inefficiency from monopoly; equal to the decrease in the market surplus.

Rent Seeking: Using Resources to Get Monopoly Power

Another source of inefficiency from a monopoly is the use of resources to acquire monopoly power. Because a monopoly is likely earn a profit, firms are willing to spend of money to persuade the government to erect barriers to entry that grant monopoly power through licenses, franchises, and tariffs. In Figure 10.4, a firm would be willing to spend up to $2,000 per hour to get a monopoly on the arthritis drug. One way to get monopoly power is to hire lobbyists to persuade legislators and other policy makers to grant monopoly power. **Rent seeking** is the process of using public policy to gain economic profit.

- **rent seeking**
  The process of using public policy to gain economic profit.

Rent seeking is inefficient because it uses resources that could be used in other ways. For example, the people employed as lobbyists could instead produce goods and services. In Figure 10.4, if the monopolist spent all its potential profit of $2,000 per hour on rent-seeking activity, the net loss to society would be areas *B* and *D*, not just area *D*. A classic study of rent seeking by economist Richard Posner found that firms in some industries spent up to 30 percent of their total revenue to get monopoly power.[2]

At the beginning of this chapter, we saw that Coca-Cola helped a state university to build a new football scoreboard and remodel its student center. Was this an act of generosity? In return for the scoreboard and the remodeled student center, Coca-Cola earned the exclusive right to sell beverages on campus. Like any monopolist, Coca-Cola will use its monopoly power to charge higher prices for beverages, so the cost of the scoreboard and student center actually comes out of the pockets of students. Although Coca-Cola has a monopoly on beverages, some of the profit from the monopoly goes to the university to pay for the scoreboard and the student center.

Monopoly and Public Policy

Given the social costs of monopoly, the government has a number of policies to intervene in markets that are dominated by a single firm or could become a monopoly. We'll examine these policies later in the book. In the case of natural monopoly—a market that can support only a single firm—the government can intervene by regulating the price charged by the natural monopolist. In other markets, the government

APPLICATION

ENDING THE MONOPOLY ON INTERNET REGISTRATION

APPLYING THE CONCEPTS #1: What happens when a monopoly ends?

For an illustration of the inefficiency of monopoly, we can look at what happens when a government-sanctioned monopoly ends. In February 1999, the U.S. government announced plans to end the five-year monopoly held by Network Solutions Inc. for registering Internet addresses. Network Solutions had an exclusive government contract to register Web addresses, also known as *domain names*, ending in .net, .org, .edu, and .com. The company registered almost 2 million names in 1998, collecting $70 for each address and charging an annual renewal fee of $35. The government's plan to introduce competition had some restrictions—an entering firm had to meet strict requirements for security and backup measures and liability insurance. Two new competitors, Register.com and Tucows.com, cut prices to between $10 and $15 per year. In addition, the new firms offered longer registration periods and permitted more characters in each domain name. Network Solutions, the original monopolist, quickly matched its competitors' lower prices and expanded service options. *Related to Exercises 2.4 and 2.5.*

SOURCE: "Tucows.com to Slash Domain Name Registration Rates," *Newsbytes News Network*, January 11, 2000; "Network Solutions Offers 10-Year.Com Registrations," *Newsbytes News Network*, January 18, 2000; "Register.com Latest to Offer Long Domain Names," *Newsbytes News Network*, January 11, 2000. *http://www.newsbytes.com*; Accessed 06/28/2006.

uses antitrust policies to break up monopolies into smaller companies and prevent corporate mergers that would lead to a monopoly. These policies are designed to promote competition, leading to lower prices and more production.

10.3 | PATENTS AND MONOPOLY POWER

One source of monopoly power is a government patent that gives a firm the exclusive right to produce a product for 20 years. As we'll see, a patent encourages innovation because the innovators know they will earn monopoly profits on a new product over the period covered by the patent. If the monopoly profits are large enough to offset the substantial research and development costs of a new product, a firm will develop the product and become a monopolist. Granting monopoly power through a patent may be efficient from the social perspective because it may encourage the development of products that would otherwise not be developed.

Incentives for Innovation

Let's use the arthritis drug to show why a patent encourages innovation. Suppose that a firm called Flexjoint hasn't yet developed the drug, but believes the potential benefits and costs of developing the drug are as follows:

- The economic cost of research and development would be $14 million, including all of the opportunity costs of the project.

- The estimated annual economic profit from a monopoly would be $2 million (in today's dollars).
- Flexjoint's competitors will need three years to develop and produce their own versions of the drug, so if Flexjoint isn't protected by a patent, its monopoly will last only three years.

Based on these numbers, Flexjoint won't develop the drug unless the firm receives a patent that lasts at least seven years. That's the length of time the firm needs to recover the research and development costs of $14 million ($2 million per year times seven years). If there is no patent and the firm loses its monopoly in three years, it will earn a profit of $6 million, which is less than the cost of research and development. By comparison, with a 20-year patent the firm will earn $40 million, which is more than enough to recover the $14 million cost.

Trade-Offs from Patents

Is the patent for Flexjoint's drug beneficial from the social perspective? The patent grants monopoly power to the firm, and it responds by charging a higher price and producing less than the quantity that would be produced in a perfectly competitive market. Looking back at Figure 10.4, a monopolist produces 200 doses per hour instead of 400. From society's perspective, 400 doses would be better than 200 doses, but we don't have that choice. Flexjoint won't develop the drug unless a patent protects the firm from competition for at least seven years. Therefore, society's choice is between the monopoly outcome of 200 doses or zero doses. Because a quantity of 200 doses is clearly better than none, the patent is beneficial from society's perspective.

What about a product that a firm would develop without the protection of a patent? Suppose we change the Flexjoint example by changing one number: The cost of research and development is only $5 million, not $14 million. Suppose that it still takes Flexjoint's competitors three years to develop a substitute, and Flexjoint's profit per year is still $2 million. Without a patent, Flexjoint would earn an economic profit of $6 million during its three-year monopoly ($2 million per year times three years), which is more than the $5 million cost of research and development. Therefore, the firm would develop the new drug even without a patent. In this case, a patent would merely prolong a monopoly, and so it would be inefficient from society's perspective.

What are the general conclusions about the merits of the patent system? It is sensible for a government to grant a patent for a product that would otherwise not be developed, but it is not sensible for other products. Unfortunately, no one knows in advance whether a particular product would be developed without a patent, so the government can't be selective in granting patents. In some cases, patents lead to new products, while in other cases patents merely prolong monopoly power.

10.4 | PRICE DISCRIMINATION

Up to this point in the book, we've assumed that a firm charges the same price to all of its consumers. As we'll see in this part of the chapter, a firm may be able to divide consumers into two or more groups and sell the good at a different price to each group, a practice known as **price discrimination**. For example, airlines offer discount tickets to travelers who are flexible in their departure times, and movie theaters have lower prices for senior citizens.

Although price discrimination is widespread, it is not always possible. A firm has an opportunity for price discrimination if three conditions are met:

1 Market power. The firm must have some control over its price, facing a negatively sloped demand curve for its product. Although we will discuss price discrimination by a monopolist, any firm that faces a negatively sloped demand curve can charge dif-

- **price discrimination**
The practice of selling a good at different prices to different consumers.

APPLICATION

BRIBING THE MAKERS OF GENERIC DRUGS

APPLYING THE CONCEPTS #2: What is the value of a monopoly?

When a patent expires, new firms enter the market, and the resulting competition for consumers decreases prices and increases quantities. In the pharmaceutical drug market, when the patent for a brand-name drug expires, other firms introduce generic versions of the drug. The generics are virtually identical to the original branded drug, but they sell at a much lower price. The producers of branded drugs have an incentive to delay the introduction of generic drugs and sometimes use illegal means to do so.

In recent years, the Federal Trade Commission (FTC) has investigated allegations that the makers of branded drugs made deals with generic suppliers to keep generics off the market. The alleged practices included cash payments and exclusive licenses for new versions of the branded drug. In 2003, the FTC ruled that Schering-Plough and Upsher-Smith Laboratories entered into an illegal agreement to keep a generic version of a heart medicine off the market. Schering-Plough paid Upsher-Smith $60 million to delay the introduction of a low-price alternative to its prescription drug K-Dur-20, which is used to treat people with low potassium.

Another tactic used by the producers of branded drugs is to claim that generics are not as good as the branded drug. DuPont has claimed that generic versions of its Coumadin (a blood thinner) are not equivalent to Coumadin, and may pose risks to patients. Because generic versions are virtually identical to the branded drugs, such claims are not based on science. *Related to Exercises 3.3 and 3.4.*

SOURCE: Federal Trade Commission, "Commission Rules Schering-Plough, Upsher, and AHP Illegally Delayed Entry of Lower-Cost Generic Drug," *http://www.ftc.gov/opa/2003/12/schering.htm*; accessed 07/09/2006.

ferent prices to different consumers. In fact, the only type of firm that cannot engage in price discrimination is a perfectly competitive price-taking firm. Such a firm faces a horizontal demand curve, taking the market price as given. For all other types of markets—monopoly, oligopoly, and monopolistic competition—price discrimination is possible.

2 Different consumer groups. Consumers must differ in their willingness to pay for the product or in their responsiveness to changes in price, as measured by the price elasticity of demand. In addition, the firm must be able to identify different groups of consumers. For example, an airline must be able to distinguish between business travelers and tourists, and a movie theater must be able to distinguish between seniors and nonseniors.

3 Resale is not possible. It must be impractical for one consumer to resell the product to another consumer. Airlines prohibit consumers from buying and reselling tickets. If airlines allowed consumers to sell discount tickets to each other, you could go into the business as a ticket broker, buying discount airline tickets one month ahead and then selling them to business travelers one week before the travel date. In general, the possibility of resale causes price discrimination to break down.

One approach to price discrimination is to offer a discount, a lower price to some types of consumers. The firm identifies a group of customers who are not willing to pay the regular price and then offers a discount to people in the group. Here are some examples of price discrimination with group discounts:

- **Discounts on airline tickets.** Airlines offer discount tickets to travelers who spend Saturday night away from home because they are likely to be tourists, not business travelers. The typical tourist is not willing to pay as much for air travel as the typical business traveler. Airlines also offer discount tickets to people who plan weeks ahead, because tourists plan longer ahead than business travelers.
- **Discount coupons for groceries and restaurant food.** The typical coupon-clipper is not willing to pay as much as the typical consumer.
- **Manufacturers' rebates for appliances.** A person who takes the trouble to mail a rebate form to the manufacturer is not willing to pay as much as the typical consumer.
- **Senior-citizen discounts on airline tickets, restaurant food, drugs, and entertainment.**
- **Student discounts on movies and concerts.**

The only legal restriction on price discrimination is that a firm cannot use it to drive rival firms out of business.

The challenge for a firm is to figure out which groups of consumers should get discounts. Firms can experiment with different prices and identify groups of consumers that are most sensitive to price. In September 2000, Amazon.com started charging different prices for different types of consumers. For example, consumers who used Netscape's browser paid $65 for the *Planet of the Apes* DVD, while Internet Explorer users paid $75 for the same DVD. Prices also varied with the consumer's Internet service provider and the number of previous purchases from Amazon. An Amazon spokeswoman said that the company varied prices in a random fashion, as part of ongoing tests to see how consumers respond to price changes. In other words, it appears that Amazon was assessing the willingness to pay of different types of consumers. In principle, Amazon could use the data collected to develop systems of price discrimination, giving discounts to the most price-sensitive consumers. After widespread protests of the Amazon pricing experiments, the company stopped the practice and issued refunds to about 7,000 consumers who paid relatively high prices.

Senior Discounts in Restaurants

Consider a restaurant whose patrons can be divided into two groups, senior citizens and others. In Figure 10.5, the demand curve for senior citizens is lower than the demand curve for other groups, reflecting the assumption that the typical senior is

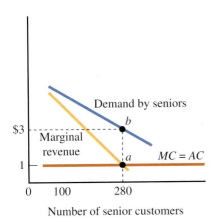

(A) Senior Citizens

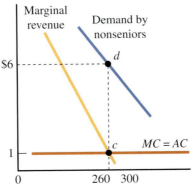

(B) Nonseniors

◀ **FIGURE 10.5**

The Marginal Principle and Price Discrimination

To engage in price discrimination, the firm divides potential customers into two groups and applies the marginal principle twice—once for each group. Using the marginal principle, the profit-maximizing prices are $3 for seniors (point *b*) and $6 for nonseniors (point *d*).

willing to pay less than the typical nonsenior. The lower willingness to pay could result from lower income or more time to shop for low prices.

Under a price-discrimination plan, the restaurant will simply apply the marginal principle twice, once for seniors and a second time for nonseniors. This approach is sensible, because the two groups have different demands for restaurant meals, so the restaurant should treat them differently. Panel A of Figure 10.5 shows how to pick a price for senior citizens. The marginal principle—marginal revenue equals marginal cost—is satisfied at point *a*, with 280 senior meals per day. Therefore, the appropriate price for seniors is $3, as shown by point *b* on the senior demand curve. In Panel B of Figure 10.5, the marginal principle is satisfied at point *c* for nonseniors, with 260 meals per day and a price of $6 per meal.

We know that the application of the marginal principle maximizes profit in each segment of the market. Therefore, price discrimination—with a price of $3 for seniors and a price of $6 for everyone else—maximizes the restaurant's total profit. If the restaurant were instead to charge a single price of $5 for both groups, the profit from each group would be lower, so the restaurant's total profit would be lower too.

Price Discrimination and the Elasticity of Demand

We can use the concept of price elasticity of demand to explain why price discrimination increases the restaurant's profit. From the chapter on elasticity, we know that when demand is elastic ($E_d > 1$), there is a negative relationship between price and total revenue: When the price decreases, total revenue (price times quantity sold)

APPLICATION

PAYING FOR A COLD SOFT DRINK ON A HOT DAY

APPLYING THE CONCEPTS #3: When does a firm have an opportunity to charge different prices to different consumers?

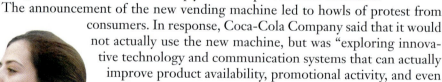

On a hot day, are you willing to pay more than you normally would for an ice-cold can of Coke? If so, you're the type of consumer Coca-Cola Company had in mind when it developed a high-tech vending machine, complete with heat sensors and microchips, that charges a higher price when the weather is hot. According to Douglas Ivester, the head of Coca-Cola, the desire for a cold drink increases when it is hot, so "it is fair that it should be more expensive. The machine will simply make the process more automatic."

The announcement of the new vending machine led to howls of protest from consumers. In response, Coca-Cola Company said that it would not actually use the new machine, but was "exploring innovative technology and communication systems that can actually improve product availability, promotional activity, and even offer consumers an interactive experience when they purchase a soft drink from a vending machine." Based on the reaction to the news of the heat-sensing vending machine, you can imagine the "interactive experience" when a hot and thirsty consumer discovers the higher price for a cold drink on a hot day. By the beginning of 2006, Coca-Cola had not used the new vending machines.

Related to Exercises 4.3 and 4.6.

SOURCE: Rance Crain, "Is Thirst for Alpha Status Behind Coke's High-Tech Talk?" *Advertising Age*, vol. 70, November 22, 1999, p. 26.

increases because the percentage increase in the quantity demanded exceeds the percentage decrease in price.

Suppose the restaurant initially has a single price of $5 for both seniors and nonseniors. Compared to other consumers, senior citizens have more elastic demand for restaurant meals, in part because they have lower income and more time to shop for low prices. A price cut for senior citizens brings good news and bad news for the restaurant:

- **Good news:** Demand is highly elastic, so total revenue increases by a large amount.
- **Bad news:** More meals are served, so total cost increases.

If the senior demand for meals is highly elastic, that is, E_d is well above 1.0, the good news will dominate the bad news: The increase in revenue will more than offset the increase in cost. Consequently, a price cut will increase the firm's profit.

For nonseniors, the firm will have an incentive to increase the price above the initial common price of $5. Suppose nonseniors have a mildly elastic demand for meals, with E_d just above 1.0. A price hike for nonseniors brings bad news on the revenue side and good news on the cost side:

- **Bad news:** Demand is mildly elastic, so total revenue decreases by a small amount.
- **Good news:** Fewer meals are served, so total cost decreases.

If the demand by nonseniors is mildly elastic, the good news will dominate the bad news: The savings in production costs will exceed the revenue loss. Consequently, the price hike for nonseniors will increase the firm's profit.

4

APPLICATION

THE PRICING OF MOVIE ADMISSION AND POPCORN

APPLYING THE CONCEPTS #4: When does price discrimination work?

Why do senior citizens pay less than everyone else for admission to a movie, but pay the same as everyone else for popcorn? As we've seen, a senior discount is not an act of generosity by a firm, but an act of profit maximization. Senior citizens are typically willing to pay less than other citizens for movies, so a theater divides its consumers into two groups—seniors and others—and offers a discount to seniors. This price discrimination in favor of senior citizens increases the theater's profit. Why don't theaters offer a senior discount for popcorn? Unlike admission to the theater, popcorn can be easily transferred from one customer to another. If senior citizens could buy popcorn at half the regular price, many nonseniors would get seniors to buy popcorn for them, so the theater wouldn't sell as much popcorn at the regular price, and the theater's profit would decrease. In contrast, as long as ticket takers check consumers' admissions tickets, admission to the movie is not transferable.

Related to Exercises 4.4 and 4.7.

APPLICATION

HARDBACK BOOKS ARE RELATIVELY EXPENSIVE

APPLYING THE CONCEPTS #5: What types of consumers pay relatively high prices?

Why is the price of the hardback edition of *The Da Vinci Code* three times the price of the paperback edition? Most books are published in two forms—hardback and paperback. Although the cost of producing a hardback book is only about 20 percent higher than producing a paperback, the hardback price is typically three times the paperback price. The hardback edition comes first, and the paperback edition is published months, or even years, later. For example, *The Da Vinci Code* by Dan Brown sold as a hardback in 2003 at a price of $25 and then three years later sold as a paperback at a price of $8. Why are hardbacks so expensive compared to paperbacks?

The key to solving this puzzle is the fact that hardback books are published first, followed by the paperback edition. Booksellers use hardbacks and paperbacks to distinguish between two types of consumers: those who are willing to pay a lot and those who are willing to pay a little. Some people are eager to read a book when it first comes out, and publishers provide them with high-price hardbacks. The more casual readers are willing to wait for the lower-priced paperback. The pricing of hardback and paperback books is another example of price discrimination, with consumers with less elastic demand paying a higher price. *Related to Exercises 4.5 and 4.8.*

SUMMARY

In this chapter, we've seen some of the subtleties of monopolies and their pricing policies. Compared to a perfectly competitive market, a monopoly charges a higher price, produces a smaller quantity, and wastes resources in the pursuit of monopoly power. On the positive side, some of the products we use today might never have been invented without the patent system and the monopoly power it grants. Firms with market power often use price discrimination to increase their profits. Here are the main points of the chapter:

1 Compared to a perfectly competitive market, a market served by a monopolist will charge a higher price, produce a smaller quantity of output, and generate a *deadweight loss* to society.

2 Some firms use resources to acquire monopoly power, a process known as *rent seeking*.

3 *Patents* protect innovators from competition, leading to higher prices for new products but greater incentives to develop new products.

4 To engage in *price discrimination*, a firm divides its customers into two or more groups and charges lower prices to groups with more elastic demand.

5 Price discrimination is not an act of generosity; it's an act of profit maximization.

KEY TERMS

barrier to entry, p. 234
deadweight loss from monopoly, p. 241
market power, p. 234

monopoly, p. 234
natural monopoly, p. 234
network externalities, p. 234

patent, p. 234
price discrimination, p. 243
rent seeking, p. 241

EXERCISES

Visit www.myeconlab.com to complete
Get Ahead of the Curve   these exercises online and get instant feedback.

10.1 | The Monopolist's Output Decision

1.1 Arrows up or down: A monopolist's marginal revenue is less than its price because to increase the quantity sold, the monopolist must _____ the price, and so the revenue from consumers who purchased the product at the higher price _____.

1.2 At a price of $18 per CD, a firm sells 60 CDs. If the slope of the demand curve is –$0.10, marginal revenue for the 61st CD is $_____. The firm should cut the price to sell one more CD if the marginal cost is less than $_____.

1.3 Arrow up or down: As the quantity produced by a monopolist increases, the gap between the marginal-revenue curve and demand curve _____.

1.4 To maximize profit, a monopolist picks the quantity at which _____ equals _____.

1.5 Arrows up or down: At a price of $18 per CD, the marginal revenue of a CD seller is $12. If the marginal cost of CDs is $9, the firm should _____ its price to _____ the quantity.

1.6 You want to determine the profit-maximizing quantity for a monopolist. You can ask the firm's accountant to draw the firm's revenue and costs curves, but each curve will cost you $1,000. From the following list, indicate which curves you will request: average total cost, average fixed cost, average variable cost, marginal cost, demand, marginal revenue.

1.7 **Textbook Pricing: Publishers Versus Authors.** Consider the problem of setting a price for a book. The marginal cost of production is constant at $20 per book. The publisher knows from experience that the slope of the demand curve is –$0.20 per textbook: Starting with a price of $44, a price cut of $0.20 will increase the quantity demanded by one textbook. For example, here are some combinations of price and quantity:

Price per textbook	$44	$40	$36	$32	$30
Quantity of textbooks	80	100	120	140	150

   a. What price will the publisher choose?
   b. Suppose that the author receives a royalty payment equal to 10 percent of the total sales revenue from the book. If the author could choose a price, what would it be?
   c. Why would the publisher and the author disagree about the price for the book?
   d. Design an alternative author-compensation scheme under which the author and the publisher would choose the same price.

1.8 **Restaurant Pricing.** Consider a restaurant that charges $10 for all you can eat and has 30 customers at this price. The slope of the demand curve is –$0.10 per meal, and the marginal cost of providing a meal is $3. Compute the profit-maximizing price and quantity, and illustrate with a complete graph.

1.9 **Empty Seats.** Consider the Slappers, a hockey team that plays in an arena with 8,000 seats. The only cost associated with staging a hockey game is a fixed cost of $6,000: The team incurs this cost regardless of how many people attend a game. The demand curve for hockey tickets has a slope of –$0.001 per ticket ($1 divided by 1,000 tickets): Each $1 increase in price decreases the number of tickets sold by 1,000. For example, here are some combinations of price and quantity:

Price per ticket	$4	$5	$6	$7
Quantity of tickets	8,000	7,000	6,000	5,000

The owner's objective is to maximize the profit per hockey game (total revenue minus the $6,000 fixed cost).
   a. What single price will maximize profit?
   b. If the owner picks the price that maximizes profit, how many seats in the arena will be empty? Why is it rational to leave some seats empty?
   c. Suppose the owner could engage in price discrimination. Would you expect the number of filled seats to increase or decrease? Explain.

10.2 | The Social Cost of Monopoly

2.1 A monopoly is inefficient solely because the monopolist gets a profit at the expense of consumers. _____ (True/False)

2.2 Consider the scoreboard story at the beginning of the chapter. The cost of the scoreboard built by

Coca-Cola is borne by _____ because getting the monopoly causes Coca-Cola to _____.

2.3 The average cost for providing off-street parking is $30 per space per day, and as a monopolist you could charge $35 per space per day for 200 spaces. The maximum amount that you are willing to pay for a monopoly is $_____.

2.4 Arrows up or down: When the government ended the monopoly on registering Internet addresses, the number of firms _____, the price _____, and the number of service options _____. (Related to Application 1 on page 242.)

2.5 **Ending a Casino Monopoly.** Consider a state that initially has a single casino for gambling. Suppose the state allows a second casino to enter the market. How would you expect the entry of the second casino to affect (a) the variety of games offered in the casinos and (b) the payout (winnings) per dollar spent? (Related to Application 1 on page 242.)

2.6 **Payoff for Casino Approval.** In 1996, developers interested in building a casino in Creswell, Oregon, placed a curious announcement in the local newspaper. If local voters approved the casino, the developers promised to give citizens $2 million per year. Given an adult population of about 1,600, each adult in Creswell would receive a cash payment of $1,250 per year. Why did the developers propose this deal? Why aren't similar deals proposed for new clothing stores, music stores, or auto repair shops?

2.7 **Consumer Compensation.** Consider the scoreboard story at the beginning of the chapter. Your job is to fully compensate each student for the cost associated with the soft-drink monopoly. Suppose the monopoly power increased the price of soft drinks by $0.20 per can and each student consumed 10 soft drinks before the monopoly was granted.
a. Kate continues to buy 10 soft drinks at the higher price. What is the appropriate compensation?
b. Elise buys only 4 soft drinks at the higher price. Her demand curve is linear. What is the appropriate compensation? Draw a graph that shows her change in consumer surplus.

2.8 **Pricing with Zero Marginal Cost.** Consider a monopolist who owns a natural spring that produces water that, according to nearby residents, has a unique taste and healing properties. The monopolist has a fixed cost of installing plumbing to tap the water but no marginal cost. The demand curve for the spring water is linear. Draw a graph to show the monopolist's choice of a price and quantity. At the profit-maximizing quantity, what is the price elasticity of demand? If the spring were owned by a government that applied the marginal principle, what price would it charge?

2.9 **Rules of Monopoly.** In the board game *Monopoly*, when a player gets the third deed for a group of properties (for example, the third orange property), the player doubles the rent charged on each property in the group. Similarly, a player who has a single railroad charges a rent of $25, while a player who has all four railroads charges a rent of $200 for each railroad.
a. Are these pricing rules consistent with the analysis of monopoly in this chapter?
b. In the game, is there a deadweight loss from monopoly? Why or why not?

2.10 **The National Park Service Monopoly.** The National Park service grants a single firm the right to sell food and other goods in Yosemite National Park.
a. What are the trade-offs associated with this policy? Who gains and who loses?
b. Does your answer to part (a) depend on whether the monopoly is granted as a political favor or auctioned to the highest bidder?

10.3 | Patents and Monopoly Power

3.1 Arrows up or down: A patent _____ the incentives to develop new products and _____ the price of the products.

3.2 Consider the arthritis drug example on page 239. If the research and development costs are $20 million, Flexjoint will develop the drug if it gets a patent that lasts at least _____ years.

3.3 To prolong their monopoly power, the producers of branded drugs pay millions of dollars to _____. (Related to Application 2 on page 244.)

3.4 **Paying to Keep a Generic Out.** Suppose your firm produces a branded drug at an average cost of $2 per dose and a price of $5 per dose. You sell 1,000 doses per day. If a generic version of the drug were introduced, your daily sales would decrease to 400 doses. How much are you willing to pay each day to prevent the entry of the generic version? (Related to Application 2 on page 244.)

3.5 **Patent for NoSmak.** A potential new drug, NoSmak, cures lip-smacking with one dose, but research and development would cost $80 million. The monopoly profit (earned while a single firm produces the product) will be $10 million per year. After a patent expires, the original developer of the drug will have sufficient brand loyalty to earn $3 million per year for another 10 years.
a. What is the shortest patent length required to induce a firm to develop the drug?
b. How would your answer to part (a) change if we ignore the profit earned after the patent expires?

10.4 | Price Discrimination

4.1 Arrows up or down: Suppose a firm starts with a single price and then switches to a price-discrimination scheme. The firm will _____ the price for the group of consumers with the less elastic demand and _____ the group with the more elastic demand.

4.2 The aspirin sold in airports is more expensive than aspirin sold in grocery stores because the demand for aspirin in airports is relatively _____.

4.3 The rationale for charging a higher price for a soft drink on a hot day is that demand is _____ (more/less) elastic on hot days. (Related to Application 3 on page 246.)

4.4 Senior citizens pay less than everyone else for admission to a movie, but pay the same as everyone else for popcorn because popcorn is _____, but admission is not. (Related to Application 4 on page 247.)

4.5 The price of the hardback edition of *The Da Vinci Code* is three times the price of the paperback edition because the eager consumers who buy hardbacks have _____ (more/less) elastic demand for the book. (Related to Application 5 on page 248.)

4.6 **Trade-Offs from a Heat-Sensing Vending Machine.** Suppose a soft-drink vending machine has a capacity of 180 cans and is filled every 10 days. The following table shows the quantities demanded on hot and cold days with different prices. The first row shows what happens with a single price of $2, and the second row shows what happens with heat-based pricing. (Related to Application 3 on page 246.)

Price on Hot Days	Price on Cold Days	Quantity of Cans Sold on Hot Days	Quantity of Cans Sold on Cold Days	Total Quantity of Cans Demanded: 5 Hot Days, 5 Cold Days	Total Quantity of Cans Demanded: 10 Hot Days
$2	$2	20	10	150	200
3	1	15	20	175	150

a. How does the switch to heat-based pricing affect the total quantity sold when there are 5 hot days and 5 cold days?

b. This occurs because the cold-weather consumers, who experience a lower price, have a _____ (more/less) elastic demand than hot-weather consumers, who experience a higher price.

4.7 **Senior Discounts for Movies.** Your movie theater charges a single price of $6. The marginal cost of each patron is $1. A recent marketing survey revealed the following information about senior citizens and nonseniors. (Related to Application 4 on page 247.)

	Price	Number of Patrons	Slope of Demand Curve
Seniors	$6	100	–$0.01 per patron
Nonseniors	6	80	–0.10 per patron

a. The marginal revenue for senior citizens is $_____, while the marginal revenue for nonseniors is $_____.

b. If your objective is to maximize profit, the marginal principle tells you to _____ the price for seniors and _____ the price for nonseniors.

4.8 **Book Pricing and Elasticity of Demand.** A publisher initially prices both hardback books and paperback books at $20 per book. The hardback version comes out first, followed two months later by the paperback version. The publisher initially sells the same number of hardbacks and paperbacks (100 each). Each book costs $2 to produce. (Related to Application 5 on page 248.)

a. Complete the following table.

	Price	Quantity	Total Revenue	Total Cost	Profit
Hardback	$20	100	_____	_____	_____
Paperback	20	100	_____	_____	_____
Total	_____	200	_____	_____	_____

b. The price elasticity of demand for hardback (eager) buyers is 0.50, and the price elasticity of demand for paperback (patient) buyers is 2.00. Suppose the publisher increases the price for hardbacks by 10 percent and decreases the price of paperbacks by 10 percent. Complete the following table.

	Price	Quantity	Total Revenue	Total Cost	Profit
Hardback	$22	_____	_____	_____	_____
Paperback	18	_____	_____	_____	_____
Total	_____	_____	_____	_____	_____

c. Does price discrimination increase or decrease the publisher's profit?

4.9 **Haircuts in Mulletville.** The town of Mulletville has a single hairstylist. The marginal cost of a haircut is the same for men and women ($10). The quantity of haircuts is 100 for men and 100 for women. The profit-maximizing price for women is $35, compared to $15 for men.

a. What explains the price difference?

b. Illustrate with a complete graph.

4.10 Tax Cuts for Discounters? Consider the following statement from a member of a city council: "Several of the merchants in our city offer discounts to our senior citizens. These discounts obviously decrease the merchants' profits, so we should decrease the merchants' taxes to offset their losses on senior-citizen discounts." Do you agree or disagree? Explain.

4.11 Airline Pricing. Consider an airline that initially has a single price of $300 for all consumers. At this price, it has 120 business travelers and 80 tourists. The airline's marginal cost is $100. The slope of the business demand curve is –$2 per traveler, and the slope of the tourist demand curve is –$1 per traveler. Does the single-price policy maximize the airline's profit? If not, how should it change its prices?

ECONOMIC EXPERIMENT

Price Discrimination

Here is an experiment that shows how a monopolist—a museum—picks different prices for different consumer groups. Some students play the roles of consumers, and others play the roles of museum managers. Here is how the experiment works:

- The instructor picks a small group of 3 to 5 students to represent the museum. There is a fixed marginal cost of each museum patron for ticket-takers, guides, cleanup, and other tasks.

- Of the 40 consumers—potential museum patrons—half are senior citizens with senior-citizen cards. Each consumer receives a number indicating how much he or she is willing to pay for a trip to a museum.

- In each round of the experiment, each museum posts two prices: one for senior citizens and one for nonseniors. Consumers then decide whether to buy a ticket at the relevant posted price.

- A consumer's score in a particular round equals the difference between his or her willingness to pay and the amount actually paid for a museum admission.

- A museum's score equals its profit, equal to its total revenue minus its total cost. The total cost is equal to $2 times the number of patrons.

- The experiment is run for 5 rounds. At the end of the experiment, each consumer computes his or her score by adding up the consumer surpluses. The museum's score equals the sum of the profits from the 5 rounds.

NOTES

1. Jeannie Donnelly, "OSU Beverages Will Be Provided Exclusively by Coca-Cola," *The Daily Barometer*, May 27, 1994, p. 1.

2. Richard A. Posner, "The Social Costs of Monopoly and Regulation," *Journal of Political Economy*, vol. 83, 1975, pp. 807–827.

3. Linda Rosencrance, "Amazon Charging Different Prices on Some DVDs," *Computerworld*, September 5, 2000, p. 23.

11

Market Entry and Monopolistic Competition

Tweeter just inherited a lot of money, enough to start her own car-stereo business. Woofer owns the only store in town selling car stereos, and he prices each stereo at $230. Woofer's average cost per stereo is $200, so he earns a profit of $30 on each one he sells. Should Tweeter use her inheritance to open her own car-stereo store? If she does, will she make a profit of $30 per stereo, just like Woofer?

Like entrepreneurs around the world, Tweeter has a difficult decision to make. Before she decides whether to enter the car-stereo market, she must predict how much she would be able to charge for her car stereos and how much it would cost her to supply them. Before she enters the market, there is a $30 gap between price and average cost per stereo, but the price is likely to drop when she enters the market and begins competing with Woofer for customers. In addition, Tweeter may have a higher average cost per stereo than Woofer. If the price she can get for her stereos drops below her average cost, Tweeter will lose money and would be better off using her inheritance some other way.

• **monopolistic competition**
A market served by many firms that sell slightly different products.

In this chapter, we explore a firm's decision to enter a market and examine the consequences of entry on prices and the profits of other firms. Firms will enter a market as long as they can make an economic profit. As we'll see, the entry of firms squeezes profit in three ways: The price decreases, the average cost of production increases, and the quantity sold per firm decreases. Eventually, the entry process stops, and we can count the number of firms serving the market. If entry stops at a single firm, we have a natural monopoly, a topic to be covered later in the book. If many firms enter the market, we have monopolistic competition, the topic of this chapter.

Monopolistic competition is a hybrid market structure, with features of both monopoly and perfect competition. The term may seem like an oxymoron—a pair of contradictory words—similar to "virtual reality" and "books on tape." However, the term actually conveys the two key features of the market.

- Each firm in the market produces a good that is slightly different from the goods of other firms, so each firm has a narrowly defined *monopoly*.
- The products sold by different firms in the market are close substitutes for one another, so there is intense *competition* between firms for consumers. For example, your local grocery store may stock several brands of toothbrushes with different design features. If the price of one brand increases, some loyal customers will continue to buy the brand, but others will switch to different brands that are close substitutes.

Some other examples of monopolistic competition are the markets for bread, clothing, restaurant meals, and gasoline. In each case, firms in the market sell products that are close, but not perfect, substitutes.

The analysis in this chapter is based on two assumptions. First, we assume there are no barriers to entry: There are no patents or government licensing programs to restrict the number of firms. Second, we assume that firms do not act strategically: Each firm acts on its own, taking the actions of other firms as given. This means that firms already in the market do not conspire to fix prices and do not try to prevent other firms from entering the market. In the next chapter, we'll explore several types of strategic behavior in an oligopoly, a market with just a few firms.

11.1 | THE EFFECTS OF MARKET ENTRY

Consider a market served by a single profitable firm, a monopolist. As we saw earlier in the book, a firm in any market can use the marginal principle to decide how much output to produce.

MARGINAL PRINCIPLE

Increase the level of an activity as long as its marginal benefit exceeds its marginal cost. Choose the level at which the marginal benefit equals the marginal cost.

Consider a firm whose activity is producing toothbrushes. On the cost side, the firm has the conventional cost curves: For small quantities produced, the average-cost curve is negatively sloped and marginal cost is less than average cost. On the benefit side, the marginal benefit of producing toothbrushes is the marginal revenue from selling one more brush. In Panel A of Figure 11.1, if a single firm produces toothbrushes, the firm-specific demand curve (the demand curve applicable to a specific firm) is the same as the market demand curve. As we saw in the chapter on monopoly, the firm's marginal-revenue curve lies below the demand curve because a monopolist must cut its price to sell more output.

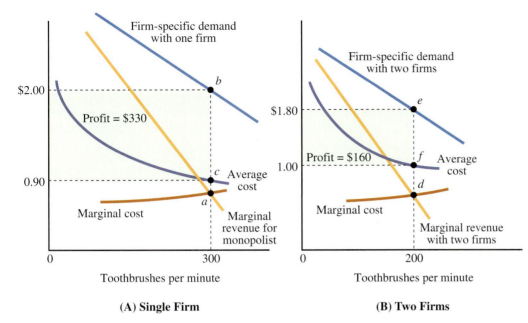

◄ FIGURE 11.1
Market Entry Decreases Price and Squeezes Profit
(A) A monopolist maximizes profit at point *a*, where marginal revenue equals marginal cost. The firm sells 300 toothbrushes at a price of $2.00 (point *b*) and an average cost of $0.90 (point *c*). The profit of $330 is shown by the shaded rectangle.
(B) The entry of a second firm shifts the firm-specific demand curve for the original firm to the left. The firm produces only 200 toothbrushes (point *d*) at a lower price ($1.80, shown by point *e*) and a higher average cost ($1.00, shown by point *f*). The firm's profit, shown by the shaded rectangle, shrinks to $160.

As we saw in the previous chapter, a monopolist maximizes profit by picking the quantity at which marginal revenue equals marginal cost. In Figure 11.1, this happens at point *a*, with a quantity of 300 toothbrushes. From point *b* on the demand curve, the price associated with this quantity is $2.00. From point *c* on the average-cost curve, we see that the average cost of this quantity is $0.90. The firm's profit, shown by the shaded rectangle, is $330:

profit = (price − average cost) × quantity = ($2.00 − $0.90) × 300 = $330

Given the large profits in the toothbrush market, will a second firm enter the market?

Entry Squeezes Profits from Three Sides

Suppose a second firm, producing a slightly different toothbrush, enters the market. When the second firm enters, the firm-specific demand curve for the original firm will shift to the left. At any particular price, some consumers will patronize the new firm, so there will be fewer consumers for the original firm: The original firm will sell fewer brushes at each price. In Panel B of Figure 11.1, the firm-specific demand curve for the original monopolist shifts to the left, and profit decreases for three reasons:

1 *The market price drops.* The marginal principle is satisfied at point *d*, so the original firm now produces 200 toothbrushes at a price of $1.80 (point *e*). The competition between the two firms causes the price to drop, from $2.00 to $1.80.

2 *The quantity produced by the first firm decreases.* The original firm produces only 200 toothbrushes, down from the 300 it produced as a monopolist.

3 *The first firm's average cost of production increases.* The decrease in the quantity produced causes the firm to move upward along its negatively sloped average-cost curve to a higher average cost per toothbrush, from $0.90 to $1.00 (point *f*).

The effects of entry are shown by comparing the profit rectangles in Panels A and B of Figure 11.1. Entry shrinks the firm's profit rectangle because it is squeezed from three directions. The top of the rectangle drops because the price decreases. The bottom of the rectangle rises because the average cost increases. The right side of the rectangle moves to the left because the quantity decreases. In this example, profit drops from $330 to $160:

profit = (price − average cost) × quantity = ($1.80 − $1.00) × 200 = $160

What about the second firm? If we assume that the second firm has access to the same production technology as the first firm and pays the same prices for its inputs, the cost curves for the second firm will be the same as the cost curves for the first firm. If the product of the second firm is nearly identical to the product as the first firm, the firm-specific demand curve for the second firm will be nearly identical to the firm-specific demand curve for the first firm. As an approximation, we can use Panel B of Figure 11.1 to represent both firms. Each firm produces 200 toothbrushes at an average cost of $1.00 per toothbrush and sells them at a price of $1.80.

Woofer, Tweeter, and the Stereo Business

For an example of the effects of entry on price, cost, and profit, recall Tweeter's hypothetical entry decision described at the beginning of the chapter. Woofer the monopolist initially sells 10 stereos per day at a price of $230 and an average cost of $200 per stereo. Suppose that if Tweeter enters the market, the price will drop to $225 and her average cost will be $205, so she could earn a profit of $20 per stereo. Although Tweeter's entry squeezes profit from both sides—decreasing the market price and increasing the average cost—there is still some profit to be made, so she will enter the market. Of course, other firms may enter the market, so Tweeter should not count on making a $20 profit per stereo for very long.

APPLICATION

1

DEREGULATION AND ENTRY IN TRUCKING

APPLYING THE CONCEPTS #1: How does market entry affect prices and profits?

What happens when the government eliminates artificial barriers to entry? The Motor Carrier Act of 1980 eliminated the government's entry restrictions on the trucking industry, most of which had been in place since the 1930s. New firms entered the trucking market, and freight prices dropped by about 22 percent. The market value of a firm's trucking license indicates how much profit the firm can earn in the market. Deregulation increased competition and decreased prices and profits, and the average value of a trucking license dropped from $579,000 in 1977 to less than $15,000 in 1982.

Empirical studies of other markets provide ample evidence that entry decreases market prices and firms' profits. In other words, consumers pay less for goods and services, and firms earn lower profits. In one study of the retail pricing of tires, a market with only two tire stores had a price of $55 per tire, compared to a price of $53 in a market with three stores, $51 with four stores, and $50 with five stores. In other words, the larger the number of stores, the lower the price of tires. *Related to Exercises 1.3 and 1.5.*

SOURCES: Theodore E. Keeler, "Deregulation and Scale Economies in the U.S. Trucking Industry: An Econometric Extension of the Survivor Principle," *Journal of Law and Economics*, vol. 32, October 1989, pp. 229–253; Thomas Gale Moore, "Rail and Truck Reform—The Record So Far," *Regulation*, November–December 1988, pp. 57–62; Leonard W. Weiss, ed., *Concentration and Price* (Cambridge, MA: MIT Press, 1989); Timothy F. Bresnahan and Peter C. Reiss, "Entry and Competition in Concentrated Markets," *Journal of Political Economy*, vol. 99, October 1991, pp. 977–1009.

APPLICATION

2

NAME BRANDS VERSUS STORE BRANDS

APPLYING THE CONCEPTS #2: How does brand competition within stores affect prices?

In many stores, nationally advertised brands share the shelves with store brands. For example, you can buy Kellogg's Frosted Flakes or Safeway's Frosted Flakes. Similarly, Bayer Aspirin shares a shelf with Safeway Aspirin. The introduction of a store brand is a form of market entry—a new competitor for a national brand—and usually decreases the price of the national brand.

The classic example of the price effects of store brands occurred in the market for lightbulbs. In the early 1980s, the price of a four-pack of General Electric bulbs was about $3.50. The introduction of store brands at a price of $1.50 caused General Electric to cut its price to $2.00. In markets without store brands, the General Electric price remained at $3.50. Similarly, in the market for disposable diapers, increased competition from store brands caused Procter and Gamble to cut its prices by 16 percent. For a wide variety of products—laundry detergent, ready-to-eat breakfast cereals, motor oil, and aluminum foil—the entry of store brands decreased the price of national brands. *Related to Exercises 1.4 and 1.6.*

SOURCE: Robert L. Steiner, "The Nature and Benefits of National Brand/Private Label Competition," *Review of Industrial Organization*, vol. 24, no. 2 (2004), pp. 105–127.

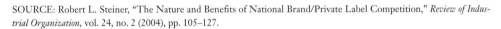

11.2 | MONOPOLISTIC COMPETITION

We've seen that the entry of a firm in a profitable market decreases the price and the profit per firm. Under a market structure called *monopolistic competition*, firms will continue to enter the market until economic profit is zero. Here are the features of monopolistic competition:

- *Many firms.* Because there are relatively small economies of scale, a small firm can produce its product at about the same average cost as a large firm. For example, a small donut shop can produce donuts and coffee at about the same average cost as a large shop. Because even a small firm can cover its costs, the market can support many firms.

- *A differentiated product.* Firms engage in **product differentiation**, the process used by firms to distinguish their products from the products of competing firms. A firm can distinguish its products from the products of other firms by offering a different performance level or appearance. For example, automobiles differ in horsepower and fuel efficiency, and toothpastes differ in flavor and their ability to clean teeth. Some products are differentiated by the services that come with them. For example, some stores provide informative and helpful salespeople, whereas others require consumers to make decisions on their own. Some pizza firms offer home delivery, and some software producers offer free technical assistance. As we'll see later in the chapter, some products are differentiated by where they are sold.

- *No artificial barriers to entry.* There are no patents or regulations that could prevent firms from entering the market.

These characteristics explain the logic behind the label "monopolistic competition." Product differentiation means that each firm is the sole seller of a narrowly

- **product differentiation**
  The process used by firms to distinguish their products from the products of competing firms.

defined good. For example, each firm in the toothbrush market has a unique design for its toothbrushes, so each is a monopolist in the narrowly defined market for that design. Because the products from different firms are close substitutes, there is keen competition for consumers. When one toothbrush maker increases its price, many of its consumers will switch to the similar toothbrushes produced by other firms. In other words, the demand for the product of a monopolistically competitive firm is very price elastic: An increase in price decreases the quantity demanded by a relatively large amount because consumers can easily switch to another firm selling a similar product.

When Entry Stops: Long-Run Equilibrium

We'll use the toothbrush example to illustrate the features of monopolistic competition. The producers of toothbrushes differentiate their products with respect to color, bristle design, handle size and shape, and durability. As we saw earlier, after a second firm enters the toothbrush market, both firms still make a profit. Will a third firm enter this lucrative market? The entry of a third firm will shift the firm-specific demand curve for each firm farther to the left. As we saw earlier, a leftward shift of a firm's demand curve decreases the market price, decreases the quantity produced per firm, and increases the average cost per toothbrush. If after the third firm enters the market profit is still positive for all three firms, a fourth firm will enter.

Because there are no barriers to entering the toothbrush market, firms will continue to enter the market until each firm makes zero economic profit. Figure 11.2 shows the long-run equilibrium from the perspective of the typical firm. Suppose a total of six firms are in the toothbrush market. Given the firm-specific demand curve in a market with six firms, the typical firm satisfies the marginal principle at point *a* by selling 80 brushes per minute at a price of $1.40 (point *b*) and an average cost of $1.40. Because the price equals the average cost, the typical firm makes zero economic profit. Each firm's revenue is high enough to cover all its costs—including the opportunity cost of all its inputs—but not enough to cause additional firms to enter the market. In other words, each firm makes just enough money to stay in business.

What are the implications of market entry for the market as a whole? In Figure 11.2, each of the six firms in the market produces 80 toothbrushes at a price of $1.40, so the total quantity produced is 480. In contrast, we started with a monopoly that had a price of $2.00 and a quantity of 300 toothbrushes. In other words, market entry decreased the price from $2.00 to $1.40 and increased the total quantity demanded from 300 to 480, consistent with the law of demand.

▶ **FIGURE 11.2**

Long-Run Equilibrium with Monopolistic Competition

Under monopolistic competition, firms continue to enter the market until economic profit is zero. Entry shifts the firm-specific demand curve to the left. The typical firm maximizes profit at point *a*, where marginal revenue equals marginal cost. At a quantity of 80 toothbrushes, price equals average cost (shown by point *b*), so economic profit is zero.

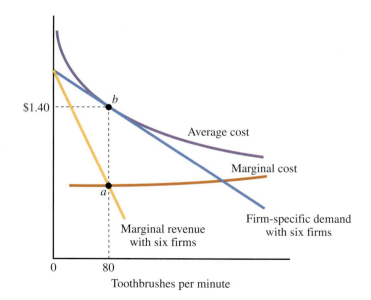

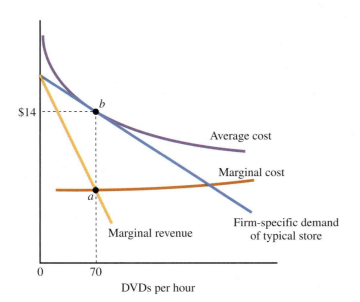

Differentiation by Location

In some monopolistically competitive markets, differentiation is simply a matter of location. Some examples are gas stations, music stores, video stores, grocery stores, movie theaters, and ice-cream parlors. In each case, many firms sell the same product at different locations. Your city probably has several video stores, each of which sells a particular DVD at about the same price. Everything else being equal, you are likely to purchase DVDs from the most convenient store, but if a store across town offers lower prices, you might purchase your DVDs there instead. In other words, each store has a monopoly in its own neighborhood, but competes with video stores in the rest of the city.

Figure 11.3 shows the long-run equilibrium in the market for DVDs. Because there are no barriers to entering the market, new video stores will enter the market until each store makes zero economic profit. The typical video store satisfies the marginal principle at point *a*, selling 70 DVDs per hour at a price of $14 per DVD (point *b*) and an average cost of $14 per DVD. The price equals the store's average cost, so the typical store makes zero economic profit. Each store's revenue is high enough to cover all its costs—including the opportunity cost of all its inputs—but not enough to cause additional stores to enter the market. In other words, the firm makes just enough money to stay in business.

11.3 | TRADE-OFFS WITH ENTRY AND MONOPOLISTIC COMPETITION

We've seen that market entry leads to lower prices and a larger total quantity in the market. At the same time, entry decreases the output per firm and increases the average cost of production. As shown in Figures 11.2 and 11.3, monopolistically competitive firms operate on the negatively sloped portion of their average-cost curves, so average cost is higher than the minimum. In other words, the average cost of production would be lower if a single toothbrush firm served the entire market by providing a single type of toothbrush. What are the other consequences of entry and monopolistic competition?

Average Cost and Variety

There are some trade-offs associated with monopolistic competition. Although the average cost of production is higher than the minimum, there is also more product variety. In a market with many toothbrush firms, consumers can choose from a wide variety

APPLICATION

OPENING A DUNKIN' DONUTS SHOP

APPLYING THE CONCEPTS #3: What does it take to enter a market with a franchise?

One way to get into a monopolistically competitive market is to get a franchise for a nationally advertised product. If you want to get into the donut market, you could pay a franchise fee of $40,000 to Allied Domecq, the parent company of Dunkin' Donuts. That gives you the right to sell donuts under the Dunkin' Donuts brand. You'll also get a few weeks training at the corporate headquarters in Massachusetts and some help in organizing a grand opening. Once you start making money, you'll pay a royalty to the parent company equal to 5.9 percent of your sales.

How much money are you likely to make in your donut shop? You will compete for donut consumers with other donut shops, bakeries, grocery stores, and coffee shops. Given the small barriers to entering the donut business, you should expect keen competition for consumers. Although your brand-name donuts will give you an edge over your competitors, remember that you must pay the franchise fee and royalties. In the monopolistically competitive donut market, you should expect to make zero economic profit, with total revenue equal to total cost. Your total cost includes the franchise fee and royalties, as well as the opportunity cost of your time and the opportunity cost of any funds you invest in the business.

Table 11.1 shows the franchise fees and royalty rates for several franchising opportunities. The fees indicate how much entrepreneurs are willing to pay for the right to sell a brand-name product. **Related to Exercises 2.4 and 2.5.**

SOURCE: *entrepreneur.com*, accessed 05/13/2006.

Table 11.1 | FRANCHISING FEES AND ROYALTIES

Brand and Product	Franchising Fee	Royalty Rate
Dunkin' Donuts: Coffee and donuts	$40,000	5.9%
Great Clips: Haircuts	25,000	6
Glass Doctor: Mobile windshield repair	20,000	4
Kabloom Flower: Cut flowers	30,000	4.5

of designs, so the higher average cost is at least partly offset by greater product variety. Here are two other examples of the benefits of product variety:

- *Restaurant meals.* The typical large city has dozens of Italian restaurants, each of which has a different menu and prepares its food in different ways. Consumers can pick from restaurants offering a wide variety of menus and preparation techniques. Although a city with a single Italian restaurant would have a lower average cost of preparing Italian meals, consumers would get less variety.

- *Shoes and clothing.* Shoes are differentiated according to their style and performance. If we all wore the same type of shoes, the average cost of producing shoes would be lower, but consumers would be unable to match their shoe preferences with suitable shoes. Similarly, if we all wore uniforms, the average cost of clothing would be lower, but that would eliminate clothing choice.

What are the trade-offs when products are differentiated by location? When firms sell the same product at different locations, the larger the number of firms, the higher the average cost of production. But when firms are numerous, consumers travel shorter distances to get the product. Therefore, higher production costs are at least partly offset by lower travel costs. If a large metropolitan area had only one video store, the average cost of DVDs would be lower, but consumers would spend more time traveling to get the DVDs.

Monopolistic Competition Versus Perfect Competition

Product differentiation is what makes monopolistic competition different from perfect competition. Perfectly competitive firms produce homogeneous products, while monopolistically competitive firms produce differentiated products. Panel A of Figure 11.4 shows the equilibrium for a perfectly competitive firm. Each price-taking firm has a horizontal demand curve. Point *a* shows the long-run equilibrium because the typical firm (1) satisfies the marginal principle, choosing the quantity where marginal revenue equals marginal cost and (2) earns zero economic profit because price equals average cost:

$$price = marginal\ cost = average\ cost$$

The only place where price equals both marginal cost *and* average cost is the minimum point of the average-cost curve, shown by point *a*.

Panel B shows the equilibrium for a monopolistically competitive firm. The firm has a differentiated product, so its demand curve is negatively sloped and marginal revenue is less than the price. With a negatively sloped demand curve, the zero-profit condition—price equals average cost—will be satisfied along the negatively sloped portion of the average-cost curve. In other words, the only place where a tangency can occur is along the negatively sloped portion of the average-cost curve. Compared to a perfectly competitive firm, a monopolistically competitive firm produces less output at a higher average cost. In Figure 11.4, the average cost for the monopolistically competitive firm is P_2, compared to P_1 for a perfectly competitive firm.

To illustrate the difference between the two market structures, imagine that product differentiation diminishes. Suppose for example that consumers decide that the distinguishing features of toothbrushes—color, shape, and bristle design—don't matter. As a result, the products of competing firms will become better substitutes, so the demand for a particular firm's product will becomes more elastic. In Panel B of Figure

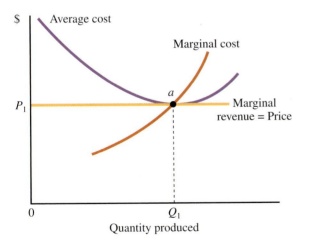 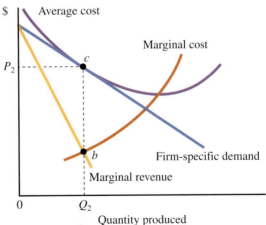

▲ **FIGURE 11.4**
Monopolistic Competition Versus Perfect Competition
(A) In a perfectly competitive market, the firm-specific demand curve is horizontal at the market price, and marginal revenue equals price. In equilibrium, price = marginal cost = average cost. The equilibrium occurs at the minimum of the average-cost curve.
(B) In a monopolistically competitive market, the firm-specific demand curve is negatively sloped and marginal revenue is less than price. In equilibrium, marginal revenue equals marginal cost (point *b*) and price equals average cost (point *c*).

11.4, the firm-specific demand curve will become flatter and will be tangent to the average-cost curve at a larger quantity, closer to the perfectly competitive quantity Q_1. As differentiation continues to diminish, the firm's demand curve will become flatter and flatter, and we will get closer and closer to the perfectly competitive outcome, where the average cost reaches its minimum.

11.4 | ADVERTISING FOR PRODUCT DIFFERENTIATION

We've seen that product differentiation is a key feature of monopolistic competition. A firm can use advertising to inform consumers about the features of its product and thus distinguish its product from the products of other firms. In addition, advertisements can inform consumers about prices. A famous study of the eyeglass market found that advertising promoted price competition between firms and reduced eyeglass prices by about 20 percent.[1]

Some advertisements don't provide any real information about a product or its price. You've seen the advertisements of beer drinkers frolicking on the beach with attractive people, cigarette smokers riding horseback, drivers of sports cars impressing classmates at high-school reunions, and sport-drink consumers performing amazing athletic feats. These sorts of advertisements are designed to promote an image for a product, not to provide information about the product's features.

Celebrity Endorsements and Signaling

An advertisement that doesn't provide any product information may actually help consumers make decisions. Firms spend millions of dollars to get celebrities like Tiger Woods and Paula Abdul to endorse their products. When a famous athlete or actor appears in an advertisement for a product, everyone realizes that the celebrity is doing the advertisement for money, not to share his or her enthusiasm for the advertised product. Nonetheless, these advertisements are effective in increasing sales. Why do they work?

By paying millions of dollars to run an advertisement, a firm sends a signal to consumers that the advertised product is appealing and likely to be popular. To illustrate this signaling effect, consider a firm that develops a new energy bar and picks a celebrity to endorse it. The purpose of a celebrity advertisement is to get people to try the product for the first time. After that, a consumer will base any repeat purchases on the taste and nutritional value of the energy bar. Suppose an advertisement with a cost of $10 million would cause 10 million consumers to try the energy bar. As shown in the first row of Table 11.2, energy bar A is an appealing product, and half of the consumers who try it will become repeat consumers. If the firm makes a profit of $4 on each repeat customer, the firm's profit of $20 million exceeds the $10 million cost of the advertisement, so the firm will run the advertisement.

Table 11.2 | ADVERTISING PROFITABILITY AND SIGNALING

Product	Number of Consumers Who Try the Product	Number of Repeat Customers	Profit per Repeat Customer	Profit from Repeat Customers	Cost of Advertisement
Energy bar A	10 million	5 million	$4	$20 million	$10 million
Energy bar B	10 million	1 million	4	4 million	10 million

What about a product that is less appealing? The second row of Table 11.2 shows the effects of an advertisement for energy bar B. Only one in 10 people who try energy bar B will become a repeat customer, so the firm's profit from an advertisement is only $4 million. That is not enough to cover the $10 million cost, so the firm won't advertise the less-appealing product. Notice that celebrity endorsements for the two products are equally effective in getting people to try the products, but what matters is repeat customers. The less-appealing product gets fewer repeat customers because it's an inferior product, and that's why it's not worthwhile to pay for an advertisement.

Celebrity endorsements and other expensive advertising send a signal to consumers that the producer expects many repeat customers. Firms undertake extensive marketing research to project the sales of their products, and when their research suggests that the product will be popular, they have an incentive to spend money on advertising to send the signal to consumers. The signal tells consumers which new products are expected to have the greatest general appeal.

APPLICATION

ADVERTISING AND MOVIE BUZZ

APPLYING THE CONCEPTS #4: What signal does an expensive advertising campaign send to consumers?

For another example of the signaling from advertising, consider movies. A movie distributor may produce several movies each year, but may advertise just a few of them. Although there are few repeat consumers for a particular movie, there is word-of-mouth advertising, also known as "buzz": People who enjoy a movie talk about it and persuade their friends and family members to see the movie. If a distributor believes that a movie will be appealing and thus generate a lot of buzz, an advertisement that gets the buzz started could pay for itself. In contrast, a distributor won't expect much buzz from a less-appealing movie, so advertising won't be sensible. In general, an expensive advertisement sends a signal that the movie will generate enough word-of-mouth advertising to cover the cost of the advertisement.
Related to Exercise 4.4.

SUMMARY

This chapter is about market entry and monopolistic competition. In a monopolistically competitive market, entry continues until each firm in the market makes zero economic profit. Firms can differentiate their products by design, level of service, location, or product image. Here are the main points of the chapter:

1 The entry of a firm into a market decreases the market price, decreases output per firm, and increases the average cost of production.

2 In a *monopolistically competitive* market, firms compete for customers by producing *differentiated products*.

3 In the long-run equilibrium with monopolistic competition, marginal revenue equals marginal cost, price equals average cost, and economic profit is zero.

4 Under monopolistic competition, the average cost of production is higher than the minimum, but there is also more product variety.

5 A firm can use celebrity endorsements and other costly advertisements to signal its belief that a product will be appealing.

KEY TERMS

monopolistic competition, p. 256

product differentiation, p. 259

EXERCISES

Get Ahead of the Curve

Visit www.myeconlab.com to complete these exercises online and get instant feedback.

11.1 | The Effects of Market Entry

1.1 A profit-maximizing firm picks the quantity of output at which _____ equals _____.

1.2 Arrows up or down: The entry of a third firm into a market with two original firms _____ the market price, _____ the average production cost, _____ the quantity produced per firm, and _____ profit of each original firm.

1.3 Arrows up or down: Changes in regulatory policy in the 1980s _____ the price of trucking services and _____ the profits of trucking firms. (Related to Application 1 on page 258.)

1.4 When grocery stores introduced their own light-bulb brands, the price of General Electric light-bulbs _____ (increased/decreased). (Related to Application 2 on page 259.)

1.5 **Bidding for Bookstore Licenses.** Paige initially has the only license to operate a bookstore in Bookville. She charges a price of $9 per book, has an average cost of $4 per book, and sells 1,001 books per year. When Paige's licenses expires, the city decides to auction two bookstore licenses to the highest bidders. Suppose the relevant variables (price, average cost, and output per firm) take on only integer values—no fraction or decimals. (Related to Application 1 on page 258.)
  a. Suppose Paige is optimistic and imagines the best possible outcome with a two-firm market. What is the maximum amount she is willing to pay for one of the two licenses?

  b. Suppose Paige is pessimistic and imagines the worst possible outcome with a two-firm market. What is the maximum amount she is willing to pay for one of the two licenses?

1.6 **Draw the Lightbulb Graph.** Consider the "Name Brands Versus Store Brands" application. Use a graph to show that the entry of store-brand lightbulbs decreased the profit-maximizing price of General Electric lightbulbs from $3.50 to $2.00. (Related to Application 2 on page 259.)

1.7 **Beware the Too-Easy Answer.** Your city initially restricts the number of pizzerias to one. The existing monopolist sells 3,000 pizzas per day. A pizzeria reaches the horizontal portion of its long-run average cost curve at an output of about 1,000 pizzas per day. Suppose the city eliminates the entry restrictions. Predict the equilibrium number of pizzerias. Beware of the TEC (too easy to be correct) answer.

11.2 | Monopolistic Competition

2.1 *Monopolistic competition* refers to a market in which old boys act naturally as they transport tight slacks in the back of Dodge Ram pickup trucks. _____ (True /False)

2.2 There are _____ oxymorons in question 2.1.

2.3 There are two conditions for a long-run equilibrium in a monopolistically competitive market:

(1) _____ equals _____ and (2) _____ equals _____.

2.4 To enter the donut market as a seller of Dunkin' Donuts, you'll pay a one-time franchise fee of $_____ and then pay _____ percent of your sales. (Related to Application 3 on page 262.)

2.5 **Willingness to Pay for a Dunkin' Donuts Franchise.** You operate a Dunkin' Donuts shop under a franchise agreement. You pay a royalty of 6 percent of your sales revenue to the parent company. Your profit-maximizing quantity is 10,000 donuts per year, and at this quantity, your price is $1.00 and your average cost per donut (including all the opportunity cost of production but not the 6% royalty) is $0.44. (Related to Application 3 on page 262.)

    a. Draw a graph with revenue and costs curves to show your profit-maximizing choice.

    b. What is the maximum amount you are willing to pay per year for the franchise?

2.6 **How Many Video Stores?** The city of Discville initially allows only one video store, which sells DVDs at a price of $20 and an average cost of $11. Suppose the city eliminates its restrictions on video stores, allowing additional stores to enter the market. According to an expert in the music market, "Each additional music store will decrease the price of DVDs by $2 per DVD and increase the average cost of selling DVDs by $1 per DVD." Predict the equilibrium number of video stores.

2.7 **Lawn-Cutting Equilibrium.** Consider the market for cutting laws. Each firm has a fixed daily cost of $18 for equipment, and the marginal cost of cutting a lawn is $4. Suppose each firm can cut up to three lawns per day. The market demand curve for lawn cuts is linear, with a vertical intercept of $70 and a slope of –$1 per lawn.

    a. If each firm in the market cuts three lawns, what is the average cost per lawn?

    b. What is the equilibrium price under monopolistic competition?

    c. How many lawns will be cut in total, and how many firms will be in the market?

2.8 **Zero Price for a Permit.** Consider a city that initially issues five licenses to pet groomers and does not allow the licenses to be bought and sold. Shortly after an economist joins the city licensing authority, the city decides to allow the licenses to be bought and sold on the open market. Much to the surprise of the licensers, the price of the licenses was zero: No one was willing to pay a positive amount for a pet grooming license.

    a. Explain why the price of grooming licenses was zero.

    b. Illustrate your answer with a complete graph.

2.9 **Auctioning Business Licenses.** The following table shows the relationships between the number of firms in the market, the market price, the quantity per firm, and the average cost of production.

Number of Firms	Price	Quantity per Firm	Average Cost
1	$20	38	$9
2	18	35	10
3	16	32	11
4	14	29	12
5	12	26	13
6	10	23	14
7	8	20	15

A business license allows a firm to operate the business for one day. The city will auction up to seven business licenses to the highest bidders, and the auctioning of licenses will continue as long as someone bids a positive amount for one of the licenses. Assume that each firm can buy only one license. What is the maximum amount you would be willing to pay for a license?

11.3 | Trade-Offs with Entry and Monopolistic Competition

3.1 The trade-off with entry is that an increase in the number of firms leads to higher _____ but greater _____.

3.2 When products are differentiated by location, the entry of firms generates benefits for consumers in the form of _____.

3.3 A perfectly competitive firm has a _____ demand curve, whereas a monopolistic competitive firm has a _____ demand curve.

3.4 In the long-run equilibrium in a perfectly competitive market, price is equal to both _____ and _____.

3.5 Arrows up or down: As product differentiation diminishes, the price elasticity of demand for the product of a monopolistically competitive firm _____ and the average cost of production _____.

3.6 **Uniform Trade-Offs.** A prominent feature of Mao's Communist China in the 1940s through the 1970s was the blue uniform worn by all citizens.

    a. Explain the trade-offs associated with the use of uniforms. What were the benefits? What were the costs?

    b. Suppose people had a choice among five uniform colors rather than being required to wear blue uniforms. Would you expect the benefits of requiring uniforms to decrease by a little or a lot?

11.4 | Advertising for Product Differentiation

4.1 Advertising for eyeglasses _____ (increases/decreases) the price of eyeglasses.

4.2 An advertisement that succeeds in getting consumers to try the product will be sensible only if the number of _____ customers is large.

4.3 In Table 11.2 on page 264, the profit from repeat customers will equal the cost of the advertisement if there are _____ repeat customers.

4.4 **Movie-Buzz Numbers.** Consider a theater that earns a profit of $2 per movie ticket sold. An advertisement that costs $3,400 would have the direct effect of getting 1,000 people to buy tickets. To make the advertisement worthwhile, how many of the original ticket buyers must each persuade just one other person to buy a ticket? (Related to Application 4 on page 265.)

4.5 **The Cost of Celebrities.** Consider a firm that hires an expensive celebrity to advertise its products. Does the firm have an incentive to prevent its customers from discovering how much it pays the celebrity?

4.6 **Word-of-Mouth Book Sales.** Consider a publisher who earns a profit of $2 per book sold. An advertisement that costs $320,000 would sell 100,000 books directly. To make the advertisement worthwhile, how many of the original buyers must each persuade just one other person to buy the book?

ECONOMIC EXPERIMENT

Fixed Costs and Entry

Here is an experiment that shows the implications of entry for prices and profits. Students play the role of entrepreneurs who must decide whether to enter the market for lawn cutting. If they decide to enter the market, they must then decide how much to charge for cutting lawns.

- There are 8 potential lawn-cutting firms, each represented by 1 to 3 students. The firms have two sorts of costs: a fixed cost per day and a marginal cost of cutting each lawn. Each firm can cut up to 2 lawns per day.
- There are 16 potential consumers. Each potential consumer is willing to pay a different amount to have his or her lawn cut.
- The experiment has two stages. In the first stage, each potential firm decides whether to enter the market. The entry decision is sequential: The instructor will go down the list of potential firms, one at a time, and give each firm the option of entering the market. The entry decisions are public knowledge. When a firm enters the market, it incurs a fixed cost of $14.
- Each firm in the market posts a price for lawn cutting, and consumers shop around and decide whether to purchase lawn care at the posted prices.
- Each trading period lasts several minutes, and each firm can change its posted price up to three times each period.
- A consumer's score in a trading period equals the difference between the amount that the consumer is willing to pay for lawn care and the price actually paid.
- A firm's score equals its profit, which is its total revenue minus its total cost (the fixed cost of $14 plus the variable cost, equal to $3 per lawn times the number of lawns cut).

NOTES

1. Lee Benham, "The Effect of Advertising on the Price of Glasses," *Journal of Law and Economics*, vol. 15, no. 2 (1972), pp. 337–352.

12

Oligopoly and Strategic Behavior

The Rock and Roll Hall of Fame and Museum in Cleveland held a raffle for four pairs of tickets to the 2006 Induction Ceremony in New York City. These tickets are usually reserved for high-level donors to the museum. Each winner also received a check for $1,000 to help offset the costs of the trip to New York City. The winners got together before the induction ceremony and talked about the artists to be inducted— Black Sabbath, Blondie, Miles Davis, Lynyrd Skynyrd, and the Sex Pistols. Then they talked about the prices of their airline tickets. Although they all traveled about the same distance to New York, they paid very different prices for their airline tickets.

1 How do firms conspire to fix prices?
   Vitamin Inc. Gets Busted

2 Does a low-price guarantee lead to higher or lower prices?
   Low-Price Guarantees and Empty Promises

3 What means do firms use to prevent other firms from entering a market?
   Legal and Illegal Entry Deterrence

4 When is it sensible for a monopolist not to take measures to prevent other firms from entering the market?
   Reynolds International Takes the Money and Leaves the Market

- Katrina was puzzled: "Brian lives in a city that's served by a single airline, and so do I. But Brian paid $200 and I paid $400."

- Jason was puzzled too: "Melissa lives in a city that's served by two airlines, and so do I. But Melissa paid $300 and I paid $400."

In this chapter, we explain these puzzling differences in prices. The monopolist in Brian's city could be charging a low price to discourage other firms from entering the market. The two airlines in Jason's city could have a price-fixing scheme under which they do not compete with one another, but instead conspire to charge the same high price.

- **oligopoly**
  A market served by a few firms.

- **game theory**
  The study of decision making in strategic situations.

- **concentration ratio**
  The percentage of the market output produced by the largest firms.

This is the fourth chapter on decision making by firms. In this chapter, we look at an **oligopoly**, a market with just a few firms. Given the small number of firms in an oligopoly, the actions of one firm have a large effect on the other firms. Therefore, firms in an oligopoly act strategically. Before a firm takes a particular action, it considers the possible reactions of its rivals. For example, before Southwest Airlines cuts its fares in an attempt to sell more tickets, it will consider the possible reactions by other airlines. If the rivals maintain their old fares, Southwest's fare cut will increase its sales and profit. But if the rivals match the lower fare, Southwest is likely to gain only a few customers, and its profit may actually decrease.

Game theory is the study of decision making in strategic situations. The theory can be applied to the game of chess as well as the decisions of oligopolists. A chess player develops a strategy to win the game, anticipating his opponent's reaction to each of his moves. Similarly, an oligopolist develops a strategy to maximize profit, anticipating the reactions of rival firms. We'll use game theory to discuss three business strategies: conspiring to fix prices, preventing another firm from entering the market, and advertising.

12.1 | WHAT IS AN OLIGOPOLY?

In an oligopoly, a few firms have market power—the power to control prices. Economists use **concentration ratios** to measure the degree of concentration in a market, computed as the percentage of the market output produced by the largest firms. For example, a four-firm concentration ratio is the percentage of total output in a market produced by the four largest firms. In Table 12.1, the four-firm concentration ratio for cigarettes is 95 percent, indicating that the largest four firms produce 95 percent of the cigarettes in the United States.

An alternative measure of market concentration is the *Herfindahl-Hirschman Index (HHI)*. It is calculated by squaring the market share of each firm in the market and then summing the resulting numbers. For example, consider a market with two firms, one with a 60-percent market share and a second with a 40-percent share. The HHI for the market is 5,200:

$$HHI = 60^2 + 40^2 = 3,600 + 1,600 = 5,200$$

In contrast, for a market with 10 firms, each with a 10-percent market share, the HHI is 1,000:

$$HHI = 10^2 \times 10 = 100 \times 10 = 1,000$$

According to the guidelines established by the U.S. Department of Justice in 1992, a market is "unconcentrated" if the HHI is below 1,000 and "highly concentrated" if it is above 1,800. For example, a market with five firms, each with a 20-percent market share, has a HHI of 2,000 and would be considered highly concentrated:

$$HHI = 20^2 \times 5 = 400 \times 5 = 2,000$$

An oligopoly—a market with just a few firms—occurs for three reasons:

1. *Government barriers to entry.* As we saw in Chapters 6 and 10, the government may limit the number of firms in a market by issuing patents or controlling the number of business licenses.

2. *Economies of scale in production.* As we saw in Chapter 10, a natural monopoly occurs when there are relatively large economies of scale in production, so a single firm produces for the entire market. In some cases, scale economies are not large enough to generate a natural monopoly, but are large enough to generate a natural oligopoly, with a few firms serving the entire market.

3. *Advertising campaigns.* In some markets, a firm cannot enter a market without a substantial investment in an advertising campaign. For example, the breakfast-cereal oligopoly results from the huge advertising campaigns required to get a foothold in the market. As in the case of economies of scale in production, just a few firms will enter the market.

Industry	Four-Firm Concentration Ratio (%)	Eight-Firm Concentration Ratio (%)
Primary copper smelting	99	Not available
House slippers	97	99
Guided missiles and space vehicles	96	99
Cigarettes	95	99
Soybean processing	95	99
Household laundry equipment	93	Not available
Breweries	91	94
Electric lamp bulbs	89	90
Military vehicles	88	93
Primary battery manufacturing	87	99
Beet sugar processing	85	98
Household refrigerators and freezers	85	95
Small arms (weapons)	84	90
Breakfast cereals	82	93
Motor vehicles and car bodies	81	91
Flavoring syrup	Not available	89

Table 12.1 | CONCENTRATION RATIOS IN SELECTED MANUFACTURING INDUSTRIES

SOURCE: U.S. Bureau of the Census, 2002 Economic Census, Manufacturing, *Concentration Ratios: 2002* (Washington, D.C.: U.S. Government Printing Office, 2006).

12.2 | CARTEL PRICING AND THE DUOPOLISTS' DILEMMA

One of the virtues of a market economy is that firms compete with one another for customers, and this leads to lower prices and larger quantities. But in some markets, firms cooperate instead of competing with one another. Eighteenth-century economist Adam Smith recognized the possibility that firms would conspire to raise prices: "People of the same trade seldom meet together, even for merriment and diversion, but the conversation ends in a conspiracy against the public, or in some contrivance to raise prices."[1] We'll see that raising prices is not simply a matter of firms getting together and agreeing on higher prices. An agreement to raise prices is likely to break down unless the firms find some way to punish a firm that violates the agreement.

We'll use a market with two firms—a **duopoly**—to explain the key features of an oligopoly. The basic insights from a duopoly apply to oligopolies with more than two firms. Consider a duopoly in the market for air travel between two hypothetical cities. The two airlines can use prices to compete for customers, or they can cooperate and conspire to raise prices. To simplify matters—and to keep the numbers manageable—let's assume that the average cost of providing air travel is constant at $100 per passenger. As shown in Figure 12.1, the average cost is constant, which means that marginal cost equals average cost.

A **cartel** is a group of firms that act in unison, coordinating their price and quantity decisions. In our airline example, the two airlines could form a cartel and choose the monopoly price. In Figure 12.1, the firm-specific demand curve for a monopolist is the market-demand curve, and the marginal-revenue curve intersects the marginal-cost curve at a quantity of 60 passengers per day (point *a*). If the two airlines act as one, they will pick the monopoly price of $400 and split the monopoly output, so each will have 30 passengers per day. The average cost per passenger is $100, so each airline earns a daily profit of $9,000:

profit = (price − average cost) × quantity per firm = ($400 − $100) × 30 = $9,000

- **duopoly**
  A market with two firms.

- **cartel**
  A group of firms that act in unison, coordinating their price and quantity decisions.

A Cartel Picks the Monopoly Quantity and Price

The monopoly outcome is shown by point *a*, where marginal revenue equals marginal cost. The monopoly quantity is 60 passengers and the price is $400. If the firms form a cartel, the price is $400 and each firm has 30 passengers (half the monopoly quantity). The profit per passenger is $300 (equal to the $400 price minus the $100 average cost), so the profit per firm is $9,000.

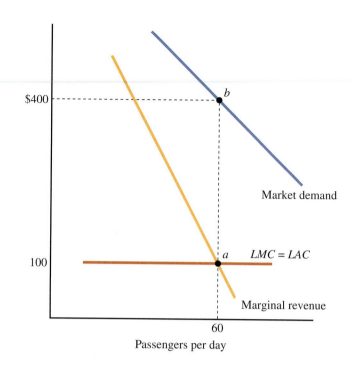

 price-fixing
An arrangement in which firms conspire to fix prices.

This is an example of **price-fixing**, an arrangement in which firms conspire to fix prices. As we'll see later in the chapter, cartels and price-fixing are illegal under U.S. antitrust laws.

What would happen if the two firms competed rather than conspiring to fix the price? If they do, each firm will have its own demand curve. As we saw in the previous chapter, the firm-specific demand curve for the typical firm lies to the left of the market demand curve because consumers can choose from two firms. At a particular price, consumers will be divided between the two firms, so each firm will serve only part of the market. In Figure 12.2, the demand curve for the typical duopolist is below the market demand curve. For example, at a price of $300, point *d* shows that the market quantity is 80 passengers, while point *b* shows that each firm has 40 passengers.

► FIGURE 12.2
Competing Duopolists Pick a Lower Price

(**A**) The typical firm maximizes profit at point *a*, where marginal revenue equals marginal cost. The firm has 40 passengers.
(**B**) At the market level, the duopoly outcome is shown by point *d*, with a price of $300 and 80 passengers. The cartel outcome, shown by point *c*, has a higher price and a smaller total quantity.

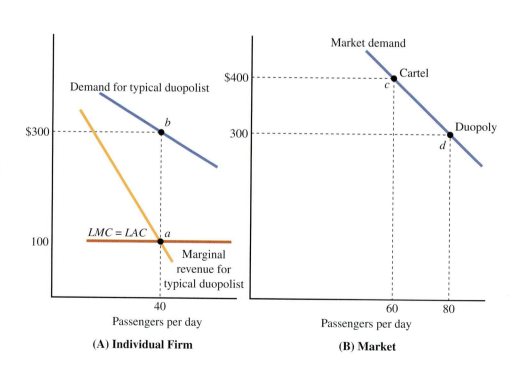

(A) Individual Firm

(B) Market

Panel A in Figure 12.2 shows the quantity and price choice of an individual firm. Given the firm-specific demand curve and marginal-revenue curve, the marginal principle is satisfied at point a, where marginal revenue equals marginal cost. The firm has 40 passengers at a price of $300 (point b). The two firms are identical, so each has 40 passengers at a price of $300. Given an average cost of $100, each firm earns a profit of $8,000:

profit = (price − average cost) × quantity per firm = ($300 − $100) × 40 = $8,000

Price-Fixing and the Game Tree

Clearly, each firm will earn more profit under a price-fixing cartel, but will a cartel succeed, or will firms cheat on a cartel agreement? We can answer this question with the help of a **game tree**, a graphical representation of the consequences of different actions in a strategic setting. Each firm must choose a price for airline tickets, either the high price (the $400 cartel price) or the low price (the duopoly price of $300). Each firm can use the game tree to pick a price, knowing that the other firm is picking a price too.

• **game tree**
A graphical representation of the consequences of different actions in a strategic setting.

Figure 12.3 shows the game tree for the price-fixing game. Let's call the managers of the airlines Jack and Jill. The game tree has three components:

- The squares are decision nodes. Each square has a player (Jack or Jill) and a list of the player's possible actions. For example, the game starts at square A, where Jill has two options: high price or low price.

- The arrows show the possible paths of the game from left to right. Jill chooses her price first, so we move from square A to one of Jack's decision nodes, either square B or square C. If Jill chooses the high price, we move from square A to square B. Once we reach one of Jack's decision nodes, he chooses a price—high or low—and then we move to one of the rectangles. For example, if Jack chooses the high price too, we move from square B to rectangle 1.

- The rectangles show the profits for the two firms. When we reach a rectangle, the game is over, and the players receive the profits shown in the rectangle. There is a profit rectangle for each of the four possible outcomes of the price-fixing game.

We've already computed the profits for two payoff rectangles. Rectangle 1 shows what happens when each firm chooses the high price. This is the cartel or price-fixing outcome, with each firm earning $9,000. Rectangle 4 shows what happens when each

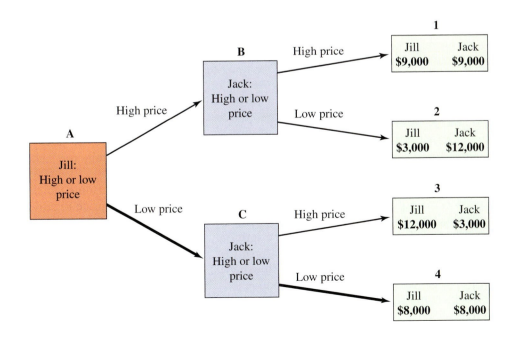

◀ **FIGURE 12.3**

Game Tree for the Price-Fixing Game

The equilibrium path of the game is square A to square C to rectangle 4: Each firm picks the low price and earns a profit of $8,000. The duopolists' dilemma is that each firm would make more profit if both picked the high price, but both firms pick the low price.

Table 12.2 | DUOPOLISTS' PROFITS WHEN THEY CHOOSE DIFFERENT PRICES

	Jill: High Price	Jack: Low Price
Price	$400	$300
Average cost	$100	$100
Profit per passenger	$300	$200
Number of passengers	10	60
Profit	$3,000	$12,000

firm chooses the low price. This is the duopoly outcome, when firms compete and each firm earns a profit of $8,000.

What would happen if the two firms chose different prices? If Jill chooses the high price and Jack chooses the low price, Jack will capture a large share of the market and gain at Jill's expense. In the first column of Table 12.2, Jill charges the high price and has only 10 passengers at a price of $400, so her profit is $3,000:

$$\text{profit} = (\text{price} - \text{average cost}) \times \text{quantity per firm} = (\$400 - \$100) \times 10 = \$3,000$$

In the second column, Jack charges the low price and has 60 passengers at a price of $300 so his profit is $12,000:

$$\text{profit} = (\text{price} - \text{average cost}) \times \text{quantity per firm} = (\$300 - \$100) \times 60 = \$12,000$$

This is shown by rectangle 2 in Figure 12.3: The path of the game is square A to square B to rectangle 2. The other underpricing outcome is shown by rectangle 3. In this case, Jill chooses the low price and Jack chooses the high price, so Jill gains at Jack's expense. The roles are reversed, and so are the numbers in the profit rectangle.

Equilibrium of the Price-Fixing Game

We can predict the equilibrium of the price-fixing game by a process of elimination. We'll eliminate the rectangles that would require one or both firms to act irrationally, leaving us with the rectangle showing the equilibrium of the game:

- If Jill chooses the high price, we'll move along the upper branches of the tree and eventually reach rectangle 1 or 2, depending on what Jack does. Although Jill would like Jack to choose the high price, too, this would be irrational for Jack. He can earn $12,000 profit by choosing the low price, compared to $9,000 with the high price. Therefore, we can eliminate rectangle 1.

- If Jill chooses the low price, we'll move along the lower branches of the tree and eventually reach rectangle 3 or 4, depending on Jack's choice. Jack won't choose the high price because he can earn $8,000 with the low price, compared to $3,000 with the high price. Therefore, we can eliminate rectangle 3.

We've eliminated the two profit rectangles that involve a high price for Jack—rectangles 1 and 3. That means that the low price is a **dominant strategy** for Jack: Regardless of what Jill does, Jack's best choice is the low price.

Two profit rectangles are left—2 and 4—and Jill's action will determine which rectangle is the equilibrium. Jill knows that Jack will choose the low price regardless of what she does. She could choose the high price and allow Jack to capture most of the market, leaving her with a profit of only $3,000 in rectangle 2. A better choice is to pick the low price and get a profit of $8,000 in rectangle 4. In other words, it would be irrational for Jill to allow herself to be underpriced, so the outcome of the game is shown by profit rectangle 4: Each player chooses the low price. The thick arrows show the equilibrium path of the game, from square A to square C to rectangle 4.

• **dominant strategy**
An action that is the best choice for a player, no matter what the other player does.

Both firms will be unhappy with this equilibrium because each could earn a higher profit with rectangle 1. To get there, however, each firm must choose the high price. The **duopolists' dilemma** is that although both firms would be better off if they both chose the high price, each firm chooses the low price. The dilemma occurs because there is a big payoff from underpricing the other firm and a big penalty from being underpriced, so both firms pick the low price. As we'll see later in the chapter, to avoid the dilemma the firms must find some way to prevent underpricing.

• **duopolists' dilemma**
A situation in which both firms in a market would be better off if both chose the high price, but each chooses the low price.

Nash Equilibrium

We have used a game tree to find the equilibrium in a price-fixing game. It is an equilibrium in the sense that each player (firm) is doing the best he or she can, given the actions of another player. The label for such an equilibrium is **Nash equilibrium**. This concept is named after John Nash, the recipient of the 1994 Nobel Prize in economics, who developed his equilibrium concept as a 21-year-old graduate student at Princeton University. His life story, which includes a 25-year bout with schizophrenia and a dramatic recovery, is chronicled in the book *A Beautiful Mind*, later made into a movie starring Russell Crowe as John Nash.[2]

• **Nash equilibrium**
An outcome of a game in which each player is doing the best he or she can, given the action of the other players.

In the price-fixing game, the Nash equilibrium is for both firms to pick the low price. Each firm is doing the best it can, given the action of the other firm:

- If Jill picks the low price, Jack's best action is to pick the low price.
- If Jack picks the low price, Jill's best action is to pick the low price.

What about the other potential outcomes? Consider first the possibility that both firms pick the high price. This is not a Nash equilibrium because neither firm is doing the best it can, given the action of the other firm:

- If Jill picks the high price, Jack's best action is to pick the low price.
- If Jack picks the high price, Jill's best action is to pick the low price.

Consider next the possibility that Jill picks the low price and Jack picks the high price. This is not a Nash equilibrium because Jack is not doing the best he can, given Jill's choice:

- If Jill picks the low price, Jack's best action is to pick the low price.

The concept of the Nash equilibrium has been applied to a wide variety of decisions. Later in the chapter, we will use it to predict the outcome of games involving entry deterrence and advertising. In addition to strategic decisions for firms, it has been used to analyze the nuclear arms race, terrorism, evolutionary biology, art auctions, environmental policy, and urban development.

12.3 | OVERCOMING THE DUOPOLISTS' DILEMMA

The duopolists' dilemma occurs because the two firms are unable to coordinate their pricing decisions and act as one. Each firm has an incentive to underprice the other firm because the low-price firm will capture a larger share of the market and earn a larger profit. The dilemma can be avoided in two ways: low-price guarantees, and repetition of the pricing game, with retaliation for underpricing.

Low-Price Guarantees

The duopolists' dilemma occurs because the payoff from underpricing the other firm is too lucrative to miss. To eliminate the possibility for underpricing, one firm can guarantee that it will match a lower price of a competitor. Suppose Jill places the following advertisement in the local newspaper:

APPLICATION

VITAMIN INC. GETS BUSTED

APPLYING THE CONCEPTS #1: How do firms conspire to fix prices?

In April 2000, four former executives of drug companies pled guilty to conspiring to fix the prices of bulk vitamins worldwide. It was the largest price-fixing case in U.S. history. The leading companies involved in the illegal cartel were Hoffman-La Roche (with 60 percent of the U.S. vitamin market), BASF AG (28 percent), and Rhone-Poulenc (7 percent). They were joined by other vitamin producers from Japan, Switzerland, and Canada. The announcement brought the number of Swiss and German executives imprisoned for the case to six, with fines for the individual executives and their companies totaling $1 billion.

For almost a decade, these executives conspired to stifle competition around the globe by fixing prices on vitamins A, B2, B5, C, E, and beta carotene. The executives called their group "Vitamin Inc." and met regularly in hotel rooms to carve up the market. Market shares for each region were specified down to a half percentage point, and prices for each vitamin were agreed upon down to the penny. For vitamin "premixes" (used for livestock feed and human food such as breakfast cereals), the executives rigged the bidding process for contracts, specifying a price and designating a "winner" for each contract. To help prevent cheating, they had "budget meetings" to check each other's data on sales and market shares. The cartel managed to boost the prices of vitamins, with markups averaging about 20 percent, or even more at the high-end of the vitamin price range. For example, the price of vitamin A nearly doubled, from about $12 per pound to $20.

Hoffman-LaRoche ultimately paid a fine of $500 million, about half of its annual revenue from its vitamin business in the United States. BASF AG paid a fine of $225 million. Rhone-Poulenc broke ranks early in the investigation, and by cooperating with U.S. Justice Department investigators the firm avoided any fines. A group of Japanese companies paid a total of $137 million. *Related to Exercises 2.8 and 2.9.*

SOURCE: David Barboza, "Tearing Down the Facade of 'Vitamin Inc.'" *New York Times*, October 10, 1999, Section 3, p. 1; Department of Justice, "Four Foreign Executives of Leading European Vitamin Firms Agree to Plead Guilty to Participating in International Vitamin Cartel," Press Release, April 6, 2000.

If you buy an airline ticket from me and then discover that Jack offers the same trip at a lower price, I will pay you the price difference. If I charge you $400 and Jack's price is only $300, I will pay you $100.

• low-price guarantee
A promise to match a lower price of a competitor.

Jill's **low-price guarantee** is a credible promise because she announces it in the newspaper. Suppose Jack makes a similar commitment to match a lower price from Jill.

Figure 12.4 shows the effect of low-price guarantees on the game tree. Jill now has two decision nodes. As before, she starts the game in square *A*. If Jill picks the high price and then Jack picks the high price, we end up at rectangle 1, as before. But if Jill picks the high price and Jack picks the low price, we get to square *D*. Jill will issue a refund of $100 to each of her consumers. In effect, she has retroactively chosen the

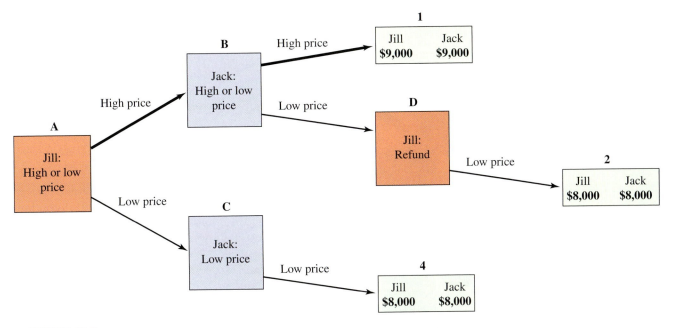

▲ FIGURE 12.4

Low-Price Guarantees Increase Prices

When both firms have a low-price guarantee, it is impossible for one firm to underprice the other. The only possible outcomes are a pair of high prices (rectangle 1) or a pair of low prices (rectangles 2 or 4). The equilibrium path of the game is square A to square B to rectangle 1. Each firm picks the high price and earns a profit of $9,000.

low price, and payoff rectangle 2 is the duopoly outcome, with both firms picking the low price. For the lower half of the game tree, recall that Jack has committed to match a lower price by Jill, so the old payoff rectangle 3 disappears, leaving us with rectangle 4, where both firms choose the low price and get the duopoly profit.

The thick arrows show the path of the game with low-price guarantees. Consider Jack's decision first:

- If Jill picks the high price, Jack chooses between payoff rectangles 1 and 2, a pair of high prices or a pair of low prices. His profit is higher at $9,000 with a pair of high prices (rectangle 1), so if Jill picks the high price, he will, too.
- If Jill picks the low price, Jack is committed to the low price, too.

Consider Jill's decision. She knows that Jack will match her price—either high or low—meaning that she chooses between profit rectangles 1 and 4. Profit is higher with rectangle 1, so she will pick the high price.

The low-price guarantee eliminates the possibility of underpricing, so it eliminates the duopolists' dilemma and promotes cartel pricing. The firms don't have to create a formal cartel to get the benefits from cartel pricing. The motto of a low-price guarantee is "Low for one means low for all," so both firms charge the high price. Once the possibility of underpricing has been eliminated, the duopoly will be replaced by an informal cartel, with each firm picking the price that would be picked by a monopolist.

Repeated Pricing Games with Retaliation for Underpricing

Up to this point, we've assumed that the price-fixing game is played only once. Each firm chooses a price and keeps that price for the lifetime of the firm. What happens when two firms play the game repeatedly, picking prices over an extended period of time? We'll see that repetition makes price-fixing more likely because firms can punish a firm that cheats on a price-fixing agreement, whether it's formal or informal.

APPLICATION

LOW-PRICE GUARANTEES AND EMPTY PROMISES

APPLYING THE CONCEPTS #2: Does a low-price guarantee lead to higher or lower prices?

If you shop around for a new car stereo, you'll notice that most sellers have a low-price guarantee. If you buy a stereo from firm A and later discover that firm B sells the same stereo at a lower price, firm A will pay you the difference in price. The guarantee typically excludes discontinued and closeout products, and the other store must be an authorized dealer of the product you bought. Will the low-price guarantee lead to lower prices? As we've seen, a low-price guarantee eliminates the possibility that one firm will underprice the other and, thus leads to high prices.

To most people, the notion that a low-price guarantee leads to higher prices is surprising. After all, if firm A promises to give refunds if its price exceeds firm B's price, we might expect firm A to keep its price low to avoid handing out a lot of refunds. In fact, firm A doesn't have to worry about giving refunds because firm B will also choose the high price. In other words, the promise to issue refunds is an *empty* promise. Although consumers might think that a low-price guarantee will protect them from high prices, it means that consumers are more likely to pay the high price. **Related to Exercises 3.5 and 3.6.**

Firms use several strategies to maintain a price-fixing agreement. Continuing our airline example, suppose Jack and Jill pick their prices at the beginning of each month. Jill chooses the cartel price for the first month and will continue to choose the cartel price as long as Jack does too. Jill could use one of the following strategies to punish Jack if he underprices her:

1 *A duopoly pricing strategy.* Jill chooses the lower duopoly price for the remaining lifetime of her firm. Once Jill is underpriced, she abandons the idea of cartel pricing and accepts the duopoly outcome, which is less profitable than the cartel outcome but more profitable than being underpriced by the other firm.

2 *A grim-trigger strategy.* When Jack underprices Jill, she responds by dropping her price to a level at which each firm will make zero economic profit. This is called the **grim-trigger strategy**, because grim consequences are triggered by Jack's underpricing.

3 *A tit-for-tat strategy.* Starting in the second month, Jill chooses whatever price Jack chose the preceding month. This is the **tit-for-tat** strategy—one firm chooses whatever price the other firm chose in the preceding period. As long as Jack chooses the cartel price, the cartel arrangement will persist. But if Jack underprices Jill, the cartel will break down.

Figure 12.5 shows how a tit-for-tat system works. Jack underprices Jill in the second month, so Jill chooses the low price for the third month, resulting in the duopoly outcome. To restore the cartel outcome, Jack must eventually choose the high price,

• **grim-trigger strategy**
A strategy where a firm responds to underpricing by choosing a price so low that each firm makes zero economic profit.

• **tit-for-tat**
A strategy where one firm chooses whatever price the other firm chose in the preceding period.

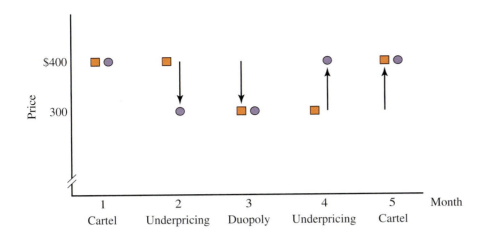

allowing Jill to underprice him for one month. This happens in the fourth month, and the cartel is restored in the fifth month. Although Jack can gain at Jill's expense in the second month, if he wants to restore cartel pricing, he must allow her to gain at his expense during some other month. Under a tit-for-tat strategy, a duopolist does exactly what his or her rival did the last round. This encourages firms to cooperate rather than compete. Several studies have shown that a tit-for-tat strategy is the most effective strategy to promote cooperation.[3]

These three pricing schemes promote cartel pricing by penalizing the firm that underprices the other firm. To decide whether to underprice Jill, Jack must weigh the short-term benefit against the long-term cost:

- The short-term benefit is the increase in profit in the current period. If Jack underprices Jill, he can increase his profit from the cartel profit of $9,000 to the $12,000 earned by a firm that underprices the other firm. Therefore, the short-term benefit of underpricing is $3,000.

- The long-term cost is the loss of profit in later periods. Jill will respond to Jack's underpricing by cutting her price, and this decreases Jack's profit. For example, if Jill retaliates with the duopoly price, Jack's future profit will be $8,000 per day instead of the $9,000 he could have earned by going along with the cartel price. The cost of underpricing is the daily loss of $1,000 in profit.

If the two firms expect to share the market for a long time, the long-term cost of underpricing will exceed the short-term benefit, so underpricing is less likely. The threat of punishment makes it easier to resist the temptation to cheat on the cartel.

Price-Fixing and the Law

Under the Sherman Antitrust Act of 1890 and subsequent legislation, explicit price-fixing is illegal. It is illegal for firms to discuss pricing strategies or methods of punishing a firm that underprices other firms. In one of the early price-fixing cases (*Addyston Pipe*, 1899), six manufacturers of cast-iron pipe met to fix prices. Several months after the Supreme Court ruled that their cartel pricing was illegal, the firms merged into a single firm, so instead of acting like a monopolist, they became a monopolist. Here are some other examples of price-fixing:

1 *Electric generators (1961)*. Executives from General Electric and Westinghouse were convicted of fixing prices for electrical generators, resulting in fines of over $2 million and imprisonment or probation for 30 corporate executives.

2 *Infant formula (1993)*. The three major U.S. producers of infant formula—Abbott Labs, Mead Johnson, and American Home Products—which together served 95 percent of the market, paid a total of $200 million to wholesalers and retailers to settle lawsuits claiming that they had conspired to fix prices.

3 *Carton-board pricing in Europe (1994).* The European Union Commission fined 19 manufacturers of carton board a total of 132 million euros ($165 million) for operating a cartel that fixed prices at secret meetings in luxury Zurich hotels.

4 *Food additives (1996).* An employee of Archer Daniels Midland (ADM), a huge food company, provided audio and videotapes of ADM executives conspiring to fix prices. ADM pleaded guilty to the charges of price-fixing and was fined $100 million.

5 *Music distribution (2000).* In exchange for advertising subsidies, music retailers agreed to adhere to the minimum advertised prices (MAP) specified by distributors. Any retailer that advertised a CD for less than the MAP would lose all of its "cooperative advertising" funds from the distributor. In May 2000, the Federal Trade Commission reached an agreement with music distributors to end the MAP scheme. The FTC estimated that the MAP scheme imposed an annual cost of $160 million on U.S. music consumers.[4]

12.4 | ALTERNATIVE MODELS OF OLIGOPOLY PRICING

We've explored a model of cartel pricing, an arrangement under which firms conspire to fix prices at the monopoly level. In this part of the chapter, we consider two alternative models of oligopoly pricing: A model of price leadership and the model of the kinked demand curve.

Price Leadership

• **price leadership**
A system under which one firm in an oligopoly takes the lead in setting prices.

Because explicit price-fixing is illegal, firms sometimes rely on implicit pricing agreements to fix prices at the monopoly level. Under the model of **price leadership**, one of the oligopolists plays the role of price leader. The leading firm picks a price, and other firms match the price. Such an agreement allows firms to cooperate without actually discussing their pricing strategies.

The problem with an implicit pricing agreement is that it relies on indirect signals that are often garbled and misinterpreted. Suppose that two firms have cooperated for several years, both sticking to the cartel price. When one firm suddenly drops its price, the other firm could interpret the price cut in one of two ways:

• *A change in market conditions.* Perhaps the first firm observed a change in demand or production cost and decides that both firms would benefit from a lower price.

• *Underpricing.* Perhaps the first firm is trying to increase its market share and profit at the expense of the second firm.

The first interpretation would probably cause the second firm to match the lower price of the first firm, and price-fixing would continue at the lower price. In contrast, the second interpretation could trigger a price war, undermining the price-fixing agreement.

The Kinked Demand Curve Model

• **kinked demand curve model**
A model in which firms in an oligopoly match price cuts by other firms, but do not match price hikes.

The **kinked demand curve model** of oligopoly gets its name from its assumptions about how firms in an oligopoly respond when one firm changes its price. The model assumes that when one firm cuts its price, the other firms will match the price cut. But if one firm raises its price, other firms don't match the price hike.

The firm-specific demand curve in Figure 12.6 incorporates the assumptions of the kinked demand curve model. The demand curve shows the demand facing Kirk, one of three firms in the oligopoly. Suppose each of the three firms starts out with a price of $6, and Kirk sells 30 units of output (point *k*). What happens if Kirk changes his price?

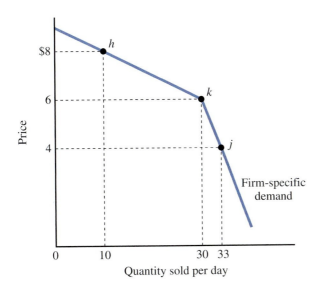

- If Kirk decreases his price, the other firms will decrease their prices too. Kirk will have the same price as the other firms, so his quantity will increase by a relatively small amount—from 30 to 33 units.

- If Kirk increases his price, the other firms will not change their prices. Kirk will have a higher price than the other firms, so his quantity will decrease by a relatively large amount—from 30 to 10 units.

In this model, the demand curve of the typical firm has a kink at the prevailing price. It is relatively flat for higher prices because other firms won't match a higher price. It is relatively steep for lower prices because other firms *will* match a lower price. Once a price has been established, it will tend to persist. The benefit of cutting the price is relatively small because the other firms will match a lower price. Moving in the other direction, the penalty for an increase in price is relatively large because the other firms won't match a higher price.

The model of kinked demand is a model of pessimism. Each firm assumes the worst about how its fellow oligopolists will respond to a change in price: The other firms will not go along with a higher price, but will match a lower price. Although this model may have some intuitive appeal, there is no evidence that firms act this way. Starting in 1947, various studies of oligopolies have failed to find compelling evidence to support the kinked demand model of oligopoly.[5]

12.5 | SIMULTANEOUS DECISION MAKING AND THE PAYOFF MATRIX

So far we have considered a game with sequential decisions. Jill chooses her price first, and then Jack observes her choice and then makes his own. An alternative scenario is that the two firms make their decisions simultaneously, so each firm picks its price without knowing the other firm's price. The analysis of a simultaneous game requires a different tool. A **payoff matrix** shows, for each possible outcome of a game, the consequences—or payoffs—for each player.

- **payoff matrix**
  A matrix or table that shows, for each possible outcome of a game, the consequences for each player.

Simultaneous Price-Fixing Game

Figure 12.7 shows the payoff matrix for the price-fixing game. Each cell in the matrix shows the payoffs from a potential outcome of the game. In the northwest corner of the matrix, if both firms pick the high price, each firm earns a profit of $9,000. In the southeast corner, if both firms pick the low price, each firm earns a profit of $8,000. If

► **FIGURE 12.7**
Payoff Matrix for the Price-Fixing Game
Jill's profit is in red, and Jack's profit is in blue. If both firms pick the high price, each firm earns a profit of $9,000. Both firms will pick the low price, and each firm will earn a profit of only $8,000.

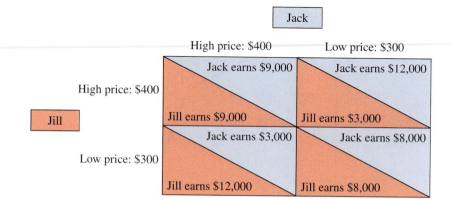

one firm picks the low price and the other picks the high price, the low-price firm earns $12,000 and the high-price firm earns only $3,000. For example, in the northeast corner, if Jill picks the high price and Jack picks the low price, Jill earns a profit of $3,000 and Jack earns a profit of $12,000.

We can use the payoff matrix to predict the equilibrium of the price-fixing game. In a simultaneous-decision game, Jack doesn't know whether Jill will pick the low price or the high price. There are two possibilities:

- If Jill picks the high price, we will be in the upper half of the matrix, and Jack's best response is the low price. In the northeast corner of the matrix, he can earn $12,000 by picking the low price. This is better than the $9,000 he can earn by picking the high price in the northwest corner.

- If Jill picks the low price, we will be in the lower half of the matrix, and Jack's best response is the low price. In the southeast corner of the matrix, he can earn $8,000 by picking the low price. This is better than the $3,000 he can earn by picking the high price in the southwest corner.

In other words, the low price is the dominant strategy for Jack. Jill knows this, so she realizes that the equilibrium will be in the eastern half of the matrix. Her best response is the low price. In the southeast corner of the matrix, she can earn $8,000 by picking the low price. This is better than the $3,000 she can earn in the northeast corner by picking the high price. Therefore, the equilibrium is the same as with the game-tree approach: Both firms pick the low price.

The Prisoners' Dilemma

We can gain some insight into the duopolists' dilemma by examining the classic prisoners' dilemma. Consider two people, Bonnie and Clyde, who have been accused of committing a crime. The police give each person an opportunity to confess to the crime. The traditional version of the story involves a simultaneous decision-making game: The two are put in separate rooms, and each makes a choice without knowing the other's choice.

The police confront Bonnie and Clyde with the payoff matrix in Figure 12.8. If both confess, each gets five years in prison, as shown in the southeast corner of the matrix. If neither confesses, the police can convict both of them on a lesser charge, and each gets two years, as shown in the northwest corner of the matrix. If only one confesses, he or she will implicate the other prisoner. The confessor is rewarded with a one-year prison sentence, while the other prisoner gets 10 years. If Bonnie confesses and Clyde does not, we are in the southwest corner of the matrix. If the roles are reversed, we are in the northeast corner.

We can use the payoff matrix to predict the equilibrium of the prisoner game. In a simultaneous-decision game, Clyde doesn't know whether Bonnie will confess or not:

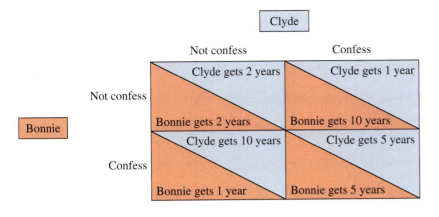

◄ FIGURE 12.8
Payoff Matrix for the Prisoners'
Dilemma
The prisoners' dilemma is that each prisoner would be better off if neither con-
fessed, but both people confess. The Nash
equilibrium is shown in the southeast corner of the matrix. Each person gets five
years of prison time.

- If Bonnie does not confess, we are in the upper half of the matrix, and Clyde's best response is to confess. In the northeast corner of the matrix, he gets one year in prison if he confesses. This is better than the two years he would get in the northwest corner by not confessing.

- If Bonnie confesses, we are in the lower half of the matrix, and Clyde's best response is to confess. In the southeast corner of the matrix, he gets five years in prison. This is better than the 10 years he would get in the southwest corner by not confessing.

In other words, confessing is the dominant strategy for Clyde. Bonnie knows this, so she realizes that the equilibrium will be in the eastern half of the matrix. Her best response is to confess. In the southeast corner of the matrix, she gets five years in prison. This is better than the 10 years she would get in the northeast by not confessing.

In the Nash equilibrium, both prisoners confess and each gets five years in prison. This is a Nash equilibrium because each prisoner is doing the best he or she can, given the actions of the other prisoner. Although both criminals would be better off if they both kept quiet, they implicate each other because the police reward them for doing so. There is an incentive for squealing, just as there is an incentive for one duopolist to underprice the other.

12.6 | THE INSECURE MONOPOLIST AND ENTRY DETERRENCE

We've seen what happens when two duopolists try to act as one, fixing the price at the monopoly level. Consider next how a monopolist might try to prevent a second firm from entering its market. We will use some of the numbers from our airline example, although we will look at a different city with a different cast of characters.

Suppose that Mona initially has a secure monopoly in the market for air travel between two cities. When there is no threat of entry, Mona uses the marginal principle (marginal revenue equals marginal cost) to pick a quantity and a price. In Figure 12.9, we start at point c on the market demand curve, with a quantity of 60 passengers per day and a price of $400 per passenger. Her profit is $18,000:

profit = (price − average cost) × quantity per firm = ($400 − $100) × 60 = $18,000

If Mona discovers that a second airline is thinking about entering the market, what will she do? Now that her monopoly is insecure, she has two options: She can be passive and allow the second airline to enter the market, or she can try to prevent the other firm from entering the market.

The Passive Approach

The passive approach will lead to the duopoly outcome we saw earlier in the chapter. In Figure 12.9, if the second firm enters the market, we move downward along the market demand curve from point c to point d. In a duopoly, each firm charges a price

Deterring Entry with Limit Pricing
Point c shows a secure monopoly, point d
shows a duopoly, and point z shows the
zero-profit outcome. The minimum entry
quantity is 20 passengers, so the entry-
deterring quantity is 100 (equal to 120 −
20), as shown by point e. The limit price is
$200.

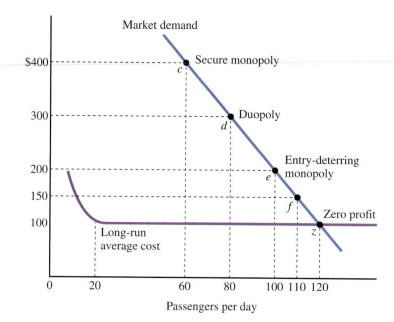

of $300 and serves 40 passengers, half the total quantity demanded at a price of $300.
For each duopolist, the daily profit is $8,000:

$$\text{profit} = (\text{price} - \text{average cost}) \times \text{quantity per firm} = (\$300 - \$100) \times 40 = \$8,000$$

Entry Deterrence and Limit Pricing

The second option is to take actions to prevent the second firm from entering the
market. To decide whether to deter the entry of the other firm, Mona must answer
two questions:

- What must she do to deter entry?
- Given what she must do to deter entry, is deterrence more profitable than being
  passive and sharing the market with the second firm?

To prevent the second firm from entering the market, Mona must commit herself
to serving a large number of passengers. If she commits to a large passenger load,
there won't be enough passengers left for a potential entrant to make a profit. Suppose
there are economies of scale in providing air travel, and the minimum entry quantity
is 20 passengers per day: That is, it would be impractical for a firm to serve fewer than
20 passengers. In Figure 12.9, the long-run average cost curve is negatively sloped for
relatively low levels of output, and the average cost for the minimum entry quantity of
20 passengers is just over $100, say $101.

Mona must compute the quantity of output that is just large enough to prevent
the second firm from entering the market. In Figure 12.9, point z shows the point of
zero economic profit in the market: If the two firms serve a total of 120 passengers per
day and split the market equally, with 60 passengers each, the price ($100) equals aver-
age cost, so each firm would earn zero economic profit. The quantity required to prevent the entry of the second firm is computed as follows:

$$\text{deterring quantity} = \text{zero profit quantity} - \text{minimum entry quantity}$$
$$100 = 120 - 20$$

If Mona commits to serve 100 passengers and a second firm were to enter with the
minimum quantity of 20 passengers, the price would drop to $100. Mona, with an
average cost of $100 to serve 100 passengers, would break even. The second firm,
with an average cost just above $100, would lose money. Specifically, if the average

cost of 20 passengers is $101, the second firm would lose $1 per passenger, or $20 in total.

It's important to note that Mona cannot simply announce that she will serve 100 passengers. She must take actions that ensure that her most profitable output is in fact 100 passengers. In other words, she must commit to 100 passengers. She could commit to the larger passenger load by purchasing a large fleet of airplanes and signing labor contracts that require her to hire a large workforce.

Which is more profitable, entry deterrence or the passive duopoly outcome? The deterrence strategy, shown by point *e* in Figure 12.9, generates a price of $200 and a profit of $10,000:

profit = (price − average cost) × quantity per firm = ($200 − $100) × 100 = $10,000

This is larger than the $8,000 profit under the passive approach, so deterrence is the best strategy.

Figure 12.10 uses a game tree to represent the entry-deterrence game. Mona makes the first move, and she considers the consequences of her two options:

- If Mona is passive and commits to serve only 40 passengers, we reach the upper branch of the game tree. The best response for Doug, the manager of the second firm, is to enter to earn a profit of $8,000, as shown by rectangle 1.
- If Mona commits to serve 100 passengers, we reach the lower branch of the game tree. If Doug enters with the minimum entry quantity of 20 passengers, his average cost will be $101, which exceeds the market price of $100. Therefore, the best response is to stay out of the market and avoid losing money.

Mona can choose between rectangles 1 and 4. Mona's profit is higher in rectangle 4, so that's the equilibrium. The equilibrium path of the game is square *A* to square *C* to rectangle 4.

Mona's entry-deterrence strategy generates a market price of $200, which is less than the $400 price charged by a secure monopolist and less than the $300 price with two competing firms. Mona can keep the second firm out of the market, but only by producing a large quantity and charging a relatively low price. This is known as **limit pricing**: To prevent a firm from entering the market, the firm reduces its price.

- **limit pricing**
  The strategy of reducing the price to deter entry.

◀ **FIGURE 12.10**

Game Tree for the Entry-Deterrence Game

The path of the game is square *A* to square *C* to rectangle 4. Mona commits to the entry-deterring quantity of 100, so Doug stays out of the market. Mona' profit of $10,000 is less than the monopoly profit but more than the duopoly profit of $8,000.

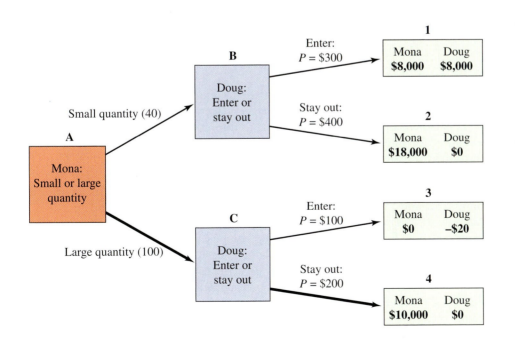

APPLICATION

LEGAL AND ILLEGAL ENTRY DETERRENCE

APPLYING THE CONCEPTS #3: What means—legal and illegal—do firms use to prevent other firms from entering a market?

When firms use limit pricing to prevent other firms from entering the market, entry deterrence is legal. For example, between 1893 and 1940, the Aluminum Company of America (Alcoa) had a monopoly on aluminum production in the United States. During this period, Alcoa kept other firms out of the market by producing a large quantity and keeping its price relatively low. Although a higher price would have generated more profit in the short run, the entry of other firms would have eventually reduced Alcoa's profit.

In recent years, the European Commission has uncovered many examples of entry deterrence that are illegal under the rules of the European Union. Van den Bergh Foods, a subsidiary of Unilever, held a dominant position in the market for ice cream in Ireland in 1998. The company provided "free" freezer cabinets to retailers, under the condition that the cabinets were to be used exclusively for the storage of Unilever's products. Irish retailers were reluctant to replace Unilever cabinets, so 40 percent of retailers sold only Unilever ice-cream products. The Commission concluded that this practice constituted an abuse of Unilever's dominant position. In 2003, the European Court of First Instance ordered Unilever to share the freezer cabinets with its competitors, including the Mars Company, which had argued that it was unable to sell its ice cream in many retail outlets in Ireland. *Related to Exercise 6.8.*

SOURCES: Leonard W. Weiss, *Economics and American Industry* (New York: Wiley, 1963), pp. 189–204; European Commission, *Report on Competition Policy 1998*, pp. 35–39.

Examples: Microsoft Windows and Campus Bookstores

For an example of limit pricing, consider the pricing of the Windows operating system by Microsoft. The Windows operating system runs about 90 percent of the world's personal computers, so it is natural to think that Microsoft has a monopoly in the market for operating systems. According to economist Richard Schmalensee, Microsoft's profit-maximizing monopoly price is between $900 and $2,000. That's the amount Microsoft would charge if it acted like a secure monopolist.[6] The fact that Microsoft charges only $99 for Windows suggests that Microsoft is an insecure monopolist, and that it picks a lower price to discourage entry and preserve its monopoly. If Microsoft charged $2,000 for its operating system, there would be a greater incentive for other firms to develop competing operating systems.

We can apply the notion of entry deterrence to your favorite monopoly: your campus bookstore. On most college campuses, the campus bookstore has a monopoly on the sale of textbooks. Other organizations are prohibited, usually by the state government or the college, from selling textbooks on campus. The recent growth of Internet commerce has given students another option: Order textbooks over the Web and have them shipped by mail, UPS, FedEx, or Airborne Express. Several Web booksellers charge less than the campus bookstore, and the growth of Web book sales threatens the campus bookstore monopoly. If your campus bookstore suddenly feels insecure about its monopoly position, it could cut its prices to prevent Web book-sellers from capturing too many of its customers. If it does this, you will pay lower prices even if you don't patronize the Web seller.

Entry Deterrence and Contestable Markets

We've seen that an insecure monopolist may cut its price to prevent a second firm from entering the market. The same logic applies to a market that has a few firms and could potentially have many firms. The mere existence of a monopoly or oligopoly does not necessarily generate high prices and large profits. To protect its market share, an oligopolist may act like a firm in a market with many firms, leading to relatively low prices.

The threat of entry faced by an insecure monopolist underlies the theory of market contestability. A **contestable market** is a market with low entry and exit costs. The few firms in a contestable market will be threatened constantly by the entry of new firms, so prices and profits will be relatively low. In the extreme case of perfect contestability, firms can enter and exit a market at zero cost. In this case, the price will be the same as the price that would occur in a competitive market. Although few markets are perfectly contestable, many markets are contestable to a certain degree, and the threat of entry tends to decrease prices and profits.

• **contestable market**
A market with low entry and exit costs.

When Is the Passive Approach Better?

Although our example shows that entry deterrence is the best strategy for Mona, it won't be the best strategy for all insecure monopolists. The key variable is the minimum entry quantity. Suppose that the scale economies in air travel were relatively small, so a second firm could enter the market with as few as 10 passengers. In this case, if Mona commits to serving only 100 passengers, that won't be enough to deter entry: A firm entering with 10 passengers will still make a profit. If the minimum entry quantity is 10 passengers, the entry-deterring quantity rises to 110 passengers:

deterring quantity = zero profit quantity − minimum entry quantity
$$110 = 120 - 10$$

Mona can commit to serving 110 passengers and thus prevent the second firm from entering the market, but is this the most profitable strategy? As shown by point f in Figure 12.9, the limit price associated with an entry-deterring quantity is $150. Mona's profit from entry deterrence would be $5,500:

profit = (price − average cost) × quantity per firm = ($150 − $100) × 110 = $5,500

This is less than the $8,000 profit she could earn by being passive and letting the second firm enter the market. In this case, the minimum entry quantity is relatively small, so the entry-deterring quantity is large and the limit price is low. As a result, sharing a duopoly is more profitable than increasing output and cutting the price to keep the other firm out.

12.7 | THE ADVERTISERS' DILEMMA

We have explored two sorts of strategic behavior of firms in an oligopoly—price-fixing and entry deterrence. A third type of strategy concerns advertising. As we'll see, firms in an oligopoly may suffer from an advertisers' dilemma: Although both firms would be better off if neither spent money on advertising, each firm advertises.

APPLICATION 4

REYNOLDS INTERNATIONAL TAKES THE MONEY AND LEAVES THE MARKET

APPLYING THE CONCEPTS #4: When is it sensible for a monopolist not to take measures to prevent other firms from entering the market?

In 1945, Reynolds International Pen Corporation introduced a revolutionary product: the ballpoint pen. The new type of pen could be produced with a very simple production technology. For three years, Reynolds earned enormous profits on this innovative product. In 1948, Reynolds stopped producing pens, dropping out of the market entirely. What happened?

The key to solving this puzzle is the fact that Reynolds earned enormous profits for a short time. The simple technology of the ballpoint pen could be copied easily by other producers, so the price required to deter entry—the limit price—was low. The limit price was so low that it was better for Reynolds to charge a high price and squeeze out as much profit as possible from a short-lived monopoly. Reynolds sold its pens for $12.50, about 16 times the average production cost of $0.80. By 1948, a total of 100 firms had entered the ballpoint market, and the price had fallen to the average cost of production, so each firm made zero economic profit. *Related to Exercises 6.9, 6.10, and 6.11.*

SOURCE: Thomas Whiteside, "Where Are They Now?" *New Yorker*, February 17, 1951, pp. 39–58.

Consider the producers of two brands of aspirin. Each firm must decide whether to spend $7 million on an advertising campaign for its product. In Table 12.3, the first two columns show what happens if neither firm advertises. Each firm earns $8 million in net revenue (revenue minus production cost) and spends no money on advertising, so each firm earns $8 million in profit. The third and fourth columns show what happens if each firm spends $7 million on advertising. The net revenue for each firm increases by only $5 million, so the profit of each firm drops by $2 million, to $6 million.

What happens if one firm advertises and the other does not? As shown in the last two columns in Table 12.3, a firm can increases its profit by advertising. If Adeline spends $7 million on advertising and Vern spends nothing, Adeline's net revenue increases to $17 million and her profit increases to $10 million. Adeline's advertisements cause some of Vern's consumers to switch to Adeline, and Vern's profit drops to $5 million.

We can use the data in Table 12.3 to construct a game tree for the advertising game. In Figure 12.11, Adeline makes her decision first, followed by Vern:

- If neither firm advertises, we go from square *A* to square *C* to rectangle 4, and each firm gets a profit $8 million.
- If both firms advertise, we go from square *A* to square *B* to rectangle 1, and each firm earns a profit of $6 million.
- If Adeline advertises and Vern does not, we go from square *A* to square *B* to rectangle 2. Adeline earns $10 million, while Vern earns $5 million. If the roles are reversed, we end up in rectangle 3, with Vern the advertiser earning $10 million and Adeline earning only $5 million.

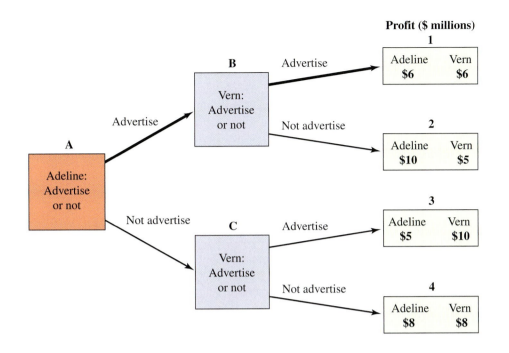

Profit ($ millions)

Game Tree for the Advertisers' Dilemma

Adeline moves first, choosing to advertise or not. Vern's best response is to advertise no matter what Adeline does. Knowing this, Adeline realizes that the only possible outcomes are shown by rectangles 1 and 3. From Adeline's perspective, rectangle 1 ($6 million) is better than rectangle 3 ($5 million), so her best response is to advertise. Both Adeline and Vern advertise, and each earns a profit of $6 million.

Table 12.3 | ADVERTISING AND PROFIT

	Neither Advertises		Both Advertise		Adeline Advertises	
	Adeline	Vern	Adeline	Vern	Adeline	Vern
Net revenue from sales ($ million)	$8	$8	$13	$13	$17	$5
Cost of advertising ($ million)	0	0	7	7	7	0
Profit ($ million)	8	8	6	6	10	5

To determine the outcome of this advertising game, let's start with Vern's possible actions:

- If Adeline advertises, we move along the upper branches of the game tree from square *A* to square *B*. Vern will earn $6 million if he advertises (rectangle 1), but only $5 million if he does not advertise (rectangle 2). Therefore, Vern's best response is to match Adeline's campaign.

- If Adeline does not advertise, we move along the lower branches from square *A* to square *C*. Vern will earn $10 million if he advertises, but only $8 million if he does not. Therefore, if Adeline does not advertise, Vern's best response is to advertise.

Advertising is Vern's dominant strategy because it is the best response no matter what Adeline does.

Consider next the options faced by Adeline. She will figure out that advertising is a dominant strategy for Vern, so she realizes that that the only possible outcomes are shown by rectangles 1 and 3. To get to rectangle 1, she advertises and gets a profit of with $6 million. This is better than not advertising and going to rectangle 3, with a profit of $5 million. So her best response is to advertise. The thick arrows show the equilibrium path of the game, from square *A* to square *B* to rectangle 1. In equilibrium, both firms advertise and each earns a profit of $6.

What is the advertisers' dilemma? Both Adeline and Vern would be better off if neither advertised. Each would get a profit of $8 million if neither advertised, compared to $6 million when they both advertise. But each firm has an incentive to use advertising to increase its sales at the expense of the other. Stuck in the dilemma, each firm earns $2 million less than it would if neither advertised.

Why does the advertisers' dilemma occur? In general, it happens when advertising causes a relatively small increase in the total sales of the industry, but allows a firm that advertises to gain at the expense of firms that don't. In our example, a pair of advertising campaigns costing a total of $14 million increases the net revenue of the entire industry by only $10 million. The increase in revenue is less than the cost of advertising, so advertising decreases total profit. Nonetheless, each firm has an incentive to advertise to take sales away from the other firm. If the increase in industry-wide net revenue were larger, advertising could benefit both firms.

SUMMARY

In this chapter, we've seen that when a few firms share a market they have an incentive to act strategically. Firms in an oligopoly try to use cartel pricing—price-fixing—to avoid competition and keep prices high. A monopolist may commit to a large quantity and a low price in order to prevent a second firm from entering the market. Oligopolists may use advertising to increase their sales at the expense of competitors. Here are the main points of the chapter:

1 Each firm in an oligopoly has an incentive to underprice the other firms, so price-fixing will be unsuccessful unless firms have some way of enforcing a price-fixing agreement.

2 One way to maintain price-fixing is a low-price guarantee: One firm chooses the high price and promises to match any lower price of its competitor.

3 Price-fixing is more likely to occur if firms choose prices repeatedly and can punish a firm that chooses a price below the cartel price.

4 To prevent a second firm from entering the market, an insecure monopolist may commit itself to producing a relatively large quantity and accepting a relatively low price.

5 The advertisers' dilemma is that both firms would be better off if neither firm advertised.

KEY TERMS

cartel, p. 273

concentration ratio, p. 272

contestable market, p. 289

dominant strategy, p. 276

duopolists' dilemma, p. 277

duopoly, p. 273

game theory, p. 272

game tree, p. 275

grim-trigger strategy, p. 280

low-price guarantee, p. 278

kinked demand curve model, p. 282

limit pricing, p. 287

Nash equilibrium, p. 277

oligopoly, p. 272

payoff matrix, p. 283

price-fixing, p. 274

price leadership, p. 282

tit-for-tat, p. 280

EXERCISES

Visit www.myeconlab.com to complete
Get Ahead of the Curve   these exercises online and get instant feedback.

12.1 | What Is an Oligopoly?

1.1 A market is considered an oligopoly if the four-firm concentration ratio is at least _____; it is considered highly concentrated if the Herfindahl-Hirschman Index (HHI) is at least _____.

1.2 For a market with four firms, each with a 25-percent market share, the Herfindahl-Hirschman Index (HHI) is equal to _____.

1.3 Oligopolies occur for three reasons: (1) the government may limit the number of firms in a market by granting _____ or limiting the number of _____; (2) large economies of _____; (3) to get a foothold in the market, large expenditures on _____ are required.

1.4 The production of breakfast cereals is not subject to large-scale economies, but the market is an oligopoly because of the barriers to entry from _____.

12.2 | Cartel Pricing and the Duopolists' Dilemma

2.1 Arrows up or down: If we move from the cartel outcome to the duopoly outcome, the price _____, the quantity per firm _____, and the profit per firm _____.

2.2 A dominant strategy is the strategy that allows one firm to dominate the market. _____ (True/False)

2.3 The duopolists' dilemma is that each firm would make more profit if both picked the _____ price, but both firms pick the _____ price.

2.4 In a Nash equilibrium, each player is doing the best he or she can, given _____.

2.5 In Figure 12.3 on page 275, rectangle 3 is not a Nash equilibrium because if _____ picks a(n) _____ price, the best response of _____ is to pick the _____ price.

2.6 In Figure 12.3 on page 275, suppose Jack promises Jill that if she picks the high price, he will, too. Is this promise credible? Explain.

2.7 Buzz and Moe are duopolists in the lawn-care market. The game tree below shows the possible pricing outcomes and their payoffs. The outcome of the pricing game is that Buzz will pick the _____ price and Moe will pick the _____ price.

2.8 The executives from the world's largest vitamin producers conspired to fix vitamin prices, increasing the prices of vitamins by an average of _____ percent. (Related to Application 1 on page 278.)

2.9 **Vitamin Market Areas.** Beta and Gamma produce vitamin A at a constant average cost of $5 per unit. Assume that low-price guarantees are illegal. Here are the possible outcomes:
- Price-fixing (cartel). Each firm sells 30 units at a price of $20 per unit.
- Duopoly (no price-fixing). Each firm sells 40 units at a price of $12 per unit.

- Underpricing (one firm charges $20 and the other charges $12). The low-price firm sells 70 units and the high-price firm sells five units. (Related to Application 1 on page 278.)

a. Suppose Beta chooses a price first, followed by Gamma. Draw a game tree for the price-fixing game and predict the outcome.

b. Suppose the firms agree to pick the high price. Once Beta picks the high price, how much more could Gamma earn if it cheated on the price-fixing agreement?

c. Suppose the firms divide the market into two areas of equal size. and assign each firm one of the areas. Each firm agrees to sell only in its assigned areas. Will this arrangement generate a successful cartel?

2.10 **Airporter Price Fixing?** Hustle and Speedy provide transportation service from downtown to the city airport. Assume that low-price guarantees are illegal. The average cost per passenger is constant at $10. Here are the possible outcomes:
- Price-fixing (cartel). Each firm has 15 passengers at a price of $25.
- Duopoly (no price-fixing). Each firm has 20 passengers at a price of $20.
- Underpricing (one firm charges $20 and the other charges $25). The low-price firm has 28 passengers and the high-price firm has five passengers.

Hustle chooses a price first, followed by Speedy. Draw a game tree for the price-fixing game and predict the outcome.

2.11 **Hotel Price Fixing?** Waikiki Beach has two hotels, one run by Juan and a second run by Tulah. The average cost of providing rooms is constant at $30 per day. Assume that low-price guarantees are illegal. Here are the possible outcomes:
- Price-fixing (cartel). Each firm has 30 customers at a price of $40.

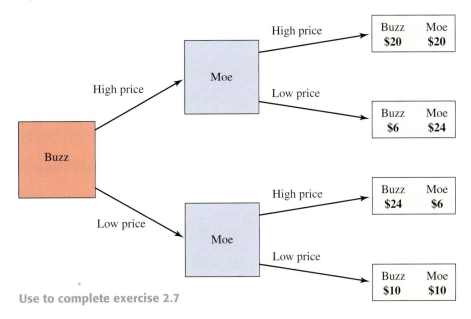

Use to complete exercise 2.7

- Duopoly (no price-fixing). Each firm has 40 customers per day at a price of $37.
- Underpricing (one firm charges $40 and the other charges $37). The low-price firm has 50 customers and the high-price firm has 10 customers.

Juan chooses a price first, followed by Tulah. Draw a game tree for the price-fixing game and predict the outcome.

12.3 | Overcoming the Duopolists' Dilemma

3.1 For firms with a low-price guarantee, the promise of matching a lower price is a(n) _____ promise, because all firms will charge the same _____ price.

3.2 Suppose that Jack and Jill use a tit-for-tat scheme to encourage cartel pricing. Jill chooses the low price for two successive months, and then switches to the high price. The two firms will deviate from cartel pricing for a total of _____ months.

3.3 If two firms expect to be in the market together for a long time, the _____ (cost/benefit) of underpricing will be large relative to the _____ (cost/benefit).

3.4 At the beginning of this chapter, we saw that Jason paid more for his plane ticket than Melissa did for hers, even though both people live in cities that are served by two airlines. Two cities with the same number of airlines could have different prices if in one city firms use a _____ guarantee to keep prices high.

3.5 If a seller promises to refund any difference between its price and the price of its competitors, this practice will lead to _____ (higher/lower) prices. (Related to Application 2 on page 280.)

3.6 **Low-Price Guarantees for a Canopy Tour.** Dip and Zip provide canopy tours in a rain forest. The average cost per rider is constant at $10. Here are the possible outcomes:
- Price-fixing (cartel). Each firm has six passengers at a price of $20.
- Duopoly (no price-fixing). Each firm has eight passengers at a price of $15.
- Underpricing (one firm charges $20 and the other charges $15). The low-price firm has 13 passengers and the high-price firm has two passengers.

Dip chooses a price first, followed by Zip. (Related to Application 2 on page 280.)
 a. Assume that the firms do not provide low-price guarantees. Draw a game tree and predict the outcome of the price-fixing game.
 b. Suppose both firms provide low-price guarantees. Draw a new game tree and predict the outcome of the price-fixing game.
 c. Is the promise to match any lower price a substantive promise or an empty promise?

3.7 **Going Out of Business Sales?** Many firms have going-out-of-business sales with remarkable bargains. What insights does the material in this chapter provide about such sales?

12.4 | Alternative Models of Oligopoly Pricing

4.1 Under a price-leadership model, a sudden drop in price by the leader is unlikely to trigger a price war if other firms believe that the price cut was caused by higher _____.

4.2 Arrows up, down, or horizontal: Under the kinked demand curve model, a firm that cuts its price expects its competitor to _____ its price, while a firm that raises its price expects its competitor to _____ its price.

4.3 An entrepreneur that acts in a manner consistent with the kinked demand curve model is a(n) _____ (optimist/pessimist).

4.4 Arrows up or down: In the kinked demand curve model, the demand for a firm's product is relatively elastic when the price _____, and relatively inelastic when the price _____.

12.5 | Simultaneous Decision Making and the Payoff Matrix

5.1 Consider a market with two firms managed by Harry and Vera. Under a cartel (both firms pick the high price), each firm earns a profit of $80. Under a duopoly (both firms pick the low price), each firm earns a profit of $60. If the two firms pick different prices, the high-price firm earns a profit of $20 and the low-price firm earns a profit of $90.

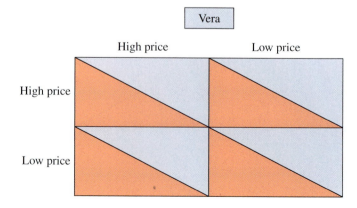

a. Fill in the payoff matrix on page 294.

b. The outcome of the pricing game is that Harry picks the _____ price and Vera picks the _____ price.

c. The outcome identified in part (b) is a Nash equilibrium because neither firm has an incentive to _____.

5.2 The prisoners' dilemma is that each prisoner would be better off if both prisoners _____, but both end up _____.

12.6 | The Insecure Monopolist and Entry Deterrence

6.1 Otto has a monopoly on limousine service, and Carla is thinking about entering the market. The outcome of the entry-deterrence game represented by the game tree below is that Otto picks the _____ quantity and Carla _____ the market.

6.2 Use the game tree in the previous exercise as a starting point. If the minimum entry quantity increases, a single number in one of the profit rectangles changes from $_____ to a smaller number. If the relevant number is reduced by half, the new outcome of the entry-deterrence game is that Otto picks the _____ quantity and Carla _____ the market.

6.3 Consider a market with an insecure monopolist. The zero-profit quantity is 60 units and the minimum entry quantity is five units. The entry-deterring quantity is _____ units. The zero-profit price is $80. The slope of the market demand curve is –$2 per unit of output. The limit price is $_____.

6.4 To deter entry, a monopolist can simply threaten that if a second firm enters, the monopolist will cut its price to the average cost. _____ (True/False)

6.5 Arrows up or down: As the minimum entry quantity decreases, the entry-deterring quantity _____, the limit price _____, and the profit from the entry-deterrence strategy _____.

6.6 In Figure 12.10 on page 287, rectangle 2 is not a Nash equilibrium because if _____ picks a small quantity, the best response for _____ is to _____.

6.7 At the beginning of this chapter, we saw that Katrina paid more for her plane ticket than Brian paid for his, even though they both live in cities that are served by a single airline. Two cities with the same number of airlines (1) could have different prices because the airline in Katrina's city could be a(n) _____ monopolist.

6.8 To prevent other firms from entering the Irish ice-cream market, Van den Bergh Foods provided free _____ to retailers on the condition that _____. (Related to Application 3 on page 288.)

6.9 In 1948, just three years after introducing a revolutionary product called the ballpoint pen, Reynolds International Pen Corporation dropped out of the market because the limit price was relatively _____, a result of relatively _____ costs of entering the market. (Related to Application 4 on page 290.)

6.10 **Ninja Turtles Versus Tai Chi Frogs.** The demand for fantasy amphibians is linear, with a slope of –$0.01 per amphibian. The average cost of production is constant at $3. The demand curve intersects the horizontal average-cost curve at a quantity of 600 amphibians. A firm selling ninja turtles currently has a monopoly, selling 300 turtles at a price of $6. A second firm is considering entering the market with tai-chi frogs, and the minimum entry quantity is 100 amphibians. If the turtle firm is passive and lets the frog firm enter, each firm will sell 200 amphibians at a price of $5. (Related to Application 4 on page 290.)

a. Draw a graph like the one shown in Figure 12.9 on page 286 with all the relevant numbers.

b. Draw a game tree like the one shown in Figure 12.10 and predict the outcome of the game. How will the turtle firm respond to the threat of entry? Will the frog firm enter the market?

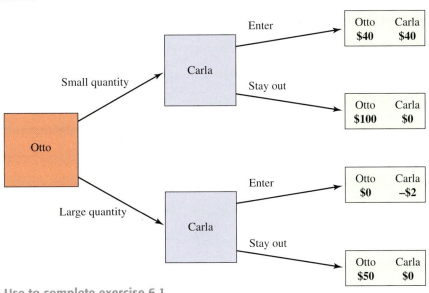

Use to complete exercise 6.1

c. How would your response to part (a) change if the minimum entry quantity dropped to 50 amphibians?

6.11 Take the Pen Money and Run? Consider the application "Reynolds International Takes the Money and Leaves the Market." Suppose the unit cost of a ballpoint pen is $1.00. Reynolds has two options.

1. *Passive.* Pick the monopoly price of $13. In the first year, Reynolds will sell 100,000 pens. Over time as other firms enter the market with lower prices, the quantity sold by Reynolds will decrease by 20,000 per year, to 80,000 in the second year, and so on, down to zero in the sixth year.
2. *Deterrence.* Commit to produce 1 million pens per year, an amount large enough to deter entry. The limit price is $1.05. (Related to Application 4 on page 290.)

   a. Under the passive strategy, the profit per year is $_____ in the first year, $_____ in the second year, and so on, down to zero in the sixth year. The total profit over the six-year period would be $_____.
   b. Under the deterrence strategy, the profit per year is $_____ . Over a 20-year period, total profit would be $_____ .
   c. Taking a 20-year perspective, which strategy is more profitable?
   d. How would your answer to part (c) change if the limit price were $1.50 rather than $1.05?

6.12 Shuttle Deterrence? Consider the market for air travel between Boston and New York. The long-run average cost is constant at $100 per passenger, and the demand curve is linear, with a slope of –$2 per passenger. The demand curve intersects the horizontal average-cost curve at a quantity of 120 passengers. The minimum entry quantity is 20 passengers. FirstShuttle currently has a monopoly, with 60 passengers at a price of $220. Another firm, SecondShuttle, is considering the market, and the minimum entry quantity is 20 passengers. If FirstShuttle is passive and lets the other firm enter, each firm will have 40 passengers at a price of $180.

   a. Draw a graph like the one shown in Figure 12.9 on page 286 with all the relevant numbers.
   b. Draw a game tree like the one shown in Figure 12.10 and predict the outcome of the game. How will FirstShuttle respond to the threat of entry? Will SecondShuttle enter the market?
   c. How would your response to (a) change if the minimum entry quantity dropped to 10 passengers?

12.7 | The Advertisers' Dilemma

7.1 The advertisers' dilemma is that _____ but _____.

7.2 The advertisers' dilemma shown in Figure 12.11 on page 291 occurs when advertising causes a relatively _____ increase in the total sales of an industry.

7.3 Consider a duopoly with two firms managed by Huck and Stella. A standard advertising campaign has a cost of $5 million per firm. If both firms run a standard campaign, the net revenue from sales increases by $4 for each firm. If only one firm runs a campaign, the advertiser's net revenue from sales increases by $8 million, and the other firm's net revenue from sales decreases by $7 million. Fill the blanks in the following table, draw a game tree, and predict the outcome of the advertising game.

	Neither Advertises		Both Advertise		Huck Advertises	
	Huck	Stella	Huck	Stella	Huck	Stella
Net revenue from sales ($ million)	$10	$10				
Cost of advertising ($ million)	0	0	5	5	5	0
Profit ($ million)						

7.4 In Figure 12.11 on page 291, rectangle 2 is not a Nash equilibrium because if _____ advertises, the best response of _____ is to _____.

7.5 Automobile Advertising. Consider two automobile companies that are considering advertising campaigns. If neither firm advertises, each will earn net revenue of $5 million. If each spends $10 million on advertising, each firm's net revenue will be $12 million. If one advertises and the other does not, the firm that advertises will earn $17 million in net revenue, while the firm that does not will earn $1 million. Draw a game tree and predict the outcome. From the industry perspective, do the benefits of advertising exceed the costs?

7.6 Got Milk? Bessie and George are milk producers, and each must decide whether to spend $7 million on an advertising campaign. If neither advertises, each will earn $10 million in net revenue from sales (net revenue). If both advertise, each will earn $20 million in net revenue and $13 million in profit ($20 million minus $7 million for advertising). If only one producer advertises, that firm will earn $16 million in net revenue, and the other firm will earn $15 million in net revenue. Prepare a game tree like Figure 12.11 on page 291. Assume that Bessie decides first. What is the outcome of this advertising game? If there is an advertisers' dilemma, how does it differ from the advertisers' dilemma discussed earlier in the chapter? How might the dairy industry solve this dilemma? (*Hint*: Think white mustaches.)

ECONOMIC EXPERIMENT

Price-Fixing

Here is a price-fixing or cartel game for the classroom. You'll have an opportunity to conspire to fix prices in a hypothetical market with five firms. The instructor divides the class into five groups. Each group represents one of five firms that produce a particular good.

Each group must develop a pricing strategy for its firm, recognizing that the other groups are choosing prices for their firms at the same time. Only two choices are possible: a high price (the cartel price) or a low price.

The profit of a particular firm depends on the price chosen by the firm and the prices chosen by the four other firms. Here is the profit matrix:

From the second row, if one of the five firms chooses the high price, and the other four firms choose the low price, the high-price firm earns a profit of $2, and each low-price firm earns a profit of $7. The game is played for several rounds. In the first three rounds, the firms make their choices without talking to each other in advance. In the fourth and fifth rounds, the firms discuss their strategies, disperse, and then make their choices. The group's score equals the profit earned by the firm.

Number of High-Price Firms	Number of Low-Price Firms	Profit for Each High-Price Firm	Profit for Each Low-Price
0	5	—	$5
1	4	$2	7
2	3	4	9
3	2	6	11
4	1	8	13
5	0	10	—

NOTES

1. Adam Smith, *The Wealth of Nations* (New York: Modern Library, 1994).

2. Sylvia Nassar, *A Beautiful Mind* (New York: Simon & Schuster, 1998).

3. Robert Axelrod, *The Evolution of Cooperation*, (New York: Basic Books, 1984).

4. Federal Trade Commission, "Record Companies Settle FTC Charges of Restraining Competition in CD Music Market," Press Release, May 10, 2000.

5. George Stigler, "The Kinked Oligopoly Demand Curve and Rigid Prices," *Journal of Political Economy*, vol. 55, 1947, pp. 432–449.

6. "Big Friendly Giant," *The Economist*, January 30, 1999, p. 72.

13

Controlling Market Power: Antitrust and Regulation

In 1997, a U.S. court blocked the proposed merger of Staples and Office Depot, the nation's two largest office-supply retailers. The judge in the case observed that the merger would eliminate Office Depot as a competitor and allow Staples to increase its prices by 13 percent. Where did the judge get that number?

APPLYING THE CONCEPTS

1 When does a natural monopoly occur?
  XM and Sirius Satellite Radio

2 How does a decrease in demand affect the price of a regulated monopoly?
  A Decrease in Demand Increases the Price of Cable TV

3 Does competition between the second- and third-largest firms matter?
  Heinz and Beech-Nut Battle for Second Place

4 How does a merger affect prices?
  Xidex Recovers Its Acquisition Cost in Two Years

When you buy groceries, hardware, or office supplies, a scanner at the checkout reads bar-code information, recording the price you pay and the quantity you purchase. The scanner system helps retailers keep track of their stock and allows them to instantly change prices without putting new price tags on their products. The scanner data can also be used to observe the pricing patterns of firms such as Staples. Economists with the Federal Trade Commission (FTC) found an interesting pattern: The prices charged by Staples were lower in cities where Office Depot also had a store. The competition generated by Office Depot led to prices that were, on average, 13 percent lower.[1]

This chapter looks at various public policies dealing with markets that are dominated by a small number of firms. We'll start with the case of natural monopoly, which occurs when the scale economies in production are so large that only a single large firm can survive. In this case, the government can intervene by regulating the price charged by the natural monopolist. Then we'll look at markets in which the government can affect the number of firms in the market by using various policies to promote competition.

The government uses antitrust policies to break monopolies into several smaller companies, prevent corporate mergers that would reduce competition, and regulate business practices that tend to reduce competition. Sometimes prior government regulations actually end up inhibiting competition, so the government later deregulates an industry to promote more competition. In the last part of the chapter, we'll look at recent deregulation of three markets: air travel, telecommunications, and electricity. In these three markets, the government reversed a long history of regulation, deregulating the industries to promote competition.

13.1 | NATURAL MONOPOLY

In an earlier chapter, we considered monopolies that resulted from artificial barriers to entry, such as patents and government licenses. In this chapter, we'll look at natural monopolies, which occur when the economies of scale for producing a product are so large that only a single firm can survive. Some examples of natural monopolies are water systems, electricity transmission, and cable TV service. It is efficient for a city to have a single supplier of water service because a second supplier would install a second set of water pipes when a single set of pipes would suffice. Similarly, it is efficient to have a single set of transmission lines for electricity and a single set of cables for TV service.

Picking an Output Level

Figure 13.1 shows the long-run average-cost curve for cable TV service in a particular city. The curve is negatively sloped and steep, reflecting the large economies of scale that occur because cable service requires a costly cable system, and the cost is the same whether the firm serves 70 subscribers or 70,000 subscribers. As the number of subscribers increases, the average cost of cable service decreases because the cost of the cable system is spread over more people.

What about the long-run marginal cost—the cost to add one subscriber—once the system is built? For each additional subscriber, a cable company incurs the cost of hooking the house into the system and the administrative cost associated with billing the subscriber. To simplify matters, we'll assume that each additional subscriber increases costs by $8 per month, so the marginal-cost curve is horizontal at $8 per subscriber.

Figure 13.1 shows how to use the cost curves and revenue curves to pick the output level that maximizes profit. Like other firms, the provider of cable TV can use the marginal principle.

MARGINAL PRINCIPLE

Increase the level of an activity as long as its marginal benefit exceeds its marginal cost. Choose the level at which the marginal benefit equals the marginal cost.

If a single firm—a monopolist—provides cable service, the firm-specific demand curve is the same as the market demand curve: The market demand curve shows, for each price, the number of subscribers for the monopolist. From the firm's perspective, the marginal benefit of a subscriber is the increase in revenue from the subscriber— the marginal revenue. The marginal principle is satisfied at point *a*, with 70,000 sub-

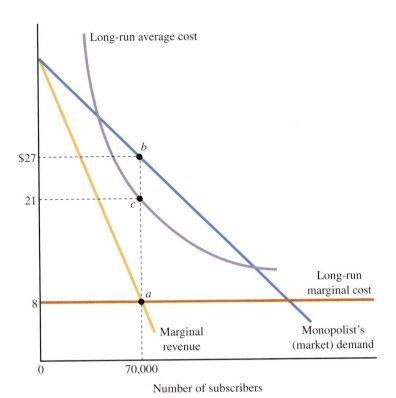

◄ FIGURE 13.1

A Natural Monopoly Uses the Marginal Principle to Pick Quantity and Price
Because of the indivisible input of cable service (the cable system), the long-run average-cost curve is negatively sloped. The monopolist chooses point *a*, where marginal revenue equals marginal cost. The firm serves 70,000 subscribers at a price of $27 each (point *b*) and an average cost of $21 (point *c*). The profit per subscriber is $6 ($27 – $21).

scribers. The price associated with this quantity is $27 per subscriber (shown by point *b*), and the average cost is $21 per unit (shown by point *c*), so the profit per subscriber is $6. The price exceeds the average cost, so the cable company will earn a profit.

Will a Second Firm Enter?

If there are no artificial barriers to entry, a second firm could enter the cable TV market. What would happen if a second firm entered the market? In Figure 13.2, the

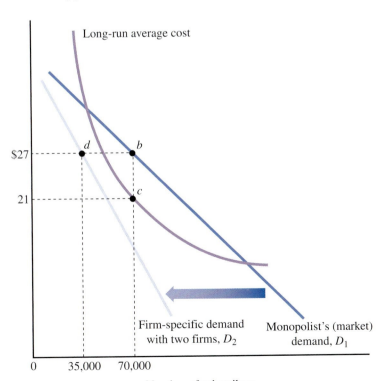

◄ FIGURE 13.2

Will a Second Cable Firm Enter the Market?
The entry of a second cable firm would shift the demand curve of the typical firm to the left. After entry, the firm's demand curve lies entirely below the long-run average-cost curve. No matter what price the firm charges, it will lose money. Therefore, a second firm will not enter the market.

entry of a second firm would shift the demand curve of the first firm—the former monopolist—to the left, from D_1 to D_2: At each price, the first firm will have fewer subscribers because it now shares the market with another firm. For example, at a price of $27, there are 70,000 subscribers, or 35,000 for each firm (point *d*). In general, the larger the number of firms, the lower the demand curve for the typical firm.

Will a second firm enter the market? Notice that the demand curve of the typical firm in a two-firm market lies entirely below the long-run average-cost curve, so there is no quantity at which the price exceeds the average cost of production. No matter what price the typical firm charges, it will lose money. The firm's demand curve lies below the average-cost curve because the average-cost curve is steep, reflecting the large economies of scale for cable service. A second firm—with half the market—would have a very high average cost and wouldn't be able to charge a price high enough to cover the cost of building the system in the first place. Therefore, the second firm will not enter the market, so there will be a single firm, a natural monopoly.

Price Controls for a Natural Monopoly

When a natural monopoly is inevitable, the government often sets a maximum price that the monopolist can charge consumers. There are many examples of natural monopolies that are subject to maximum prices. Local governments regulate utilities and firms that provide water, electricity, cable service, and local telephone service. Many state governments use public utility commissions (PUCs) to regulate the electric power industry.

We can use the cable TV market to explain the effects of government regulation on a natural monopoly. Suppose the government sets a maximum price for cable service and forces the cable company to serve all consumers who are willing to pay the maximum price. In other words, the government—not the firm—picks a point on the market demand curve. Under an *average-cost pricing policy*, the government picks the price at which the market demand curve intersects the monopolist's long-run average-cost curve. In Figure 13.3, the average-cost curve intersects the demand curve at point *e*, with a price of $12 per subscriber. This is much lower than the profit-maximizing price of $27. As a

▶ **FIGURE 13.3**

Regulators Use Average-Cost Pricing to Pick a Monopoly's Quantity and Price

Under an average-cost pricing policy, the government chooses the price at which the demand curve intersects the long-run average-cost curve—$12 per subscriber. Regulation decreases the price and increases the quantity.

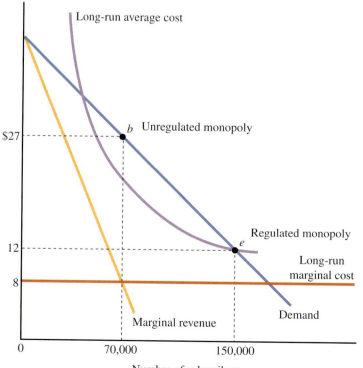

APPLICATION

XM AND SIRIUS SATELLITE RADIO

APPLYING THE CONCEPTS #1: When does a natural monopoly occur?

The biggest development in radio since the emergence of the FM band is satellite radio. Two firms—Sirius Satellite Radio and XM Satellite Radio—provide dozens of national radio channels that can be accessed by special radio receivers for cars and homes. The quality of the reception is on par with compact discs and is the same throughout the continental United States. Both firms provide dozens of channels, including music channels with rock and roll, punk, pop, country/western, R&B, and classical music. The information channels include the Bloomberg News Radio, CNBC, C-SPAN, BBC WorldService, NPR Talk, and Public Radio International.

The advantage of satellite radio is that most stations are free of annoying commercials that clutter most broadcast radio stations. The music channels on the Sirius system are commercial-free, and the information channels air just a few minutes of commercials every hour. About half the XM channels are commercial-free, and the others have no more than six minutes of commercials every hour (compared to 20 minutes at the typical broadcast radio station). The monthly charge for Sirius is $13. XM radio has a lower price—$10 per month—because it has more commercials.

How many satellite radio systems can the market support? The cost of the infrastructure to set up a single system—satellites and ground stations—is about $2 billion. In addition, both systems added to their setup costs by signing contracts with radio personalities, news organizations, and sports information sources. For example, Sirius agreed to pay Howard Stern $679 million over a five-year period. To cover the cost of the Stern contract, Sirius needs an additional 2.4 million subscribers. In early 2006, both firms were gaining subscribers but still losing money. If subscriptions continue to grow rapidly, both firms will become profitable in the next few years. But if subscription growth slows, there will be enough demand to support one satellite radio firm, but not two. *Related to Exercises 1.4 and 1.6.*

SOURCES: Associated Press Wire News, "Satellite Radio Takes Off in U.S.," June 1, 2003; David Ng, "Stern Compensation at Sirius Higher Than Estimated." Forbes.com, January 27, 2006 (*http://www.forbes.com/markets/2006/01/27/sirius-howard-stern-0127markets03.html*; accessed 06/28/2006); Ed Lin. "Sirius Seen Reaching Breakeven Before XM," Forbes.com, December 20, 2005. (*http://www.forbes.com/markets/2005/12/20/sirius-xm-satellite-radio-1220markets10.html*; accessed 06/28/2006).

result, the number of subscribers is much larger—150,000 compared to 70,000. The purpose of the average-cost pricing policy is to get the lowest feasible price. The cable company would lose money at any price less than $12, so a lower price isn't feasible.

How will this regulatory policy affect the monopolist's production costs? Under average-cost pricing, a change in the monopolist's production cost will have little effect on its profit, because the government will soon adjust the regulated price to keep the price equal to the average cost. The government will increase the regulated price when the monopolist's cost increases and decrease the price when the monopolist's cost decreases. Because the monopolist has no incentive to cut costs and faces no penalty for higher costs, its costs are likely to creep upward. As average cost increases, the regulated price will, too.

APPLICATION

A DECREASE IN DEMAND INCREASES THE PRICE OF CABLE TV

APPLYING THE CONCEPTS #2: How does a decrease in demand affect the price of a regulated monopoly?

When the population of a city decreases, the demand for all sorts of goods—including housing and cable TV service—decreases. The decrease in the demand for housing decreases the price of housing, consistent with the laws of supply and demand. In contrast, the price of cable TV service, a regulated natural monopoly in the city, increases.

A higher price for cable service seems to defy the laws of supply and demand. What explains the puzzling increase in price?

The key to solving this puzzle is that cable TV is a regulated natural monopoly, with a price equal to the average cost of providing cable service. A decrease in the number of subscribers will cause the cable company to move upward along its negatively sloped average-cost curve to a higher average cost and a higher regulated price. In graphical terms, the demand curve for cable service shifts to the left, so it will intersect the negatively sloped average-cost curve at a higher average cost. Intuitively, there are fewer subscribers to share the large fixed cost of the cable system, so each subscriber must pay more. *Related to Exercises 1.5 and 1.7.*

13.2 | ANTITRUST POLICY

- **trust**
  An arrangement under which the owners of several companies transfer their decision-making powers to a small group of trustees.

A **trust** is an arrangement under which the owners of several companies transfer their decision-making powers to a small group of trustees. The purpose of antitrust policy is to promote competition among firms, which leads to lower prices for consumers.

Two government organizations, the Antitrust Division of the Department of Justice and the Federal Trade Commission, are responsible for initiating actions against individuals or firms that may be violating antitrust laws. The courts have the power to impose penalties on the executives found to be in violation of the laws, including fines and prison sentences. In some cases, the government seeks no penalties but directs the firm to discontinue illegal practices and take other measures to promote competition. We'll explore three types of antitrust policies: breaking up monopolies, blocking mergers, and regulating business practices.

Breaking Up Monopolies

One form of antitrust policy is to break up a monopoly into several smaller firms. The label "antitrust" comes from the names of the early conglomerates that the government broke up. The classic example is John D. Rockefeller's Standard Oil Trust, which was formed in 1882 when the owners of 40 oil companies empowered nine trustees to make the decisions for all 40 companies. The trust controlled over 90 percent of the market for refined petroleum products, and the trustees ran it like a monopoly. In 1911, the government ordered its breakup. The Supreme Court found that Rockefeller had used "unnatural methods" to maintain his monopoly power and drive his rivals out of business. In addition to forming the trust, he coerced railroads to give him special rates for shipping, and he spied on his competitors. The government broke up Standard Oil into 34 separate companies, including the corporate ancestors of Exxon, Mobil, Chevron, and Amoco.

The American Tobacco Company started in 1890 as a merger of several tobacco firms. By 1907, the company had acquired over 200 rival firms and controlled 95 percent of the U.S. cigarette market. The Supreme Court found that American Tobacco maintained its monopoly power by driving rivals out of business and agreeing to exclusive contracts with wholesalers that prevented them from purchasing cigarettes from other companies. The court-ordered breakup in 1911 led to several new companies, including several of today's big cigarette companies: Reynolds, Liggett and Meyers, and P. Lorillard.

In 1982, the government broke up American Telephone and Telegraph (AT&T) into seven regional phone companies. AT&T had used its legal monopoly in local telephone service to prevent competition in the markets for long-distance service and communications equipment. After an eight-year legal battle, AT&T agreed to form seven Regional Bell Operating Companies, transforming "Ma Bell" into seven "Baby Bells." The new AT&T was allowed to compete in the market for long-distance service, where it faced competition from newcomers MCI and Sprint. AT&T was also allowed to operate in the market for communications equipment, where it faced competition from newcomers Mitel and Northern Telecom.

Blocking Mergers

A **merger** occurs when two or more firms combine their operations. A *horizontal merger* involves two firms producing a similar product, for example, two producers of pet food. A *vertical merger* involves two firms at different stages of the production process, for example, a sugar refiner and a candy producer. A second type of antitrust policy is to block corporate mergers that would reduce competition and lead to higher prices. We saw in an earlier chapter that as the number of firms in a market increases, competition among firms drives down prices. Because a merger decreases the number of firms in a market, it is likely to lead to higher prices. In 1994, Microsoft tried to purchase Intuit, the maker of Quicken, a personal-finance software package that was a substitute for a similar Microsoft product. The merger would have reduced competition in the personal-finance software market, so the government blocked it.

Of course, the government does not oppose all corporate mergers. One possible benefit from a merger is that the new firm could combine production, marketing, and administrative operations, producing products at a lower average cost. Consumers might reap the rewards in the form of lower prices. In 1997, the Justice Department and the Federal Trade Commission (FTC) released new guidelines for proposed mergers. The new guidelines allow companies involved in a proposed merger to present evidence that the merger would reduce costs and lead to lower prices, better products, or better service. If the evidence for greater efficiency is convincing, the government might allow a merger that reduces the number of firms in a market. The chairman of the FTC assessed the effects of the new guidelines as follows[2]:

> There may be some deals that go through which otherwise would not have. But it won't change the result in a large number of cases [rather it will have] the greatest impact in a transaction where the potential anticompetitive problem is modest and efficiencies that would be created are great.

The new guidelines will bring the U.S. antitrust rules closer in line with those of Europe and Canada and could help U.S. companies compete in those markets.

• **merger**
A process in which two or more firms combine their operations.

Pricing by Staples in Cities With and Without Competition
Using the marginal principle, Staples picks the quantity at which its marginal revenue equals its marginal cost. In a city without a competing firm, Staples picks the monopoly price of $14. In a city where Staples competes with Office Depot, the demand facing Staples is lower, so the profit-maximizing price is only $12.

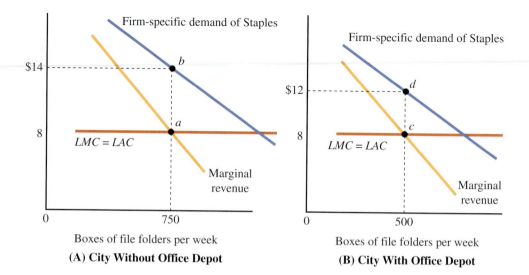

(A) City Without Office Depot

(B) City With Office Depot

In recent years, the analysis of proposed mergers has shifted from counting the number of firms in a market to predicting how a particular merger would affect prices. The data generated by retail checkout scanners provide an enormous amount of information about prices and quantities sold. Using these data, economists can determine how one firm's pricing policies affect the sales of that firm and its competitors. Economists can use this information to predict whether a merger would lead to higher prices.

As we saw in the chapter opener, the FTC used pricing data to support its decision to block a proposed merger between Staples and Office Depot. The data showed that Staples charged lower prices in cities where Office Depot also had stores. Figure 13.4 shows Staples' revenue and cost curves for one specific product: file folders. Panel A shows what happens when Staples faces no competition from an Office Depot, and Panel B shows what happens when it does. The demand curve of Staples is lower in the city where it faces competition with Office Depot because the two firms share the market. Using the marginal principle, Staples picks the quantity and price where its marginal revenue equals its marginal cost. The profit-maximizing price is $14 in a city without an Office Depot and $12 in a city with one.

The FTC used this logic to convince the court that the proposed merger of Staples and Office Depot would lead to higher prices. The judge in the case observed that,

> direct evidence shows that by eliminating Staples' most significant, and in many markets, only, rival, the merger would allow Staples to increase prices or otherwise maintain prices at an anticompetitive level.

Evidence from the companies' pricing data showed that the merger would have allowed Staples to increase its prices by about 13 percent. According to an FTC study, blocking the merger saved consumers an estimated $1.1 billion over five years.

Merger Remedy for Wonder Bread

In some cases, the government allows a merger to happen but imposes restrictions on the new company. In 1995, Interstate Bakeries, the nation's third-largest wholesale baker, tried to buy Continental Baking, the maker of Wonder Bread. Based on grocery store scanner data, the government concluded that Wonder Bread is a close substitute for Interstate's bread: The demand for Wonder Bread increases when the price of Interstate's bread increases, and vice versa.[3] The scanner data showed that when Interstate increased its price, many consumers switched to Wonder Bread, so their bread money went to Continental instead of Interstate. The substitutability of the two brands discouraged Interstate from increasing its prices.

APPLICATION

HEINZ AND BEECH-NUT BATTLE FOR SECOND PLACE

APPLYING THE CONCEPTS #3: Does competition between the second- and third-largest firms matter?

In 2001, H.J. Heinz Company announced plans to buy Milnot Holding Company's Beech-Nut for $185 million. The merger would combine the nation's second- and third-largest sellers of baby food, with a combined market share of 28 percent. The combined company would still be less than half the size of the market leader, Gerber, with its 70-percent market share. The FTC successfully blocked the merger, based on two observations:

- Most retailers stock only two brands of baby food, Gerber and either Heinz or Beech-Nut. The two smaller companies compete vigorously for shelf space, with discounts, coupons, and other programs that lead to lower prices for consumers. After the merger, the Heinz brand would disappear, leaving Beech-Nut as a secure second brand on the shelves next to Gerber. The elimination of competition for second place would lead to higher prices.

- The smaller the number of firms in an oligopoly, the easier it is to coordinate pricing. The FTC argued that "significant market concentration makes it easier for firms in the market to collude, expressly or tacitly, and thereby force price above or farther above the competitive level." In other words, in a market with two firms instead of three, it would be easier for the baby-food manufacturers to fix prices. *Related to Exercises 2.5 and 2.7.*

SOURCES: "Baby-Food Makers Heinz, Beech-Nut Call Off Merger Following Court Ruling," *Wall Street Journal*, April 27, 2001, p. A13; United State District Court for the District of Columbia, "*Federal Trade Commission v. H. J. Heinz Company*: Memorandum in Support of Plaintiff's Motion for Preliminary Injunction," July 24, 2000.

Table 13.1 shows an example of a merger leading to higher prices and smaller quantities. Let's assume that the average cost per loaf of bread is $1.50, and this doesn't change with a merger. The situation before the merger is shown in columns 1 and 3: For each brand, the price per loaf of bread is $2.00, the quantity is 100 loaves, and the profit is $50 (the profit $0.50 per loaf times 100 loaves).

How would a merger affect the incentives to raise prices? After a merger, a single company would earn the profits from both brands (Wonder and Interstate) and pick both prices. Suppose the new company increased the price of Interstate bread to $2.20 but kept the price of Wonder Bread at $2.00. The price hike would bring bad news and good news for the new company:

- Bad news: Less profit on Interstate Bread. As shown in columns 3 and 4, the price hike decreases the quantity of Interstate bread from 100 to 70 loaves. Although the profit per loaf increases to $0.70 (the new price of $2.20 minus the average cost of $1.50), only 70 loaves are sold, so the profit from the brand drops to $49, down from $50. The bad news is the $1 loss of profit on Interstate Bread.

Table 13.1 | A MERGER INCREASES PRICES

	Wonder Brand		Interstate Brand		Total	
	1 Before Merger	2 After Merger	3 Before Merger	4 After Merger	5 Before Merger	6 After Merger
Average cost	$1.50	$1.50	$1.50	$1.50		
Price	$2.00	$2.00	$2.00	$2.20		
Quantity	100	110	100	70	200	180
Profit	$50	$55	$50	$49	$100	$104

- Good news: More profit on Wonder Bread. As shown in columns 1 and 2, the increase in the price of Interstate Bread increases the quantity of Wonder Bread sold from 100 to 110 loaves. The profit per loaf is still $0.50 per bread, so the profit on Wonder Bread increases to $55, up from $50. The good news is the extra $5 of profit on Wonder Bread.

In this case, the good news ($5 more profit from Wonder) exceeds the bad news ($1 less profit from Interstate), so the price hike increases the total profit of the merged company. This is shown in columns 5 and 6. Although the total quantity drops, total profit increases by $4. A merger means that the good news from a price hike stays within the larger firm, encouraging that firm to increase prices.

The lesson from this example is that a merger of two firms selling close substitutes may lead to higher prices. That's what the Department of Justice concluded in the case of Interstate Bakeries and Continental Bakery. The government allowed the merger between the two companies but forced Interstate to sell some of its brands and bakeries. For example, Interstate sold the rights to sell its Weber brand bread to Four-S Baking Company. The idea was to ensure that other companies would be able to compete with the newly merged company.

Regulating Business Practices: Price-Fixing, Tying, and Cooperative Agreements

The third type of antitrust policy involves the regulation of business practices. The government may intervene when a specific business practice increases market concentration in an already concentrated market. A **tie-in sale** occurs when a business forces the buyer of one product to purchase another product. The FTC recently charged a pharmaceutical company with tying the sale of clozapine, an antipsychotic drug, to a blood testing and monitoring system. Another illegal business practice is a cooperative agreement to limit advertising. The FTC recently charged a group of auto dealers with restricting comparative and discount advertising.

The Robinson–Patman Act prohibits the selling of products at "unreasonably low prices" with the intent of reducing competition, a practice known as **predatory pricing**. A firm engages in predatory pricing when it sells a product at a price below its production costs, with the objective of driving a rival out of business. Once the predator's rivals drop out of the market, the firm then charges a monopoly price, well above its production cost. This strategy will be profitable if the firm can charge the monopoly price for a long enough period to offset the losses it experienced while driving its rivals out of business.

But is predatory pricing really practical? Consider a market with two firms, one of which is determined to have the market to itself. By cutting its price below its cost, the firm can drive its competitor out of business, losing perhaps $10 million in the process. If it increases its price next year, there may be nothing to prevent a new firm from entering the market. If so, it would have to cut its price below its cost again to drive the new firm out. The problem with predatory pricing is that it never ends. The firm must repeatedly lose money to drive out an endless series of competitors.

- **tie-in sales**
  A business practice under which a business requires a consumer of one product to purchase another product.

- **predatory pricing**
  A firm sells a product at a price below its production cost to drive a rival out of business and then increases the price.

APPLICATION

XIDEX RECOVERS ITS ACQUISITION COST IN TWO YEARS

APPLYING THE CONCEPTS #4: How does a merger affect prices?

In 1981, the FTC brought an antitrust suit against Xidex Corporation for its earlier acquisition of two rivals in the microfilm market. By acquiring Scott Graphics, Inc., in 1976 and Kalvar Corporation in 1979, Xidex increased its market share of the U.S. microfilm market from 46 to 71 percent. As a result, the price of microfilm increased: The price of one type of microfilm (diazo) increased by 11 percent, and the price of a second type (vesicular) increased by 23 percent. These price hikes were large enough that Xidex recovered the cost of acquiring its two rivals ($4.2 million for Scott Graphics and $6 million for Kalvar) in less than two years. To settle the antitrust lawsuit, Xidex agreed to license its microfilm technology—at bargain prices—to other firms. The idea was that if other firms have access to the microfilm technology, the competition between Xidex and the competing firms would decrease the price of microfilm. **Related to Exercises 2.6 and 2.8.**

SOURCE: David M. Barton and Roger Sherman, "The Price and Profit Effects of Horizontal Merger: A Case Study," *Journal of Industrial Economics*, vol. 33, December 1984, pp. 165–177.

The Microsoft Cases

In recent years, the most widely reported antitrust actions have involved Microsoft Corporation, the software giant. Microsoft receives royalties from computer makers that install the Microsoft operating software on their computers. The curious—and illegal—feature of the original arrangement was that Microsoft received a royalty for every computer made by the firm, even if the firm installed other operating systems on some of its computers. This scheme discouraged computer makers from using software from Microsoft's rivals, and the courts declared the practice illegal in 1994.

In the case of *United States v. Microsoft Corporation*, the judge concluded that Microsoft stifled competition in the software industry. Specifically, Microsoft tried to use its monopoly in the market for operating systems to get a monopoly in the browser market. Under an initial ruling, the judge's remedy was to break up the corporation into two companies, one producing the Windows operating system and a second producing application software. On appeal, the U.S. Justice Department rejected this remedy, and in 2002 directed Microsoft to accommodate rival browsers on the Windows desktop and release more technical information about its operating system.

A Brief History of U.S. Antitrust Policy

Table 13.2 provides a brief summary of the history of antitrust policy. The first legislation was the Sherman Antitrust Act of 1890, which made it illegal to monopolize a market or to engage in practices that result in a restraint of trade. Because the act did not specify which practices were illegal, it led to conflicting court rulings.

Many of the ambiguities of the Sherman Act were resolved by the Clayton Act of 1914. The Clayton Act outlawed specific practices that discourage competition, including tie-in sales contracts and price discrimination that reduces competition.

Table 13.2 | KEY ANTITRUST LEGISLATION

Law	Date Enacted	Regulation Enacted
Sherman Act	1890	Made it illegal to monopolize a market or to engage in practices that result in a restraint of trade.
Clayton Act	1914	Outlawed specific practices that discourage competition, including tie-in sales contracts, price discrimination for the purpose of reducing competition, and stock-purchase mergers that would substantially reduce competition.
Federal Trade Commission Act	1914	Created a mechanism to enforce antitrust laws.
Robinson–Patman Act	1936	Prohibited selling products at "unreasonably low prices" with the intent of reducing competition.
Celler–Kefauver Act	1950	Outlawed asset-purchase mergers that would substantially reduce competition.
Hart–Scott–Rodino Act	1980	Extended antitrust legislation to proprietorships and partnerships.

The act also outlawed mergers resulting from the purchase of a competitor's stock when such a merger would substantially reduce competition.

More recent legislation clarified and extended antitrust laws. The Robinson–Patman Act of 1936 prohibited predatory pricing. The Celler–Kefauver Act of 1950 closed a loophole in the Clayton Act by prohibiting one firm from purchasing another firm's physical assets, such as buildings and equipment, when the acquisition would reduce competition substantially. The Hart–Scott–Rodino Act of 1980 extended antitrust legislation to proprietorships and partnerships. Before this act, antitrust legislation applied only to corporations.

13.3 | DEREGULATION: AIRLINES, TELECOMMUNICATIONS, AND ELECTRICITY

We have discussed government policies that address the problems that result from market concentration. When a monopoly is inevitable, the government can regulate a natural monopoly to prevent excessive prices. When the merger of two firms would increase concentration, the government can prevent the merger and thereby promote competition. We now shift the emphasis and look at situations in which government regulations inhibit competition rather than promote it. When a regulation inhibits competition, government can use deregulation to reverse the course and promote competition. We explore the deregulation of two markets: air travel and telecommunications. The Airline Deregulation Act of 1978 eliminated entry restrictions and price controls in the market for air travel. The Telecommunications Act of 1996 eliminated most price controls for cable television and established a framework for entry into the markets for cable television service, local telephone service, and Internet service.

Deregulation of Airlines

Consider first the deregulation of airline service.[4] Before 1978, the Civil Aeronautics Board (CAB) regulated interstate air travel by limiting entry into the market and controlling prices. About 90 percent of the markets were monopolized, and studies indicated that prices were 30 to 50 percent higher than they would have been in a more competitive environment. The Airline Deregulation Act of 1978 eliminated most of the entry restrictions and price controls, and the CAB eventually disappeared.

Deregulation led to lower prices, which fell by about 28 percent, on average. By 1998, deregulation had generated $24 billion in savings for passengers. Here are the factors that contributed to the lower prices and the percentage of savings for each:

Factor	Percentage of Savings
Competition from incumbent carriers	18%
Competition from Southwest Airlines	31
Competition from other entrants	10
Improvements in operating efficiencies	41

Although prices fell on most routes, about a quarter of routes actually experienced price increases. In general, prices were lower on long routes and higher on short routes. This is not surprising, because the CAB had a policy of setting long-haul fares above average cost and short-haul fares below average cost. In addition, many airports are dominated by just one or two airlines. In 1998, the fares at 12 hub airports with a two-firm concentration ratio of at least 85 percent were 23 percent higher than at other airports with more competition, including low-cost carriers like Southwest Airlines.

Deregulation of Telecommunication Services

Consider next the deregulation of telecommunication services.[5] The Telecommunications Act of 1996 established new rules to promote competition among firms that transmit video, voice, and data. Several provisions of the act affect the Regional Bell Operating Companies (the Baby Bells) that were formed as a result of the breakup of AT&T in 1982. Here are the most important provisions of the act:

- *Local telephone service.* The act opened local telephone service to competition. New firms will now compete with the Baby Bells for local-service customers. In addition, cable TV firms might eventually provide telephone service over their cables.
- *Cable TV service.* Price controls for cable TV services were eliminated, and telephone companies will now be allowed to enter the market for cable TV services.
- *Long-distance service.* Once there is sufficient competition for local telephone service, the Baby Bells will be allowed to enter the long-distance market.

The challenge in deregulating local telephone service is to develop a set of rules giving competitors access to the wires and cables leading into residences. That access is currently controlled by the Baby Bells. After a slow start, there has been some progress in opening up local telephone service to competition, with most of the progress in large cities. As competition spreads, we can expect lower prices for local service, just as we saw in 1984 with the deregulation of long-distance service.

Deregulation of Electricity

Consider next the deregulation of electricity. The electricity industry has been regulated as a natural monopoly since its early days. There are three stages of producing electricity: generation in power plants, transmission along high-voltage lines, and distribution to final users along low-voltage lines. The transmission stage is subject to economies of scale because a city can be served by one set of transmission lines from power plants. There are substantial fixed costs associated with laying the transmission lines, so it is sensible to lay one set of lines and regulate the single firm as a natural monopolist. The same economies of scale occur when it comes to the distribution of power to individual users.

Until recently, there were also substantial economies of scale in electricity generation. The minimum efficient scale for power plants was large relative to the size of the markets they served, meaning that a single firm could supply the market more efficiently than several small firms. Under traditional electricity regulation, public and private utilities were responsible for all three phases of electricity production: They generated electricity in their own power plants and then used their own transmission and distribution systems to deliver electricity to consumers. State and local governments granted each utility a monopoly over a particular geographical area and set the price of electricity at a level so the utility earned a reasonable or "fair" accounting profit, including a fair return on capital investment. This is the average-cost pricing we discussed earlier in the chapter. Because utilities were responsible for all three stages of production, there was just one price to control—the retail price charged to consumers.

In the 1990s, there was growing pressure to deregulate the electricity market for two reasons. First, technological innovations reduced the economies of scale in electricity generation, so generation was no longer a true natural monopoly. For example, the minimum efficient scale for combined cycle gas turbine technology (CCGT) is about one-fifth the scale of a traditional power plant. Instead of a single power source for a city, there could be many generators, with competition among alternative producers leading to lower prices. A second factor in the pressure to deregulate was the substantial variation in electricity prices across states. For example, the price was 10 cents per kilowatt-hour (kWh) in some northeastern states (Massachusetts, Connecticut, and New York), 6 cents in some central states (Indiana and Wisconsin), and 5 cents in northwestern states (Oregon and Washington). In California, the price was 9.5 cents per kWh. Consumers in high-price states called for deregulation to allow electricity to be transmitted across state lines.

Electricity Deregulation in California

The state of California reformed its electricity regulation program in 1998. Although the plan is often labeled "California's Deregulation Plan," the label is inaccurate, because although some regulations were eliminated, others remained in force. In an attempt to foster competition at the generation level, the state's utilities sold off their generating facilities to the highest bidders. California allowed the wholesale price of electricity (the price utilities pay to generators) to fluctuate with market forces. In contrast, the retail price was subject to strict controls: California rolled back the retail price by 10 percent and maintained this level for several years.

Two years after the reform program was implemented, the California electricity market was in disarray. Because of growing demand and a delay in getting new generation facilities up and running, utilities did not have enough power to meet demand and were forced to implement rolling blackouts—cutting off the power supply for an hour in alternating areas. The wholesale price for electricity soared above $200 per megawatt-hour (MWh) while the retail price remained at about $60 per MWh. Electric utilities lost money on each kilowatt they sold, totaling billions of dollars. By 2001, the retailer/utilities had lost $12 billion, and in early 2001 one of the state's largest utilities, Pacific Gas and Electric, filed for bankruptcy.

The higher wholesale price was caused by a combination of higher fuel costs for generators, a drought that decreased supply from hydroelectric generators in the Pacific Northwest, and price manipulation by generating companies. The objective of the reform plan had been to promote competition in the generating market, but after the utilities sold their power plants to the highest bidders, just a few companies controlled most of the power generated in the state. As we saw earlier in the book, firms in oligopolies have the power to charge a price higher than the competitive price, and there is evidence that is what happened in California. One study suggests that the market price was almost twice the competitive price, and that generating companies used a strategy of withholding supply (taking plants off line to create an artificial shortage) to manipulate prices.[6] The California energy crisis is an example of the "perfect storm" explanation of disasters. Although no one factor that contributed to the problem—an increase in demand for electricity, stagnant supply, rising fuel costs, retail price controls, price manipulation, or the drought in the Pacific Northwest—by itself would have caused major problems, their convergence in 2001 led to an electricity crisis.

Electricity Deregulation in Other U.S. States

In the mid-1990s, Pennsylvania and New York restructured their electricity markets, with both moving toward deregulation. Consumers in both states can now choose from several electricity retailers. Some retailers also generate their own power, whereas others buy power from generating companies and transmit it to business and residential users. Consumers can get on the Internet and type in their zip codes to get a list of alternative suppliers. By April 2001, almost 800,000 Pennsylvanians had selected alternative electricity suppliers.

The early experience with electricity deregulation in the two states is mixed. Prices are lower in Pennsylvania but much higher in New York. Under the New York plan, utilities sold off their generating plants to the highest bidders. The plants were sold to a small number of firms, and the purchase prices were much higher than expected, reflecting the expectations that in the deregulated market with a small number of firms, each could charge a high price. Over a one-year period, the average bill from Con Ed, a generating company in New York, increased by about 38 percent as a result of higher fuel costs and perhaps some exercise of market power by Con Ed.

It is too early to determine the long-term effects on electricity deregulation. The energy debacle in California has provided some important lessons for policy makers in other states. Many other states are at earlier stages of the deregulation process and may modify their plans to avoid some of the problems generated by the perfect storm in California.

SUMMARY

In this chapter, we've explored public policies for markets with a few dominant firms. In the case of natural monopoly, the government can regulate prices. In other industries, the government uses antitrust policies to affect the number of firms in the market, encouraging competition that leads to lower prices. Here are the main points of the chapter:

1 A natural monopoly occurs when there are large-scale economies in production, so the market can support only one firm.

2 Under an average-cost pricing policy, the regulated price for a natural monopoly is equal to the average cost of production.

3 The government uses antitrust policy to break up some dominant firms, prevent some corporate mergers, and regulate business practices that reduce competition.

4 The modern approach to merger policy uses price data to predict the effects of a merger.

5 In most circumstances, predatory pricing is unprofitable because the monopoly power is costly to acquire and hard to maintain.

6 The deregulation of the airline industry led to more competition and lower prices on average, but higher prices in some markets.

KEY TERMS

merger, p. 305

predatory pricing, p. 308

tie-in sales, p. 308

trust, p. 304

EXERCISES

Get Ahead of the Curve

Visit www.myeconlab.com to complete these exercises online and get instant feedback.

13.1 | Natural Monopoly

1.1 A natural monopolist picks the quantity of output at which _____ equals _____.

1.2 The entry of a second firm shifts the demand curve of the original firm to the _____, so that at each price the original firm will sell a(n) _____ quantity.

1.3 A natural monopoly occurs when the long-run cost curve lies entirely _____ (above/below) the demand curve of the typical firm in a two-firm market.

1.4 If subscriptions to satellite radio continue to grow rapidly, the market will support _____ satellite radio systems. (Related to Application 1 on page 303.)

1.5 Arrows up or down: When the demand for cable TV service decreases, the price _____, because as the number of subscribers _____ the average cost of production _____. (Related to Application 2 on page 304.)

1.6 **Duopoly Versus Monopoly Satellite Radio.** Suppose the demand for satellite radio levels off at the number of subscribers reached in early 2006. (Related to Application 1 on page 303.)
   a. Use a graph to show the average-cost curve and firm-specific demand curve for one of the two satellite radio firms.
   b. Suppose the two firms merge into a single profitable firm. Draw the average-cost curve and firm-specific demand curve for the monopolist. Then use the marginal principle to show the profit-maximizing quantity and price. Would you expect the price to be higher or lower than the prices charged in 2006 by XM ($10) and Sirius ($13)?

1.7 **Decrease in Cable Demand.** Consider a cable TV company that has a fixed cost of $48 million and a marginal cost of $5 per subscriber. The company is regulated with average-cost pricing policy. (Related to Application 2 on page 304.)
   a. The first two columns of the following table show three points on the initial demand curve. For example, at a price of $15 the quantity demanded is 6 million subscribers. For each $2 reduction in price, the number of subscribers increases by 1 million. Fill the blanks in the following table. The regulated price is _____.

Price	Subscribers (millions)	Average Cost
$15	6	_____
13	7	_____
11	8	_____

   b. Suppose the demand for the product decreases, with the demand curve shifting to the left by 1 million subscribers. Fill the blanks in the following table. The new regulated price is $_____.

Price	Subscribers (millions)	Average Cost
$15	_____	_____
13	_____	_____
11	_____	_____

1.8 **Environmental Costs for Regulated Monopoly.** The Bonneville Power Administration (BPA) is a regulated monopoly in the Northwest that uses dozens of hydroelectric dams to generate electricity. Unfortunately, the BPA's dams block the paths of migrating fish, contributing to the decline of several species. Suppose that BPA spends $100 million to make its hydroelectric dams less hazardous for migrating fish. Who will bear the cost of this program?

13.2 | Antitrust Policy

2.1 The purpose of antitrust policy is to promote _____, which leads to lower _____.

2.2 In the Staples case discussed in this chapter, the data showed that competition with Office Depot led to _____ prices, suggesting that a merger would harm _____.

2.3 In the Interstate Baking case discussed in this chapter, scanner data showed that the products of Interstate and Continental Baking were _____, so a merger would lead to higher _____.

2.4 Predatory pricing provides a practical and effective means of getting and keeping a monopoly. _____ (True/False)

2.5 The government blocked the proposed merger between Heinz and Beech-Nut because a merger would eliminate competition for _____ (first/second/third) place in the baby-food market. (Related to Application 3 on page 307.)

2.6 After Xidex Corporation acquired two of its rivals for $10 million, it _____ (increased/decreased) prices and recovered the acquisition cost in _____ years. (Related to Application 4 on page 309.)

2.7 **Incentive to Raise Prices After a Merger.** Consider the application "Heinz and Beech-Nut Battle…" Suppose the merger of two firms will reduce the price elasticity of demand for each firm's product from 3.0 to 1.50. For each firm, the average cost of production is constant at $5 per unit. Suppose Heinz initially has a price of $10 and is considering raising the price to $11. (Related to Application 3 on page 307.)
   a. Fill the blanks in the following table, showing the payoffs from raising the price before the merger (elasticity = 3.0) and after the merger (elasticity = 1.50).

Price	Quantity	Total Revenue	Total Cost	Profit
Initial: $10	100	$1,000	$500	$500
New: $11 Before merger: Elasticity of demand = 3.0				
_____	_____	_____	_____	_____
New: $11 After merger: Elasticity of demand = 1.50				
_____	_____	_____	_____	_____

   b. Before the merger, raising the price would _____ the firm's profit. After the merger, raising the price would _____ the firm's profit.
   c. Why is it reasonable to assume that the merger will decrease the elasticity of demand for each firm's products?

2.8 **Recovering the Acquisition Cost.** The long-run average cost of production is constant at $6 per unit. Suppose firm X acquires Y at a cost of $24 million and increases the price to $14. At the new price, X sells 1.5 million units per year.

a. How does the acquisition affect X's annual profit?

b. How many years will it take for X to recover the cost of acquiring Y? (Related to Application 4 on page 309.)

2.9 Check the Yellow Pages? On Yellin's first day on the job as an economist with the FTC, she was put on a team examining a proposed merger between the country's second- and fourth-largest hardware store chains. Her job was to predict whether a merger would increase hardware prices. Her boss handed her some CDs with checkout scanner data from the second-largest chain. Each CD contained scanner data from one small town, listing the prices and quantities of hammers, wrenches, nuts, bolts, rakes, glue, drills, and hundreds of other hardware products. Her boss also gave her the telephone Yellow Pages for each small town. How can she use the information in the disks and the Yellow Pages to make a prediction?

2.10 Cost Savings from a Merger. Consider the following statement from a firm that has proposed a merger between two companies: "The two companies could save about $50 million per year by combining our production, marketing, and administrative operations. In other words, we could realize substantial economies of scale. Therefore, the government should allow the merger." In light of the new guidelines concerning mergers, how would you react to this statement?

2.11 Deadweight Loss from a Merger. Consider a market that is initially served by two firms, each of which charges a price of $10 and sells 100 units of the good. The long-run average cost of production is constant at $6 per unit. Suppose a merger increases the price to $14 and reduces the total quantity sold from 200 to 150. Compute the consumer loss associated with the merger. How does it compare to the increase in profit? What is the net loss from the merger?

13.3 | Deregulation: Airlines, Telecommunications, and Electricity

3.1 The deregulation of the airline industry led to _____ prices on average, but _____ prices in cities.

3.2 One source of pressure to deregulate electricity market was new technology that _____ the scale economies in power generation.

3.3 The following three factors contributed to the increase in the wholesale price of electricity during the California energy crisis: (1) _____; (2) _____; and (3) _____.

3.4 Willingness to Pay for New Airport Gates. Your city is considering an airport-expansion project that would increase the number of airport gates and allow additional airlines to serve your city. According to a recent report, the additional competition made possible by the new gates would decrease the average airline fare from $220 to $200 and increase the number of passengers from 400 to 600 per day. The city would borrow money to finance the project, and the daily payment required to pay off the loan over 20 years would be $8,100. How does the benefit to consumers compare to the cost of the project?

3.5 Gates to Gotcha? A construction project at your city's airport is nearing completion, and your job is to decide how to use the 10 new airport gates. The city is currently served by Gotcha Airlines, which has offered the city $20 million to help cover the cost of the airport construction project. In return, the new gates would be designated for the exclusive use of Gotcha. What trade-offs are associated with accepting Gotcha's offer?

NOTES

1. "The Economics of Antitrust: The Trustbuster's New Tools," *The Economist*, May 2, 1998, pp. 62–64; *Federal Trade Commission v. Staples, Inc.*, 970 F. Supp. 1066 (D.D.C. 1997, Hogan, J); U.S. Federal Trade Commission, *Promoting Competition, Protecting Consumers: A Plain English Guide to Antitrust Laws*, available online at www.ftc.gov/bc/compguide/index.htm, accessed 06/28/2006.

2. John R. Wilke, "New Antitrust Rules May Ease Path to Mergers," *Wall Street Journal*, April 9, 1997, pp. A3–A4.

3. "The Economics of Antitrust: The Trustbuster's New Tools," *The Economist*, May 2, 1998, pp. 62–64.

4. William G. Shepherd and James W. Brock, "Airlines," Chapter 10 in *The Structure of American Industry*, edited by Walter Adams and James W. Brock (Upper Saddle River, NJ: Prentice Hall, 1995); Clifford Winston, "U.S. Industry Adjustment to Economic Deregu-

lation," *Journal of Economic Perspectives*, vol. 12, no. 3, Summer 1998, pp. 89–110; Paul MacAvoy, *Industry Regulation and the Performance of the American Economy* (New York: W. W. Norton, 1992); Alfred E. Kahn, "Airline Deregulation—A Mixed Bag But a Clear Success Nonetheless," *Transportation Law Journal*, vol. 16, 1988, pp. 229–252; Steven A. Morrison, "Airline Service: The Evolution of Competition Since Deregulation," Chapter 6 in *Industry Studies*, 3d ed., edited by Larry Duetsch (New York: Sharpe, 2002).

5. Susan McMaster, "Telecommunications: Competition and Network Access," Chapter 14 in *Industry Studies*, 3d ed., edited by Larry Duetsch (New York: Sharpe, 2002).

6. Paul Joskow and Edward Kahn, "A Quantitative Analysis of Pricing Behavior in California's Wholesale Electricity Market During Summer 2000," NBER Working Paper 8157, March 2001.

14

Imperfect Information: Adverse Selection and Moral Hazard

"So, why are you selling this used car?"

The buyers of used cars ask this question frequently and then listen carefully to the answer. Assuming the car seller is honest, the answer the buyer hopes for is, "Because I need a different car for my new job," or "I buy a new car every three years." The buyer is trying to avoid sellers who

1 Why does a new car lose about 20 percent of its value in the first week?
   The Resale Value of a Week-Old Car

2 How can government solve the adverse-selection problem?
   Regulation of the California Kiwifruit Market

3 Does the market for baseball pitchers suffer from the adverse-selection problem?
   Baseball Pitchers Are Like Used Cars

4 Who benefits from better information about risks?
   Genetic Testing Benefits Low-Risk People

5 How does insurance change behavior?
   People with Insurance Take More Risks

are trying to get rid of a "lemon"—a car that breaks down frequently and generates large repair bills. People don't ask this sort of question in other markets. For example, no one ever asks, "So, why are you selling this pizza?"

"Does my insurance policy cover accidental death from bungee jumping?"

Life is risky, and people buy insurance to decrease the financial losses from events such as theft, sickness, injury, and death. This question above from the potential bungee jumper reveals an important fact about insurance: It causes people to take greater risks because they know insurance will cover part of the cost of an accident.

Thinmthis chapter explores the role of information in markets and what happens when one side of the market has better information than the other. In the market for used cars, sellers know more about the quality of the product than buyers do. In the market for life insurance, buyers know more about the risks they face than sellers do. As we saw earlier in the book, the model of supply and demand is based on several assumptions, one of which is that buyers and sellers have enough information to make informed choices. In a world of fully informed buyers and sellers, markets operate smoothly, generating an equilibrium price and an equilibrium quantity for each good. In a world with imperfect information, some goods will be sold in very small numbers, or not sold at all. In addition, buyers and sellers will use resources to acquire information to help make better decisions. The 2001 Nobel Prize in economics was awarded to three economists—George Akerlof, Michael Spence, and Joseph Stiglitz—who studied the effects of imperfect information on all sorts of markets.

14.1 | THE LEMONS PROBLEM

The classic example of a market with imperfect information is the market for used cars.[1] Suppose there are two types of cars, low quality and high quality. A low-quality car, also known as a "lemon," breaks down frequently and has relatively high repair costs. A high-quality car, also known as a "plum," is reliable and has relatively low repair costs. Suppose buyers cannot distinguish between lemons and plums. Although a buyer can get some information about a particular car by looking at the car and taking it for a test drive, the information gleaned from this kind of inspection is not enough to determine the quality of the car. In contrast, a person selling a car after owning it for a while knows from experience whether the car is a lemon or a plum. We say that there is **asymmetric information** in a market if one side of the market—either buyers or sellers—has better information than the other side. Because buyers cannot distinguish between lemons and plums, there will be a single market for used automobiles: Both types of cars will be sold together in a **mixed market** for the same price.

• **asymmetric information**
A situation in which one side of the market—either buyers or sellers—has better information than the other.

• **mixed market**
A market in which goods of different qualities are sold for the same price.

Uninformed Buyers and Knowledgeable Sellers

How much is a consumer willing to pay for a used car that could be either a lemon or a plum? To determine a consumer's willingness to pay in a mixed market with both lemons and plums, we must answer three questions:

1 How much is the consumer willing to pay for a plum?

2 How much is the consumer willing to pay for a lemon?

3 What is the chance that a used car purchased in the mixed market will be of low quality?

Suppose the typical buyer is willing to pay $4,000 for a plum and $2,000 for a lemon. The buyer is willing to pay less for a lemon because it is less reliable and has higher repair costs. For someone who is willing to put up with the hassle and repair expense, a lemon is a reasonable car. That's why the typical buyer is willing to pay $2,000, not zero, for a low-quality car that we tag with the label "lemon." Someone who pays $2,000 and gets a lemon is just as happy as someone who pays $4,000 and gets a plum.

Consumer expectations play a key role in determining the market outcome when there is imperfect information. Suppose that half the used cars *on the road* are lemons, and consumers know this. A reasonable expectation for consumers is that half the cars *on the used-car market* will be lemons, too. In other words, buyers initially expect a

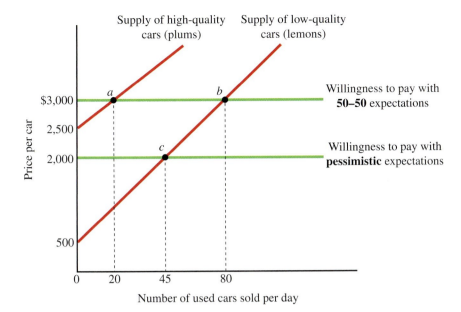

If buyers assume that there is a 50–50 chance of getting a lemon or a plum, they are willing to pay $3,000 for a used car. At this price, 20 plums are supplied (point *a*) along with 80 lemons (point *b*). This is not an equilibrium because consumers' expectation of a 50–50 split are not realized. If consumers become pessimistic and assume that all cars on the market will be lemons, they are willing to pay $2,000 for a used car. At this price, only lemons will be supplied (point *c*). Consumer expectations are realized, so the equilibrium is shown by point *c*, with an equilibrium price of $2,000.

50–50 split between the two types of cars. A reasonable assumption is that a buyer in the mixed market is willing to pay the average value of the two types of cars, or $3,000. In other words, a buyer is willing to pay $3,000 for a 50–50 chance of getting either a plum or a lemon.

The current owner of a used car knows from everyday experience whether the car is a lemon or a plum. For each owner, the question is, given the single market price for all used cars, lemons and plums alike, should I sell my car? The answers to this question are shown by the two supply curves in Figure 14.1, one for lemons and one for plums:

- *Lemon supply.* As shown by the lower curve, the minimum supply price for lemons is $500: At any price less than $500, no lemons will be supplied. Lemons have a lower minimum price because they are worth less to their current owners. The number of lemons supplied increases with price. For example, 80 cars will be supplied at a price of $3,000 (point *b*).

- *Plum supply.* As shown by the upper curve, the minimum supply price for plums is $2,500: At any price less than $2,500, no plums will be supplied. Consistent with the law of supply, the higher the price of used cars, the larger the number of plums supplied. For example, 20 plums will be supplied at a price of $3,000 (point *a*).

Equilibrium with All Low-Quality Goods

Table 14.1 shows two scenarios for our hypothetical used-car market, based on the supply curves shown in Figure 14.1. In the first column, we assume that buyers have 50–50 expectations about the quality of used cars. As we saw earlier, if buyers expect a 50–50 split between lemons and plums, the typical buyer will be willing to pay $3,000 for a used car. From the supply curves in Figure 14.1, we know that at this price 20 plums and 80 lemons will be supplied, so 80 percent of the used cars (80 of 100) will be lemons. In this case, consumers are too optimistic and underestimate the chance of getting a lemon.

The experiences of these 100 consumers show that the actual chance of getting a lemon is 80 percent, not 50 percent as initially assumed. Once future buyers realize this, they will of course become more pessimistic about the used-car market. Suppose they assume that all the used cars on the market will be lemons. Under this assumption, the typical buyer will be willing to pay only $2,000 (the value of a lemon) for a used car. As shown in Figure 14.1, this price is less than the $2,500 minimum price for

Table 14.1 | EQUILIBRIUM WITH ALL LOW-QUALITY GOODS

	Buyers Initially Have 50–50 Expectations	Equilibrium: Pessimistic Expectations
Demand Side of Market		
Amount buyer is willing to pay for a lemon	$2,000	$2,000
Amount buyer is willing to pay for a plum	$4,000	$4,000
Assumed chance of getting a lemon	50%	100%
Assumed chance of getting a plum	50%	0%
Amount buyer is willing to pay for a used car in mixed market	$3,000	$2,000
Supply Side of Market		
Number of lemons supplied	80	45
Number of plums supplied	20	0
Total number of used cars supplied	100	45
Actual chance of getting a lemon	80%	100%

supplying plums, so plums will disappear from the used-car market. At a price of $2,000, the quantity of plums supplied is zero, but the quantity of lemons supplied is 45 (point *c*). In other words, all the used cars will be lemons, so consumers' pessimism is justified. Because consumers' expectations are consistent with their actual experiences in the market, the equilibrium price of used cars is $2,000. The equilibrium in the used-car market is shown in the second column of Table 14.1.

In this equilibrium, no plums are bought or sold, so every buyer will get a lemon. People get exactly what they pay for: They are willing to pay $2,000 for a serviceable but low-quality car, and that's what each consumer gets. The domination of the used-car market by lemons is an example of the **adverse-selection problem**. The uninformed side of the market (buyers in this case) must choose from an undesirable or adverse selection of used cars. The asymmetric information in the market generates a downward spiral of price and quality:

• The presence of low-quality goods on the market pulls down the price that consumers are willing to pay.

• A decrease in price decreases the number of high-quality goods supplied, decreasing the average quality of goods on the market.

• The decrease in the average quality of goods on the market pulls down the price that consumers are willing to pay again.

In the extreme case, this downward spiral continues until all the cars on the market are lemons.

A Thin Market: Equilibrium with Some High-Quality Goods

The disappearance of plums from our hypothetical used-car market is an extreme case. The plums disappeared from the market because informed plum owners decided to keep their cars rather than selling them at a relatively low price in the used-car market. This outcome would change if the minimum supply price of plums were lower, specifically if it is below $2,000. In this case, most but not all the used cars on the market will be lemons, and some lucky buyers will get plums. In this case, we say that asymmetric information generates a **thin market**: Some high-quality goods are sold, but fewer than would be sold in a market with perfect information.

Figure 14.2 shows the situation that leads to a thin market. The minimum supply price for plums is $1,833, and the quantity of plums supplied increases with the price of used cars. Suppose that consumers are initially pessimistic, assuming that

• adverse-selection problem
A situation in which the uninformed side of the market must choose from an undesirable or adverse selection of goods.

• thin market
A market in which some high-quality goods are sold but fewer than would be sold in a market with perfect information.

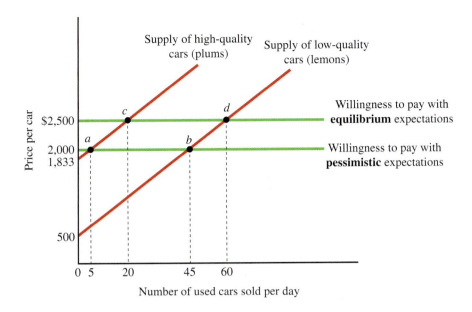

The Market for High-Quality Cars (Plums) Is Thin

If buyers are pessimistic and assume that only lemons will be sold, they are willing to pay $2,000 for a used car. At this price, 5 plums are supplied (point *a*), along with 45 lemons (point *b*). This is not an equilibrium because 10% of consumers get plums, contrary to their expectations. If consumers assume that there is a 25% change of getting a plum, they are willing to pay $2,500 for a used car. At this price, 20 plums are supplied (point *c*), along with 60 lemons (point *d*). This is an equilibrium because 25% of consumers get plums, consistent with their expectations. Consumer expectations are realized, so the equilibrium is shown by points *c* and *d*.

all cars for sale will be lemons. This means that consumers are willing to pay only $2,000 for a used car. Because the minimum supply price for plums ($1,833) is now less than the willingness to pay for a lemon, some plums will be supplied at a price of $2,000. In Figure 14.2, 5 plums and 45 lemons are supplied at this price, so 1 out of every 10 buyers will get a plum. In this case, pessimism is not an equilibrium, because some buyers will get plums when they expect lemons. This is also shown in the first column of Table 14.2.

In equilibrium, consumer expectations about the chances of getting the two types of cars are realized. Suppose that consumers expect 1 of every 4 cars to be a plum. Let's assume that each consumer is willing to pay $2,500 for a used car under these circumstances. Consumers are willing to pay a bit more than the value of a lemon because there is a small chance of getting a plum. In Figure 14.2, at this price 20 plums are supplied (point *c*) and 60 lemons are supplied (point *d*), so in fact 1 in 4 consumers actually gets a plum. This is an equilibrium because 25 percent of the cars sold are plums and 75 percent are lemons, consistent with consumers' expectations. This is also shown in the second column of Table 14.2.

Table 14.2 | A THIN MARKET FOR HIGH-QUALITY GOODS

	Initial Pessimistic Expectations	Equilibrium: 75–25 Expectations
Demand Side of Market		
Amount buyer is willing to pay for a lemon	$2,000	$2,000
Amount buyer is willing to pay for a plum	$4,000	$4,000
Assumed chance of getting a lemon	100%	75%
Assumed chance of getting a plum	0%	25%
Amount buyer is willing to pay for a used car in mixed market	$2,000	$2,500
Supply Side of Market		
Number of lemons supplied	45	60
Number of plums supplied	5	20
Total number of used cars supplied	50	80
Actual chance of getting a lemon	90%	75%

14.2 | RESPONDING TO THE LEMONS PROBLEM

In a market with asymmetric information, there are strong incentives for buyers and sellers to solve the lemons problem. In our example of a thin market, the price of a used car is $2,500, but consumers are willing to pay $4,000 for a plum. This $1,500 gap between the willingness to pay for a plum and the price in the mixed market provides an incentive for buyers to acquire information to help identify plums. It also provides an incentive for plum owners to prove that they are selling high-quality cars.

Buyers Invest in Information

In our model of the thin market, 1 of 4 buyers pays $2,500 to get a plum worth $4,000. The more information a buyer has, the greater the chance of picking a plum from the cars in the mixed market. Suppose a buyer gets enough information to identify the plums in a market. The buyer could purchase a plum worth $4,000 at the prevailing price of $2,500, generating a gain of $1,500. A buyer can get information about individual cars by taking the car to a mechanic for a careful inspection. In addition, a buyer can get general information about the reliability of different models from magazines and the Internet. *Consumer Reports* publishes information on repair histories of different models and even computes a "Trouble" index, scoring each model on a scale of 1 to 5. By consulting these information sources, a buyer improves the chances of getting a high-quality car.

Consumer Satisfaction Scores from ValueStar and eBay

The problem of asymmetric information in consumer goods such as cars also occurs for some types of consumer services. Most consumers can't easily determine the quality of service they will receive from an auto repair shop, a landscaper, or a plumber. How can a high-quality service provider distinguish itself from low-quality providers?

If you live in the San Francisco Bay area, you can get information about the performance of firms providing consumer services such as medical and dental care, gardening and landscaping, pet grooming, auto repair, and home improvement. ValueStar is a consumer guide and business directory that uses customer satisfaction surveys to determine how well a firm does relative to its competitors in providing quality service. To earn the right to display a Customer-Rated seal from ValueStar, a firm must prove that it has all the required licenses and insurance and must agree to pay for a survey of its past customers. ValueStar uses consumer surveys to compute a consumer-satisfaction score for each company. Any company receiving a score of at least 85 out of 100 has the right to display a Customer-Rated Gold seal for a one-year period.

Another example of consumer satisfaction scores is evident on eBay, the Internet auction site. On eBay, buyers must rely on sellers to honestly disclose the quality of the goods they are auctioning and to promptly ship them once a consumer pays. Buyers help other purchasers distinguish "good" from "bad" sellers on eBay by rating them online with "stars," indicating their satisfaction with their transactions.

Guarantees and Lemons Laws

Used-car sellers also have an incentive to solve the lemons problem. If a plum owner persuades a buyer that her car is a plum and then sells the car for $4,000 rather than $2,500, the seller's gain is $1,500. Sellers can identify a car as a plum in a sea of lemons by offering one of the following guarantees:

- *Money-back guarantees.* The seller could promise to refund the $4,000 price if the car turned out to be a lemon. Because the car is in fact a plum—a fact known by the seller—the buyer will not ask for a refund, so both the buyer and the seller will be happy with the transaction.

- *Warranties and repair guarantees.* The seller could promise to cover any extraordinary repair costs for one year. Because the car is a plum, there won't be any extraordinary costs, so both the buyer and the seller will be happy with the transaction.

Many states have laws that require automakers to buy back cars that experience frequent problems in the first year of use. For example, under California's Song–Beverly Consumer Warranty Act, also known as the "Lemons Law," auto dealers are required to repurchase vehicles that have been brought back for repair at least four times for the same problem or have been in the mechanic's shop for at least 30 calendar days in the first year following purchase. A vehicle repurchased under the lemons law must be fixed before it is sold to another customer and must be identified as a lemon with a stamp on the title and a sticker on the car that says "lemons law buyback." One problem with enforcing these laws is that lemons can cross state lines without a paper trail. The interstate commerce in lemons has led to new laws in some states requiring the branding of lemons on vehicle titles to follow the car when it crosses state lines.

14.3 | EVIDENCE OF THE LEMONS EFFECT

The lemons model makes two predictions about markets with asymmetric information. First, the presence of low-quality goods in a market will at least reduce the number of high-quality goods in the market and may even eliminate them. Second, buyers and sellers will respond to the lemons problem by investing in information and other means of distinguishing between low-quality and high-quality goods. What's the evidence for the lemons model?

APPLICATION

THE RESALE VALUE OF A WEEK-OLD CAR

APPLYING THE CONCEPTS #1: Why does a new car lose about 20 percent of its value in the first week?

If you buy a new car for $20,000 today and then try to sell it a week later, you probably won't get more than $16,000 for it. Even if you drove it just a couple hundred miles, cleaned it up, and returned it to the dealer with that new-car smell, the car will lose about 20 percent of its value in the first week. You won't fare any better by putting an advertisement in the newspaper or trying to sell the car on eBay. Why does the typical new car lose so much of its value in the first week?

A potential buyer of a week-old car might believe that a person who returns a car after only one week could have discovered it was a lemon and may be trying to get rid of it. Alternatively, the seller could have simply changed his or her mind about the car. The problem is that buyers don't know why the car is being sold, and as long as there is a chance that the car is a lemon they won't be willing to pay the full "new" price for it. In general, buyers are willing to pay a lot less for a week-old car, and so the owners of high-quality, week-old cars are less likely to put them on the market. This downward spiral ultimately reduces the price of week-old cars by about 20 percent. *Related to Exercises 3.1 and 3.6.*

Used Pickup Trucks

Studies of the market for used pickup trucks have provided mixed results concerning the lemons problem.[2] It appears that for trucks less than 10 years old, those sold on the market are just as reliable, on average, as those that remain with their current owners. These studies provide support for the second implication of the theory of lemons, that people acquire information and develop effective means to deal with the problem of asymmetric information. In contrast, there does seem to be a lemons problem for trucks at least 10 years old, which represent about one-third of transactions. Compared to old trucks that remain with their current owners, old trucks that are sold have significantly higher repair costs, with a difference in cost of about 45 percent. Old trucks that are sold have a much higher probability of requiring engine and transmission repairs.

2 APPLICATION

REGULATION OF THE CALIFORNIA KIWIFRUIT MARKET

APPLYING THE CONCEPTS #2: How can government solve the adverse-selection problem?

Kiwifruit is subject to imperfect information because buyers cannot determine its sweetness—its quality level—by simple inspection. The sweetness level at the time of consumption is determined by the fruit's "maturity"—its sugar content at the time of harvest. Kiwifruit continues to convert starch into sugar after it is picked, so a harvest-time sugar content of 6.5 percent leads to a sugar content of about 14 percent at the time of consumption. Fruit that is picked early has a low sugar content at harvest time and never tastes sweet. There is asymmetric information because producers know the maturity of the fruit, but fruit wholesalers and grocery stores, who buy fruit at the time of harvest, cannot determine whether a piece of fruit will ultimately be sweet or sour.

Before 1987, kiwifruit from California suffered from the "lemons" problem. Maturity levels of the fruit varied across producers. On average, the sugar content at the time of harvest was below the industry standard, established by kiwifruit from New Zealand. Given the large number of "lemons" among California kiwifruit, grocery stores were not willing to pay as much for California fruit. In other words, the presence of low-quality (immature) fruit in the mixed market pulled down the price of California fruit. Mature kiwifruit is more costly to produce than immature fruit, and the low price decreased the production of mature fruit. This is similar to low used-car prices decreasing the number of high-quality used cars on the market. In general, adverse selection led to low prices and a relatively large volume of low-quality kiwifruit from California.

In 1987, California producers implemented a federal marketing order to address the lemon–kiwi problem. The federal order specified a minimum maturity standard (6.5 percent sugar content at the time of harvest), and as the average quality of California fruit increased, so did the price. Within a few years, the gap between California and New Zealand prices had decreased significantly.

Related to Exercises 3.3 and 3.7.

SOURCE: Christopher Ferguson and Hoy Carman, "Kiwifruit and the 'Lemon' Problem: Do Minimum Quality Standards Work?" Working Paper, 1999. International Food and Agribusiness Management Association.

APPLICATION

BASEBALL PITCHERS ARE LIKE USED CARS

APPLYING THE CONCEPTS #3: Does the market for baseball pitchers suffer from the adverse-selection problem?

Professional baseball teams compete with each other for players. After six years of play in the major leagues, a player has the option of becoming a free agent and offering his services to the highest bidder. A player is likely to switch teams if the new team offers him a higher salary than his original team. One of the puzzling features of the free-agent market is that pitchers who switch teams are more prone to injuries than pitchers who don't. On average, pitchers who switch teams spend 28 days per season on the disabled list, compared to only 5 days for pitchers who do not switch teams. This doesn't mean that all the switching pitchers are lemons; many of them are injury-free and are valuable additions to their new teams. But on average, the switching pitchers spend five times longer recovering from injuries.

This puzzling feature of the free-agent market for baseball players is explained by asymmetric information and adverse selection. Because the coaches, physicians, and trainers from the player's original team have interacted with the player on a daily basis for several years, they know from experience whether he is likely to suffer from injuries that prevent him from playing. In contrast, the new team has much less information. Its physicians can examine the pitcher, and the team can check league records to see how long the pitcher has spent on the disabled list, but these measures do not eliminate the asymmetric information. The original team has several years of daily experience with the pitcher and has better information about the pitcher's physical health.

To illustrate the lemons problem for pitchers, consider the incentives for a team to outbid another team for a pitcher. Suppose the market price for pitchers is $1 million per year, and a pitcher who is currently with the Detroit Tigers is offered this salary by another team. If the Tigers think the pitcher is likely to spend a lot of time next season recovering from injuries, they won't try to outbid the other team for the pitcher: They will let the pitcher switch teams. But if the Tigers think the pitcher will be injury-free and productive, he will be worth more than $1 million to the Tigers, so they will outbid other teams and keep him. In general, an injury-prone pitcher is more likely to switch teams. As in the used-car market, there are many "lemons" on the used-pitcher market. The market for baseball players playing other positions does not suffer from the adverse selection, perhaps because the injuries that affect their performance are easier for other teams to detect.

Although you may think it's bizarre to compare baseball pitchers to used cars, people in baseball don't think so. They recognize the similarity between the two markets. Jackie Moore, who managed a free-agent camp where teams looking for players can see free agents in action, sounds like a used-car salesman: "We want to get players off the lot. We want to cut a deal. How many camps can you go into where you can look at a player and take him home with you?" *Related to Exercises 3.4 and 3.8.*

SOURCES: Kenneth Lehn, "Information Asymmetries in Baseball's Free Agent Market," *Economic Inquiry*, vol. 22, January 1984, pp. 37–44; Chris Sheridan, "Free Agents at End of Baseball's Earth," Associated Press, printed in *Corvallis Gazette-Times*, April 15, 1995, p. B1.

14.4 | UNINFORMED SELLERS AND KNOWLEDGEABLE BUYERS: INSURANCE

So far, we have explored the effects of asymmetric information when sellers are more knowledgeable than buyers. The same sort of problems occur when buyers are more knowledgeable than sellers. The best example of superior knowledge on the demand side of the market is insurance. A person who buys an insurance policy knows much more about his or her risks and needs for insurance than the insurance company knows. For example, when you buy an auto insurance policy, you know more than your insurance company about your driving habits and your chances of getting into an accident. We'll see that insurance markets suffer from the adverse-selection problem: Insurance companies must pick from an adverse or undesirable selection of customers.

Health Insurance

To illustrate the information problems in the market for insurance, consider health insurance provided to individual consumers. Suppose there are two types of consumers: low-cost consumers with relatively low medical expenses of $2,000 per year and high-cost consumers with relatively high medical expenses $6,000 per year. The amount a consumer is willing to pay for an insurance policy covering all medical expenses increases with the anticipated medical expenses, so high-cost people are willing to pay more for health insurance.

The insurance company cannot distinguish between high-cost and low-cost people, but it still must pick a price for its coverage. To simplify matters, let's assume that there are no administrative costs, so the only cost for the insurance company is the medical bills it pays for its customers. Let's also assume that the insurance company sets the price equal to its average cost per customer, equal to the total medical bills paid by the insurance company divided by the number of customers. These assumptions simplify the math without affecting the basic results.

What is the insurance company's average cost per customer? To determine the average cost in a mixed market, we must answer three questions:

- What is the cost of providing medical care to a high-cost person?
- What is the cost of providing medical care to a low-cost person?
- What fraction of the customers are low-cost people?

Suppose that half the population is high cost and the other half is low cost. Let's assume that the insurance company is somewhat naive and initially assumes that the mix of insurance buyers will be the same as the population mix. In other words, the insurance company initially assumes that half its customers will be high cost and half will be low cost. In this case, the average cost per customer is $4,000, that is, the average of $2,000 for each low-cost customer and $6,000 for each high-cost customer.

There is asymmetric information in the insurance market because potential buyers know from everyday experience and family histories what type of customer they are, either low cost or high cost. For each person, the question is: Given the single market price for all insurance, for low-cost and high-cost people alike, should I buy insurance? The answers to this question are shown in two demand curves in Figure 14.3. The demand curve for the high-cost people is higher than the curve for the low-cost people, reflecting their larger benefits from having medical insurance.

Equilibrium with All High-Cost Consumers

Table 14.3 shows two scenarios for our hypothetical insurance market, with numbers based on the demand curves shown in Figure 14.3. In the first column, we assume that firms initially assume a 50–50 mix of customers. As we saw earlier, if sellers expect a

◄ **FIGURE 14.3**

All Insurance Customers Are High-Cost People

If insurance companies assume there will be a 50–50 split between high-cost and low-cost customers, the average cost of insurance and its price is $4,000. At this price, there are 25 low-cost customers (point *a*) and 75 high-cost customers (point *b*). This is not an equilibrium because 75 percent of insurance buyers are high-cost customers, contrary to the expectations of a 50–50 split. If insurance companies become pessimistic and assume that all buyers will be high-cost consumers, the average cost and price is $6,000. The insurance company's expectations are realized, so the equilibrium is shown by point *c*.

Table 14.3 | EQUILIBRIUM WITH ALL HIGH-COST CUSTOMERS

	50–50 Expectations	Equilibrium: Pessimistic Expectations
Supply Side of Market		
Cost of serving a high-cost customer	$6,000	$6,000
Cost of serving a low-cost customer	$2,000	$2,000
Assumed fraction of high-cost customers	50%	100%
Assumed chance of low-cost customers	50%	0%
Expected average cost per customer (price)	$4,000	$6,000
Demand Side of Market		
Number of high-cost customers	75	40
Number of low-cost customers	25	0
Total number of customers	100	40
Actual fraction of high-cost customers	75%	100%
Actual average cost per customer	$5,000	$6,000

50–50 split between the two types, the average cost per customer is $4,000, and that's the price they charge for medical insurance. From the demand curves in Figure 14.3, we know that at this price 25 low-cost people will buy insurance (point *a*), along with 75 high-cost people (point *b*). In this case, insurance companies are too optimistic and underestimate the fraction of customers with large medical bills. The actual fraction of high-cost customers is 75 percent, and the actual average cost is $5,000 (equal to 0.25 times $2,000, plus 0.75 times $6,000). The company's average cost of $5,000 exceeds its price of $4,000, so the firm will lose money.

Suppose that after observing the outcome in the first column, insurance companies become very pessimistic. They assume that all their customers will be high-cost people. Under this assumption, the average cost per customer is $6,000, the average cost per high-cost customer, and that's the pessimistic price. As shown in Figure 14.3, this price exceeds the maximum that low-cost people are willing to pay for insurance ($5,200), so none of the low-cost consumers will buy insurance at this price. But a total of 40 high-cost consumers will buy insurance at this price (point *c*). In other words, all the customers will be high-cost people, so the company's pessimism is justified. The price chosen by the insurance company equals the actual average cost of providing service, so the equilibrium is shown by point *c*, with an equilibrium price of $6,000. This equilibrium is shown in the second column of Table 14.3.

The domination of the insurance market by high-cost people is another example of the adverse-selection problem. The uninformed side of the market (sellers in this case) must choose from an undesirable or adverse selection of consumers. The asymmetric information in the market generates an upward spiral of price and average cost of service:

- The presence of high-cost consumers in the market pulls up the average cost of service, pulling up the price.

- An increase in price decreases the number of low-cost consumers who purchase insurance.

- The decrease in the number of low-cost consumers pulls up the average cost of insurance.

- In the extreme case, this upward spiral continues until all insurance customers are high-cost people.

Our example of health insurance indicates that only high-cost people buy insurance. A more realistic outcome is a thin market, with a relatively small number of low-cost people buying insurance. The adverse-selection problem could be less severe, but still will be present as long as insurance companies cannot distinguish perfectly between low-cost and high-cost people.

Responding to Adverse Selection in Insurance: Group Insurance

Insurance companies use group insurance plans to diminish the adverse-selection problem. By enrolling all the employees of an organization in one or two insurance plans, they ensure that all workers, not just high-cost people, join the pool of consumers.

In our example, group insurance would generate a 50–50 mix of low-cost and high-cost customers, and the break-even price would be $6,000. In contrast, when a firm sells insurance to individuals, the low-cost people have an incentive to go without insurance, leading to the adverse-selection problem and higher prices.

Most insurance companies use **experience rating** to set their prices for group insurance. They charge different prices to different firms, depending on the past medical bills of the firm's employees. A firm whose employees have low medical bills pays a low price for its employees' health insurance. Experience rating gives firms an incentive to decrease the health costs of their workers. As a result, they have an incentive to invest in safety and health programs for their workers. They also have an incentive to avoid hiring applicants with health problems. Under experience rating, a firm that hires a worker with above-average medical costs will ultimately pay a higher price for its group insurance.

- **experience rating**
  A situation in which insurance companies charge different prices for medical insurance to different firms depending on the past medical bills of a firm's employees.

The Uninsured

One implication of asymmetric information in the insurance market is that many low-cost consumers who are not eligible for a group plan will not carry insurance. Given the adverse-selection problem, the price for an individual insurance plan is relatively high, and many consumers go without insurance. This is a contributing factor to the problem of the "uninsured." In 2004, about 46 million people (about 14 percent of the U.S. population) were not covered by health insurance. About 70 percent of working-age people have private insurance, and another 10 percent have some sort of government insurance, leaving 20 percent without health insurance. In general, the uninsured are the people and their families who do not receive insurance through their employers, are unemployed or between jobs, or are poor but do not qualify for

Medicaid. The uninsured obtain care for medical emergencies but typically do not receive routine—and less costly—preventive care.

The problem of uninsured people does not show any signs of improving. A proposal for universal coverage from the national government, which would have required each employer to provide health insurance for all its workers, was soundly defeated. Stanford health economist Victor Fuchs has suggested a plan under which everyone would receive a voucher—a coupon from the government they could use toward the purchase of their own health insurance.[3] The difficulty with any voucher plan is that new taxes would be necessary to finance it. Most European countries that provide universal coverage to their citizens finance it with a value-added tax—essentially a national sales tax. Clearly, introducing a new tax or raising existing tax rates to finance a voucher plan would be very controversial.

APPLICATION

GENETIC TESTING BENEFITS LOW-RISK PEOPLE

APPLYING THE CONCEPTS #4: Who benefits from better information about risks?

You probably know someone who is impulsive and excitable, a thrill seeker who keeps life interesting for those of us who are more relaxed and mellow. Scientists recently identified one of the genes responsible for novelty-seeking behavior and discovered that about 15 percent of the people in Israel, Europe, and the United States carry the gene. Scientists estimate that about half of novelty-seeking behavior among people is linked to their genes, which might make them more inclined to take up skydiving or bungee jumping and engage in other risky behavior.

If you managed a life insurance company, would you like to know whether each customer has the novelty-seeking gene? It would reduce the problem of asymmetric information and allow you to charge different prices for insurance, leading to lower prices for people who are less inclined to take risks. In other words, people who don't have the novelty-seeking gene benefit from genetic testing because they will pay lower prices for life insurance.

The same logic applies to genetic tests that reveal an individual's likelihood of developing heart disease. In principle, an insurance company that has genetic information for its customers could distinguish between high-cost and low-cost customers and charge different prices to the two types of consumers. This is good news for people with a favorable genetic makeup because they would pay lower prices. But it's bad news for people whose genetic makeup makes them more likely to develop heart disease, because they would pay a higher price.

The development of genetic tests has led to fears that insurance companies will use the results of the tests to engage in genetic discrimination—denying insurance or charging higher prices to people with unfavorable genes. Federal employees are protected by an executive order that forbids genetic discrimination. Most states have laws that prevent insurance companies from using genetic information in determining prices and eligibility for insurance coverage. *Related to Exercises 4.3 and 4.4.*

SOURCE: "Genetic Discrimination Feared," Associated Press Online, June 26, 2000 www.ap.org, accessed 01/29/2001; Malcolm Ritter, "A Thrill a Minute: Geneticists Find Personality Link," The *Oregonian*, January 2, 1996, p. A1; National Conference of State Legislatures, "Genetics and Health Insurance: State Anti-Discrimination Laws," June 2005, available online at www.ncsl.org/programs/health/genetics/ndishlth.htm, accessed 07/05/2006.

Other Types of Insurance

The same logic of adverse selection applies to the markets for other types of insurance, including life insurance, home insurance for theft and property damage, and automobile insurance. Buyers know more than sellers about their risks, so there is adverse selection, with high-risk individuals more likely to buy insurance. Life insurance companies provide group coverage to get a broader base of consumers and also try to distinguish between high-risk and low-risk people with physical exams. But because the companies are unable to distinguish between high-risk and low-risk people with sufficient precision, the adverse-selection problem persists.

14.5 | INSURANCE AND MORAL HAZARD

Does insurance affect people's risk-taking behavior? The answer is, yes. Insurance causes people to take greater risks because they know part of the cost of an undesirable outcome will be borne by their insurance companies. Here are some examples of people taking greater risks because they have insurance:

- Will Irma buy a fire extinguisher for her kitchen? If she had to pay for any property damage caused by a fire, she would definitely buy a fire extinguisher. But because her homeowner's insurance covers property damage from fires, she doesn't buy a fire extinguisher.
- Will Harry drive his car carefully? If he had to pay for all repairs resulting from a collision out of his own pocket, he would drive very carefully. But because his auto insurance covers some of the repair costs, he drives fast and recklessly.
- Will Flo fly on a commercial airline or hitch a ride with her pilot friend in a four-seat airplane? Traveling in small airplanes is much riskier. If Flo dies in an airplane crash, her family will lose the income she would otherwise earn. If she didn't have life insurance to offset these income losses, she would be less likely to risk harming her family by flying on the small plane instead of the commercial airline. But because she knows her family will collect $1 million in life insurance, she is willing to take the risk.

• **moral hazard**
A situation in which one side of an economic relationship takes undesirable or costly actions that the other side of the relationship cannot observe.

The risky behavior triggered by insurance is an example of the moral-hazard problem. **Moral hazard** occurs when one side of an economic relationship takes undesirable or costly actions that the other side of the relationship cannot observe. For example, Irma's insurance company doesn't know whether she has a fire extinguisher. She doesn't buy an extinguisher because her insurance will cover the cost of a kitchen fire. If there is a fire, Irma's hidden action—going without an extinguisher—is costly for the insurance company. Similarly, Harry's insurance company doesn't know how fast and recklessly he drives, and insurance encourages him to drive recklessly. His hidden action of reckless driving increases the likelihood of a costly accident. Just as collision insurance encourages risky driving, life insurance encourages risky activities such as flying small airplanes, parachuting, and bungee jumping. Similarly, health insurance encourages risky behavior such as smoking, drinking, and unhealthy diets.

Insurance companies use various measures to decrease the moral-hazard problem. Many insurance policies have a deductible—a dollar amount that a policy holder must pay before getting compensation from the insurance company. For example, if your car insurance policy has a $500 deductible and the damage from a collision is $900, the insurance company will pay you only $400. To compute its payment, the insurance company deducts your $500 deductible from the $900 damage figure, and then pays you $400. Deductibles reduces the moral-hazard problem because they shift part of the cost of a collision to the policy holder. Like a deductible, an insurance copayment shifts part of the cost of risky behavior to policy holders and thus reduces the moral-hazard problem.

Deposit Insurance for Savings & Loans

For another example of moral hazard, consider the insurance provided for bank deposits. When you deposit money in a Savings and Loan (S&L), the money doesn't just sit in a vault. The S&L will invest the money, loaning it out and expecting to make a profit when loans are repaid with interest. Unfortunately, some loans are not repaid, and the S&L could lose money and be unable to return your money. To protect people who put their money in S&Ls and other banks, the Federal Deposit Insurance Corporation (FDIC) insures the first $100,000 of your deposit, so if the S&L goes bankrupt, you'll still get your money back. The government enacted the federal deposit insurance law in 1933 in response to the bank failures of the Great Depression.

How does deposit insurance affect you and the people who manage the S&L? If you know you'll get your money back no matter what happens to the S&L, you may deposit your money there without evaluating the performance of the S&L and the riskiness of its loans to borrowers and investments in the stock market. The manager of an S&L will also be more likely to make risky investments knowing that if it doesn't pay off and the S&L goes bankrupt, the federal government will reimburse depositors. Recognizing this moral hazard problem, the federal government has historically limited S&Ls to relatively safe investments.

In the 1980s, the federal government loosened some of the investment restrictions on S&Ls, and S&L managers began investing in volatile securities, including high-risk commercial mortgages and junk bonds. When these risky investments failed, many of the S&Ls went into bankruptcy. The government then bailed out the failed S&Ls, at a total cost to taxpayers of about $200 billion.

APPLICATION

5

PEOPLE WITH INSURANCE TAKE MORE RISKS

APPLYING THE CONCEPTS #5: How does insurance change behavior?

At fictional Wheeler State University, 1 out of every 10 bicycles was stolen in 2004. When a group of young entrepreneurs discovered that no one on campus had bicycle theft insurance, they decided to go into the insurance business, offering one-year theft insurance for $15 per bike. They sold 100 policies in 2005 and expected 10 of their 100 customers (10 percent of them) to lose their bicycles to theft. The entrepreneurs figured that their total revenue would more than cover the cost of replacing 10 bicycles, leaving a tidy profit. By the end of 2005, a total of 20 insured bicycles had been stolen, and the students lost a bundle of money on their little enterprise. What happened?

The key to solving this puzzle is the fact that the 10-percent theft rate occurred in 2004 when *no one* had theft insurance. When the entrepreneurs offered theft insurance the next year, they expected the same theft rate. Because of moral hazard, however, the students who bought theft insurance were less careful in protecting their bikes, perhaps using less secure locks or leaving their bikes on campus overnight. As a result, the theft rate for insured bikes was 20 percent, not 10 percent. The entrepreneurs lost money because they did not anticipate that insurance would increase risk-taking. *Related to Exercise 5.5.*

SUMMARY

In this chapter, we've seen what happens when one of the assumptions underlying most supply and demand analysis—that people make informed decisions—is violated. If either buyers or sellers don't have reliable information about a particular good or service, the market will suffer from the adverse-selection problem. The uninformed side picks from an adverse selection of goods or customers. Here are the main points of the chapter:

1 The *adverse-selection problem* occurs when one side of the market cannot distinguish between high-quality and low-quality goods. The presence of low-quality goods pulls down the price that buyers are willing to pay, which decreases the quantity of high-quality goods supplied, which further

decreases the average quality and the price. In the extreme case, only low-quality goods are sold.

2 A *thin* market occurs when the sellers of high-quality goods have a relatively low minimum supply price, so some high-quality goods are sold.

3 In a market subject to *asymmetric information*, buyers have an incentive to invest in information to help make better choices and sellers have an incentive to provide quality guarantees.

4 Insurance markets suffer from adverse selection because compared to insurance sellers, buyers have better information about the risks they face.

5 Insurance encourages risky behavior because part of the cost of an unfavorable outcome will be paid by an insurance company.

KEY TERMS

adverse-selection problem, p. 320
asymmetric information, p. 318

experience rating, p. 328
mixed market, p. 318

moral hazard, p. 330
thin market, p. 320

EXERCISES

Visit www.myeconlab.com to complete
Get Ahead of the Curve these exercises online and get instant feedback.

14.1 | The Lemons Problem

1.1 There is asymmetric information in the used-car market because _____ (buyers/sellers) cannot distinguish between lemons and plums but _____ (buyers/sellers) can.

1.2 In the used-car market, suppose the typical consumer is willing to pay $4,000 for a plum and $1,000 for a lemon. If there is a 50-percent chance of getting a lemon, the consumer is willing to pay $ _____ for a used car.

1.3 The following table shows the prices and quantities in three different used-car markets. Complete the table by filling in the last two rows.

	Market A	Market B	Market C
Assumed chance of getting a lemon	60%	80%	95%
Willingness to pay for a used car	$6,000	$5,000	$4,500
Number of lemons supplied	70	40	90
Number of plums supplied	30	10	10
Total number of used cars supplied	100	50	100
Equilibrium: Yes or No?			
If disequilibrium, will price then rise or drop?			

1.4 We will have a thin market for used cars if the minimum supply price for plums (high quality) is _____ (greater than/less than) the willingness to pay for a lemon.

1.5 Arrows up or down: As the minimum supply price of plums (high quality) decreases, the number of plums supplied at each price will _____, so the likelihood of getting a plum will _____.

1.6 The typical consumer is willing to pay $1,000 for a low-quality 1995 Z13 car and $5,000 for a high-quality 1995 Z13 car. If equilibrium price for such a car is $1,800, the likelihood of getting a lemon is _____ chances in 5, and the likelihood of getting a plum is _____ chances in 5.

1.7 *Consumer Reports.* You want to buy a used car, specifically a 1999 Zephyr. According to *Consumer Reports*, half of the 1999 Zephyrs now on the road are lemons, meaning that they break down frequently and generate large repair bills. Consumers are willing to pay $2,000 for a lemon, but $5,000 for a plum. According to Ms. Wizard, "The equilibrium price of used 1999 Zephyrs will be $2,000 in Sourland but $2,600 in Sweetland."
   a. Illustrate with a complete graph for each market.
   b. What is the fundamental difference between the two markets?

1.8 Fashion and Prices. You are in the market for a used car and have narrowed your options to two types of cars, type F and type P. According to *Consumer Reports,* the two types of cars have roughly the same frequency of lemons (50 percent). Like other consumers, you are willing to pay $1,000 for a lemon and $7,000 for a plum. The people who buy new F cars are fashion-conscious and purchase a new car every three years. The people who buy new P cars are insensitive to the whims of fashion. Predict the equilibrium prices of the two types of cars and defend your answer with two graphs, one for each type of car.

1.9 Double Ignorance. Suppose both buyers and sellers of used cars are ignorant: No one can distinguish between lemons and plums. Would you expect the market to be dominated by lemons? Illustrate with a completely labeled graph.

1.10 Groucho Club. Consider a classic quip from Groucho Marx: "I won't join any club that is willing to accept me as a member." Suppose Groucho wants to associate with high-income people (the higher the income the better) and everyone else has the same preferences as Groucho.
   a. Use the notion of adverse selection to explain this quip.
   b. Relate the quip to the adverse-selection problem.

1.11 Purchasing a Fleet of Used Cars. You are responsible for buying a fleet of 10 used cars for your employees and must pick either brand B or brand C. For your purposes, the two brands are identical except for one difference: Based on your experience with the two brands, you figure that 50 percent of B cars in the market are lemons and only 20 percent of C cars in the market are lemons. You are willing to pay $1,000 for a known lemon and $3,000 for a known plum. If the price of B cars is $1,800 and the price of C cars is $2,200, which brand of car should you pick?

1.12 Adverse Selection of Furbies. Consider the market for used Furbies, with knowledgeable sellers and ignorant buyers. Half of the Furbies in existence are plums and half are lemons. Each buyer is willing to pay $50 for a plum or $20 for a lemon. The minimum supply price for a plum is $10 and the minimum supply price for a lemon is $2.
   a. In equilibrium, will the market be "thin" or will all the used Furbies in the market be lemons? Explain and illustrate your answer with a complete graph.
   b. Suppose that at a price of $26, the quantity of plums is 20 and the quantity of lemons is 80. Is this an equilibrium? Explain and illustrate your answer with a complete graph.

14.2 | Responding to the Lemons Problem

2.1 Suppose the price of a used car in a thin market is $2,800 and you are willing to pay $5,000 for a plum.

You would be willing to pay up to $ _____ for information that identifies a true plum.

2.2 Consider a thin used-car market. Someone just developed a device that can instantly identify the nearest plum in a used-car lot. The device works only once. The maximum amount that a consumer would be willing to pay for the device equals _____ minus _____.

2.3 The price of a used car in a thin market is $2,800, and consumers are willing to pay $2,000 for a lemon and $5,000 for a plum. Suppose two sellers, a lemon owner and a plum owner, each provide a money-back guarantee when they sell their cars for $5,000.
   a. If the lemon owner sells the car with the guarantee, the net gain for the seller will be $ _____.
   b. If the plum owner sells the car with the guarantee, the net gain for the seller will be $ _____.

2.4 Paying for Information. You are willing to pay $7,000 for a high-quality car—a plum. The current price of used cars is $4,000, and 4 of 5 cars in the market are lemons, meaning that 1 in 5 is a plum.
   a. Suppose you could pay a finder's fee to a personal shopper/mechanic who will find you a plum at a price of $4,000. What is the maximum you are willing to pay as a finder's fee?
   b. As you shop for a used car, you will bring each car you consider to your mechanic, who will thoroughly inspect the car and tell you for certain whether it is a plum or a lemon. If the price per inspection is $400, is it worth the money?
   c. How would your answer to part (b) change if only 1 out of 10 used cars was a plum?

14.3 | Evidence of the Lemons Effect

3.1 A new car loses about _____ percent of its value in the first week because recent buyers are more likely to want to sell a _____ (lemon/plum). (Related to Application 1 on page 323.)

3.2 Recall the discussion of the market for used pickup trucks. There is an adverse-selection problem for _____ trucks.

3.3 Arrows up or down: Government regulations for kiwifruit _____ the average quality and _____ the price of kiwifruit. (Related to Application 2 on page 324.)

3.4 Professional baseball pitchers are like used _____ because there is _____ information: A player's _____ has better information about the pitcher's health and likelihood of injury. (Related to Application 3 on page 325.)

3.5 Your favorite baseball team just announced that it signed a new pitcher from the free-agent market. We expect the new pitcher to be injured _____ (more/less) often than free-agent pitchers who returned to their old teams.

3.6 Mix of Lemons and Plums in the Week-Old Car Market. Recall the application, "Resale Value of a Week-Old Car." Suppose the value of a high-quality week-old car (a plum) is $20,000 (the same as the purchase price of a new car), while the value of a low-quality week-old car (a lemon) is $10,000. Suppose that at a price of $16,000 per car, 6 of 10 cars on the used market are plums and 4 of 10 are lemons. (Related to Application 1 on page 323.)

a. How much is the typical buyer willing to pay for a used car in the mixed market?

b. Is the $16,000 price an equilibrium price? Why or why not?

c. Suppose that for every 10 new cars sold by new-car dealer, 9 are plums and only 1 is a lemon. Why is the equilibrium mix in the used car market different from the mix of new cars sold?

3.7 Equilibrium in the Kiwifruit Market. Consumers are willing to pay 10 cents for a sour kiwifruit and 30 cents for a sweet kiwifruit. The minimum supply price for sour kiwifruit is 6 cents and the minimum supply price for sweet kiwifruit is 18 cents. The slope of each supply curve is 1 cent per thousand kiwifruit. (Related to Application 2 on page 324.)

a. Suppose consumers initially expect a 50–50 mix of sweet and sour kiwifruits. Is this an equilibrium? Illustrate with a graph.

b. Suppose consumers are pessimistic, expecting all sour kiwifruit. Is this an equilibrium? Illustrate with a graph. What is the price of kiwifruit?

c. Suppose the state outlaws sour kiwifruit, and they disappear from the market. What happens to the equilibrium price of kiwifruit? What is the equilibrium quantity of sweet kiwifruit?

3.8 Willingness to Pay for Used Baseball Pitchers. Suppose a healthy baseball pitcher is worth $5 million per year to his team, compared to only $1 million per year for an unhealthy pitcher. Suppose that half the pitchers in the league are healthy, and half are unhealthy. According to an executive of a baseball team, "If my assumptions are correct, our team is willing to pay a maximum of $3 million for a pitcher in the free-agent market." (Related to Application 3 on page 325.)

a. What are the executive's assumptions?

b. Are these assumptions realistic?

14.4 | Uninformed Sellers and Knowledgeable Buyers: Insurance

4.1 Suppose that the average annual malpractice cost is $40,000 for reckless doctors and $2,000 for careful doctors. If half of an insurance company's insured doctors are reckless, the company will earn zero economic profit if the price of insurance is $ _____. If careful doctors are not willing to pay any more than $5,000 for insurance, the price required for zero economic profit is $ _____.

4.2 Arrows up or down: In an insurance market, the presence of high-cost consumers _____ the average cost of providing insurance. The resulting _____ in the number of low-cost consumers _____ the average cost of providing insurance and _____ the price.

4.3 Arrows up or down: If a life insurance company gets access to genetic information about its customers, the company will _____ the price for customers with favorable genetic characteristics and _____ the price for customers with unfavorable characteristics. (Related to Application 4 on page 329.)

4.4 Genetic Testing and Insurance Prices. Suppose the likelihood that a person will get disease X is determined in large part (but not exclusively) by his or her genes. Initially, it is impossible to determine who carries the gene for the disease, and many people spend $500 on special health insurance to cover the costs of treatment for the disease. Suppose scientists uncover the gene responsible for the disease and develop a simple test for the gene. (Related to Application 4 on page 329.)

a. Suppose the government passes a law that prevents insurance companies from getting the results of a customer's genetic test for X. Will the new price of X insurance be greater than or less than $500?

b. Suppose insurance companies have access to the results of genetic tests and they require all customers to get the test. How will the insurance company change its price of X insurance?

4.5 Rising Insurance Rates. Consider an insurance company that provides group medical coverage for university employees. The company discovered that some of its younger employees had switched to other insurance companies. The company responded to the loss of customers by increasing its price. This is puzzling because you might think the insurance company would drop its price to prevent other employees from switching to other companies.

a. What is the rationale for increasing the price?

b. If you change one word in the second sentence, it would be logical for the insurance company to decrease rather than increase its price. What's the word, and why is it decisive?

4.6 State Auto Insurance Pool. Consider a state in which automobile drivers are divided equally into two types of drivers: careful and reckless. The average annual auto insurance claim is $400 for a careful driver and $1,200 for a reckless driver. Suppose the state adopts an insurance system in which all drivers are placed in a common pool and allocated to insurance companies randomly. An insurance company cannot refuse coverage to any driver it is assigned, but a driver who is unhappy with the insurance company has the option of being randomly reassigned to another insurance company. By law, each insurance company must charge the same price to all its customers. Predict the price of auto insurance under the two alternative policy scenarios:

a. Under Policy M, auto insurance is mandatory.

b. Under Policy V, auto insurance is voluntary.

14.5 | Insurance and Moral Hazard

5.1 In the market for insurance, the moral-hazard problem is that insurance encourages _____.

5.2 While shopping for office equipment, an office manager sees a display of fire extinguishers. After making a single phone call, the manager decides not to buy a fire extinguisher. The manager called her _____ and asked, "_____?"

5.3 Many professional athletes purchase insurance against career-ending injuries. We expect the insured players to experience _____ (more/fewer) injuries than uninsured players.

5.4 If you offer insurance against bicycle theft and base your price on last year's theft rate, you are likely to lose money because insurance _____ theft rates.

5.5 **Selling iPod Insurance.** On the campus of Klepto College, half the iPods are expensive (replacement value is $400) and half are cheap (replacement value is $100). There is a 20-percent chance that any particular iPod—expensive or cheap—will be stolen in the next year. Suppose a firm offers iPod-theft insurance for $50 per year: The firm will replace any insured iPod that is stolen. Suppose the firm sells 20 insurance policies. (Related to Application 5 on page 331.)

a. Assume for the moment that the theft rate remains at 20 percent for both types of iPods. The firm's total revenue equals _____. The firm's cost—the money paid out to replace stolen iPods—will be $ _____ to replace expensive iPods and $ _____ to replace cheap iPods, for a total of $ _____. The insurance firm will make zero economic profit with a price of $ _____.

b. Is it realistic to assume that the introduction of insurance will not affect the theft rate? Which is a more plausible assumption, that the theft rate will decrease to 10 percent or that it will increase to 30 percent? For the more plausible theft rate, compute the zero-profit insurance price when insurance is purchased exclusively by the owners of expensive iPods.

5.6 **Skydiver Question.** Several of your friends have offered to take you on a tandem skydiving adventure: Strapped together with a single set of parachutes (main and emergency), you jump out of an airplane and then either float to earth or crash. All your skydiving friends are equally skillful, and none of them has the thrill-seeker gene. You can ask each of them a single question.

a. What's your question?

b. Provide the answer you're looking for in a skydiving mate.

5.7 **Insurance and Fire Prevention.** In a given year, there is a 10-percent chance that a fire in Ira's warehouse will cause $100,000 in property damage. If Ira spends $4,000 on a fire-prevention program, the probability of a fire would drop to zero.

a. If Ira doesn't have fire insurance, will he spend the money on the prevention program?

b. If Ira has an insurance policy that covers 80 percent of the property damage from a fire (covering $80,000 of the $100,000 worth of damage), will he spend the money on the prevention program?

ECONOMIC EXPERIMENT

Rolling for Lemons

In this experiment, students play the role of consumers purchasing used cars. Over half the used cars on the road (57 percent) are plums, and the remaining cars (43 percent) are lemons. Each consumer offers a price for a used car and then rolls a pair of dice to find out whether he or she gets a lemon or a plum. In general, rolling a big number is good news: To get a plum, you need to roll a big number. The higher the price you offer, the smaller the number you must roll to get a plum. Here is how the experiment works:

- Each consumer tells the instructor how much he or she is offering for a used car and then rolls the dice.

- The instructor tells the consumer whether the number rolled is large enough to get a plum. If the number is not large enough, the consumer gets a lemon.

- The consumers' scores equal the difference between the maximum amount they are willing to pay for the type of car they got ($1,200 for a plum and $400 for a lemon) and the price they actually paid. For example, if Otto offers $500 and gets a plum, his score is $700. If Carla offers $600 and gets a lemon, her score is –$200.

- The instructor announces the result of each transaction to the class.

- There are three to five buying periods. At the end of the last trading period, each consumer adds up his or her score.

ECONOMIC EXPERIMENT

Bike Insurance

This experiment shows the effect of asymmetric information on the market for bicycle insurance. Consider a city with two types of bike owners: some face a relatively high probability of bike theft, and others face a relatively low probability of bike theft. Bike owners know from experience whether they face a high probability or a low probability of theft, but the insurance company cannot distinguish between the two types of owners. For the city as a whole, 20 percent of bicycles are stolen every year. Here is how the experiment works:

- The class is divided into small groups. Each group represents an insurance company that must pick a price at which to offer bike-theft insurance. The insurance company must pay $100 for each insured bike that is stolen.

- The instructor has a table that shows for each price of bike insurance how many owners of each type (high probability and low probability) will purchase insurance. Using the numbers supplied by the instructor, each insurance company can compute its total revenue (the price per bike insured times the number of insured bikes), the number of bikes stolen, and the company's total replacement cost.

- The group's score for a trading period equals the company's profit, which is the total revenue less the total replacement cost for stolen bikes.

- The experiment runs for several trading periods, and a group's score equals the sum of its profits over these trading periods.

NOTES

1. George Akerlof, "The Market for 'Lemons': Quality Uncertainty and the Market Mechanism," *Quarterly Journal of Economics*, August 1970, pp. 488–500.

2. Eric Bond, "A Direct Test of the Lemons' Model: The Market for Used Pickup Trucks," *American Economic Review*, September 1982, 72, pp. 836–840; Michael Pratt and George Hoffer, "Test of the Lemons Model: Comment," *American Economic Review*, September 1984, 74, pp. 798–800; Eric Bond, "Test of the Lemons' Model: A Reply," *American Economic Review*, September 1984, 74, pp. 801–804.

3. Victor Fuchs, "Economics, Values, and Health Reform," *American Economic Review*, March 1996, pp. 1–26.

15

Public Goods and Public Choice

Here is the text from a TV newscast in the year 2070: Boomer, the 200-meter asteroid on a collision path with the earth, is expected to land at about 10:00 A.M. in the heart of the world's breadbasket, the American Midwest. The energy expected to be released by the impact will exceed the total explosive yield of all the nuclear weapons on the planet. Although Boomer is much smaller than the asteroid that caused the extinction of the dinosaurs about 65 million years ago, it is large enough to cause significant changes in the world's climate. The collision will generate a stratospheric dust cloud that will inhibit photosynthesis and retard plant growth, resulting in lower agricultural yields and higher food prices throughout the world.

Could this catastrophe have been averted? Yes, according to scientists at the National Aeronautics and Space Administration (NASA). In 1996, scientists developed the technology for an asteroid-diversion system: Large optical telescopes would detect an asteroid on a collision course with the earth, and an orbiting gossamer mirror of coated polyester would focus a tight beam of sunlight on the asteroid, vaporizing enough of its surface to change its path. In a United Nations debate over the asteroid-diversion system, the representatives of all nations agreed that the potential benefits of the system would outweigh the costs, but no one was willing to pay for the system. Why couldn't the nations of the world agree on such an important program, one that would have prevented tomorrow's catastrophe?

I n this chapter, we'll see that if a particular good generates external benefits, government intervention can make beneficial transactions. For example, although everyone on earth would benefit from an asteroid-diversion system, the cost of an asteroid-diversion program is so high that no single person would provide such a system. We will never have such a program—even if its benefits exceed its costs—unless we make a collective decision about what sort of diversion system to develop and how to pay for it. One purpose of government is to help make this sort of collective decision. The hypothetical newscast suggests that a multinational arrangement may be necessary to launch an asteroid-diversion program.

This chapter explores the challenges associated with providing goods that generate external benefits. After an overview of government spending programs and tax sources, we'll look at the differences between private goods, such as housing, and public goods, such as levees. We'll discuss various responses to the problem of free riders—people who benefit from public goods but don't pay for them. We'll also discuss the external benefits from education and other private goods. Then we'll show how the preferences of citizens affect elections and decisions in the public sector. Finally, we'll look at some alternative theories on government decision making.

Although it's convenient to talk about "the" government, there are thousands of governments in the United States, and each citizen deals with at least three different levels of government. Figure 15.1 shows the budget breakdown for the three levels of government. The United States has more than 80,000 local governments, including municipalities (city governments), counties, school districts, and special districts responsible for providing services such as water, fire protection, and libraries. Local governments spend most of their money on education (kindergarten through high school), public welfare and health (payments to poor households and support for public hospitals), highways, fire protection, and police and corrections. For states, the biggest spending programs are education (including colleges and universities), public welfare, highways, health and hospitals, and corrections (state courts and prisons). For the federal government, the biggest spending programs are programs for the elderly (Social Security and Medicare), national defense, income security (payments to the poor), and interest on the national debt.

Figure 15.2 shows the revenue sources for local governments, states, and the federal government. About two-fifths of local government revenue comes from higher levels of government in the form of intergovernmental grants. The other major revenue source for local governments is the property tax, which is a fixed percentage of the value of residential, commercial, or industrial property. At the state level, the most important revenue sources are intergovernmental grants from the federal government, the sales tax, and the individual income tax. A person's state income tax liability is based on how much he or she earns, with tax rates that typically increase as income increases. At the federal level, the major revenue sources are individual income taxes and employment taxes, which include taxes collected to support Social Security and Medicare.

15.1 | EXTERNAL BENEFITS AND PUBLIC GOODS

As we saw earlier in the chapter on market efficiency, when there are neither external benefits nor external costs, the market equilibrium is efficient. When a government intervenes in an efficient market, the result is inefficiency. In this chapter, we'll see that a market with external benefits is inefficient, so there is an opportunity for government to promote efficiency.

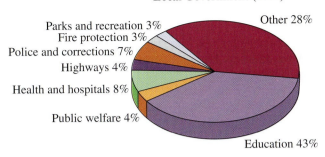

Local Government (2002)

Parks and recreation 3%
Fire protection 3%
Police and corrections 7%
Highways 4%
Health and hospitals 8%
Public welfare 4%
Other 28%
Education 43%

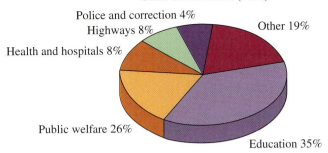

State Government (2002)

Police and correction 4%
Highways 8%
Health and hospitals 8%
Public welfare 26%
Other 19%
Education 35%

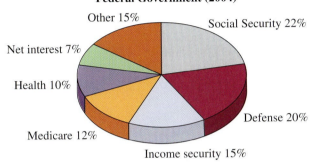

Federal Government (2004)

Other 15%
Net interest 7%
Health 10%
Medicare 12%
Income security 15%
Social Security 22%
Defense 20%

▲ **FIGURE 15.1**
Spending Programs for Local, State, and Federal Governments
SOURCE: Statistical Abstract of the United States, *2006*

For most goods, the benefits of consumption are confined to the person who buys the good. The benefit experienced by a buyer is called a *private benefit*. In contrast, when someone else benefits from a good, the good generates an **external benefit**. To illustrate the idea of external benefits and inefficiency, consider a dam built for flood-control purposes. One thousand people would be protected by the dam, and each person gets a $50 benefit. If one person builds a dam, the private benefit is $50 and the external benefit is $49,950, or $50 for each of the 999 other people who benefit from the dam. If the cost of building the dam is $20,000, no single person will build it because the cost exceeds the $50 private benefit. In other words, if we rely on the forces of supply and demand, with each person considering only private benefits and the costs of the dam, it won't be built.

When there are external benefits from a good, collective decision making generates more-efficient choices. In the case of the dam, the total benefit of $50,000 exceeds the $20,000 cost, so the dam is efficient and society as a whole will be better off if it is built. The government can solve this problem by collecting enough tax revenue to pay for the dam. Suppose the government proposes to collect $20 per person to pay for the dam. The tax raises $20,000 in tax revenue ($20 per person times 1,000 people), which is just high enough to pay the $20,000 cost of the dam. Most people will support this proposal because the $20 tax per person is less than the $50 benefit per person. The government can use its taxing power to provide a good that would otherwise not be provided.

Public Goods and the Free-Rider Problem

The dam is an example of a *public good*. A **public good** is available for everyone to utilize, regardless of who pays for it and who doesn't. More precisely, a public good is *nonrival* in consumption: The fact that one person benefits from a good does not prevent another person from benefiting. For example, the fact that I benefit from a flood-control dam doesn't reduce your benefit from the dam.

• **external benefit**
A benefit from a good experienced by someone other than the person who buys the good.

• **public good**
A good that is available for everyone to consume, regardless of who pays and who doesn't; a good that is nonrival in consumption and nonexcludable.

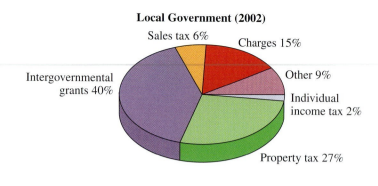

Local Government (2002)

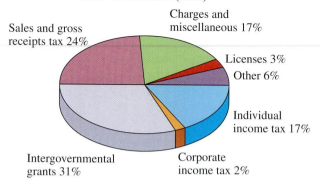

State Government (2002)

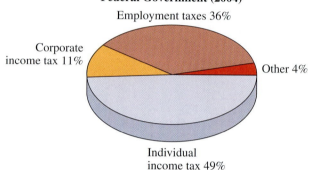

Federal Government (2004)

▲ **FIGURE 15.2**
Revenue Sources for Local, State, and Federal Governments
SOURCE: Statistical Abstract of the United States, *2006*

• **private good**
A good that is consumed by a single person or household; a good that is rival in consumption and excludable.

• **free rider**
A person who gets the benefit from a good but does not pay for it.

Public goods are also *nonexcludable*: It is impractical to exclude people who don't pay. Some examples of public goods are national defense, law enforcement, space exploration, the preservation of endangered species, the protection of the earth's ozone layer, and fireworks shows. If someone refuses to pay for one of these public goods, it would be impractical to prevent that person from consuming or benefiting from the good.

In contrast with public goods, each unit of a **private good** is consumed by a single person or household. For example, only one person can eat a hot dog, so it is a private good. If a government hands out free cheese to the poor, is the free cheese a public good or a private good? Although anyone can get in line for the cheese, only one person can actually consume a particular piece of cheese, so the free cheese is a private good that happens to be available free of charge from the government. Similarly, an apartment in a public housing project can be occupied by a single household, so it is a private good provided by the government.

Most public goods are supported by taxes. What would happen if we eliminated taxes and asked people to contribute money to pay for national defense, dams, city streets, and the police? Would people contribute enough money to support these programs at the efficient level? The problem with using voluntary contributions to support public goods is known as the *free-rider problem*. A **free rider** is a person who gets the benefit from a good but does not pay for it. Each person has a financial incentive to try to get the benefits of a public good without paying for it. That is, some people will try to get a "free ride" at the expense of others who do pay. Of course, if everyone tries to get a free ride there will be no money to support the public good, so it won't be provided.

The flip side of the free-rider problem is the chump problem: No one wants to be the chump—the person who gives free rides to other people—so no one contributes any money. The free-rider problem suggests that if taxes were replaced with

APPLICATION

FREE RIDERS AND THE THREE-CLOCK TOWER

APPLYING THE CONCEPTS #1: What is the free-rider problem?

Back in the days before inexpensive wristwatches, most people did not carry their own timepieces. Many towns built clock towers to help their citizens keep track of time. The towns paid for the clock towers with voluntary contributions from citizens. One town in the northeastern United States built a four-sided tower but put clock faces on only three sides of the tower. To most people, this seems bizarre. If you build a clock tower, why not put clock faces on all four sides? It turns out that one of the town's wealthy citizens refused to contribute money to help build the clock tower. The town officials decided not to put a clock face on the side of the tower facing the wealthy citizen's house. In other words, the citizen tried—unsuccessfully—to get a free ride. The problem is that other citizens on the same side of town also suffered from not seeing the clock. In this case, preventing a free ride by one citizen caused problems for other citizens. *Related to Exercise 1.5.*

voluntary contributions, the government would be forced to cut back or eliminate many programs.

Overcoming the Free-Rider Problem

Many organizations, including public radio and television, religious organizations, and charitable organizations, raise money through voluntary contributions. So it appears that some people overcome their inclination to be free riders and contribute voluntarily to organizations that provide public goods. The successful organizations use a number of techniques to encourage people to contribute:

- *Giving contributors private goods such as coffee mugs, books, musical recordings, and magazine subscriptions.* People are more likely to contribute if they get something for it.

- *Arranging matching contributions.* You are more likely to contribute if you know that your $30 contribution will be matched with a contribution from another person or your employer.

- Appealing to a person's sense of civic or moral responsibility.

It's important to note, however, that these organizations are only partly successful in mitigating the free-rider problem. Public radio is one of the success stories, even though the typical public-radio station gets contributions from less than a quarter of its listeners.

APPLICATION

PAYING LANDOWNERS TO HOST WOLVES

APPLYING THE CONCEPTS #2: How can we pay for public goods?

We can apply the concepts of public goods and free riding to the issue of preserving wildlife. There are some trade-offs associated with preserving wolves and other wildlife in Yellowstone Park. To environmentalists, wolves are a part of the natural ecosystem. To ranchers, wolves are predators that eat livestock. In other words, there are costs as well as benefits associated with the preservation of wolves, just as there are costs and benefits associated with other public goods such as dams, fireworks, national defense, and space exploration.

One response to the wolf-preservation problem comes from Defenders of Wildlife, an environmental group in Montana. The organization collects money from its members and uses the money to reward landowners who allow wolves to live on their properties. The host landowner receives a payment of $5,000 for each litter of wolf pups reared on the property. In addition, the organization compensates ranchers for livestock killed by wolves. As a result of these programs, ranchers in the Yellowstone area are more likely to support efforts to maintain the wolves as part of Yellowstone Park's ecosystem. The programs treat preservation as a public good, one that is supported by money contributed by people who benefit from preservation. The organization has collected contributions from thousands of people despite the free-rider problem. The success of Defenders of Wildlife illustrates one of the key principles of economics. *Related to Exercise 1.6.*

PRINCIPLE OF VOLUNTARY EXCHANGE

A voluntary exchange between two people makes both people better off.

SOURCE: Terry L. Anderson, "A Carrot to Save the Wolf," *The Margin*, Spring 1992, p. 28.

Asteroid Diversion as a Public Good

Consider the issue of protecting the earth from catastrophic collisions with asteroids. On average, the earth is hit by a 200-meter asteroid every 10,000 years, by a 2-kilometer asteroid every million years, and by a 10-kilometer asteroid every 100 million years.[1] As we saw at the beginning of the chapter, we have the technology to divert approaching asteroids.

The diversion of asteroids is a public good in the sense that it is available for everyone's benefit, regardless of who pays and who doesn't. As with any public good, the key to developing an asteroid-diversion program is to collect money to pay for the program. According to NASA scientists, the program would require several new telescopes, which would cost about $50 million to install and about $10 million per year to operate.[2] The cost of the gossamer mirror or the nuclear weapons required to change the path of the asteroid would be $100 million to $200 million. Although it would be sensible to finance the program with contributions from all earthlings, it may be impossible to collect money from everyone. A more likely outcome is that one or more developed countries will finance their own diversion systems.

15.2 | PRIVATE GOODS WITH EXTERNAL BENEFITS

In contrast to a public good, a private good can be utilized by a single person or household. However, some private goods generate benefits for people who do not directly consume the good. For example, suppose I replace the peeling paint on my house with a fresh coat of paint. I benefit from the new paint because it protects my house from decay and my house will look better, at least to me. Assuming that I've avoided an obnoxious color, my neighbors will also benefit from the improved appearance of the neighborhood. Similarly, if I buy a fire extinguisher and install fireproof roofing, my neighbors benefit because a fire is then less likely to spread to their houses.

External Benefits from Education

Education is another private good that generates external benefits. Most of the benefits of education go to the student because education increases productivity and income, and presumably makes everyday life easier and more interesting. Education generates three sorts of external benefits:

1 *Workplace externalities.* In most workplaces, people work in groups and teamwork is important. A well-educated person understands instructions readily and is more likely to suggest ways to improve the production process. As a result, when a well-educated person joins a work team, the productivity of everyone on the team increases. Higher productivity generally leads to higher profits for firms, and members of the team are likely to earn higher salaries.

2 *Civic externalities.* Citizens in a democratic society make collective decisions by voting in elections, and each citizen must live with these decisions. A well-educated person is more likely to vote intelligently, so there are external benefits for other citizens.

3 *Crime externalities.* Educated people earn higher legal incomes and thus commit less crime. High-school dropouts have relatively low wages and high crime rates, so increasing the high-school graduation rate generates large reductions in crime.

A recent study estimates the external benefits of education related to lower crime rates.[3] For every high-school student who graduates rather than dropping out after 11th grade, the cost of crime decreases by about $1,600 per year for the rest of the graduate's working life. The average cost of one year of high school is about $6,000, so for a one-time expense of $6,000 society gets a crime-reduction benefit of $1,600 per year for 30 or 40 years.

External Benefits and the Marginal Principle

Consider a parent's decision about how much time and money to spend on a child's education. Suppose that the parent bases the decision on the parent's cost and the child's private benefits—the increase in potential earnings as an adult. To be specific, consider the decision on how many books to buy for the child. In Figure 15.3, the marginal private benefit curve shows the extra benefit to the child from each additional book, measured as the increase in future income. Assume that the marginal cost of books is constant at $8 per book. Applying the marginal principle, the parent will choose point *a*, where the marginal benefit equals the marginal cost, and buy 9 books.

External Benefits and the Marginal Principle
Education (represented here as the number of books read) generates external benefits, so the marginal social benefit exceeds the marginal private benefit. Using books as an example of education, an individual picks point *a*, where the marginal private benefit equals the marginal cost. Point *b* is the socially efficient point, where the marginal social benefit equals the marginal cost.

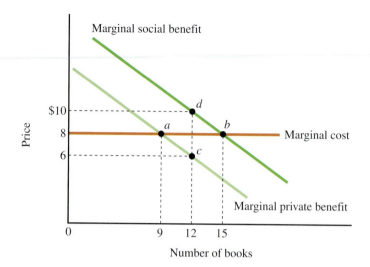

MARGINAL PRINCIPLE

Increase the level of an activity as long as its marginal benefit exceeds its marginal cost. Choose the level at which the marginal benefit equals the marginal cost.

The higher of the two negatively sloped curves is the marginal social benefit of education. The marginal social benefit equals the marginal private benefit plus the marginal external benefit. As we've seen, there are external benefits from education, so the social benefit exceeds the private benefit. From society's perspective, the best point is *b*, where the marginal social benefit equals the marginal cost. The socially efficient quantity is 15 books. As an illustration, consider the 12th book. The marginal private benefit is $6 (shown by point *c*) and the external benefit is $4, so the marginal social benefit is $6 plus $4, or $10 (shown by point *d*). The social benefit exceeds the $8 cost, so providing the book is efficient from the social perspective. The private benefit of $6 is less than the $8 cost, however, so the parent won't buy the 12th book, but instead will stop with 9 books. The lesson is that when there are external benefits, decisions based on private benefits will generate an inefficiently small quantity of the good.

Because of the external benefits from education, the government uses various policies to encourage people to become educated. Local governments provide free education through high school. States subsidize students at public colleges and universities, providing college education at a fraction of its actual cost. In addition, the federal government provides financial aid to students in both public and private schools.

Other Private Goods That Generate External Benefits

The government subsidizes other goods that generate external benefits. Subsidies for on-the-job training and education encourage workers and firms to invest in human capital and increase labor productivity. It is sensible for the government to subsidize training and education because some of the benefits are transferred to other firms when workers change employers. Another example of external benefits is research at universities and other nonprofit organizations. If a research project provides knowledge or technology that leads to the development of new products or the improvement of old ones, the benefits from the project spill over onto consumers and producers. When there are external benefits, the government can encourage people to take actions that benefit other people. By making beneficial transactions happen, the government can increase efficiency.

APPLICATION

EXTERNAL BENEFITS FROM LOJACK

APPLYING THE CONCEPTS #3: What private goods generate external benefits?

LoJack, a system used to recover stolen vehicles, is a private good that generates external benefits. A small, silent transmitter hidden in a vehicle allows police to track a stolen car. The name is a play on words, meant to convey the idea that LoJack will recover vehicles that are hijacked or stolen. A thief who steals a LoJack-equipped car won't keep the car for long and is likely to get caught, so LoJack is an effective deterrent to car theft. Car thieves cannot distinguish between cars with and without LoJack, so the system decreases the payoff from car theft in general, and criminals steal fewer cars. People who install LoJack systems in their cars generate benefits for themselves and external benefits for other car owners who don't have LoJack.

A study by two economists estimated the private and external benefits from LoJack. The annual cost of a LoJack system is about $100. For a car owner who carries theft insurance, the benefit from a LoJack system is the discount offered by an insurance company, typically well below the $100 annual cost. For every three LoJack systems installed, the number of auto thefts decreases by one car per year. The external benefit from fewer vehicle thefts is about $1,300 per LoJack per year. The benefits are experienced by people who don't buy their own LoJack systems, but benefit because thieves can never be sure whether a particular car is protected by LoJack or not. *Related to Exercises 2.5 and 2.6.*

SOURCE: Ian Ayres and Steven Levitt, "Measuring Positive Externalities from Unobservable Victim Precautions: An Empirical Analysis of Lojack," *Quarterly Journal of Economics*, vol. 113 (1998), pp. 43–77.

15.3 | PUBLIC CHOICE

We have discussed the challenges associated with providing and paying for goods that generate external benefits. In this part of the chapter, we study **public-choice economics**, a field that uses models of rational-choice to explore decision making in the public sector. We'll start with a model of government decisions based on voting and then look at some alternative models.

> • **public-choice economics**
> A field of economics that uses models of rational choice to explore decision making in the public sector.

Voting and the Median-Voter Rule

As citizens in a democracy, we pick people to make public decisions. We vote for people to represent our viewpoints in legislative bodies (city council members, state legislators, and congressional representatives), and we vote for people in executive positions (mayors, governors, and presidents). The basic idea of a democracy is that the government will take actions that are approved by the majority of citizens. If governments are responsive to voters, the voting public

• **median-voter rule**
The choices made by government will match the preferences of the median voter.

ultimately makes all the important decisions, and the actions of the government will reflect their preferences.

One concept of public-choice economics is known as the **median-voter rule**. According to this rule, the choices made by government will match the preferences of the median voter, defined as the voter whose preferences lie in the middle of the set of all voters' preferences: Half the voters want more of something (for example, a larger government budget) and half want less (a smaller government budget). As we'll see, this rule has some important implications for decision making and politics.

To see the logic of the median-voter rule, consider a state where there are two candidates for governor—Penny and Buck—and the only issue in the election is how much the state should spend on education. Each citizen will vote for the candidate whose proposed education budget is closest to the citizen's preferred budget. Figure 15.4 shows citizens' preferences for education spending, with different preferred budgets on the horizontal axis and the number of voters on the vertical axis. For example, two citizens have a preferred budget of $1 billion, four have a preferred budget of $2 billion, and so on. The median budget, which splits the rest of the voters into two equal groups (20 voters on each side), is $5 billion.

Suppose the two candidates start out with very different proposed education budgets. Penny proposes a budget of $3 billion, and Buck proposes $7 billion. The 20 citizens with preferred budgets less than or equal to $4 billion will vote for Penny because her proposed budget is closest to their preferred budgets. Buck's supporters include the 20 citizens with preferred budgets greater than or equal to $6 billion. The two candidates will split the 10 voters with a preferred budget of $5 billion (halfway between the two proposed budgets), so each candidate will get a total of 25 votes, resulting in a tie.

Penny could increase her chance of being elected by increasing her proposed budget. Let's say she proposes $4 billion instead of $3 billion. All the voters with a preferred budget of $5 billion will vote for Penny because Penny's $4 billion proposal is now closer to their $5 billion preferred budget than Buck's $7 billion proposal. Penny won't lose any of her other votes either, so she will win the election by a vote of 30 (equal to 2 + 4 + 6 + 8 + 10) to 20 (equal to 8 + 8 + 4). If Buck is smart, he will realize that he could get more votes by moving toward the median budget. For example, if he decreases his proposed budget to $6 billion, the election would result in a tie vote again. Penny and Buck will continue to move their proposed budgets toward the median budget ($5 billion) until they both propose budgets that are very close to the median budget.

▶ **FIGURE 15.4**

The Median-Voter Rule

If Penny proposes a $3 billion budget and Buck proposes a $7 billion budget, the election will result in a tie. By moving toward the median budget, Penny can increase her chance of being elected. In equilibrium, both candidates will propose a budget close to the $5 billion preferred budget of the median voter.

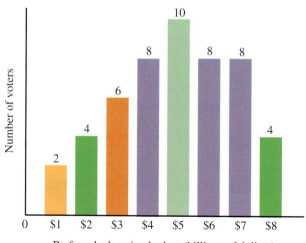

Powerful forces pull the two candidates toward the preferences of the median voter. As long as Penny proposes a smaller budget than Buck, the people with small preferred budgets will continue to vote for her. The benefit of moving toward the median is that she can take some votes from Buck. Similarly, Buck doesn't have to worry about people with large preferred budgets, but can concentrate instead on the battle for voters in the middle. The result is that by election day the two candidates have adopted virtually the same position: The position of the median voter. Voters trying to choose between two candidates may feel they don't have much choice. In fact, the median-voter rule says that the choices made by government will match the preferences of the median voter, regardless of who wins the election.

Although we usually think that people make political decisions by voting in elections, it is also possible to "vote with your feet." In 1956, economist Charles M. Tiebout suggested that a household's choice of which community to live in is based in part on the tax and spending policies of different communities.[4] Households express their preferences by moving to communities that offer the best package of services and taxes. A community with inefficient public services will experience a loss in population, perhaps causing the local officials to make the public services more efficient.

It is clear that people vote with their ballots *and* with their feet. In both cases, citizens can express their preferences for public goods, taxes, and public policies. These two sources of citizen power limit the ability of governments to take actions that are inconsistent with the preferences of most voters.

Alternative Models of Government: Self-Interest and Special Interests

Several economists, including Nobel laureate James Buchanan, have suggested a model of government that focuses on the selfish behavior of government officials. According to this view, politicians and bureaucrats pursue their own narrow interests, which, of course, may differ from the public interest. For example, politicians or bureaucrats may gain prestige from starting a new spending program even if the cost of the program exceeds its social benefit. Because voters don't have much information about the costs and benefits of public services, they may not be in a position to evaluate the actions of politicians or bureaucrats and vote accordingly.

The self-interest theory of government explains why voters sometimes approve explicit limits on taxes and government spending. For example, most states have limits on the amount of property taxes that can be raised, and many states also limit total government spending. According to the self-interest theory of government, limitations on taxes and spending are necessary safeguards against politicians and bureaucrats who benefit from larger budgets.

Another model of government is based on the idea that small groups of people manipulate government for their own gain. Suppose the total benefit of a dam is less than its total cost, so the project is inefficient, but a few farmers reap large benefits from the dam, while the costs are spread over a million taxpayers. The farmers have a strong incentive to spend time and money to convince policy makers to build the dam. In contrast, if the tax is only $1 per person, few taxpayers will make their preferences known to policy makers because the marginal benefit (the $1 tax savings) is less than the marginal cost (the opportunity cost of their time). If politicians listen to people who express their preferences and contribute money to political campaigns, the inefficient project may be approved. This is an example of a special-interest group (farmers) manipulating the government at the expense of a larger group (all taxpayers). In general, when a few people share the benefit from a project and a large number of people share the cost, the government is more likely to approve inefficient projects.

In general, whenever benefits are concentrated on a few citizens but costs are spread out over many citizens, we expect special-interest groups to form. Special-interest organizations often use lobbyists to express their views to government officials and policy makers.

APPLICATION

POLITICIANS ARE LIKE ICE-CREAM SELLERS

APPLYING THE CONCEPTS #4: What is the economic logic of the median-voter rule?

The logic of the median-voter result also applies to competition among some types of sellers. Imagine a one-mile stretch of beach with 120 swimmers and sunbathers distributed evenly along the beach. Suppose each person on the beach will purchase one ice-cream cone, and is willing to travel up to a mile. If there are two ice-cream vendors on the beach selling an identical product, where will they locate?

The most efficient arrangement is to locate the two vendors a half mile apart. We could divide the beach into two half-mile territories and locate each vendor at the middle of a territory. As shown in Panel A of Figure 15.5, Lefty would be at the quarter-mile mark, and Righty would be at the three-quarter-mile mark. If beachgoers patronize the closer vendor, each vendor would sell 60 ice cream cones. This arrangement will minimize the total travel costs of ice-cream patrons.

Is this an equilibrium arrangement? If Lefty were to move to the right—to the half-mile mark, the median location that splits consumers into two equal halves—he would not lose any of his customers to his left but would capture part of Righty's market. As shown in Panel B of Figure 15.5, Lefty would then be the closer vendor for the people located between the half-mile mark and the five-eighths mark. Therefore, Lefty would sell 75 cones (up from 60) and Righty would sell only 45 cones. To protect her market, Righty would move to the median location, too, locating right next to Lefty. By doing so, Righty can recover her 50-percent share of the market, again serving the consumers on the right half of the beach. At any other location, she would get less than half the market, given Lefty is at the median location. In equilibrium, shown in Panel C of Figure 15.5, both vendors pick the median location and each serves half the market.

The outcome of the ice-cream vendors' game is the same as the politicians' game. Like the politicians, the vendors have an incentive to move to the median location, so there is no real difference between the two vendors. *Related to Exercise 3.5.*

If the two sellers start at the 1/4 and 3/4 mile marks, each has a territory of 1/2 mile and sells 60 cones:

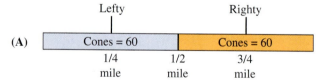

(A)

▲ FIGURE 15.5

Competition on a Beach Leads to a Median Location for Both Sellers

(**A**) If one seller starts at the 1/4 mile mark and the other starts at the 3/4 mile mark, each has a territory of one-half mile and sells 60 cones. (**B**) If Lefty moves to the median location, his territory increases to the 5/8 mile mark, and he sells 75 cones, compared to 45 for Righty. (**C**) Righty can recover her lost territory by moving to the median location. In equilibrium, both sellers locate at the median location and each has half the market.

If Lefty moves to the median location, his territory increases to the 5/8 mile mark, and he sells 75 cones, compared to 45 for Righty:

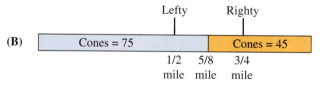

(B)

Righty can recover her lost territory by moving to the median location. In equilibrium, both sellers locate at the median location and each has half the market:

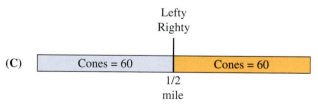

(C)

Which Theory Is Correct?

Which of these theories or viewpoints best describes the actual practices of governments? This is a very difficult question. Economists and political scientists have studied many dimensions of the decision-making processes underlying tax policies and spending policies. There is evidence that people do vote with ballots and with their feet, and that these two forms of voting make a difference. There is also evidence that government officials sometimes pursue their own interests and those of special-interest groups. The field of public choice is a very active area of research involving both economists and political scientists.

SUMMARY

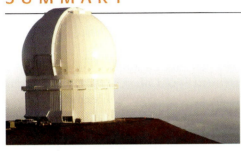

In this chapter, we've seen why the government provides public goods. The free-rider problem means that we can't rely on voluntary contributions to support public goods and subsidies, so taxes are necessary to support public programs. We've also examined different views on how governments actually make decisions. Here are the main points of the chapter:

1 When a good generates *external benefits*, collective decision making generates more-efficient choices.

2 A *public good* is available for everyone to consume (nonrival in consumption), regardless of who pays and who doesn't (nonexcludable).

3 A system of voluntary contributions suffers from the *free-rider problem*: People do not have a financial incentive to support public goods.

4 Education generates external benefits in the workplace and in elections and reduces crime.

5 The *median-voter rule* suggests that government choices will match the preferences of the median voter, defined as the voter whose preferences lie in the middle of voter preferences.

KEY TERMS

external benefit, p. 341

free rider, p. 342

median-voter rule, p. 348

private good, p. 342

public-choice economics, p. 347

public good, p. 341

EXERCISES

Get Ahead of the Curve

Visit www.myeconlab.com to complete these exercises online and get instant feedback.

15.1 | External Benefits and Public Goods

1.1 Suppose 1,000 people would each get a benefit of $40 from a levee. Building the levee is socially efficient if its cost is less than $_____. If the cost is $30,000, a tax of $ _____ per person would generate unanimous support for the levee.

1.2 An external benefit is experienced by _____.

1.3 A public good is _____ (rival/nonrival) in consumption and _____ (excludable/nonexcludable).

1.4 A free rider is someone who _____.

1.5 **Paying for a WiFi Network.** Consider a small town with 1,000 households. The town could install a wireless WiFi network that would give everyone in town access to the Internet. Each household is willing to pay a maximum of $50 per year for the network, and

the cost of the system is $20,000 per year. (Related to Application 1 on page 343.)

a. Is the WiFi system efficient?

b. Suppose the town asks for voluntary contributions to support the network. Would you expect the total contributions to cover the $20,000 cost?

c. Suppose the town keeps track of the contributions and issues passwords to people who contributed at least $20. Would you expect the total contributions to cover the $20,000 cost?

1.6 **Defenders of Wildlife.** Each of the 80,000 citizens in a particular county is willing to pay $0.10 to increase the number of wolf litters by one. Each litter of wolves imposes a cost of $5,000 in livestock losses to ranchers. (Related to Application 2 on page 344.)

a. Is the provision of an additional litter of wolves efficient from the social perspective?

b. Design a system that will generate the socially efficient outcome.

1.7 **Class Participation.** Consider a course with 40 students, some of whom are confused after the professor explains a concept. The professor doesn't know whether students are confused, but will clarify the concept if one student asks a question. A student who asks a question—and reveals his or her confusion—loses 10 utils. When the professor clarifies the concept in response to a question, each confused student gets a benefit of 2 utils.

a. At what level of confusion (measured by the number of confused students) is a question from a confused student socially efficient?

b. In the absence of participation incentives, will a confused student ask a question when it would be socially efficient to do so?

c. Design an incentive system to generate efficient questioning.

1.8 **Fireworks as Public Goods.** A three-person city is considering a fireworks display. Bertha is willing to pay $100 for the proposed fireworks display, Marian is willing to pay $30, and Sam is willing to pay $20. The cost of the fireworks display is $120.

a. Will any single citizen provide the display on his or her own?

b. If the cost of the fireworks display is divided equally among the citizens, will a majority vote in favor of the display?

c. Describe a transaction that would benefit all three citizens.

1.9 **Stream Preservation.** Consider a trout stream that is threatened with destruction by a nearby logging operation. Each of the 10,000 local fishers would be willing to pay $5 to preserve the stream. The owner of the land would incur a cost of $20,000 to change the logging operation to protect the stream.

a. Is the preservation of the stream efficient from the social perspective?

b. If the landowner has the right to log the land any way he wants, will the stream be preserved?

c. Propose a solution to this problem. Describe a transaction that would benefit the fishers and the landowner.

15.2 | Private Goods with External Benefits

2.1 Education generates three types of external benefits: _____ ; _____ ; and _____ .

2.2 The external benefit of transforming a high-school dropout into a graduate is about $ _____ per year.

2.3 A parent chooses the level of education where the marginal _____ benefit equals marginal cost and

chooses _____ (more/less) than the socially efficient level because the parent ignores the _____ .

2.4 It is sensible for the government to subsidize worker training and education because some of the benefits from training go to _____ .

2.5 The external benefit of a LoJack is about $ _____ per year, compared to an annual cost per LoJack of $ _____ . (Related to Application 3 on page 347.)

2.6 **LoJack and Insurance Companies.** Consider the application "External Benefits from LoJack." Suppose that all vehicles in a state carry theft insurance. The benefit from reduced vehicle theft goes to insurance companies because they replace fewer stolen vehicles. Insurance companies do not offer any discounts for customers who install LoJack. The cost of LoJack is $100 per vehicle per year. To simplify matters, assume that the private benefit of LoJack is zero, so the social benefit equals the external benefit. (Related to Application 3 on page 347.)

a. Suppose a single insurance company provides automobile insurance to all vehicles in the state. Will the insurance company provide free LoJacks to at least some of its customers? Explain.

b. Suppose that there are 20 companies in the state, each with a market share of 5 percent. Will the insurance company provide free LoJacks?

c. What is the threshold number of insurance companies—the number at which each insurance company will be indifferent about providing free LoJack systems?

2.7 **External Benefits from Education and Deadweight Loss.** Using Figure 15.3 on page 346 as a starting point, compute the deadweight loss associated with reaching the market equilibrium at point *a* rather than the socially efficient outcome at point *b*. Notice that the marginal external cost is constant at $4 per book, so the gap between the marginal private benefit curve and the marginal social benefit curve is $4.

15.3 | Public Choice

3.1 According to the model of voting developed in the chapter, the choices made by government match the preferences of the _____ voter.

3.2 In the example of ice-cream vendors, the vendors choose the _____ location, and this is an _____ (efficient/inefficient) choice.

3.3 The self-interest theory of government explains why many states have limits on _____ and _____ .

3.4 The special-interest theory of government suggests a government will approve an inefficient project if the costs of the project are paid by a _____ (large/small) number of citizens and the benefits go to a _____ (large/small) number of citizens.

3.5 **Alienation and the Median-Voter Rule.** Consider the application, "Politicians Are Like Ice-Cream Sellers." Suppose that people are unwilling to walk more than 1/4 mile for an ice-cream cone. As a starting point, suppose both sellers locate at the median location, at the 1/2 mark. (Related to Application 4 on page 350.)

a. Fill the blanks in the following table.

	Location Lefty	Location Righty	Quantity Lefty	Quantity Righty
Starting point: Median location	1/2	1/2	_____	_____
Lefty moves to 1/4 mile mark	1/4	1/2	_____	_____
Righty moves to 3/4 mile mark	1/4	3/4	_____	_____

b. Does Lefty have an incentive to move to the left, to the 1/4 mile mark?

c. If Lefty moves to the 1/4 mile mark, does Righty have an incentive to move to the right, to the 3/4 mile mark?

d. What are the equilibrium locations for the two sellers? How does it differ from the equilibrium when everyone bought an ice-cream cone, regardless of the distance to the nearest seller?

e. Recall the discussion of the median-voter rule. Suppose that voters are subject to alienation: A citizen will not vote in a budget election if the difference between the voter's preference and the politician's position is too large. Does the median-voter rule still hold?

3.6 **More Voters.** Consider the example of the governor's election shown in Figure 15.4 on page 348. Suppose 18 new people move into the state and each newcomer has a desired education budget of $9 billion. Predict the proposed education budgets for the two candidates.

3.7 **Change in Preferences and Proposed Budgets?** Consider the example of the governor's election shown in Figure 15.4 on page 348. Suppose that the preferences of the 4 voters who prefer a budget of $8 billion change, with each person preferring $15 billion instead. Will this change in preferences change the proposed budgets of the two candidates?

ECONOMIC EXPERIMENT

Voluntary Contributions

Do people really try to get free rides? Or would most people contribute at least some money to support a public good? Here is a classroom experiment that helps to answer this question:

- The instructor selects 10 students and gives each student 10 dimes.

- Each student can contribute money to support a public good by dropping 1, 2, or 3 dimes into a public-good pot. Each student has the option of keeping all the dimes and not contributing anything. The contributions are anonymous: No one knows how much a particular student contributes.

- For each dime in the pot, the instructor adds 2 dimes. For example, if the students contribute a total of 40 dimes, the instructor adds 80 dimes, for a total of 120 dimes in the pot. The two-for-one match represents the idea that the benefits of public goods exceed the costs. In this case, the benefit–cost ratio is three to one.

- The instructor divides the money in the public-good pot equally among the 10 students. For example, if there are 120 dimes in the pot, each student receives 12 dimes.

- Steps 2 through 4 can be repeated four or five times.

We can change the experiment to mimic the compulsory tax system. The instructor could require each student to contribute 3 dimes, the maximum amount, each. Would a switch to a compulsory tax system make the students better or worse off?

Experiment Debriefing

After completing the experiment, do the following exercise:

Consider the contribution incentives for Margie, one of the 10 students in the experiment. She thinks in marginal terms, and asks herself, "If I contribute one more dime, how would that affect my payoff from the experiment?

a. Answer Margie's question, assuming that her contribution does not affect the contribution of other students.

b. If Margie uses the marginal principle to make all her decisions, will she contribute the extra dime?

NOTES

1. Carl Sagan, "A Warning for Us?" *Parade*, June 5, 1994, p. 8; John Boudreau, "Collision Course: Scientists Say There's a Big Asteroid Bang in Our Future," *Washington Post*, April 6, 1994, p. C1.

2. "Mirror Beam Could Deflect Killer Asteroid, Theory Says," *New York Times*, November 9, 1994, p. C6.

3. Lance Lochner and Enrico Moretti, "The Effect of Education on Crime: Evidence from Prison Inmates, Arrests, and Self Reports," *American Economic Review*, vol. 94 (2004), pp. 155–189.

4. "A Pure Theory of Local Public Expenditures," *Journal of Political Economy*, vol, 64 (1956), pp. 416–424.

16

External Costs and Environmental Policy

In 2001, a group of students from an economics course at Hobart and William Smith Colleges joined an auction for the right to discharge sulfur dioxide into the atmosphere. Sulfur dioxide is an important ingredient in air pollution and acid rain. It causes thousands of premature deaths each year and destroys vegetation, damages buildings, and kills

1 How do we determine the optimum level of pollution?
    The Optimum Level of Sulfur Dioxide Emissions

2 What is the economic approach to global warming?
    The Effects of a Carbon Tax

3 Are there different ways to reduce pollution or mitigate its effects?
    Dear Abby and Environmental Policy

4 What determines the price of a marketable pollution permit?
    Marketable Permits for Sulfur Dioxide

5 What are the benefits of giving firms options for reducing greenhouse gases?
    Chicago Climate Exchange

6 What is the external cost of young drivers?
    Young Drivers and Collisions

fish. Among the other bidders for the sulfur dioxide permits were energy giants Enron and Ohio Power Company. The students paid $181 for a permit and promised to hold it rather than use it. As a result, there is one less ton of sulfur dioxide in the air.

The auction for sulfur dioxide permits is an example of the economic approach to reducing pollution. Earlier in the book in the chapter on market efficiency, we introduced the notion of market failure, which happens when production generates external costs, such as air or water pollution. The sulfur dioxide discharged by electricity producers imposes an external cost on society, and because producers ignore these costs in their decisions, the market fails to operate efficiently. As we'll see in this chapter, the best response to market failure is not to abandon markets, but instead to use markets to reduce pollution in the most efficient manner. We'll discuss two market-oriented policies: pollution taxes and auctions for pollution permits. The chapter's theme is that often the economic solution to market failure is to create markets where they do not currently exist.

16.1 | THE OPTIMAL LEVEL OF POLLUTION

Should we eliminate all pollution? Although a pristine environment with pure water and air sounds appealing, there would be some very unappealing consequences. To reduce air pollution, we could eliminate trucks, but shipping goods by horse-drawn wagon would result in higher freight costs and higher prices for most products—and a different sort of pollution. We could reduce water pollution by shutting down all the paper mills, but reverting to parchment and slate boards would be unwieldy. Given the consequences of eliminating pollution, it is sensible to allow some pollution to occur. What's the optimal level of pollution?

Using the Marginal Principle

The most convenient way to discuss pollution policies is in terms of pollution abatement, that is, reductions in pollution from some starting level. We can use the marginal principle to determine the optimal level of pollution abatement.

MARGINAL PRINCIPLE

Increase the level of an activity as long as its marginal benefit exceeds its marginal cost. Choose the level at which the marginal benefit equals the marginal cost.

According to this principle, we should cut pollution to the level where the marginal benefit of abatement equals its marginal cost.

The marginal principle focuses our attention on the trade-offs from pollution—its costs and benefits. From society's perspective, there are many benefits from pollution abatement:

- **Better health.** Cleaner water means less sickness from waterborne pollutants, and cleaner air means fewer respiratory problems and thus lower health-care costs and fewer sick days taken by workers.

- **Increased enjoyment of the natural environment.** Improving the air quality increases visibility and improves the health of trees. Improving the water quality enhances recreational activities, such as swimming, boating, and fishing.

- **Lower production costs.** Some firms are dependent on clean water for survival: Farmers use water for irrigation, and some manufacturers use clean water as part of the production process. Cleaner water means lower production costs for these firms.

On the other hand, pollution abatement is costly because resources—labor, capital, and land—are used in the abatement process. Using the marginal principle, we look for the level of pollution abatement where the marginal benefit equals the marginal cost.

APPLICATION 1

THE OPTIMAL LEVEL OF SULFUR DIOXIDE EMISSIONS

APPLYING THE CONCEPTS #1: How do we determine the optimum level of pollution?

Sulfur dioxide (SO_2) emissions contribute to health problems such as upper respiratory illness, bronchitis, coughing episodes, and chest discomfort. SO_2 is a contributing factor—along with nitrogen oxide and other pollutants—in thousands of premature deaths each year. When sulfur dioxide is combined with nitrogen oxides and other chemicals in the atmosphere, the result is acid rain, which damages vegetation and buildings and kills aquatic life.

A recent study estimated the marginal benefits and marginal costs of reducing SO_2 emissions from electricity generation facilities, looking ahead to the year 2010. Figure 16.1 shows the marginal-benefit and marginal-cost curves for SO_2 abatement. Notice that along the horizontal axis, abatement increases as we move to the right, while the amount of SO_2 discharged decreases. The sum of abatement and discharges is 9.1 million tons:

- The marginal-benefit curve is horizontal at $3,500, because for each additional ton of SO_2 discharged into the atmosphere, the costs associated with premature deaths and health problems increase by about $3,500.

- The marginal-cost curve is positively sloped, because the more pollution we abate, the higher the marginal cost of abatement. The first 2 million tons can be abated at a relatively low cost—$500 per ton—by switching to coal with a lower sulfur content. The next several million tons can be abated at a higher cost by installing scrubbers that remove sulfur from coal smoke. Further abatement requires a switch from coal to natural gas, a more expensive fuel. For the last million tons abated, the marginal cost is about $6,000 per ton.

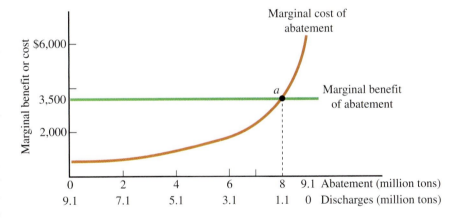

The marginal-cost curve intersects the marginal-benefit curve at 8 million tons of abatement, leaving 1.1 million tons of SO_2 to be discharged in 2010. The current level of emissions is about 10 million tons per year. Under the provisions of the Clean Air Act passed by the U.S. government in 1990, emissions are scheduled to drop to 1.25 million tons by 2010, just above the optimal level shown in Figure 16.1. *Related to Exercises 1.4 and 1.5.*

▲ **FIGURE 16.1**
The Optimal Level of Sulfur Dioxide Emissions in 2010
The optimum level of pollution abatement is shown by point *a*, where the marginal benefit of abatement equals its marginal cost.

SOURCE: Spencer Banzhaf, Dallas Burtraw, and Karen Palmer, "Efficient Emission Fees in the U.S. Electricity Sector," Resources for the Future Discussion Paper 02-45, October 2002.

• **private cost of production**
The production cost borne by a producer, which typically includes the costs of labor, capital, and materials.

• **external cost of production**
A cost incurred by someone other than the producer.

• **social cost of production**
Private cost plus external cost.

• **pollution tax**
A tax or charge equal to the external cost per unit of pollution.

16.2 | TAXING POLLUTION

The economic approach to pollution is to get producers to pay for the waste they generate, just as they pay for labor, capital, and materials. The costs of labor, capital, and materials are the **private cost of production**, the cost borne by the producer of the product. The **external cost of production** is the cost incurred by someone other than the producer, for example, the cost associated with health problems and premature deaths from sulfur dioxide. The **social cost of production** is the sum of the private cost and the external cost. The idea of a **pollution tax** equal to the external cost per unit of pollution is to "internalize" the externality—to make the producer responsible for the external cost of production. When the tax equals the external cost imposed on others, the externality is internalized. In the example of sulfur dioxide pollution, the appropriate pollution tax is the external cost of $3,500 per ton.

A Firm's Response to a Pollution Tax

A polluting firm will respond to a pollution tax in the same way as it responds to the prices of labor and materials. The firm will use the marginal principle to decide how much waste to generate and how much to abate. The firm will increase the level of abatement as long as the marginal benefit exceeds the marginal cost and stop when the marginal benefit equals the marginal cost.

Figure 16.2 shows an electricity producer's marginal benefits and costs of abating SO_2. The marginal cost is $2,200 for the first ton abated (point *a*), and the marginal cost increases with the level of abatement, to $3,500 for the sixth ton abated (point *c*) and $4,500 for the seventh ton (point *d*). The marginal cost increases with the amount abated because the firm must use progressively more costly means to cut emissions. From the firm's perspective, the benefit of abating pollution is that it can avoid paying the pollution tax. The marginal benefit of abatement is the $3,500 savings in pollution taxes from abating a ton of SO_2 rather than discharging it into the air. The firm satisfies the marginal principle at point *c*, with 6 tons of abatement. For the first 6 tons abated, the marginal benefit of abatement—avoiding the $3,500 tax—is greater than or equal to the marginal cost. The firm stops at 6 tons because the marginal cost of abating a seventh ton ($4,500, as shown by point *d*), exceeds the marginal benefit (the $3,500 tax avoided). Instead of paying $4,500 to abate one more ton, the firm will instead pay the $3,500 tax.

The Market Effects of a Pollution Tax

Consider the effect of a pollution tax on the market for the product produced by polluting firms. For example, a tax on SO_2 increases the cost of producing electricity because firms pay for abatement and also pay pollution taxes on any remaining waste

▶ **FIGURE 16.2**

The Firm's Response to a SO₂ Tax
From the perspective of a firm subject to a pollution tax, the marginal benefit of abatement is the $3,500 pollution tax that can be avoided by cutting pollution by 1 ton. The firm satisfies the marginal principle at point c, with 6 tons of abatement, leaving 2 tons of SO_2 discharged into the atmosphere.

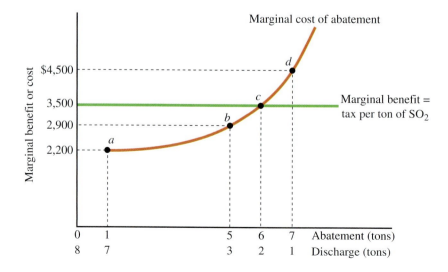

they generate. As we saw in an earlier chapter on market efficiency, a tax shifts the supply curve upward by the amount of the tax, decreasing the equilibrium quantity and increasing the equilibrium price.

Consider the effects of pollution taxes on the market for electricity. The production of electricity generates two major pollutants:

- **Sulfur dioxide.** Electric power plants are responsible for about two-thirds of SO_2 emissions. As we saw earlier in the chapter, the marginal damage from SO_2 is $3,500 per ton, so that's the appropriate pollution tax.

- **Nitrogen oxides (NO$_x$).** Power plants are also responsible for about one-quarter of the nation's NO_x emissions, a contributing factor in acid rain and the most important factor in urban smog. The study cited earlier in the chapter estimated that the appropriate tax for NO_x is about $1,100 per ton.

Figure 16.3 shows the effects of pollution taxes in the market for electricity. The taxes increase the cost of producing electricity, shifting the supply curve upward. The equilibrium moves from point *a* to point *b*, where the demand curve intersects the new supply curve. According to the electricity study, the pollution taxes would increase the price of electricity from $64.90 to $67.60 per megawatt-hour, an increase of 4 percent. The price elasticity of demand for electricity is 0.28, so the 4-percent increase in price decreases the quantity of electricity demanded by 1.1 percent, from 4,294 to 4,247 megawatt hours. Like other taxes, the pollution tax is shifted forward to consumers in the form of a higher price, and they respond by consuming less of the polluting good. When consumers face the full cost of producing electricity, they buy less of it.

A pollution tax also changes the production process as firms switch to cleaner technology. Figure 16.4 shows the effects of pollution taxes on the energy sources used to generate electricity. Producers respond to the taxes by switching to low-sulfur coal, which is more expensive but reduces their SO_2 taxes. The share of power generated with low-sulfur coal increases from 0.43 to 0.53. The taxes increase the cost of using coal relative to the cost of using natural gas and nuclear power, so the share of electricity from these other sources increases while the share of power from coal decreases. As firms shift to cleaner energy sources, the amount of SO_2 and NO_x emissions per unit of electricity generated decreases.

These pollution taxes decrease the total amount of air pollution for two reasons. First, as shown in Figure 16.3, the increase in the price of electricity decreases the quantity of electricity demanded by 1 percent. Second, as shown in Figure 16.4, the shift to cleaner energy sources means that each unit of electricity generates less pollution. The combined effect of these two changes is a substantial reduction in pollution: SO_2 decreases to 11 percent of its initial volume, and NO_x decreases to 30 percent of its initial volume. An added bonus of the pollution tax is that the government could use the revenue from the tax to cut other taxes, for example, the payroll tax or the income tax.

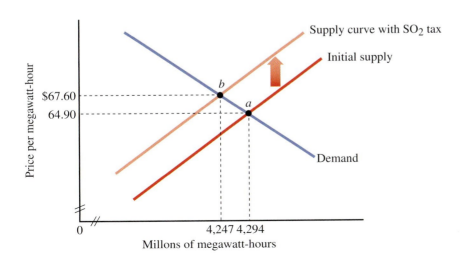

◄ FIGURE 16.3

The Effects of SO$_2$ and NO$_x$ Taxes on the Electricity Market

The pollution tax increases the cost of producing electricity, shifting the market supply curve up. The equilibrium moves from point *a* to point *b*. The tax increases the equilibrium price from $64.90 to $67.60 per megawatt -hour and decreases the equilibrium quantity.

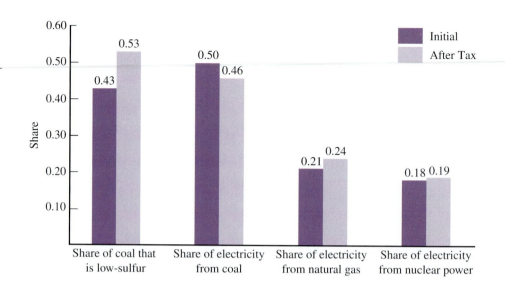

16.3 | TRADITIONAL REGULATION

Although the economic approach to pollution is to get polluters to pay for the waste they generate, governments often take a different approach. Under a traditional regulation policy, the government tells each firm how much pollution to abate and what abatement techniques to use.

Uniform Abatement with Permits

To illustrate the effects of regulation, consider an area with two electricity generators, firm L (for low cost) and firm H (for high cost). Suppose that in the absence of pollution-abatement efforts, each firm would discharge 5 tons of pollution per hour. Suppose the government sets a target abatement level of 2 tons of SO$_2$ per hour, divided equally between the two firms. Under this *uniform abatement policy*, the government will issue 4 pollution permits to each firm, forcing each firm to cut pollution from 5 tons to 4 tons. Suppose the marginal abatement cost of firm L is $2,000 and the marginal abatement cost for firm H is $5,000.

A uniform abatement policy is likely to be inefficient because it does not take advantage of the differences in abatement costs between the two firms. The cost of abating 2 tons is $7,000, including $2,000 for firm L and $5,000 for firm H. To show the inefficiency of the uniform abatement policy, imagine that the low-cost firm did all the abating, incurring a cost of $4,000 to abate 2 tons ($2,000 per ton times 2 tons). The total cost of abating 2 tons has dropped from $7,000 to $4,000. It's not a coincidence that the savings in abatement cost equals the difference in the abatement costs of the two firms. By shifting abatement responsibility to the low-cost firm, the savings in abatement cost equals the gap between the marginal abatement costs of the two firms. The basic problem with the uniform abatement policy is that it treats firms equally with respect to pollution abatement, even though the firms are unequal in terms of their abatement costs.

In contrast, a pollution tax would exploit the differences in abatement costs. Suppose the pollution tax is $3,500 per ton. Firm L, with a marginal abatement cost of only $2,000, will abate pollution rather than paying the tax. In contrast, firm H, with a marginal abatement cost of $5,000 will pollute and pay the tax. The tax is superior to the uniform abatement policy because it gets the low-cost firm to do more abating. The low-cost firm abates more but also pays less in pollution taxes.

APPLICATION

THE EFFECTS OF A CARBON TAX

APPLYING THE CONCEPTS #2: What is the economic approach to global warming?

A report from the National Academy of Sciences, the nation's most prestigious scientific body, concluded that "greenhouse gases are accumulating in the Earth's atmosphere as a result of human activities" and that the "human-induced warming and associated sea level changes are expected to continue through the twenty-first century." The most important greenhouse gas is carbon dioxide, which is generated when we burn carbon-based fuels such as oil, coal, and gas. The report notes that there is considerable uncertainty about how our ecosystems will respond to a rapid increase in carbon dioxide and temperatures.

One approach to dealing with the problem of greenhouse gases is to tax carbon-based fuels. A carbon tax of $100 per ton of carbon content would translate into taxes of $0.28 per gallon of gasoline, $12 per barrel of oil, and $70 per ton of coal. The tax on coal would be relatively high because of its higher carbon content. A carbon tax would reduce greenhouse emissions in several ways:

- The price of gasoline would increase, causing people to drive less and buy more energy-efficient vehicles.
- The tax would increase the price of electricity, decreasing the quantity of electricity demanded and the quantity of fossil fuels burned.
- The higher price of home heating would cause people to turn down their thermostats and improve the heating efficiency of their homes, perhaps by installing energy-efficient windows or more insulation.
- Some electricity producers would switch from coal to natural gas, which has a lower carbon content, and thus a lower carbon tax. Others would switch to noncarbon energy sources such as the wind, the sun, and geothermal sources.

In 2002, New Zealand announced plans to implement a tax of $12 per ton of carbon, starting in 2007. New Zealand ranks fourth (behind the United States, Australia, and Canada) in per capita carbon emissions. About half of the greenhouse gases come from the methane emitted from the country's 50 million sheep and cattle during digestion. However, New Zealand farmers and ranchers will be exempt from the tax, over the strenuous objection of coal producers, who will pay a 20-percent tax. *Related to Exercise 2.6.*

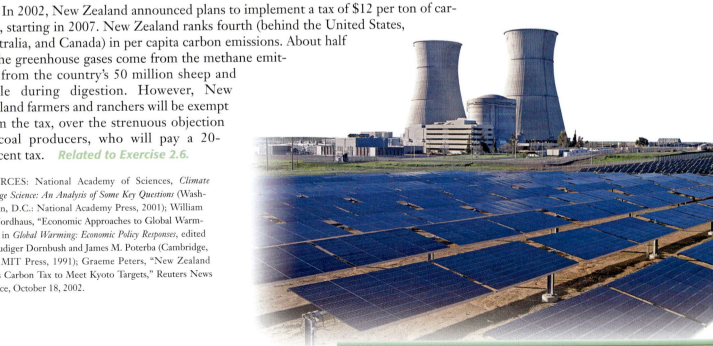

SOURCES: National Academy of Sciences, *Climate Change Science: An Analysis of Some Key Questions* (Washington, D.C.: National Academy Press, 2001); William D. Nordhaus, "Economic Approaches to Global Warming," in *Global Warming: Economic Policy Responses*, edited by Rudiger Dornbush and James M. Poterba (Cambridge, MA: MIT Press, 1991); Graeme Peters, "New Zealand Plans Carbon Tax to Meet Kyoto Targets," Reuters News Service, October 18, 2002.

Command and Control

Traditional regulation policies have another dimension that contributes to higher compliance costs. Under a command-and-control policy, the government requires each firm to produce no more than a certain volume of pollution and requires the abatement be done with a particular technology. The problem with this approach is that the mandated abatement technology—the control part of the policy—is unlikely to be the most efficient technology for two reasons:

- The regulatory policy specifies a single abatement technology for all firms. Because the producers of a polluting good often use different materials and production techniques, an abatement technology that is efficient for one firm may be inefficient for others.
- The regulatory policy decreases the incentives to develop more efficient abatement technologies. The command part of the policy specifies a maximum volume of waste for each firm, so there is no incentive to cut the volume of waste below the maximum allowed. In other words, the benefit of developing new technologies is relatively small because there is no payoff from using them. In contrast, a pollution tax provides the right incentives: If the firm develops a new technology that cuts pollution, it will pay less in pollution taxes.

A command-and-control policy causes firms to use inefficient abatement technologies, so production costs will be higher than they would be under a pollution tax.

Market Effects of Pollution Regulations

How do the market effects of pollution regulation compare to the effects of a pollution tax? Recall that the uniform abatement policy achieves the same reduction in pollution at a higher cost because it doesn't exploit differences in abatement costs across firms. In addition, the control part of command and control may lead to relatively costly abatement techniques because there's no incentive to develop better ones. This will cause the supply curve for the polluting good to shift upward by a larger amount than it would with a tax. A larger supply shift causes a larger increase in the equilibrium price and a larger reduction in quantity. The inefficiency of regulations is passed on to consumers, who pay higher prices.

One advantage of the command-and-control policy is its predictability. The policy specifies how much waste each firm can produce, so we can predict the total volume of waste. In contrast, we don't know exactly how firms will respond to the pollution tax—they could pollute a little or a lot, depending on the tax and the cost of abating pollution—so it is difficult to predict the total volume of waste that will be emitted.

16.4 | MARKETABLE POLLUTION PERMITS

In recent years, policy makers have developed a new approach to environmental policy. The approach uses **marketable pollution permits**, sometimes called *pollution allowances*. Here is how a government runs a system of marketable pollution permits:

- Pick a target pollution level for a particular area.
- Issue just enough permits to meet the pollution target.
- Allow firms to buy and sell the permits.

In the policy world, this is known as a *cap-and-trade system*: The government "caps" the total emissions by issuing a fixed number of permits, and then allows firms to trade the permits.

> • **marketable pollution permits**
> A system under which the government picks a target pollution level for a particular area, issues just enough pollution permits to meet the pollution target, and allows firms to buy and sell the permits; also known as a *cap-and-trade system*.

APPLICATION

3

DEAR ABBY AND ENVIRONMENTAL POLICY

APPLYING THE CONCEPTS #3: Are there different ways to reduce pollution or mitigate its effects?

We've seen that one problem with traditional environmental policy is that it is inflexible. It doesn't allow firms to use the most efficient abatement methods available. An example of different abatement strategies comes from the column of advice columnist Abigail Van Buren. A person with the moniker "Dreading Winter" sought advice about how to deal with a pollution problem. Her neighbors heated their home with a wood-burning stove, and the smell and smoke from the wood fire gave Dreading Winter burning eyes, a stuffy nose, and painful sinuses. She offered the neighbors $500 to stop burning wood, but they declined the offer. The readers of "Dear Abby" offered the following suggestions to Dreading Winter:

- Buy the neighbors a catalytic add-on for the wood stove or a wood-chip gasifier for an oil furnace. In either case, there would be much less air pollution from burning wood.
- Soak a towel in water, swish it around the room, and watch the smoke disappear.
- Leave a saucer of vinegar in each room to eliminate the smoke odor.
- Pay your neighbors to hire a chimney sweep to clean their flue.
- Seal and caulk your windows to keep the smoke outside at a cost of less than $500.
- Use the $500 to purchase an air purifier for your home.

These suggestions demonstrate a fundamental idea behind environmental economics: There is usually more than one way to deal with a pollution problem. The economic question is: What is the most efficient and least costly way to reduce the problem? In some cases, it may be more efficient to prevent the pollution by switching to an alternative fuel or installing a catalytic add-on to the stove than to clean up the environment after it has been polluted by installing an air purifier. In other cases, cleanup will be more efficient than prevention.
Related to Exercises 3.4 and 3.5.

SOURCE: Abigail Van Buren, "Aid for Reader's Winter Woe," *Sacramento Bee*, February 15, 1984, p. XX.

363

Voluntary Exchange and Marketable Permits

Making pollution permits marketable is sensible because it allows mutually beneficial exchanges between firms with different abatement costs. This is another illustration of the principle of voluntary exchange.

THE PRINCIPLE OF VOLUNTARY EXCHANGE

A voluntary exchange between two people makes both people better off.

Firms will buy and sell pollution permits only when an exchange will make both firms better off. This happens when the firms have different abatement costs.

To illustrate the effects of marketable permits, let's return to the example of the two electricity generators with different abatement costs. Suppose the government issues each firm several pollution permits, one less than the initial level of pollution. In other words, the government will reduce pollution by two tons. Can the two firms make a deal for a permit?

- Firm H is willing to pay a maximum of $5,000 for a permit because that's how much it costs to abate a ton of pollution.
- Firm L is willing to accept a minimum of $2,000 for a permit because that's how much it costs to abate a ton of pollution.

Firm H is willing to pay up to $5,000 and firm L is willing to accept as little as $2,000, so there is an opportunity for mutually beneficial exchange. If the two firms split the difference, the price of a permit is $3,500, and each firm gains $1,500 from the transaction. Firm H pays $3,500 to save $5,000 on abatement cost, for a savings of $1,500. Firm L gets $3,500 but pays an additional $2,000 in abatement cost, for a benefit of $1,500.

How does the marketability of permits affect the total cost of abatement? In our example, the total cost with nonmarketable permits is $7,000, including $2,000 for firm L and $5,000 for firm H. In contrast, when a single firm does all the abating, the cost for 2 tons of abatement is $4,000 (2 tons times $2,000 per ton). The savings of $3,000 equals the gap between the abatement cost of the high-cost and low-cost firm. Making the permits marketable exploits differences in abatement costs across firms, so we as a society can achieve the same level of abatement at a lower total cost.

The first program of marketable pollution permits, started in 1976 by the U.S. Environmental Protection Agency, allowed limited trading of permits for several airborne pollutants. Trading was later extended to lead in gasoline (in 1985) and then to the chemicals responsible for the depletion of the ozone layer (in 1988). As we'll see later in the chapter, there are now active markets for permits to discharge sulfur dioxide, carbon dioxide, and nitrogen oxides.

Supply, Demand, and the Price of Marketable Permits

We can use a model of supply and demand to represent the market for pollution permits. Figure 16.5 depicts a trading system introduced in the Los Angeles basin for smog pollutants such as NO_x. The supply curve for permits is vertical at the fixed number of permits provided by the government. The demand for permits comes from firms that can use a permit to avoid paying for pollution abatement, and the willingness to pay for a permit equals the savings in abatement costs. In Figure 16.5, the demand curve for permits is negatively sloped, meaning that the larger the number of permits available, the lower the willingness to pay for a permit. This is sensible because with more permits and pollution, the marginal cost of abatement will be relatively low. With a fixed supply of 100 permits in 1994, the equilibrium price, shown by the intersection of the demand curve and the 1994 supply curve at point *a*, is $7.

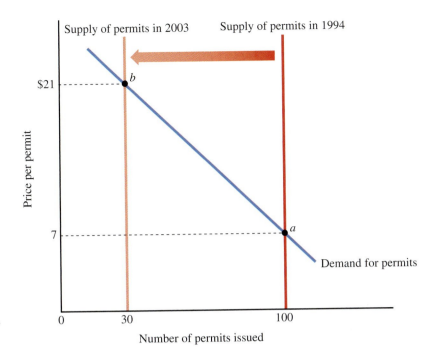

Under Los Angeles' smog program, the number of NO_x permits decreased each year, and in 2003 reached its goal of cutting NO_x discharges to 30 percent of the level attained nine years earlier.[1] In Figure 16.5, the decrease in the number of permits from 100 to 30 shifts the supply curve to the left, increasing the equilibrium price of permits from $7 at point *a* to $21 at point *b*. Polluters in Los Angeles responded to the higher permit prices by abating more. The Los Angeles Department of Water and Power installed abatement equipment—at a cost of $40 million—because abatement was cheaper than buying pollution permits. Libbey Glass Company installed low-pollution burners in its plant, dropping its emissions below the volume allowed by its permits. The company sold its extra permits to other firms, generating income for Libbey. The firms that bought the permits from Libbey were able to continue production using their existing abatement equipment.

How do technological advances in abatement technology affect the price of pollution permits? A pollution permit allows a firm to avoid paying for abatement, and the higher the abatement cost that can be avoided, the larger the amount a firm is willing to pay for a permit. A technological innovation that decreases abatement costs will encourage firms to use the new technology to abate pollution rather than buying permits that allow pollution. As a result, the demand curve for permits shifts downward and to the left, and the equilibrium price of permits will decrease.

16.5 | EXTERNAL COSTS FROM AUTOMOBILES

The use of automobiles generates three types of external costs. First, as we saw in Chapter 1, a person who uses a congested highway slows down other travelers, imposing time costs on other people. Second, automobiles generate air pollution, so drivers impose external costs on people sensitive to air pollutants. The third externality is motor-vehicle accidents—collisions with other vehicles, bicycles, and pedestrians. In this part of the chapter, we'll explore various policy responses to these externalities.

External Costs from Pollution

Ozone pollution, more commonly known as smog, is one of our most persistent environmental problems. Smog results from the mixing of several pollutants, including nitrogen oxides, sulfur dioxide, and volatile organic compounds. Smog causes health

4

APPLICATION

MARKETABLE PERMITS FOR SULFUR DIOXIDE

APPLYING THE CONCEPTS #4: What determines the price of a marketable pollution permit?

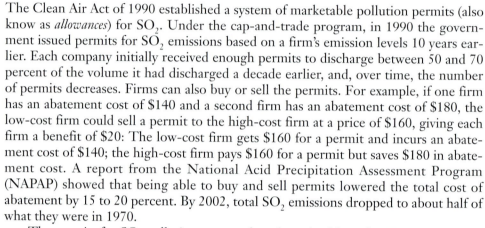

The Clean Air Act of 1990 established a system of marketable pollution permits (also know as *allowances*) for SO_2. Under the cap-and-trade program, in 1990 the government issued permits for SO_2 emissions based on a firm's emission levels 10 years earlier. Each company initially received enough permits to discharge between 50 and 70 percent of the volume it had discharged a decade earlier, and, over time, the number of permits decreases. Firms can also buy or sell the permits. For example, if one firm has an abatement cost of $140 and a second firm has an abatement cost of $180, the low-cost firm could sell a permit to the high-cost firm at a price of $160, giving each firm a benefit of $20: The low-cost firm gets $160 for a permit and incurs an abatement cost of $140; the high-cost firm pays $160 for a permit but saves $180 in abatement cost. A report from the National Acid Precipitation Assessment Program (NAPAP) showed that being able to buy and sell permits lowered the total cost of abatement by 15 to 20 percent. By 2002, total SO_2 emissions dropped to about half of what they were in 1970.

The permits for SO_2 pollution are now bought and sold on the Chicago Board of Trade. Each year the Environmental Protection Agency issues permits to existing SO_2 sources but withholds some permits for auction. Utilities can also put their permits up for bid on the Chicago Board of Trade. In 2002, a total of 127,388 permits were auctioned at an average price of $167 per ton. Individuals and environmental groups are allowed to buy the permits and, if they wish, reduce pollution by withdrawing them from the market. In 2001, a total of 31 permits went to schools and environmental groups, including the students mentioned in the chapter opener, who paid $181 for a permit. *Related to Exercise 4.5.*

SOURCES: http://www.epa.gov/airmarkets/auctions/; accessed 07/09/06.

problems, triggering asthma attacks in the 15 million people in the United States who suffer from asthma and worsening other respiratory problems, leading to premature deaths. Smog also retards plant growth and decreases agricultural productivity. Because of health and other problems created by smog, the EPA has established standards for smog concentrations in urban areas. Nonetheless, in many cities ozone pollution levels rise above these healthful levels.

The Breathmobile provides a visible reminder of the health effects of smog. Started in Los Angeles in 2000, the mobile asthma clinic, housed in a 34-foot recreational vehicle, provides free diagnosis and treatment for asthmatic schoolchildren. The clinic identifies and treats children who experience aggravated asthma symptoms on smoggy days. The Breathmobile program started in low-income neighborhoods in Los Angeles in 2000 and since then has spread to other cities.[2]

The automobile is by far the biggest source of smog-causing pollutants. We currently use a command-and-control approach to regulate automobile pollution: The EPA tells automakers what abatement equipment to install in cars. The equipment does not control the total emissions of the car, just the pollution per mile driven. If people buy cleaner cars but then drive more miles, total emissions can actually increase.

APPLICATION

CHICAGO CLIMATE EXCHANGE

APPLYING THE CONCEPTS #5: What are the benefits of giving firms options for reducing greenhouse gases?

The Chicago Climate Exchange (CCX) allows firms to cut their emissions of greenhouse gases in different ways. When a firm joins CCX, it agrees to reduce its contribution to greenhouse gases by 4 percent within four years by (1) cutting its own emissions, (2) paying for extra reductions by other firms, or (3) paying for projects such as reforestation that offset the firm's emissions. Among the members of CCX are Ford Motor Company, DuPont, Motorola, IBM, American Electric Power, the City of Chicago, and Tufts University. In the first auctions in 2003, the price for carbon dioxide emissions was about $1 per ton.

The experience of American Electric Power (AEP), the nation's largest electricity producer, illustrates how CCX works. AEP bought 10,000 acres of fallow land and planted walnut trees, which each year will withdraw about 71,000 tons of carbon dioxide from the air and convert it into solid wood. As long as the wood doesn't burn or decompose, AEP can use the trees to offset some of its carbon emissions. The cost of tree farming is $1.25 per ton of carbon absorbed, or "sequestered," which is small relative to the alternative—converting the company's generators from coal to natural gas at a cost of about $50 per ton of carbon abated. *Related to Exercise 4.6.*

SOURCE: Thomas Kellner, "Got Gas?" *Forbes*, March 17, 2003, p. 56.

The economic approach to air pollution is to internalize the external cost with a pollution tax. Under such a tax, a car owner would have the car tested at the end of the year to determine how much pollution it generated per mile and then pay a tax equal to the miles driven times the external cost per mile. For example, if the external cost for a particular car is $0.02 per mile and the mileage for the year is 10,000 miles, the pollution tax for the year would be $200. The pollution tax would encourage people to buy cleaner cars, maintain their emissions equipment, drive less, and use alternative modes of transportation. The tax is consistent with the idea that people should pay the full cost of driving their automobiles, including the external costs.

One alternative to a direct pollution tax on automobile travel is a gasoline tax. According to a recent study, smog-related damages from automobiles average about $0.02 per mile driven, which translates to an average of $0.40 per gallon of gasoline.[3] Burning gasoline also contributes to global warming, and if the appropriate carbon tax is $100 per ton of carbon, the associated gasoline tax would be about $0.28 per gallon. Adding the $0.40 tax for smog damage and the $0.28 tax for global warming, the gasoline tax would be $0.68 per gallon. This tax would be added to the current gasoline taxes (a federal tax of $0.18 and state taxes that average about $0.22), which pay for highway construction and maintenance. A gasoline tax would be inferior to a real pollution tax because a driver's gasoline tax bill would not depend directly on pollution, so there would be less incentive to drive cleaner cars.

Figure 16.6 shows the market effects of a gasoline tax equal to $0.68 per gallon. The tax shifts the supply curve upward by the amount of the tax, as shown by points *a* and *b*. The new equilibrium is shown by point *c*, with an equilibrium price of $2.00 (up

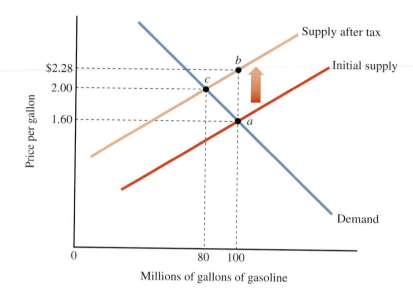

► **FIGURE 16.6**

The Market Effects of a Gasoline Tax

A gasoline tax of $0.68 per gallon shifts the supply curve upward by the amount of the tax and increases the equilibrium price by $0.40. The tax is shifted forward onto consumers, who pay $0.40 more per gallon, and backward onto input suppliers, who receive lower prices for crude oil.

from $1.60) and an equilibrium quantity of 80 million gallons (down from 100 million gallons). The increase in price decreases the quantity demanded as consumers drive fewer miles, switch to alternative travel modes—bus, train, bicycle, walking—and switch to more fuel-efficient cars.

The equilibrium price rises by $0.40, which is less than the $0.68 tax. As we saw earlier in the book, a tax is shifted forward to consumers in the form of a price hike ($0.40 in this example) and backward onto input suppliers in the form of lower prices for inputs. The decrease in the quantity of gasoline produced will decrease the demand for crude oil, decreasing its price. In other words, part of the gasoline tax will be borne by the people and governments who own crude oil.

External Costs from Congestion

As we saw in Chapter 1, the typical urban commuter wastes about 47 hours per year in slow traffic and wastes $84 worth of fuel. The economic approach to congestion is to internalize the external cost by imposing a tax on drivers equal to the external costs they impose on others. To compute the appropriate tax per mile driven, we compute the change in total travel time caused by one additional car on the highway and multiply the change in travel time by the opportunity cost of travel time. For peak travel in the typical large metropolitan areas, the external cost is about $0.21 per mile traveled, so a commuter who makes a 10-mile trip during peak travel times would pay a congestion tax of $2.10. During off-peak periods when highways are less crowded, the external cost is much lower, around $0.04 per mile driven. When traffic volume is low enough that everyone can travel at the legal speed limit, the external cost is zero, so there would be no congestion tax.

Modern technology allows the efficient collection of congestion taxes. Under a vehicle identification system (VIS), each car is equipped with a transponder—an electronic device that allows sensors along the road to identify a car as it passes. The system records the number of times a vehicle uses a congested highway and sends a congestion bill to the driver at the end of the month. For example, a driver who travels 10 miles along a congested highway 20 times per month would pay a monthly congestion bill of $42.00 (20 times $2.10). The alternative approach is to use anonymous debit cards to charge for driving on congested roads.

The use of congestion taxes and other time-sensitive pricing of highways is spreading. Singapore uses Electronic Road Pricing (ERP), a debit-card system with charges that increase with the level of congestion. In Toronto, users of the Express Toll Road pay fees that depend on the distance traveled and time of day. The per-kilometer toll is $0.10 (Canadian) during peak periods, $0.07 during other weekday times, and $0.04 cents on the weekend. Along some highways in Southern California, drivers can pay a fee to use lanes normally reserved for carpools. The toll varies in "real time" from $0.50 to $4.00, depending on the level of congestion, and is highest from 7 A.M. to 8 A.M. and 4 P.M. to 5 P.M.

External Costs from Collisions

A third externality from the use of the automobile comes from motor-vehicle accidents—collisions with other vehicles, bicycles, and pedestrians. In the United States, the annual cost of property damage, injuries, and deaths from traffic collisions is about $300 billion per year. About two-thirds of these costs are incurred by the driver who causes the accident, and the other third is borne by someone else. In other words, traffic collisions have substantial external costs. On average, the collision-related external cost of travel is about 4.4 cents per mile driven. By way of comparison, the fuel cost per mile is about 10 to 15 cents. The direct approach to internalize this externality would be to impose a tax of 4.4 cents per vehicle mile traveled, a VMT tax. Such a tax would improve traffic safety by reducing the number of miles driven.

Consider two alternatives to the VMT tax. First, the premium for automobile insurance could be based on miles driven rather than being a fixed amount per year. A person who drove less would pay less for insurance, which is sensible because he or she would be less likely to have an accident and impose an external cost on someone else.

Second, a gasoline tax could be imposed. The basic problem is that a person's gas-tax bill depends on the amount of gasoline consumed, not the number of miles driven and the external cost of collisions. Gas mileage varies across vehicles, and a person in a car with better gas mileage would pay less than the external cost of collisions.

6

APPLICATION

YOUNG DRIVERS AND COLLISIONS

APPLYING THE CONCEPTS #6: What is the external cost of young drivers?

A VMT tax of 4.4 cents per mile would internalize the external cost from collisions on average, but the external cost varies with the age of the driver. As shown in Table 16.1, the external cost of young drivers is over three times the external cost of middle-aged drivers. A precise VMT tax would have higher tax rates for the drivers with higher external cost. For example, the tax for young drivers would be 11 cents per mile, compared to 3.4 cents per mile for a middle-aged driver. Such a tax would reduce the miles driven by all drivers, but the reductions would be larger for young drivers, the group with the highest collision rates and external costs. *Related to Exercise 5.6.*

SOURCE: Ian W.H. Parry, "Comparing Alternative Policies to Reduce Traffic Accidents," *Journal of Urban Economics*, vol. 56 (2004), pp. 346–368.

Table 16.1 | THE EXTERNAL ACCIDENT COSTS FOR DIFFERENT VEHICLES AND DRIVER AGES

	Younger than age 25	Between the ages of 25 and 70	Over age 70
Cents per mile	11	3.4	5.4

SUMMARY

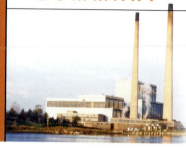

The theme of this chapter is that the best way to control pollution and other external costs is to rely on the exchange principle and markets. A *pollution tax* internalizes the external cost of pollution, causing firms to cut the pollution per unit of output and consumers to buy less of a polluting product. A *cap-and-trade system* for emissions achieves a pollution target at the lowest possible cost because the firms with the lowest cost do most of the abatement. The external costs from automobiles could be internalized with taxes on pollution, congestion, and miles driven. Here are the main points of the chapter:

1 The optimum level of pollution abatement is where the marginal benefit equals the marginal cost.

2 A tax on the emissions of electricity generators decreases total emissions as firms switch to cleaner fuels and consumers buy less electricity at the higher price.

3 Compared to a pollution tax, traditional pollution regulations lead to higher production costs and higher product prices.

4 Allowing firms to buy and sell pollution permits reduces the cost of abatement because low-cost firms do more of the abatement.

5 Urban smog is a continuing problem, in part because the traditional command-and-control policies are less effective than an annual automobile pollution tax.

6 The external cost from traffic congestion could be internalized with a tax that varies with the level of traffic congestion.

7 The external cost from traffic collisions could be internalized with a tax that varies with the likelihood of causing a collision.

KEY TERMS

external cost of production, p. 358

marketable pollution permits, p. 362

pollution tax, p. 358

private cost of production, p. 358

social cost of production, p. 358

EXERCISES

Visit www.myeconlab.com to complete these exercises online and get instant feedback.

Get Ahead of the Curve

16.1 | The Optimal Level of Pollution

1.1 The optimal level of pollution abatement is the level at which the _____ of abatement equals the _____ of abatement.

1.2 The marginal cost of abatement typically _____ (increases/decreases) with the level of abatement.

1.3 In the case of sulfur dioxide pollution, the marginal benefit curve is _____ (positively sloped/negatively sloped/ horizontal/vertical).

1.4 The estimated optimal level of sulfur dioxide emissions for 2010 is roughly _____ million tons (1/8/12). (Related to Application 1 on page 357.)

1.5 **Optimal Pollution Abatement.** Suppose the marginal benefit of pollution abatement is constant at $12 per unit. The marginal cost of abatement is $2 for the first unit abated and increases by $2 for each additional unit, to $4 for the second unit, $6 for the third unit, and so on. (Related to Application 1 on page 357.)
   a. What is the optimal level of pollution abatement?
   b. What is the appropriate pollution tax?

1.6 **Optimal Noise Pollution.** Vivian is trying to learn to play the violin, much to the dismay of her housemates. Her marginal benefit from the first hour of practice is $8, and the marginal benefit decreases by $1 per hour, to $7 for the second hour, $6 for the third hour, and so on. For her housemates, the external cost from the noise pollution is $4 per hour.
   a. In the market equilibrium (no restrictions), how many hours will Vivian play? Illustrate with a graph.
   b. What is the socially efficient practice time?
   c. What is the economic approach to noise pollution, and how would it be applied in this case?

16.2 | Taxing Pollution

2.1 The social cost of production equals the _____ cost plus the _____ cost.

2.2 In the presence of a pollution tax, the marginal benefit of abating pollution equals _____. A firm will respond to a pollution tax by picking the level of abatement where the pollution tax equals _____.

2.3 Arrows up or down: A pollution tax shifts the supply curve _____, which _____ the equilibrium price and _____ the equilibrium quantity of the polluting product.

2.4 A pollution tax decreases the volume of pollution in two ways, by decreasing _____ and decreasing _____.

2.5 Arrows up or down: A carbon tax will shift the supply curve for home heating oil _____, causing the equilibrium price to _____ and the equilibrium quantity to _____.

2.6 **The Market Effects of a Carbon Tax.** Consider the market for gasoline. In the initial equilibrium, the price is $2.00 per gallon and the quantity is 100 million gallons. The price elasticity of demand is 0.70, and the price elasticity of supply is 1.0. Suppose a carbon tax shifts the supply curve upward by $0.34 and to the left by 17 percent. (Related to Application 2 on page 361.)
  a. Use a graph to show the effects of the tax on the equilibrium price and quantity of gasoline.
  b. After reviewing the price-change formula in the earlier chapter on elasticity, compute the new price and quantity. The new price is $ _____ per gallon and the new quantity is _____ million gallons.
  c. Consumers pay $ _____ of the $0.34 tax and producers pay the remaining $ _____ of the tax.

2.7 **Shifting a Tax on Home Heating Oil.** You are an economic consultant to a member of Congress. Someone just introduced a bill that would impose a carbon tax of $100 per ton, which would shift the supply curve for heating oil upward by $0.30 per gallon and to the left by 15 percent. The initial (pretax) price of heating oil is $2.00.
  a. Use a graph to show the effects of the tax on the price and quantity of heating oil. Will the entire tax to be paid by consumers? If not, who else will bear part of the tax?
  b. Suppose the price elasticity of supply of heating oil is 1.0 and the price elasticity of demand is 0.50. Use the price-change formula developed in the chapter on elasticity to predict the new equilibrium price. What fraction of the tax is passed forward to consumers?

16.3 | Traditional Regulation

3.1 Compared to a pollution tax, a uniform-abatement policy is _____ (more/less) efficient because it does not exploit differences in _____ across firms.

3.2 A command-and-control policy is likely to be inefficient because it causes firms to use _____.

3.3 Arrows up or down: A switch from a pollution-tax policy to a uniform-reduction policy will shift the supply curve of the polluting product _____ and _____ the equilibrium price.

3.4 The lesson from the application, "Dear Abby and Environmental Policy" is that sometimes _____ is less costly than _____, and sometimes the reverse is true. (Related to Application 3 on page 363.)

3.5 **Options for Abating Noise Pollution.** Radiohead enjoys loud music and is willing to pay $9 for the first song and $1 less for each succeeding song ($8 for the second, $7 for the third, and so on). For her dorm mates, the external cost from the noise pollution is $4 per song. (Related to Application 3 on page 363.)
  a. Suppose initially the price of songs is zero. How many songs will Radiohead play? Illustrate with a graph.
  b. Suppose the government imposes a pollution tax of $4 per song. How many songs will Radiohead play? Compute the loss in consumer surplus from the tax, which increases the price of songs from zero to $4.
  c. Radiohead could soundproof her room, eliminating the noise pollution and her responsibility to pay the pollution tax. If the soundproofing costs $30, is it worthwhile?
  d. Radiohead could compensate her dorm mates for each unit of noise pollution—each song played. How much compensation would be required? From Radiohead's perspective, is paying compensation better than paying the tax, worse, or the same?

3.6 **Regulations Eliminate a Market?** Consider a market in which the initial equilibrium quantity of a polluting good is 20 tons.
  a. Use a graph to show the effects of a pollution tax that decreases the equilibrium quantity to 12 tons.
  b. Consider a command-and-control policy that generates the same volume of pollution as the pollution tax but decreases the equilibrium quantity of the polluting good to zero. Use a graph to show the effects of the command-and-control policy.

16.4 | Marketable Pollution Permits

4.1 Under a system of marketable pollution permits, a firm with _____ (low/high) abatement costs will buy permits from a firm with _____ (low/high) abatement costs.

4.2 Arrows up or down: A switch from regular pollution permits to marketable permits _____ the total cost of abatement.

4.3 A decrease in the supply of marketable pollution permits will shift the supply curve for permits to the _____ and _____ the equilibrium price of permits.

4.4 Arrows up or down: A technological advance that decreases abatement costs will _____ the demand for marketable pollution permits and _____ the equilibrium price.

4.5 **Split the Difference for a Pollution Permit.** Consider two firms, each of which is issued 3 marketable pollution permits. For firm H, the marginal cost of abatement is $190. For firm L, the marginal cost of abatement is $130. (Related to Application 4 on page 366.)

   a. Is there room for a mutually beneficial exchange of one permit? If so, which firm will buy a permit and which firm will sell a permit?

   b. If the two firms split the difference, what's the price of a permit?

   c. Suppose that after the exchange of one permit, the marginal cost of abatement for the firm that sold the permit is $170 and the marginal cost of the firm that bought the permit is $150. Will the firms exchange another permit, or are they done trading?

   d. What is the savings in abatement cost from allowing firms to buy and sell a permit?

4.6 **Reforestation Versus Abatement.** Suppose your firm joins the Chicago Climate Exchange and commits to reducing greenhouse gases by 11 tons per year. You can pay for a reforestation project that offsets your emissions at a cost of $7 per ton of carbon offset. Or you can modify your production cost to abate pollution. Your marginal cost of abating the first ton is $3; the marginal cost increases by $1 for each additional ton, to $4 for the second ton, $5 for the third ton, and so on. (Related to Application 5 on page 367.)

   a. What's the best combination of reforestation offsets and abatement?

   b. How much money does your firm save by using the offsets?

4.7 **No Permits Exchanged?** A state issued marketable permits for sulfur dioxide emissions to several electric-

ity generators. Most of the permits were given to the utilities with the oldest generating facilities. One year later, none of the permits had been bought or sold. What could explain the absence of permit exchanges?

4.8 **Lower Abatement Cost and Permit Prices.** Suppose new technology decreases the cost of abating pollution by half. Depict graphically the implications of the decrease in abatement cost on the equilibrium price of marketable permits. Use Figure 16.5 on page 365 as a starting point, with an initial permit price of $21 (point *b*). What's the new equilibrium price?

16.5 | External Costs from Automobiles

5.1 A pollution tax on automobiles provides an incentive to buy _____, maintain _____, drive _____, and use alternative _____.

5.2 Arrows up or down: A gasoline tax will shift the supply curve for gasoline _____, causing the equilibrium price to _____ and the equilibrium quantity to _____.

5.3 A gasoline tax will be shifted forward to _____ and backward to _____, such as the suppliers of _____.

5.4 To internalize the external cost associated with automobile emissions that cause urban smog, the appropriate gasoline tax is about _____ ($0.20/$0.40/$0.80/$1.00) per gallon.

5.5 To internalize the external cost associated with traffic collisions, the appropriate VMT tax is about _____ ($0.01/$0.02/$0.04/$0.20) per mile.

5.6 **Youngsters Pay to Drive.** The demand for automobile travel by the typical young driver (age less than 25 years) is linear, with a vertical intercept of $1.00 per mile and a horizontal intercept of 200 miles per week. Initially, the cost of automobile insurance is a fixed weekly sum, independent of mileage. The average cost of driving—for gasoline, oil, maintenance, and repair—is constant at $0.20 per mile. (Related to Application 6 on page 369.)

   a. Use a graph to show the driver's choice of how many miles to drive, labeled as point *a*

   b. Use the data in the application, "Young Drivers and Collisions," in Table 16.1 on page 369 to show the socially efficient outcome, labeled as point *b*.

ECONOMIC EXPERIMENT

Pollution Permits

In this pollution-permit experiment, students play the role of paper firms that buy or sell pollution permits. The class is divided into groups of three to five students, with each group representing a firm that produces one ton of paper per period. The instructor provides each firm with data about its cost of production. The cost depends on how much waste the firm generates: The smaller the volume of waste, the higher the production cost. Here is an example:

Gallons of waste generated	2	3	4
Production cost per ton	$36	$26	$20

Each firm receives 3 pollution permits for each of the five trading periods. A firm that does not sell any of its permits to other firms has the right to generate 3 gallons of waste in that period. A firm that sells one of its 3 permits can generate only 2 gallons of waste, and a firm that buys a permit from another firm can generate 4 gallons of waste.

At the beginning of each of the five trading periods, firms meet in the trading area to buy or sell pollution permits for that day. Each firm can buy or sell one permit per day. Once a transaction has been arranged, the buyer and the seller inform the instructor of the transaction, record the transaction on their report cards, and then leave the trading area. The firm's objective is to maximize profit, and in each trading period we compute the firm's profit with the following equation:

$$\text{profit} = \text{price of paper} - \text{production cost} + \text{revenue from permit sold} - \text{cost of permit purchased}$$

In each period, a firm will either buy or sell a permit, so we compute the firm's profit with just three numbers. For example, using the production cost numbers shown in the table, if the price of paper is $50 per ton and a firm buys a permit for $5 and generates 4 gallons of waste, the firm's profit is:

$$\text{profit} = \$50 - \$20 + 0 - \$5 = \$25$$

If another firm sells a permit for $5 and generates 2 gallons of waste, the firm's profit is:

$$\text{profit} = \$50 - \$36 + \$5 - 0 = \$19$$

For the fourth and fifth trading periods, several environmental groups have the option of buying pollution permits. Each environmental group is given a fixed sum of money to spend on permits, and its objective is to get as many permits as possible, reducing the total volume of pollution in the process.

NOTES

1. Gary Polaroid, "Cost of Clean Air Credits Soars in Southland," *Los Angeles Times*, September 5, 2000, page B.

2. South Coast Air Quality Management District, "New Mobile Asthma Clinic to Serve L.A. County Children," May 12, 2000.

3. Kenneth Small and Camilla Kazimi, "On the Costs of Air Pollution from Motor Vehicles," *Journal of Transport Economics and Policy*, vol. 29 (1995), pp. 7–32.

17

The Labor Market, Income, and Poverty

Recent reports on the earnings of college graduates have made the jobs of college recruiters easier[1]:

- In 1972, the typical college graduate earned 43 percent more than a high-school graduate.

- In 2002, the typical college graduate earned roughly twice as much as a high-school graduate.

These facts raise two questions: First, why do college graduates earn so much more than high-school graduates? Second, why did the earnings gap almost double during the last three decades?

U p to this point in the book, we have discussed the markets for final goods and services. In this chapter, we switch to the market for one of the factors of production—labor. Labor costs are responsible for about three-fourths of production costs, and for most people labor income is by far the most important source of income. We'll use a model of demand and supply to see how wages are determined and why wages differ between college graduates and high-school graduates, men and women, and people in different occupations. We'll also take a look at the distribution of income and the problem of poverty.

17.1 | THE DEMAND FOR LABOR

We can use demand and supply curves to show how wages are determined and examine how changes in the labor market affect wages and employment. We'll start with the demand side of the labor market, looking first at how an individual firm can use the key principles of economics to decide how many workers to hire.

The demand for labor and other productive inputs is different from the demand for consumer products such as iPods, books, haircuts, and pizza. Firms use workers to produce the products demanded by consumers, and so economists say that labor demand is a "derived demand." That is, it is determined by, or derived from, the demand for the products produced by workers. As we'll see in this chapter, the demand for labor is determined by the demand for consumer products and the price of those products.

Labor Demand by an Individual Firm in the Short Run

Consider a perfectly competitive firm that produces rubber balls. Because this firm is perfectly competitive, it takes the price of its output and the prices of its inputs as given. Because it hires a tiny fraction of the workers in the labor market, it takes the market wage as given and can hire as many workers as it wants at that wage. In addition, the firm produces a tiny fraction of the rubber balls sold in the market, so it takes the price of its output as given. Let's say the price of rubber balls is $0.50.

Consider the firm's hiring decision in the short run, defined as the period during which at least one input—for example, its factory—cannot be changed. We can use two of the key principles of economics to explain the firm's hiring decision. Recall the marginal principle.

MARGINAL PRINCIPLE

Increase the level of an activity as long as its marginal benefit exceeds its marginal cost. Choose the level at which the marginal benefit equals the marginal cost.

The firm will pick the quantity of labor at which the marginal benefit of labor equals the marginal cost of labor. It can hire as many workers as it wants at the market wage, so the marginal cost of labor equals the hourly wage. If the wage is $8 per hour, the extra cost associated with one more hour of labor—the marginal cost—is $8, regardless of how many workers the firm hires.

What is the marginal benefit of labor? The firm hires labor to produce balls, so the marginal benefit equals the monetary value of the balls produced with an additional hour of labor. Table 17.1 shows how to compute the marginal benefit associated

Table 17.1 | USING THE MARGINAL PRINCIPLE TO MAKE A LABOR DECISION

(1) Workers	(2) Balls	(3) Marginal Product of Labor	(4) Price	(5) Marginal Revenue Product of Labor (*MRP*)	(6) Marginal Cost When Wage = $8
1	26	26	$0.50	$13	$8
2	50	24	0.50	12	8
3	72	22	0.50	11	8
4	92	20	0.50	10	8
5	108	16	0.50	8	8
6	120	12	0.50	6	8
7	128	8	0.50	4	8
8	130	2	0.50	1	8

with different quantities of labor. The first two columns show the relationship between the number of workers and the quantity of balls produced. Recall the principle of diminishing returns.

PRINCIPLE OF DIMINISHING RETURNS

Suppose that output is produced with two or more inputs and we increase one input while holding the other inputs fixed. Beyond some point—called the *point of diminishing returns*—output will increase at a decreasing rate.

As we saw earlier in the book, the **marginal product of labor**, the change in output from one additional unit of labor, typically rises for the first few workers and then eventually decreases. To simplify matters, we'll assume diminishing returns start to occur with the second worker. As shown in the third column of Table 17.1, the marginal product of labor decreases as the number of workers increases, from 26 for the first worker, to 24 for the second worker, and so on.

The marginal benefit of labor equals the **marginal-revenue product of labor (*MRP*)**, which is defined as the extra revenue generated by one additional unit of labor. To compute the *MRP*, we multiply the marginal product of labor by the price of output ($0.50 per ball in this example):

$$MRP = \text{marginal product} \times \text{price of output}$$

Figure 17.1 shows the marginal-revenue product curve. Because the marginal product drops as the number of workers increases, the *MRP* curve is negatively sloped, falling from $11 for the third worker (point *a*) to $8 for the fifth worker (point *b*), and so on.

A firm can use its *MRP* curve to decide how much labor to hire at a particular wage. In Figure 17.1, the marginal-cost curve is horizontal at the market wage ($8). The perfectly competitive firm takes the wage as given, so the marginal-cost curve is also the labor-supply curve faced by the firm. The marginal principle is satisfied at point *b*, where the marginal cost equals the marginal-revenue product. The firm will hire 5 workers because for the first 5 workers, the marginal benefit (the *MRP*) is greater than or equal to the marginal cost (the $8 wage). It would not be sensible to hire another worker, because the additional revenue from the sixth worker ($6) would be less than the $8 additional cost of that worker. If the wage increases to $11, the firm will satisfy the marginal principle at point *a*, hiring only 3 workers.

The *MRP* curve is also the firm's **short-run demand curve for labor**, which shows the relationship between the wage and the quantity of labor demanded in the short run, when the firm cannot change its production facility. The demand curve answers

- **marginal product of labor**
  The change in output from one additional unit of labor.

- **marginal-revenue product of labor** (*MRP*)
  The extra revenue generated from one additional unit of labor; *MRP* is equal to the price of output times the marginal product of labor.

- **short-run demand curve for labor**
  A curve showing the relationship between the wage and the quantity of labor demanded over the short run, when the firm cannot change its production facility.

The Marginal Principle and the Firm's Demand for Labor
Using the marginal principle, the firm picks the quantity of workers at which the marginal benefit (the marginal revenue product of labor) equals the marginal cost (the wage). The firm's short-run demand curve for labor is the marginal revenue product curve.

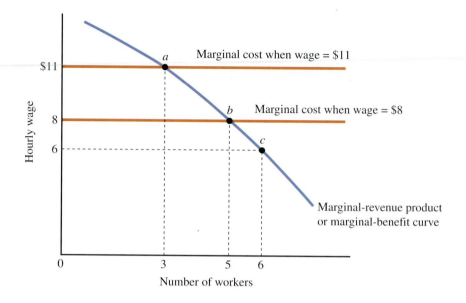

the following question: At each wage, how many workers does the firm want to hire? We've already used the *MRP* curve to answer this question for two different wages ($11 and $8), and we can do the same for any other wage. Because the *MRP* curve is a marginal-benefit curve, and the firm uses the marginal principle to decide how much labor to hire, the *MRP* curve is the same as the firm's demand curve for labor. If you pick a wage, the *MRP* curve tells you exactly how much labor the firm will demand at that wage.

What sorts of changes would cause the demand curve to shift? To draw the labor-demand curve, we fix the price of the output and the productivity of workers. Therefore, an increase in the price of the output will increase the *MRP* of workers, shifting the entire demand curve for labor to the right: At each wage, the firm will hire more workers. This is shown in Figure 17.2. An increase in the price of balls shifts the labor-demand curve to the right. At a wage of $8, the firm hires 7 workers instead of 5. Similarly, if workers become more productive, the increase in the marginal product of labor will increase the *MRP* and shift the demand curve to the right. Conversely, a decrease in price or labor productivity would shift the demand curve to the left.

► **FIGURE 17.2**

An Increase in the Price of Output Shifts the Labor-Demand Curve
An increase in the price of the good produced by workers increases the marginal revenue product at each quantity of workers, shifting the demand curve to the right. At each wage, the firm will demand more workers. For example, at a wage of $8, the demand for labor increases from 5 workers (point *b*) to 7 workers (point *d*).

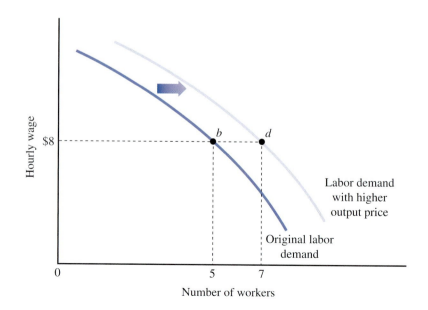

Market Demand for Labor in the Short Run

To draw the short-run market demand curve for labor, we add the labor demands of all the firms that use a particular type of labor. In the simplest case, all firms are identical, and we simply multiply the number of firms by the quantity of labor demanded by the typical firm. If there were 100 firms and each hired 5 workers at a wage of $8, the market demand for labor would be 500 workers. Similarly, if the typical firm hired 3 workers at a wage of $11, the market demand would be 300 workers.

Labor Demand in the Long Run

Recall that in the long run, firms can enter or leave the market and firms already in the market can change all of their inputs, including their production facilities. The **long-run demand curve for labor** shows the relationship between the wage and the quantity of labor demanded over the long run, when the number of firms in the market can change and firms in the market can modify their production facilities.

Although there are no diminishing returns in the long run, the market demand curve is still negatively sloped. As the wage increases, the quantity of labor demanded decreases for two reasons:

- The **output effect.** An increase in the wage will increase the cost of producing balls, and firms will pass on at least part of the higher labor cost to their consumers: Prices will increase. According to the law of demand, firms will sell fewer balls at the higher price, so they will need less of all inputs, including labor.
- The **input-substitution effect.** An increase in the wage will cause the firm to substitute other inputs for labor. At a wage of $4, it may not be sensible to use much machinery in the ball factory, but at a wage of $20 it may be sensible to mechanize the factory, using more machinery and fewer workers. This substitution of other inputs for labor decreases the labor input per unit of output.

The input-substitution effect decreases the labor input per unit of output while the output effect decreases total output. The two effects operate in the same direction, so the market demand curve is negatively sloped.

The notion of input substitution applies to other labor markets as well. For the most graphic examples of factor substitution, we can travel from a developed country, such as the United States, Canada, France, Germany, or Japan, to a less-developed country in South America, Africa, or Asia. Wages are much lower in the less-developed countries, so production tends to be more labor intensive. In other words, labor is less costly relative to machinery and equipment, so labor is substituted for these other inputs. Here are some examples:

- *Mining.* U.S. firms use huge earthmoving equipment to mine for minerals; firms in some less-developed countries use thousands of workers, digging by hand.
- *Furniture.* Firms in developed countries manufacture furniture with sophisticated machinery and equipment; firms in some less-developed countries make furniture by hand.
- *Accounting.* Accountants in developed countries use computers and sophisticated software programs; some accountants in less-developed countries use simple calculators and ledger paper.

Short-Run Versus Long-Run Demand

How does the short-run demand curve for labor compare to the long-run demand curve? There is less flexibility in the short run because firms cannot enter or leave the

- **long-run demand curve for labor**
A curve showing the relationship between the wage and the quantity of labor demanded over the long run, when the number of firms in the market can change and firms can modify their production facilities.

- **output effect**
The change in the quantity of labor demanded resulting from a change in the quantity of output produced.

- **input-substitution effect**
The change in the quantity of labor demanded resulting from an increase in the price of labor relative to the price of other inputs.

market and they cannot modify their production facilities. As a result, the demand for labor is less elastic in the short run. That means the short-run demand curve is steeper than the long-run demand curve. You may recall that we used the same logic to explain why the short-run supply curve for a product (plain cotton T-shirts) was steeper than the long-run supply curve for the product.

17.2 | THE SUPPLY OF LABOR

The labor-supply curve answers the following question: How many hours of labor will be supplied at each wage? When we speak of a labor market, we are referring to the market for a specific occupation in a specific geographical area. Consider the supply for nurses in the hypothetical city of Florence. The supply question is: How many hours of nursing services will be supplied at each wage? To answer that question, we must think about how many nurses are in the city and how many hours each nurse works.

The Individual Labor-Supply Decision: How Many Hours?

Let's start with an individual's decision about how many hours to work. The decision to work is a decision to sacrifice some leisure time for money: Each hour of work reduces leisure time by one hour. Therefore, the demand for leisure is the flip side of the supply of labor. The price of leisure time is the income sacrificed for each hour of leisure, that is, the hourly wage. We know from earlier chapters that an increase in the price of a good has two effects: a substitution effect and an income effect. An increase in the wage—the price of leisure—has two effects on the demand for leisure.

• **substitution effect for leisure demand**
The change in leisure time resulting from a change in the wage (the price of leisure) relative to the price of other goods.

Consider first the **substitution effect for leisure demand**. The worker faces a trade-off between leisure time and consumer goods such as music, books, food, and entertainment. For each hour of leisure time Leah takes, she loses one hour of work time, and her income drops by an amount equal to the wage. Therefore, she has less money to spend on consumer goods. For example, if the wage is $8 per hour, each hour of leisure decreases the amount of income available to spend on consumer goods by $8. When the wage increases to, say, $10, Leah will sacrifice more income—and consumer goods—for each hour of leisure she takes. Given the larger sacrifice of consumer goods per hour of leisure time, she will demand less leisure. That means that she will work more hours and earn more money for consumer goods. In other words, as the wage increases, she will substitute income—and the consumer goods it buys—for leisure time.

• **income effect for leisure demand**
The change in leisure time resulting from a change in real income caused by a change in the wage.

Consider next the **income effect** of an increase in the wage. For most people, leisure is a normal good in the sense that the demand for leisure increases as real income increases. An increase in the wage increases Leah's real income in the sense that she can afford more of all goods, including leisure time. Suppose Leah has a total of 100 hours per week to divide between leisure and work. At a wage of $10, she works 36 hours and has 64 hours of leisure. She also earns $360 ($10 per hour times 36 hours of work) and spends that amount on consumer goods. If her wage increases to $15, her real income increases because she can have more consumer goods and more leisure time. For example, if she worked only 30 hours, she could buy $450 worth of consumer goods ($15 per hour times 30 hours) and have 70 hours of leisure (100 hours per week minus 30 hours of work). The increase in real income causes Leah to consume more of all normal goods, including leisure time. The increase in real income causes her to demand more leisure and supply less labor.

In the labor market, the income and substitution effects of an increase in wages operate in opposite directions. The substitution effect decreases the desired leisure time, while the income effect increases the desired leisure time. Therefore, we can't predict whether an increase in the wage will cause a worker to demand more leisure time (supply less labor) or less leisure (supply more labor).

APPLICATION 1

DIFFERENT RESPONSES TO A HIGHER WAGE

APPLYING THE CONCEPTS #1: When the wage increases, will the typical person work more hours or fewer hours?

A simple example will show why we can't predict a worker's response to an increase in the wage. Suppose each nurse in Florence initially works 36 hours per week at an hourly wage of $10 and the wage increases to $12. The following are three reasonable responses to the higher wage:

1 *Lester works fewer hours.* If Lester works 30 hours instead of 36 hours, he gets 6 hours of extra leisure time and still earns the same income per week ($360 = 30 hours × $12 per hour).

2 *Sam works the same number of hours.* If Sam continues to work 36 hours per week, he gets an additional $72 of income ($2 per hour × 36 hours) and the same amount of leisure time.

3 *Maureen works more hours.* If Maureen works 43 hours instead of 36 hours, she sacrifices 7 hours of leisure time but earns a total of $516, compared to only $360 at a wage of $10 per hour.

Empirical studies of the labor market confirm that each of these responses is reasonable. When the wage increases, some people work more, others work less, and others work about the same amount. In most labor markets, the average number of hours per worker doesn't change very much as the wage changes because the increases in work hours from people like Maureen are nearly offset by decreases in work hours from people like Lester. *Related to Exercise 2.6.*

SOURCE: Ronald Ehrenberg and Robert Smith, *Modern Labor Economics* (Boston: Pearson Addison Wesley, 2005).

The Market Supply Curve for Labor

Now that we know how individual workers respond to changes in wages, we're ready to consider the supply side of the labor market. The **market supply curve for labor** shows the relationship between the wage and the quantity of labor supplied. In Figure 17.3, the market supply curve for labor is positively sloped, consistent with the law of supply: There is a positive relationship between the wage (the price of labor) and the quantity of labor supplied, *ceteris paribus*. An increase in the wage affects the quantity of nursing supplied in three ways:

- **market supply curve for labor**
  A curve showing the relationship between the wage and the quantity of labor supplied.

1 *Hours worked per employee.* When the wage increases, some nurses will work more hours, some will work fewer hours, and some will work the same number of hours. We don't know for certain whether the average number of work hours will increase, decrease, or stay the same, but the change in the average number of hours worked is likely to be relatively small.

2 *Occupational choice.* An increase in the nursing wage will cause some workers to switch from other occupations to nursing and motivate more new workers to pick nursing over other occupations.

381

► **FIGURE 17.3**

Supply, Demand, and Labor Market Equilibrium

At the market equilibrium shown by point *a*, the wage is $15 per hour and the quantity of labor is 16,000 hours. The quantity supplied equals the quantity demanded, so there is neither excess demand for labor nor excess supply of labor.

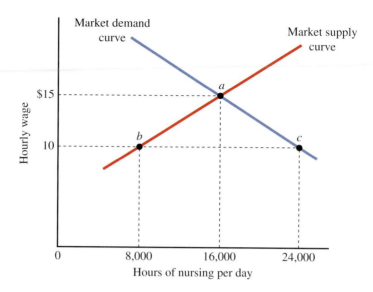

3 *Migration.* Some nurses in other cities will move to Florence to earn the higher wages offered there.

The second and third effects reinforce one another, so an increase in the wage causes movement upward along the market supply curve. If the wage of Florence nurses increases from $10 to $15 per hour, the quantity of nurses supplied increases from 8,000 hours per day (point *b*) to 16,000 hours per day (point *a*). Although individual workers may not work more hours as the wage increases, the supply curve is positively sloped because an increase in the wage changes workers' occupational choices and causes migration.

17.3 | LABOR MARKET EQUILIBRIUM

We're ready to put demand and supply together to think about equilibrium in the labor market. A market equilibrium is a situation in which there is no pressure to change the price of a good or service. Figure 17.3 shows the equilibrium in the market for nurses. The supply curve intersects the demand curve at point *a*, so the equilibrium wage is $15 per hour and the equilibrium quantity is 16,000 hours of nursing per day. At this wage, there is neither an excess demand for labor nor an excess supply of labor, so the market has reached an equilibrium.

Changes in Demand and Supply

How would a change in the demand for nurses affect the equilibrium wage of nurses? We know from Chapter 4 that a change in demand causes the equilibrium price and the equilibrium quantity to move in the same direction: An increase in demand increases the equilibrium price and quantity, whereas a decrease in demand decreases the equilibrium price and quantity. For example, suppose that the demand for medical care increases. Nurses help to provide medical care, so an increase in the quantity of medical care demanded will shift the demand curve for nurses to the right: At each wage, firms will demand more hours of nursing services. As shown in Figure 17.4, an increase in demand increases the equilibrium wage and the equilibrium quantity of nursing services.

How would a change in supply of nurses affect the equilibrium wage of nurses? We know from Chapter 4 that a change in supply causes price and quantity to move in opposite directions: An increase in supply decreases the equilibrium price but increases the equilibrium quantity, whereas a decrease in supply

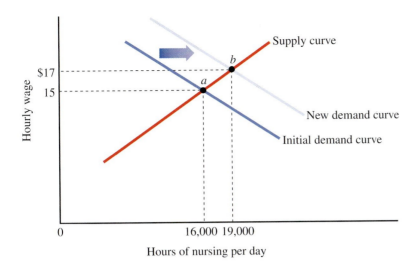

◀ **FIGURE 17.4**
The Market Effect of an Increase in Demand for Labor
An increase in the demand for nursing services shifts the demand curve to the right, moving the equilibrium from point *a* to point *b*. The equilibrium wage increases from $15 to $17 per hour, and the equilibrium quantity increases from 16,000 hours to 19,000 hours.

increases the equilibrium price but decreases the equilibrium quantity. Suppose a new television program makes nursing look like an attractive occupation, causing a large number of young people to become nurses rather than accountants, lawyers, or doctors. The supply curve for nurses will shift to the right: At each wage, more nursing hours will be supplied. The equilibrium wage will decrease, and the equilibrium quantity will increase.

The Market Effects of the Minimum Wage

We can use the model of the labor market to show how various public policies, such as the federally mandated minimum wage, affect total employment. In 2006, the federal minimum wage was $5.15 per hour. Figure 17.5 shows the effects of a minimum wage on the market for restaurant workers. The market equilibrium is shown by point *a*: The supply of restaurant workers equals demand at a wage of $4.70 and a quantity of 50,000 worker hours per day. Suppose a minimum wage is established at $5.15 per hour. At this wage, the quantity of labor demanded is only 49,000 hours (point *b* on the demand curve). In other words, the minimum wage decreases the quantity of labor restaurants use by 1,000 hours per day.

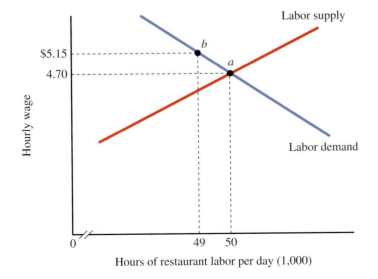

◀ **FIGURE 17.5**
The Market Effects of a Minimum Wage
The market equilibrium is shown by point *a*: The wage is $4.70 per hour, and the quantity of labor is 50,000 hours. A minimum wage of $5.15 decreases the quantity of labor demanded to 49,000 hours per day (point *b*). Although some workers receive a higher wage, others lose their jobs or work fewer hours.

APPLICATION

CODES OF CONDUCT AND LIVING WAGES

APPLYING THE CONCEPTS #2: Does a living wage have the same effects as a minimum wage?

In recent years, several widely publicized reports have documented poor working conditions and low wages in foreign factories that produce shoes, soccer balls, clothing, and toys for U.S. corporations. On college campuses, the United Students Against Sweatshops developed a code of conduct for companies that produce products bearing university logos. The code requires the companies to follow local laws concerning child labor, workplace safety, and minimum wages. The code also calls for producers to pay a "living wage," defined as a wage high enough to support a family.

How will a "living wage" affect overseas workers who produce T-shirts with a university logo? An increase in the wage will increase the cost of producing T-shirts, so the price of T-shirts will increase. Consumers will respond to the higher price by purchasing fewer T-shirts, consistent with the law of demand. Firms will produce fewer T-shirts, so they will employ fewer workers. In other words, a living wage is similar to a minimum wage in its effects on labor income: Some workers will earn higher wages, but others will lose their jobs.

Is there any way to avoid job losses when the wage increases? One possibility is that consumers are willing to pay a higher price for goods that are produced by living-wage workers. In this case, the increase in the price of shirts would cause a smaller decrease in the quantity of T-shirts demanded, so fewer workers would lose their jobs. Given the uncertainty about how much more consumers are willing to pay for living-wage products, it is difficult to predict the actual effects of living wages on overseas workers.
Related to Exercises 3.5 and 3.7.

What are the trade-offs associated with the minimum wage? For restaurant workers and restaurant diners, there is good news and bad news:

- *Good news for some restaurant workers.* Some workers keep their jobs and receive a higher wage ($5.15 per hour instead of $4.70 per hour).

- *Bad news for some restaurant workers.* Some workers lose their jobs. If the typical workday for restaurant workers is five hours, the loss of 1,000 hours of restaurant work per day translates into a loss of 200 jobs.

- *Bad news for diners.* The increase in the wage increases the cost of producing restaurant meals, increasing the price of meals.

There are winners and losers from the minimum wage. Workers who keep their jobs gain at the expense of other workers and at the expense of diners. A recent study suggests that a 10-percent increase in the minimum wage decreases the number of minimum wage jobs by about 1 percent.[2]

APPLICATION

3

TRADE-OFFS FROM IMMIGRATION

APPLYING THE CONCEPTS #3: Who benefits from the immigration of low-skilled workers?

Since about 1850, international migration has played an important role in labor markets. In the first wave of immigration, from 1850 to 1913, over a million people migrated to the Americas each year. Most of the immigrants were from European countries. After several decades of war and economic depressions, massive immigration resumed in 1945, and most of the immigrants were from less-developed countries. The most recent wave of immigration started in 1990 and has increased the supply of labor to the U.S. economy by about 10 percent per decade.

Immigration creates winners and losers within the economy. The increase in the supply of labor decreases wages for the native workers who have the same skill level as the immigrants. Because the average U.S. immigrant has less education and earns less income than the average native, immigrants compete with low-skill natives, decreasing their wages. On the benefit side, the decrease in the wages of low-skill labor decreases production costs and product prices, so consumers benefit. In general, we expect low-skill workers to lose as a result of immigration because the lower wages will dominate the benefits of lower consumer prices. In contrast, we expect high-skill workers to benefit from lower prices.

Economists have estimated the net effect of immigration on the U.S. economy. George Borjas shows that immigration to the United States has a small positive effect, with the losses in wages of low-skilled workers more than offset by gains to consumers and firms. This conclusion is consistent with the idea that exchange increases efficiency and the size of the overall economic pie. Studies of the most recent wave of immigration suggest that immigration decreases the wages of high-school dropouts and other low-skilled workers. *Related to Exercises 3.6 and 3.8.*

SOURCES: George Borjas, "The Economics of Immigration," *Journal of Economic Literature*, vol. 32 (1994), pp. 1667–1717; George Borjas, "The Labor Demand Curve Is Downward Sloping: Reexamining the Impact of Immigration on the Labor Market," *Quarterly Journal of Economics*, vol. 108 (2003), pp. 1335–1374; Gianmarco Ottaviano and Giovanni Peri, "Rethinking the Gains from Immigration: Theory and Evidence from the U.S.," NBER Working Paper 11672 (2005).

17.4 | EXPLAINING DIFFERENCES IN WAGES AND INCOME

Now that we know how the equilibrium wage for a particular occupation is determined, we're ready to explain why wages vary from one job to another. Let's think about why some occupations pay more than others, why women earn less than men, and why college graduates earn more than high-school graduates.

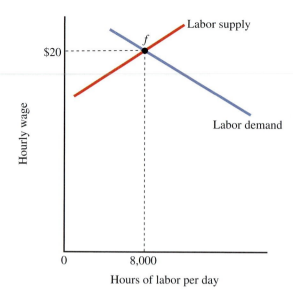

Why Do Wages Differ Across Occupations?

There is substantial variation in wages across occupations. Most professional athletes earn more than medical doctors, who earn more than college professors, who earn more than janitors. We'll see that the wage for a particular occupation will be high if the supply of workers in that occupation is small relative to the demand for those workers. This is shown in Figure 17.6, where the supply curve intersects the demand curve at a high wage. The supply of workers in a particular occupation could be small for four reasons:

1 *Few people with the required skills.* To play professional baseball, people must be able to hit balls thrown at them at about 90 miles per hour. The few people who have this skill are paid a lot of money, because baseball owners compete with one another for skillful players, bidding up the wage. The same logic applies to other professional athletes, musicians, and actors. The few people who have the skills required for these occupations are paid high wages.

2 *High training costs.* The skills required for some occupations can only be acquired through education and training. For example, the skills that are required of a medical doctor can only be acquired in medical school, and legal skills can only be acquired in law school. If it is costly to acquire these skills, a relatively small number of people will become skilled, and they will receive high wages. The higher wage compensates workers for their training costs.

3 *Undesirable working conditions.* Some occupations have undesirable working conditions, and workers demand higher wages as compensation. Wages are higher for jobs that are dangerous, dirty, stressful, or require people to work at odd hours.

4 *Artificial barriers to entry.* As we'll see in the next chapter, government and professional licensing boards restrict the number of people in certain occupations, and labor unions restrict their membership. These supply restrictions increase wages.

The Gender Pay Gap

Why do women, on average, earn less than men? In the United States, the typical woman earns about 75 percent as much as the typical man. The gender gap is smaller in European nations but much larger in Japan. An important factor in the gender gap is the concentration of women in occupations that pay low wages. Given the distribution of men and women in different occupations, about half of female workers would have to change occupations to achieve equal gender representation in all occupations.[3] A recent study explored several factors that contribute to the gender pay gap.[4] The

APPLICATION

WAGE PREMIUMS FOR DANGEROUS JOBS

APPLYING THE CONCEPTS #4: Do dangerous occupations pay higher wages?

Workers who choose dangerous occupations receive high wages, so they are compensated for the danger associated with their jobs. The workers with the greatest risk of losing their lives on the job are lumberjacks, boiler-makers, taxicab drivers, and mine workers. To compensate for the higher risk of getting killed on the job, steelworkers receive a wage premium of 3.7 percent. In the United States, the average job fatality rate is 1 in 25,000 workers per year. For a worker who faces twice the average fatality rate, the wage is about 1 percent higher.

The same logic applies to occupations with other undesirable features. The wage premium for jobs with an annual injury rate of 2 percent is 1.15 percent for men and 3.68 percent for women. Workers receive higher wages for night shifts, jobs in noisy environments, and jobs that cause mental stress, in part because stress contributes to health problems such as heart disease and stroke. *Related to Exercise 4.5.*

SOURCES: Craig Olson, "An Analysis of Wage Differentials Received by Workers on Dangerous Jobs," *Journal of Human Resources*, vol. 16, Spring 1981, pp. 167–185; John Leeth and John Ruser, "Compensating Wage Differentials for Fatal and Nonfatal Injury Risk by Gender and Race," *Journal of Risk and Uncertainty*, vol. 27 (2003), pp. 257–277; Michael French and Laura Dunlap, "Compensating Wage Differentials for Job Stress," *Applied Economics*, vol. 30 (1998), pp. 1067–1075; Ronald Ehrenberg and Robert Smith, *Modern Labor Economics* (Boston: Pearson Addison Wesley, 2005).

study observed a gap of about 20 percent among workers aged 26 to 34. The study identified four factors that contribute to the gender gap:

- *Difference in worker skills and productivity.* On average, women have less education and work experience, so they are less productive and thus receive lower wages. An important factor in the lower-than-men-level of work experience among women is that many women interrupt their careers to raise children. The study concluded that lower productivity is the most important factor in the gender gap.

- *Differences in occupational preferences.* Wages vary across occupations: Clerical and service occupations receive lower wages than craft and professional occupations. Compared to men, women express stronger preferences for low-wage occupations, such as clerical and service occupations, and weaker preferences for some high-wage occupations, such as craft and operator occupations. In contrast, women have slightly stronger preferences for high-wage professional and technical occupations. On balance, the general orientation of women toward low-wage occupations contributes to the gender gap.

- *Occupational discrimination.* Given the variation in wages across occupations, if employers have a bias against hiring women for high-paying occupations, women will receive lower wages. The study shows that on average, women are less successful than men in attaining their desired occupations, and this occupational discrimination by employers explains between 7 and 25 percent of the gender gap.

• *Wage discrimination.* If employers pay women less than their equally productive male counterparts, women's wages will be lower. The results of the study on this issue are mixed, with some evidence that wage discrimination is a significant factor in the gender pay gap.

The general conclusion of the study is that differences in productivity and occupational status are the most important factors in the gender pay gap. It appears that the relatively large number of women in low-paying occupations results both from the occupational preferences of women and employer discrimination that inhibits occupational attainment for women.

Racial Discrimination

What about differences in earnings by race? In 1995, African American males who worked full time earned 73 percent as much as their white counterparts earned, while African American females earned 86 percent as much as their white counterparts. Hispanic males earned 62 percent as much as white males, while Hispanic females earned 73 percent as much as white females.[5] For both males and females, part of the earnings gap is caused by differences in productivity: On average, whites have more education and work experience, so they are paid higher wages. Part of the wage gap is caused by racial discrimination. Some African American and Hispanic workers are paid lower wages for similar jobs, and others are denied opportunities to work in some high-paying jobs.

How much of the earnings gap is caused by discrimination? A recent study suggests that racial discrimination decreases the wages of African American men by about 13 percent.[6] Another study shows that these earnings differences have decreased over the last few decades and that the differences are now small enough that "most of the disparity in earnings between blacks and whites in the labor market of the 1990s is due to the differences in skills they bring to the market, and not to discrimination within the labor market."[7] The differences in skills brought to the labor market are caused by a number of factors, including past discrimination that has inhibited the acquisition of job skills and differences in educational opportunities. For example, in urban areas about one-third of African American high-school students have above-average scores on reading and math exams, compared to about two-thirds of white students.

Why Do College Graduates Earn Higher Wages?

In 2002, the typical college graduate earned roughly twice as much as the typical high-school graduate. There are two explanations for the college premium.

The first explanation is based on supply and demand analysis. A college education provides the skills necessary to enter certain occupations, so a college graduate has more job options than a high-school graduate. Both high-school grads and college grads can fill jobs that require only a high-school education, so the supply of workers for these low-skill jobs is plentiful, and the equilibrium wage for these jobs is low. In contrast, there is a smaller supply of workers for jobs that require a college education, so the wages in these high-skill jobs are higher than the wages for low-skill jobs. This is the **learning effect** of a college education: College students learn the skills required for certain occupations, increasing their human capital.

• **learning effect**
The increase in a person's wage resulting from the learning of skills required for certain occupations.

The second explanation of the college premium requires a different perspective on college and its role in the labor market. Suppose certain skills are required for a particular job, but an employer cannot determine whether a prospective employee has these skills. For example, most managerial jobs require the employee to manage time efficiently, but it is impossible for an employer to determine whether a prospective employee is a good manager of time. Suppose that these skills are also required to complete a college degree. For example, to get passing grades in all your classes, you must be able to use your time efficiently. When you

APPLICATION

LAKISHA WASHINGTON VERSUS EMILY WALSH

APPLYING THE CONCEPTS #5: How does racial discrimination affect the labor market?

Imagine that two recent high-school graduates apply for low-skill jobs advertised in the newspaper. The jobs include waiting tables, dishwashing, and working in warehouses. One man is white and admits to serving 18 months in prison for selling cocaine. The other applicant is an African American man without a criminal record. Which applicant has a greater chance of being called back for a second interview? In a carefully designed experiment with college students posing as job applicants, the white applicant with a criminal record was called back 17 percent of the time, while the crime-free African American applicant was called back only 14 percent of the time. In other words, the study implies that the disadvantage of being African American is roughly equivalent to the disadvantage of spending 18 months in prison.

This experiment in Milwaukee revealed substantial racial discrimination in hiring for low-skill jobs. According to Devah Pager, the researcher who conducted the experiment,

> *In these low-wage, entry-level markets, race remains a huge barrier. Affirmative-action pressures aren't operating here. Employers don't spend a lot of time screening applicants. They want a quick signal whether the applicant seems suitable. Stereotypes among young black men remain so prevalent and so strong that race continues to serve as a major signal of characteristics of which employers are wary.*

In another experiment, economists responded in writing to help-wanted ads in Chicago and in Boston, using hypothetical names that were likely to be identified by employers as either white or African American. Applicants named Greg Kelly or Emily Walsh were 50 percent more likely to be called for interviews than those named Jamal Jackson or Lakisha Washington. Having a white-sounding name on an application was equivalent to about eight additional years of work experience. The researchers experimented with different resumes for both types of applicants. Adding work experience and computer skills increased the likelihood of interviews by 30 percent for white-sounding applicants but only 9 percent for those whose names suggested an African American background. ***Related to Exercise 4.6.***

SOURCE: David Wessel, "Racial Discrimination Is Still at Work in U.S.," *Wall Street Journal*, September 4, 2003, p. A2.

get a college degree, firms will conclude that you have some of the skills they require, so they may hire you instead of a high-school graduate. This is the **signaling effect** of a college education: People who complete college provide a signal to employers about their skills. This second explanation suggests that colleges simply provide a testing ground where students can reveal their skills to potential employers.

• **signaling effect**
The information about a person's work skills conveyed by completing college.

389

Over the last three decades, this wage gap, or "college premium," has almost doubled. The most important factor in doubling the college premium is technological change. Changes in technology have increased the demand for college graduates relative to the demand for other workers. In all sectors of the economy, firms are switching to sophisticated machinery and equipment that require highly skilled workers. Consequently, the share of jobs that require a college education has increased steadily, increasing the demand for college graduates. Of course, the supply of college graduates has increased, too, but not by as much as demand. Because the increase in demand is large relative to the increase in supply, the wages of college graduates have increased. Another factor in the growing college premium is the pace of technological change. Workers with more education can more easily learn new skills and new jobs, so firms are willing to pay more for college graduates.

17.5 | THE DISTRIBUTION OF INCOME

In 2004, the median household income in the United States was $44,389—half of households earned more income and half earned less. There is substantial variation in household income, with some households earning much more and others earning much less. In this part of the chapter, we'll discuss the extent of income inequality in the United States and explore some of the reasons why the households with the highest income are receiving a larger share of total income.

Income Distribution Facts

Income can be measured in different ways, and two income measures are relevant for our discussion. *Market income* is defined as all earnings received from labor and capital markets. It includes wages and salaries, as well as earnings from bonds, stocks, and real estate. *Disposable income* equals market income, plus government transfers, minus taxes paid. The transfers include income supplements, Social Security payments, food stamps, and housing assistance. The taxes include state and federal income and payroll taxes, as well as local property taxes.

Table 17.2 shows the distributions of income before and after the effects of government transfer programs and taxes. To compute the numbers in the second column of the table (Percent of Market Income), we take four steps:

1 Rank the nation's households according to market income: The household with the highest income is at the top of the list, and the household with the lowest income is at the bottom of the list.

2 Divide the households into five groups, or "quintiles": The lowest fifth includes the poorest 20 percent of households (the lowest 20% of the list), the second fifth is the next poorest 20 percent, and so on.

3 Compute each group's income by adding up the income received by all the households in the group.

4 Compute each group's percentage of total income (the number in the third column of the table) by dividing the group's income by the nation's total income.

Table 17.2 | SHARES OF INCOME EARNED BY DIFFERENT U.S. GROUPS, 2004

Income Group	Percent of Market Income	Percent of Disposable Income
Lowest fifth	1.48%	4.68%
Second fifth	7.36	10.34
Middle fifth	14.10	16.08
Fourth fifth	23.63	24.02
Highest fifth	53.44	44.88

SOURCE: U.S. Census Bureau, *The Effects of Government Taxes and Transfers on Income and Poverty: 2004.*

By repeating this process for disposable income, we can compute the numbers in the third column of the table.

Consider first the distribution of market income, shown in the second column of Table 17.2. The lowest fifth earns only 1.48 percent of the total market income, while the highest fifth earns over half the total market income. If we combine the lowest two fifths, the lowest 40 percent of households earn only 8.84 percent of total market income. Three key factors explain these substantial differences in market income:

1 *Differences in labor skills and effort.* Some people have better labor skills—more human capital—than others, so they earn higher wages. Labor skills are determined by innate ability and education. In addition, some people work longer hours or at more demanding jobs, so they earn more income.

2 *Luck and misfortune.* Some people are luckier than others in investing their money, starting a business, or picking an occupation. Among the unlucky people are those who develop health problems that make it difficult to earn income. Among the lucky people are those who inherit wealth and earn income by investing the inherited wealth.

3 *Discrimination.* Some people are paid lower wages or have limited opportunities for education and work because of their race or gender.

Consider next the distribution of disposable income, which includes the effects of government redistribution and tax polices. Going from market income to disposable income, the largest changes occur at the top and the bottom of the income distribution. The share of the lowest fifth increases by just over 3 percentage points, while the share of the highest fifth decreases by almost 9 percentage points. In other words, government transfer and tax policies reduce income inequality.

Recent Changes in the Distribution of Income

Table 17.3 shows the changes in the distribution of money income (total pretax cash income) between 1970 and 2004. The share of the top fifth rose from 43.3 to 50.0 percent, while the share of every other group dropped. By historical standards, these changes in the distribution of income were very rapid. What caused these changes in the distribution in money income?

It appears that the most important reason for growing inequality is what labor economists call an "increase in the demand for skill."[8] In the labor market, the demand for highly skilled (highly educated) workers has increased relative to the demand for less-skilled (less-educated) workers. As a result, the wage gap between the two groups has widened. As we saw at the beginning of the chapter, in the last three decades the college premium has increased significantly. At the same time, the premium for advanced degrees increased. Finally, the dropout penalty (the wage gap between high-school graduates and dropouts) has nearly doubled.

Table 17.3 | CHANGES IN U.S. INCOME SHARES, 1970–2001

Year	Lowest Fifth	Second Fifth	Third Fifth	Fourth Fifth	Highest Fifth
2004	3.4%	8.7%	14.8%	23.0%	50.0%
2000	3.6	8.9	14.8	23.0	49.8
1995	3.7	9.1	15.2	23.3	48.7
1990	3.9	9.6	15.9	24.0	46.6
1985	4.0	9.7	16.3	24.6	45.3
1980	4.3	10.3	16.9	24.9	43.7
1975	4.4	10.5	17.1	24.8	43.2
1970	4.1	10.8	17.4	24.5	43.3

SOURCE: U.S. Bureau of the Census, *Current Population Reports, Selected years.*

Why did the demand for skill increase over the last three decades? There are two main reasons:

- **Technological change.** Advances in technology have simultaneously decreased the demand for less-educated workers and increased the demand for college graduates and people with advanced degrees. While the new technology has made it possible to replace many low-skilled workers with "smart" machines and computers, it has increased the demand for workers who have the education and skills required to produce the new technology and use it.

- **Increased international trade.** An increase in international trade means more exports and imports. Trade allows developed countries like the United States to easily export goods produced with high-skilled labor and import goods produced with low-skilled labor. As a result, the expansion of international trade in the last three decades has increased the demand for high-skilled workers and decreased the demand for low-skilled workers in the United States.

Economists have not yet reached a consensus on the relative importance of these two factors.

Changes in the Top End of Income Distribution: 1920–1998

Figure 17.7 shows the trends in the income shares of the several groups at the top of the income distribution. The upper line shows the share for the top decile (top 10 percent) of income earners. The income share was just over 40 percent in 1917 and just under 45 percent at the start of World War II. The share plunged during the war and leveled out in the postwar period at about 33 percent. The share started increasing in 1970, rising from 32 to 42 percent by 1998. The middle line shows the income share for the top 5 percent of earners. It follows a similar pattern, with lower shares after the war, a long period of relative stability, and then increases starting in 1970. The lower line, showing the income share for the top 1 percent of the distribution, shows a similar pattern.

What caused these patterns? Recent studies of the trends for the top decile generated the following observations[9]:

1 During World War II, the income share of the top decile decreased because government wage controls compressed wages. In addition, the government increased tax rates on invested money (stock dividends, interest earnings, and entrepreneurial income) to support the war effort, and these rates remained relatively high until the 1980s. The higher tax rates decreased the return that could be earned on investments and slowed the rate at which fortunes were amassed.

► **FIGURE 17.7**

Top Income Distribution Shares, 1920–1998

SOURCE: Author's computation based on Thomas Piketly and Emmanuel Sace, "Income Inequality in the United States, 1913–1998," Quarterly Journal of Economics, 118 (2003), pp. 1–39.

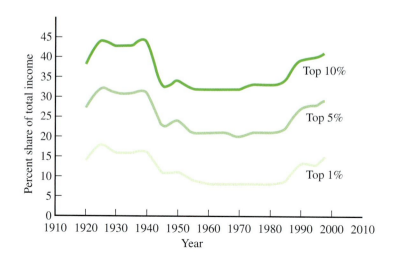

2 The stability of the income share in the period 1945–1970 is puzzling because one would expect wages to rebound after wage controls ended following World War II. During this time period, there *was* a postwar rebound in top-decile wages in France and other countries, but not in the United States.

3 Between 1920 and 1998, the share of income from wages increased at the expense of income from investments. For the top decile, the share of income from wages rose from 58 to 84 percent. For the top 1 percent, the wage share rose from 42 to 70 percent.

4 The increase in the income shares since 1970 has been caused by rapid increases in the compensation of the highest-wage workers—the executives of large corporations and other organizations. Most of the action in the top decile is in the top 1 percent of earners, and most of the action at the top is in rising wages, not increases in investment income. After adjusting for inflation, the salaries of top executives increased by about 6 percent per year in the 1990s, much more rapidly than average salaries.

5 Chief executives in the United States are paid much more than their counterparts in other developed nations. For example, U.S. executives receive three to four times more than their counterparts in Britain, Germany, and France. In the United States, the average pay for a chief executive is 24 times the pay of the average production worker. In Germany, the average executive is paid only eight times as much as the average production worker.

6 The U.S. experience in the last 30 years contrasts sharply with that of France, where the income share of the top decile actually decreased between 1970 and 1998, from 33 to 32 percent.

17.6 | POVERTY AND PUBLIC POLICY

The U.S. government defines a poor household as one with a total income less than the amount required to satisfy the "minimum needs" of the household. The government estimates a minimum food budget for each type of household and multiplies the food budget by three to get the official poverty budget. A household with income lower than the official poverty budget is considered poor. In 2004, the poverty budget was $15,067 for a three-person household and $19,307 for a four-person household, compared to a median income of $44,389. In 2004, almost 37 million people were below the poverty line, or 12.7 percent of the population.

Poverty Rates for Different Groups

Table 17.4 shows the incidence of poverty among different groups of people. For each group, the poverty rate equals the percentage of people in that group who live in households with incomes lower than the official poverty budget. In 2004, the overall poverty rate was 12.7 percent, and there was substantial variation in poverty rates among the listed groups:

1 *Race.* The poverty rates for both blacks and Hispanics are more than twice the poverty rates for whites.

2 *Type of family.* The poverty rate for female-headed households is about five times the poverty rate for households headed by a married couple.

3 *Age.* One of the successes in the war on poverty has been the decrease in poverty among the aged; their poverty rate dropped from 35 percent in 1959 to 9.8 percent in 2004, largely as a result of increased Social Security benefits. About one-sixth of children lived in poverty in 2004, with much higher poverty rates for racial minorities.

Table 17.4 | POVERTY RATES FOR DIFFERENT GROUPS, 2004

Characteristic	Poverty Rate in 2004
All	12.7%
Race	
White	10.8
Black	24.7
Hispanic	21.9
Asian	9.8
Type of Family	
Married couple	5.5
Female-headed household	28.4
Age	
Under 18 years	17.8
65 years and older	9.8

SOURCE: U.S. Census Bureau, *Poverty in the United States* (2004).

Education is a key factor in determining wages, and poverty rates are lower for more-educated workers. As we saw earlier in the chapter, college graduates earn roughly twice as much as high-school graduates. The poverty rate for college graduates is 3 percent, compared to 9 percent for high-school graduates. For high-school dropouts, the poverty rate is 22 percent.

Redistribution Programs for the Poor

• **means-tested program**
A government spending program that provides assistance to those whose income falls below a certain level.

The government uses a number of programs to provide assistance to the poor. These programs, broadly defined as "welfare programs," are **means-tested programs**, meaning that only people whose incomes fall below a certain level receive assistance. These programs reduce the poverty rate by a substantial margin. In 2004, the poverty rate based on market income—before accounting for government tax and spending programs—was 19.4 percent. The poverty rates shown in Table 17.4 incorporate the effects of cash transfers to poor households, indicating that cash transfers decreased the overall poverty rate from 19.4 to 12.7 percent. As a final calculation, we can compute poverty rates for disposable income, which includes taxes as well as the value of noncash programs, such as food stamps. With this definition of income, the poverty rate is 10.6 percent. To summarize, government tax and spending programs reduced the 2004 poverty rate from 19.4 to 10.6 percent.

Table 17.5 shows the government expenditures on means-tested programs in 2002. As shown in the second row, cash assistance is responsible for only about one-fifth of total spending, while medical care makes up over half of total spending.

Welfare Reform and TANF

In 1996, the overhaul of federal antipoverty programs ended decades of policy based on the notion that poor families are entitled to cash and in-kind assistance. The Personal Responsibility and Work Opportunity Reconciliation Act of 1996 eliminated the entitlement of poor families to receive cash assistance. The federal government now provides block grants to states to provide Temporary Aid to Needy Families (TANF), with restrictions on what recipients must do to qualify for assistance and limits on how long they can receive assistance:

• A recipient must participate in work activities, defined as employment, on-the-job training, work experience, community service, or vocational training.

• After a total of 60 months of cash assistance (consecutive or nonconsecutive), assistance stops. States can allow exceptions to the 60-month rule for up to 20 percent of recipients.

Table 17.5 | EXPENDITURES ON MEANS-TESTED PROGRAMS, 2002

	Spending ($ billion)		
	Federal	*State and Local*	*Total*
Medical care	$164	$119	$282
Cash aid	82	20	102
Food benefits	37	2	39
Housing aid	35	1	36
Education	29	2	30
Services	18	5	22
Jobs/training	7	1	8
Energy aid	2	0	2
Total	**373**	**149**	**522**

SOURCE: Vee Burke, *Cash and Noncash Benefits for Persons with Limited Income*, Congressional Research Service (2003).

The general thrust of welfare reform was to change an entitlement program into a program that requires work in exchange for time-limited assistance.

In the years since welfare reform was implemented, the number of people receiving assistance has decreased dramatically. Between 1994 and 2002, the national welfare caseload dropped by over 50 percent, and the employment of single mothers increased. During this period, the economy grew rapidly, increasing employment opportunities for all households. Although the rapidly growing economy was partly responsible for the reduction in welfare caseloads, the implementation of TANF certainly played a role in reducing the number of people on welfare. It also was an important factor in reducing poverty among children, from 23 percent in 1993 to 18 percent in 2004.[10]

Welfare and Work Incentives

How does cash assistance to the poor affect their incentives to work? Two features of an assistance program affect work incentives. The first feature is the base cash payment. The larger the amount provided as a base—the payment to someone who earns no market income—the lower the incentive to work to supplement the base income. There is considerable variation across states in the base payment. In Alabama, the monthly payment for a single-parent family of three is $164, compared to $801 in Minnesota.[11]

The second feature that affects work incentives is the benefit reduction rate for market income. When a recipient earns market income, the welfare payment decreases. For example, if the benefit reduction rate is 40 percent, each dollar of market income reduces the welfare payment by $0.40, so the net income from a dollar of market income is $0.60. There is considerable variation across states in benefit reduction rates. In about a third of states, the benefit reduction rate is 100 percent: Each dollar of market income reduces the welfare payment by a dollar. California allows recipients to earn $225 without any benefit reduction, and each additional dollar reduces the welfare payment by 50 cents. About one-third of states have reduction rates of 50 percent or less. The larger the reduction rate, the lower the payoff for each hour of market income, and the lower the incentive to earn additional income. There is evidence that in states with relatively large work incentives, welfare recipients work more hours and earn more market income.[12]

SUMMARY

In this chapter, we've seen how wages are determined in perfectly competitive labor markets and why wages differ from one occupation to another. We've also looked at the distribution of income in the United States and explored possible reasons for growing inequality. Here are the main points of the chapter:

1 The *long-run demand curve for labor* is negatively sloped because the output and input-substitution effects operate in the same direction: An increase in the wage decreases labor per unit of output and decreases the total output produced.

2 An increase in the wage triggers *income* and *substitution effects* that operate in opposite directions, so an increase in the wage has an ambiguous effect on the quantity of labor supplied.

3 The wage in a particular occupation will be relatively high if supply is small relative to demand. This will occur if (1) few people have the skills required for the occupation, (2) training costs are high, or (3) the job is dangerous or stressful.

4 College graduates earn more than high-school graduates because a college education provides new skills and allows people to reveal their skills to employers.

5 The trade-off with a minimum wage is that some workers earn higher income, but others lose their jobs.

6 The wealthiest 20 percent of families in the United States earn about half of total income, while the wealthiest 10 percent earn 42 percent of total income. At the other end of the income distribution, the poorest 20 percent earn only 3.5 percent of total income.

7 Poverty rates are relatively high among African Americans, Hispanics, high-school dropouts, and female-headed households.

KEY TERMS

income effect for leisure demand, p. 380

input-substitution effect, p. 379

learning effect, p. 388

long-run demand curve for labor, p. 379

marginal product of labor, p. 377

marginal-revenue product of labor (*MRP*), p. 377

market supply curve for labor, p. 381

means-tested programs, p. 394

output effect, p. 379

short-run demand curve for labor, p. 377.

signaling effect, p. 389

substitution effect for leisure demand, p. 380

EXERCISES

Visit www.myeconlab.com to complete these exercises online and get instant feedback.

Get Ahead of the Curve

17.1 | The Demand for Labor

1.1 The marginal revenue product of labor equals _____ times _____.

1.2 A profit-maximizing firm will hire the number of workers where _____ equals _____.

1.3 Your favorite professional team is considering hiring a new player for $3 million per year. It will be sensible (profitable) to hire the player if his _____ is greater than the $3 million cost.

1.4 Arrows up or down: The logic of the output effect is that a decrease in the wage will _____ production costs, so the price of output will _____ and the quantity of output demanded will _____. As a result, the quantity of labor demanded will _____.

1.5 The logic of the input-substitution effect is that a decrease in the wage causes the firm to _____.

1.6 The long-run market demand curve for labor is _____ (steeper/flatter) than the short-run market demand curve for labor.

1.7 **Demand for News Kids.** Consider the market for newspaper delivery kids in Kidsville. Each news kid receives a piece rate of $2 per subscriber per month and has a fixed territory that initially has 100 subscribers. The price elasticity of demand for subscriptions is 2.0. Suppose the new city council of Kidsville passes a law that establishes a minimum piece rate of $3 per subscriber per month. As a result, the publisher increases the monthly price of a subscription by 20 percent. How will the new law affect the monthly income of the typical news kid?

1.8 **Demand for Airline Pilots.** Comment on the following: "There is no substitute for an airline pilot: Someone has to fly the plane. Therefore, an increase in the wage of airline pilots will not change the number of pilots used by the airlines."

17.2 | The Supply of Labor

2.1 Arrows up or down: The logic of the substitution effect for leisure is that an increase in the wage _____ the opportunity cost of leisure time, which tends to _____ leisure time and _____ labor time.

2.2 Arrows up or down: The logic of the income effect for leisure is that an increase in the wage _____ real income, and if leisure is a normal good this tends to _____ leisure time and _____ labor time.

2.3 We cannot predict a worker's response to an increase in the wage because the _____ effect and the _____ effect work in _____ direction(s).

2.4 Your objective is to earn exactly $120 per week. If your wage decreases from $6 to $4 per hour, you will respond by working _____ hours instead of _____ hours. In other words, your labor-supply curve is _____ sloped.

2.5 If every worker in a particular occupation works exactly 40 hours per week, regardless of the wage, the individual supply curve is vertical. _____ (True/False)

2.6 **Income and Substitution Effects.** Sabrina works for a workers' cooperative that initially pays her a lump sum of $200 per week (as long as she works at least 15 hours per week) and a wage of $20 per hour of work. She initially works 40 hours per week. Suppose the cooperative changes its pay plan by increasing the lump-sum payment to $280 and decreasing the hourly wage to $18. (Related to Application 1 on page 381.)
   a. If Sabrina continues to work 40 hours per week, how does the change in the pay plan affect her total income?
   b. Use the concepts of the income and substitution effects to predict whether Sabrina will work more hours, fewer hours, or the same number of hours. (*Hint:* Is there an income effect to consider?)

2.7 **City Versus National Carpenter Supply.** Consider two markets for carpenters: the city of Portland and the United States. Draw two supply curves for carpenters: one for the city of Portland and one for the United States. In which market would you expect a more elastic supply of carpenters?

2.8 **Tax Rate and Tax Revenue.** Critically appraise the following statement: "The law of supply says that an increase in price increases the quantity supplied. A decrease in the income tax rate will increase the worker's net wage, so each worker will work more hours. As a result, the revenue from the income tax will increase."

2.9 **Personal Labor Supply.** We discussed the responses of Lester, Sam, and Maureen to a wage increase. Which person's response is closest to your own? If your wage increased, would you work more hours, fewer hours, or about the same number of hours?

17.3 | Labor Market Equilibrium

3.1 Arrows up or down: A decrease in the supply of nurses will _____ the equilibrium wage and _____ the equilibrium quantity of nursing services.

3.2 Arrows up or down: An increase in the demand for nursing services will _____ the equilibrium wage and _____ the equilibrium quantity of nursing services.

3.3 A minimum wage for restaurant workers brings good news to _____, but bad news to _____ and _____.

3.4 Arrows up or down: The immigration of low-skill workers _____ the supply of low-skill labor, which _____ the wages of low-skill natives and _____ consumer prices.

3.5 Arrows up or down: Suppose that a code of conduct for firms producing apparel overseas increases the wage paid to workers. The code will _____ the firms' cost of production, _____ the price of apparel products, _____ the quantity of apparel products demanded, and _____ the quantity of labor demanded. (Related to Application 2 on page 384.)

3.6 The immigration of low-skill workers generates net benefits for _____ workers because they benefit from lower _____ without bearing the cost associated with lower _____. (Related to Application 3 on page 385.)

3.7 **Living Wage and Labor Income.** Consider a university that has sweatshirts bearing its logo produced overseas by a contractor who initially pays a wage of $8 per sweatshirt and has other costs of $12 per sweatshirt, resulting in a price of $20 per sweatshirt. At this price, the university sells 100 sweatshirts per week. Suppose a student group succeeds in getting the contractor to increase the wage to $10 per shirt and the other costs of production don't change. (Related to Application 2 on page 384.)
   a. The price per sweatshirt will increase from _____ to _____, an increase of _____ percent.
   b. Suppose the price elasticity of demand for the university's sweatshirts is 3.0. At the higher price, a total of _____ sweatshirts will be purchased and the total spending on sweatshirt labor (total labor income) will change from $_____ to $_____.

c. Suppose consumers are willing to pay a higher price for sweatshirts made by workers receiving a higher wage. How would this change the numbers in part (b)? Provide an example in which the higher wage actually increases the total spending on sweatshirt labor.

3.8 Wage and Price Effects of Immigration. In the initial equilibrium in the market for farm workers, the wage is $10 per hour. The elasticity of supply of farm workers is 2.0, and the elasticity of demand for farm workers is 1.0. Suppose that immigration increases the supply of farm workers by 12 percent: The supply curve shifts to the right by 12 percent. (Related to Application 3 on page 385.)

a. Use the price-change formula discussed in an earlier chapter on elasticity to compute the change in the equilibrium wage.

b. Suppose that farm workers are responsible for one-fourth of the production cost of food. What are the implications of immigration for the cost of producing food and its price?

3.9 Payroll Tax. You are an economic consultant to a city that just imposed a payroll tax of $1 per hour of work. This payroll tax is paid by workers through a payroll deduction: For each hour of work, the employer deducts $1 and sends the money to the city government. The initial wage (before the tax) is $10, and total employment is 20,000 hours per day. Use a graph to show the effect of the tax on the equilibrium wage and employment.

3.10 Higher Teacher Salaries. Advocates of higher salaries for teachers point out that most teachers have college degrees and that teaching children is an important job.

a. Why aren't teachers' salaries higher, given the importance of the job and the education required?

b. Suppose a new law establishes a minimum teacher salary that is 20 percent higher than the prevailing salary. How would expect this law to affect the average quality of teachers and the taxes paid by the typical household?

17.4 | Explaining Differences in Wages and Income

4.1 The wage for a particular occupation will be relatively low if labor _____ (demand/supply) is small relative to labor _____ (demand/supply).

4.2 If a city has a relatively high crime rate, we would expect the wage for taxi drivers to be relatively _____ (high/low).

4.3 In some countries, it is customary to tip restaurant waiters. We would expect the wages paid to waiters to be _____ (higher/lower/the same) in countries where tips are customary.

4.4 If a worker switches from a relatively safe factory job to a job in a steel mill, the wage will increase by roughly _____ (2/4/10/30) percent.

4.5 Improved Safety and Wages. Consider an occupation that initially has a relatively high rate of nonfatal injuries. The equilibrium wage is $20 per hour, and the equilibrium quantity is 100,000 hours. Suppose a new safety device cuts the injury rate in half, and the supply of labor increases by 12 percent: The labor supply curve shifts to the right by 12 percent. (Related to Application 4 on page 387.)

a. Use a graph to show the effects of the safety device on the equilibrium wage and employment.

b. Suppose the elasticity of supply of labor is 3.0 and the elasticity of demand is 1.0. Use the price-change formula discussed in an earlier chapter on elasticity to compute the change in the equilibrium wage.

c. Suppose the demand curve you've drawn is a long-run demand curve. Explain the roles of the output effect and substitution effect on the change in the quantity of labor demanded.

4.6 Quick Signals from High School. Consider the application, "Lakisha Washington Versus Emily Walsh." According to the researcher, "They (employers) want a quick signal whether the applicant seems suitable." Suppose a firm hiring workers cannot distinguish between high-productivity and low-productivity applicants. But the firm knows whether an applicant graduated from high-school H, where the average achievement level is relatively high, or high-school L, where the average achievement level is relatively low (Related to Application 5 on page 389.).

a. If the firm will hire one of two applicants, one from high-school H and a second from high-school L, which is the better choice?

b. What insights does this exercise provide about why firms are more likely to interview and hire applicants with white-sounding names?

4.7 Waiter Tips and Income. Consider a city where the typical waiter has a five-hour shift and daily "sales" (total bills presented to customers) of $400. The customary tip is 15 percent, so tips add up to $60 per day (15% of $400). The initial wage is $10 per hour, so the typical waiter initially earns $50 in wages paid directly by the restaurant. Suppose a local waiter association runs a successful campaign to get the city's restaurant patrons to increase the average tip from 15 to 20 percent.

a. Use a supply and demand graph with wage (excluding tips) on the vertical axis to show the effects of the new tip rate on the labor market.

b. How will the new tip rate affect the daily income (wages plus tips) of the typical waiter?

17.5 | The Distribution of Income

5.1 Government transfer and tax policies increase the income share of the lowest quintile of the income distribution from about _____ percent to about _____ percent.

5.2 The college premium is defined as the percentage difference between the incomes of _____ and _____. It is currently about _____ percent.

5.3 Arrows up or down: Since 1970, the income share of the top fifth of the income distribution has _____, while the shares of the lowest and middle fifths have _____.

5.4 Arrows up or down: An important factor in growing inequality over the last 30 years is technological change that has _____ the demand for college graduates and _____ the demand for less-educated workers.

17.6 | Poverty and Public Policy

6.1 For each of the following pairs of population groups, indicate which group has a higher poverty rate:
_____ White, _____ Hispanic
_____ White, _____ Asian
_____ Married couple, _____ Female-headed household
_____ Under 18 years, _____ 65 years and older

6.2 Government spending and tax policies reduce the overall poverty rate from roughly _____ (25/20/15/10) percent to roughly _____ (15/10/5/2) percent.

6.3 Cash aid to the poor makes up roughly _____ (90/50/30/20) percent of the total spending on means-tested programs.

6.4 A low-income person receiving cash aid under TANF receives a fixed sum per month for an unlimited length of time. _____ (True/False)

NOTES

1. W. Michael Fox and Beverly J. Fox, "What's Happening to Americans' Income?" *The Southwest Economy, Federal Reserve Bank of Dallas*, Issue 2, 1995, pp. 3–6; *U.S. Bureau of the Census, Statistical Abstract of the United States 2006* (Washington, D.C.: U.S. Government Printing Office, 2006).

2. Victor R. Fuchs, Alan B. Krueger, and James M. Poterba, "Why Do Economists Disagree About Policy? The Role of Beliefs About Parameters and Values," *Journal of Economic Literature*, vol. 36, no. 3 (1998), pp. 1387–1426.

3. Suzanne Bianchi and Daphne Spain, "Women, Work, and Family in America," *Population Bulletin*, vol. 51, no. 3 (1998), pp. 2–48.

4. Eric J. Solberg, "Occupational Assignment, Hiring Discrimination, and the Gender Pay Gap," *Atlantic Economic Journal*, vol. 32 (2004), pp. 11–27.

5. U.S. Department of Labor, *Employment and Earnings* (Washington, D.C.: U.S. Government Printing Office, 1996).

6. William Darity and Patrick Mason, "Evidence on Discrimination in Employment: Codes of Color, Codes of Gender," *Journal of Economic Perspectives*, vol. 12, no. 2 (1998), pp. 63–90.

7. James Heckman, "Detecting Discrimination," *Journal of Economic Perspectives*, vol. 12, no. 2 (1998), pp. 101–116.

8. Finis Welch, "In Defense of Inequality," *American Economic Review*, vol. 89, no. 2 (1999), pp. 1–17.

9. Thomas Piketty and Emmanuel Saez, "Income Inequality in the United States, 1913–1998," *Quarterly Journal of Economics*, vol. 118 (2003), pp. 1–39; Alan Krueger, "Attempting to Explain Income Inequality," *New York Times*, April 4, 2002, p. C2.

10. Rebecca Blank and Robert Schoeni, "Changes in the Distribution of Children's Family Income over the 1990s," *The American Economic Review*, vol. 93 (2003), pp. 304–308.

11. Robert Moffitt, "The Temporary Assistance to Needy Families Program," Working Paper No. 8749, National Bureau of Economic Research (2002).

12. Rebecca Blank and Robert Schoeni, "Changes in the Distribution of Children's Family Income over the 1990s," *The American Economic Review*, vol. 93 (2003), pp. 304–308.

18

Unions, Monopsony, and Imperfect Information

In the early days of the automobile industry, the early 1900s, the prevailing wage for autoworkers was $3 per day. Assembly-line jobs were repetitive and tedious, and the turnover rate of workers was very high. When Henry Ford decided to increase the daily wage for his workers from $3 to $5 in 1914, most observers were baffled. They predicted that Ford's labor costs would be almost twice as high as those of his rivals, so he would lose a lot of money and quickly go out of business. The wage hike appeared to be a great act of generosity but

APPLYING THE CONCEPTS

1 Is there a trade-off between union wages and the number of union jobs?
Truckers Trade Off Wages and Jobs

2 How does competition in the product market affect union wages?
Competition Reduces Trucker Wages

3 Do firms face a positively sloped labor-supply curve?
Pubs and the Labor-Supply Curve

4 When does an increase in the wage increase profit?
Efficiency Wages at Ford Motor Company

very bad business. You can imagine their surprise when Ford's profit doubled from $30 million to $60 million. How was this possible? How can higher wages lead to higher profits?

T his chapter continues our discussion of labor markets, exploring three topics that take us beyond the simple model of perfect competition in the previous chapter. One of the assumptions of perfect competition in the labor market is that each worker acts independently of other workers, taking the market wage as given. In this chapter, we start by explaining how labor unions allow workers to act collectively, controlling the supply of labor and negotiating wages. A second assumption of perfect competition is that each firm takes the wage as given, so a firm can hire an unlimited number of workers at the prevailing market wage. In this chapter, we'll see what happens when a single firm dominates the demand for labor. A third assumption of perfect competition is perfect information: Each firm knows the productivity level of each worker. In this chapter, we see what happens when firms cannot distinguish between workers with different productivities. We'll use the notion of imperfect information in the labor market to explain Henry Ford's puzzling wage hike.

18.1 | LABOR UNIONS

A **labor union** is a group of workers organized to increase job security, improve working conditions, and increase wages and fringe benefits. Acting as a group, union members have some control over the wages and fringe benefits they receive. There are two types of labor unions:

- A **craft union** includes workers with a specific skill or trade in particular occupations, such as plumbers, bakers, or electricians.
- An **industrial union** includes all types of workers from a single industry, such as steelworkers or autoworkers.

Umbrella organizations include many individual unions. The largest of these "unions of unions" is the American Federation of Labor–Congress of Industrial Organizations (AFL-CIO). Unions use **collective bargaining** to negotiate contracts covering wages, fringe benefits, job security, and working conditions.

A Brief History of Labor Unions in the United States

As shown in Panel A of Figure 18.1, about one in eight workers in the United States belongs to a union, down from about one in three workers in the 1950s. The unionization rate is 7.8 percent for private-sector workers, compared to 36.5 percent for public-sector workers. As shown in Panel B, unionization rates are higher in most other industrial countries.

Let's take a brief look at the history of labor organizations in the United States. Labor unions arose largely in response to long work hours and awful working conditions. The long workweek was not new to those who had worked on farms, but the working conditions were. For the early union organizers, the key demands were higher wages, shorter hours, and safer work environments. The main umbrella organizations were the Knights of Labor (founded in 1869) and the AFL (founded in 1886). The CIO (formed in 1935) was a collection of industrial unions that represented semiskilled workers in mass production, including workers in the automobile, rubber, and steel industries. The CIO merged with the AFL in 1955, forming the AFL-CIO.

The states and the federal government have empowered labor unions. The most important labor legislation gave workers the right to form unions, but limited their power:

- The National Labor Relations Act (Wagner Act) of 1935 guaranteed workers the right to join unions and required each firm to bargain with a union formed by a majority of its workers. The National Labor Relations Board (NLRB) was established to conduct certification elections in which workers could pick a union to represent them and to investigate claims that employers violated election rules or refused to negotiate with union officials.

- **labor union**
  A group of workers organized to increase job security, improve working conditions, and increase wages and fringe benefits.

- **craft union**
  A labor organization that includes workers from a particular occupation, for example, plumbers, bakers, or electricians.

- **industrial union**
  A labor organization that includes all types of workers from a single industry, for example, steelworkers or autoworkers.

- **collective bargaining**
  Negotiations between a union and a firm over wages, fringe benefits, job security, and working conditions.

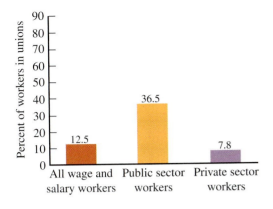

(A) Unionization Rates in the United States, 2002

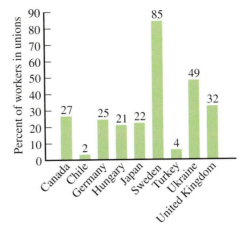

(B) Unionization Rates in OECD Countries, 1994

▲ **FIGURE 18.1**
Unionization Rates in the United States and Other Countries
SOURCES: U.S. Bureau of Labor Statistics; International Labor Organization.

- The Labor Management Relations Act (Taft–Hartley) of 1947 gave government the power to stop strikes that "imperiled the national health or safety" and allowed states to pass **right-to-work laws**. These laws, which are currently in force in 22 states (most in the South, Southwest, and Plains states), make it illegal to require a worker to join a union as a condition of employment.

- The Labor Management Reporting and Disclosure Act (Landrum–Griffin Act) of 1959 was a response to allegations of corruption and misconduct by union officials. This act guaranteed union members the right to fair elections, made it easier for them to monitor union finances, and made the theft of union funds a federal offense.

• **right-to-work laws**
Laws that prohibit union shops, where union membership is required as a condition of employment.

Labor Unions and Wages

There is evidence that unions raise the wages of union workers. For the United States, the consensus is that union workers earn 10 to 20 percent more than nonunion workers doing the same work.[1] Most other industrialized countries have a smaller union wage differential. The differential is 10 percent in the United Kingdom, 8 percent in Canada, and 4 percent in Germany.

What are the trade-offs between wages and employment? Suppose workers in a particular industry form an industrial union and agree on a union wage that exceeds the equilibrium wage. As we saw in the previous chapter, an increase in the wage decreases the quantity of labor demanded because of the output effect and the input-substitution effect.

- *Output effect.* An increase in the wage increases the cost of production, and a firm will pass on the higher cost to consumers by increasing its product price. Consumers respond to the higher price by purchasing a smaller quantity, so the firm will produce less output and employ fewer workers.

- *Input-substitution effect.* An increase in the wage increases the cost of labor relative to the cost of capital, and the firm will substitute capital for labor, reducing the quantity of labor demanded.

Given the trade-off between wages and employment, an increase in the union wage increases the income of the workers who keep their jobs, but also decreases the number of union jobs.

APPLICATION

TRUCKERS TRADE OFF WAGES AND JOBS

APPLYING THE CONCEPTS #1: Is there a trade-off between union wages and the number of union jobs?

In recent decades, the union wage differential has decreased in many industries, including trucking services. Between 1978 and 1996, the union differential decreased from 40 percent to 23 percent. The deregulation of the industry in the 1980s allowed many small firms to enter the market, and many of the new firms were not unionized. As a result, the demand for union truckers decreased, and unions faced a trade-off between wages and employment. If they maintained the relatively high union wage, total employment of union truckers would decrease by a large amount. In contrast, if they tried to maintain the same level of union employment, union truckers would be forced to accept much lower wages.

Figure 18.2 shows the response of union truckers to the entry of nonunion firms. In 1978, the union wage was $20 per hour and union employment was 526,000 truckers (point *a*). The entry of nonunion firms shifted the demand curve facing union truckers to the left. If the wage had remained at $20, total union employment would have dropped by half, to 263,000 workers (point *b*). Rather than accepting such a large reduction in union employment, truckers accepted a wage of $14 per hour, and total union employment in 1996 was 439,000 (point *c*). In other words, union truckers accepted lower wages in exchange for more jobs—or a smaller reduction in jobs. **Related to Exercise 1.5.**

SOURCE: Dale Belman and Paula Voos, "Changes in Union Wage Effects by Industry: A Fresh Look at the Evidence," *Industrial Relations* 43 (2004), pp. 491–519.

▶ **FIGURE 18.2**
Deregulation of Trucking and the Trade-Off Between Employment and Wages
The entry of nonunion firms decreased the demand for union truckers, shifting the demand curve to the left. At a wage of $20, the quantity of union truckers demanded would have decreased from 526,000 (point *a*) to 263,000 (point *b*). Union truckers accepted a lower wage of $14, generating total union employment of 439,000 (point *c*).

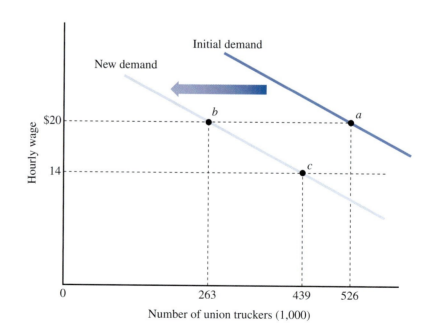

Market Structure and the Wage–Jobs Trade-Off

We've seen that one factor in the trade-off between wages and employment is the output effect. An increase in the wage increases the product price and decreases the firm's output, so the firm hires fewer workers. When will the output effect be relatively large?

- *Large fraction of costs from labor.* If labor is responsible for a relatively large fraction of production costs, an increase in the wage will cause a relatively large increase in the product price and, thus, a relatively large decrease in output and the quantity of labor demanded.
- *Elastic demand.* If the price elasticity of demand for the product is relatively large, a given increase in price will cause a relatively large reduction in output.

Under these conditions, a given increase in the union wage will cause a relatively large decrease in the number of union jobs. Given the large loss of jobs from a higher wage, we expect the union workers to accept a relatively small wage premium over nonunion workers. In contrast, when the output effect is small—when labor costs are a relatively small fraction of production costs and product demand is relatively inelastic—an increase in the wage leads to a relatively small loss of jobs, and we expect a relatively large union wage differential.

The price elasticity of demand for a product depends, in part, on the degree of market competition. As we saw earlier in the book, a firm with just few competitors faces a relatively inelastic demand for its product because consumers have few options. The inelastic demand means that an increase in the union wage will cause a relatively small loss in union jobs. Therefore, we expect relatively large union wage differentials in a monopoly or an oligopoly. In more-competitive markets, consumers have more options and the demand for a firm's output is relatively elastic. An increase in the union wage causes a relatively large loss of union jobs, so we expect a relatively small union wage differential.

The Effects of Unions on Worker Productivity and Turnover

One response to the trade-off between wages and jobs is to impose work rules that increase the amount of labor required to produce a given quantity of output. This is called **featherbedding**. One example of featherbedding is requiring a minimum crew size, which forces a firm to hire more workers than it needs to perform a particular task. For example, the typical unionized airline hires three workers to guide an airplane into the gate, while nonunion airlines use only two workers. In the past, railroad unions forced railroads to use firemen (whose job was to shovel coal) on diesel-powered engines, which don't use coal.

Featherbedding may actually decrease the demand for labor. Although featherbedding forces the firm to use more labor per unit of output, it also decreases the quantity of output produced. A firm that hires workers it doesn't need will have higher production costs, resulting in a higher price for its product. Consumers respond to a higher price by purchasing less output, so although the firm may use more labor per unit of output, it sells less output. If output falls by a large amount, the quantity of labor demanded by the firm will actually decrease.

We've seen that unions lead to higher wages and may impose work rules that reduce productivity. In other words, unions increase production costs. What are the possible benefits of unions? First, unions may increase worker productivity by facilitating communication between workers and managers. A second possible benefit of unions is lower turnover among workers. If a worker is unhappy with a job, one option is to quit. From the firm's perspective, this is costly because the firm loses an experienced worker and must train a new one. A dissatisfied worker who belongs to a union has a second option: The worker can use the union as an intermediary to discuss job issues with managers. This sort of communication can solve problems before they become so severe that the worker quits. There is evidence that firms whose workers

• **featherbedding**
Work rules that increase the amount of labor required to produce a given quantity of output.

APPLICATION

COMPETITION REDUCES TRUCKER WAGES

APPLYING THE CONCEPTS #2: How does competition in the product market affect union wages?

Two sectors of the trucking industry differ in the degree of competition. In the full-truckload (TL) sector, firms transport full truckloads of freight, with direct trips from a shipper to a destination. Entry is relatively easy in the TL sector because the production process is so simple: All you need to enter the market is a truck and a valid license. As a result, firms in the TL sector are small and numerous, and the highly competitive environment means that the demand facing each firm is relatively elastic. An increase in the union wage causes a relatively large loss of union jobs, so we expect a small gap between union and nonunion wages. In the TL sector in 1991, the union wage differential was 23 percent: On average, union workers earned 23 percent more than nonunion workers.

The less-than-truckload (LTL) sector handles smaller shipments, with each truck delivering multiple shipments. A firm in the LTL sector must be large enough to support a complex system of coordinated routes and maintain large facilities to store and transfer shipments from one route to another. There is less competition in the LTL market, and the demand facing each firm is relatively inelastic. An increase in the union wage leads to a relatively small loss of union jobs, so we expect a relatively large gap between union and nonunion wages. In the LTL sector in 1991, the union wage differential was 34 percent: On average, union workers earned 34 percent more than nonunion workers. *Related to Exercise 1.6.*

SOURCE: Michael Belzer, "Collective Bargaining After Deregulation: Do the Teamsters Still Count?" *Industrial and Labor Relations Review*, vol. 48 (1995), pp. 636–655; Michael Belzer, *Paying the Toll: Economic Deregulation of the Trucking Industry* (Washington, D.C.: Economic Policy Institute, 1994).

are in unions have lower turnover rates, in part because they facilitate communication between workers and managers.[2] These lower turnover rates lead to lower training costs and a more experienced workforce. The savings from less turnover is equivalent to a 1 to 2 percent reduction in costs.

18.2 | MONOPSONY POWER

In the previous chapter, we assumed that each employer is such a small part of the labor market that the employer takes the market wage as given. In graphical terms, a perfectly competitive firm faces a labor-supply curve that is horizontal at the market wage. In other words, each firm is a wage taker. In contrast, in a labor market with a single employer the firm is a wage maker, choosing what wage to pay its workers. Of course, the lower the wage, the smaller the quantity of labor supplied to the firm. For example, if your city has a single hospital, there will be a single employer of surgical nurses. This is the case of **monopsony**: There is a single buyer of an input. The classic example of monopsony is a company town, where most workers are employed by a

• **monopsony**
A market in which there is a single buyer of an input.

single firm. For example, a coal-mining firm could employ most of the workers in an isolated town in West Virginia, or a pineapple plantation could employ most of the workers on a small Hawaiian island.

Marginal Labor Cost Exceeds the Wage

A monopsonist faces a positively sloped market supply curve of labor. If the firm wants to hire more workers, it must pay a higher wage to attract them away from other firms. In Figure 18.3, the firm can hire 7 workers at a wage of $10 (point *a*) and 8 workers at a wage of $12 (point *b*). The firm's **marginal labor cost** (also known as *marginal factor cost*) is defined as the increase in the firm's total labor cost from one more unit of labor. When the firm decides to hire 8 workers instead of 7, its total labor cost increases from $70 per hour ($10 per worker per hour times 7 workers) to $96 per hour ($12 per worker per hour times 8 workers), an increase of $26. Therefore, the firm's marginal labor cost for the eighth worker is $26 (shown by point *c* in Figure 18.3).

As shown in Figure 18.3, the marginal labor cost exceeds the wage. When a firm increases the wage to hire one more worker, it must increase the wage for all of its workers. For example, to hire the eighth worker, the firm pays $12 to the new worker, but it also pays an extra $2 for each of the 7 workers who were willing to work at the lower wage of $10. We compute the marginal labor cost as follows:

marginal labor cost = wage paid to new worker + (change in wage
× original quantity of labor)
$26 = $12 + ($2 × 7)

In this example, the marginal labor cost is $26, including $12 for the new worker and $14 extra for the original workers.

Picking a Quantity of Labor and a Wage

Figure 18.4 shows the hiring decision of the monopsonist. The firm can use the marginal principle to determine how many workers to hire.

- **marginal labor cost**
The increase in a firm's total labor cost resulting from one more unit of labor.

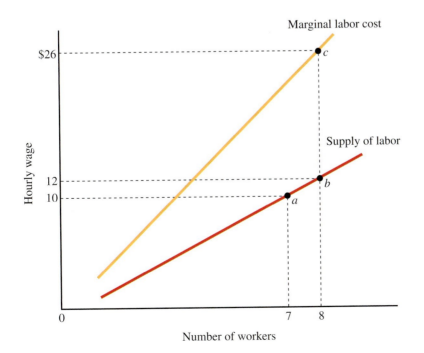

◄ **FIGURE 18.3**

The Supply of Labor and Marginal Labor Cost for a Monopsonist

To hire more workers, the monopsonist must pay a higher wage, so the marginal labor cost exceeds the wage. To hire the eighth worker, the firm increases the wage from $10 (point *a*) to $12 (point *b*). The marginal labor cost for the eighth worker is $26 (point *c*), equal to $12 paid to the eighth worker plus $14 extra paid to the 7 original workers, each of whom receives $2 more per hour.

▶ FIGURE 18.4

The Hiring Decision of a Monopsonist

The monopsonist satisfies the marginal principle at point *a*, where the marginal benefit of labor (marginal revenue product) equals the marginal labor cost, so the firm hires 40 workers. The labor-supply curve indicates that to hire 40 workers, the monopsonist must pay a wage of $4 (point *b*).

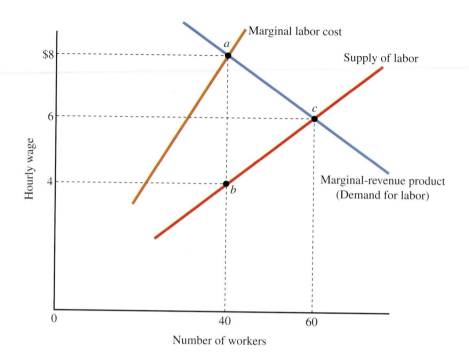

MARGINAL PRINCIPLE

Increase the level of an activity as long as its marginal benefit exceeds its marginal cost. Choose the level at which the marginal benefit equals the marginal cost.

The firm chooses the quantity of labor at which the marginal benefit of labor equals the marginal cost. As we saw in the previous chapter, the marginal benefit of labor equals the marginal-revenue product of labor—the increase in revenue generated by an additional worker. The marginal-revenue product curve is also the demand curve for labor. In Figure 18.4, the marginal-labor cost curve intersects the marginal revenue product curve at point *a*, so the monopsonist hires 40 workers. As shown by the labor supply curve, to hire 40 workers the firm must pay a wage of $4 (shown by point *b*).

Why does the monopsonist stop at 40 workers when it could hire an additional worker for just over $4, and the 41st worker would have a marginal revenue product of just under $8? To hire one more worker, the monopsonist must increase the wage to $4.10. The marginal labor cost of the 41st worker incorporates the higher wages that must be paid to the first 40 workers:

marginal labor cost = wage paid to new worker + (change in wage ×
quantity of original workers)
$8.10 = $4.10 + ($0.10 × 40)

Because a higher wage must be paid to the 40 original workers, the marginal labor cost of the 41st worker ($8.10) exceeds the marginal revenue product (less than $8.00). Therefore, the firm stops at 40 workers.

Monopsony Versus Perfect Competition

How does the monopsony outcome compare to the perfectly competitive outcome? Any firm that hires workers—either a monopsonist or perfect competitor—will continue to hire more workers until the marginal cost equals the marginal benefit (the marginal revenue product). A perfectly competitive firm is both a price taker and a

Table 18.1 | MONOPOLY VERSUS MONOPSONY

Monopoly	Monopsony
Single seller of output	Single buyer of labor
Produces a relatively small quantity of output	Hires a relatively small quantity of labor
High price of output	Low price of labor (wage)

wage taker: Each firm is too small to affect either the price of output or the price of labor. Therefore, the marginal cost of labor is simply the wage. In Figure 18.4, the perfectly competitive equilibrium is shown by the intersection of the demand curve (marginal-revenue product curve) and the supply curve at point c. The equilibrium wage is $6, and the equilibrium quantity is 60 workers.

For a monopsonist, the marginal cost of labor exceeds the wage because the firm must increase its wage to hire more workers. Compared to a perfectly competitive firm, a monopsonist has a higher marginal cost of labor. As a result, a firm will hire fewer workers than a collection of perfectly competitive firms. In Figure 18.4, the monopsonist hires only 40 workers because its higher marginal cost equals the marginal benefit at a smaller quantity of labor.

You may have noticed the similarity between a monopsonist and a monopolist. As shown in the first column of Table 18.1, a monopolist in a product market produces a relatively small quantity of output and charges a relatively high price. In the second column of the table, a monopsonist in the labor market demands a relatively small quantity of labor and pays a relatively low wage. In both cases, market power generates a relatively small quantity of either output (monopoly) or labor (monopsony)

What is the role of a labor union in a labor market with a single buyer? Monopsony leads to an artificially low wage, and a union may lead to an artificially high wage. A market with both a union and a monopsonist will have a wage somewhere between the two extremes, with the actual value of the wage determined by the bargaining power of the two sides. In such a market, the market powers on the two sides of the market counteract each other, leading to a wage between the artificially low monopsony wage and the artificially high union wage.

Monopsony and a Minimum Wage

In the previous chapter, we showed that a minimum wage decreases the quantity of labor demanded below the perfectly competitive level. In this case, there is a trade-off between higher wages and total employment. How does this analysis change when a monopsonist has market power on the demand side of the market?

Figure 18.5 shows the effects of a minimum wage of $7. This wage exceeds the monopsony wage of $4 as well as the perfectly competitive wage of $6. The minimum wage rules out wages below $7, so the supply curve facing the monopsonist is horizontal up to 70 workers. The first 70 workers are willing to work at the minimum wage, so to hire the 41st worker, the firm doesn't have to pay any more than it did for the first 40 workers. For the first 70 workers, the marginal labor cost is the minimum wage of $7. If the firm wants to hire more than 70 workers, it must pay a wage higher than the minimum, as shown by the market supply curve beyond point d. But for fewer than 70 workers, the supply curve facing the firm is horizontal, so the marginal labor cost is constant at the minimum wage of $7.

To maximize its profit, the firm will pick the quantity of labor at which the marginal benefit equals the marginal cost. At point e, the marginal labor cost (shown by the horizontal portion of the new supply curve) equals the marginal benefit (shown by the marginal revenue product curve), so the monopsonist hires 50 workers, up from 40 workers before the minimum wage. In other words, the minimum wage increases the quantity of labor demanded.

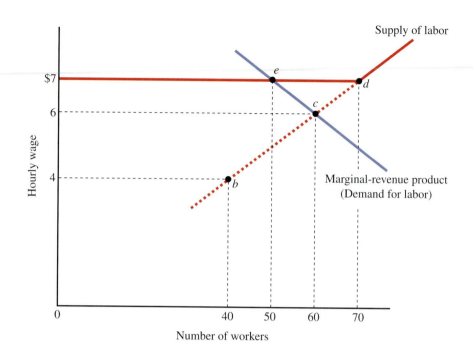

► **FIGURE 18.5**

A Minimum Wage Increases Employment by a Monopsonist

With a minimum wage, the labor-supply curve is horizontal at the minimum wage ($7) up to the point where the minimum-wage line intersects the original supply curve. For the first 70 workers, the marginal labor cost for the monopsonist equals the minimum wage. The monopsonist chooses point *e*, where the marginal benefit of labor (the marginal revenue product) equals the marginal labor cost. The minimum wage increases the quantity of labor hired from 40 workers to 50.

How does this analysis compare to the analysis of the minimum wage in the previous chapter? Recall that in a perfectly competitive market, the minimum wage decreases the quantity of labor. In Figure 18.5, the competitive outcome is shown by point *c*, with 60 workers. So a minimum wage of $7 generates less than the competitive quantity but more than the monopsony quantity (40 workers). Starting from the monopsony outcome, a minimum wage of $7 moves the market closer to the perfectly competitive outcome. In fact, if the minimum wage were set at $6, the market would reach the competitive quantity of 60 workers. The minimum wage makes the monopsonist a wage-taking firm, so the quantity of labor demanded increases.

Monopsony and the Real World

Although a pure monopsony, such as a company town, is rare, the insights from the monopsony model are relevant for actual labor markets. The essential feature of the model is that if an individual firm wants to hire additional workers, it must increase its wage to attract more workers. In other words, the firm faces a positively sloped supply curve for workers, not a horizontal curve. We saw that a positively sloped supply curve generates a marginal labor cost curve above the supply curve, and the profit-maximizing quantity of labor is less than the perfectly competitive quantity.

British economist Joan Robinson (1903–1983), a leader in the modeling of imperfect competition, listed several reasons why a firm could face a positively sloped labor-supply curve:

> There may be a certain number of workers in the immediate neighbourhood and to attract those from farther afield it may be necessary to pay a wage equal to what they can earn near home plus their fares to and fro; or there could be workers attached to the firm by preference or custom and to attract others it may be necessary to pay a higher wage. Or ignorance may prevent workers from moving from one to another in response to differences in the wages offered by the different firms.[3]

Because of these frictions in the labor market, a firm must pay a higher wage to get more workers: The labor supply curve facing a firm is positively sloped. With a positively sloped supply curve, the marginal labor cost exceeds the wage, and the quantity of labor will be less than occurs in a perfectly competitive market.

APPLICATION

PUBS AND THE LABOR-SUPPLY CURVE

APPLYING THE CONCEPTS #3: Do firms face a positively sloped labor-supply curve?

Labor economist Alan Manning provides some unconventional evidence of positively sloped labor-supply curves. He notes that "people go to the pub to celebrate when they get a job, rather than greeting the news with a shrug of the shoulders. . . ." In other words, a new job is a big deal.

   If a pub celebration seems like the obvious response to a new job, consider what happens when each firm faces a horizontal supply curve for labor, with a single market wage. A firm has no incentive to pay a higher wage because it can hire as many workers as it wants at the market wage. And if the firm paid a lower wage, all its workers would instantly switch to other firms paying the market wage. In this perfectly competitive environment, a worker won't celebrate a new job because the new job pays the same as any other job the worker could get. The wage paid by an employer equals the worker's opportunity cost.

   Suppose instead that the supply curve facing a firm is positively sloped. To hire more workers, the firm must pay a higher wage. Most workers will receive a wage that exceeds the opportunity cost of their time, so each worker gets a producer surplus. Workers switch jobs to get a bigger surplus, so they celebrate new jobs. Manning also notes that people also "go to the pub to drown their sorrows when they lose their jobs." This response wouldn't be sensible with a horizontal supply curve, because someone who loses a job could instantly get another one at the same wage. But with a positively sloped supply curve, losing a job means losing a producer surplus.
Related to Exercise 2.5.

SOURCE: Alan Manning, *Monopsony in Motion: Imperfect Competition in Labor Markets* (Princeton, NJ: Princeton University Press, 2003).

18.3 | IMPERFECT INFORMATION AND EFFICIENCY WAGES

Up to this point, our discussion of labor markets has been based on the assumption of perfect information. Each employer knows the productivity level of each worker and only hires a worker if the marginal benefit exceeds the marginal cost. In some markets, workers differ in their skill levels and the amount of effort they exert on the job. At the time of hiring, employers cannot always distinguish between skillful and unskillful workers or between hard workers and lazy workers. In other words, there is asymmetric information in the labor market.

The Mixed Market for Labor

In the chapter on imperfect information, we saw that in a market with asymmetric information, high-quality and low-quality goods are sold in a mixed market at a single price. In the labor market, workers differ in their productivity, but a potential employer may not be able to distinguish between workers with high or low productivity. As shown in Table

Table 18.2 | DIFFERENCES IN PRODUCTIVITY AND EFFICIENCY WAGES

	Low-Productivity Worker	High-Productivity Worker
Marginal revenue product	$40	$80
Opportunity cost	25	50

18.2, suppose that low-productivity workers have half the marginal revenue product of high-productivity workers, and also half the opportunity cost. Suppose employers are perfectly competitive and cannot distinguish between low-skill and high-skill workers before hiring them. Each firm offers a single wage to all workers, realizing that its workforce may include some workers of each type. What is the equilibrium wage?

In a perfectly competitive labor market, competition among firms will bid up the wage to equal the marginal revenue product (*MRP*) of hired workers. Therefore, the equilibrium wage will be at least $40 because that's the *MRP* of the least productive workers. Consider a wage of $40, which exceeds the opportunity cost of low-productivity workers ($25) but not the opportunity cost of high-productivity workers ($50). As a result, only low-productivity workers will apply for jobs and be hired. As shown in the first row of Table 18.3, the wage equals the *MRP* of the workers hired, so each firm makes zero economic profit. In other words, $40 is an equilibrium wage.

In this market with asymmetric information, there is actually a second equilibrium wage, equal to $60. This wage is high enough to exceed the opportunity costs of both types of workers, so both types apply for jobs and are hired. Suppose the number of low-productivity workers equals the number of high-productivity workers. In this case, the average labor productivity of the hired workers will be the average of $40 (for low-productivity workers) and $80 (for high-productivity workers), or $60. As shown in the last row of Table 18.3, the wage equals the average productivity of the hired workforce, so each firm will make zero economic profit. In other words, $60 is another equilibrium wage.

What about wages between $40 and $60? The second row of Table 18.3 shows the effects of a $45 wage. The wage is below the opportunity cost of high-productivity workers, so all the hired workers will have an *MRP* of $40 and firms will lose $5 on each worker hired. Economic profit is negative, so this is not an equilibrium. The third row of the table shows the effects of a $55 wage, which exceeds the opportunity cost of high-productivity workers. Half the workers have an *MRP* of $40, and half have an *MRP* of $80, for an average of $60. Firms earn an average profit of $5 per worker, and the positive economic profit will cause competing firm to bid up the wage. The wage will continue to rise until it reaches $60, the wage at which economic profit is zero, and we have an equilibrium.

We've seen that paying a higher wage may increase the average productivity of workers. This is known as **paying efficiency wages**. Productivity increases because a higher wage makes it possible to hire workers with higher opportunity costs. There are two other reasons for paying efficiency wages:

- *Reduce shirking.* When a high wage is combined with a policy of firing workers who shirk—putting in less than a full effort—the firm can encourage hard work. The penalty associated with being fired will be much greater if the firm pays a wage above the worker's opportunity cost.

• **paying efficiency wages**
The practice of paying a higher wage to increase the average productivity of the workforce.

Table 18.3 | EQUILIBRIUM WAGES WITH ASYMMETRIC INFORMATION

Wage	Worker Mix	Average Productivity (*MRP*)	Profit per Worker
$40	**All low**	**$40**	**$0**
45	All low	40	−5
55	Half of each	60	+5
60	**Half of each**	**60**	**0**

APPLICATION

4

EFFICIENCY WAGES AT FORD MOTOR COMPANY

APPLYING THE CONCEPTS #4: When does an increase in the wage increase profit?

Recall the chapter opener about Henry Ford's puzzling wage hike. Ford increased the daily wage for his workers from $3 to $5, and his profit doubled from $30 million to $60 million. Why did higher wages lead to more profit? When Ford raised the wage, the average productivity of Ford workers increased by about 50 percent because of several changes in the workforce:

- The pool of job applicants improved, so Ford could choose better workers.
- Fewer workers were fired for shirking.
- Fewer workers quit voluntarily.
- The rate of absenteeism was cut in half.

In the words of Henry Ford, "There was no charity in any way involved. . . . The payment of five dollars a day for an eight-hour day was one of the finest cost cutting moves we ever made." *Related to Exercise 3.5.*

SOURCES: J. R. Lee, "So-Called Profit Sharing System in the Ford Plant," *Annals of the American Academy of Political and Social Science*, May 1915, pp. 297–310; David Halberstam, *The Reckoning* (New York: William Morrow, 1986), pp. 91–92; Daniel M. G. Graff and Lawrence H. Summers, "Did Henry Ford Pay Efficiency Wages?" *Journal of Labor Economics*, vol. 5 (1987), pp. 557–586.

- ***Reduce turnover.*** A wage above the worker's opportunity cost will reduce worker turnover. A firm that pays a higher wage than its competitors discourages workers from switching employers. The firm paying the higher wage will have lower turnover and thus incur smaller costs in hiring and training workers.

SUMMARY

In this chapter, we extended our discussion of labor markets beyond the simple world of perfectly competitive labor markets, where each side of the labor market takes the market wage as given. *Labor unions* have market power—the ability to affect wages—on the supply side of the market, while a *monopsonist* has market power on the demand side of the market. When workers know more about their productivity than employers, this asymmetric information provides an incentive for firms to increase wages in order to increase the average productivity of workers. Here are the main points of the chapter:

1 A union faces a trade-off between wages and total employment: An increase in the wage causes an output effect and an input-substitution effect that combine to decrease the quantity of labor demanded.

2 The gap between the union wage and the nonunion wage will be relatively large when the price elasticity of demand for a product is relatively low. Demand is relatively inelastic in less competitive product markets.

3 A firm facing a positively sloped labor supply curve must pay a higher wage to hire more workers, and the marginal labor cost exceeds the wage.

4 The equilibrium employment in a monopsony is less than the equilibrium employment in a perfectly competitive market.

5 In a labor market with asymmetric information about worker productivity, an increase in the wage may increase the average productivity of hired workers and increase profit.

413

KEY TERMS

collective bargaining, p. 402

craft union, p. 402

featherbedding, p. 405

industrial union, p. 402

labor union, p. 402

marginal labor cost, p. 407

monopsony, p. 406

paying efficiency wages, p. 412

right-to-work laws, p. 403

EXERCISES

Visit www.myeconlab.com to complete these exercises online and get instant feedback.

Get Ahead of the Curve

18.1 | Labor Unions

1.1 In the United States, union workers earn _____ to _____ percent more than nonunion workers doing the same work. The union wage differential is _____ (larger/smaller) in most other industrialized countries.

1.2 Arrows up or down: Featherbedding may decrease the demand for labor because it _____ production costs and _____ the price of the output, which _____ the quantity of the product demanded and produced.

1.3 Arrows up or down: Unions tend to _____ turnover rates and thus _____ training costs and _____ the average experience level of workers.

1.4 Unions decrease productivity. (True/False/ Uncertain)

1.5 **Maximizing Labor Income.** Consider a union that faces a linear demand for its workers. The vertical intercept is $40 and the slope is –$0.20 per worker, so the horizontal intercept is 200 workers (Related to Application 1 on page 404.)

   a. The union faces a trade-off between the wage and employment: For every $2 increase in the wage, employment decreases by _____ workers.

   b. Suppose the union tentatively picks a wage of $30, where the elasticity of demand for labor is 3.0 (in absolute value). If the union decreases the wage by 5 percent, by how much will the quantity of labor demanded increase? Will total labor income increase or decrease?

   c. Suppose the union's objective is to maximize total labor income. What is the income-maximizing wage and quantity of labor demanded?

1.6 **Product Elasticities and the Wage–Job Trade-Off.** Consider two unions, one in an industry where the price elasticity of demand for the product is 3.0 (industry E), and one where the price elasticity of demand is 2.0 (industry I). In both industries, the initial wage is $30 and labor is responsible for half the cost of production, so the percentage change in the product price is half the percentage change in the wage. In each industry, the initial employment is

100 workers. Suppose each union increases its wage by 10 percent. (Related to Application 2 on page 406.)

   a. Compute the output effect of the wage increase for each industry: Total employment in industry E drops from 100 to _____; total employment in industry I drops from 100 to _____.

   b. Assume that there is no substitution effect from changes in wages. Use two graphs to show the effects of the increase in the wage on the quantity of labor demanded.

1.7 **Trade-Offs from Featherbedding.** Suppose that featherbedding increases the labor time per unit of output from 5 hours to 6 and increases the firm's production cost and its price by 15 percent. The firm initially produces and sells 100 units of output. If the price elasticity of demand for the firm's product is 2.0, how will featherbedding affect the firm's total demand for labor?

1.8 **Labor Demand Elasticity and Total Income.** Suppose a union's objective is to maximize the total income of nurses (total money spent by firms on nurses). At the current wage, the price elasticity of demand for nurses is 0.75 (in absolute value).

   a. Should the union increase or decrease the union wage? Explain.

   b. Is there a trade-off between wages and total employment?

18.2 | Monopsony Power

2.1 For a monopsonist, the marginal labor cost exceeds the wage because to hire more workers, the firm must _____.

2.2 A monopsonist hires workers to the quantity at which _____ equals _____.

2.3 A monopolist sells its output at a relatively _____ (high/low) price, while a monopsonist buys its inputs at a relatively _____ price.

2.4 Arrows up or down: If several hospitals in a city merge into a single hospital, we expect a _____ in the nurse wage and a _____ in citywide nurse employment.

2.5 Elasticity of Supply. Consider the application, "Pubs and the Labor-Supply Curve," which suggests that workers switch jobs to get a bigger producer surplus. Consider two types of workers, janitors in a large city and radiology technicians in a medium-size city with two hospitals (Related to Application 3 on page 411.)

  a. Which type of worker is likely to get a larger change in producer surplus when switching jobs?

  b. What are the implications for the supply curves facing the employers—janitorial firms and hospitals?

2.6 Competition Versus Monopsony. Consider the following data on the supply of labor and the demand for labor. The first three rows show the supply side of the market, and the last two rows show the demand side.

Wage	$5	$6	$7	$8	$9	$10	$11
Quantity of labor supplied	1	2	3	4	5	6	7
Marginal labor cost	$5	$7	$9	$11	$13	$15	$17
Quantity of workers demanded	1	2	3	4	5	6	7
Marginal-revenue product	$20	$18	$16	$14	$12	$10	$8

  a. In the perfectly competitive outcome, the equilibrium wage is _____ and the equilibrium quantity is _____.

  b. In the monopsony outcome, the monopsonist chooses a quantity of _____ and pays a wage of _____.

2.7 Effects of a Minimum Wage. Consider the monopsony depicted in Figure 18.4 on page 408 and Figure 18.5 on page 410. Note that the curves are linear with constant slopes.

  a. Fill the blanks in the following table, providing the relationship between the minimum wage and the number of workers hired.

Minimum wage	$4	$5	$6	$7	$8	$9
Number of workers hired						

  b. Provide a general rule for the relationship between the minimum wage and the number of workers hired. As the minimum wage increases, the number of workers hired will increase if _____, but will decrease if _____.

18.3 | Imperfect Information and Efficiency Wages

3.1 The asymmetry in the labor market is that _____ know more than _____ about a worker's skills.

3.2 Arrows up or down: In a labor market with asymmetric information, a firm will hire only low-productivity workers if the firm's _____ is less than the _____ of high-productivity workers.

3.3 In a labor market with asymmetric information, an increase in the wage _____ (increases/decreases) the average productivity of the workforce if the wage rises above the _____ of high-productivity workers.

3.4 Paying efficiency wages increases the average productivity of a firm's workers by discouraging _____ and reducing worker _____.

3.5 Higher Wages for Landscaping Workers. Suppose that half of landscaping workers have a marginal-revenue product of $40 and an opportunity cost of $30 and the other half have a marginal-revenue product of $60 and an opportunity cost of $45. A landscaping firm cannot distinguish between the two types of workers (Related to Application 4 on page 413.)

  a. Suppose a landscaping firm offers a wage equal to $41. What is the average productivity of its workforce? On average, what is the firm's profit per worker?

  b. Suppose the firm increases its wage to $47. What is the average productivity of its workforce? On average, what is the firm's profit per worker?

  c. What are the equilibrium wages?

3.6 Equilibrium with Efficiency Wages. Consider a labor market with asymmetric information: Each worker knows his or her marginal-revenue product, but firms cannot distinguish between low-skill and high-skill workers. Each low-skill worker has an opportunity cost of $80 and a marginal revenue product of $100, and each high-skill worker has an opportunity cost of $130 and a marginal revenue product of $200. The workforce is divided equally between the two types of workers. Fill the blanks in the following table.

Wage	$100	$120	$140	$150
Average profit per worker				

NOTES

1. Ronald Ehrenberg and Robert Smith, *Modern Labor Economics: Theory and Public Policy* (Boston: Pearson Addison Wesley, 2006).

2. Richard B. Freeman and James Medoff, *What Do Unions Do?* (New York: Basic Books, 1985).

3. Joan Robinson, *The Economics of Imperfect Competition* (London: Macmillan, 1933), p. 296.

19

International Trade and Public Policy

Look at the label on your shirt or your tie. Chances are it was made in China, Indonesia, or another developing country. If you own a $100 pair of brand-name athletic shoes it was probably assembled somewhere in the Far East, perhaps Vietnam or Cambodia. We are no longer surprised to learn this, because many major companies locate their key production facilities abroad.

But somehow, we are still astonished that when we make a service call to fix a problem on our personal computer, we may eventually be

1 Do tariffs (taxes) on imported goods hurt the poor disproportionately?
The Impact of Tariffs on the Poor

2 How much does it really cost to "save" a job that might be lost under free trade?
Measuring the Costs of Protecting Jobs

3 Does the concept of "unfair" competition make sense?
Protection for Candle Makers

4 What are the most pressing current issues in today's trade negotiations?
Ongoing Trade Negotiations

speaking to a technical representative in Bangalore, India. And certainly many sophisticated jobs are now performed outside the United States. High-tech firms in Silicon Valley in California often have their computer code written in India or other countries around the globe. How will these changes in our global economy affect our lives in the United States?

As the world economy grows, U.S. policies toward international trade become ever more important. Many people view trade as a "zero-sum game." They believe that if one country gains from international trade, another must lose. Based on this belief, they advocate restricting trade with other countries. The United States does restrict trade to protect American jobs in many sectors, such as those in the apparel and steel industries. One lesson from this chapter is that free trade could make everyone better off. The challenge for government officials is to create policies that accomplish, or come close to accomplishing, this goal.

In this chapter, we discuss the benefits of international trade and the effects of policies that restrict trade.

19.1 | BENEFITS FROM SPECIALIZATION AND TRADE

What if you lived in a nation that could produce everything it consumed and didn't depend on any other country for its economic livelihood? If you were put in charge of your nation, would you pursue a policy of national self-sufficiency? Although self-sufficiency might sound appealing, it would actually be better for your country to specialize in the production of some products and then trade some of those products to other countries. You saw in Chapter 3 that specialization and exchange can make both parties better off. In this chapter, we use a simple example to explain the benefits of specialization and international trade between two nations.

Let's say there are two nations, Shirtland and Chipland. Each nation produces computer chips and shirts, and each consumes computer chips and shirts. Table 19.1 shows the daily output of the two goods for the two nations. In a single day, Shirtland can produce a maximum of either 108 shirts or 36 computer chips, whereas Chipland can produce a maximum of either 120 shirts or 120 computer chips. The last two rows of the table show the opportunity costs of the two goods. Recall the principle of opportunity cost.

• **production possibilities curve**
A curve that shows the possible combinations of products that an economy can produce, given that its productive resources are fully employed and efficiently used.

 PRINCIPLE OF OPPORTUNITY COST
The opportunity cost of something is what you sacrifice to get it.

In Chipland, the trade-off between shirts and chips is one to one: The opportunity cost of one shirt is one chip, and the opportunity cost of one chip is one shirt. In Shirtland, people can produce three times as many shirts as chips in a given amount of time: The opportunity cost of one chip is three shirts. Conversely, the opportunity cost of one shirt is one-third of a chip.

Production Possibilities Curve

Let's start by seeing what happens if Shirtland and Chipland are each self-sufficient. Each nation can use its resources (labor, land, buildings, machinery, and equipment) to produce its own shirts and chips. The **production possibilities curve** shows all the possible combinations of products that an economy can produce, given that its productive resources are fully employed and efficiently used. This curve, which we discussed in

Table 19.1 | OUTPUT AND OPPORTUNITY COST

	Quantity Produced Per Day	Opportunity Cost of Shirts	Opportunity Cost of Chips
Shirtland	108 shirts 36 chips	1/3 chip	3 shirts
Chipland	120 shirts 120 chips	1 chip	1 shirt

Production Possibilities Curve
The production possibilities curve shows the combination of two goods that can be produced with a nation's resources. For Chipland, the trade-off between the two goods is one to one. For Shirtland, the trade-off is three shirts for every computer chip. In the absence of trade, Shirtland can pick point c—28 chips and 24 shirts—and Chipland can pick point f—60 chips and 60 shirts.

Shirtland Possibilites

Point	Shirts	Chips
a	108	0
b	54	18
c	24	28
d	0	36

Chipland Possibilities

Point	Shirts	Chips
e	120	0
f	60	60
g	0	120

Chapter 2, provides a menu of production options. To keep things simple, we assume that the curve is a straight line, indicating a constant trade-off between the two goods. As shown by Shirtland's production possibilities curve in Figure 19.1, the following combinations of chips and shirts are possible:

1 *All shirts and no chips:* point *a*. If Shirtland uses all of its resources to produce shirts, it will produce 108 shirts per day.

2 *All chips and no shirts:* point *d*. If Shirtland uses all of its resources to produce chips, it will produce 36 chips per day.

3 *Equal division of resources:* point *b*. Shirtland could divide its resources between shirts and chips to produce 54 shirts and 18 chips each day.

All the other points on the line connecting points *a* and *d* are also feasible. One option is point *c*, with 28 chips and 24 shirts. The steepness of the curve's slope—3.0— shows the opportunity cost of computer chips: one chip per three shirts. Figure 19.1 also shows the production possibilities curve for Chipland. Chipland can produce daily 120 shirts and no chips (point *e*), 120 chips and no shirts (point *g*), or any combination of chips and shirts between these two points. In Chipland, the trade-off is one shirt per computer chip: The opportunity cost of a chip is one shirt, so the slope of the production possibilities curve is 1.0.

Each nation could decide to be self-sufficient, picking a point on its production possibilities curve and producing everything it wants to consume. For example, Shirtland could pick point *c*, producing daily 28 chips and 24 shirts, and Chipland could pick point *f*, producing daily 60 chips and 60 shirts. In the language of international trade, this is a case of *autarky*, or self-sufficiency (in Greek, *aut* means "self" and *arke* means "to suffice").

Comparative Advantage and the Terms of Trade

Would the two nations be better off if each nation specialized in the production of one good and traded with the other nation? To decide which nation should produce

• **comparative advantage**
The ability of one person or nation to produce a good at a lower opportunity cost than another person or nation.

• **absolute advantage**
The ability of one person or nation to produce a good at a lower resource cost than another person or nation.

• **terms of trade**
The rate at which units of one product can be exchanged for units of another product.

• **consumption possibilities curve**
A curve showing the combinations of two goods that can be consumed when a nation specializes in a particular good and trades with another nation.

a particular good, we need to look at each good and figure out which nation has the lower opportunity cost of producing it. As you saw in Chapter 3, the nation with the lower opportunity cost has a **comparative advantage** in producing that good. As we emphasized in Chapter 3, it is comparative advantage that matters for trade—not **absolute advantage**, the ability of a nation to produce a particular good at a lower absolute cost than that of another nation. Let's see how it works.

1 *Chips produced in Chipland.* The opportunity cost of one chip is one shirt in Chipland, and the opportunity cost of one chip is three shirts in Shirtland. Chipland has a comparative advantage in the production of chips. Because Chipland sacrifices fewer shirts to produce one chip, Chipland should produce chips.

2 *Shirts produced in Shirtland.* The opportunity cost of one shirt is one chip in Chipland, and the opportunity cost of one shirt is one-third of a chip in Shirtland. When it comes to producing shirts, Shirtland has a comparative advantage because it sacrifices fewer chips to produce one shirt. Shirtland should therefore produce shirts.

Trade will make it possible for people in each specialized nation to consume both goods. At what rate will the two nations exchange shirts and chips? To determine the **terms of trade**, the rate at which units of one product can be exchanged for units of another product, let's look at how much Shirtland is willing to pay to get one chip and how much Chipland is willing to accept to give up one chip.

1 To get one chip, Shirtland is willing to pay up to three shirts. That's how many shirts it would sacrifice if it produced its own chip. For example, if the nations agree to exchange two shirts per chip, Shirtland could rearrange its production, producing one fewer chip but three more shirts. After exchanging two of the newly produced shirts for one chip, Shirtland will have the same number of chips but one additional shirt.

2 To give up one chip, Chipland is willing to accept any amount greater than one shirt. For example, if the nations agree to exchange two shirts per chip, Chipland could rearrange its production, producing one more chip and one fewer shirt. After it exchanges the newly produced chip for two shirts, Chipland will have the same number of chips but one additional shirt.

The potential for mutually beneficial trade between the two countries is possible because the willingness to pay—three shirts by Shirtland—exceeds the willingness to accept—one shirt by Chipland. It's possible for Shirtland and Chipland to split the difference between the willingness to pay and the willingness to accept, exchanging two shirts per chip. This will actually make both countries better off in terms of the total amount of goods they can consume. We'll see why next.

The Consumption Possibilities Curve

A nation that decides to specialize and trade is no longer limited to the options shown by its own production possibilities curve. The **consumption possibilities curve** shows the combinations of two goods (computer chips and shirts in our example) that a nation can consume when it specializes in one good and trades with another nation.

Figure 19.2 shows the consumption possibilities curve for our two nations, assuming that they exchange two shirts per chip:

• In Panel A, Chipland specializes in chip production, the good for which it has a comparative advantage. It produces 120 chips and no shirts (point *g*). Given the terms of trade, Chipland can exchange 40 of its 120 chips for 80 shirts, leading to point *h*. At point *h*, Chipland can consume 80 chips and 80 shirts.

• In Panel B, Shirtland specializes in shirt production. It produces 108 shirts and no chips (point *a*). Given the terms of trade, it can exchange 80 of its 108 shirts for 40 chips, leading to point *k* on its consumption possibilities curve. Shirtland can consume 28 shirts and 40 chips.

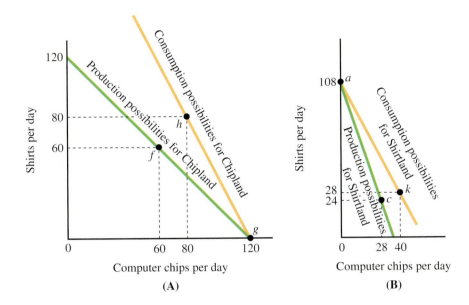

Consumption Possibilities Curve
The consumption possibilities curve shows the combinations of computer chips and shirts that can be consumed if each country specializes and trades. In Panel A, Chipland produces 120 chips and trades 40 of these chips to Shirtland for 80 shirts. In Panel B, Shirtland produces 108 shirts and trades 80 of these shirts to Chipland for 40 chips. The trade allows each nation to consume more.

How do the outcomes with specialization and trade compare to the autarky outcomes? Chipland moves from point *f* (autarky) to point *h*, so trade increases the consumption of each good by 20 units. Shirtland moves from point *c* to point *k*, so this nation consumes 12 additional chips and 4 additional shirts.

In Figure 19.2, each consumption possibilities curve lies above the nation's production possibilities curves, meaning that each nation has more options about how much to consume under specialization and trade. In most cases, a nation picks a point on the consumption possibilities curve that provides more of each good. Of course, this is a very simple example. In the actual world market, there are many countries producing and trading many goods. The marketplace determines what the terms of those trades will be depending upon supply, demand, and pricing.

How Free Trade Affects Employment

You've now seen that trade allows each nation to consume more of each good. But we haven't yet discussed the effects of trade on employment. Under free trade, each nation will begin to specialize in a single good, causing considerable changes in the country's employment in different industries. In Chipland, the chip industry doubles in size—output increases from 60 to 120 chips per day—while the shirt industry disappears. Workers and other resources will leave the shirt industry and move to the chip industry. In Shirtland, the flow is in the opposite direction: Workers and other resources move from the chip industry to the shirt industry.

Is free trade good for everyone? Switching from self-sufficiency to specialization and trade increases consumption in both nations, so on average, people in each nation benefit from free trade. But some people in both nations will be harmed by free trade. In Chipland, for example, people in the shirt industry will lose their jobs when the shirt industry disappears. Some workers can easily move into the expanding computer-chip industry. For these workers, free trade is likely to be beneficial. However, other shirt workers will be unable to make the move to the chip industry and will be forced to accept lower-paying jobs or face unemployment. Free trade is likely to make these displaced workers worse off. There is a saying, "Where you stand on an issue depends on where you sit." In our example, a worker sitting at a sewing machine in Chipland is likely to oppose free trade because that worker is likely to lose a job. A worker sitting at a workstation in a computer-chip fabrication facility is likely to support free trade because the resulting increase in computer-chip exports will generate more employment opportunities in that industry.

19.2 | PROTECTIONIST POLICIES

Now that you know the basic rationale for specialization and trade, we can explore the effects of public policies that restrict it. All the restrictions we explore limit the gains from specialization and trade. We will consider four common import-restriction policies: an outright ban on imports, an import quota, voluntary export restraints, and a tariff.

Import Bans

To show how an import ban affects the market, let's start with an unrestricted market—no import ban. Figure 19.3 shows the market for shirts in Chipland, a nation with a comparative advantage in producing computer chips, not shirts. The domestic supply curve shows the quantity of shirts supplied by firms in Chipland. Looking at point *b*, we see that Chipland firms will not supply any shirts unless the price is at least $17 per shirt. The total supply curve for shirts, which shows the quantity supplied by both domestic firms and foreign firms (in Shirtland), lies to the right of the domestic supply curve. At each price, the total supply of shirts exceeds the domestic supply because foreign firms supply shirts, too. Point *c* shows the free-trade equilibrium. The demand curve from domestic residents intersects the total supply curve at a price of $12 per shirt and a quantity of 80 shirts. Because this price is below the minimum price for domestic firms, domestic firms produce no shirts, and all the shirts in Chipland are imported from Shirtland.

What will happen if Chipland bans imported shirts? Foreign suppliers will disappear from the shirt market, so the total supply of shirts will be the domestic supply. In Figure 19.3, point *a* shows the equilibrium when Chipland bans imported shirts: The domestic demand curve intersects the domestic supply curve at a price of $23 per shirt and a quantity of 60 shirts. In other words, the decrease in supply resulting from the import ban increases the price consumers have to pay for shirts and decreases the quantity available for them to buy.

Quotas and Voluntary Export Restraints

• **import quota**
A government-imposed limit on the quantity of a good that can be imported.

An alternative to an import ban is an **import quota**—a government-imposed limit on the quantity of a good that can be imported. An import quota is a restrictive policy that falls between free trade and an outright ban: Imports are cut, but not eliminated.

▶ **FIGURE 19.3**

Effects of an Import Ban

In the free-trade equilibrium, demand intersects the total supply curve at point *c*, with a price of $12 and a quantity of 80 shirts. If shirt imports are banned, the equilibrium is shown by the intersection of the demand curve and the domestic supply curve (point *a*). The price increases to $23.

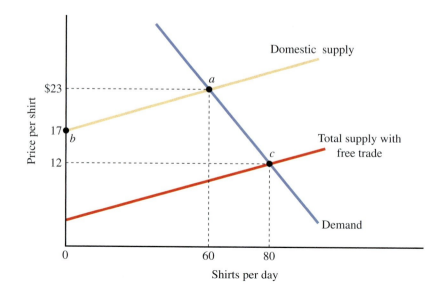

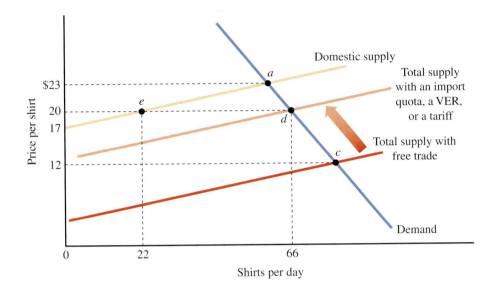

◄ **FIGURE 19.4**
Market Effects of a Quota, a VER, or a Tariff
An import quota shifts the supply curve to the left. The market moves upward along the demand curve to point *d*, which is between point *c* (free trade) and *a* (an import ban). We can reach the same point with a tariff that shifts the total supply curve to the same position.

For example, if a quota were put on shirts, the price consumers would have to pay would fall somewhere between the price they would pay with free trade ($12 per shirt, as in our example) and the price they would pay if imported shirts were banned ($23 per shirt). Where exactly the price would fall would depend on how high or low the quotas are.

Import quotas are illegal under international trading rules. To get around these rules, an exporting country will sometimes agree to a **voluntary export restraint (VER)**. A VER is similar to an import ban. When an exporting nation adopts a VER, it decreases its exports to avoid having to face even more restrictive trade policies importing countries might be tempted to impose on them. Although VERs are legal under global-trade rules, they violate the spirit of international free-trade agreements. In any case, quotas and VERs have the same effect. Like a quota, a VER increases the price of the restricted good, making it more feasible for domestic firms to participate in the market.

Figure 19.4 shows the effect of an import quota or VER. Starting from the free-trade equilibrium at point c, an import quota will shift the total supply curve to the left: At each price there will be a smaller quantity of shirts supplied because foreign suppliers aren't allowed to supply as many. The total supply curve when there is an import quota or VER will lie between the domestic supply curve and the total supply curve under free trade. The equilibrium under an import quota or VER occurs at point *d*, where the demand curve intersects the total supply curve under an import limitation. The $20 price per shirt with the import quota exceeds the $17 minimum price of domestic firms, so domestic firms supply 22 shirts (point *e*). Under a free-trade policy, they would have supplied no shirts.

A quota or a VER produces winners and losers. The winners include foreign and domestic shirt producers. In our example, foreign firms can sell shirts at a price of $20 instead of $12 each, and the price is high enough for domestic firms to participate in the market. This generates benefits for the firms and their workers. The losers are consumers, who pay a higher price for shirts. In some cases, the government issues **import licenses** to some citizens, who can then buy shirts from foreign firms at a low price, such as $12, and sell the shirts at the higher domestic price, $20. Because import licenses provide profits to the holder, they are often awarded to politically powerful firms or individuals. Moreover, because they are so valuable, some people may bribe government officials for the licenses.

We know that consumers pay higher prices for goods that are subject to protectionist policies, but how much more? Here is one example. In the United States, voluntary export restraints on Japanese automobiles in 1984 increased the price of a Japanese car by about $1,300 and the price of a domestic car by about $660.[1]

• **voluntary export restraint (VER)**
A scheme under which an exporting country voluntarily decreases its exports.

• **import licenses**
Rights, issued by a government, to import goods.

• **tariff**
A tax on imported goods.

An alternative to a quota or a VER is an import **tariff**, which is a tax on an imported good. Tariffs have the same effect as quotas and VERs. We know from our earlier discussions that a tax shifts the supply curve to the left and increases the equilibrium price. In Figure 19.4, suppose the tariff shifts the total supply curve with free trade so that it intersects the domestic demand curve at point *d*. In other words, we reach the same point we reached with the quota: Consumers pay the same $20 price per shirt, and domestic firms produce the same quantity: 22 shirts.

There is one fundamental difference between a quota and a tariff. An import quota allows importers to buy shirts from foreign suppliers at a low price—say, $12 per shirt—and sell them for $20 each, the artificially high price. In other words, importers make money from the quota. Under a tariff, the government gets the money, collecting $8 per shirt from foreign suppliers. Citizens in Chipland will prefer the tariff to the quota because the government can use the revenue from the tariff to cut other taxes or expand public programs.

In the real world, tariffs can have major effects. One trade expert estimated that cutting industrial tariffs by 50 percent would increase the output of the world's economy by $270 billion per year. Similar easing of tariffs on agricultural products would cut the world's food bill by $100 billion.[2] Tariffs also appear to disproportionately affect the poor.

Responses to Protectionist Policies

A restriction on imports is likely to lead to further restrictions on trade. For example, if Chipland bans shirt imports, Shirtland might retaliate by banning computer chips from Chipland. A trade war of this sort could escalate to the point where the two

APPLICATION

THE IMPACT OF TARIFFS ON THE POOR

APPLYING THE CONCEPTS #1: Do tariffs (taxes) on imported goods hurt the poor disproportionately?

Economists have found that tariffs in the United States fall most heavily on lower-income consumers. In the United States, tariffs are very high on textiles, apparel items, and footwear. These goods represent a higher fraction of the consumption of lower-income households than higher-income households. For example, footwear accounts for 1.3 percent of the expenditure of lower-income households, as compared to 0.5 percent for higher-income households.

Moreover, even within these categories of goods for which tariffs are high, the highest tariffs fall on the cheapest products—precisely those that will be purchased by lower-income consumers. For example, low-price sneakers face a 32-percent tariff whereas expensive track shoes face only a 20-percent tariff. In general, to protect U.S. industries, tariffs are highest on labor-intensive goods; goods that use relatively more labor than capital. But these goods tend to be lower priced. That is why tariffs do fall disproportionately on the poor. *Related to Exercise 2.7.*

SOURCE: *Economic Report of the President 2006,* Chapter 7, available online at *www.gpoaccess.gov/eop/download.html*, accessed June, 2006.

nations return to self-sufficiency. If this happens, the two countries would be forced to scale back their consumption. We can see that by looking back at Figure 19.2: Chipland will move from point *b* to point *f*, and Shirtland will move from point *k* to point *c*. This sort of retaliatory response is common. Because it is, we know that protecting one industry in a nation is likely to harm that nation's other exports. Chipland's shirt industry, if protected from imports, may grow, but it will be at the expense of its computer-chip industry.

There are many examples of import restrictions that have led to retaliatory policies and substantially lessened trade. The most famous was the Smoot–Hawley tariff of 1930. When the United States increased its average tariff on imports to 59 percent, its trading partners retaliated with higher tariffs on U.S. products. The resulting trade war reduced international trade and deepened the worldwide depression of the 1930s.

The threat of retaliatory policies may persuade a nation to loosen its protectionist policies. For example, in 1995 the United States announced that it would impose 100-percent tariffs on Japanese luxury cars if Japan didn't ease its restrictions on imported auto parts. Just hours before the tariffs were to take effect, the two nations reached an agreement that was expected to increase the sales of U.S. auto parts to Japanese firms. In 2002, President Bush imposed tariffs on steel. However, when faced with the threat of retaliatory policies in Europe, he ended the sanctions in 2003.

Import restrictions also create an incentive to smuggle goods. The restrictions create a gap between the cost of purchasing the restricted goods abroad and the price goods can be sold for in the protected economy, so there is a profit to be made.

19.3 | WHAT ARE THE RATIONALES FOR PROTECTIONIST POLICIES?

Why would a government impose protectionist policies such as an import ban, quota, VER, or tariff? There are three possible reasons:

1 To shield workers from foreign competition

2 To nurture infant industries until they mature

3 To help domestic firms establish monopolies in world markets

To Shield Workers from Foreign Competition

One of the most basic arguments for protectionism is that it shields workers in industries that would be hurt by trade. Suppose that relative to the United States, nations in the Far East have a comparative advantage in producing textiles. If the United States were to reduce existing tariffs on textiles, domestic manufacturers could not compete. They would have to close their factories and lay off workers. In an ideal world, the laid-off workers would take new jobs in other sectors of the economy. In practice, this is difficult. Many workers don't immediately have the skills to go to work in other sectors, and obtaining those skills takes time. Moreover, the textile industry is heavily concentrated in the southeastern part of the United States. Politicians from that region will try to keep tariffs in place to prevent the temporary unemployment and changes in employment patterns in their areas—they have an incentive to protect their own constituents, even though it may cause major economic losses for the economy. The result of this protection will be less-efficient production, higher prices, and lower consumption for the United States. How much does it cost to protect a job?

To Nurture Infant Industries

During World War II, the United States built hundreds of boats, called Liberty ships, for the Navy. As more and more of these ships were built, each required fewer hours to complete, because workers acquired knowledge during the production process and

2

APPLICATION

MEASURING THE COSTS OF PROTECTING JOBS

APPLYING THE CONCEPTS #2: How much does it really cost to "save" a job that might be lost under free trade?

The Federal Reserve Bank of Dallas recently examined the cost to the United States to protect jobs in 20 different industries. Below are the top five industries in terms of costs per job saved:

Protected Industry	Jobs Saved	Annual Cost per Job Saved	Total Annual Cost
Benzenoid chemicals	216	$1,376,436	$ 297,310,176
Luggage	226	1,285,078	290,427,628
Softwood lumber	605	1,044,271	631,783,955
Sugar	2,261	826,104	1,867,821,144
Polyethylene resins	298	812,928	242,252,544

The annual cost of saving only one job in these industries is staggering—in three of these industries the cost is over a million dollars a year! In other industries, the costs per job may be a bit lower, but the total cost to the economy is much higher because the number of jobs saved is much greater. In textiles and apparels, the annual cost per job is "only" $199,241, but the total cost of protecting this industry is $33.6 billion a year. *Related to Exercise 3.5.*

SOURCE: Federal Reserve Bank of Dallas, *Annual Report 2002*, p. 19.

- **learning by doing**
  Knowledge and skills workers gain during production that increase productivity and lower cost.

- **infant industries**
  Industries that are at an early stage of development.

got better at it. Engineers and economists call this phenomenon **learning by doing**. To learn a new game, such as Ping-Pong, you learn by doing. At first, you may find it difficult to play, but your skills improve as you go along.

Tariffs and other protectionist policies are often defended on the grounds that they protect new or **infant industries** that are in the early stages of development and can benefit from learning by doing. A tariff shields a young industry from the competition of its more mature rivals. After the infant industry "grows up," the tariff can eventually be eliminated because the industry is able to compete. In practice, infant industries rarely become competitive with their foreign rivals. During the 1950s and 1960s, many Latin American countries used tariffs and other policies to protect their young manufacturing industries from foreign competition. Unfortunately, the domestic industries never became as efficient as foreign suppliers, and the Latin American countries that tried this policy suffered. Another problem with protecting an infant industry is that once an industry is given tariff protection, it is difficult to take that protection away. More generally, even some established companies also complain about "unfair competition," but this concept does not always make sense.

To Help Domestic Firms Establish Monopolies in World Markets

If the production of a particular good requires extremely large economies of scale, the world market will support only a few, or perhaps just one, firm. In this case, a nation

APPLICATION

PROTECTION FOR CANDLE MAKERS

APPLYING THE CONCEPTS #3: Does the concept of "unfair" competition make sense?

In response to the spread of protectionism, the French economist Frédéric Bastiat (1801–1851) wrote the following fictitious petition, in which French candle makers asked for protection from "unfair" competition:

> *We are suffering from the intolerable competition of a foreign rival, placed, it would seem, in a condition so far superior to ours for the production of light, that he absolutely inundates our national market at a price fabulously reduced. The moment he shows himself, our trade leaves us—all of our customers apply to him; and a branch of native industry, having countless ramifications, is all at once rendered completely stagnant. This rival . . . is none other than the sun.*
>
> *What we pray for is, that it may please you to pass a law ordering the shutting up of all windows, sky-lights, dormer windows, curtains, blinds, bull's eyes; in a word all openings, holes, chinks, clefts, and fissures, by or through which the light of the sun has been in use to enter houses, to the prejudice of the meritorious manufactures with which we . . . have accommodated our country—a country which, in gratitude, ought not to abandon us now.*
>
> *Does it not argue to the greatest inconsistency to check as you do the importation of coal, iron, cheese, and goods of foreign manufacture, merely because . . . their price approaches zero, while at the same time you freely admit, and without limitation, the light of the sun, whose price is during the whole day at zero?* **Related to Exercise 3.7.**

SOURCE: Frédéric Bastiat, *Economics Sophisms* (Edinburgh: Oliver & Boyd, 1873), pp. 49–53.

might be tempted to adopt policies to ensure a company within its borders will end up being the world monopolist. Suppose the commercial aircraft industry can support only one large firm. If two firms enter the industry, both will lose money. A nation could agree to provide financial support to a domestic firm to guarantee that the firm will make a profit. With such a guarantee, the domestic firm will enter the industry. Knowing this, a foreign firm will be reluctant to enter, so the domestic firm will capture the monopoly profit. The country where the successful firm is located will benefit from higher production and more jobs for its citizens.

One famous example of this is the case of Airbus, an airplane-manufacturing consortium in Europe. Several European countries provided large subsidies for the firms producing the Airbus line of planes. These subsidies allowed the firms associated with Airbus to underprice some of their rivals in the United States, and at least one U.S. manufacturer of commercial airplanes was forced out of business.

What could go wrong with these monopoly creation policies? First, if both nations subsidize their domestic firms, both firms will enter the market and lose money. The taxpayers in both countries will then have to pay for the subsidies. Second, a nation may pick the wrong industry to subsidize. Together, the British and French subsidized an airplane known as the Concorde, which flew at supersonic speeds, rapidly shuttling passengers between Europe and the United States. Although the Concorde captured the market, the market was not worth capturing. The venture lost money because the Concorde was very costly to develop and fly and few people were willing to pay a large premium for supersonic travel. The Concorde stopped flying in 2003. Finally, the subsidized firm may not perform well. As an example, in 2006, Airbus was facing severe problems with its planes and losing business to its competitors.

19.4 | A BRIEF HISTORY OF INTERNATIONAL TARIFF AND TRADE AGREEMENTS

Today, the average U.S. tariff is 4.6 percent of the value of imported goods, a rate that is close to the average tariffs in Japan and most European nations but very low by historical standards. As we noted earlier, when the Smoot–Hawley tariffs were implemented in the 1930s, the average U.S. tariff was a whopping 59 percent of a product's price. Tariffs are lower today because several international agreements subsequently reduced them.

The first major international trade agreement following World War II was the **General Agreement on Tariffs and Trade (GATT)**. This agreement was initiated in 1947 by the United States and 23 other nations and now has over 149 members. Nine rounds of GATT negotiations over tariffs and trade regulations have taken place, resulting in progressively lower tariffs for the member nations. The last completed set of negotiations, the Uruguay round (1994), decreased tariffs by about one-third of the previous level. In 1995, the **World Trade Organization (WTO)** was formed to enforce GATT and other international trade agreements. Under GATT's "most favored nation" provision, a country that reduces tariffs for one nation must do so for all members of GATT. This provision helps reduce tariffs throughout the world.

A new round of trade negotiations began in Doha, Qatar, in 2001. This round focused on many issues especially relevant to developing countries.

In addition to the large group of nations involved in the WTO, other nations have formed trade associations to lower trade barriers and promote international trade. Here are some of the most well-known agreements:

- The North American Free Trade Agreement (NAFTA) took effect in 1994 and will be implemented over a 15-year period. The agreement will eventually eliminate all tariffs and other trade barriers between Canada, Mexico, and the United States.

- The European Union (EU) was designed to remove all trade barriers within Europe and create a single market. Initially, the EU consisted of just six countries: Belgium, Germany, France, Italy, Luxembourg, and the Netherlands. Denmark, Ireland, and the United Kingdom joined in 1973; Greece in 1981; Spain and Portugal in 1986; and Austria, Finland, and Sweden in 1995. In 2004, the biggest ever enlargement took place with 10 new countries joining the EU.

- The leaders of 18 Asian nations have formed an organization called Asian Pacific Economic Cooperation (APEC). In 1994, APEC signed a nonbinding agreement to reduce trade barriers among these nations.

- The proposed U.S.-Central America Free Trade Agreement (CAFTA) would promote trade liberalization between the United States and five Central American countries: Costa Rica, El Salvador, Guatemala, Honduras, and Nicaragua. Modeled after the North American Free Trade Agreement (NAFTA), CAFTA must be approved by the U.S. Congress and by National Assemblies in the Central American countries before it becomes law.

- **General Agreement on Tariffs and Trade (GATT)**
  An international agreement established in 1947 that has lowered trade barriers between the United States and other nations.

- **World Trade Organization (WTO)**
  An organization established in 1995 that oversees GATT and other international trade agreements, resolves trade disputes, and holds forums for further rounds of trade negotiations.

APPLICATION

ONGOING TRADE NEGOTIATIONS

APPLYING THE CONCEPTS #4: What are the most pressing current issues in today's trade negotiations?

The focus of the latest round of trade negotiations was to help the developing countries by opening up trade in agriculture, as well as to continue to reduce barriers in manufacturing throughout the globe. The comparative advantage of many developing countries lies in agriculture, but the developed countries, such as those in both Europe and the United States, still provide subsidies and protection to their agriculture industries. Subsidies to exports lower world prices, and thereby make it more difficult for developing countries to compete in world markets. Although the number of farmers has decreased in developed countries, they remain politically powerful, particularly in Europe.

The Doha rounds have proceeded through a number of meetings of negotiators in Cancun, Geneva, Paris, and Hong Kong. In the Hong Kong meeting in December 2005, negotiators agreed in principle to eliminate all export subsidies for agriculture exports by the year 2013. This was an important accomplishment, but many more details and issues need to be negotiated before the Doha round can come to a fruitful conclusion. *Related to Exercise 4.7.*

Some economists are concerned that these regional trade agreements may stand in the way of broader international trade agreements under GATT. Although regional agreements may lead to reduced tariffs for neighboring or member countries, they do little to promote efficiency across the globe. For example, a Belgian firm may find it easier to sell goods in France than a firm from South America that has a lower cost of production.

19.5 | RECENT POLICY DEBATES AND TRADE AGREEMENTS

We're now ready to discuss three recent policy debates concerning international trade:

1 Are foreign producers dumping their products?
2 Do trade laws inhibit environmental protection?
3 Does outsourcing and trade cause income inequality?

Are Foreign Producers Dumping Their Products?

Although tariff rates have been reduced in recent years, a number of controversies surrounding free trade remain. One of these controversies relates to *dumping*. A firm is **dumping** when the price it charges in a foreign market is either lower than the price it

• **dumping**
A situation in which the price a firm charges in a foreign market is lower than either the price it charges in its home markets or the production cost.

• **price discrimination**
The process under which a firm divides consumers into two or more groups and charges a different price for each group buying the same product.

• **predatory pricing**
A pricing scheme under which a firm decreases the price to drive rival firms out of business and increases the price when rival firms leave the market.

charges in its home market or lower than its production cost. Dumping is illegal under international trade agreements. Hundreds of cases of alleged dumping are presented to WTO authorities each year. Here are some recent cases in which the WTO concluded that dumping had occurred: Hong Kong VCRs sold in Europe; Chinese bicycles sold in the United States; Asian TV sets sold in Europe; steel from Brazil, India, Japan, and Spain sold in the United States; U.S. beef sold in Mexico; and Chinese computer disks sold in Japan and the United States. Under the current provisions of the WTO, a nation can impose antidumping duties, a tax, on products that are being dumped within its borders.

Why would a firm dump—charge a low price in the foreign market? The first reason is price discrimination. **Price discrimination** occurs when a firm charges a different price to different customers buying the same product. If a firm has a monopoly in its home market but faces strong competition in a foreign market, it will naturally charge a higher price in the home market. What the firm is doing is using its monopoly power to charge higher prices to consumers at home and charge lower prices to consumers abroad where it faces competition. This strategy maximizes the firm's profits.

To illustrate how international price discrimination works, let's look at the case of Korean VCRs.[3] In the 1980s there were only three firms, all Korean, selling VCRs in Korea, but there were dozens of firms selling VCRs in Europe. The lack of competition in Korea generated very high prices for Korean consumers: They paid much more than European consumers paid for identical Korean VCRs and VCRs produced by firms in other countries. Essentially, Korean firms used their market power to discriminate against consumers in their own country. When international trade authorities concluded these companies were, indeed, dumping VCRs in Europe, the Korean firms responded by cutting prices in their home market. However, they didn't increase their prices in Europe—much to the delight of European consumers and the dismay of European producers, who had sought relief from the dumping in the first place.

The Korean VCR example brings up a second reason for dumping: **predatory pricing**—cutting prices in an attempt to drive rival firms out of business. The predatory firm sets its price below its production cost. The price is low enough that both the predator and its prey (a firm in the foreign market) lose money. After the prey goes out of business, the predator increases its price to earn a monopoly profit.

Although the rationale for antidumping laws is to prevent predatory pricing, it is difficult to determine whether low prices are the result of this or price discrimination. Many economists are skeptical about how frequently predatory pricing actually occurs versus price discrimination. They suspect that many nations use their antidumping laws as protectionist policies in disguise. Because WTO rules limit tariffs and quotas, some nations may be tempted to substitute antidumping duties for these protectionist policies.

Until the 1990s, antidumping cases were brought almost exclusively by Australia, New Zealand, Europe, Canada, and the United States. However, starting in the 1990s, the number of antidumping cases alleged by developing countries began to rise. Today, approximately half of the cases are brought by developing countries. Professor Thomas Prusa of Rutgers University has studied antidumping and has found that it is a potent weapon for protecting domestic industries. If an antidumping case is settled and a tariff is imposed as a result, imports typically fall by 50 to 70 percent during the first three years of the protection period. Even if a country loses a claim, imports still fall by 15 to 20 percent.[4]

Do Trade Laws Inhibit Environmental Protection?

In recent trade negotiations, a new player—environmental groups—appeared on the scene. Starting in the early 1990s, environmentalists began to question whether policies that liberalized trade could harm the environment. They were concerned that increased trade would lead to worldwide environmental degradation. An important issue that attracted their attention was the killing of dolphins by tuna fishers.

Anyone who catches tuna with a large net will also catch the dolphins that swim with the tuna, and most of the dolphins will die. In 1972, the United States outlawed the use of tuna nets by U.S. ships. However, ships from other nations, including Mexico, were still catching tuna with nets and selling that tuna in the United States. The

United States responded with a boycott of Mexican tuna caught with nets. The Mexican government complained to an international trade authority that the tuna boycott was an unfair trade barrier. The trade authority agreed with Mexico and forced the United States to remove the boycott.

Under current WTO rules, a country can adopt any environmental standard it chooses, as long as it does not discriminate against foreign producers. For example, the United States can limit the exhaust emissions of all cars that operate in the United States. As long as emissions rules apply equally to all cars, domestic and imports, the rules are legal according to the WTO. An international panel upheld U.S. fuel efficiency rules for automobiles on this principle.

The tuna boycott was a violation of WTO rules because killing dolphins does not harm the U.S. environment directly. For the same reason, the United States cannot ban imported goods produced by factories that generate air or water pollution in other countries. It is easy to understand why WTO rules do not allow countries to restrict trade on the basis of the methods that are used to produce goods and services. Countries differ in the value they place on the environment. For example, a poor nation may be willing to tolerate more pollution if it means attaining a higher standard of living for its citizens.

If trade restrictions cannot be used to protect the dolphins and deal with other global environmental problems, what else can we do? Shouldn't we have the right to protect dolphins? International agreements have been used for a variety of different environmental goals, from limiting the harvest of whales to reducing the chemicals that deplete the ozone layer. These agreements are difficult to reach, however, so some nations will be tempted to use trade restrictions to pursue environmental goals. If they do, they will encounter resistance because WTO rules mean that a nation can pursue its environmental goals only within its own borders.

Trade disputes about environmental issues are part of a larger phenomenon that occurs when trade issues and national regulations collide. At one time, most trade disputes were simply matters of protecting domestic industries from foreign competition. Agriculture, textile, and steel industries around the world frequently benefited from various forms of protection. But in recent years, a new breed of trade disputes has erupted revolving around social problems and the role that government regulation should play in solving them.

The EU, for example, has banned imports of hormone-treated beef. The United States and Canada successfully challenged this ban with the WTO. They argued that there was no scientific evidence that concluded hormone-treated beef adversely affected human health. The EU refused to rescind the ban and, as a consequence, the United States and Canada were permitted to impose tariffs on a wide range of European products that affected many of its industries.

The EU's ban on hormone-treated beef was intended to protect European farmers from imports, but it also reflected the nervousness of Europeans about technology. After all, Europe banned all hormone-treated beef, not just imported beef. Shouldn't a country have a right to pursue this policy, even if it is not based on the best science of the day? Although the costs of the policy are straightforward in terms of higher beef prices, the benefits, in terms of potential safety and peace of mind, are much more difficult to assess. Similar issues will arise as genetically modified crops become more commonplace. As a world trading community, we will have to decide at what point we allow national policy concerns to override principles of free trade.

Do Outsourcing and Trade Cause Inequality?

Inequality in wages has been growing in the United States since 1973. The wages of skilled workers have risen faster than the wages of unskilled workers. World trade has also boomed since 1973. Could there be a connection between the two?

Trade theory suggests a link between increased trade and increased wage inequality. Here is how they might be linked. Suppose the United States produces two types of goods: one using skilled labor (say, airplanes) and one using unskilled labor (say, textiles). The United States is likely to have a comparative advantage in products that use skilled labor, and developing countries are likely to have a comparative advantage in products that use unskilled labor. An increase in world trade will increase both exports and imports. An increase in U.S. exports means we'll need to produce more goods requiring skilled labor, so the domestic demand for skilled labor will increase, and so will the wages of these workers. At the same time, an increase in U.S. imports means that we'll be buying more goods produced by unskilled laborers abroad, so the demand for unskilled workers here will decrease, and these people's wages will fall. As a result, the gap between the wages of the two types of workers in the United States will increase.

• **outsourcing**
Firms producing components of their goods and services in other countries.

In addition, U.S. firms will produce some components of their goods and services overseas, which is known as **outsourcing**. If a firm outsources products that use unskilled labor, the demand for unskilled labor in the United States will decline, and this will also increase the gap between wages for the skilled and the unskilled.

Economists have tried to determine how much trade has contributed to growing wage inequality in the United States. As usual, other factors make such a determination difficult. It is difficult, for example, to distinguish between the effects of trade and the effects of technical progress. Technical change, such as the rapid introduction and use of computers, will also tend to increase the demand for skilled workers and decrease the demand for unskilled workers. Economists have noted, however, that the exports of goods using skilled labor and the imports of goods using unskilled labor have both increased, just as the theory predicts. Nonetheless, at least some of the increased wage inequality is caused by international trade.

One response to this undesirable side effect of trade is to use trade restrictions to protect industries that use unskilled workers. Another approach is to make the transition to an economy with more skilled than unskilled jobs less traumatic. In the long run, of course, workers will move to industries that require skilled labor, and they will eventually earn higher wages. However, in the short run the government could facilitate the transition by providing assistance for the education and training of unskilled workers.

More recently, there has been another concern. In our chapter-opening story, we discussed how jobs such as providing technical support or writing computer code may be shipped overseas. What this means is that not all jobs that are outsourced will be low-skilled jobs. It is possible that more-skilled jobs can also be outsourced. Not all services, however, can be outsourced and, in general, more routine services are the ones that will be outsourced. In the coming years, we will gain better insights into how international trade and outsourcing affect the wages of skilled workers.

Why Do People Protest Against Free Trade?

We have seen that there are important policy issues surrounding trade. Under current international trade rules, a country cannot dictate the terms under which another country actually produces the goods and services that it sells—even if it harms the environment. It is also possible that free trade can contribute to inequality within the United States. But do these reasons explain the passion we sometimes see in protests against free trade, such as the riots in 1999 in Seattle at a WTO meeting or the protestors dressed in death masks gathering at world trade meetings? Possibly, but it is more likely that the protestors are driven by something more basic. As we have seen in this chapter, trade and specialization provide important opportunities to raise living standards throughout the globe. But they also mean that individuals and nations surrender some of their independence and sovereignty. By not producing precisely what we consume, we become dependent on others to trade. By cooperating with other nations, we need to develop agreed-upon rules that, at times, limit our own actions.

The protestors may simply not understand the principles of trade, but they also may fear loss of cultural identity and independence. But in today's world, "no man is an island." Nations have become increasingly dependent on one another. Multinational corporations are the ultimate symbol of this interdependence, producing and distributing goods on a global scale. As symbols, companies such as McDonald's, Starbucks, or Nike can come under attack by the protestors. The benefits of trade, however, are so vast that countries will need to find ways to address issues of sovereignty and control while retaining an open and prosperous trading system.

SUMMARY

In this chapter, we discussed the benefits of specialization and trade, and we explored the trade-offs associated with protectionist policies. There is a basic conflict between consumers who prefer free trade because free trade decreases prices and workers in the protected industries who want to keep their jobs. Here are the main points of the chapter:

1 If one country has a *comparative advantage* vis-à-vis another country in producing a particular good (a lower opportunity cost), specialization and trade will benefit both countries.

2 An import ban or an *import quota* increases prices, protecting domestic industries, but domestic consumers pay the price.

3 Because the victims of protectionist policies often retaliate, the protection of a domestic industry can harm an exporting industry.

4 A *tariff*, a tax on imports, generates revenue for the government, whereas an *import quota*—a limit on imports—generates revenue for foreigners or importers.

5 In principle, the laws against *dumping* are designed to prevent *predatory pricing*. In practice, predatory pricing laws are often used to shield domestic industries from competition. Allegations of it are hard to prove.

6 Under *World Trade Organization (WTO)* rules, each country may pursue its environmental goals only within its own borders.

7 International trade has contributed to the widening gap between the wages of low-skilled and high-skilled labor.

KEY TERMS

absolute advantage, p. 420

comparative advantage, p. 420

consumption possibilities curve, p. 420

dumping, p. 429

General Agreement on Tariffs and Trade (GATT), p. 428

import licenses, p. 423

import quota, p. 422

infant industries, p. 426

learning by doing, p. 426

outsourcing, p. 432

predatory pricing, p. 430

price discrimination, p. 430

production possibilities curve, p. 418

tariff, p. 424

terms of trade, p. 420

voluntary export restraint (VER), p. 423

World Trade Organization (WTO), p. 428

EXERCISES

Get Ahead of the Curve

Visit www.myeconlab.com to complete these exercises online and get instant feedback.

19.1 | Benefits from Specialization and Trade

1.1 A country has a comparative advantage if it has a lower _____ cost of producing a good.

1.2 The _____ of trade is the rate at which two goods can be exchanged for one another.

1.3 Suppose a country has a comparative advantage in shirts but not computer chips. Workers in the chip industry will be _____ with trade.

1.4 Trade requires absolute advantage to make both parties better off. _____ (True/False)

1.5 **Finding Comparative Advantage.** In one minute, Country B can produce either 1,000 TVs and no computers or 500 computers and no TVs. Similarly, in one minute Country C can produce either 2,400 TVs or 600 computers.
  a. Compute the opportunity costs of TVs and computers for each country. Which country has a comparative advantage in producing TVs? Which country has a comparative advantage in producing computers?
  b. Draw the production possibilities curves for the two countries.

1.6 **Benefits from Trade.** In Country U, the opportunity cost of a computer is 10 pairs of shoes. In Country C, the opportunity cost of a computer is 100 pairs of shoes.
  a. Suppose the two countries split the difference between the willingness to pay for computers and the willingness to accept computers. Compute the terms of trade, that is, the rate at which the two countries will exchange computers and shoes.
  b. Suppose the two countries exchange one computer for the number of shoes dictated by the terms of trade you computed in part (a). Compute the net benefit from trade for each country.

1.7 Measuring the Gains from Trade. Consider two countries, Tableland and Chairland, each capable of producing tables and chairs. Chairland can produce the following combinations of chairs and tables:

    All chairs and no tables: 36 chairs per day
    All tables and no chairs: 18 tables per day

Tableland can produce the following combinations of chairs and tables:

    All chairs and no tables: 40 chairs per day
    All tables and no chairs: 40 tables per day

In each country, there is a fixed trade-off of tables for chairs.

a. Draw the two production possibilities curves, with chairs on the vertical axis and tables on the horizontal axis.

b. Suppose that each country is initially self-sufficient and divides its resources equally between the two goods. How much does each country produce and consume?

c. Which country has a comparative advantage in producing tables? Which country has a comparative advantage in producing chairs?

d. If the two countries split the difference between the buyer's willingness to pay for chairs and the seller's willingness to accept, in terms of chairs per table, what are the terms of trade?

e. Draw the consumption possibilities curves.

f. Suppose each country specializes in the good for which it has a comparative advantage, and they exchange 14 tables for some quantity of chairs. Compute the consumption bundles—*bundles* mean the consumption of tables and chairs—for each country.

19.2 | Protectionist Policies

2.1 If a country bans the importation of a particular good, the market equilibrium is shown by the intersection of the _____ curve and the _____ curve.

2.2 The equilibrium price under an import quota is _____ (above/below) the price that occurs with an import ban and _____ (above/below) the price that occurs with free trade.

2.3 From the perspective of consumers, a _____ (tariff/quota) is better.

2.4 Threatening to impose a tariff on a country's exports if it doesn't open up its markets to trade is an example of a _____ policy.

2.5 Incentives for Smuggling. If a country bans imports, smugglers may try to penetrate its markets. Suppose Chipland bans shirt imports, causing some importers to bribe customs officials who "look the other way" as smugglers bring shirts into the country. Your job is to combat shirt smuggling. Use the information in Figure 19.3 on page 422 to answer the following questions:

a. Suppose importers can sell their shirts on the world market at a price of $12 per shirt. How much is an importer willing to pay to get customs officials to look the other way?

b. What sort of change in trade policy would make your job easier?

2.6 Tariffs on Steel Imports. When the United States placed a tariff on steel imports in 2002, foreign producers naturally complained. But there were also complaints from U.S. firms operating in other industries. Why would other types of firms strongly object to the tariffs on U.S. steel imports?

2.7 Tariffs and the Poor. Historically, apparel and textiles were subject to high tariffs. Explain why this might hurt low-income consumers more than high-income consumers. (Related to Application 1 on page 424.)

2.8 The Political Dynamics of Tariffs and Quotas. Suppose the president of a nation proposes that it switch from a system of import quotas to a system of tariffs, with the idea that the switch will not affect the quantity of goods imported. Who will be in favor of the switch? Who will oppose it? Would you expect the proponents and the opponents to have the same political influence on the president?

19.3 | What Are the Rationales for Protectionist Policies?

3.1 The _____-industry argument is often given to provide a rationale for tariffs for new firms.

3.2 Knowledge gained during production is known as _____ by doing.

3.3 If only one firm can exist in a market, a government may try to subsidize the firm so that the country can share in the _____ profits.

3.4 In the 1950s and 1960s, countries in _____ used tariffs and other policies to nurture domestic industries.

3.5 Protecting Jobs. What is the cost to consumers for each sugar industry job protected by import restrictions? In your opinion, is protecting these jobs worthwhile at this cost? If not, how much should we as a society be willing to pay for each job that is protected? (Related to Application 2 on page 426.)

3.6 Infant Industries and Productivity. Many economists argue that industries that are protected from international competition are slower to innovate than industries that face worldwide competition. Assuming this fact is true, how does it affect the argument for tariff protection for infant industries?

3.7 Unfair Competition. We are amused by candle makers asking for protection from the sun under the guise of unfair competition. How does this differ from U.S. producers of clothing claiming there is unfair competition from low-wage countries? (Related to Application 3 on page 427.)

19.4 | A Brief History of International Tariff and Trade Agreements

4.1 The latest trade round is called the _____ round.

4.2 The _____ was formed in 1995 to oversee GATT.

4.3 NAFTA is a free trade agreement between the United States, Mexico, and _____.

4.4 The average tariff rate in the United States is roughly _____ percent.

4.5 **A Major Change in U.S. Trade Policy?** In Chapter 7 of the 2006 *Economic Report of the President* (*www.gpoaccess.gov/eop/download.html*), the authors of the report discuss the important changes that occurred in 1934 under the Reciprocal Trade Agreements Act. They contend that it began to move the United States to a policy of more open trade after the Smoot–Hawley tariffs. Identify the key changes enacted in 1934.

4.6 **Expansion in the European Union.** When the EU originated, member countries generally had similar standards of living. However, with the most recent expansion of the EU, countries that were less developed joined the developed countries. What implications might the entry of the new countries have for wage inequality within the more established European countries?

4.7 **Tracking Current Trade Talks.** Go to the Web site for the World Trade Organization (*www.wto.org*) and briefly summarize the current status of ongoing trade negotiations. (Related to Application 4 on page 429.)

19.5 | Recent Policy Debates and Trade Agreements

5.1 Pricing below production cost or selling at prices in foreign markets less than domestic markets is known as _____.

5.2 Under global trade rules, the United States was allowed to boycott Mexican tuna because they used fishing nets that killed dolphins. _____ (True/False)

5.3 Suppose the United States has a comparative advantage in goods that use skilled labor. If we trade with a country that has a comparative advantage in goods using unskilled labor, the wage differences between skilled and unskilled labor in the United States will _____.

5.4 Under a scheme of _____ pricing, a firm cuts its price to drive out rivals and then raises its price later.

5.5 **Trade in Genetically Modified Crops.** Suppose the residents of a country become fearful of using genetically modified crops in their food supply. Consider the following two possible scenarios:
 a. Aware of consumer sentiment, the largest supermarket chains in the country vow they will not purchase food products that use genetically modified crops.
 b. The government, aware of voter sentiment during an election year, bans the import of the food products that use genetically modified crops.

In both cases, no genetically modified crops enter the country. Does either of these cases run afoul of WTO policies?

5.6 **Fears of Biotechnology and Trade Policy.** Suppose residents of one nation are very fearful of biotechnology and they pass a law prohibiting the sale of all genetically altered foods in their country. Another nation, which produces these foods, claims that this law is an unfair trade barrier.
 a. Give one reason why the first nation should be allowed to prevent these imports.
 b. Give one reason why the first nation should not be allowed to prevent these imports.

5.7 **Issues in U.S. Trade Policy.** Go to the Web site for the U.S. Trade Representative (*www.ustr.gov*), which is an office within the executive branch of the government. From the Web site, what are some of the key trade issues for the U.S. government today?

NOTES

1. *A Review of Recent Developments in the U.S. Automobile Industry, Including an Assessment of the Japanese Voluntary Restraint Agreements* (Washington, D.C.: U.S. International Trade Commission, February 1985).

2. Gary C. Hufbauer, "The Benefits of Open Markets and the Costs of Trade Protection and Economic Sanction," ACCF Center for Policy Research, available online at www.accf.org/ publications/reports/sr-benefits-openmarkets1997.html, accessed June, 2006.

3. Taeho Bark, "The Korean Consumer Electronics Industry: Reaction to Antidumping Actions," Chapter 7 in *Antidumping: How It Works and Who Gets Hurt*, edited by J. Michael Finger (Ann Arbor, MI: University of Michigan Press, 1993).

4. Virginia Postrel, "Curb Demonstrates Faults of Courting Special Interests," *New York Times*, June 14, 2001, p. C1.

Glossary

absolute advantage The ability of one person or nation to produce a product at a lower resource cost than another person or nation.

accounting cost The explicit costs of production.

accounting profit Total revenue minus accounting cost.

adverse-selection problem A situation in which the uninformed side of the market must choose from an undesirable or adverse selection of goods.

asymmetric information A situation in which one side of the market—either buyers or sellers—has better information than the other.

average fixed cost (AFC) Fixed cost divided by the quantity produced.

average variable cost (AVC) Variable cost divided by the quantity produced.

barrier to entry Something that prevents firms from entering a profitable market.

break-even price The price at which economic profit is zero; price equals average total cost.

budget line The line connecting all the combinations of two goods that exhaust a consumer's budget.

budget set A set of points that includes all the combinations of two goods that a consumer can afford, given the consumer's income and the prices of the goods.

cartel A group of firms that act in unison, coordinating their pricee and quantity decisions.

centrally planned economy An economy in which a government bureaucracy decides how much of each good to produce, how to produce the good, and who gets them.

ceteris paribus The Latin expression meaning other variables being held fixed.

change in demand A shift of the demand curve caused by a change in a variable other than the price of the product.

change in quantity demanded A change in the quantity consumers are willing and able to buy when the price changes; represented graphically by movement along the demand curve.

change in quantity supplied A change in the quantity firms are willing and able to sell when the price changes; represented graphically by movement along the supply curve.

change in supply A shift of the supply curve caused by a change in a variable other than the price of the product.

collective bargaining Negotiations between a union and a firm over wages, fringe benefits, job security, and working conditions.

comparative advantage The ability of one person or nation to produce a good at a lower opportunity cost than another person or nation.

complements Two goods for which a decrease in the price of one good increases the demand for the other good.

concentration ratio The percentage of the market output produced by the largest firms.

constant returns to scale A situation in which the long-run total cost increases proportionately with output, so average cost is constant.

constant-cost industry An industry in which the average cost of production is constant; the long-run supply curve is horizontal.

consumer surplus The amount a consumer is willing to pay for a product minus the price the consumer actually pays.

consumption possibilities curve A curve showing the combinations of two goods that can be consumed when a nation specializes in a particular good and trades with another nation.

contestable market A market with low entry and exit costs.

craft union A labor organization that includes workers from a particular occupation, for example, plumbers, bakers, or electricians.

cross-price elasticity of demand A measure of the responsiveness of demand to changes in the price of a another good; equal to the percentage change in the quantity demanded of one good (X) divided by the percentage change in the price of another good (Y).

deadweight loss The decrease in the total surplus of the market that results from a policy such as rent control.

deadweight loss from monopoly A measure of the inefficiency from monopoly; equal to the decrease in the market surplus.

deadweight loss from taxation The difference between the total burden of a tax and the amount of revenue collected by the government.

demand schedule A table that shows the relationship between the price of a product and the quantity demanded, *ceteris paribus*.

diminishing returns As one input increases while the other inputs are held fixed, output increases at a decreasing rate.

diseconomies of scale A situation in which the long-run average cost of production increases as ouput increases.

dominant strategy An action that is the best choice for a player, no matter what the other player does.

dumping A situation in which the price a firm charges in a foreign market is lower than either the price it charges in its home markets or the production cost.

duopolists' dilemma A situation in which both firms in a market would be better off if both chose the high price, but each chooses the low price.

duopoly A market with two firms.

economic cost The opportunity cost of the inputs used in the production process; equal to explicit cost plus implicit cost.

economic model A simplified representation of an economic environment, often employing a graph.

economic profit Total revenue minus economic cost.

economics The study of choices when there is scarcity.

economies of scale A situation in which the long-run average cost of production decreases as output increases.

efficiency A situation in which people do the best they can, given their limited resources.

elastic demand The price elasticity of demand is greater than one.

entrepreneurship The effort used to coordinate the factors of production—natural resources, labor, physical capital, and human capital—to produce and sell products.

equimarginal rule Pick the combination of two activities where the marginal benefit per dollar for the first activity equals the marginal benefit per dollar for the second activity.

excess burden of a tax Another name for deadweight loss.

excess demand (shortage) A situation in which, at the prevailing price, the quantity demanded exceeds the quantity supplied.

excess supply (surplus) A situation in which at the prevailing price the quantity supplied exceeds the quantity demanded.

experience rating A situation in which insurance companies charge different prices for medical insurance to different firms depending on the past medical bills of a firm's employees.

explicit cost The actual monetary payment for inputs.

export A product produced in the home country and sold in another country.

external benefit A benefit from a good experienced by someone other than the person who buys the good.

external cost of production A cost incurred by someone other than the producer.

factors of production The resources used to produce goods and services; also known as *production inputs*.

featherbedding Work rules that increase the amount of labor required to produce a given quantity of output.

firm-specific demand curve A curve showing the relationship between the price charged by a specific firm and the quantity the firm can sell.

fixed cost (FC) Cost that does not vary with the quantity produced.

free rider A person who gets the benefit from a good but does not pay for it.

game theory The study of decision making in strategic situations.

game tree A graphical representation of the consequences of different actions in a strategic setting.

General Agreement on Tariffs and Trade (GATT) An international agreement established in 1947 that has lowered trade barriers between the United States and other nations.

grim-trigger strategy A strategy where a firm responds to underpricing by choosing a price so low that each firm makes zero economic profit.

human capital The knowledge and skills acquired by a worker through education and experience.

implicit cost The opportunity cost of inputs that do not require a monetary payment.

Import A product produced in a foreign country and purchased by residents of the home country.

import licenses Rights, issued by a government, to import goods.

import quota A government-imposed limit on the quantity of a good that can be imported.

income effect The change in quantity consumed that is caused by a change in real income, with relative prices held constant.

income effect for leisure demand The change in leisure time resulting from a change in real income caused by a change in the wage.

income elasticity of demand A measure of the responsiveness of demand to changes in consumer income; equal to the percentage change in the quantity demanded divided by the percentage change in income.

increasing-cost industry An industry in which the average cost of production increases as the total output of the industry increases; the long-run supply curve is positively sloped.

indifference curve A curve showing the different combinations of two goods that generate the same level of utility or satisfaction.

indifference curve map A set of indifference curves, each with a different utility level.

individual demand curve A curve that shows the relationship between the price of a good and quantity demanded by an individual consumer, *ceteris paribus*.

individual supply curve A curve showing the relationship between price and quantity supplied by a single firm, *ceteris paribus*.

indivisible input An input that cannot be scaled down to produce a smaller quantity of output.

industrial union A labor organization that includes all types of workers from a single industry, for example, steelworkers or autoworkers.

inelastic demand The price elasticity of demand is less than one.

infant industries Industries that are at an early stage of development.

inferior good A good for which an increase in income decreases demand.

input-substitution effect The change in the quantity of labor demanded resulting from an increase in the price of labor relative to the price of other inputs.

kinked demand curve model A model in which firms in an oligopoly match price cuts by other firms, but do not match price hikes.

labor   The physical and mental effort people use to produce goods and services.

labor union   A group of workers organized to increase job security, improve working conditions, and increase wages and fringe benefits.

law of demand   There is a negative relationship between price and quantity demanded, *ceteris paribus*.

law of diminishing marginal utility   As the consumption of a particular good increases, marginal utility decreases.

law of supply   There is a positive relationship between price and quantity supplied, *ceteris paribus*.

learning by doing   Knowledge and skills workers gain during production that increase productivity and lower cost.

learning effect   The increase in a person's wage resulting from the learning of skills required for certain occupations.

limit pricing   The strategy of reducing the price to deter entry.

long-run average cost (LAC)   The long-run cost divided by the quantity produced.

long-run demand curve for labor   A curve showing the relationship between the wage and the quantity of labor demanded over the long run, when the number of firms in the market can change and firms can modify their production facilities.

long-run marginal cost (LMC)   The change in long-run cost resulting from a one-unit increase in output.

long-run market supply curve   A curve showing the relationship between the market price and quantity supplied in the long run.

long-run total cost (LTC)   The total cost of production when a firm is perfectly flexible in choosing its inputs.

low-price guarantee   A promise to match a lower price of a competitor.

Macroeconomics   The study of the nation's economy as a whole; focuses on the issues of inflation, unemployment, and economic growth.

marginal benefit   The additional benefit resulting from a small increase in some activity.

marginal change   A small, one-unit change in value.

marginal cost   The additional cost resulting from a small increase in some activity.

marginal labor cost   The increase in a firm's total labor cost resulting from one more unit of labor.

marginal product of labor   The change in output from one additional unit of labor.

marginal rate of substitution (MRS)   The rate at which a consumer is willing to trade or substitute one good for another.

marginal revenue   The change in total revenue from selling one more unit of output.

marginal utility   The change in total utility from one additional unit of a good.

marginal-revenue product of labor (MRP)   The extra revenue generated from one additional unit of labor; *MRP* is equal to the price of output times the marginal product of labor.

market demand curve   A curve showing the relationship between price and quantity demanded by all consumers, *ceteris paribus*.

market economy   An economy in which people specialize and exchange goods and services in markets.

market equilibrium   A situation in which the quantity demanded equals the quantity supplied at the prevailing market price.

market power   The ability of a firm to affect the price of its product.

market supply curve   A curve showing the relationship between the market price and quantity supplied by all firms, *ceteris paribus*.

market supply curve for labor   A curve showing the relationship between the wage and the quantity of labor supplied.

marketable pollution permits   A system under which the government picks a target pollution level for a particular area, issues just enough pollution permits to meet the pollution target, and allows firms to buy and sell the permits; also known as a *cap-and-trade system*.

means-tested program   A government spending program that provides assistance to those whose income falls below a certain level.

median-voter rule   The choices made by government will match the preferences of the median voter.

merger   A process in which two or more firms combine their operations.

microeconomics   The study of the choices made by households, firms, and government and how these choices affect the markets for goods and services.

minimum efficient scale   The output at which scale economies are exhausted.

minimum supply price   The lowest price at which a product will be supplied.

mixed market   A market in which goods of different qualities are sold for the same price.

monopolistic competition   A market served by many firms that sell slightly different products.

monopoly   A market in which a single firm sells a product that does not have any close substitutes.

monopsony   A market in which there is a single buyer of an input.

moral hazard   A situation in which one side of an economic relationship takes undesirable or costly actions that the other side of the relationship cannot observe.

Nash equilibrium   An outcome of a game in which each player is doing the best he or she can, given the action of the other players.

natural monopoly   A market in which the economies of scale in production are so large that only a single large firm can earn a profit.

natural resources Resources provided by nature and used to produce goods and services.

negative relationship A relationship in which two variables move in opposite directions.

network externalities The value of a product to a consumer increases with the number of other consumers who use it.

nominal value The face value of an amount of money.

normal good A good for which an increase in income increases demand.

normative analysis Answers the question "What *ought to be?*"

Oligopoly A market served by a few firms.

opportunity cost What you sacrifice to get something.

output effect The change in the quantity of labor demanded resulting from a change in the quantity of output produced.

outsourcing Firms producing components of their goods and services in other countries.

Patent The exclusive right to sell a new good for some period of time.

paying efficiency wages The practice of paying a higher wage to increase the average productivity of the workforce.

payoff matrix A matrix or table that shows, for each possible outcome of a game, the consequences for each player.

perfectly competitive market A market with many sellers and buyers of a homogeneous product and no barriers to entry.

perfectly competitive market A market with so many buyers and sellers that no single buyer or seller can affect the market price.

perfectly elastic demand The price elasticity of demand is infinite.

perfectly elastic supply The price elasticity of supply is equal to infinity.

perfectly inelastic demand The price elasticity of demand is zero.

perfectly inelastic supply The price elasticity of supply equals zero.

physical capital The stock of equipment, machines, structures, and infrastructure that is used to produce goods and services.

pollution tax A tax or charge equal to the external cost per unit of pollution.

positive analysis Answers the question "What is?" or "*What will be?*"

positive relationship A relationship in which two variables move in the same direction.

predatory pricing A pricing scheme under which a firm decreases the price to drive rival firms out of business and increases the price when rival firms leave the market.

price ceiling A maximum price set by the government.

price discrimination The practice of selling a good at different prices to different consumers.

price discrimination The process under which a firm divides consumers into two or more groups and charges a different price for each group buying the same product.

price elasticity of demand (E_d) A measure of the responsiveness of the quantity demanded to changes in price; equal to the absolute value of the percentage change in quantity demanded divided by the percentage change in price.

price elasticity of supply A measure of the responsiveness of the quantity supplied to changes in price; equal to the percentage change in quantity supplied divided by the percentage change in price.

price floor A minimum price set by the government.

price leadership A system under which one firm in an oligopoly takes the lead in setting prices.

price ratio The price of the good on the horizontal axis divided by the price of the good on the vertical axis.

price taker A buyer or seller that takes the market price as given.

price-fixing An arrangement in which firms conspire to fix prices.

private cost of production The production cost borne by a producer, which typically includes the costs of labor, capital, and materials.

private good A good that is consumed by a single person or household; a good that is rival in consumption and excludable.

producer surplus The price a producer receives for a product minus the marginal cost of production.

product differentiation The process used by firms to distinguish their products from the products of competing firms.

production possibilities curve A curve that shows the possible combinations of products that an economy can produce, given that its productive resources are fully employed and efficiently used.

public good A good that is available for everyone to consume, regardless of who pays and who doesn't; a good that is nonrival in consumption and nonexcludable.

public-choice economics A field of economics that uses models of rational choice to explore decision making in the public sector.

quantity demanded The amount of a product that consumers are willing and able to buy.

quantity supplied The amount of a product that firms are willing and able to sell.

real value The value of an amount of money in terms of what it can buy.

rent seeking The process of using public policy to gain economic profit.

right-to-work laws Laws that prohibit union shops, where union membership is required as a condition of employment.

scarcity The resources we use to produce goods and services are limited.

short-run average total cost (ATC) Short-run total cost divided by the quantity of output; equal to *AFC* plus *AVC*.

short-run demand curve for labor A curve showing the relationship between the wage and the quantity of labor demanded over the short run, when the firm cannot change its production facility.

short-run marginal cost (MC) The change in short-run total cost resulting from a one-unit increase in output.

short-run market supply curve A curve showing the relationship between market price and the quantity supplied in the short run.

short-run supply curve A curve showing the relationship between the market price of a product and the quantity of output supplied by a firm in the short run.

short-run total cost (TC) The total cost of production when at least one input is fixed; equal to fixed cost plus variable cost.

shut-down price The price at which the firm is indifferent between operating and shutting down; equal to the minimum average variable cost.

signaling effect The information about a person's work skills conveyed by completing college.

slope of a curve The vertical difference between two points (the *rise*) divided by the horizontal difference (the *run*).

social cost of production Private cost plus external cost.

Substitutes Two goods for which an increase in the price of one good increases the demand for the other good.

substitution effect The change in quantity consumed that is caused by a change in the relative price of the good, with real income held constant.

substitution effect for leisure demand The change in leisure time resulting from a change in the wage (the price of leisure) relative to the price of other goods.

sunk cost A cost that a firm has already paid or committed to pay, so it cannot be recovered.

supply schedule A table that shows the relationship between the price of a product and quantity supplied, *ceteris paribus.*

tariff A tax on imported goods.

terms of trade The rate at which units of one product can be exchanged for units of another product.

thin market A market in which some high-quality goods are sold but fewer than would be sold in a market with perfect information.

tie-in sales A business practice under which a business requires a consumer of one product to purchase another product.

tit-for-tat A strategy where one firm chooses whatever price the other firm chose in the preceding period.

total revenue The money a firm generates from selling its product.

total surplus The sum of consumer surplus and producer surplus.

total-product curve A curve showing the relationship between the quantity of labor and the quantity of output produced, ceteris paribus.

trust An arrangement under which the owners of several companies transfer their decision-making powers to a small group of trustees.

unit elastic demand The price elasticity of demand is one.

util One unit of utility.

utility The satisfaction experienced from consuming a good.

utility-maximizing rule Pick the combination that makes marginal rate of substitution equal to the price ratio.

variable A measure of something that can take on different values.

variable cost (VC) Cost that varies with the quantity produced.

voluntary export restraint (VER) A scheme under which an exporting country voluntarily decreases its exports.

willingness to accept The minimum amount a producer is willing to accept as payment for a product; equal to the marginal cost of production.

willingness to pay The maximum amount a consumer is willing to pay for a product.

World Trade Organization (WTO) An organization established in 1995 that oversees GATT and other international trade agreements, resolves trade disputes, and holds forums for further rounds of trade negotiations.

Photo Credits

Index